LETTERS OF E. B. WHITE

LETTERS OF
E. B. White

COLLECTED AND EDITED BY Dorothy Lobrano Guth

PERENNIAL LIBRARY

Harper & Row, Publishers, New York
Cambridge, Philadelphia, San Francisco
London, Mexico City, São Paulo, Singapore, Sydney

A hardcover edition of this book was published by Harper & Row, Publishers, Inc.

First PERENNIAL LIBRARY edition published 1989.

LIBRARY OF CONGRESS CATALOG CARD NUMBER 73-18660

ISBN 0-06-091517-X

89 90 91 92 93 HC 10 9 8 7 6 5 4 3 2 1

CONTENTS

ILLUSTRATIONS

Following page 176

Family portrait, taken a few months after Elwyn Brooks White's birth.

Clara and Elwyn White with their mother.

101 Summit Avenue, Mount Vernon, New York.

Lillian and Elwyn.

Beppo, an Irish setter, and Elwyn.

Lillian, Elwyn, and their mother at Great Pond, North Belgrade, Maine.

The White family at Great Pond.

High-button shoes, about 1910.

Elwyn posing with a cast-iron dog.

The Model T, "Hotspur," in North Dakota, Howard Cushman in the driver's seat.

White and Cushman in Walker, Minnesota, where White dislocated his elbow.

"Hotspur" on a detour through the sage in Montana.

Between Choteau and Browning, Montana, in the Blackfeet Indian Reservation.

The S.S. *Buford*.

Cushman and White in the fruit harvest in Yakima, Washington.

INTRODUCTION

The gentle arts of conversation and letter writing have largely given way, nowadays, to the intrusive urgency of the telephone. E. B. White grew up, however, in a time that favored those arts and with talents that suited them. His writing not only reads well but rings agreeably in the reader's inner ear, just as good and graceful conversation does. Reading his essays, novels, short stories, and poems is like hearing him talk to you, and his letters have the same quality. They're good company.

In March 1972, Ursula Nordstrom, then chief editor of the children's book division of Harper & Row, wrote to E. B. White suggesting that his letters be collected and published in book form. As editor of White's three children's books, she had thirty years of letters on which to base this suggestion, and Cass Canfield, editor of his adult books, concurred in it. White wrote back that he didn't really consider himself much of a letter writer. But he thought about the idea and talked it over with Katharine White, his wife. When Mrs. White produced a cache of letters that he had written to her in the twenties and thirties, he began to look more favorably on the project. A collection of letters has the appeal of being both previously unpublished material and something of an unself-conscious autobiography. Letters show the direction of a person's life. They capture, in an informal but immediate way, many of its episodes. They also reveal, sometimes in a way that is embarrassing to the letter writer, quite a lot about his character, his relationships with others, his hopes and disappointments.

Katharine White would have been the obvious choice for editor of a volume of E. B. White letters, but her poor health made that impossible. I was another natural candidate, for reasons of both familiarity and experience. My father, the late G. S. Lobrano, was a close friend of E. B.

White's and since he also worked at *The New Yorker*, I knew something of the atmosphere and cast of characters at the magazine. Mr. White, moreover, is my godfather and he is my close friend, too.

Though I have worked for a publishing house and *The New Yorker*, letter collecting, selecting, and annotating were all new to me, and even with the help of the Whites, putting this book together has been a large job that has taken longer than anticipated. I have advertised for letters in newspapers and magazines; I've made two trips to the Cornell University Library and many to the New York Public Library; I've written hundreds of letters and read thousands of them—and even helped my mother and Mrs. Clarence Day search their attics!

I carried the final selection to Maine in a very large suitcase. The sheer volume of the letters has been both a blessing and a bother. They cover more than sixty years and touch on growing up, marriage, fatherhood, *The New Yorker*, town and country life, a world war, the atom bomb, growing old—and many of the intellectual and political controversies of the last forty years. This book is about a man's life and his times, the development of an individual and his country from the years of the Model-T Ford to the Bicentennial.

As the collector of the letters, being sleuth as well as judge, I have had a great deal of help from librarians and from private individuals. Some people save letters and some don't, and so of course the collection just can't be completely representative: E. B. White's son Joel, for example, was a thrower-outer, his stepson Roger Angell was a saver. Naturally enough, two or three letters written on the same day or even during the same week would be to some extent repetitious when read together, so that some of the letters had to be left out or cut. Many of the letters that were eliminated, with the help and advice of E. B. and Katharine White, seem to me to be wonderful ones; many of them came from cellars and attics where friends and strangers had searched hard for them. Almost every time I left out a letter I did it regretfully.

Condescending references to blacks in a few of the early letters may come as a surprise to the reader. "I find these references embarrassing but not surprising," White says. "I was born in a WASP's nest and learned to speak by listening to my elders. When I was a child, my bigotry—if you want to call it that—was benign, built-in, and standard. And although I began, early on, to question the social structure, it is quite apparent from these letters that I did nothing about revising the vocabulary of implied condescension. Not until mid-century, when I was a lad of fifty, did America finally get around to questioning its complacent attitudes and objectionable speech."

Because simplicity and informality are the essence of E. B. White's style as a letter writer, my editor at Harper, Corona Machemer, and I have tried to keep editorial intrusions to a minimum. Persons, places, and things have been identified whenever identification seemed called for, but in ways which we hope will contribute to the reader's pleasure without distracting him. When writing a letter, White can be as carefree as any of the rest of us about spelling and seldom corrects typographical errors. We have corrected misspellings in all except the childhood letters, unless the error seemed from its context to have special significance. Letters written over a long period of time for many different reasons, to family, to friends and strangers, to adults and children, are not likely to conform to any standard "style" in such matters as the use of italics or quotation marks to identify the titles of books, and we have not made White's letters conform for publication, choosing instead to retain the variations in the originals. Dots of ellipses indicate where material has been cut from the text of a letter. Most of these cuts represent material that is repetitive, but occasionally a cut has been made to spare someone's feelings. To the best of my knowledge, we have made no cuts to spare the feelings of Mr. White.

In these technical matters, and in many other editorial matters as well, Corona Machemer's sharp eye and good sense of direction have been invaluable, and I am very grateful for her expert assistance.

From a writer who has won many literary honors, one might expect a book of "literary" letters. This collection is hardly that. To E. B. White, everyday life has always been fully as absorbing as the world of letters, and his delight in bringing off a successful hatch of goose eggs is as real as his satisfaction at bringing off a good sentence or a good book.

Dorothy Lobrano Guth

AUTHOR'S NOTE

Ideally, a book of letters should be published posthumously. The advantages are obvious: the editor enjoys a free hand, and the author enjoys a perfect hiding place—the grave, where he is impervious to embarrassments and beyond the reach of libel. I have failed to cooperate in this ideal arrangement. Through some typical bit of mismanagement, I am still alive, and the book has had to adjust to that awkward fact. But since I *am* still around, I shall seize the chance to thank the three people who brought the book into being: Dorothy Guth, my goddaughter; Corona Machemer, my Harper editor; and Katharine White, my wife. Mrs. Guth proved as resourceful and as tireless as a hound dog in finding letters; Miss Machemer knocked herself out in a remarkable show of dedication and organizational frenzy; and Katharine White gazed steadily and skeptically at the whole mess with a patience born of her long years of dealing with unruly writers and untidy manuscripts. I salute all three and send my love.

E. B. W.

July 19, 1976

LETTERS OF E. B. WHITE

I

MOUNT VERNON

1908-1917

● *(Elwyn Brooks White was born in Mount Vernon, New York, on July 11, 1899, the youngest of the six children of Samuel and Jessie Hart White. Mount Vernon was a quiet, leafy suburb in the early years of the new century, and Elwyn, sometimes called "En," grew up in a child's paradise of backyards and skating ponds, bicycles and pets. He attended public schools, where he got good grades, and he did some writing for the* Oracle, *the high school paper. White himself can best supply the details and introduce the characters, and the following introduction is, therefore, in his own words.—Ed.)*

If an unhappy childhood is indispensable for a writer, I am ill-equipped: I missed out on all that and was neither deprived nor unloved. It would be inaccurate, however, to say that my childhood was untroubled. The normal fears and worries of every child were in me developed to a high degree; every day was an awesome prospect. I was uneasy about practically everything: the uncertainty of the future, the dark of the attic, the panoply and discipline of school, the transitoriness of life, the mystery of the church and of God, the frailty of the body, the sadness of afternoon, the shadow of sex, the distant challenge of love and marriage, the far-off problem of a livelihood. I brooded about them all, lived with them day by day. Being the youngest in a large family, I was usually in a crowd but often felt lonely and removed. I took to writing early, to assuage my uneasiness and collect my thoughts, and I was a busy writer long before I went into long pants.

Our big house at 101 Summit Avenue was my castle. From it I emerged to do battle, and into it I retreated when I was frightened or in trouble. The house even had the appearance of a fortress, with its octagonal tower room for sighting the enemy and its second-story porches *for gun emplacements. Just inside the massive front door was the oak hatrack, next to the umbrella stand. On the left the parlor, where the action was; on the right the "reception room," where no one was ever received but where I found my mother one day stretched out on the settee, recovering from an accident with a runaway horse. I thought she was dead.*

I remember the cellar, its darkness and dampness, its set tubs, its Early American water closet for the help, its coal furnace that often tried to asphyxiate us all, and the early sound of the Italian furnace man who crept in at dawn and shook the thing down. As a very small boy, I used to repair to the cellar, where I would pee in the coal bin—for variety. Out back was the stable, where I spent countless hours hobnobbing with James Bridges, the coachman, watching him polish harness and wash carriages.

My father, Samuel Tilly White, was born in Brooklyn, the son of a carpenter and the grandson of a contractor. I don't know a great deal about my father's upbringing and home life. I don't think there was much money there, and there may have been some rough times. My father was, all his life, a sober and abstemious man, but I'm not sure his father was. His mother, Mary Ann Elizabeth Tilly, was an admirable woman. She came of "landed Gentry" in England but was deprived of her share of her father's estate because she married a tradesman. At any rate, young Samuel, my father (he always wrote his name "Sam'l"), felt obliged to quit school at thirteen and go to work. He found a job as "bundle boy" (wrapping packages) with the piano firm of Horace Waters & Company, at 134 Fifth Avenue, Manhattan. This company had a factory in Harlem, where the cases for uprights, squares, and baby grands were manufactured by a crew of beer-drinking Germans, skilled artisans. The actions (keyboard, hammers, dampers, etc.) were bought from a company that specialized in that and were installed at the Horace Waters factory.

Sam White not only wrapped bundles for his employer, he began pulling at his own bootstraps. He informed himself about every aspect of the business, learned bookkeeping, learned to play the piano, kept his eyes and ears open, and was soon climbing life's ladder. He was successively a clerk, a salesman, a branch manager (there were two or three retail stores scattered about the city), an officer of the company, finally president. When I was a child, I used to watch parades from a front-row seat next to the big plate glass window on the second floor of 134 Fifth Avenue—a splendid vantage point. I was "Mr. White's boy," marked for the special treatment. I made many visits to 134 and remember particularly the wonderful sad sound of a piano being tuned somewhere in the building.

Old Horace Waters, who founded the company, was an active temperance man. This may have had some effect on Father's life—I don't know. I do know that he spent most of his life as a teetotaler; only near the end did he occasionally treat himself to a glass of wine. He was a man of great probity, scrupulously honest and fair, a wing-collar, starched-cuff man, whose speech was never blurred by obscenities or profanities. He had a sentimental turn of mind, which led him into songwriting, and two or three of his compositions were published in the form of sheet music. But essentially he was a man of affairs, of business. He was what we call "well to do," a moderately successful businessman who ran both his company and his private life with caution and thrift. Over the years he accumulated enough money to build a house in Mount Vernon in the district called Chester Hill, which was classy. I have no idea how he met Mother. Their backgrounds were quite different. Father was forty-five years old when I was born; Mother was forty-one. So my parents and I were separated by almost two generations. I never knew my grandparents—they were all either dead or dying when I came along.

One of the fringe benefits of being the son of a piano man was that our parlor at 101 Summit Avenue was well supplied with musical instruments: a Waters grand, a reed organ with phony pipes, and, at one period, a Waters player piano called an "Autola." There were six of us children, and we were practically a ready-made band. All we lacked was talent. We had violins, cellos, mandolins, guitars, banjos, and drums, and there was always a lot of music filling the air in our home, none of it good. We sang, composed, harmonized, drummed, and some of us took lessons for brief spells in an attempt to raise the general tone of the commotion. My brother Stanley was a fiddler. I played piano, picked at the mandolin, and at one point acquired a three-quarter-size cello and took lessons. But I failed to develop musical curiosity, learned nothing about the works of the great, and was content to make a noise, whether ragtime or schmalz or Czerny. Like my father, I liked the sound of music but was too lazy to follow it to its source.

My mother, Jessie Hart White, was also born in Brooklyn. She was of Scottish ancestry. Her father, William Hart, left Scotland for America in 1831. A Bible that survives in our family had belonged to James Hart, of Paisley, father of William. The inscription, after noting the union of James Hart and Marion Robertson, gets right into the swing of marriage.

We have a great work to do and but a short time to do it.
Get this principle wrought in your heart
That there is nothing got by sin but misery
Nothing lost by holiness but Hell.

*With only a short time allotted them, James and Marion speedily pro-
duced ten children, two of whom, William (my grandfather) and his
younger brother James, managed to make a name for themselves in
American art. William was a redhead. He began his career as a painter
in Troy, New York, where he was apprenticed to a coachmaker, helping
to decorate the carriages and coaches and fire trucks of that horse-drawn
era. He would tie three brushes together, spin a wheel, and produce three
decorative stripes. An Albany man named Armsby, who was a doctor,
took an interest in William Hart and helped him get his start as a professional painter. For a while, my grandfather was an itinerant portrait
painter, traveling about and doing portraits for a small fee. After a bit,
he was drawn to landscape painting and ended up as one of the pillars
of the Hudson River school. He was particularly excited by a landscape
that contained cows. Many of his best and most ambitious oils featured
cattle. I have seen some of his sketch books: they are loaded with the
details of udders, rear ends, heads, horns, and hooves.*

*William Hart became known in art circles, got good prices for his
large canvases, and was the first president of the Brooklyn Academy of
Design. My mother, although a shy and simple person, liked being the
daughter of an illustrious father, and she often referred to him as "an
Academician." The word gave her a lift. She worshiped my father, but I
think in a subtle way she pulled rank on him, now and then, by pulling
William Hart on him. After all, Father was just a businessman, son of a
carpenter. Her father was an artist. Mother herself had no knowledge of
art beyond the limits of her father's studio. She had no artistic pretensions
or gifts. But it meant something to her to have an artist for a parent—an
artist was special. Toward the end of his life and before I was born,
Grandfather Hart moved from Brooklyn to Mount Vernon, to a house on
Sidney Avenue. I presume this influenced my father to make the same
move. It enabled Mother to be near her own family.*

*In the order of our arrival, we were Marion Robertson White, Clara
Frances White, Albert Hunt White, Stanley Hart White, Lillian White,
and Elwyn Brooks White. There was a seventh child—Mother's second
—who died in infancy. Father and Mother almost never mentioned her,
and it was as though she had never existed.*

*Marion was red-haired. She was a quiet, gentle girl—soft-spoken
and long-suffering. When I was three years old, she married a Mount
Vernon man named Arthur Brittingham. They had five children—Arthur
Jr., Frank, Jessie, Stanley, and Sam, who was tragically killed in a bicycle
accident. Arthur Brittingham was a brisk, opinionated man with a pene-
trating voice, a jolly manner, and the ability to do practically anything.
Father complained that he didn't bring home the bacon. He brought a lot*

of other things home, though: firecrackers, jack o'lanterns, toys, baby alligators, cameras, tools, magic sets, and the ingredients for candy. He
made the best candy of anyone in Westchester County. He irritated the
life out of my father, who soon found himself contributing regularly to
the support of the rapidly increasing Brittingham family. Arthur was a
Bull Mooser—loved Teddy Roosevelt and carrying the big stick. Father
was a Woodrow Wilson man, and the clash of political ideas was intense.
Children found Arthur completely fascinating. He was always ready to
drop anything to build a kite, spin a top, set up a toy railroad, or whoop
up a batch of candy. Halloween and the Fourth of July, occasions that
simply made Father uneasy, were practically designed for Arthur Brittingham, who prepared for them well in advance and gave them everything he had. He was a greatly gifted photographer and a dedicated
gardener. The Brittinghams lived first in Mount Vernon, then in Tucka-
hoe, then moved to Bridgeport, where Arthur went to work in a factory
and brought home a paycheck. At one time, the family acquired a couple
of baby alligators. Many American families have enjoyed a short interlude with baby alligators, but the Brittingham alligators were no tran-
sients: they settled right in. When they were six or seven feet long, they
were moved down cellar and dwelt there in morose seclusion, terrorizing
the man who was supposed to read the meter.

Marion died of cancer in 1959 and was buried in Arlington Cemetery, to await her husband. Arthur, desolated but courageous, lived on
alone in the Bridgeport house until his death at ninety. He was the king
of the neighborhood children. He never slacked up on celebrating the
great occasions and fete days. The last time I was in his house (it was just
before Halloween) there was a large stuffed alligator on the hearth, its
wicked jaws slowly opening and closing, to reveal a red interior glow.

Clara was the second child in our family. We called her "Tar." She
was brown-haired, high-spirited, handsome, with not a care in the world.
When a young attorney named Manton Marble Wyvell, from Wellsville,
New York, took a look at Clara he decided he had seen it all, and they
were married. She bore him nine children, of whom seven—Marion,
Manton Jr., Dorothy, Conrad, Eleanor, Janet, and Donald—survived.

Manton was an ambitious fellow, impressive to look at—a large,
commanding man with a massive head, who often seemed utterly
oblivious of the presence of others. Oil was in his blood. He drilled wells,
and speculated. He practiced law, dabbled in politics, and made money.
He was a Democrat and a devotee of William Jennings Bryan. When
Bryan became Secretary of State, Manton became Bryan's personal
secretary and front man. At one time he was worth a good deal, and the
Wyvells lived in a big house in Washington, D.C. He loved Clara but was

so preoccupied with his own intricate affairs (of which she knew nothing) he had little time for family life. It often seemed to me that he hadn't really learned the names of his own children. Manton overreached himself, the bubble burst, he went broke and then collapsed mentally. Tar, cheerful and imperturbable, placed him in an institution and turned her home into a boardinghouse. Manton died in the thirties. Clara, at this writing, is still living, almost blind, cared for by one of her children.

My two brothers, Albert and Stanley, were near of an age though not at all alike. As teen-agers they were close pals and were a pair of busy boys. They built a boat in our barn, they built the first skis to be seen in Mount Vernon (if they weren't the first they were easily the most unmanageable), they constructed a cable aerial railway from our barn loft to our pear tree, they entered Cornell together, founded a fraternity there, graduated together in 1912, and married sisters—the Bigney girls of Brockton, Mildred and Blanche.

When Albert was born, my father and mother were tickled to have a boy child for a change. It was the era of Little Lord Fauntleroy, and as soon as little Albert was ambulatory, my doting parents dressed him up in a Fauntleroy suit. He was a handsome child, kindly and with winning ways. He had a tough time adjusting to life, nonetheless, and never managed to carve out a career that brought him much satisfaction or ease. He had two children, a son Bill and a daughter Frances. Al died in 1964 at the age of seventy-one, well loved and still busy trying to solve the riddle of this difficult world.

Stanley, nicknamed "Bunny," was number four. He was a redhead like his grandfather Hart, tall and rangy and bespectacled. Of all my brothers and sisters, Stan was the one I was most with. Although eight years older, he latched onto me because he liked to have someone to instruct. He was a born teacher and spent most of his life on the faculty of the University of Illinois, professor of Landscape Architecture. He is alive, retired, and living in Denver with his wife Blanche, whom he married in 1916. They have one daughter, Janice, an artist.

Stan taught me to read when I was in kindergarten and I could read fairly fluently when I entered the first grade—an accomplishment my classmates found annoying. I'm not sure my teacher, Miss Hackett, thought much of it, either. Stan's method of teaching me was to hand me a copy of the New York Times and show me how to sound the syllables. He assured me there was nothing to learning to read—a simple matter. He imparted information as casually as a tree drops its leaves in the fall. He taught me the harmonic circle on the pianoforte. He gave me haphazard lessons in the laws of physics: centrifugal force, momentum, inertia, gravity, surface tension, and illustrated everything in a clowning way. He taught me to paddle a canoe so that it would proceed on a straight course instead of a series of zigzags. He showed me how to hold the scissors for trimming the fingernails of my right hand. He showed me how to handle a jackknife without cutting myself. Hardly a day passes in my life without my performing some act that reminds me of something I learned from Bunny. He was called Bunny because he wiggled his nose like a rabbit. He resembled Grandfather Hart and, like his grandfather, he liked to draw and paint. Both Stanley and Albert took Agriculture at Cornell—perhaps because New York State residents got free tuition in that college. It was on my visits to Ithaca to see my older brothers that I fell wildly in love with the trolley car that ran up and down the hills and across the gorges on the high bridges, and so chose Cornell for myself when the time came.

Lillian, also a redhead, was the fifth child. I got on pretty well with Lil and still do (we are not far apart in age). She was a pretty girl and had many beaux. She liked dances and parties and gaiety. Neither Marion nor Clara went to college, but Lil made it to Vassar and graduated, daisy chain and all. Socially, I was a backward boy, and Lil would occasionally take a stab at getting me going with my peers. It never worked. I never went to dances or took girls out. The nearest I came to that, in my high-school days, was skating with a girl I met on an ice pond.

Lil had a hard time deciding whom to marry among her many suitors. She kept putting the matter off and for a while went to work in New York as a secretary and became a commuter. But after a few years of this, she met another commuter—Arthur Illian, a Wall Street broker —and married him, thus becoming Lillian Illian, a dubious triumph in alliteration. She and Arthur had three girls, Carol, Noel, and Sidney. I grew very fond of my brother-in-law, who was, among other things, a railroad buff. He died (appropriately) in Penn Station, in middle life, and Lil has been a widow for many years. She lives in Northport, Long Island, near her three married daughters.

On the summer morning when I arrived in this world, there was a breakdown in communications. Dr. Archibald Campbell was supposed to come to the house and deliver me, but he couldn't be reached. At the last minute, some member of the family looked out of a front window, saw Dr. Campbell driving by in his buggy, flagged him down, and hustled him up to Mother's bedroom, where he took over. My numbers were lucky ones: July is the seventh month, and I appeared on the eleventh day. Seven, eleven. I've been lucky ever since and have always counted heavily on luck.

When the time came for me to enter kindergarten, I fought my parents with every ounce of my puny strength. I screamed and carried on. *The idea of school terrified me—I wanted to stay home and live peacefully in familiar surroundings. My parents, of course, won, after a showdown, and I was bundled off to P.S. 2 on Lincoln Avenue. The name of my kindergarten teacher was Miss Greene. We sat in little chairs in a circle. There was a pudgy girl who thought I was cute and wanted to hold my hand. I hated her with all my heart and would pull my hand away in revulsion.*

I spent the next nine years in P.S. 2. I covered the distance on foot or on a bicycle. There were no school buses, and there was no nonsense in the classroom, either. Nothing was called "language arts" or "social studies." Everything went by its simple name: reading, writing, spelling, arithmetic, grammar, geography, history, music. I was a diligent scholar —more from fear of falling behind than from intellectual curiosity— and got good marks. School opened with an assembly, in a big room where we saluted the flag, listened to the principal read a passage from the Bible, heard one student recite a piece from the platform, and then marched out to piano music by Mrs. Schuyler, with whom I was in love. It was in P.S. 2 that I contracted the fear of platforms that has dogged me all my life and caused me to decline every invitation to speak in public. For the assembly performances, pupils were picked in alphabetical order, and since there were a great many pupils and my name began with W, I spent the entire term dreading the ordeal of making a public appearance. I suffered from a severe anticipatory sickness. Usually the term ended before my name came up, and then the new term started again at the top of the alphabet. I mounted the platform only once in my whole career, but I suffered tortures every day of the school year, thinking about the awesome—if improbable—event.

By 1908, our household was beginning to thin out. Marion and Clara had married and were having children. In the fall, Albert and Stanley went off to college. That left just Father and Mother and Lillian and me, plus the domestics.

For me the golden time of year was summertime, when we all went for one month to a rented camp on the shore of Great Pond, one of the Belgrade Lakes, in Maine. This Belgrade era began, I think, in 1904, when I was five years old. It was sheer enchantment. We Whites were city people—everything about Belgrade was a new experience: the big fresh-water lake, the pines and spruces and birches, the pasture with its sweetfern and juniper, the farmhouse where we took our meals, the rough camp with its sparsely furnished bedrooms, the backhouse with its can of chloride-of-lime, the boating, the swimming, and the company of other campers along the shore. The month of August was four solid weeks of heaven. Father took exactly one month's vacation, always the month of August. July was a waiting time at 101 Summit Avenue—

sultry summer nights in a hammock on the screened porch, games in the street just before dark, the smell of honeysuckle and of the dust laid by the sprinkling cart. Families stayed together in that innocent era— the young were less apt than they are now to go off on their own or to take a summer job. Resort places always had a liberal supply of young bucks in ice-cream pants and young girls in pretty frocks. America's nomadic life had not begun—the campers and the trailers and the out- board boats and the minicycles lashed to the top.

The journey to Belgrade was by rail and was a miracle of planning and execution. The packing of the trunks began weeks in advance of the target date. Father, who spent thousands of hours commuting between Mount Vernon and New York in a day coach, embraced Pullman travel with a real passion—a once-a-year affair, when he shot his wad and bought overnight accommodations on the Bar Harbor Express for his entire family. It must have run into a lot of money, but Father was no pinchpenny, once he had a dream firmly in mind. The Bar Harbor Ex- press left New York in the evening and got to Belgrade at about nine the next morning. Since it did not stop at Mount Vernon, we all had to pile into New York on a late afternoon train, after a great business about the trunks. Father was everywhere, masterminding everything. Mother looked after the younger children. And when we reached Grand Central, we went in a swarm to Mendel's restaurant for dinner, and Mr. Mendel himself, who also lived on Summit Avenue, would come to our table to greet us and we would all jump to our feet, including Mother, at the excitement of being recognized and singled out in a great public dining hall by the proprietor himself. Then the boarding of the fashionable train, and the green delights of compartments and drawing rooms and uppers and lowers. The fan had three speeds, with little Elwyn at the controls, happy with anticipation of the morrow and the fatigue of today. Mother always slept in her clothes, to be ready for the derailing.

The delicious smells and sounds of Belgrade are still with me after these many years of separation. I spent much of my time in a canoe, exploring bogs and streams, netting turtles. At night in bed, I fell asleep to the distant thump of a single-cylinder engine far out on the lake—a benign passage on dark waters. The little launch Al and Stan had built in Mount Vernon was shipped to Belgrade, and we would all crowd into her, nestling together in the tiny cockpit like barn swallows in their nest, and cross the pond in all kinds of weather. She was named Jessie, after Mother, who couldn't swim and who hated and feared the water. Only through the indulgence of Providence did my family survive those crossings, for the Jessie was almost always in a seriously overloaded condition, gamely dragging her ensign in the wake and right on course for disaster. Father would be in his round white flannel hat, Mother shading herself with a parasol, Lillian in ribbons and bows, Albert and Stanley nursing the brave little engine. Leaving the Gleason shore, we would steer straight for Horse Point a mile away, give the Point a berth of only twelve feet to take advantage of the deep water, then veer in a westerly direction for the long two-mile hitch to Allen Point, passing between Wentworth Shoal and the Ledges, then on to the well-concealed mouth of Belgrade Stream, which led to the Mills. At Bean's store, Father would treat us to a round of Moxie or birch beer, and we could feed the big bass that hung around the wharf and then head back across the lake, sometimes adding to the boat's already intolerable burden a case of Moxie— Father's favorite drink. (There was a new drink out called Coca-Cola, but Father assured us it was a cheap imitation of Moxie and without virtue.)

From P.S. 2, I went on to the Mount Vernon High School. I liked Latin pretty well but never was able to get a modern language and am still monolingual. Some of the girls were beginning to wear silk stockings, and this got my thoughts moving. I didn't care for athletics, being skinny and small, but I liked ice ponds and skating, and on winter afternoons and evenings I would visit a pond (a fifteen-minute ride on a trolley car) and skate with a girl named Mildred Hesse. Her eyes were blue and her ankles were strong. Together we must have covered hundreds of miles, sometimes leaving the pond proper and gliding into the woods on narrow fingers of ice. We didn't talk much, never embraced, we just skated for the ecstasy of skating—a magical glide. After one of these sessions, I would go home and play Liebestraum *on the Autola, bathed in the splendor of perfect love and natural fatigue. This brief interlude on ice, in the days of my youth, had a dreamlike quality, a purity, that has stayed with me all my life; and when nowadays I see a winter sky and feel the wind dropping with the sun and the naked trees against a reddening west, I remember what it was like to be in love before any of love's complexities or realities or disturbances had entered in, to dilute its splendor and challenge its perfection.*

To **ALBERT HUNT WHITE**

101 Summit Ave.
Mt. Vernon, N.Y.
Oct. 21, 1908

Dear Albert,

I am sure it is a long time since your post came, but I have been waiting for something to say. I think it will be about eight or nine years before I go to Cornell. Hope so anyway. Yesterday I received a letter from

Kezzie.[1] She says Elwyn, her little boy, don't like Sunday school. One day Kezzie asked him why he didn't and he answered that he s'posed he'd never been brought up that way.

To-day the big Albany day-boat "New York" was into the pier being repaired when it caught on fire and burned up. The paper does not say whether or not anyone was killed. . . . It isn't a very nice day and I've got a cold so I didn't go to school. Mamma brought me a tennis ball and if I be very careful can I use your racket? I just heard now while I'm writing this letter that Philis Goodwin [a neighbor's child] died. They wouldn't have a doctor and so you see. Pa bought me a new book of music. I know eight pieces out of it already. I am also composing pieces too. There isn't much more to say except we are all well.

Lovingly,
Elwyn

To ALBERT HUNT WHITE

[Mount Vernon, N.Y.]
[1910]

Dear Ally,

Oh! The hill by our house is simply grand for coasting. I got a hitch on a sleigh down to the postoffice and back.

I am taking music lessons of Miss Ihlefeld.

We have certainly enjoyed that book of pieces you gave Lill for Xmas.

I know you're going to laugh when I tell you I got 98% in Physiology exam.

Tell Bun I thank him awfully much for the use of his skis (which I use every day).

Well I'll certainly be glad to see you Easter.

Lovingly, En

To ALBERT HUNT WHITE

Chester Hill
Mount Vernon, N.Y.
April 21, '10

Dear Ally,

Received your letter with much rejoicing. I had to ask ma how to spell rejoicing and I don't know as I have it right yet. Please excuse me if I didn't or rather excuse ma.

---

1. Kezzie Simpson was an English girl who had been employed by the Whites to help care for the infant Elwyn. Later, when she had children of her own, she named her firstborn Elwyn.

Well I got over the comet pretty well although Esther and Winnie were scared out of their skin.[1]

Our garden is coming along pretty durn well

CONSIDERING

The cosmos and sweet peas and nasturtiums and poppies are up and thriving. We just put in more seeds a couple of days ago. We put in enough so that some, at least, will come up. I had to much ink on my pen when I dotted those eyes. As you see and I had to rub them out and put new ones in their place.

This letter is beeing writed—that's pronounced (rītĕd)—before school in the morning so you must excuse my careless writing.

Wallace Hart still keeps on eating night walkers and live flies and cotton and paper and still looks as well as usual.[2] I guess he takes to his pa for an appetite. I didn't have to ask any body how to spell appetite cause it was in my spelling lesson.

Well there haint much more to say so I'll have to close—anyway I have to scoot to that blessed school.

From
Master Elwyn Brooks White

To STANLEY HART WHITE

[Mount Vernon, N.Y.]
[April 1915]
Friday night

Dear Stan,

There have been several topics of local interest lately arisen which I will try in a few words to enumerate:

I received your letter and the box of ground coverings, but you didn't say what to do with the extra tree which I mentioned, from the last lot. Please tell me.[1]

The ground coverings are safe between the two beech trees, and I might add that Matilda's pastry doesn't compare with the texture of my mud. I will do my utmost to make them grow.

The place is looking just grand in fresh green leaves. The grand plan is beginning after my years of labor to eventuate. It's just in time,

---

1. Esther and Winnie were domestics in the Whites' house. The comet was Halley's.
2. Wallace Hart Wyvell was the infant son of White's sister Clara. Clara was a permissive parent, according to White. She let her children eat practically anything they wanted to.

---

1. Stanley had just launched himself as a landscape architect, and had dragooned his young brother into giving the home place a face lift.

too, for the house, as you know, is in the market.[2] Grass appears by the front piazza, two blossoms burst on the magnolia bush, red tulips and little white flowers line the side walk, and yellow jonquils proclaim the official boundary line. But as Kenneth Walters says, "Rome was not made in a day."

My camelian thrives and grows tamer day by day, that is, providing I don't go near him. Also I have other live stock to the amount of one large, grey, ill-tempered hen, and thirteen eggs. They are in the same box, and my hopes are high.

Spinach, parsley, and lettuce are up with the rest of the maple seedlings, violets, and lilies-of-the-valley.

I finished the pen drawing of the camp, and made less of a mess of it than I thought I would, which isn't saying much. However, I like that kind of stuff because it's so easy.

Having sold all the junk in the barn to the junkman, and the two front vases to a private party, I am now in funds to the amount of $9.80. Father raved because you busted his $10 vase stones. I vividly narrated (when he asked me) how you got so mad at them that you mercilessly smashed them to pieces with a pick. Indeed, my boy, considering the load of manure, etc, I think that if you break one more pebble on the place, or spend about fifty cents more, you're going to get in Dutch with the paternal end of the family. Let that suffice.

For the last few days, I have been blamed for every disagreeable thing which has happened in the last few years: me and the hen have. The other morning when I came home from school, Ma would hardly speak to me, because she said I had deliberately locked her and Peter out of the barn when I knew she wanted to clean it. I had merely shut the sliding doors after taking my wheel out, as I have been instructed hundreds of times by Father; and Ma and Peter were mentally and physically incapable of opening them (there's sort of [a] combination to them as you probably know). I did it one handed when I came from school. I thought it was pretty hard on the hen, seeing as she wasn't in the barn at all.

Oh well!

They have adopted a plan for fixing up the ground in back of the High School for an athletic field. Five hundred dollars has been appropriated by some guy, and the fellows are to do the work. You volunteer for 3 hours work some afternoon in the week, and are put in a certain squad. The work for the boys consists of running wheelbarrows,

2. White's father sold the house at 101 Summit Avenue shortly before White left for college, and the family moved to 48 Mersereau Avenue, a much smaller and more modern house.

spading dirt, and lifting[?] heavy bricks; the girls serve lemonade. It will be some job to grade the place, but with fifty fellows working every afternoon, it can probably be accomplished.

Only seventeen days till Brünhilde comes off the eggs.

Faithfully,
Buttercup

P.S.   You said a mouthful when you wrote, "Clear the nursery of old roots and things."

•   *In 1916 Stanley was employed as landscape architect by the Lake Placid Club. White was looking for a summer job and wrote to Stanley, sounding him out. He eventually did find work at the club, caddying on the golf course and working as chainman for a surveyor who was mapping the place.*

To STANLEY HART WHITE

Chester Hill
Mount Vernon, N.Y.
[May 14, 1916]
Saturday

Dear Stan,

I'm not sure what I'm going to do this summer. If I can get a good job, I'd rather work than anything else. If not I will probably spend my vacation with father. He has suggested several places—Muncie Island, Muskoka Lakes, Canada, Moosehead Lake, and 101 Summit.

My Sunday-school teacher is the pastor's assistant at the 1st Baptist Church. Last night I was at a class meeting, and found out he had been a bell hop at the Lake Placid Club two or three summers ago, that he also had been head clerk, and that he knows Mr. Dewey[1] and all the others very well. His name is Clausen. His brothers have worked there too, and I think are going to be there this summer.

I have an idea that it would be very nice if I could get a job as bell hop there during the busy months in the summertime. It's light work and pretty good pay, besides which, being rather novel. Don't you think brass buttons would show me off to good advantage?

Here's where you can help me. Look around and size up the situation on paper for me. Without saying anything to anybody you can write me and tell me about it. I haven't mentioned it to anybody here: in fact I

_____
1. Melvil Dewey, founder of the Lake Placid Club and pioneer of Simplified Spelling.

only just thought of it about an hour ago. Please let me know soon because the sooner I get in my application the better.

Mr. Clausen lent me the 1914 handbook. I think the simplified spelling is the most complicated affair I ever saw. The place must be pretty good if that hasn't queered it. I suppose you will soon be writing home to "get ready, the end iz cuming!" Here is a sentence from the handbook: "Juj the distanse and pich the ball az high az you can consistentli with accurasi."

The place here looks great—some of the bulbs around the well have come up and the east flower borders look fine with their many colored tulips and green stalks. The new grass sprung into existence suddenly and is doing well. Father is greatly pleased with it and said that it was worth all it cost just to make the place look green if only for a couple of weeks. I thought that showed enthusiasm, if not faith. The lilacs and pansies and iris are out, also the floribunda by the well, and in fact everything but the two little aques viteres who always are tardy. Someone asked Mother the other day about the floribunda, and Mother exclaimed with pride: "Why that's our little apple tree!" The pear tree is full of blossoms and promises good fruit next fall.

Al bought a car the other day. It's a 1910 Buick four. The machine itself is funny in itself, but the reason why he bought it, plus the car constitutes the real humor. He said it was "to get in right with the girls." He took it out of the garage last night with the help of George Cottrell, and the thing gave forth such immense clouds of smoke that one man came running up and asked me where the fire was. It stood in the driveway over night, and this morning, Al went out to try to take it back to the garage. I held a little wire while he turned the handle round and round. About every third turn he cussed, and that kept it from getting monotonous. Finally it wheezed a little, and then broke into a loud rattle. This lasted for a little while (I calculated that it was just about long enough to wake up the Eddies) and then it gave a couple of coughs, a muffled sob, and died. However, it is certainly a good investment—it's so different from other cars!

I have four pairs of large, mated Homer pigeons out in the chicken coop. One pair already has a nest and two eggs which will hatch into squabs the 30th of May provided Mac[2] doesn't scare the germ out of them with barking.

Pigeons are much easier and more profitable to keep than chickens. They take up far less time, and they cost far less to bring up. The parent birds feed the squabs which stay in the nest till they are four weeks old

---

2. A collie—White's first dog.

(killing age). The squabs which my birds will raise weigh from ¾ to 1 lb. at 4 weeks and sell at from $1.00 to $1.50 per pair. I tried to pan off an egg laid by another hen, on the pair which have the nest, but they took it and smashed it outside in the fly pen.

Don't forget to write me about Lake Placid, will you?

As before,
En

To STANLEY HART WHITE

118 Archer Avenue[1]
[Mount Vernon, N.Y.]
[May 26, 1916]
Thursday morning

Dear Stan:

I got a letter from Mother telling me that you were going to ask Mr. Dewey if he had a job for me. I'm glad you are thinking about me, but what I had intended you to do (perhaps I didn't make it clear in the letter) was to tell me what work seemed favorable, and then I would make an application for that position myself. This may seem to you to be a finicky notion, but I think I would stand a better chance if it were done this way. It would be more like a business deal, and less like a frame up; more as if I was just looking for a vacation.

I appreciate your trying to help me a lot, but if you have not already spoken to Mr. Dewey, please do not do it.

Last night I had a good time. After supper I went to the library to try to make up some Virgil. Mac tagged along and I let him come in and lie by me in the reading room because I had done it twice before successfully. About quarter to eight a dead silence hung about the whole room. Learned men pored over ponderous volumes; sentimental ladies were engrossed in the latest best seller; white haired old men quietly turned the pages of a magazine; and I was lost in Virgil. From a distance there came a scarcely audible yap-yap of a far off poodle. Mac gave a dive for the window through which the sound came, and let out a succession of his deepest barks, which echoed and re-echoed throughout the whole big room and which ruthlessly tore the learned men, the sentimental ladies, the white-haired old gentlemen, and me from their respective pieces of literature. Words cannot adequately describe it— I leave the rest to you.

Always
$970[2]

1. White was staying with relatives on Archer Avenue for a few days while his parents were away.
2. The signature is in a code that the youngest White had invented.

II

CORNELL AND THE OPEN ROAD

1917–1925

• *In January 1917, White graduated from Mount Vernon High School, where he had done well enough to win two scholarships totaling $1,000—a significant sum in those days, when the tuition at Cornell was $100 a year. He waited until fall to enter the university, meantime occupying himself with a course in bookkeeping and with raising pigeons.*

"When I landed in Ithaca," White writes now, "I was a green boy if ever there was one." He stepped off the train three days earlier than other entering freshmen and took a room downtown in the Ithaca Hotel, where he became so engrossed in the ebb and flow of life on Main Street that he failed to present himself on the campus for registration until a day or two after classes had begun. When he finally got straightened around, however, he settled into college life and began enjoying it all. He tried out for the Cornell Daily Sun *and made it, joined a fraternity (Phi Gamma Delta), and acquired a new name, "Andy," after Cornell's first president, Andrew D. White. It was a nickname commonly bestowed on Cornell students named White and one that Elwyn Brooks was pleased to have, since he had always disliked his given name. Because of his association with the* Sun, *he gradually became a Big Man on Campus, and by the end of his college career, as he puts it, "glowed with a fraudulent self-confidence, alight with love, full of importance."*

The Sun *was, for a college paper, unusually large, prosperous, and influential—a seven-column, eight-page sheet that appeared six days a week. It was free of faculty control and carried AP news that came in over a nightly telephone hookup. White made it to the* Sun *Board as a result of winning the freshman competition, a grueling race that began in the fall and ended in the spring. One of the freshmen competing against him was Allison Danzig, who later made a name for himself as a sports writer on the* New York Times. *According to White, the com-*

petition was supposed to be decided on the basis of space filled in the paper, and a daily record was kept of the inches each competitor amassed. Danzig ended up with the most inches, but White was named winner. "I never knew why," White says. "Danzig was so sore he left Cornell in a huff. I suspect that my victory had something to do with campus or fraternity politics, and I strongly suspect that the late Peter Vischer, who was both a Sun man and a member of Phi Gamma Delta, masterminded it. I did not feel any guilt about it, as I had nothing to do with it, but I sympathized with Danzig just the same and still think he got a raw deal."

White's career on the Sun was interrupted briefly at the beginning of his sophomore year, when he joined the Army and did a stretch in the Student Army Training Corps. But the war ended in November, and by the first of the new year he was back in mufti and back with the Sun. Near the end of his junior year, he was elected editor-in-chief and during the following year wrote most of the editorials. Academic life faded into the background. Although the young editor attended classes and got passing marks, there was nothing of the scholar in him and his education, he says, suffered from his being submerged in printer's ink. Nevertheless, he was tapped for Aleph Samach, the Junior Honorary Society. He became president of his fraternity and was elected to the Senior Honorary Society, Quill and Dagger.

Of all the friendships White made in college, the two that were to prove most solid and lasting were the ones with Howard Cushman, editor of the Widow, and with Gustave Lobrano, whom White got to know at his fraternity house and also at the Sun. For a year, Lobrano ran the column in the Sun called The Berry Patch, to which both White and Cushman contributed—"a chatty, pseudo-literary column" according to White, patterned after the famous newspaper columns in New York: Franklin P. Adams's Conning Tower, Christopher Morley's Bowling Green, and Don Marquis's Sun Dial.

White made three good friends among the faculty—Bristow Adams, Martin Sampson, and William Strunk, Jr. He came to know them intimately through his membership in the Manuscript Club, a group that met informally on Saturday nights at Sampson's house on Buffalo Street. Each member arrived bearing something he had written—a sketch, a poem—which was then deposited, unsigned, in a cardboard box. After a round of shandygaff and some light conversation, Professor Sampson would open the box and read the compositions, a ritual followed by a discussion period. It was at the MS Club that White first encountered Morris Bishop, an alumnus at that time working for an advertising agency in New York (he went back to Cornell to teach in the fall of 1921).

Adams, who was known as "B.A.," was a professor in the College of

*Agriculture. He had liberal arts leanings, however, and liked to enter-
tain students at his home on Fall Creek Drive every Monday night, for
cocoa and talk. His house became a second home for White, a friendly
place where he was always welcome. Among the students he often encountered there was Russell Lord. Sampson taught English literature
courses, and Strunk gave a course called English Usage and Style. It was
Strunk's small textbook,* The Elements of Style, *that White, years later,
revised with such success for the Macmillan Company.*

To JESSIE HART WHITE

[Ithaca, N.Y.]
[December 1918]
Wednesday

Dear Ma,

It is time, so I see, for my mid-week's effusion which I'll start
with the sad news that, through some delusion, you've been led to believe
that our Christmas vacation has entirely escaped from war's grim
depredation. The date of my homecoming, if you remember, is Saturday
morn—21st of December.

This error corrected, I gracefully turn to the topics of interest, and
first you should learn that in spite of the Ithaca weather's contortions
(this topic alone might assume large proportions), I now—this is really
a subject for prose—am entirely rid of my cold in the nose. My health
is restored—I am chipper and brisk, to be brief I'm convinced that it's
taking no risk to give to the world—though you never can tell—the as-
tounding report that I'm perfectly well.

This morning came news of my utter redemption from deepest of
gloom, for I got an exemption from any more of those weekly abortions
which the English Department deals out in large portions—which is
merely to say in a casual way, that I don't have to write so much stuff
every day.

There's been nothing extraordinary happened of late—there'll be
lots more to do when we're able to skate. Just at present the pond is quite
infirm of purpose and it wouldn't be I that would step on its surface.

It's time I was leaving to go to the town; through the tortuous graveyard I'll shamble down, twixt tombs to the right of me, tombs to the left
of me, tombs in front of me, gaping in silence.

I make this last statement with naught of compunction, that, if in
these lines you perceive aught of unction, you must know that this vile
deed (I see you are frowning) is due to an over abundance of Browning.

Thanking you lots for the interest money, I beg to remain

Most lovingly
Sonny

• *In White's senior year a freshman named Morelli defied tradition by refusing to wear the little gray beanie that every first-year student was expected to wear. Public opinion, including editorial opinion in the* Sun, *was strongly against him. He was twice attacked by mobs of students: once he was chained to a tree; another time he was tossed into Beebe Lake. But Morelli had his champions, chief among them the famous George Lincoln Burr, professor of medieval history and hater of anything that smacked of orthodoxy and of lynch law. It would appear from the following letter that Professor Burr had written to the* Sun *defending Morelli; when the* Sun *failed to publish his letter, Burr took his complaint to the Ithaca* Journal News. *Whereupon White, though his term as editor-in-chief had expired, felt called upon to defend the* Sun.

To GEORGE LINCOLN BURR

[Ithaca, N.Y.]
April 24, 1921

Dear Professor Burr:

As a former editor of the Cornell *Sun*, I have a most intense interest in everything which pertains to the *Sun* and to the University.

When I read your communication to the editor of the *Journal News*, my interest was naturally awakened. When I read the part which expressed your hope that the article would prove "less unwelcome" to the *Journal* than to the *Sun*, my interest stretched to the point of investigation, for, after all, it goes pretty deep to hear the journal for which I feel a sense of loyalty accused of editorial bias and a tendency toward the suppression of news. As far as I have been able to learn, your article failed to appear in Saturday's issue because of a misunderstanding and not because of the dereliction of editorial duty on the part of any one connected with the *Sun*.

My ideas on freedom of speech and of the press coincide very closely with yours and they are the ideas and principles which I have tried, during my regime, to pass on to the *Sun*.

Sun editors, Professor Burr, sometimes commit journalistic errors, but *Sun* editors are not journalistic miscreants, and your article, I feel very sure, was not "unwelcome."

Very sincerely yours,
E. B. White

• *In the summers of 1920 and 1921 White worked as a counselor at Camp Otter, near Dorset, Ontario—a boys' camp owned by Professor C. V. P. Young, Cornell's physical education director. Canoe trips were*

*the big thing, and the woods and lakes of Ontario opened White's eyes
to a wilderness far removed from the Belgrade Lakes region of his childhood summers in Maine. He loved the life. Almost fifty years later, he
drew on his memories of Camp Otter in his account of "Camp Kookoos-
koos" in* The Trumpet of the Swan.

*The camp had a strong Cornell flavor: Howard Ortner, varsity bas-
ketball star, was a counselor, along with C. E. (Bugs) Ackerly, feather-
weight wrestling champion at the 1920 Olympics, and Howard Cushman.
Abram T. Kerr, a teacher in the Cornell Medical College, was camp
doctor. Another counselor, not from Cornell, was Robert (Hub) Hubbard. He and White became good friends and in later years became
joint owners of the camp, a partnership that turned out to be ill-fated.*

*During his junior year, White had fallen in love with a Cornell
coed, Alice Burchfield, a Buffalo girl. She was petite and by all accounts
pretty. Their romance, rather cautious and ill-starred, lasted a long
time, and many letters passed between them.*

To **ALICE BURCHFIELD**

Dorset, Ontario
[July 1921]
Sat.—almost Sunday

Dear Alice:

You're right about the mails improving—nothing like practice,
you know. Thanks for the snapshots. Your idea was pretty good but the
execution was rotten.[1] I was prepared for a back view, anyway. But I
thought you could pick out someone not a decided brunette. And how tall
you are growing, Alice! Oh well. . . . I'll try to get my moustaches registered on a film, although that's as tough a job as you and your bobs.
Until last night my moustaches have been spread all over my face—a
six foot growth during the trip. The poor things were all gnarled and
matted when I returned. But my whiskers were perfectly beautiful—
everyone agreed that I looked like Saint Peter, except Brad,[2] who said
I resembled the man who used to take his garbage up. And Art Treman[3]—
who had just arrived—failed to recognize me for the first three minutes.

Our return to camp was phenomenal—and the cookies played a
vital part which is getting ahead of the story. The trip was awfully good
—the best I've taken this year. Hub and I pushed hard the first couple

1. Alice had fudged a picture to show how she looked with bobbed hair.
2. Bradley Fisk, a junior counselor.
3. A visiting fireman—cousin of Robert E. Treman, who was the proprietor of
an Ithaca sporting goods store and the husband of Irene Castle.

of days to get the work done and the ground covered, and then lay on our backs and absorbed sunlight. We swatted bullfrogs whenever we hit a swamp, and kept ourselves supplied with legs. The second afternoon out we left the canoes at Big Trout Lake and walked through to Wolf Lake to look the trail over. Hub will be leading a trip through that way next week and I am scheduled to take one the week after. The trail is a good five miles and pretty bad. We had to go most of the way by the blazes, the trail itself being overgrown. It used to be a lumber road forty years ago when the pines were still standing in this country. At Wolf we came out on a little sand beach that ended in a marsh. There were fresh deer tracks all along the shore and the woods were crisscrossed with runs. It was the grimmest lake I've seen yet. On the morning of the third day I took the coldest pre-breakfast plunge of the summer. (Hub and I are under a silent agreement to go in every morning.) . . . That day one of the kids got sick. He had been a little low when we started, but seemed to revive as we went on. But when he began to develop a temperature and had passed out a couple of times, we began to hit for camp. We ate lunch at a lake that was about eleven miles north of camp, and put the kid to sleep. When he woke up late that afternoon, his eyes looked queer and he was too weak to stand. Hub and I decided that it wasn't safe to keep him out over night. And the only way to get him to camp was to leave the three other kids and the grub and to come through with him and one canoe. The sun had been down fifteen minutes, and the only light was the glow in the west. There were four lakes and three portages between us and camp, and then a two mile walk from the last lake. We got three teaspoonfuls of tea down the kid's throat, took a little snack ourselves, lifted him into the canoe, and beat it. It was a weird journey. We had to make time to get to the last portage while there was still a vestige of light. On the carries, Hub took the boy and I took the canoe. On one of the lakes I stepped too far over toward the log where the trail ended, and went down to my hips, being prevented from going any further by the canoe. We were in too much of a hurry to even laugh— although we did the next day when I was combing the mud from my pants. We made the last portage just in time to get through without missing the trail. The kid had just strength enough to sit on Hub's shoulders without falling off. Luckily he only weighed about 90 pounds. The last two miles were darker than hell's cellar. We left the canoe and took turns with the kid, picking our way along. We reached camp just as Mr. Young was putting the fire out—a record trip of a little over two hours. And this is where you come in. After giving the kid to Doctor Kerr, Hub and I went into the shack to look for something to set us up. We had come all the way from the Boundary of the Reserve that day, and all we had tasted since lunch was a bowl of tea. The kitchen was locked as usual. Ackerly had eaten the last of a community pie that we had cached under the stairs. Cush donated a thimbleful of cheese— but that didn't help much. When life was at lowest ebb, Cush mentioned that a couple of packages had come for me and that he had put 'em in my tent. Good Lord if you knew what those cookies meant in our lives. . . . You can bob your hair and grow a moustache and a couple double chins and I'll still love you—you can have my last shirt, and I've only got two.

It's pretty lucky we brought the boy in when we did. He's been delirious ever since we got back (forty-eight hours). One of my jobs is to sit with him down in the little isolation tent, and listen to him ramble. . . .

Gosh I envy you if you got to New York. I don't know where I'll be headed from here. Guess I'll go wherever there is a job—and from the things I hear there aren't any of them. . . .

Must close before the pen runs dry. Do I hear a sigh of relief? My letters are full of ego, I know, but that's the only thing I can write from here, except philosophical ruminations—which of course would be worse.

> For the cookies, thanks.
> Yours,
> Andy

• *When camp closed in the fall of 1921, White went to New York to find work. Like all job hunters, he looked up his friends—in this case three Cornellians who were journalists in the big city: Frank Sullivan, Henry F. Pringle, and Peter Vischer.*

To ALICE BURCHFIELD

[Mount Vernon, N.Y.]
[September 15, 1921]
Wednesday

Dear Alice:

Gosh, it's good to write again. That flip remark I made in parting about writing "when I got a job" certainly saved me a lot of stationery. But it gives me great pleasure to report that at 3:32 on the afternoon of the sixth day I secured a position. At 4:32 I had a date to jump off Brooklyn bridge, so it came in plenty of time.

Taking it all in all, this has been the gol darndest week I ever put in. When I arrived in the city last Wednesday, I parked my suitcase and

Corona, shaved, and started pounding the pavements before even going out to greet the family. I took lunch with Frank Sullivan, Pete Vischer, and Hank Pringle—who are all on the [New York] Sun—and that afternoon I interviewed the managing editor of the Post and the city editor of the Sun. They both said that they were carrying about six men more than they needed on their staff. Which didn't leave much room for argument. And which didn't increase my appetite for dinner any. Going out to Mount Vernon on the train, the first article I chanced upon in the paper was

ALL SIGNS POINT
TO HARD WINTER

and after reading it grimly through to the end I turned to the Post and read

Who's Who Among
The Unemployed
Where They Came From
And Why They're Here

This was also in a bright and cheerful vein, recounting that there were approximately four hundred thousand persons in the city unable to find a job. I had visions of writing you a letter to say hello along about 1924. It did me a lot of good, though, to turn back to the Sun and see

WHY MEN DISLIKE BOBBED HAIR
Shorn Locks Make Wives More Efficient Than
Their Husbands

Well, anyway, I've been at it for a week, and I now have a speaking acquaintance with every stenographer in lower New York, I call all the elevator boys by their first name, I buy subway tickets in three foot lengths, I feel perfectly at home in all the benches along Park Row, and I haven't given a single managing editor a moment's rest. It's been very gruesome and somber—New York was naturally a bit grey and inhospitable after a day in Ithaca, not to mention an evening at Percy Field —but it was, I suppose, what is technically known as "good experience." You must have often looked in a dictionary and been directed to "see such and such" and when you looked there you were again directed to see such-and-such. And so on. That's what I've been doing the past week—I go to one person and he says hello and shoots me on to another.

The job I took today is with the United Press—an organization similar to and rivalling the Associated Press. I start feeding wires in the

subjects. The only way I could get there would be to just go without notice, and get fired the following Monday. I'm supposed to work twelve hours on Saturdays. I varied it a little yesterday: the boss [Hugh Baillie] sent me flying to Valley Forge with the instructions to phone a story of the [Senator] Knox funeral to the Philadelphia bureau. I got there just in time to see the box being lowered into a hole in the ground while a band of relentless camera men ground noisily away at their machines and a group of seedy looking Senators in high hats stood by, bored by the curious gaze of about a thousand hangers-on who crowded in toward the grave. Afterwards I took dinner with the Philadelphia bureau manager and I saw the lead sentence he had written: "Valley Forge, Oct. 15 (United Press)—With simple ceremony, Philander C. Knox was consigned to the earth from which he sprang here this afternoon."

I have been spending my thirty minute lunch periods looking for jobs this week. I wouldn't mind going without the food if I could have a little luck with the jobs, but it's damn hard to have neither success nor sandwiches at noon. I tried the Sun and the Herald; and this week I am going to concentrate on the Times. It's a weary life, these here first ten years. . . .

I feel bed coming on. I always end my nightly prayer with "And may the alarm clock stick during the night." God hasn't heard me yet.

Yours very truly,
Andy

• *Although White kept pestering city editors for a job, he was unsure of his ability to cope with the pace and complexity of newspaper work in the big city. Most of his attempts to land a job followed a timid routine that was bound to fail: unaccompanied by friendly sponsor or letter of introduction, White would simply walk into a newspaper city room and blurt out his request to the city editor. When he visited the* Times, *however, he had an interview with the publisher himself, Adolph Ochs. The meeting had been arranged—not at White's request—by "Aunt Ruby" Smith, wife of Cornell's much loved dean of engineering and then acting president, Albert W. ("Uncle Pete") Smith. Mrs. Smith thought highly of White, she was acquainted with Ochs, and she took matters into her own hands. White felt he had to keep the date as a matter of courtesy, but before he was ever ushered into Ochs' office he had decided not to ask for a job. His ambivalence about newspaper work— and sheer fright—almost certainly played a part in his decision.*

Luella Adams had been the hostess on those Monday nights at Pro-

fessor Bristow Adams' house during White's years as an undergraduate —she made the cocoa and poured it, a small, good-looking, friendly woman well loved by all B.A.'s students.

To LUELLA ADAMS

[Mount Vernon, N.Y.]
[December 6, 1921]
Sunday

Dear Mrs. Adams:

In reply to yours of September 30th. . . . Never mind, I've read your letter over more than once even if it has taken me two months to get down to answering it. This is the night of nights for the job because I am in the midst of a tremendous blue spell and must have relief in some fashion. I would be out in the garden eating worms only it has been snowing and the worms are moulting down where it's too deep to find 'em.

Well, a lot of things have happened since the last letter. I am now a dirty publicity person[1]: I am the person at whom the city editors shy their paper weights and other missiles. I sneak into their office when the desk-boy isn't looking and hand them stories that they don't like. I don't blame them for not liking them. I am the person who furnishes the material that keeps the janitors employed. If it wasn't for me there would be thousands of janitors out of work in New York City. I write the stories, the city editors brush 'em onto the floor, and the janitors sweep 'em up. So you see I am actually doing a very valuable work—the janitors *must* live. The reason I haven't been fired is because my boss hasn't got round to it yet. It's one of the things he has on his desk calendar, to be done when he finds the time. I am convinced that my boss is a rascal—and I've only seen him three times since I've had the job. Such perception!

Pete [Vischer] is going to the World next week—did you know that? And Hank Pringle has gone to the Globe. That's nothing, I've gone to all of them.

Had a good time last Thursday afternoon when Adolph Ochs and I had a date. Aunt Ruby wrote him, you know, and told him to see me. She was very modest in her letter—after I read a copy of it I wondered how it happened that Adolph hadn't resigned in my favor long ago.

Mr. Ochs has an office on the top floor of the Times Annex on 43 Street. It is well fortified by moats and draw-bridges and things. You have to have a letter from President Harding in order to even be allowed to speak to Mr. Ochs' secretary. I had a letter with Adolph's very signa-

---

1. In November White had left UP and gone to work for a public relations man, George S. Wheat. One of his tasks was to write "human interest" stories for the papers publicizing the efforts of the Municipal Employment Bureau on behalf of the unemployed.

ture, which was, of course, even better. Leaving my office earlier than usual on Thursday afternoon I proceeded uptown, conning the answers to a possible list of questions he might ask. This proved very dangerous, for twice I was almost run down at the crossings because of my deep absorption. While in the elevator on the way to the eleventh floor I arrived at the decision not to ask Mr. Ochs for a job. Dropping my cherished list in my pocket with one last, fond, lingering glance, I stepped out and approached the colored gate keeper with excellent savoir faire. I desired to see Mr. Ochs' secretary relative to an appointment which had been arranged between us. The colored party looked suspiciously at my informal street garb as though comparing it with his tailored uniform, and then ushered me in to the secretary, casting a contemptuous look back over his shoulder as he glided decorously back to his post. The secretary pretended she didn't see me at first—but I recognized that as old stuff, and before we got through I had her admitting that her home was in Trumansburg and that Ithaca was the best town in North America. She was at least 50. From where I sat I could see through a lavishly furnished reception room into the private office of Ochs. I could even see one of Mr. Ochs' ears. Yet I realized I was still a long way from the Presence. The secretary kept casting her eye around to ascertain the moment when it would be most expedient to announce me. Whether she did this to impress me with the necessity for discreet handling[?] of the case or merely because she was still a bit timid herself is hard to say. Finally she arrived at a conclusion, and buzzed for the colored party. He entered, still disgusted at my clothes, and was instructed to announce me. Immediately all his poise vanished, and he tiptoed into the Presence as if he were headed for a graveyard. For a long while he skulked around the reception room and then finally delivered the news in suppressed tones but with a tremendous effort. Then he tiptoed back, tried vainly to regain his dignity, and was instructed by the secretary to show me in. That gave me my chance, and I fooled him by leading the way stoutly myself, leaving him fawning in the rear and very much embarrassed.

The great Ochs shook hands with me. I noticed that his necktie and his left eye were both a little off center. This composed me to a certain extent. I could almost remember what Answer #1 was. Andy White and Adolph, I thought—a little talk. Ha, ha. Then Ochs began to strain visibly trying to place me. Mrs. Smith. That's right. Then silence for a moment. He seemed to be straining again. I heard Broadway's wheeze filtering through the window.

Turning quickly, he said in loud, distinct tones: "Now just what do you want me to do for you, Mr. White?" It was as if I had told a person that my mother had died and that person had said, "What are you going to do about it?" It was a hard question to answer. I felt about to say,

"Not a thing, brother," but I gulped instead and said, "I'm looking for advice." I couldn't very well say, Please Mr. Ochs, I'm only a frail young college boy, lost in the naughty city.

I stated my case. I was dumfounded to learn that he didn't understand what publicity work meant at all. You probably won't believe this, but it's a fact. Mr. Ochs seemed a man wise but not keen. He is interesting but not interested.

His advice was to get connected with a paper in a small town, in order to learn every department of journalism before attempting to get with a metropolitan sheet. He explained to me that I knew nothing about practical paper work, illustrating his point by saying, "You don't know what a stick rule is or how a column is measured, do you?" When I said, Yes, he looked very disappointed in me. I guess I should have said, No.

Anyway, he said good bye and good luck when I left, and also handed me a copy of the History of the New York Times, with the remark, "This may interest you." It sounded like a vendor at the circus handing out a dodger extolling the merits of a patent medicine.

Believe me I had a wonderful time—I had a much better time than Adolph did. On the way out I spurned the colored party, and he looked much taken down.

I don't know why I'm writing all this bunk to you—you don't have to believe it. . . .

Best regards to all—yours,
Andy

• *In January 1922, White joined the American Legion News Service, where his immediate boss was Carl Helm, an Indianapolis reporter turned PR man. The office was in a dingy loft building on West 43rd Street near Eleventh Avenue. At work in the same building, oddly enough, was Harold Ross, then editor of the comic weekly* Judge. *White knew who Ross was—he had first encountered the name "H. Ross" in Franklin P. Adams' "Diary of Our Own Samuel Pepys" in the* Herald Tribune— *but the two did not meet until some years later.*

To ALICE BURCHFIELD

[Mount Vernon, N.Y.]
[February 1922]

Dear Alice:

. . . My job with the News Service of the Legion is very good in many respects. It gives me the opportunity to learn publicity by practising it on a very large scale—the Legion covers an awful lot of ground and the stuff I turn out reaches in the neighborhood of 15,000 papers—and there is the chance, in the spring, of my being handed the boss's job, inasmuch as he contemplates moving west. He doesn't like New York City. The disadvantages are chiefly that publicity work pains me most of the time—when it doesn't bore me. Publicity is new, and, like other new things, it is overpaid and consequently has been exploited. That's particularly the case around New York City. The result is it has a black eye in journalistic circles. Take this for instance—last Tuesday I had a talk with the editor of *Editor and Publisher*, whom I know. He offered me a job, first of all, with his publication—which I didn't take for certain reasons. Then he asked me what I was doing—he thought I was still with the United Press—and when I told him that I was in publicity he gave me a beautiful calling down—"a man of your ideals in a tainted profession." All that kind of stuff. That was at ten minutes to nine—nice pleasant way to start the day having a person like that inform you that you're tainted. I had a mental picture of Mother sniffing me when I came home at night, the way she does butter to see if it is all right. . . .

Sold a story to the N.Y. Sun last week, so I'm not entirely rancid yet. . . .

How's life in Ithaca? Or aren't you in Ithaca? I'm not quite sure. Anyway, how is life? . . .

Andy

• *White's restlessness and his disenchantment with publicity work continued unabated. In February his friend Howard Cushman, then a senior at Cornell, turned up unexpectedly in New York, having flunked out of the university. White was glad to see him, and together they spent several evenings exploring the night spots of Greenwich Village and discussing their common plight. Although temperamentally quite different, the two men had a number of things in common. Each was a former college editor and they shared an interest in belles lettres and in journalism. Both were men of stature recently shrunk, and they were looking for a way to escape their present condition.*

Happily, White had recently bought (for about $400) a Model-T roadster, and the two men decided to "go West" and see America—an adventure that in those days still posed a challenge. Motoring was in its early stages, the great West was still largely uncharted territory, roads were bad, signs few. The early tourist carried a "Blue Book" and followed stripes painted on telephone poles to mark the route.

Although their decision to make the trip was impulsive, the two men planned carefully. White took the Ford, which he had named Hot-

spur, to a blacksmith and got him to rivet two iron brackets for a foot locker to the left running board. "In the back compartment," White wrote at the time, "is a big telescopic suitcase full of shirts and things that will soon be dirty judging by the present rate of consumption, two Coronas, a can of grease, 40 foot of rope, a jack, two pairs of shoe-packs, and a brief case. On the left running board is the Army trunk full of sweaters, notebook paper, stationery, Corona tripod and sixty-two what-nots, including one money belt (Cush's, but he can't wear it because it itches so), one complete lottery set, one hunting knife, eighteen pairs of heavy socks, two journal covers, three issues of the Greenwich Village Quill, and a whetstone. Also on the left running board is a book-box within easy reach of the driver so that he may lean over and bring up the Holy Bible or Putnam's Word Book without slackening the pace. Jammed in in front of the spare on the rear is the bed-roll —our pride and joy—tent, blankets, and ponchos all neatly contained within a buckled duck ground cloth. Hanging one on either side of the windshield are spacious bags—one of 'em is an S bag to catch the eye of Cornellians along the route. These are catch-alls, and incidentally hold such things as percolators, double boilers, grills, pans, and one fiddle. Cush harbors a mouth organ about his person, which he blows into without success I think."

Their strategy was simple: they would drive from one college town to another, scrounging bed and board from fraternity brothers and friends. Between the college towns they would camp out. They would get jobs when necessary, but for the most part would cultivate idleness —and literary ambition. They left Mount Vernon on the afternoon of March 9, and reached Cushman's hometown, East Aurora, New York, nine days later.

To JESSIE AND SAMUEL WHITE

East Aurora, New York
Saturday, March 18, 22.

Dear Family:

A robin awoke me this morning, but he should have held his peace, for he is a false prophet. The weather is beautiful though wintry. Spring dallies somewhere in the offing, like a backward child asked to perform.

We have come about four hundred and fifty miles, I reckon— through Albany, Schenectady, Utica, Cortland, Ithaca, Geneva, and Batavia. We left the Beta house at Union College, Schenectady, just a week ago this morning, and arrived in Ithaca that night in time to drop in at the Manuscript Club meeting. The road along the Mohawk Valley to Utica was rutted seven inches deep with frozen snow. We covered almost as much territory backing up to let other cars through as we did advancing to let ourselves through. Fords are always the goats in that respect—and besides Cush and I are essentially good humored and make it a point never to dispute passage with other cars larger than ours. Utica we found in the midst of Spring. And an hour later, turning south from Chitanango, we toiled up a rise of seven or eight hundred feet and flew through a countryside buried under two inches of new-fallen snow. The hills, all bonneted, were like little Alps; and, toward twilight, everything turned blue—hills, snow, and sky.

We were in Ithaca until Thursday morning. Although we slipped into town darkly and without noise, people seemed to find out quickly that we were there. Scandal travels fast on the Hill. Monday night at B.A.'s house we took up a collection and got 61 cents for singing a very brief song, entitled "Father's a hand-organ man is he." We were also presented with a very small stove. Enclosed is a Berry Patch which we wrote one day as a diversion.

We left in a blizzard, donning Army underwear and sheep-coats for protection. Confining our remarks to a few well-frozen words (Cush's, not mine) we arrived completely paralyzed in Geneva on Thursday noon. After shopping round a bit we lodged in a back room of a commercial hotel and sat down by a simmering radiator and wrote things on Spring. It was a very pleasant room, I thought, for it made you think you were aboard ship. The dresser was heeled over at a pretty good angle, and the wash-stand and bed listed to port also. You could almost feel the sails drawing and hear the swish of the scuppers.

From Geneva to East Aurora the ride was smooth and without wind. This is really a most cheery and exciting time of year—the world holds its breath, anticipating the great event. Farm animals stand motionless against the mows, which at this season are gutted all round the base from being eaten into so much; country schools hold session with doors tight shut and windows; streams, silent beneath a thin crisp coat of ice, throw back the mild grey glare of the sky; cats, hunting in brown fields, are poised in the midst of motion, as though caught by the cold; and sad-eyed loungers at the cross-road inns stand blankly up against the outworn bar, awaiting the provocation to spit. A most cheery time of year. Sheep stand in barnyards, boasting new-born lambs who also stand, musing upon the day when they shall gambol. Our one annoyance was the recurrence of Rotary Club signs. Just when we would be settled into our skins, wrapped in complacency, we would come upon an enormous poster bearing a legend such as this: "Work hard today!—Rotary Club of Rochester," or "Give your best to the work before you.—Rotary Club of Canandaigua." It was most irritating to be continually harassed by these busy clubs, lashing us to an industry which we purposely shunned. I advocate the destruction of these signs, which will not allow an idle man to ride along in peace.

Waiting for me in East Aurora was your fine letter. Also my check from the American Legion. They paid me for two weeks instead of one (sort of bonus idea, I guess). Nice of Mr. Helm, though. In spite of my assiduous attempt to become poor for this occasion, I am acquiring wealth. The Masque [Cornell dramatic society] handed me fifty dollars which they owed me, when I was in Ithaca. What chance has a poor man to become penniless when ruthless debtors beset him on all sides with payments.

I am sorry that there was a certain abruptness about my departure. It was not entirely without reason—the fact was I wished to avoid saying anything about going until I knew for sure that I *was* going. And I didn't know until the day of departure. (No one ever does.) I don't blame Mother for being shocked. I really thought that she would be home for luncheon and that we could eat together.

The trip is not without purpose, although I doubt that I could make it plain to you. It was planned deliberately on my part and hence is no passing fancy or thoughtless escapade. It may be a success, of a sort, and it may be a sort of failure.

But it's going great.

Better just set aside a drawer somewhere and into it throw whatever comes to me in the way of mail, as I don't expect to acquire a forwarding address.

With most affectionate regards,
Andy

P.S. The laundry and suitcase have arrived—which is very nice of you.

• *White, who was in love, occasionally tried to press his suit, but always cautiously and sometimes ambiguously. There were several misunderstandings. Miss Burchfield, although fond of him and attracted to him, was wary of his intentions and at this juncture worked to keep their relationship relaxed. White, in poetical fashion, savored the sadness of being an unsuccessful suitor, all the while knowing that his "unsuccess" was the result of his own irresolution. On his way through Ithaca with Cushman, he attempted to see Alice by waylaying her on a bridge on her way to classes—a tactic that probably appealed to him because it introduced the element of chance. The attempt failed, and they did not meet. A couple of weeks later, during his long stay in East*

Aurora, he went to see Alice in Buffalo when she was home from college for a few days, and he proposed to her—proposed in so guarded a manner as to cause any sensible girl to hesitate. The following letter was written after this encounter.

To ALICE BURCHFIELD

[East Aurora, N.Y.]
[April 1922]
Wednesday Night

Dear Alice:

Having so many things that will be said, I hesitate where to begin. You know, I've been sitting here with my dreadful pipe, trying to get straightened out, and it seems like the realization of an early dream that I should be writing you, because I used to wonder—coming up late from town through the cemetery—whether I'd ever have as a friend the one that grinned so cheerfully in Goldwin Smith.[1] And here we are.

There are a few things that I want to get down on paper—and then after this I promise that all my letters will be in the most orthodox friendly vein. I don't want you to think me a bad loser because I went ahead and said the things that were in my head even after you had explained my role to me. I think you'll forgive me that much, won't you?

One thing I'm not sure you know is that I called you up before ever receiving Mrs. Adams' letter, so that had nothing to do with the case so far as I was concerned. I managed to get myself to a telephone Thursday night, and the letter didn't come until Saturday morning. If that ill-conceived missive did anything, it deterred me rather than urged me to renew our much mangled relationship. Ever since Sunday night, Alice, I've been almost out of my mind because you gave me the impression, by something that you said then, that you thought the only reason I asked you to marry me was because of something in that letter. Good Lord I've been looking forward ever since Senior Week to it—you don't suppose I had to be told by a well meaning friend, do you? I came so near to it that night at Percy Field that I've been wondering ever since how I held my breath so long. In everything I wrote I hoped I was making you understand how I felt; and up until February the only reason I never said anything was because, like a fool, I believed I had no right to, having no money nor immediate prospect of getting any. . . .

It's only now that I realize what a despicable performance I gave in Ithaca by not seeing you. I did intend to see you, and Sunday afternoon someone said you were engaged, and Monday morning I developed a funny looking boil on my nose, and between the two I quit entirely

---

1. The principal building of the Arts College at Cornell.

and spent the rest of the time trying to convince myself I was having a fine time "back at college." Those morbid berries in the Patch testify to the splendid time I was having. Wednesday night I put some salve on the boil, set my alarm for seven o'clock, and the next morning I was up on the bridge sitting in the Ford waiting for you to come across. I was going to ask you to cut your eight o'clock and go out to Forest Home,[2] and from there I was willing to go anyplace.

I suppose you wonder why I don't act like a normal person. I wonder too. Instead, I wait on bridges for people and when they don't come, I pack up and go on to Geneva. I hope I get over it some day.

And now when I look back at the last few days, what I marvel at most is the conceit I must have nourished in supposing that you could like me after the way I had kicked you around. Only a very conceited person could have thought that. I must have thought you were like the Mutt. But actually, Alice, I was so completely absorbed in you that it never occurred to me that you might have other ideas. I guess I had always sort of thought that when anybody felt the way I did, it was bound to be mutual, and when I found out otherwise by what you said, it took it a few minutes to sink in. For that I apologize. I spent all the next morning allowing it to sink in, in spite of opposition from one song sparrow, one warm breeze, one patch of wild flowers, and about a million little frogs.

You once gave me a card that read: "Never explain—your friends don't need it and your enemies won't believe you any way." And here I've waded through three pages of explanation. But it's just that I can't bear to think that you're thinking things that aren't so about me. You see, I thought things that weren't so about you, and look where I got!

Friends believe each other, so I'm happy in being confident that you believe what I have said and that you will continue to believe me. I'm a born idealist, Alice, and when I sometimes seem blue it's because the pictures that I paint in my mind are often disappointing when they appear in the bald cold colors of every day life. One of the pictures that I used to paint in school was of you. I was content to look on from a distance, partly because I was afraid it would vanish if I came any nearer, and partly because at the time I didn't know how to come any nearer. And then one night a year ago, when I was all ready for the disappointment, I discovered that instead of appearing less wonderful you increased in loveliness when I knew you. It wasn't any wonder that last spring was the happiest time I had ever known, because I began to renew what faith I had in ideals! I used to write things about you and not show them to you because such a thing as marriage seemed a thou-

---

2. A hamlet east of Ithaca.

sand years away and I didn't think it was fair [to] say things promiscuously. In New York I guess I failed because instead of being full of ambition I was full of doubt all the time.

This letter is all ego. You must be tremendously disgruntled at my rambling on about myself. But it's about you too, which vindicates me. Besides, from now on, as I said, my notes will pass any censor, and I'll write of the weather and similar gol darn things. And everything I write about you will be stuck all proper in some dusty journal, unless you want 'em for light Sunday afternoon reading.

It's time I began getting some sort of conclusion under way—conclusion to this letter I mean. Please keep the pin just as a pledge of my good faith and of my friendship. I'm going to get a lot of fun out of being a friend of yours. Don't forget what you promised me—I mean about calling me up when you need someone to bail you out or to cheer you up by bringing you a lollypop. And remember, too, what you said about writing. I'm going to write as often as I can, but maybe you can figure out why it won't be as often as ink allows.

I'm wishing you lots of luck this spring with Bianca and chemistry and whatever else you take it into your head to get interested in. Once in a while take a lazy look down the valley when the train is whistling and remember this: that there are some things in the world that I never change my mind about, and one of 'em's you.

Sincerely,
Andy

P.S. Hope you wear the blue suit when you invite me to tea. I can take my tea with or without sugar.

To PETER VISCHER

159 Park Place
East Aurora, N.Y.
[April 1922]

Dear Pete:

A letter from Mother mentioned that you phoned some time ago. In the hope that you owe me money I hasten to reply. Actually, it's been on my mind to write for quite a while, for no other reason than that we used to play golf together.

Cush and I start Monday in a Ford. We've been hanging round Buffalo quite a while, transacting business and buying double boilers. Cush busted—I guess you heard. I wrenched myself from the ill-smelling press agenting job, somewhat to the dismay of my boss, who offered me $50 to stay and said it would be $75 in June if I continued to write good stuff. We stopped in at Ithaca for a week coming up—the town was still murmuring something about your having been there shortly before to get a Farmers' Week story or something. Pretty low, boy—we used to make freshman competitors write about the Ag hens and the calving rate.

But I certainly hand it to you, selling the World on a story of up-state rural pleasures, with round trip ticket and everything. You and Herb[1] must be hitting it off.

If you're so damn influential, you might show him—or whoever handles features—the enclosed travelogues as samples of what the Cushman-White syndicate are going to turn out. Let me explain:

We happened to hit on the idea of parodying travel lingo. At first we just sent a couple to the Berry Patch for the fun of doing it. Then we showed samples to John D. Wells, managing editor and columnist of the Buffalo Times. He's a brisk, snappy individual that never cracks a smile. He read 'em carefully, told us he thought they were good, said he would use 'em as a daily feature at a dollar a throw, and suggested we attempt to syndicate them to ten or a dozen papers so that we could afford to write them at that price. You now find us attempting.

Mostly rejection slips so far (from a somewhat hit-and-miss list of eastern dailies), but we are pleased to offer the World the privilege of contributing, confident that nothing more brilliant will ever be offered to their columns. The editors will die laughing. All that is necessary is to sign up for our stuff, and they will never know another unhappy moment.

We supply copy, six travelogues at a time, one dollar each, to be released daily except Sunday (one a day) beginning April 24, and to run for three or four months. As you observe two fictitious characters are created, who will travel completely round the world, starting from New York, and visiting such interesting places as Marion, O., Death Valley, San Moritz, the Hinterland, Yonkers, Hollywood, Korea, Punxatawney, Mauch Chunk, Filbert Islands, and the rubber fields of Akron. There will be hot stuff about the coolies and cold dope about China; there will be just enough psychology to make it suitable for women readers, and positively no mention of William Jennings Bryan.

You can tell Herbert that Cush was the best editor the Widow ever had and that everyone thinks I'm funny. Autographed photos of the authors supplied free of charge.

Do what you think best, and above all things don't get thrown from the World on our account. But let us know as soon as possible, will ya? Hell, we don't want to starve along the roadside. A letter addressed here will be forwarded. . . .

Wish I could tell you more about the real purpose of the trip, Pete, and about the good time that we've had thus far. Cush and I are both

---

1. Herbert Bayard Swope, editor of the New York *World*, where Vischer was a reporter.

bent on the profession of writing, and just now we are interested in seeing all sorts of people and all kinds of country, so that we will at least know where to begin. It sounds pompous, I guess, to talk abstractly of "background" and "experience" and "travel—the great educator" and all that sort of stuff—but we are both convinced that now, if ever, is the time to bum about a bit, so here we go, jogging leisurely from one free meal to the next, taking a general westerly direction, and bothered neither with road maps nor collapsible buckets, writing a lot, selling a little maybe, and chopping proverbial wood to eke out a supper. Wish you could see the Ford. . . . We're equipped for any exigency (except making a respectable living), and can appear properly dressed for any sort of party, from an antelope hunt to a Charity Ball. I don't know when we'll be back, or how far we'll get. There is, of course, the chance that we might like the West, or China, well enough to linger.

Cush sends his best.

Andy

To JESSIE HART WHITE

Beta Theta Pi house
Ohio State University
Columbus, Ohio
26 April 1922

Dearest Mum:

I am hoping this will arrive on April 27 to greet you on your 42nd wedding anniversary, but I am a little late in starting it as usual. Your letter reached me at Mansfield, O. a couple of days ago where it was forwarded from East Aurora. I guess I told you in one of my previous letters that the way to reach me by mail is via 159 Park Place, East Aurora. Mr. Cushman does the forwarding.

> So you've been gay for forty years
>   For forty years and two—
> Been jolly all through smiles and tears
> So you've been gay for forty years:
> A thing one very seldom hears.
>   I send my love to you.
> So you've been gay for forty years
>   For forty years and two.

I hardly think I have written you since we left East Aurora a week ago Monday in the afternoon. We remained over Easter at the Cushmans' and had Easter Sunday dinner at the Roycroft. The next day we left, clanking merrily out of town with our bed upon our back as goes the turtle. . . .

Spring has arrived in Ohio. This is a flat state where red pigs graze in bright green fields and where farms are neat and prosperous—not like New York farms. We roll along through dozens of villages and cities whose names we never heard. They are typical of the middle west. The oldest inhabitant is generally standing somewhere pulling a long white beard, the smithy door is generally open and the sound of the anvil to be heard, the village flapper is generally flapping up and down along Main Street in front of a group of jobless youths who help hold the drug store up, and somewhere there is always a housewife sweeping off a porch or carrying a spadeful of manure to the garden. Toward evening the country scenes become idyllic—the sort of thing you have seen in the moving pictures and never quite believed in. Sheep come drifting up long green lawns where poplars throw interminable shadows, come drifting up and stand like statues beneath white plum blossoms, while far down the lane and off in the fields a little Ford tractor moves like a snail across the furrows. Lilacs are in full bloom and the lavender ironwood blossoms are coloring all the roads.

I've given up cigarettes until I get to California. Isn't that a good idea? Cush thinks it's great. I also am looking forward soon to giving up clean shirts. They're worse than cigarettes. I'm on my last one now.

The Ford is a tremendous expense. Repairs have cost us 75 cents since we left New York—50 cents for a busted radiator and 25 cents for a fan belt. Pretty heavy going.

New York is the state for roads. Here there are pikes, which are cement on one side and dirt on the other. When you meet another car if you are on the cement side all is well, and when you are on the dirt side you steer to one side, sink down indefinitely, and then get out and lift the car back onto the road again. That's why Fords can go places where heavier cars have difficulty. Whenever your Ford shows signs of weakening, you can lift it back where it belongs.

Tell Father he ought to read Benchley's *Of All Things* if he wants a good time. I read it the other day in Mansfield. It's about as funny as anything there is on the market today with the exception, of course, of the Cushman-White travelogues which are simply killing.

We'll be leaving for Kentucky on Friday morning. This place is so beautiful we want to stay for a day or so to become acquainted with it.

Congratulations again on your anniversary. Have a good time at Atlantic City honeymooning. Love to Father—tell him I received his letter and thank you. I mailed the slip to the Trust Company the other day in Mansfield.

Yours,
Andy

To JESSIE HART WHITE

Highland Springs Free Camping Ground
Campers' Supplies. Fresh Butter Eggs
and Milk. Refreshments Routing and
Cave Information Free.
Western Kentucky—Monday May 8 [1922]

Dear Mother:

We are now within 950 miles of St. Petersburg, Florida. Every sign along the road gives us that information, due probably to an active Chamber of Commerce in the above city. "Whereabouts are you-all goin'?" ask various persons whom we meet along the way. "West," we answer. "Then what are you-all doin' down round here?" "Oh, we just dropped down," we answer in a kindly voice.

I have no doubt that the last place from which I wrote was Columbus, Ohio. Since that time we have journeyed by devious means down into Kentucky, West Virginia, back into Kentucky, back into Ohio, back into Kentucky, and here we are, three miles west of Cave City and all primed to see one of the seven wonders of the world. This part of Kentucky is full of caves—no home is complete without one.

About the first thing we did out of Columbus was try and join Spark's Circus, which was playing Circleville, O. It was a bright, warm noon when we encountered Circleville, and one of the first things we saw was a big steam calliope. The big top and painted wagons were visible down a side street—so we parked, dismounted, and drew near afoot. One side show was open to take care of the early afternoon visitants that filtered in, and the red-necked barker was cajoling patrons, garnered from the ring of idlers who gazed in sheepish bewilderment at the picture of Joe, the man eating gorilla, at the picture of Toto, the seven-year old tot who fondles boa-constrictors, at the picture of Gunder, the rhinoceros straight from the heart of Africa—wondering whether the moans that emanated at regular intervals from within the show were made by Joe, Toto, or Gunder, or by a small colored boy pulling a rasp-string. "There he is," sobbed the barker, pointing to the incomparable Joe on the billboard. "That's Joe—that's the gorilla that makes men quail with terror. He's in there. They're all in there; and they're all alyuve." The fact that the parties in question were alive was too much for the impressionable man, and he broke down. "It's only a dime, and they're all alyuve." Whether because of the man's tears or because of the moans from within, two or three more individuals would weaken and pass inside, followed by the envious gaze of the others.

Mr. Spark felt that we would be a redundancy in his troupe, unfavorably impressed as he was with Cush's inability to turn handsprings,

—so we passed on to see what remained of Circleville. "A woman sawed in half—bring your own saw" read Mr. Spark's signs along Main Street, and the populace clearly had nothing else on its mind that day. I have read of the middle west and heard it talked of, but I first met it in Circleville. It is a town that enjoys a mild industrial prosperity of a sort, and it is near enough what we call civilization (Columbus) to know that its Main Street should be nicely paved and its stores glass fronted. It does all these things and smacks its lips with civic pride. . . .

We kept going south, and that afternoon began to run across turtle-doves—always in pairs. We slept that night on a little hill in the Ohio Valley, east of Portsmouth.

Eastern Kentucky has queer stubby hills which rise quite abruptly from the Ohio River. A week ago today we recrossed the Ohio at Ashland, taking the indolent ferry boat "City of Ashland," which is without shape and without ambition, and which is gently propelled—at the expense of an enormous quantity of native coal—by a stern-wheel made from farm-planks. Queer how rivers are like the people along their banks—or vice-versa. There you have the well-groomed Hudson, hustling business-like and blue about its business, flanked by docks and store-houses and factories and estates, and bearing on its shoulders men-of-war and punctual ferries and doughty tugs and splendid excursion steamers with their shiny decks and well-oiled, throbbing engines. Here, where the populace drawls and sits leisurely on front-porches, we have the muddy Ohio, creeping indolently down a smiling valley, blending its pretty brown with the greens of the field, and floating little old flat boats sculled by calm country men. Cush and I watched a gala craft, the Homer Smith, come drifting down from Pittsburgh, announcing himself by the charmed calliope—come drifting down and swing informally in to the mud bank, scornful of wharves, and stand to, held by an ancient mud hook, and taking passengers over a long plank from shore.

From Portsmouth to Maysville was along a dirt road on the Ohio side of the river. We went as far as we could, in and out of holes the like of which you never have seen, and finally ended in a creek bed at eight o'clock, without lights, without food, and without much conception of where we were. So we slept. The next morning a farmer said he had heard us and thought we were revenue officers come to investigate the family whose children had been coming to school drunk from moonshine.

It took us in all about three hours and a half to go from where we had slept to Maysville—a distance of eighteen miles. What few rattles were still latent in Hotspur developed rapidly, and he now clatters along with the orchestration of a mature car. We made him clatter up the mile-long hill in Maysville, from which point we turned and had a wonderful view of the Ohio and the town below, and of the stubby hills of Kentucky, and of the brown and green fields across the river, white in splotches with the blossoms of locust trees. We were not to see the Ohio again until Louisville.

. . . The Blue Grass is hard to describe. The region must be very like parts of England. There are rolling downs where sheep, duroc pigs, and horses and cows graze. The grass is a luxurious blueish-green, and the heavy oaks and beeches give the landscape a park-like effect. At first we couldn't figure out what made the region so different from anything we had ever seen, and finally we realized that it was because of the complete absence of weeds, underbrush, and indiscriminate foliage. It is as if there were a great gardener stalking through with a magic trowel, pruning and hoeing. The homes are led up to by long arbors, and the houses themselves are usually set way back from the road. The stables are more elaborate and beautiful than the dwellings—great brick buildings (in the case of breeders who have a racing string) covered with vines and surrounded by blossoming trees. . . .

It rained as we drew into Lexington (we passed up the sights of Paris) so we took a room at the Lafayette and led Hotspur to a fashionable garage. It was the first time the little fellow had been among other cars in so long that he was much embarrassed, Cush says, and little beads of oil stood out all over him.

The races were on in Lexington. We soon discovered that. The lobby of the hotel was full of horsey men, in stripes and checks, who looked as though they knew the record of every filly of any account back to 1880. And full of racy women—wives of the horsey men. And full of small colored bell-hops in purple uniforms and enormous gold buttons, going about carrying strawberry cocktails to the guests.

In the morning we acquired a Chicago racing form for ten cents. "I think I'll back Sweet Cookie," sighed Cush, "she ought to roll in." I noticed that one race was scheduled for virgins, and I was for picking out a likely looking one and staking our all. As a matter of fact we were much chagrined at our inability to decipher the pages of statistics. I read the leading editorial and an advertisement entitled "Get yourself behind a veteran horseman," and made no appreciable gain. The former consisted of a list of names, tabulated, of which I understood nothing but the weather report. The latter informed you that one George Black would let you in on something neat, for fifty dollars. . . .

[Cush] spent the whole morning poring over asterisks and past performances, and even read the advice of sporting writers in the morning papers. "A little knowledge is a dangerous thing," said I, quoting from my good Pope. "I shall maintain my chaste ignorance, and pick some paradoxical mare such as Hopeless." . . . Two o'clock found us, flushed with the ecstasy of being near a Kentucky course, parting with a hard earned two dollars to get inside the gate. "Show me whar ah do mah bookin'," I demanded of Cushman in my best accent.

Refreshed by two hamburgers we paraded up and down in front of the mutuel machines, and read the selections for the first race. I saw Cush stealthily pull a memorandum from his pocket and consult it privately. "They all give it to John F. Turner, with Rapid Stride to place," he mused. "Nonsense," I replied, glancing at the list. I was strangely attracted by the very first name (there were eight in all). It was "Auntie May." There was something conservative about it—something quieting amidst the fury of the gambling atmosphere. "Auntie May is the animal," I breathed, much to Cushman's disgust, who was averse to my throwing away my money on a creature that not one sporting writer had so much as mentioned and that didn't figure in the dope. "All you have to do is look at the machine," he cautioned. There were the figures being rung up as the betting progressed—and for every hundred on John F. Turner there were only about fifteen on Auntie May. All the others were in between.

I approached my booking stall, clutching another two dollars tightly and wondering whether I should call out "One on Auntie May," or "One on Number 1312," which was the corresponding mutuel number. Fear seized my heart that when I should finally be face to face with my clerk my voice would waver. No such thing occurred. I rose well to the crisis. "One on Auntie May," I called vigorously, as though she were my closest relative. The bookie garnered in my two dollars and handed me a small green ticket marked 1312-straight—which meant that I was signifying my belief that the good animal was coming in none other than first. By this time I was so suffused with charitable emotions and a sudden love for this mare that I only now dimly remember placing the ticket in an inside pocket. Cush was visible in the next aisle, buying a ticket on John F. Turner.

An Eskimo pie apiece settled our hamburger, and we reached the grandstand fit and hearty. Cush had bought a program. Betting was quickening in the stalls below and the crowds were pressing out and up into the seats beside us. . . . "Let me see the program," I demanded.

The race was scheduled, I observed, for "maidens three years old and upward." By carefully tracing down the page I found that Auntie May's number was 8. This was a needless effort, for when a moment later I looked up and gazed down the track I knew her immediately. The race was, as I have said, for maidens three years old and upward. Auntie May looked upward of thirty-five. Probably the first thing I noticed about her was her color. The other maidens were all of uniform hue—that is, each had her own uniform shade. There were sleek bays and sleek browns and one beautiful black. Not so Auntie May. She was a sort of brindle— as though she had once been brown until the moths got in. I had never before seen quite such a marking on any animal—not even on a bird. Cush was impolite enough to laugh outright.

Probably the next thing I noticed about Auntie May was her composure. The other maidens were all life, all zest. They were frisking and sidling in the most maidenly fashion. One even kicked up her heels in an attempt to unseat her jockey, and had to be calmed by the groom on the lead-pony. You could tell by looking at them that the race had been on their minds all night and that they had been chafing in their stalls. You could tell by looking at them that the happiest moment in their lives would be when they should go to the barrier. You could tell by looking at them that each one nursed the spirit of competition that goes with Kentucky horseflesh. . . .

Not so Auntie May. She not only had no personal enthusiasm for the race, but she had actually lost interest in life. The sight of the eager stands failed to thrill her; the feel of the turf under hoof failed to send a gladdening beat to her heart. She never once even so much as glanced at the other seven maidens. They all wore blinkers on their eyes to keep their high-strung nerves from being shattered at a passing object. All but Auntie May, who needed no eyeshade.

I was sobbing quietly in my seat in the stands, beating gently upon my breast. Suddenly the starter cried "Come On," the barrier leapt up, and we were aware that the action had begun.

There never was such a change in any animal. Folks at home, I wish you could have seen my Auntie May! Thirty-five years of maidenly experience had taught her that prancing and showing enthusiasm in front of the stands before starting time required just so many vitamines, and that the real dope was to save 'em for the performance. . . . I should have said before that from the first I had noticed that Auntie May sported a wonderful looking pair of legs. They were legs that any maiden could be proud of. And the upshot of it all was that when the starter yelled "Come On" and the barrier flew up, my good animal suddenly uncoiled like a watch spring, and with a super-maidenly leap cast herself clear over the heads of the enthusiastic frisking competitors, and landed about a quarter of a mile down the track, with both pairs of legs beating indomitable time.

And it is to the credit of the other seven maidens that they stuck it out and ran the whole mile to the finish line. And it is to my own credit that I deported myself as a gentleman should deport himself when his pony comes home several lengths ahead of the nearest rival. I merely said quietly, "Good animal, Good May," and again, "Good animal, excellent relative," and went downstairs to present my little green ticket. And haply the odds had been so awful against this motley maiden that they handed me $24.60—twenty-four dollars and sixty cents, good mother, in the currency of our nation. And there was much moaning in the ranks of the backers of John F. Turner, as well there might be, for he failed even to place.

And that is what is known as "upsetting the dope" or "a bad day for the followers of form." And I would write you many more things about nights in the Blue Grass, with the heavy breathing of asthmatic cows next our tent, and about the high bridge across the Kentucky River south of Willmore, and about the remarkable beauty of the women of Louisville, and about the road from West Point to Cave City, and about Elizabethtown, and about the hospitality of the people of the state, and about little fires at dusk—but it is now seven of the clock in the morning, and Cush will be awakening in about ten minutes and we will be wanting our breakfast, which is lying before me on the ground, in its natural state, and which I must set about preparing. Haven't heard from you in a long while, but we haven't heard from anyone in a long while, not hitting the right post-offices.

Andy

• *The two young horse players, flushed with their success in Lexington, tried again at Churchill Downs, where they were a complete flop. White, in the hope of recouping their losses at the track, wrote a sonnet to the winning horse, Morvich, right after the race, and sold it the same evening to the Louisville* Herald *(after being turned down by the* Courier*). The poem appeared the next morning in a two-column box on the front page, under the byline "Elwyn Brooks White." The sonnet began, "Bold son of Runnymede . . ." It is conceivable that this is the only time in the history of horse racing that a gambler managed to recoup his losses by selling a sonnet.*

To ALICE BURCHFIELD

Chicago, Ill.
[May 1922]
Monday night

Dear Alice:

I waited over the week-end before writing hoping I'd hear from you, but no letter came today, so I've decided to write anyway.

. . . From Cave City we went back up the Dixie Highway toward Louisville. We landed the night before the Kentucky Derby, on the outskirts of the city in the dark. Picking out a nice soft spot near the road we went comfortably to sleep and arose the next morning to find ourselves in the municipal dumping grounds. That's the joy of picking beds in the dark. Another time we awoke and found we had come darn close to sleeping on the lawn of the Governor of Kentucky, near Frankfort.

The Derby was a sight worth going all the distance for. I picked up a sudden spasm of hayfever at the vital moment, but saw a good deal notwithstanding. It's Kentucky's big day. Everyone gets all dolled up and excited in the morning, and drunk at night. After a vigorous afternoon of betting on various animals I came out only 60 cents to the good. Cush lost six dollars. We rode dejectedly in to Childs on a dumpy street car, and I told Cush that I felt a sonnet coming on—indited to Morvich, the winning horse. He worked strenuously to dissuade me, but I wrote it on a paper napkin while he was busy with chicken giblets, and then afterward we went round and got Hotspur and drove to a street light in front of the public library where I pulled out my loyal Corona and typed it off. "Now I shall sell it," I cried, while Cush sat on the curbing and tried to act as though he didn't know me. "Do you do this for glory or for money?" the editor of the Louisville Herald wanted to know when I presented the gem. "I do it for money," I replied, coming quickly to the point. So I took the five dollars and Cush celebrated with glass after glass of Coca Cola, drowning his guilt thus. We left town that night (sleeping next to a cow that suffered from some chronic disorder that caused her to cry all night) and the next morning bought a Herald in Shelbyville and found the sonnet jumping at us from the front page, next to the news story of the big race. My name was in such large type I could hardly eat my fried egg. I now claim the distinction of being the only person that ever wrote a sonnet to a race horse and got away with it.

. . . Today is rainy. Chicago in the rain is a forlorn prospect. Hope the post office has something to offer—and one thing in particular.

Yours,
Andy

• *Enclosed with the following letter was a clipping from the Minneapolis* Journal *listing E. B. White as "Last Week's Winner" of the limerick contest the paper was running at the time. With the $25 prize for*

the best last line in their pockets, the wayfarers were able to shake the
dust of Minneapolis from their feet.

To JESSIE AND SAMUEL WHITE

Billings, Montana
25 June 1922

Dear Folks:

Little Falls, Brainerd, Walker, Akeley, Park Rapids, Detroit, Moor-
head, Fargo, Mapleton, Buffalo, Tower City, Oriska, Valley City, Sanborn,
Jamestown, Cleveland, Medina, Crystal Springs, Tappen, Dawson, Steele,
Driscoll, Sterling, McKenzie, Mencken, Bismarck, Mandan, New Salem,
Glen Ullin, Hebron, Almont, Richardton, Taylor, Gladstone, Dickinson,
South Heart, Bofield, Fryburg, Medora, Sentinel Butte, Beach, Yates,
Wibaux, Glendive, Fallon, Terry, Miles City, Rosebud, Forsyth—these
will fill out your map for you. By these have I come circuitously and
stoutly to Billings.

South of Hardin, Montana
27 June 1922

I am now seated in the shade of one of Montana's seven trees. When
you are in Montana you can say, "You know that tree near Helena . . ."
Trees and water scarcely exist in this state, and when you do find them
they are always together. A thin line of foliage running between the
hills forty miles in the distance means that there is a creek there. It is
quite likely dried up. But that is not all I could say about Montana.

From St. Cloud—which was our camp at last writing—we journeyed
north through the fertile river-bottom country of Minnesota. Gradually
the open fields of grain were left behind and lakes with wooded shores
began to appear. Brainerd is a county seat, where fishing tackle and
canvas buckets are on sale to north-bound tourists. We picked up some
grub there, and some flour bags for containers. That afternoon we
washed dirt from ourselves and our clothes in Ten Mile Lake and slept
there in a little pine grove. Slipping on a pine needle, I tumbled on my
right elbow the next day, and dislocated it. The mayor of Walker, who
is also the president of the Board of Education and the town physician,
gave me a good manly sniff of ether, and when I again awakened to the
world some four hours later, I found the elbow neatly done up in a
plaster cast. The next morning Cush and I drove over to a T.B. sanitorium
on Leech Lake and I had an X-ray taken of the wayward member to see
what the Doctor had been doing in my temporary absence. The fellow
there was a sort of photographic bug, and he took a wonderful stereo-
scopic picture. It showed the bones to be uninjured and properly set. The

principal damage of course was to the ligaments, muscles, soft tissues, and other items constituting an arm. The Doctor, who incidentally was a very capable sort of person—having taken care of the whole town of Walker for 29 years single handed—advised me against too much idleness, so I ripped the plaster cast off the following morning at 4 o'clock, and now after twelve days am pleased to report that all that remains of this dark and terrible chapter in my life is an empty bottle of Sloan's liniment—which we still keep with us when we sleep because the smell keeps mosquitoes away.

Walker is on Leech Lake. It is a decadent lumber town of a thousand souls. The two big days of the year are the days when the Indians from a nearby reservation get paid off by the Government. For a week prior to these days the shop windows of Walker are dressed in Christmas splendor. We had a lot of fun in Walker, lingering there over the weekend to clear up the Doctor's bill and allow my arm to get under way. Saturday morning Uncle Tom's Cabin came to town—a genuine little road company, heralded by a genuinely superlative handbill depicting the ferocity of the bloodhounds and the departure of the soul of little Eva. It was a big day for Walker. The two railroad cars which carried the troupe were shunted off onto the freight siding across from the depot at an early hour; long before the town—with the exception of the male population age 8 through 14—was bestirred. The cars had seen better days. Even in the midst of early morning, long before the first Siberian bloodhound had commenced to bark—even before the fat cook had yawned and rolled over, preparatory to starting breakfast—one could see that they were the merest shadow of their former selves. . . . Despite the playbill's adequate announcement that the company would arrive "in their own private palace cars" there was a lack of lustre somewhere. One doubted not the lineage of these cars but their fortune.

By nine o'clock things were getting under way for the noon parade. The small, fat ponies were grazing on the little grass plot next to the siding, rolling their pink, vicious eyes at the town boys who edged in to take a stealthy pat. The bloodhounds were leashed to the side of the car, napping and growling by turns. They were the sort of mongrel mastiffs which you see in any Italian quarter, evidently picked up by the astute manager for a petty farthing. Through the dirty windows of the car, little Eva's mother was discernible. She was washing her hair. Colored gentlemen practised laconically on cornets and trombones, sounding the meaningless, isolated notes dear to the hearts of horn-blowers. The success of one small town boy in setting off a string of fire-crackers under the nose of one of the bloodhounds marked a little crisis in the hot, tense morning. By ten o'clock the flunkeys were fussing with harness and with bolts and coupling pins and traces. Things fitted together in the easy, exact way which denotes long weeks of packing and unpacking, buttoning and unbuttoning. There was no shouting of orders. You felt that things would come naturally and normally to a head at twelve o'clock. The manager appeared in a grey suit. He unleashed the hounds personally, and the Siberian animals were frantic with joy. They recognized real blood when they saw it. Fifteen town boys stood proudly in line and were fitted with faded red jackets to augment the parade.

By five minutes of twelve the horn-notes of the negro band had increased almost to the fervor of a symphony. The miniature cabin had been assembled and was lined up behind a span of mules. The brown pony had been put into the tiny red buggy with gold trimmings, and all eyes were turned ready for the advent of little Eva. She came unabashed before the worshipful gaze of a hundred urchins—pink-befrocked and thirteen. What a sight to see her climb daintily and demurely into her tiny buggy and raise her pink parasol above the golden curls that had been so carefully tied with pink ribbon! What a growling the bloodhounds set up! What a stamping of ponies' hoofs and beating of negro drums! What a race for the curb on the part of Walkerites! Where was Uncle Tom? No one knew. I had a suspicion he was the second cornetist from the right, but it was a thing I said nothing about. What a flutter of banners!—And what am I writing all this for . . .

Monday we made fifteen dollars. Cush had been talking with the editor of the Cass County Pioneer—a typical country weekly. The editor put him next to some dope—so the editor said. Anyway, it worked. A new hotel had recently been erected on Leech Lake. Cush went to the manager and told him that he (Cush) would supply the room cards, containing rules and regulations, free of charge if the manager would let him solicit small ads for the margins. So we drew up a dummy, and out of about thirty business men in Walker (you ought to see a Walker business man) we sold fifteen. That netted $26.50 and the printing bill was $11.00. The whole thing consumed less than twenty-four hours, and we shook the dust of Walker Tuesday noon.

The region around Walker used to be wonderful lumber country. It has now all been either lumbered or burnt over—a thing, however, which has not marred its beauty but simply given it a new kind of beauty. South of Walker there used to be a town called Lothrop, which was a lively gambling center, full of the business of lumbering and of lumbermen. Today there is not a stick left of the town. Natural dirt roads crisscross the state. They are smooth and beautiful. Along one of these we went, through Akeley and Detroit—which people in Minnesota really call

"De-trō-it." Every curve in the road brought forth a new lake to view, shining blue and peaceful and unmolested. It was a day of very white clouds, and very blue skies, and very dark green spruces behind the lighter hardwoods. Wild roses lined the road timidly all of the way.

It was Tuesday noon, hot and bright, when we left Walker; and it was Saturday noon, hotter and brighter, when we dismounted and stretched before the post office in Billings. Eight or nine hundred miles. To attempt to tell you about it would be like attempting to tell you how a piece of music sounds. But I wish you could have been with us. If you have never rushed along through eastern North Dakota, mile after mile, with never a turn, with never a landmark in all the great sea of grain— rushed along on a two track road that comes from the sky thirty miles behind and leads to the sky thirty miles ahead—why then you ought to drop your task and do it.

There are so many things about the west which you learn and un-learn. Your popular conception of a national highway would be blasted were you to ride, as we rode, into the capital of North Dakota on a road which had grass in the center just as the roads of North Belgrade used to. With the exception of city streets, we have not been on a single artificial road since the marvelous concrete highway from Minneapolis to St. Cloud. All the roads here are "natural." Of course they are what is called "improved," but they are nothing more nor less than the old trunks worn down with the passing of centuries of hoofs and wheels.

Just as we got to Bismarck, the capital, Hotspur coughed, wheezed, and died of malnutrition. It was late at night and we had been running since early morning, having come all the way from Fargo. Being suffi-ciently tired ourselves we automatically climbed into the bed roll, and awakened the next morning on an island in the middle of a boulevard. But we hadn't bothered to take our trousers off, so the embarrassment was slight. That is the beauty of our equipment—it works right in the heart of cities.

A stern-wheeler carried us across the rushing Missouri, and at Mandan we ran upon a tremendous sign which said, "This is where the west begins." Not much farther, out on the prairies, we passed our first prairie schooner. It was a man and his young wife—moving from west to east. First came the cattle—ambling slowly along at the insistent pushing of a clever pony which the man rode splendidly. Then came the schooner, drawn by two sturdy horses, and driven by the girl. She was very sun-burned and very beautiful. She stared, wide-eyed, and seemed very much a part of things. You felt she could stand motionless all day, like a horse dozing by pasture bars. Behind the schooner—which con-tained all their worldly estate—were a couple of ponies, a mule, and a colt. We took a picture of the outfit, and drove on. Then we turned and watched it crawling steadily along, like a ship at sea, steadily on to the horizon.

I'm drawn up by the road as I write this, with my Corona set up in Hotspur's tonneau. (Did you know he had a tonneau?) An Indian with his family just passed in a buckboard drawn by two spotted ponies. I am on the Crow reservation. As he passed he asked me to take a picture, and I have just performed that duty, handing the three-months old baby a quarter. The Indian spoke effortless, correct English. "My name is Fred Oldhorn," he said, and, squatting, quickly wrote it in the dust. He said this was the only independent Indian reservation—the only one in which the Indians are not paid by the government. . . .

There is a magic to this state of Montana. Of course we have not yet come to the mountains, nor to the "scenery." But there is something about Montana ranch country so wildly enchanting as to be almost fearsome. Stand on the plains in the valley of the Yellowstone; watch great herds advancing grimly, like the ranks of an army, into the sun. The leaves of the aspens quiver down by the banks of the Yellowstone. And you don't know anything of what they whisper. And the herd which you thought was a mile away you now know is three miles away. You look at the painted buttes, silhouetted majestically, and you don't know whether they are a hundred feet high or a hundred thousand. . . .

Yesterday noon we turned south from Billings toward Hardin. I spent two hours helping a fat red-headed family up a hill with their Ford. It was a screamingly funny outfit. The day was hot and the Ford was hot and all the red-headed fat people were hot and the hill was steep. The total weight must have been in the neighborhood of forty thousand pounds. They were typical tourists—left their house home when they started but took everything else with them in a trailer and hung promiscuously about the flanks of the Ford. When I got there, the Ford had refused to puff any longer and the red-headed baby had taken to wailing because he had been so long without a drink of water. Out of the sticky mass of debris I excavated the trailer, unhooked it, and laid it aside. Then I excavated the entire family one by one from the back seat, the fenders, the front seat, and the hood. I laid that too aside, including a faint son-in-law who was the only thin thing in the outfit. Then I hailed three cars in succession and milked a gallon of gasoline from each, and placed these in the belly of the Ford. And I wiped his timer, and patted him gently on the hood, and gave him cool water. Then I hailed a fourth car and tied the trailer to its rear and let it pull the trailer to the top, which it could do easily, being a good robust car. Then, having got the Ford reduced pretty well to simple terms, I mounted and rode easily and swiftly to the top of the hill. And pretty soon the family came panting up from where I had laid them aside, and after we had got the trailer hooked on again and all the wash-basins, fine-tooth combs, handy tool-kits, collapsible chairs, and patent tent pegs too, why then the family got in and were off in clouds of dust and exhilaration. And truly it was a splendid sight, and well worth the effort.

Hardin is a genuine western town. I can't write you about it at this sitting because I am due at my labors very shortly. Cush and I both have jobs. Cush is a hay hand in the fields, and I play the piano at "Becker's Cafe." I now close this account, such as it is, with love and greetings to all.

Yours,
Andy

To JESSIE AND SAMUEL WHITE

Hart's Ranch
near Melville, Mont.
Sunday, July 16 [1922]

Dear Folks:

Green and crisp they fluttered from their cozy envelopes, green and crisp and strong—out onto the counter of White's Lunch. And I almost changed my order from egg sandwich to ham and eggs, but held myself in check as an exercise in self-control in the face of riches. I felt that had I changed the order to ham and eggs the short-order man would have thought I was putting on airs.

One of the coyest jokes was the little joke in Father's letter about our accepting it as a mute reminder although of course we had no need for it. Well, I celebrated by buying myself a fine big pair of boots for five and a half, and a fine grey shirt for ninety cents, and a haircut twelve days overdue, and a little stove for seven and a half, and a tank full of gasoline at 45 cents a gallon, and an admission to Yellowstone for seven and a half, and a malted milk for 20 cents, and a new timer for Hotspur for 60 cents (Hotspur's total internal repairs to date amount to about a dollar and a half from New York City), and then we were off up the valley of the Shoshone, off to the west along a road that wound up and up—up so steeply that Hotspur many times had to blow his little horn to make the big lumbering cars get out of his way. Up past the Shoshone Dam, which is so high that the bottom of it, viewed from the top of it, seems like no part of it at all. So high as that—and yet hardly high at all compared to Sylvan Pass through which we must go to enter the Park. When we had mounted 8,500 feet we jumped over Hotspur's side and made snowballs and threw them at the white-tailed deer and the marmots. And we looked across to where the Teton mountains were twenty miles away—and we couldn't quite see them because the day was not clear enough.

Near Hardin, Montana—which is the point from which I last wrote—is the ranch of Frank Heinrich, the largest cattle man in America. Ranching has changed greatly in the past generation. In the old days the cattle were turned out on vast ranges to forage for themselves. They were not fed—neither in summer nor in winter—and there were no fences. Each rancher sent out a wagon and riders twice a year to round up the herds. In the spring the men branded the calves, and in the fall they brought in the beeves for shipment. No one in particular owned any land in particular. Now the land is fenced and owned, and with the exception of Heinrich and one other man ranchers operate in the new style—that is, the cattle are ranged within definite bounds and in the winter they are fed occasionally on hay.

Monday

I was interrupted yesterday in order to drive the ranch children to a party next door. Next door in this case was six miles. In this country no one thinks to go even to the gate without taking the car. The beauty of it is you can sit on your front porch and see your company coming ten miles away. You have plenty of time to leisurely dust off the piano and start the eggs. It might seem to you that treeless country such as this would be painfully monotonous to the view. That's because you have not seen the shadows, the buttes, the clouds, the herds, the riders, and the nights. . . .

We slept on a little hill above Cody, and the next morning descended into town to partake of the last breakfast. Cody was preparing for the annual stampede—which is a sort of western county fair. Instead of having merry-go-rounds, balloon ascensions, and stock judging Cody goes in for bucking, bull dogging (steer throwing), roping, racing, and six-shooting. Everybody between the Mississippi and the Pacific drops round for the show, which lasts three days—July 4, 5, and 6.

Cody was hot. The sun becomes indignant at the broad-brimmed hats of the boys, so it curls down round them, and up under them. It ripples and crackles along the curbing at noon. . . . Dead worms on the side walks fry and sizzle, and the upholstery of autos left in the street bakes and cracks and burns your breeches. The little thermometers on store fronts mount as best they can, and then give it up as a bad job and settle down to a steady 100°.

We sandpapered a dance floor that afternoon—a roofless, open air thing. At night we were not broke by five dollars. We shaved, down by the river. We ate, and found the five was lost. Cush lost it from his breeches.

Lots of things happened. Cush washed dishes. . . . I bought a concession on the curb. With small boys I built a skin game, and later a wheel, and ran them on the hot days and the freezing nights.

Yellowstone is like an aquarium—all sorts of queer specimens, with thousands of people pressing in to get a glimpse. The Park is spectacular beyond my Corona (I should say beyond Cush's Corona—I sold mine to a bystander one time in a moment of starvation), and it is well and unobtrusively policed. But it is so obviously "on exhibition" all the time. Inspiration Point, for instance—on the rim of the wonderful Yellowstone canyon. Everything has a stupid name like that. Railings have initials on them.

They tried to fine us $500 for leaving a fire going in the upper basin. We were glad of the compliment, for at the moment we were well under three dollars. I told the ranger that it was perfectly absurd, the charge that I had left a fire. I told him that during sixteen weeks in the Canadian woods I hadn't left any fires, and if there was any fire where we had stopped the day before it was built up by one or more of the twenty tourist parties who had encircled us when we boiled an egg. He telephoned these statements in a loud voice to the United States District court at Mammoth, and the court answered, "Oh hell, let them go."

. . . The Hart Ranch, where I am working for grub by proving myself a factotum, looks across to the white peaks of the Crazy Mountains. There is Mr. Harry (Harry Hart) who came here from England in the eighties, and who calls out to me after every meal, "I say, help yourself to my tobacco there, will you?" Mr. Harry and his long moustaches can be found at 6 a.m., garbed in a tremendous straw sombrero and leather puttees, fussing with bridles and ring bolts in the horse stable, and at 6 p.m., garbed in immaculate tweeds, sitting down merrily to dinner. There is Nan (Mrs. Harry Hart), who works like Mae Gleason and talks like Mrs. McCarten,[1] and who has bobbed hair. Nan is the genius of the ranch—she bakes chocolate cake and grinds Ford valves with equal vigor and success. And there is Mrs. Brown, a person of doubtful nationality and practically no parentage, who just arrived yesterday to take charge of cooking for the hay crew. Mrs. Brown never got to go to any school, she says. Her outlook on life is of the darkest. "I sometimes wish it had been the good Lord's will that I die along with my mother," she so often says. . . . And there is Al, who

---

1. Mae Gleason was a waitress at Gram Gleason's in Belgrade. White's garrulous "Auntie Blanche" McCarten was the second wife of his Uncle Arthur McCarten.

sits with Fred in the evenings and talks about flea-bitten mares. And there is Fred, who sits with Al in the evenings and talks about the same thing. Al shaves only once a week, because the whiskers sort of keep the mosquiters away, he says. Fred shaves every day, and sits up very straight because he was two years in the Army. Al and Fred are hay hands. We eat hot cakes with them at 6 o'clock every morning. And there is Torvald, another hay hand, who just got in from Oregon. Torvald has too few teeth. And there is Nipper, who is lying at my feet at this very moment. . . .

Today is Friday

Well, Cush got fired yesterday, so I guess we will be moving on toward the north. It will be hard to leave this wonderful ranch, but it will be better to leave before we are asked to leave.

My thanks for the birthday gifts, and my love.

Yours entirely,
Andy

• *Frank E. Morse was the head of the Morse Chain Works in Ithaca. He had developed a pocket-sized calculating machine, or "arithmometer," and had slipped a few to Cushman and White when they stopped in Ithaca on their way west, hoping they could peddle them in the course of their wanderings. They tried—with no great success.*

To FRANK E. MORSE

Spokane, Wash.
9 August 1922

Dear Mr. Morse:

This is to acknowledge the receipt of the two adding machines. With the exception of twelve cans of evaporated milk, one gallon of gas, and sixty-four cents they represented our worldly estate when we drew in at Glacier Park Station.

I don't know whether you have ever been in that town. It consists mainly of four stores and an excellent view of the mountains. Garbed splendidly in our last white shirts and armed to the teeth with arithmometers we set boldly forth. It soon became apparent that the town fairly seethed with adding machines. The smallest log cabin had one. I never saw a town so well equipped to add anything at a moment's notice. One lady listened patiently to me for some thirty-five minutes and then remarked, timidly, "I think I like my electric Burroughs better."

My most enjoyable session was at the butcher shop. The butcher was a small man who carried an enormous knife. After forty minutes of demonstration, during which time I added up to seventy-three thousand and back again, he gazed wistfully up from the counter and murmured, "Come in tomorrow when I'm not so rushed."

It occurred to us that with one gallon of gas remaining we could make Browning, a town, as Cush says, of a thousand souls and several hundred Blackfeet Indians. So we went back. At two o'clock I consummated a sale with a gentleman who sat eating fish in an extremely small short-order cafe. He had his mouth so full of fish when he bought the arithmometer that I hardly knew whether he said Yes or No.

We left town, after putting the receipts from the sale into gas, oil, rice, and oatmeal. On the strength of it we were able to take a five-day walking trip through Glacier Park, crossing the continental divide twice. . . .

If I ever have a child I shall name it Arithmometer in loving memory of your kindness. This small typewriter cannot adequately express my very sincere appreciation of your interest—it can only beg pardon for delaying this long in acknowledging it.

We are enclosing a money order for ten dollars and would be glad to have three or four more machines if you could send them to us General Delivery, Olympia, Washington.[1] We owe you a lot more than ten dollars, but at the present time we can do no more than merely admit it openly. I wish you would let us know if you ever go broke so that we can ship you a couple of wash boilers or a brace of player-pianos or something to keep you going. . . .

Very sincerely,
E. B. White

To JESSIE AND SAMUEL WHITE

[Yakima, Wash.]
[August 1922]

. . . Everywhere water is trickling in tiny ditches. There is no rain— the weather is entirely dependable: perfect for church picnics.

In my last letter I believe I ended abruptly on Gunsight Pass—left you high and dry, so to speak. It was high, in truth. The trail led across a snow field near the summit, and growing next the snow were wild flowers. On the other side of the continental divide the trail led down to the border of Lake Ellen Wilson, then up over another mountain to Sperry chalet. I am sending you under separate cover a booklet which I ran across, containing good pictures of the Park.

---

1. If the machines were sent, they are probably still there. The two travelers never got to Olympia.

From Sperry we descended three or four thousand feet through spruce forests to Lake McDonald, stopping an hour during the afternoon to pick huckleberries for supper. We slept that night on the edge of the lake, and were up early the next morning to begin the climb to Granite— a distance of twenty miles. All morning we went up an easy grade, following along the creek. We stopped for lunch where the real climb began, and had about seven grape nuts apiece and a can of tomato soup. I never experienced such an altitudinous mountain. At about six or seven thousand feet we began to run out of calories: the tomatoes in the soup had disappeared through the pores of our respective skins and the grape nuts had begun to rattle. The height of the Woolworth Building is about five hundred feet. We did that ten times over. (Pause a moment to get the full effect of the thing.) What's more, we were traversing a southern slope, which meant no water. You see, the snows do not last on the southern slopes through the summer so they are dry. The opposite slopes have streams every few feet along the trail. I did come to a tiny rill near the top, however. Cush was ahead on the trail, and I arrived at the place together with a black-tailed deer who was just as thirsty as I was. It was a beautiful doe—she had a nice wet black nose and attractive eyes. Together we tippled at the tiny water hole, and had many a long drink. . . .

In the morning we crossed back over the divide through Swiftcurrent Pass, and made Many Glaciers by noon. So you see we hadn't wasted much time, for it was Monday morning when we crossed Gunsight and Wednesday morning when we crossed back over Swiftcurrent. We were five days in the Park. . . . We covered about sixty miles—which is the equivalent of about 160 miles counting the ups and downs.

Hotspur was where we had left him. He was probably glad of the rest. Camel-like, he had retained enough gas to make the Canadian border—so we started from Bab straight north. I made a dollar and a half by accident. We spent the half for delicacies and kept the dollar for luck. A small half-breed girl took it away from us at the U.S. customs. She said it was the fee for crossing. She lied most dreadfully—but we didn't find that out until a week or so later. At Cardstom we discovered we still had two gallons left, so we took a look at the Mormon temple and started for Macleod, fifty miles away. Through Alberta's plains went our small car, and flew without a pause into the very heart of Macleod. From a little distance you would think Macleod had about a hundred thousand people. It is built up in the shape of a square—but there is nothing in the center. We had nothing in our center either when we got there. We loafed around the Dominion Employment Agency for a while and then went down the creek about a mile, crossed a bridge, and swam and ate cocoa or something and went to bed. The next day the town was all closed up on account of a traveling fair which was coming through. Blackfeet had come in for miles around. They were camped next to us on the creek—they and all their horses and dogs and women. Indians never go anywhere without taking everything that they own along with them. In the afternoon Cush took a job digging an irrigation ditch somewhere to the north about twenty miles. I hocked my Sun charm[1] for a couple of dollars and bought a steak. Next day I dressed up and sold an arithmometer to a man in a notion store. After three or four nights Cush showed up. We bought gas at 55 cents a gallon and oil at 60 cents a quart and sped through Crow's Nest Pass in the Canadian Rockies. Two punctures and two blowouts in as many hours left us again penniless and our tireless car tireless indeed. We gazed about and observed that we were at Galloway, British Columbia. Galloway boasted only one structure —the railway station on the C.P.R. Even that was closed permanently. Forest fires were burning in desultory fashion through the country, and a ranger said he would give us a job putting them out if we wanted it. We slept on the station platform. At seven the next morning I set out afoot with Cush's Corona, toward Cranbrook—thirty-two miles away. I walked and walked and recited blank verse to the ancestral mountains for my own amusement. At four I was back at Galloway without the Corona, in whose stead I produced a Goodyear tire and seven dollars and a half. We mended Hotspur's tired feet and started riding. By the moon we rode until 2:30 the next morning, at which time we both fell asleep for the sixth time. The next morning we were waked up by being walked upon by cows. We drove to Kingsgate—only a few miles away, and waited two hours for the customs to open up. Then upon a road unsurfaced, ungroomed, and uncouth to Bonners' Ferry, Idaho, where we halted for breath and ice-cream before plunging down to Sandpoint and Spokane.

Eleven miles out of Spokane we glided upon a concrete road—the first pavement since Minnesota.

I got seventeen letters in Spokane, and Cush got only one, so it was a tremendous victory. News from home was very welcome, and you should see the amount of waffles we bought with Father's Postscript. Spokane goes in for waffles—there are waffle houses all down the street. We also bought a spare tire and a room at the Y.M.C.A. . . .

The next day we went south, and crossed the Snake River to Walla Walla. Cush calls it Walladitto. You would marvel at the wheat country —very different from Alberta and the Dakotas. It is rolling, like New York State, except that it rolls less frequently and with a grander motion.

---

1. A gold charm worn on their watch chains by board members of the *Cornell Sun*.

We passed through the Peleuse region just at harvest time. The yellow grain was in little cocks in the fields, like polka dots.

Hotspur had internal injuries the next day at noon. He broke down and cried on the banks of the Columbia River. It was Kennewick. "It's the rear end," said the silent ferryman, sagely. "Yes," I whispered.

So I took a bucket, down by the banks of the Columbia, and I began taking parts out of Hotspur. I took and took and took. . . . I removed everything south of the front seat. "Come on on the boat," said the silent ferryman. So we took the rear end aboard the stern-wheeler, and placed it and the bucket next the boiler. Plump, plump, went the parts into the bucket, while my busy pliers took out cotter-pin after cotter-pin.

"It's the main drive pinion," murmured the silent ferryman. "Yes," I said.

So I bought a new main drive pinion for a dollar. And we bought something to eat. And there was left a dollar and a half. And in the gloaming I dove off the stern of the ferry into the cool waters of the Columbia. And the dollar and a half, being hot also, dove too when I wasn't looking. We slept that night on the ferry-wharf, and observed many shooting stars—for the Heaven was full of them. Rosy-fingered dawn found me at work with my bucket by my side, giving each part its due, and replacing it in its allotted place. Twenty-four hours after I had started the previous day I was through. (I smell something ungrammatical in that sentence.) We took three baths, one right after the other, and shaved.

"Got anything to eat on?" inquired the silent ferryman. "Yes," we said, playing with the truth woefully. "They found your eight bits—the kids were diving," he said, lying incontinently and handing us a silver dollar.[2]

Off went Hotspur, airily on his brand new pinion. And here we are at Yakima.

"Heigh, ho; heigh, ho; heigh, ho!" calls Mr. Van Vliet at six thirty in the morning. And we get up and eat tremendous cantaloupes and innumerable bacon and eggs and then hie us to the pear orchards, where we pick bartlett pears at 30 cents an hour for ten hours. Or else we roll over and go to sleep again, awakening in time to go swimming in the afternoon.

I haven't any idea where you all spent your vacation this summer, because the last letter I had from you was dated in July. Cush's family

---

2. This was the only serious trouble the travelers had with their car. White drew on the incident in the piece "Farewell, My Lovely," which appeared in *The New Yorker* over the pseudonym Lee Strout White and which was published as a book in 1936 by G. P. Putnam's Sons under the title *Farewell to Model T*.

were at Cotuit. I am awfully glad that Stan got his job at Illinois—it is a fine university and it should be the sort of work that Stan is best fitted for. . . .

I am so sleepy tonight I can't write anything very lucid or legible. But asleep or awake I am unreservedly

Yours faithfully,
Andy

• *In Seattle, White landed a job with the Seattle* Times *that paid $40 a week, and he promptly traded Hotspur for a coupe. After he had been with the* Times *as a reporter for a few months, he was offered the chance to conduct a daily column, and jumped at it. However, it soon turned out that the purpose of the proposed "literary" column was to promote classified advertising—the lifeblood of most newspapers. The* Times's *publisher, Colonel C. B. Blethen, informed White that the column would be set in the style of the want ads, would carry the title "Personal Column," and would be unsigned. The first column in the series was largely rewritten by the colonel himself, and ran on the first page. It began, "I want what I want when I want it." A day or two later the column disappeared from page one and surfaced in the want-ad section, where it was typographically indistinguishable from the ads. This would have discouraged most self-respecting columnists, but White was young and eager and glad of any chance. He continued to knock out the "Personal Column" every day until he was laid off as part of a general cutback in June 1923.*

To ALICE BURCHFIELD

1222-17th Ave. N.
Seattle, Washington
[October 1922]

Dear Alice:

. . . At last I again have a local habitation. You see it above. I am pretty firmly rooted now in Mrs. Donohue's boarding house, and already owe her a month's rent. A week and a half ago I succeeded in getting a job on the Seattle Times (afternoon paper) so I am again engaged in what might be termed honest labor. I'm not sure about the honesty, but can vouch for the labor.

The Times is very highbrow, very conservative, very rich, and entirely unreadable. It is one of the most splendidly equipped newspaper organizations in the country—wonderful big new building occupying an entire block in the center of the city; and five enormous rotary presses.

When you are sent out to get a story, you go in as much style as the Prince of Wales. It's like this: You are sitting at your typewriter, simulating work. The city editor approaches rapidly. He speaks a name and a location, turns on his heel, and is gone. You press the elevator button and land downstairs, where a staff photographer and a staff automobile await you at the door.—Can you beat that for service?

I work from 7:30 a.m. until I'm through—which is anywhere from 2:30 to 11:30 p.m., according to what my assignments have been. At present I have no regular beat, but am on general assignment and rewrite, which means that one minute I am reporting a drowning at the waterfront, and the next minute interviewing a member of the Japanese Embassy. This afternoon I ran a children's football contest.

Cush is still in Seattle but will probably be going south shortly, being unable to find a job here.

This is a very peculiar city. It rains here every day all winter long— and it has begun already. I find it a trifle depressing. . . . But I guess I'll stay here, for I've at last got a job on a newspaper. . . .

Andy

To STANLEY HART WHITE

[Seattle, Wash.]
[January 2, 1923]

Dear Stan:

Glad to get your letter. You are right about my not shining spittoons: all editors spit on the floor.

Received your Christmas present, and have not got round to reading it yet because, as the title suggests, it requires not less than half an hour. This would be as good a place as any delicately to mention that I didn't buy you any present. I didn't go in heavily for that sort of thing this year, principally because I am at my daily stint long before the stores open in the morning, and I stay at it intermittently until long after they close at night.

Even at this moment I am supposed to be out gathering material for a Sunday magazine story on what goes on in Seattle in the dead hours of night when all honest citizens slumber in their legitimate beds. With photographs.

The Times sicks me on feature stuff because the city editor discovered early in the game that city politics appear only in humorous light to me.

That's all right. I get $4 extra for every story I write for the magazine, and at the same time avoid getting into controversy with the mayor and city councilmen.

Somehow or other I am afraid that I am doomed to be a newspaper reporter all my life—with all the dire connotations. I never could get up enough enthusiasm for marketing paper bags or building up effective sales representation for Dry-foot Shoes to warrant my going into any business that pays a living wage.

You are absolutely correct about becoming a professor. Next to being a ferryman it is the finest life.

I'll endeavor to write you a letter sometime. Reply requested.

Yours,
En

To ALICE BURCHFIELD

[Seattle, Wash.]
[February 1923]
Friday night

Dear Alice:

. . . There isn't anything new. We had a snowstorm a while ago. It wasn't very much of a one, but Seattle thought it was terrible. It was the worst blizzard in seven years, and all the streetcar lines were dead for three days. Employees of the Times were billeted in downtown hotels, and it was very dramatic. If it had been in any eastern city, nobody would have known that it was snowing. But out here, people take the weather seriously.

Last night I heard Carl Sandburg speak, and was so pleased I wanted to go right to Chicago. The contrast was all the more striking because of all the businessmen's luncheons I have gone to in the last five months.

. . . I'm quite sick of the Times and of the dark skies of Seattle, and will be on my way to sunnier places if the spring fever hits me again the way it did the other day. Soon I'll be out of a job again—which seems to be my native state. I had a lot of fun tonight making out my Income Tax report for the past year. My earnings amounted to $1,002.55. My exemption was $1,000. Therefore the tax was computed on $2.55. Four percent of that equals 10 cents. So I owe my country one dime, and will present myself tomorrow at the Bureau of Internal Revenue and settle up.

. . . I think if I should walk into the Phi Gam house I'd get kicked out for an old clothes man.—And I just bought a new suit the other day, too: $28.85. Oh, a stunning suit—real western cut, with peg top pants and everything. I've got it on now, and can hardly write for looking at myself. I bet if I had known my income tax was going to be so slight I would have really splurged and bought one for $32.50 instead. As it is I'm going to spend the difference for licorice chewing gum, for which I have a great passion. . . .

Yours,
Andy

• *Cushman had left White in Seattle and returned to the East by way of California and Texas. The following letter refers to the burlesque travelogues the two men had written during their coast-to-coast journey. "In retrospect," White says now, "my belief is that no publisher in his right mind would have published those travelogues."*

On their way west, while they lay over in Ithaca, Cushman and White had been asked to write a "Berry Patch" column for the Sun. *As a lark, they divided the task. First White would write a poem, and sign it "Ho." Then Cushman would add a paragraph, and sign it "Hum." And so on, in alternation. Afterward the two men often used "Ho" (White) and "Hum" (Cushman) in their correspondence.*

To **HOWARD CUSHMAN**

[Seattle, Wash.]
[April 23, 1923]
Monday

Hum:

Without attempting to answer your recent letter I jump into the heart of things. As follows.

In re travelogues, I have suddenly undergone a change of heart. It seems to me, after a cold-blooded critical reading, that our scant efforts— however lacking in some of the subtler virtues—are not without a certain merit. And as long as nothing with merit has any place in the Times, it occurs to me that my Column would not do justice to these articles.

In short, I really believe that, properly revised and cleverly illustrated, they would make, sir, a saleable BOOK. I say it seriously, deliberately, and with suitable genuflections.

It would be a small book. Each article would be a chapter. Instead of the asterisks, the sentences would be paragraphed. The book would be of pretty tough heavy paper, with ample type. Each chapter would have one full paged cartoon illustration.

The book, then, like the Rootabaga Stories of Carl Sandburg, would serve three generations—infancy, boredom, and senescence. That is, the subject matter seems to me, on careful reading, to be ludicrous and fanciful enough to hold a child's imagination; and on the o.h. the treatment is facile enough to please a reading public on the watch for pen gymnastics. . . .

One supreme virtue which seems to redeem the whole series in my mind is the belief that THE IDEA IS DIFFERENT—it hasn't been done. The nearest thing seems to be the Kawa,[1] which, after all, is not so very similar.

---

1. *The Cruise of the Kawa* by "Professor Walter E. Traprock" (George Shepard Chappell of *Vanity Fair*), a burlesque on the South Sea school of writers.

At any rate, don't dally with this thought, but be full of strong vigorous action. Let's hear at a near date what your reaction is, and also what the chances would be—if you favor the scheme—to secure illustrations.

One other thing—I think the name is very valuable: Westward Ho Ho. It is a saleable name, methinks.

Yours till we're both immortal,

Ho

• *When he was let go by the Seattle* Times, *White again found himself adrift, but instead of heading back east he boarded a ship, the* S.S. Buford, *bound for Alaska and Siberia. With money saved from his newspaper job, he was able to purchase first-class passage as far as Skagway. He counted on being able to work his way after that. Years later, White wrote an account of his Alaska experience, which he called "The Years of Wonder." It is the final chapter of his book* The Points of My Compass.

To JESSIE HART WHITE

Aboard S.S. Buford
Alaskan Gulf—light sea
Friday, August 3 or 4 [1923]

Darling Mother:

I shall mail this in Seward, trusting that it will catch a southbound ship. We are due there in a few hours.

It was the evening of July 24 that I put to sea in this ponderous vessel. With forty dollars I bought myself a first class passage to Skagway. I liked the name.

This is a sort of excursion cruise of the San Francisco Chamber of Commerce, made in the interest of extending trade relations. We have with us the Six Brown Brothers—who you remember played the saxophone with Fred Stone—also H. A. Snow, African big game hunter who made movies of wild animals. The ship is in command of Capt. L. L. Lane, well known whaleman and stampeder of the Northland. It is an ex-transport, and makes eleven knots.

In a small bay off Vancouver Island one evening we passed the Henderson. President Harding waved his handkerchief, and we stopped for a salute. In Cordova yesterday we heard news of his death.

A great change came over me at Skagway. I suddenly appeared in a white coat. I suddenly became associated with brooms, mops, pails of slop water, and other paraphernalia of the great service world. I suddenly—without warning the delightful wives and sisters of the members of the Chamber of Commerce—began to serve night lunch to them in the dining saloon. The shock to the company was terrific. Many of them had thought I was orthodox, socially. Lord, they had danced with me on those nights from Seattle to Skagway in the dance hall. I shall not attempt to describe in this letter my extreme enjoyment of all this. I don't know how I happened to think of such a funny thing to do, but I did, and I am having a wonderful time.

We are going to the Pribiloff Islands, the ice pack of the Arctic, East Cape, Nome, and are going to lower the whaleboat after a whale.

I work from 8 p.m. to 6 a.m. in the saloon. Saloon, Mother dear, has to do with eating, not drinking. I set table and prepare lunch for thirty, serve the lunch (with marvelous dexterity in heavy weather), clean off the tables, wash and wipe and put away all dishes, silver, and glasses, sweep down the companion way to the social hall, and shine the brass. The sun sets for a few hours around midnight. At 3 o'clock, when I step out on the forward deck to smoke a pipe, the north is bright. Up on the bridge, the mate paces back and forth, or peers through binoculars. The ship moves along with a swish and a throb. The headlands rise black in the east. The sun pops out, and snores grow throaty from the staterooms. I wipe a few more dishes, and pretty soon I flop. Flop is what the second steward calls going to bed.

This must be all. If I don't mail this here, it will not arrive eastward. There is no mail service at the ice pack.

Love to all,
Andy

• *When the* Buford *called at Seattle on her way back to San Francisco, White left the ship. After an evening on the town, he sold his car, paid his debts, and entrained for New York, with a stopover in Buffalo to see Miss Burchfield. He then returned to the house in Mount Vernon he had left abruptly a year and a half before and to the same problem from which he had tried to win a reprieve: how to earn a living in the world of letters.*

To ALICE BURCHFIELD

[September 17, 1923]
Mount Vernon, N.Y.
48 Mersereau Avenue

Dear Alice:

I have just been sent to bed. But as long as there is a little tobacco left in the can and as long as the obliging cricket outside the window continues to sing queer little ballads, I think bed is not to be considered. The cricket must be a kinsman of the one I heard in your back garden: he knows the same tunes.

Well—I went to Ithaca. If ever you want something to warm the cockles of your heart, stay away from the campus about a year and a half—then amble back at leisure, when nothing stirs in the long halls and only a few of the old inhabitants are about to make it real. I was so glad it was not a reunion—I didn't have to wear a colored hat or get drunk.

There was a light in Adams. Mrs. Adams and a couple of friends were there. The notorious professor was in Washington, D.C., I was told. Sunday was a sunny day; and I had hardly started on a stroll when Uncle Pete [Albert W. Smith] came stepping along, a newly completed biography under his arm, a book of verse in his pocket. He beguiled me to his cubbyhole in Sibley, where he read me little things and then he sauntered out again with me and showed me the sights.

I had dinner at the Adamses'. About twenty persons, as usual. Ev and Tote were at least three feet taller than I'd ever seen them before. Gertrude was in bed with a pain, and there was talk of appendicitis.[1] Mrs. Adams' mother was there—a very ancient little person whom I'd never met. After dinner I wandered across to Willie Strunk's house. Did I tell you I had sent him a post card from Medicine Hat, just as I'd promised a year ago? Anyway, Willie grasped his coat lapels in the orthodox Strunkish fashion and mumbled: "What do they do in Medicine Hat? What do they do in Medicine Hat?" It was wonderful. He told me (among other bits of news) that D— S— had completed an extraordinary romance with the daughter of a coal baron. There was mention of a lightning courtship, of at least two trips to Europe, and of $50 bills being passed under the table from the coal baroness to the groom. . . .

This is the third page, and I haven't started yet to tell you that it was good to be in Buffalo again—and that's what this letter is supposed to be all about: and is, really. You were like the first channel light in a passage East, and the first is always the most welcome to mariners.

It seemed a shame that you were in the midst of tonsils, and I've been wondering whether walking about in the street did you any harm. I'm a very bum sympathizer when I'm around persons that have something wrong with them—probably because when I get low myself I don't like to have people snooping around and suggesting things—so if I didn't keep talking about your throat, it was just a habit I have, and didn't mean that I wasn't sorry. Tell me when you are going to have an

1. Everett, Bristow, Jr. (Tote), and Gertrude were Bristow Adams's children.

operation and I'll come up and keep the nurse from giving you too much ether.

Sitting on this porch is great. The laundryman comes down the street with the same shambling horse that I used to know (wait till he sees the filth of some of my clothes). Across the street a house is going up; and nice fundamental, creative sounds come from there. The locust trees shiver a bit, even in the sunlight; and the poplars are talking together in such loud whispers I can hear them way over here. They are discussing September (if you must know). The laundryman's horse adjusts his ears and approves of the month: the flies are not bad and it's cooler up the hills.

Pretty soon I hope to get the letter from you that went to Seattle. And maybe an answer to this one as well. Please get well again and start to eat things.

Andy

• *When White drifted away from the East in 1922, he also drifted away from Alice Burchfield. He was gone a year and a half on his search for adventure, and the long separation put a great strain on the relationship. The two continued to correspond, but the bloom was off, and the romance, thanks to the young man's fear of entanglement, was obviously on dead center. Alice had had about enough of her suitor's footlessness and irresolution, and their long-drawn-out affair finally collapsed when White, back east again, dispatched the letter that follows—a letter that must have caused him much anguish to write and that must have caused Miss Burchfield even more pain to receive. She took it in her stride, allowed the correspondence to drop, and eventually married a less errant Cornellian, James F. Sumner, with whom she had been associated as an undergraduate in Cornell's Dramatic Club.*

To ALICE BURCHFIELD

[New York]
[Spring 1924]
Sunday

Dear Alice:

Today I returned from Florida and found your letter. . . . If you think I have treated you badly, I guess it is true; but things turned out the way they did because of my stupidity and not because of any subtle intentions. If I had been a normal person two years ago, I would have either besieged your doorstep, or else I'd have gone off and sent you a polite note saying, "My dear Lady: Having besought your hand without success, I shall consider the incident jolly well closed and hoping you are the same . . ." But I was more of a dub. I went away and proceeded to consider the incident jolly well closed on Tuesdays, Thursdays, and Saturdays; and on the other days (being both chicken hearted and ignorant) I felt qualms of conscience, and remembering youthful vows of constancy I proceeded to indite safe-and-sane letters under the guise of friendship—they turned out to be as safe as rattlesnakes and as sane as could be expected from me. We weren't friends, so the friendly letters were flivvers. The strange part is that you failed to discover how ridiculous I was a long while ago. You even answered the letters. You mustn't forget that. I hope I'm not being more blunt than's necessary, but I don't want misunderstanding to run along any further. When I saw you last fall, it seemed to me that any doubts which you might have had concerning my "status" (if you want to call it that) were cleared up. I certainly talked about the weather. And then I began to receive letters from you saying that you were tearing up your initial attempts. I wasn't too dense to comprehend—but I don't think you realized that I did comprehend. At any rate, the postscript to Ruth's [Alice's sister's] letter didn't leave much to the imagination. It was a very wonderful thing to receive, but a rather awkward thing for me to acknowledge. I virtually answered it by omitting to answer it. You see, you (and not I) were the one who continued to row after the boat had sunk.

I don't think you can mistake my meaning, and I'm not going to let you. If there were anything to talk about, I would certainly come to see you. But there's nothing that I can't say or won't say in this letter. After all, what you may think of me now will be no worse than what you have been thinking. Your imagination has overemphasized things: I'm not as bad as you think, and I'm not as good. I didn't intend to play any trick on you or to take any advantage; I have too much respect for your intelligence to suppose that you want any sort of apology or sidestepping. I think you wanted a lot of facts, and I guess they're all set down. It wasn't exactly easy. If I had to write another letter like this I'd turn my few little hairs quite grey. The only unfortunate part is that your letter was not forwarded so that I could have answered right away.

Andy

Monday
I was so tired last night, my letter didn't contain quite all that I wanted. It sounds chopped off at the end. The thing I want you to believe is that I am sorry. It isn't hard for me to endure my bungling ways because I am used to them by this time; but I can understand that it's

hard on the other people. My thoughts, like persons in a doorway, crowd forward and won't let each other through. It's strange that you—the last person in the world I'd wish to hurt—are the one I've treated worst. And of course the damnable part is that there's nothing that can be done about it. If there had been, I would have come to Buffalo a long while ago whether you invited me or not.

I haven't the slightest suspicion that I played fair with you; but I don't want you to have the slightest suspicion that I tried anything else. Failing to understand the game, I should have kept out. Nobody ever does keep out, though, and that's why it remains perpetually interesting and eternally comic. It's lucky you wrote me letters enough to precipitate this one, because it's better written than unwritten, and it's certainly going to be *sent.*

Make lots of money and treat me to a show when you come to New York: I haven't got a job.

A.

●   *On his return from the West in the fall of 1923, White went to
work in the advertising business, first with Frank Seaman & Company
at $25 a week, then with J. H. Newmark at $30. For two years he lived
with his parents in Mount Vernon and commuted to work, but life at
home was irksome and White did not like commuting. One of his first
poems in* The New Yorker *was a quatrain about the commuting life:*
COMMUTER—*one who spends his life/ In riding to and from his
wife;/ A man who shaves and takes a train/ And then rides back to
shave again.*

*In November 1925, he moved into 112 West 13th Street, which he
describes as "a Manhattan refuge for struggling Cornellians." For quite
a while, the four occupants of the apartment were White, Gus Lobrano,
Burke Dowling (Bob) Adams, and Mitchell T. (Mike) Galbreath. The place
was a typical Pullman flat—living room on the street side, bedroom in
back with two double-decker beds, and, in between the two rooms, an
illegal kitchen. This was White's first experience of life in Manhattan. "Everything was great," he says now, "everything was exciting,
except that for much of the time I didn't have a job, having drifted out
of advertising, which I hated. Galbreath worked for McGraw-Hill, Adams
and Lobrano worked for the Cunard Line. They would depart for work
in the morning, leaving me to do the breakfast dishes and tidy up the
joint. I acquired a caged bird to keep me company and tried my hand
at free lancing—nothing new for me, as I had been submitting poems
and sketches to newspapers and magazines for years. F. P. A. had used
a poem or two in the* Conning Tower, *Christopher Morley had published
a sonnet to a bantam rooster—for which I won a prize, competing with
other sonneteers. To appear in the* Conning Tower *gave a young poet
a great lift to the spirit: it did not give him any money. The arrival on*

*the scene of Harold Ross's New Yorker, February 21, 1925, was a turn-
ing point in my life, although I did not know it at the time. I bought a
copy of the first issue at a newsstand in Grand Central, examined Eustace Tilley and his butterfly on the cover, and was attracted to the new-
born magazine not because it had any great merit but because the items
were short, relaxed, and sometimes funny. I was a 'short' writer, and I
lost no time in submitting squibs and poems. In return I received a few
small checks and the satisfaction of seeing myself in print as a pro."*

By 1926, Ross was encouraging White to join the staff and asking
him to drop in at the office. One day, he remembers, he did drop in, and
the editor who came into the reception room to greet him was Katharine
(Mrs. Ernest) Angell. *"I noted that she had a lot of back hair and the
knack of making a young contributor feel at ease. I sat there peacefully
gazing at the classic features of my future wife without, as usual, knowing what I was doing."*

For a writer the lowliest job on the magazine was the newsbreak
job—editing the little fillers from other papers and writing punchlines
for them. White was given a batch to try, and Ross was so pleased with
the results he phoned White to tell him so. In 1926, however, White
was not chiefly preoccupied either with The New Yorker or with his
future wife—he was preoccupied with a dark-haired girl from Birmingham, Alabama, named Mary Osborn. She lived on Jones Street. He was
in love again, and, true to form, spent a good bit of time that year avoiding love's entanglements. He visited Ithaca, he walked through the
Shenandoah Valley, he made a trip to Washington, D.C., and finally,
in July, he sailed for Europe aboard the Cunard Line's Andania—a free
trip abroad in return for his writing the script for a promotional film for
Cunard. He says that he communicated his more passionate feelings to
Mary chiefly in poems, which he dispatched to the newspaper columnists
of the day in hopes that they would be published and that she would
see them. At least two of these love poems—"The Circus" and "Coldly,
to the Bronze Bust of Holley in Washington Square"—were published and
(presumably) seen by the lady in question; both were subsequently included in his first book, The Lady Is Cold. After more than a year of
trying to figure White out, the young woman resolved the matter by
marrying a West Point cadet.

Ross kept after White, and in January 1927 they worked out an
arrangement. White agreed to work half-time for the magazine, keeping
a half-time job with J. H. Newmark as insurance. The New Yorker gave
him $30 a week and a desk on the thirteenth floor at 25 West 45th
Street. Newmark paid him another $30, and he considered himself in
clover. Gradually he increased his work at the magazine until it
amounted to a full-time job, and then quit Newmark.

White did almost no editing. But like everyone else in those early days at the magazine, he was plunged into a wild variety of duties. He wrote the taglines for newsbreaks and the captions for pictures. He wrote Comment and original pieces for Talk of the Town. He was a re-write man on Talk, and a consultant on verse. He substituted, when called on, for the drama and movie critics, and did a great deal of writing to fill the gaping holes in every issue. He never, however, construed "full-time" to mean that he was obliged to sit in the office all day, which he seems to have been temperamentally incapable of doing. Other staffers at the magazine toiled from ten to six. White worked long hours or short, when and if he felt like it—and Ross accepted the arrangement. For although footloose, White was conscientious about deadlines, and Ross never had to worry that White would let him down, even though he often did not know where he was.

"The cast of characters in those early days," White writes, "was as shifty as the characters in a floating poker game. People drifted in and drifted out. Every week the magazine teetered on the edge of financial ruin. Katharine Angell arrived in 1925. Fillmore Hyde, from the Peapack hunting set, arrived. James Kevin McGuiness, Charles Baskerville, Herman J. Mankiewicz, Joseph Moncure March. Then Ralph McAllister Ingersoll arrived, right out of the social register. Lois Long, Peter Arno, Rogers Whitaker arrived, right out of the subway. Rea Irvin, the art editor, arrived before anybody else. He was the one person around the place who seemed to know what he was doing. Philip Wylie, Morris Markey, Carmen Peppe, Ralph Paladino, Elsie Dick, Oliver Claxton. Ross fumed, fussed, broke down partitions, changed the format every issue, strove and strove, cursed and raged. It was chaos, but it was enjoyable. I dropped the name James Thurber, and Ross hired him immediately. 'I hire anybody,' he remarked, gloomily. Thurber and I shared a sort of elongated closet, just big enough to hold two desks, two typewriters, and a mountainous stack of yellow copy paper, which the two of us set about covering with words and pictures. Raoul Fleischmann poured money in, Ross fought with Fleischmann and erected an impenetrable barrier between the advertising department and the editorial department. It was known as the Ross Barrier."

A key figure in those desperate years was Katharine Angell. She was a pleasant, soft-spoken, hard-headed woman who, unbeknownst to herself or anybody else, was starting an important career in an era when that was rare for women. More and more, Ross found himself turning to her for the solutions to the myriad things that bothered him.

Forty years later, in an interview with the Paris Review, *White said of his wife: "I have never seen an adequate account of Katharine's role with* The New Yorker. . . . *She was one of the first editors to be hired, and I can't imagine what would have happened to the magazine if she hadn't turned up. Ross, though something of a genius, had serious gaps. In Katharine he found someone who filled them. No two people were ever more different than Mr. Ross and Mrs. Angell; what he lacked, she had; what she lacked, he had. She complemented him in a way that, in retrospect, seems to me to have been indispensable to the survival of the magazine. She was a product of Miss Winsor's and Bryn Mawr. Ross was a high school dropout. She had a natural refinement of manner and speech; Ross mumbled and bellowed and swore. She quickly discovered, in this fumbling and impoverished new weekly, something that fascinated her: its quest for humor, its search for excellence, its involvement with young writers and artists. She enjoyed contact with people; Ross, with certain exceptions, despised it—especially during hours. She was patient and quiet; he was impatient and noisy. Katharine was soon sitting in on art sessions and planning sessions, editing fiction and poetry, cheering and steering authors and artists along the paths they were eager to follow, learning makeup, learning pencil editing, heading the Fiction Department, sharing the personal woes and dilemmas of innumerable contributors and staff people who were in trouble or despair, and, in short, accepting the whole unruly business of a tottering magazine with the warmth and dedication of a broody hen.*

"I had a bird's-eye view of all this because, in the midst of it, I became her husband. During the day I saw her in operation at the office. At the end of the day, I watched her bring the whole mess home with her in a cheap and bulging portfolio. The light burned late, our bed was lumpy with page proofs, and our home was alive with laughter and the pervasive spirit of her dedication and her industry. . . . I suspect that one of Ross's luckiest days was the day a young woman named Mrs. Angell stepped off the elevator, all ready to go to work."

To **HOWARD CUSHMAN**

112 West 13 Street
[September 1926]
Fridee

Sweet Hum:

Now that the harvest moon is on the way, now that I am back from across the sea, now that Yakima pears are being hawked in the quiet cool gutters of Thirteenth Street—I can write you a letter. I got yours in which you avowed you had a swell daughter,[1] and really if the truth were

---

1. While working on a paper in New Rochelle, Cushman had courted and married one of his co-workers in the city room. They had a daughter, Nancy. The marriage ended in divorce shortly afterward.

known I have been hankering for a sight of her, but seldom get round to calling on other people's daughters, what with earning my living and keeping the apartment picked up after the boys, and walking round and about in my beloved city, and taking moving pitchers of the Zuider Zee.

Once in a while I meet Gert,[2] brisking around a corner in blue, or lolling beneath the Elevated in black, and I say how is Cush and she says he is fine, and that is all the news I get. In fact I don't even know what paper you are with, or why. I have no job but strange as it may seem I have got along fairly well since the first of the year, partly with the New Yorker, partly with the Cunard Line, and here and there a publicity job or something. The New Yorker has been quite receptive, rejecting little, buying much, and even asking me to lunch once in a while.

Who lives around the corner? Carl Helm and Harriett. They arrived from San Francisco[3] via the canal a couple of weeks ago, with the usual amount of dunnage—parakeets, machete, tapestries, piano, and things Nicaraguan for interior decoration. As usual Carl spent the first day writing a musical comedy, a novel, a short story, and a sentimental magazine article—and then gravitated naturally down to Mr. Hearst's American and got a job on rewrite. They have a room on Twelfth Street.

Yes I have been Europe, or similar goddam phrases. Bob Adams was commissioned by the Cunard Line to make a four reel movie to advertise student tours, or college cabin, or whatever they call the tendency. He was presented with a real live cameraman from Hearst International Newsreel, and was instructed to do something to take the sting out of a travelogue. So one day we went out to the Princeton campus (this was toward the end of June) and we took some preliminary shots, and then Bob hired me to write the gags and the titles and to carry the tripod. I decided to go at nine o'clock one morning and left that afternoon on the Andania at five. Frank Mueller—Phi Gam, little mustache, chin like Jack Holt—was impressed into service as leading man; and the four of us were off, the cameraman and Bob in the saloon cabin, Frank and I in steerage. It was a serene, comical, pleasantly eventful voyage—unique in a way, for we made an honest to god movie with continuity and plot and heart interest and stark realism by the simple (and occasionally complicated) process of conscripting actors and actresses from among the passengers, feeding them rye highballs until they got to the point where they didn't care whether they were acting for the cinema or not. It's too bad

2. Gertrude Lynahan, who had been the women's editor of the *Cornell Sun*. She later married Joel Sayre.

3. Carl Helm, White's boss at the American Legion News Service, had been so impressed by his young assistant's carefree departure for the West that he had quit his own job and, with his wife, headed for the Coast.

you can't be on hand for the premiere. In Europe we followed one of the tours, out of necessity, and made a grand hurried march through the usual points of interest—a dreamlike journey, leaving tiny bright memories: the glint of sun on the Avon, late in the day; the Cornish coast in the blue of morning; the melodious voice of a concierge in Berne, phoning; the way gravel feels under your feet; drinking beer in a garden in Köln; a hayfield above the Lake of Thun; hors d'oeuvres for eight francs. You should have been along, tramping along.

Bob is so infected with the cinema that he has resigned from the Cunard Line and sets out for Hollywood in a new blue Dodge about the first of October. He warns you that he expects a meal in East Aurora, playing your own game on you, sir. Be kind to him—he is only a boy touring the country as others have done before him. I have instructed him in many things. I shall present him with a shiny bowl and my blessing, and advise him of the device of sending post cards on ahead.

Saw B.A. for a fleeting moment at Stamford Bridge in London. He was officiating at the Princeton-Cornell-Oxford-Cambridge affair, manfully pushing the bar up for the pole vault, stoutly rushing forward to catch the pole as it fell, all business, all sincerity. I was in Ithaca last spring and committed the unpardonable sin of NOT continuing to Buffalo, which I would like to have done, for I pine for a sight of Nancy-Elizabeth-Howard. I pine for the tranquility of Casenovia Creek, for the warm hospitality of the house of Cushman. Life is much the same. Probably I shall get a job soon, at something or other. I have been approached by a small publisher who wants me to write a small book; but I seem to have small taste for it, so I guess nothing much will come of that. This very moment I must go to bed, for tomorrow will be full of polo on Long Island with Peter Vischer and others, and my eyes must be bright and sparkling after eight hours' sleep. I am a bachelor and we crotchety bachelors are fretted if we miss our Postum in the morning, and if we are cheated out of our beauty sleep at night.

> With love to all and a prayer for
> a letter,
> Thine,
> Ho

I see you are in *Life*. I meet people on the street and they nod and bow and say "I see your friend Cushman is in *Life*."

• *In April 1927 Gus Lobrano married Jean Flick, who ran a travel bureau in Albany, and soon thereafter he left New York City and joined his wife in running the business. About a year later, with Bob Adams in*

California and Lobrano in Albany, the apartment at 112 West 13th
Street was vacated. White and Mike Galbreath moved into a two-room
apartment at 23 West 12th Street.

To JEAN FLICK

The New Yorker
25 West 45th Street
[February? 1927]
Wednesday

Dear Jean—

Gus has TOLD ALL (in strict confidence) and I would like—even
this early—to send you my excited greetings and wish you joy. Having
deeply pondered over the whole felicitous affair, I can see that it is surrounded with the greatest happiness—and I know that when you have
lived in the vicinity of this Mr. Lobrano for as long a time as I have you
will discover that *it alone* is almost boon enough to make life worth living
twenty-four hours of the day. At any rate this hurried note is just to assure you that all these parlous and sudden goings-on have the UN-
QUALIFIED ENDORSEMENT of this wizened old roommate—who is
not merely willing but eager to have his most precious charge ship off
and get married when he selects so delightful a lady.

With love to you both,
Andy

To HAROLD ROSS

c/o Bert Mosher
Oakland, Me.
[September 1927]

Dear Mr. Ross—

. . . I am on my vacation.[1] The reason I chose Maine is because there
is a lady here who gets the *N.Y. Times* and she lets me have it after she is
through. She uses P.1 to light fires with, but I never cared much for
aviation. Also I have a cricket. I will bet you haven't got a cricket. All you
have is Ralph.[2] I have named my cricket "Ralph" and he sings to me by
scraping his legs together.

My vacation has done me a world of good: I have taken off about
fifteen pounds and am gradually getting back my old pulmonary trouble.

---

1. The "vacation" was unauthorized—White simply disappeared without telling
anyone where he was going. He stayed at Bear Spring Camps on one of the Belgrade
Lakes. The proprietor of the camps was Bert Mosher, whom White had known
since his early days in Maine.
2. Ralph Paladino, Ross's secretary.

There is a spare bedroom in my shack, and I trust that if you are ever up this way you will feel free to drop in.

Very sincerely yours,
E. B. White

Ralph is trying to get out underneath the door. I think he wants to make water.

To **HAROLD ROSS**

[New York]
[December? 1927]

Dear Mr. Ross:

Here is the address book you were hinting for. Perhaps a few words of explanation would not be amiss. It was bought at Brentano's and cost seven fifty, a little more than I had expected to pay. It is of hand-tooled leather, as opposed to the ordinary machine-tooled kind which is every bit as good probably. It is a "red" book with a decorative border of "gold" and has a little pencil at the side which you will never use because it isn't practical. There is a good chance that you will never use the book either, but I took that into consideration when I bought it and will not be emotionally affected one way or the other. The filler or "pack" is removable, which is a handy wrinkle except that Brentano's have none of them in stock and it would be a lot of work to hunt one up any place else. The filler is indexed, the letters of the alphabet being alternately blue and red, possibly for some reason which you can figure out.

Now as to spirit of the gift. The spirit of the gift is very good. At first I resented the idea of having to give anything my employer. I don't owe you anything! Everything I have had at your hands I have worked for, often twice. But then it occurred to me that it might be worth my while to give you an address book in order to "get in strong" with you. And I might add that all my previous employers, when Christmas came round, received from me a little package of ground glass and porcupine quills. But my relations with you have always been pleasant, and as Ring Lardner so aptly put it you are a wonderful friend you. With a lot of hard work and honest effort on your part, I see no reason why we cannot continue on this friendly basis almost indefinitely. Please enter my name in your address book 12 W. 113 St. Chelsea 5276[1] and believe me

Merry Christmas,
E. B. White

Thank you for your many courtesies, which I often brood over.

---

1. The address was intentionally wrong—White was still living at 112 West 13th Street. The telephone number is scrambled, too.

To HAROLD ROSS

16 Juin [1928]
Guaranty, France

Dear Friend-across-the-Sea:

I will enclose a couple of clippings from the Paris Herald—which is the most entertaining morning newspaper I've ever read (probably because reading it is not a preface to going to work). I am also sending under separate cover a little article of some 35,000 words, called "Dr. Vinton."[1] After you are through laughing at it and wondering why I ever bothered to write it, give it to Morton [an office boy]—who once told me he enjoyed everything I wrote regardless of whether he quite understood it. I often think of that when I am lonely.

I am alone in Paris and evidently look it. Immoral women approach me and lay their hand on my arm (which is derived from a ceremony in the Roman church called "the laying on of the hands"). Three of them in an automobile approached me the other evening and asked me if I was lonely and wanted to go somewhere for a drink. I said "No man is lonely who has Jesus on his side," and they evidently saw my point for they drove away, pouting.

I want to go down to the Coast somewhere swimming but am prevented from doing so by my inability to speak French, and hence my inability to get to the railroad station. When I try to say the words I become ridiculous and when I don't try to say them I come to a standstill. English is not spoken at my hotel, but they serve me breakfast in bed and I get through the rest of the day by wandering from one cafe to another and saying the single word "Beer!" which is very sustaining and amusing. As soon as Gus gets back from Amsterdam I will get him to put me on a train for Nice, and then I will spend the rest of my life trying to talk my way out of the railroad station at Nice—which might make a little Talk item.

Best love,
White

To HOPE CROUCH

25 West 45th Street
[October 1928?]
Friday

Dear Hope:

I can't find anything the matter with Baby, which is very unusual after he has been visiting, and I have been trying to get round to thanking

---

1. "Dr. Vinton" was rejected by Ross, who said he didn't understand it. It was published in England in *The Adelphi* magazine in January 1931. White later included it in his collection of pieces, *Quo Vadimus?*

you for same.[1] Also fish delivered in good condition. Sorry it was necessary for me to break window to get them, but when I want my animals I want my animals.

As you probably know, I have very definite rates of payment for animal trouble, and other domestic inconveniences. It is a sliding scale which runs something like this: Bird overnight, ice cream soda; fish overnight, bon bons; dusting and sweeping, flowers; bird one week, evening at a moving picture theater; bird *and* fish one week, morning in Wanamaker auditorium; alligator one month, week-end in Atlantic City; laying rugs and making curtains, ermine coat; laying rugs and making curtains *and* keeping bird and fish and alligator for one month, offer of marriage or equivalent. Your case comes under head of keeping bird and fish two weeks, which according to my scale merits either an evening at the legitimate drama or an afternoon at the Columbia-Cornell football game (Nov. 3), whichever the lady designates.

My animal invitations always prove embarrassing to the lady, because she always suspects (and rightly so) that the invitation is tendered merely in line of duty, and spends the evening grousing quietly to herself. Therefore, I always extend the invitation with the definite understanding that if the lady wishes to consider it a perfunctory affair, she is at perfect liberty to do so and can spend all or part of the evening grousing quietly to herself if she wants to, without in any way impairing the general quality of the entertainment. So I trust you will be good enough to reply, choosing roughly between the football game and the legitimate drama, and I hope from the bottom of my perfunctory heart that you will favor me with an acceptance. Until I hear from you I shall be living on tenterhooks—and you know what fun that is.

EBW

To **HAROLD ROSS**

[1928?]
[Interoffice memo]

MR. ROSS:

Re progress of my efficiency.

You will note that in this week's batch of newsbreaks, the break "A blackjack in the hands of a colored choirmaster" was prepared by the "paste on the sheet" method, instead of the old "type and relax" method. Following is a report of the experiment, which I conducted only because you had specifically requested it.

---

1. Hope Crouch (now Mrs. Ray Nash), a friend who lived nearby, had been looking after White's pets during one of his periodic absences from the city. "Baby" was White's canary, the subject of several pieces in *The New Yorker*.

Time elapsed looking for paste: 4 min.

Loosening paste with water to make it sticky: 2 min.

Trimming the clipping so it would look neat: 5 min.

Applying paste to clipping and fingers 1 min.

Pressing clipping to paper and withdrawing sticky fingers 1½ min.

Trip to men's comfort room to wash hands 2 min.

Time elapsed in men's room talking to friend I met there 30 min.

Trip back ½ min.

Time elapsed trying to get paste-up break into typewriter to write line 1 min.

Re-pasting clipping because it came off 5 min.

Time spent thinking up witty note to send you about experiment 1 min.

Time spent writing   "   "   to you   "   "   8 min.

Total elapsed time on newsbreak "A blackjack in the hands" one hour 1 min.

Conclusion re efficiency: Hooey.

EBW

I V

"THE MOST BEAUTIFUL DECISION"

1929-1930

•   *Nineteen twenty-nine was a big year for White—his first two books were published (one in collaboration with Thurber) and he and Katharine Angell were married. The year, however, did not start on a note of either literary triumph or domestic felicity. Here are the first two entries in his journal:*

> January 1—23 W. 12. In the morning rain—sorrowing on the broad flat roof outside my window, in the afternoon heavy fog, turning the trees to plumes, the buildings to castles, and the lights to balloons. Walking twice around the reservoir this afternoon in the fog, resolving a problem: whether to quit my job and leave town telling no one where I was going. I got no sleep last night trying to resolve it. . . . This year I dread—it will make me thirty before it's done with me.
>
> January 3. Yesterday hard at work, dutiful at the office, for all my great fuss the day before about going away. But I thought of a funny drawing, and so was reconciled to my lot. Besides, one of the persons I like best in the world is Thurber. Just being around him is something. I have just walked to the corner and bought tomorrow's paper and found my poem ["Rhyme for a Reasonable Lady," a love poem to K. S. Angell, in F.P.A.'s Conning Tower] . . .

On a tip from Mrs. Angell, Eugene Saxton of Harper & Brothers had become interested in White's writings and had agreed to publish him. The Lady Is Cold, a collection of his poems, came out in the spring. Is Sex Necessary?, a spoof on the heavy sex books of that day, came out in the fall. On November 3, White noted in his journal: "Tonight at Mount Vernon I overheard Mother and Father discussing the sex book. Father said, 'Well, I don't know what you think about it, but I'm ashamed of it.'" It was a sobering moment for a young writer. Ten days later, he gave his parents a second jolt—he married a divorcee with two children.

Katharine Sergeant Angell, the bride, was a transplanted Bostonian, youngest of three daughters of Charles S. Sergeant, vice-president of the Boston Elevated Street Railway. Her mother had died when she was five years old, and she had been mothered by Mr. Sergeant's unmarried sister Caroline, "Aunt Crully," who came to Brookline to take charge of the household. Katharine went from Miss Winsor's school to Bryn Mawr, graduated in 1914, and a year later married Ernest Angell, a young lawyer in Cleveland. When the United States got into the war, Angell joined up, won a commission, and disappeared overseas for the duration, leaving his young wife in Cleveland with their infant daughter, Nancy —not an auspicious beginning for a marriage. Katharine took a job and stayed on in Cleveland until the house got too cold to survive in, then returned to her father's in Brookline. On Angell's return from the war, the couple lived briefly in Cleveland, then moved to New York, where he went to work with a law firm.

When Mrs. Angell joined the staff of The New Yorker *in August 1925, she realized that her marriage was breaking up. She had taken the editorial job partly to keep her mind off problems at home and partly to develop some skills against the day when she might have to be self-supporting. There were two children now—Roger was born in 1920. In the winter of 1929, with the magazine celebrating its fourth birthday, she moved out of her house on the Upper East Side and took an apartment at 16 East 8th Street; and when summer arrived she went to Reno for a divorce. On November 13, she married E. B. White. They were both back at their desks the next day, preferring to delay until springtime the honeymoon they planned in Bermuda.*

Although they had been aware of their growing attachment to each other long before her divorce became final, the courtship was not smooth. White, always wary of entanglements, found himself in love with an older woman, mother of two. Katharine, with her New England background, was reluctant to accept the failure of her first marriage and was concerned about the problems a divorce and remarriage would create for her children, and whether marriage to White made sense anyway, considering the disparity in their ages. Finally, they managed to shed their anxieties long enough to drive out to Bedford Village, New York, and get married in the Presbyterian church on the village green. They had told no one of their plan, for fear the news would start an endless round of debates. Only Katharine's dog, Daisy, went along as an attendant. White, who hates ritualistic occasions of all kinds, remembers the ceremony with pleasure. "It was a very nice wedding—nobody threw anything, and there was a dog fight."

He adds: "I soon realized I had made no mistake in my choice of a wife. I was helping her pack an overnight bag one afternoon when she said, 'Put in some tooth twine.' I knew then that a girl who called dental floss tooth twine was the girl for me. It had been a long search, but it was worth it."

To STANLEY HART WHITE

[New York]
[January 1929]
Tuesday

Dear Stan:

I was moderately pleased to receive a letter from a personal follower and brother, on this cold day. Brothers, I have noticed, never write each other, which is a good thing. I have been meaning to send you a note, however, explaining the wire requesting your Plaza sketches—that having probably come as a surprise and an annoyance. Also expressing regret that you left town when you did. Harper's is publishing, in the spring, a volume of my poetry, and you had hardly been out of town ten minutes when I wanted you back here to submit some sketches on New York subjects, to be used as little decorative illustrations of the poems which are on New York subjects. The jacket of the book, for instance, will be the lady at the fountain in the Plaza, the title of the book being: "The Lady Is Cold." My reason for getting you to send me those sketches was that I wanted to show them to the artist who did the drawing. As things stand now, the book will contain three or four little spot drawings, in the wood-cut manner, but nothing of much consequence, because they were done by a high-powered artist who was not particularly interested in the task. I think if you had been here, with more leisure and sympathy, our collaboration might have been effective.

I appreciated your critical estimate and praise of my writing— a special kind of writing which has always amused me. I discovered a long time ago that writing of the small things of the day, the trivial matters of the heart, the inconsequential but near things of this living, was the only kind of creative work which I could accomplish with any sincerity or grace. As a reporter, I was a flop, because I always came back laden not with facts about the case, but with a mind full of the little difficulties and amusements I had encountered in my travels. Not till *The New Yorker* came along did I ever find any means of expressing those impertinences and irrelevancies. Thus yesterday, setting out to get a story on how police horses are trained, I ended by writing a story entitled "How Police Horses Are Trained" which never even mentions a police horse, but has to do entirely with my own absurd adventures at police headquarters. The rewards of such endeavor are not that I have acquired an audience or a following, as you suggest (fame of any kind being a Pyrrhic victory), but that sometimes in writing of myself—which is the only subject anyone knows intimately—I have occasionally had the exquisite thrill of putting my finger on a little capsule of truth, and heard it give the faint squeak of mortality under my pressure, an antic sound.

I predict that a man of your digestion and parts will go far in the art of picture-making, and I suspect that it will eventually take some such form as the drawings and paintings by my friend Walter King Stone,[1] which adorn Country Life and things like that, and which must give him much satisfaction in the making. One nice thing about either writing or drawing is that it is both a direct and an uncertain way of making a living. To write a piece and sell it to a magazine is as near a simple life as shining up a pushcart full of apples and vending them to passersby. It has a pleasing directness not found in the world of commerce and business, where every motion is by this time so far removed from the cause and the return, as to be almost beyond recognition.

Give my love to the chameleon that comes out from behind a vine on the porch of the Ponce de Leon,[2] leers at you for a moment in the sunlight, and races back again.

Yours,

En

Needless to say, if you will mention a suitable address, I will perpetuate your *New Yorker* subscription, which is a mere gesture frequently made in order to hold my public, which I must keep at any cost.

To HAROLD ROSS

[Dorset, Ont.]
[July? 1929]
Friday

Dear Ross:

Report on me, as requested in your letter of uncertain date.

I am getting back to New York later than I expected due to the fact that I'm acquiring an interest in this camp [Camp Otter], and that takes time. My mild participation in the belles lettres of New York will probably be less this year than formerly (I'm working out a tentative schedule

---

1. Cornell professor and artist, brother-in-law of Bristow Adams.
2. Stanley was working as landscape architect at the Hotel Ponce de Leon in St. Augustine.

of 10 minutes a week for poesy, 25 minutes for prose, and a half hour before breakfast for answers to hard questions), a consummation designed to improve the state of the local b.l. as well as my own general condition. On account of the fact that The New Yorker has a tendency to make me morose and surly, the farther I stay away the better. I appreciate very much your extraordinary capacity to endure, and in fact cope with, my somewhat vengeful attitude about The New Yorker and my crafty habit of slipping away for long intervals (these intervals wouldn't have cost you a cent if you hadn't been a damn fanciful bookkeeper— this last one has cost you some $420, but if you insist on being ridiculous, it's out of my control). Next to yourself and maybe one or two others, I probably have as tender a feeling for your magazine as anybody. For me it isn't a complete life, though, and that's one reason why returning to this place where I worked during the summers of 1920-21 has been such a satisfying experience. In ten years Dorset hasn't changed—it's almost the only place I've ever come back to that hasn't given me an empty feeling from discovering that nothing can be the same again. The fellow that I first came here with [Robert Hubbard] is now running the camp, and we're working on a plan for going in business together. At the moment I don't know just what this amounts to, but it's a lucky break for me because it's a realization of an old desire of mine. Sometime next week I'm going to Ithaca via Fairport with the Hubbards. I don't know exactly when I'll be in New York.

I'm worried about old man Thurber and hope you can make him take a decent vacation. He needs fancy bookkeeping more than I do, who don't need it at all. . . .

This report on me is a bit sketchy, but you asked for it and it's the best I can do in the hour between breakfast and the time I have to row over and get the milk.

Yrs with love,
White

Tell Thurber to write me.

To KATHARINE SERGEANT ANGELL

[Dorset, Ont.]
[August 1929]
Tuesday

Dear Katharine:

If my calculations are correct (one arrives at the day of the month by taking shots at the stars and computing from old newspapers discovered in the privy) you are on the way home [from Reno]. Probably none too soon. I have an anguished letter from Ross that sounds as though he could only hang on three days longer. He takes things too hard. If he thinks the New Yorker is complicated he ought to see a boys' camp. Lost blankets, heart-aches, fallings-in-the-lake—a marvelous confusion, always comical because kids are so funny. Hub just showed me a letter he received from a frightened parent; the letter enclosed another that the parent had got from his small son in camp: "Dear Daddy, Please come up at once as I am so homesick and I will die if you don't come up here right away." Hub, on investigating, found out that the boy had written the letter just after being hit on the head with a broom by a tent-mate, and had forgotten the whole affair ten minutes later. But he had mailed the letter home, just as a matter of routine.

The boys leave a week from today and grown people begin to drift in. Hub and I are going into the bush again, probably with Hub's wife and a kid who is staying after camp closes because of hay fever. Our trip last week was grand, through the most beautiful country I've ever seen. Nights are freezing now (frost almost every night) but the days heat up just as in July. The trees are turning early this year, and it looks like fall already. I haven't heard from you in a dog's age, but my mail seems to be scattered around a bit anyway. I have succeeded in losing track of about everything—people, dates, friends, mail, jobs, home. And it feels good. The sun beats in. Yesterday Hubbard gave me a haircut with the camp clippers. Things are much as they were in the days when I was here before—the clanging gong that gets you up, the kids trading desserts for nickel candy bars, the still shore where you brush your teeth, the little lakes nearby where you can watch blue herons catch frogs, the lumber camp and the peat bog. Ontario is wonderful (haven't you been up here, I seem to remember that you have). I envy Hub his job even though it is a lot of work and a lot of responsibility. . . .

There's a marvelous doubles game going on right outside, making it impossible to write. It's impossible to write up here anyway. Love to everybody, and keep the home fires burning.

Andy

To KATHARINE SERGEANT ANGELL

[Dorset, Ont.]
[September 11, 1929]
Wednesday

Dear Katharine:

I once started a letter to you (date uncertain) but it dried up and got crumbly. Later I started another, but it got wet and mouldy. I intend to get this one down on the floor with my knees on it and push it into an envelope even if it's got maggots. The last letter I wrote was a beauty—four typewritten pages, which so exhausted me I couldn't reach for a stamp—vivid word pictures of lakes, streams, fish, men and women, seasonal changes, statistical matter, references, addenda, all kinds of advice, charts, marginal notations, and brisk passages designed to stimulate and exalt. It got wet.

This afternoon I get the last trout of the year and carry the canoe back from Harvey Lake (one mile through swamp). Tomorrow the third coat will be dry on my handsome new canoe which Hughie McEachern [a local craftsman] has built for me. I've decided to go in business with Hubbard and we're going to Ithaca to settle matters. He's going to incorporate, and we are going to hold directors' meetings on top of the diving tower. This camp is much better than it used to be, and it used to be very good. It's got everything now, including a live Chippewa Indian, a sugar bush, a 1917 Dodge truck, a marauding bear, and a family of worms in the tennis court. If I can, I'm going to leave [the car] in Ithaca with Bob [Hubbard] and paddle my shiny new canoe down the Erie canal and Hudson to surprise central New York people and to give myself a good time.

Camp has been wonderful the last couple of weeks. No adults came (I misunderstood what Bob said about adults—he meant that some of the grown-up persons in camp would remain) and the woods are beautiful. Ray Wattles (age nine) lives with me in my shack. Hunting will start soon and Bob is coming back up for deer season. He hunts with Sam Beaver, his private Indian.[1] Sam lives in camp the year round to keep the snow off the roofs. Ray's hunting season has started already: he has his eye on woodchuck—wants the fur.

Give my best to Jim.

Andy

• *Because they worked in the same building, the Whites often communicated by interoffice memo. Soon after their marriage, White cut from an old issue of* The New Yorker *a fragment of a Rea Irvin drawing whose caption was a quote from Albert Einstein—"People slowly accustomed themselves to the idea that the physical states of space itself were the final physical reality." White wrote a new caption and placed the result on his wife's desk.*

---

1. White liked the name Sam Beaver and years later gave the name to the boy in *The Trumpet of the Swan.*

To KATHARINE S. WHITE

[November 1929]
[Interoffice memo]

E.B. White slowly accustomed himself
to the idea that he had made the
most beautiful decision of his life.

• The first few weeks of married life were not easy. Because of a "joint custody" arrangement, Katharine's children stayed with their father during the school week, with their mother on weekends, holidays, and during their summer vacations—a great deal of shuttling about. Nancy was thirteen, Roger nine. White's worldly goods were at 23 West 12th Street, and he and Katharine decided to set up housekeeping a few blocks away in her apartment, 16 East 8th Street, which was larger and more attractive.

To KATHARINE S. WHITE

[New York]
[Late November 1929]
Saturday night

Dear Katharine (very dear):

I've had moments of despair during the last week which have added years to my life and put many new thoughts in my head. Always, however, I have ended on a cheerful note of hope, based on the realization that you are the person to whom I return and that you are the recurrent phrase in my life. I realized that so strongly one day a couple of weeks ago when, after being away among people I wasn't sure of and in circumstances I had doubts about, I came back and walked into your office and saw how real and incontrovertible you seemed. I don't know whether you know just what I mean or whether you experience, ever, the same feeling; but what I mean is, that being with you is like walking on a very clear morning—definitely the sensation of belonging there.

This marriage is a terrible challenge: everyone wishing us well, and all with their tongues in their cheeks. What other people think, or wish, or prophesy, is not particularly important, except as it tends to work on our minds. I think you have the same intuitive hesitancy that I have—about pushing anything too hard, and the immediate problem surely is that we recognize & respect each other's identity. That I could assimilate Nancy overnight is obviously out of the question—or that she could me. In things like that we gain ground slowly. By and large, our respective families had probably best be kept in their respective places during the pumpkin weather—and gradually, like the Einstein drawing of Rea Irvin's, people will become accustomed to the idea that etc. etc.

I'm just writing this haphazard for no reason other than that I felt like writing you a letter before going to bed.

I love you. And that's a break.

Andy

To KATHARINE S. WHITE

[King Edward Hotel]
[Toronto]
[November 30, 1929]

Natural History

The spider, dropping down from twig,
Unwinds a thread of his devising:
A thin, premeditated rig
To use in rising.

And all the journey down through space,
In cool descent, and loyal-hearted,
He builds a ladder to the place
From which he started.

Thus I, gone forth, as spiders do,
In spider's web a truth discerning,
Attach one silken strand to you
For my returning.

• *White sometimes engaged Daisy, the Scottish terrier, to write to Katharine, "thus enabling me to refer to myself in the third person—a common device of politicians and tyrants." Daisy was, according to White, "an opinionated little bitch," the daughter of a female named Jeannie, owned by Thurber.*

To KATHARINE S. WHITE

[Bedford Village, N.Y.]
[Spring 1930]

Dear Mrs. White:

I like having Josephine[1] here in the morning, although I suppose I will get less actual thinking done—as I used to do my thinking mornings in the bathroom. White has been stewing around for two days now, a little bit worried because he is not sure that he has made you realize how glad he is that there is to be what the column writer in the Mirror calls a blessed event. So I am taking this opportunity, Mrs. White, to help him out to the extent of writing you a brief note which I haven't done in quite a long time but have been a little sick myself as you know. Well, the truth is White is beside himself and would have said more about it but is holding himself back, not wanting to appear ludicrous to a veteran mother. What he feels, he told me, is a strange queer tight little twitchy feeling around the inside of his throat whenever he thinks that something is happening which will require so much love and all on account of you being so wonderful. (I am not making myself clear I am afraid, but on the occasions when White has spoken privately with me about this he was in no condition to make himself clear either and I am just doing the best I can in my own way.) I know White so well that I always know what is the matter with him, and it always comes to the same thing—he gets thinking that nothing that he writes or says ever quite expresses his

---

1. Josephine Buffa, the cook, a North Italian woman who was crazy about puppies. According to White, she was the only person he ever knew who, when a dog got sick on the floor and she had to clean up the mess, felt sorry for the dog.

feeling, and he worries about his inarticulateness just the same as he does about his bowels, except it is worse, and it makes him either mad, or sick, or with a prickly sensation in the head. But my, my, my, last Sunday he was so full of this matter which he couldn't talk about, and he was what Josephine in her simple way would call hoppy, and particularly so because it seemed so good that everything was starting at once—I mean those things, whatever they are, that are making such a noise over in the pond by Palmer Lewis's house,[2] and the song sparrow that even I could hear from my confinement in the house, and those little seeds that you were sprinkling up where the cut glass and bones used to be—all starting at the same time as the baby, which he seems to think exists already by the way he stands around staring at you and muttering little prayers. Of course he is also very worried for fear you will get the idea that he is regarding you merely as a future mother and not as a present person, or that he wants a child merely as a vindication of his vanity. I doubt if those things are true; White enjoys animal husbandry of all kinds including his own; and as for his regard for you, he has told me that, quite apart from this fertility, he admires you in all kinds of situations or dilemmas, some of which he says have been quite dirty.

Well, Mrs. White, I expect I am tiring you with this long letter, but as you often say yourself, a husband and wife should tell each other about the things that are on their mind, otherwise you get nowhere, and White didn't seem to be able to tell you about his happiness, so thought I would attempt to put in a word.

White is getting me a new blanket, as the cushion in the bathroom is soiled.

Lovingly,
Daisy

To KATHARINE S. WHITE

Hotel Genosha
Oshawa, Ontario
[July 4, 1930]
Friday night

Dear K:

We are in Oshawa, suffering from Oshawa. Across the street a Tiny Tim miniature golf course is being constructed, the men working overtime, pushing hand rollers and installing small hazards. This morning we crossed Lake Ontario and would have gone right on to camp but the Pierce, after some brilliant road work, burned out a generator—

2. Palmer Lewis owned the cottage the Whites had rented in Bedford Village so they would have a place in the country to take Nancy and Roger on weekends.

which will cost me a pretty penny and will land us in Dorset tomorrow night. God is also striking me a full blow across the eyes—the hay being ripe on every side.

You really should have seen the Pierce being put aboard the S.S. *Ontario* of the B.R.&R. this morning at the Genesee Dock in Rochester. The ship is built to carry railroad freight cars, and when occasionally someone comes along wanting to take his automobile, the automobile (even if there's only one, as there was this morning) is loaded onto a freight car, and the whole business is pushed by a steam locomotive onto the boat. The Pierce never looked so small and I never felt so impressive as when I found the locomotive and one car waiting for me, steam up, engineer at attention, and a crew of three to do the switching and the coupling. All this—services of a private standard-size locomotive at both ends plus trip across—only $10.50.

The boy we took on in Ithaca is eleven, a squirming jumpy little brat who seems never to go to the bathroom. He is in bed beside me, after having refused a Milnesia wafer. Yesterday's ride to Ithaca was fine—a swell day, cool and sunny—and we went at a good clip, the Pierce's tin horn shrill in the green valleys. Conrad Wyvell[1] was equipped with torpedoes for the dull silences of Sullivan County.

Love to you, Serena, Daisy, Roger, Nancy, Josephine, Willy, Miss Heyl, your father, and the two cats.[2] Or is it eleven cats?

A.

To KATHARINE S. WHITE

Camp Otter
Dorset, Ontario
[July 10, 1930]

Dear K:

Just have time for a small greeting before taking some parents across the lake. Jim [Thurber] is here, wandering aimlessly about camp, a tall misty visitor about whom nothing much is known. He arrived yesterday in Bracebridge, his suitcase collapsing on the platform just as he detrained. I found him picking up shirts and neckties, the blood rushing to his head.

He brought your letter and also tidings, and I'm so glad you are well, you and yours. I want Little Joe[1] and Serena up here with me: the place is all reserved in the green canoe for you and them. This morning

---

1. One of White's nephews, who spent the summer of 1930 at Camp Otter.
2. Serena was a name the Whites used for the unborn baby. Willy was the son of Josephine Buffa, and Miss Heyl a governess on loan from Katharine's sister.

1. Another name for the unborn baby.

I took Jim across the lake to see about a loon's nest on Huckleberry Island. . . . I took the movie camera and set up the birthday tripod right in the canoe in back of Thurber's head, where I could operate it. There was just a faint east wind, and when we got round the other side of the island, the mother was on the nest. I got the canoe in close and she came off like a streak and I could see the day-old chick and the unhatched egg. Then the loon, calling at the top of her lungs, splashed up and down right in front of the camera, trying to attract us away from the nest. I got a lot of shots and then the chick, hearing his mother crying, came off the nest and set out on his first big trip. His mother joined him (all this just a few yards away from the canoe where I could photograph everything that went on) and together they beat it down the lake. I don't see how I can wait to see the picture.

Jim and I are going to walk up the Hollow Lake road this afternoon in hopes of finding Sam Beaver home. Somebody saw him in Dorset the other day and the report is that he wants to come back to camp.

Bob still hasn't showed up, and the camp lacks the gaiety that he supplies. He is due tonight.

The parents are waiting. I love you too.

Andy

To KATHARINE S. WHITE

[Dorset, Ont.]
[July 1930]
Wednesday night

Dear K:

This has been a wonderful day, full of great doings. All morning with Allan [camp handyman], pulling the propeller shaft out of the motor boat, and this afternoon driving Allan and his small son Arnold to Bracebridge—Arnold with his tiny country voice and his little country smell. In Bracebridge I went to the foundry to get a new shaft and in the middle of things a terrific storm broke—hail, thunder and lightning. One of the workmen came running in to show off a hailstone, and just as I reached the doorway and stood for a moment, a beautiful green-blue bolt of lightning crackled down and struck a telegraph pole about two hundred feet away, setting fire to the transformer, which went up in a green flame. We all jumped out of the doorway and one of the men ran and threw the switch in the foundry, cutting off the current. The thunder clap that accompanied the flash was simply deafening and I could feel the electricity. About three minutes later we heard people running and somebody shouted that Shier's lumber mill was on fire. All the men in the foundry piled into the Pierce and I drove them to the mill, with the whole town of Bracebridge streaming along. The fire gong in the town was ringing a steady call, and all the sky was red with flames. The mill had caught like so much kindling, and the place was shooting into the air higher than the four tall black smokestacks that still stood upright. The Bracebridge fire department arrived—a hose cart towed behind a Studebaker sedan, and a horse drawn pumper. All it could do was spray water on nearby buildings. The blaze was so hot that although I stood in the rain, my clothes stayed dry. Finally the heat melted the guy wires that supported the chimneys, and all four of them went toppling down together.

Afterwards Allan and Arnold and I to dinner at Keeler's [a restaurant], and then driving home through the clear storm-cooled evening a red sunset sky and white mist rising in all the swamps around the trunks of the birches and tamaracks. Crossing the lake, the red glow had gone, the full moon had come up, and the northern lights were sending bright shafts high into the dome.

Your letters came in the reverse order from which they were written and I have pieced together the news. How marvelous that you are in the midst of kittens and calendulas, and Daisy safe[1]—but it is foolish of you to be anywhere but here, with your tumultuous little Joe whom I love so and who must hear the great frogs of July at their love-making and see the lights in the north. Even at long distance it's so good to know you.

A.

To KATHARINE S. WHITE

[Dorset, Ont.]
[July 21, 1930]
Monday morning

Dear K:

It is a gray morning. Thurber is drawing animals for Harper's, the tennis court is being rolled with the squeaky roller, and Gretchen has lost a red ball in the calm lake. The trips are back in camp and preliminary swimming races start this afternoon.

In Peterborough we bought a rowing skiff and a small sail boat and I had hay fever pretty bad from driving all afternoon through the hay harvest. I was so tickled to get your letter with the drawing of Daisy's insides. Have they set the bone, and will she be well enough to come up here with us? I feel very guilty to have been away through it all, when it must have been so much work and so upsetting to you. But I am glad she is alive and you are alive. . . .

---

1. Daisy had been hit by a car in Bedford Village but had escaped with a broken leg.

Parents drift in and out of camp, always with minor discomforts or accidents. Bob Howe's people came for a day last week, didn't know how to get to camp, tried to drive their car around the lake on an old lumber road, finally got out and walked right on past camp two miles through the woods and landed at another lake to the north of here. Saturday Joe Archibald's mother and father showed up: their car had blown a gasket in Gravenhurst and they had hired another car to bring them the rest of the way. I drove them back to Gravenhurst last night in the Pierce. Bob and Louise [Hubbard] went along for the ride . . . and coming back I ditched the Pierce trying to pass another car in the narrow dark rainy road, and we had to get pulled out.

Camp is really going very well and everybody is happy. The morning dip parties have started at Sandy Beach, and the whole camp rushes naked into the still cold lake to Hubbard's bellowing. The weather has been warm and good, with the most beautiful skies at night. I took Jim over to the peat bog the other evening (the first time I had carried my own canoe) and we drifted around in the twilight hopeful of seeing a deer. The white water lilies are out in the streams, and the huckleberries will be ready on the island in a few days. Another trip goes out this afternoon, into Algonquin. I want you up here for all these things. Friday night I wished you could be here . . . Jim Wright and John Duerr and I went to a private dance at the Russells' on the Hollow Lake road.[1] (Thurber didn't go because he was afraid of getting shot.) The party was given for one of the Russells who showed up after being gone thirty years. (He has gone away again, this time, he says, never to come back.) I had been to several dances at the grange but this was the first private dance I'd ever seen. It was marvelous, all square dances, with women feeding their babies in the kitchen and the men drinking home-made beer in the dirt cellar. Mr. Cameron, of the fire tower, was one of the fiddlers, and a Russell was the other. We arrived at the party at half past eleven and it was just beginning to get under way. The rooms of the old house had been cleared of furniture, and planks had been laid along chairs along the wall for people to sit on. The men wore suspenders and some of them had on clean shirts. Hughie McEachern called the dances, wearing a jacket and tie. When we arrived Len Russell took us over and introduced us to the Russell who was fiddling. He shook hands very solemnly, and said he was happy to meet us and we should make ourselves at home. At one o'clock some of the men were beginning to get lively with beer, and the women passed refreshments. First they passed a wash tub filled with empty cups. Then they came around with hot tea and plates of

1. Wright and Duerr were camp counselors. Wright, a Canadian, and White took many canoe trips together and became lifelong friends.

canned salmon sandwiches. A shy . . . boy, lately out of jail for raping his cousin, passed the sugar. "Have some sugar?" he said, in a soft, almost inaudible voice. At one thirty Bruce Crewson, age 12, wandered in to see how the party was getting on. He shook hands with me and I asked him how his father was. "All right the last time I saw him," he replied gravely.

Old Mrs. McEachern, mother of Hughie, spelled one of the fiddlers along about midnight, holding the fiddle down on her breast. She wore a black dress and a lace collar and sat rigid and unsmiling, not even tapping her toe, but playing very fast and always right in time with the fiddler. Mr. Dagg was there, in peg top trousers, his seventy years adding finish to his dancing. After a while he lost track of Mrs. Dagg, and went about looking for her with a flashlight. Since the death of Freddie McKey, Mr. Dagg has taken over the burden of bootlegging for Dorset. At half past one we descended into the cellar and were offered a bottle of the yeasty beer while somebody held a match.

I wish you could have accompanied us to that dance.

Bob has just passed by my cabin and asked me if I want to drive to Rochester with him tomorrow, but I am afraid of hay fever and think I'll wait a day or two and come on the train. At any rate, I'll be seeing you this week. (Thurber has just been discussing his bowels and comparing them to mine, claiming that his are better than mine, adding that of course he is older and taller than I am.) . . .

We are building a ping pong table down in Tent 8.

The first issue of the *Otter Bee*[2] was out Saturday, containing a special Thurber rotogravure section. . . .

Love to you all.

Andy

I will be awfully glad to see you.

To JAMES A. WRIGHT

St. Luke's Hospital,
overlooking Harlem,
New York City,
Sept. 12, 1930

Dear Jim,

They've got me down now and the only escape from a hospital is the grave. I got sick the second day after returning to New York, and

---

2. The camp paper. With James Thurber contributing drawings, it was in a peculiarly happy position.

after a good deal of sparring the doctor pronounced it Paratyphoid[1] and shipped me to this dump, where I made an instant hit with the day-nurse by kicking over a basin of trichloride solution. My room commands a very pretty view of Harlem, including the Hell Gate railroad bridge, a Castoria sign, and the Sixth Avenue "L." Every two hours a Greek orderly named Nick comes wandering into the room and takes my temperature by pushing a thermometer up my bunghole. My temperature is normal. The chances of my recovery are said to be good, although there is a whispering campaign among the internes to the effect that I have pernicious anemia and am a goner. They took my blood-count and found it was only 3,600 when it should be 8,000, thus strengthening their theory that I wouldn't last long.

We had a great trip down in the Pierce, which developed a strange and alarming ineffectualness just after leaving Orillia. It finally burned out its two little resistance coils and we missed the Cobourg boat, and spent the night in Oshawa. The Pierce is at the moment in the hands of the Bedford police, who confiscated it after it had stood three days parked on the main street by the railroad station, where I left it on the morning I took sick.

I hope Paul[2] remembered to give you the half bottle of Golden Wedding which I cached for you in a roll of roofing paper in the boathouse. You better try to get down to New York this fall—we will put you up at the best hospital in town. We received your pretty card of Highland Inn and were glad to know you were still alive at that point. I will never forget the merry scene at Hardwood where you stood surrounded by 3 women, each applying a tourniquet. I pray God I may live to see such sights again.

Yrs,
Andy

To KATHARINE S. WHITE

[October? 1930]
[Interoffice memo]

K.

My publishers settled up this morning, & the 5th Avenue shops could hardly hold me.

This flower was bought with the smaller of the 2 checks—the one for $13.30 "Lady Is Cold."

Love

Andy

---

1. It was probably hepatitis.
2. Paul Hartzell, who conducted religious services at Camp Otter.

To GUSTAVE S. LOBRANO

[New York]
[December 1930]
Sunday

You lie, you rotter—I write you all the time. It's a crime the way I'm always writing you. Katharine was saying only yesterday: "All you ever do is write that Mr. Lobrano." We both think you ought to come down again, as it would save us all a lot of trouble and I could take you to the Cameo again, an experience which I know you must have thoroughly enjoyed. I met Jack Koffler on the street yesterday—he said the yacht was going fairly well in spite of people being broke.[1] He asked for you and I said you were fine. Said you were up in Albany cutting your teeth out of whole cloth.

K. is fine and young White will turn up in a fortnight, at the Harbor hospital, 61st and Madison. The suitcases are packed, and the nursery is in order—ping pong table, commode, drawers with little shirts laid neatly. All that remains to be done is for me, the father, to construct some bathing facilities for the baby, which is to have a bath every day. If it is a girl it is to be Serena; if a boy heaven knows what name he will go by. We thought of Gustave and dropped it like a hot iron. Please check one:

Joel	Seth
Cornelius	Shepley
Samuel	Angus
Oliver Partridge	James
Matthew	Eric

I remember the letter you wrote me when Dottie was born, on the excitements and limitations of sudden fatherhood, and I am beginning to feel something of it already. Aside from the simple satisfaction which most parents derive from seeing a new person created more or less in one's own image, I seem to enjoy a warm glow at the idea of helping to people the earth—this despite the tricks earth knows how to play on its people, despite even some of the people themselves. Also, to a writer, a child is an alibi. If I should never in all my years write anything worth reading, I can always explain that by pointing to my child. I was concerned with larger affairs than literature: I was peopling the earth. A soothsayer out west told K. last year that this child (not even conceived,

---

1. Koffler, a travel agent, had chartered a royal yacht and converted it to a cruise ship.

I might add, at that time) was destined to become a good musician, and would take us, its parents, to all the capitals of Europe. Courtesy of the Flick Travel Service, maybe? . . .

Love,
Andy

Remember "Dr. Vinton"? I've just resurrected it and sold it to *The Adelphi* (London). Hah!

•   *The years at 16 East 8th Street—the first six years of his marriage—are remembered by White as among the happiest and busiest of his life. His wanderings were over, he had acquired a lovely wife and an amiable infant son, and he was enjoying the cachet of being published in* The New Yorker.

The Village was home to him. Eighth Street, with its crosstown streetcar, was a relatively tranquil spot in that decade, and good friends, old and new, lived nearby: Jim and Althea Thurber, Jap and Helen Gude, Bob and Elsa Coates, Russell and Kate Lord, Joel Sayre, St. Clair McKelway.

White liked to begin the day on the top deck of a Fifth Avenue bus, riding uptown to the office. The Depression was on, but The New Yorker, *perversely, had begun to prosper. When many publications were plunging downhill or hanging on by their fingernails,* The New Yorker *was climbing steadily, gaining literary acclaim and enjoying a moderate financial success.*

The staff of the magazine grew and became more specialized. Robert Benchley was theater critic and started The Wayward Press *department. Clifton Fadiman reviewed books. Geoffrey Hellman joined up as staff writer and contributor in the Fact department, which in 1935 was separated from Fiction and edited by St. Clair McKelway. Frequent contributors to the magazine included Frank Sullivan, Clarence Day, S. J. Perelman, Lewis Mumford, Robert Coates, John O'Hara, Ogden Nash, Dorothy Parker, Phillis McGinley, Ring Lardner, John McNulty. Artists included, besides the redoubtable Thurber, Arno, and Irvin, Mary Petty and her husband, Alan Dunn, Whitney Darrow, Gluyas Williams, Helen Hokinson. Alexander Woollcott's Shouts and Murmurs department was the only feature in the history of the magazine that was cut to fit. One critical addition, for the Whites, was Daise Terry, who arrived in 1929 as secretary to Katharine and later headed a pool of stenographers and*

typists. Other notable arrivals were John Mosher, first reader and con-
tributor of fiction; William Shawn, who signed on as a Talk reporter and
was soon Ross's right-hand man in the Fact department; and Wolcott
Gibbs, who gave up a job as brakeman on the Long Island Railroad to
help Katharine edit fiction.

In January 1931, White's weekly pay check was $240. For this sum
he wrote the Comment page, edited the Newsbreaks, did some Talk re-
write, and doctored picture captions. By turning out a couple of pieces,
he could double his weekly take. Katharine, too, was earning well and
liking her work more and more. "It was a peculiarly lucky time for us,"
White says now. "Both of us were so busy with writing and editing, we
had little time or inclination for spending money. We just took our
money and turned it over without comment to the bank. Later, when we
decided to buy a house in Maine, there the money was." In 1934 White's
third book, Every Day Is Saturday—*a collection of Comments from* The
New Yorker—*was published.*

In the summer of 1930, the Whites rented a cottage in East Blue
Hill, Maine, on a property called "the Granite." Miss Nila Slaven was
their landlady; Percy Moore and Herman Gray, caretakers for Miss
Slaven, became their friends. Here, in coastal Maine, the children—
Nancy and Roger Angell and Joel White—were united for the summer.
Both the Whites carried their work along with them: Katharine edited
manuscripts by day and by night, White ground out Comment pages and
Newsbreaks from a small room over the garage. Maine worked well as
a retreat, and after three years of renting, the Whites drifted a few miles
south into Brooklin and bought the farm where they have spent a good
part of their lives.

To GUSTAVE S. LOBRANO

16 East 8 Street
[Early 1931]
Monday

Dear Gus:

Sex is male, color white, and a dandy son all right all right. First
name Joel, then McCoun, and all in all he's such a boon. Now I'll slip
into prose, naturally and easily. I should, yes I should, have told you all
about this before, but I have not had a minute. You know how fathers
are when they are pressed for time. Kay had a miserable time on December 21st; the doctor discovered in the midst of things that she would
have to have a Caesarian operation, so they bustled her up to the operating room, produced a live baby, and then later gave her a blood transfusion to save her life. It was pretty agonizing for everybody concerned
except Little Joe, who got out easy. Kay made a quick recovery and came
home ten days ago, only to be laid low by a strange malady called pilitis,

accent on second syllable. She had to return to the hospital, or rather to another hospital, and is still there—feeling defeated, whipped, and mad. She runs a low fever, but isn't in any particular pain or danger. Just awfully blue from being six weeks in bed.

. . . Was it really true about that pewter cup? Joe has a cup made from old silver coins—quite a beautiful thing and a genuine antique, but I don't know how good it would be to drink from. I can now mix his formula—no harder than mixing a good Martini—and am in complete charge of his life and character; he has plenty of both. He weighs, at this writing, eleven pounds no ounces. Much of the time he spends in Washington Square, with the rest of the unemployed. When, after a cry, he stares at me with a critical and resentful gaze, just out of focus, I feel the mixed pride and oppression of fatherhood in the very base of my spine. This small man, so challengingly complete and so devastatingly remote! But you know about that. In fact I think it was you who told me about it.

When are you coming to town? Being in business I should think you would have plenty of excuses to come to New York, whereas the only reason I could give for visiting Albany outside of paying a social call would be unemployment relief. "I got to see the Governor about something." You know how well *that* gets across. . . .

Yrs,
Andy

•   *The Whites were off for their first summer in Maine. It was decided that White would drive the car, taking along their cook, Mrs. Lardner, their Scottish terrier, Daisy, and most of the luggage. Katharine and the baby would follow in a day or two by train, which in those days, White remembers, "was a far easier and quicker journey than the motor trip. Mrs. Lardner, an elderly Irish woman with strong maternal feelings, was quite vague about where this place called 'Maine' was, and it seemed unlikely to her that I really knew where I was going. Crossing the Penobscot River on the little scow ferry to Bucksport, she closed her eyes and prayed aloud until we reached the far shore."*

To KATHARINE S. WHITE

Rockingham Hotel
Portsmouth, N.H.
[June 27, 1931]
Saturday night

Dear K:

We are camped here for the night, Daisy and Mrs. L. in their Sink of Loneliness, #37; I in quieter diggings one flight up. The two women dined in their room, as the expedient solution of their special wants: a pot of tea and a beef bone. I dined alone in the Oak Room, below. This being my first major trip with a terrier and a domestic, I have got along fairly well—thus far the chief difficulty is that they roam away from the main body and are found far afield, fooling with each other. It is as hard to catch Mrs. L. in a field of buttercups as it is to catch a butterfly.

Luncheon (at Stafford Springs) was a great personal triumph, if not a moral victory. The restaurant insisted that the dog be tied outside, to a tree. Mrs. L. would hear of no such arrangement—said Daisy would be prostrated with fright and loneliness, the little darlin', and insisted that I eat my lunch while she waited outside with D. and then I could wait with Daisy while she ate. It was clear to me that a double-shift arrangement like that would increase our running time to about two weeks; but Mrs. L. was adamant. Luckily I discovered a table so situated that Daisy could be tied on the porch yet separated from Mrs. L. by only the thickness of a screen door. This worked perfectly.

The two of them have just passed through the lobby on their way out for their evening walk. It is raining, and D. is constipated by travel, I suspect—so they will probably be back about midnight.

Also registered at the Rockingham is a span of Cairns.

See you Tuesday—Love,

Andy

•   *White had come to New York for a few days to catch up on work when the following was written, while his wife and infant son stayed in Maine. The Broadway show to which White took his sister Lillian was a revue called "Shoot the Works," put together by Heywood Broun. White's New Yorker piece "The Near-Demise of Mrs. Coe" was used as one of the sketches.*

To KATHARINE S. WHITE

[Mount Vernon, N.Y.]
[July 21, 1931]
Tues morn

Dear K

They say it isn't hot, but the salt sticks and the windows stick and the air smells like factory exhaust. Even the roaches have turned their feet up and lie on their backs, breathing heavily. Last night I slept in father's flannel pajamas on the velvet couch in the living room. Father has nothing but flannel pajamas.

Here is an item from this morning's Tribune, daughter to Mr. Pepys [Franklin P. Adams]—a surprise to me. Noel [Illian] is enchanting—

quite petite and feminine, trying hard to say something and not quite saying it. Won't eat and never has.

The usual vapors hang over the office, Mosher has another red face from physical exposure, Ross full of interminable accounts of Hollywood. He says he's only been out once to Bedford but everything is all right. Mosher took me at once to lunch in an effort to learn bits of news: he has sold three stories to the North German Lloyd magazine in partial exchange for passage, and says they represent his best work—all of them New Yorker rejections. . . .

The folks leave tomorrow morning for a hotel in Lake George, chosen by the usual methods—writing the Chamber of Commerce to get the names of hotels, then corresponding at great length with about six, finally choosing one because of the way the correspondent expressed himself. It is a stucco building, meals on the European plan. They won't say anything about coming to Maine. I'm taking Lilly to the show tonight, and she has presented us with a two-piece hand-knitted white suit for Joe, bought in England when Mother was there, and no good for Noel.

I am cordially hated at the office, treated in a surly manner as the perpetual vacationist. Last night [in a dream] the timber at the top of the gangway split in two, the bottom slid off the float, and the float foundered. I'll be loving you always.

A.

To KATHARINE S. WHITE

[New York]
[July 23, 1931]
Thurs morn

Dear K

Saw the Toy Bulldog fight the Sailor to a draw at Ebbet's Field last night—my first prize fight. Honey[1] went with me and enjoyed the spectacle. Tonight Mr. R is taking me to Private Lives, and I suppose I will have to go through the ordeal of going backstage with him to pay court to Madge,[2] always a dreaded experience. The Broun show—to which I took Lilly—is not much. The critics were fairly kind to it, on the score of its being a benevolent adventure, but the entertainment value isn't so high. Broun messes around in his old pants, sweating and filling stage waits with patter. The E. B. White–Sig Herzig–Mrs. Coe sketch was about par with the rest of the show. Collaborator Herzig has completely re-

---

1. Ann Honeycutt, later married to St. Clair McKelway.
2. Madge Kennedy, an actress whom Ross was courting. White's New Yorker casual "The Doily Menace," which later appeared in Quo Vadimus? was based on an incident at dinner at Madge Kennedy's.

written it, putting in a couple of dirty lines to make it in tone with the rest of the performance, and adding a rather bright ending: the doctor inadvertently swallows a glass of sterile solution, and realizing that he has been poisoned, calls for the whites of two eggs. This pleases Mr. Coe (who is in the egg business) and he tells the stricken doctor that he deals only in the yolks. Curtain.

The weather is fiendish—humid and hot, the air unbreathable. I've been able to get a fair amount of work done, nevertheless: more than two weeks' batch of comment, and some Talk rewrite. Benchley is going to do a couple of Comment departments for me, Ross thinks. Apparently he backed out of going to the Broun show, as being too embarrassing. I wrote a review of it, as nothing embarrasses me.

It's been fun being in town for a few days. The apartment is a sanctuary, still and dark and cool. Yellow cannas and zinnias attest the diligence of Mr. Gerard [the super] in the garden, and a perennial border of cockroach powder around the bowl in the bathroom shows that Mrs. Carroll has passed that way. From the ground floor I have heard, now and then, the tick of R. Lord's typewriter, but haven't paid a call yet. In this slumberous, midsummer condition, one has time to wander about the rooms, taking root and enjoying the memories of activity. The amaryllis went up a foot, and then fell away, despairing.

. . . It still seems a long time till Saturday morning when I'll see you all again. I miss Joe's comical face and his STRAIGHT white hair and his gaiety. Hope he will recall having seen me before, when I return.

Love,
Andy

• *The following letter was written when Katharine White was at the Ellsworth Bunkers' in Putney, Vermont, where her son Roger had come down with pneumonia while visiting the Bunker children. White had attended the Danbury Fair with his friends Robert and Elsa Coates.*

To KATHARINE S. WHITE

Cross River Road—Tues morn
[Bedford Village, N.Y.]
[October 6, 1931]

Dear K

Another excellent day, with P. Lewis up already whacking the shingles from the roof of the littlest cottage and making a mighty noise out of it. The only louder thing in the neighborhood is Joe, who doesn't need any shingles. In my dream last night, Joe had chicken pox; so I awoke to the extra pleasure of finding that his face wasn't covered with welts.

The Fair was very diverting, Coateses and myself having eaten well under the same tree where you and I parked the Pierce last year. Bob was in white trousers and blue work-shirt open at the throat, Elsa in a close fitting white cap with no hair showing. Two autogiros circled above, completing the ensemble. Bob had never seen a giro before, and was trembling with excitement. During the races, one of the machines kept dropping down to within a few yards of the infield, and then whisking away again—apparently the pilot wanted to watch the trotting. The races were without incident, but the track was in such good shape and there were so many fine horses entered that two track records were broken. The vaudeville attractions were marvelous: Max Kruger and his oddities (elephant, zebra, and Great Dane), a "combination never before seen in any ring together"; also a troupe introduced by the announcer as "a famous Artex explorer and his huskies," several malamutes and a man in a white parka; also a pickaninny band, the pickaninnies so small that the one who played the bass horn had to sit on the floor beside his instrument.

On the way to the Coateses', we stopped at Sears Roebuck in Danbury, where Mr. Coates bought a furnace for $116, and I bought Joe a pair of sandals for 78¢. Then we sped on to the Coateses' little wilderness home, through country that I hadn't imagined existed so near at hand—beautiful valleys and quite good sized hills, almost mountains, and very little sign of any human settlement. Their house is on a steep hillside, looking down a valley, and with a brook at the foot of the slope. The house has one large room, finished roughly, like a camp; also kitchen, bedroom, and attic. A steak was broiled on a grate made out of an old horse manger, water was pumped up from the well by Bob, who ran down the slope to the well beside the brook, and gave a few lusty pulls at a long handle, and we dined well though late. Matthew Josephson was a guest, quite deaf; and we all talked at great length on modern education, Josephson championing it, and the Coateses and I taking a middle course.

Have just driven in town, carrying our cook and our cook's dog. Gave the one $300 in currency and placed the other in the infirmary, with eczema. What an odd pair they are, wandering happily together on the brink of sanity! It was all I could do to keep Mrs. L. from registering at Speyer's overnight too.

I forgot to tell you that Coates was held up at two o'clock the other morning on Waverly Place, just off Sixth. He was coming back from Sam Schwartz's [the restaurant] with Jap Gude's wife, and a man stepped out and asked them to step into the nearest doorway. The man held his right hand in his coat pocket, as though concealing a gun. Bob took a few steps toward Sixth Avenue, hoping to get nearer some traffic, but the man kept edging him in, and saying "Get into a doorway before I plug you full of lead." So Bob said: "L-et me se-ee-ee the gun." Stuttering very hard. The man said he didn't need to see the gun. "But," said Bob, "I re-ee-really think we ought-ought to have a lo-oook at the gun." With that the man pulled his hand out of his pocket and showed Bob that he didn't have any gun, and then put on a great cock-and-bull story about his sick wife and no work and so forth. It ended by Bob and he walking arm and arm up Sixth Avenue, and Bob giving him two dollars from sheer gratitude at his not having a gun.

Joe has a new trick—he feeds crackers to Daisy, chuckling softly to himself. A very pretty sight. The Sears Roebuck sandals fit him excellently.

. . . Gibbs is in, looking healthy and happy. Thurber is in carrying a stick. He is entertaining this p.m. for Mr. Nash.[1] A letter is at hand from Bob Hubbard, unintelligible and asking for five hundred dollars which I shall not send. . . .

I hope Roger is getting on, and please give him my best. Joe and I send lots of love, and hope you'll be back soon.

A—

To GUSTAVE S. LOBRANO

[New York]
[December 1931]
Monday

Dear Gus:

The only Earp I ever knew was neither Wyatt nor Henry—he was Fred Earp, a copyreader on the Seattle *Times*. All this is getting us nowhere, all this Earp business. It earps me. I suspect it earps you, too.[1] . . .

Since you have visited us we have made certain amusing alterations in the apartment. By chopping a hole in the ceiling of the living room, we effected an entrance into the apartment directly above ours, dispossessed the tenants, and moved in ourselves with much noise and flourish. Thus we now live more compactly, more like a family—and are seen less frequently wandering about the hallways trying to establish communication between upstairs and downstairs. It would be worth your while to

---

1. Paul Nash, British art critic, who was full of praise for Thurber's drawings.

1. In fact, Henry C. Earp is a character in "The Key of Life," one of the pieces in *Quo Vadimus?*

come to New York, to study our abode. I wish you would. I have some sherry wine that is excellent, and we could sit around drinking it and making merry.

Hard times have dealt lightly with *The New Yorker,* and I still find myself in comfortable circumstances, with a soft seat under my bottom. While Mr. Benchley is away, I am attempting the theater job in addition to my other duties—mostly in the hopes of earning a vast store of wealth against the time when I will be too indigent, or too inept, to be able to make a farthing. Incidentally, it looks as though there is a good show in the offing—the Kaufman-Gershwin musical comedy (light opera, rather) called "Of Thee I Sing." I have heard from people in Boston, where it now is, that it comes closer to being a Gilbert & Sullivan show than anything this land has yet produced. Wouldn't it be nice if you could be here for the opening? Which, I may add, is an invitation and not just a piece of whimsy. The date hasn't been fixed definitely, but it is some day next week.

Among the people who have turned up recently out of a job, is B. D. Adams, whose aircraft company is in a state of collapse.[2] Bob hasn't changed much—is still tall, healthy, uneasy. He's living at the Phi Gamma Delta Club somewhat dismally, and talks of starting a manufacturing business in Brooklyn.

Joe thrives, on a well rounded diet of small objects that he picks up and swallows—cigarette butts, erasers, wooden letters from the anagram set, and the like. He walks now, a bit of mischief he picked up only last week—from associating with elders. He is a handsome, enthusiastic son and we get on well. We celebrate his first birthday next Monday with cake, prayers, and thanksgiving.

K sends her love, which includes the hope that you can come down soon. We dined the other evening with Mr. and Mrs. Galbreath in their Abingdon Square apartment, very new and tidy, with *Mr.* Galbreath doing most of the cooking, and pretty good too.[3] Mostly we have been going to the theater a good deal, in line of duty. Many bad shows, and one or two good ones. I am discovering that criticism is about the most difficult kind of writing—has to be more accurate, more just, and less self-conscious than most scrivening. Takes a lot out of a man.

Best to Jean and the wee bairns. Write soon.

Andy

---

2. Adams had launched the aircraft company after an interlude in Hollywood. He eventually found his niche in advertising in Atlanta.

3. Mike Galbreath, seemingly the steadiest and most solid of the quartet of roommates from 112 West 13th Street, was at this time still working for McGraw-Hill. A few years later he suddenly became mentally ill—victim of schizophrenia. He was placed in a mental hospital, languished there and, years later, died there.

To HAROLD ROSS

[January? 1932]
[Interoffice memo]

Mr. Ross:

As a small, worried stockholder, and as the author of one of the pieces quoted, I feel impelled to say that this ad makes the current issue of the New Yorker sound strangely dull. I don't think we should present reasons why an Alva Johnston profile is good, or draw a diagram of a Gluyas Williams drawing, or pull one sentence out of an obituary, or describe Woollcott as having "a considerable playgoing following."

In other words, it seems in bad taste to have the contents of one issue of the New Yorker *described* by someone who seems not to catch its meaning. I think weekly ads cataloguing the contents of the issue are good; but the contents should be catalogued, and not described—unless by someone whose powers of description are greater than in the attached.

Yrs in deep purple,
Mr. W

To GUSTAVE S. LOBRANO

[New York]
Feb. 10 [1932]

Dear Gus:

On the back of the envelope containing your last letter, I find the following two lines.

Gall, amant de la reine, alla, tour magnanime
Gallamment de l'Arène à la Tour Magne, à Nîmes.

The lines are in the meticulous hand of Will Strunk, who was a visitor here, and who carries a little store of such oddities about with him in his head for the entertainment of his hosts. A French poet, after thinking hard, composed the lines to prove to his satisfaction the possibility of two lines of Alexandrine verse which would be identical, syllable for syllable. Poets were less busy then. . . .

K and I are just back from Lake Placid, which is not so much a sign of great wealth as it is a sign of daddy's willingness to write a long, rather tedious, story about the winter games for the New Yorker. Daddy gladly did it, however, for we had a grand time and enjoyed Nature's Masterpiece very much. You in Albany are doubtless visited with snow and ice occasionally, but we in New York have to go and find ours. We had good skiing and good weather, we wore long woollies, we saw the patinage de vitesse and the skisprünglauf, we saw a sled dog team stop short in mid-race to allow the pole dog to go to the b-thr—m, we stayed at the Club where everything is spelled in simplified spelling and where "the liquor law can not be treated as a joke or defyd by any Club member, gest, or employe," we defyd the liquor law, we walked in the chill dusk and made scrunchy noises in the well-packed snow, and we wished you were along. This is just a line to let you know. Love from all.

Andy

To BERNARD BERGMAN

[East Blue Hill, Me.]
[Summer 1932?]
Sunday

Dear Bergie:

I have taken up the matter of my vacation payment with all the natives here, and they think it is perfectly satisfactory.[1] On the strength of it, Les Eaton is going to rig a mooring for me provided I cut the cedar for the pole, Mrs. Dan Trewargy is going to continue letting us have eggs Tuesdays and Fridays if the hens think well of the arrangement, and I am going to make a rent payment on the Christopher Columbus—a black sloop built by a man with no fingers. To cross the Atlantic. She tends to broach to in heavy weather, but is tight.[2]

There is an east wind today and Mrs. White has taken advantage of it to drive the cook to mass. I always hang a medallion of St. Christopher right next to the gear-shift, as they say he watches over women drivers; but I worry a good bit, and the cook uses the whole mass praying for her safe return. The hay is all in, and the county agents are busy condemning the blueberry crop, on account of maggots. There is no more granite shipped out, and it is simply used locally for grave stones. I hope everybody is well but I have never seen the time when they were. Anyway I am glad to know that you have straightened out my vacation payment, as it must have been a courageous move, with Lippmann holding out for cancellation.

Yrs,
Andy

---

1. Bergman was managing editor of *The New Yorker*, and had to cope with the financial aspects of White's comings and goings.

2. The "man with no fingers" was Howard Blackburn, a sailor of great renown. While fishing out of Gloucester in 1883, his dory became separated from the mother ship. Blackburn deliberately let his hands freeze around the oars so he could continue to row. He made it to shore, losing his fingers in the ordeal. Later, he crossed the Atlantic in a sloop called *Great Republic*. White had been told that his chartered boat was *Great Republic* with her name changed. This wasn't so—she was a Blackburn sloop but a later one.

To KATHARINE S. WHITE

[January? 1933]
[Interoffice memo]

Dear Mrs. White—

Sympathizing with you in your recent dilemma when you found yourself sandwiched in between two old-line coupon clippers, and aware of your humiliation, I made so bold as to seek out the enclosed pamphlet from the Fifth Avenue Bank, explaining how such embarrassments may be avoided—at a slight charge. A cheerful fire was burning in the hearth, and it was warm and cozy inside the Bank even though I was immediately under suspicion because of my odd clothes. I do not know that it is at all necessary for you to have a Custody Account, but what with Mrs. Lardner so sick and Willy [Buffa] growing up and Daisy dead[1] and Nancy off to school and Joe's cough and everything I didn't know but what you might like to consider it. Ever since I found the railroad tickets in with the sliced bananas and yesterday's melons, I have wondered.[2]

Yrs lovingly,
Mr. White

To GUSTAVE S. LOBRANO

[New York]
[March 1933]
Saturday afternoon

Dear Gus:

A moment's calm has settled like dust over this apartment, and it looks as though I might be able to manage a letter before sunset gun. I was glad to get yours, and to learn of your increasing influence in the life of the state capital—memorable as the city from which emerged the superman who quietly picked up the pieces of our shattered republic. All through the campaign I thought Mr. R. was something of a pain; but the pain is gone, and it feels so good. You talk of stirring times: you should have been in New York that crazy March 4. There was, all through the town, the feeling not so much of financial disintegration, as of disunion. It was a question of who was your friend any more. Was the cop

1. Daisy was run over on December 22, 1931, by a yellow cab that jumped the curb at the corner of University Place and 8th Street. Mrs. Lardner, who had been walking the dog and who loved her dearly, was so upset by the accident that she left the Whites' employ. An account of Daisy's death appears in "Obituary," a *New Yorker* piece later included in *Quo Vadimus?*

2. Katharine White had once absent-mindedly thrown the family's Maine–to–New York railway tickets in the garbage pail. A search of the local dump followed, and the tickets were recovered.

on the corner on your side, or on the other side? I found myself busy with all sorts of fantastic conjectures and solutions, and mostly very envious of my remote grandsires, who could attack the problem of existence directly, with plow and musket. At noon I happened to be driving north on Fourth Avenue, and got held up in a traffic snarl caused by the parade of the radical groups. There were thousands of them, and with the usual ill-assorted banners and slogans, flaunting the most various and diverse complaints and demands. There was no common enemy, as there is in war; and I have never seen a red demonstration that seemed to hold so much dynamite ready to go off. The cops were as polite as ladies at a garden party. I really believe that if anything untoward had happened, some minor spark somewhere, New York would have had one of the damndest riots in history—not because anybody knew what he wanted, but because *nobody* did. Driving my capitalistic limousine through the town, I felt like a noble in the French revolution, and expected at any minute to run down a child and have to use my whip on the rabble.

A little later, standing on a street corner in Lexington Avenue and reading the President's inaugural address, I got the sort of lift that I guess our ancestors occasionally felt in great moments during the early days of the country—the love-of-fatherland, which ordinarily we take pains to keep ourselves intellectually independent of. It was a great day and I won't forget it.

. . . Kay and I are seriously thinking of taking to the land: we cut out farm ads. Also we think often of your antique invitation to visit you. I can imagine your curious feelings if we ever showed up; for we now occupy in your minds the comfortable berth accorded those who have proved, through the years, that They Never Come. I do want to go fishing, though, and maybe I could work that. How about naming a day and hour and telling me to be there, in my reefer and cap? I am knitting a tiny creel.

Andy

To CLARENCE DAY

25 West 45th Street
New York
[January 4, 1934]
Thurs

Dear Clarence:

. . . I called up the NY Times on Tuesday morning, when I received your letter, and said I wanted to insert a Public Notice. "How does it go?" the clerk asked. "It goes," I replied, " 'E. B. White sends New

Year's greetings to Clarence Day exactly.' " Well, the clerk said, you will have to come into the office, we can't take that over the telephone. Come in and see either Mr. McNamara or Mr. Kaufman. This sounded like a challenge, so I went around to the Times office and gained an audience with Mr. McNamara. I showed him the typewritten copy. "E. B. White sends New Year's greetings to Clarence Day exactly." He studied it a long time. "What does it mean?" he asked finally. "Means what it says," I snapped. "It's kind of a greeting." "Well," he said, "we can't run that as a Public Notice; it might mean something." Then he got up and took the matter up with Mr. Kaufman. I saw Mr. Kaufman study the slip of paper for a long time, then shake his head. Mr. McNamara came back. "What does this mean here—Clarence Day *exactly*? What do you mean 'exactly'?" "I put that in," I explained, "to prevent a great many inconsiderable and nosey people, in whom I haven't the slightest charitable interest, from horning in on the New Year's wishes I am sending my good friend Mr. Day." Mr. McNamara gazed at me in alarm. "However," I went on, "if you object to the word 'exactly' I will take it out. Just make it read: 'E. B. White sends New Year's greetings to Clarence Day.' " Again Mr. McNamara studied the notice, in a kind of reverie. He shook his head. "You mean," I asked, "that the Times won't accept my greetings?" "We can't," he said. "It might mean something." "Really," I said, "the Times is magnificent!" I rose, shook hands and departed. Happy new year *anyway!*

Andy

•   *After Christmas, 1933, White went to Camden, South Carolina, for a short time to work on a piece away from the distractions of office and home. He selected Camden because he had been there with his parents and remembered it as a peaceful place.*

To KATHARINE S. WHITE

Court Inn,
Camden, S.C.
[January 20, 1934]
Saturday night

Dear Kay:

The sound of these keys seems like sacrilege in this noiseless tavern where everybody tiptoes except the mice in the writing room. There are about a dozen guests, of which I am the least probable. The men shoot quail, I gather from snatches of dinner table conversation; and the ladies buy comforters made by the blind, on display in the room across from the writing room. I actually recognized the head-waiter—I was ten when I first came here, and he is still pulling chairs back. . . .

An east wind blew today, rather chilling, but I took a long walk this afternoon, and South Carolina has the same gentle sadness that I knew and liked as a child. This garden, with its heavy, lonely arbors, its sandy paths, its formal maze, its jays and tanagers and mocking birds, hasn't changed a particle—except that the goat is gone. In its place there seems to be a small furtive fox terrier, with little puppy mongrel ears. I will try to catch him (or her) and bring him (her) home; but so far the animal follows at a distance of forty paces and peers at me from behind holly trees. The dogs of Camden are showing the effects of northern visitors: the hound is the native dog, but the winter influx of the standard Park Avenue breeds has left its mark, and the place is full of Scotch hounds, bull hounds, Sealyham hounds, spaniel hounds—curious, medium sized slack-tail dogs, as aimless as everything else here. I was attacked by a bull hound this afternoon, but not damaged. I haven't found a bicycle yet, but will have to get one, as the distances are rather gruelling for footwork. I had forgotten that Camden has a Jim Crow Main Street—the east side is for niggers, the west side for whites—and I walked up the black side absent-mindedly until I heard remarks being passed . . . "white man." You really don't know America until you have experienced the dreamy shiftlessness of this south, the mules, the cabins, the brown cotton fields, the slow voices. There are intimations in the air here that you don't get other places, special mysteries and suggestions of life dying on its feet. The state seems to be dry, from a cursory inspection; and I will have to ration my pint of Golden Wedding to make it stretch the week.

I am feeling fine, pleasantly drowsy and disconnected—the way you sometimes do feel, alone in empty inns, as though you never had known anybody, might never know anybody. I saw announcements of a polo match for tomorrow afternoon, and there seem to be plenty of churches in town, so I guess my Sabbath is all cut out for me. The water in my toilet runs a dribble continuously, which gives life a continuity, or flux. In the flurry of my departure from New York I failed to thank you adequately for the wool vest. I am wearing it at the moment and enjoying not only its warmth (the inn is sketchily heated as all southern inns are) but also the middleclass, middleage feeling that sweater vests produce. It is just that feeling, I presume, which has caused the sweater vest to go out. Last night in the smoking room, aided by the train clicking, I wrote a prayer for Joe to say, to start his career as a petitioner, but this morning couldn't remember a line of it so it couldn't have been good.

Also wrote hundreds of lines of my magnum opus and forgot them too. Trains are tantalizing that way—they give you great power, then complete forgetfulness.

I remembered something today I hadn't thought of in years. When I was here as a child I saw a town boy shoot a songbird with a slingshot. I was impressed with his marksmanship, as I didn't think anybody could really bring anything down with a slingshot; and when I asked him why he had shot the bird, I was again impressed. "To eat, of course," he answered. I remembered it when I saw some boys shooting birds today. They are still at it, although these had an air gun. I must say goodnight now, and try to catch up the sleep I didn't get last night. With a hound baying outside, and a moon, it should be full of dream. All my love, and for Joe a hug.

Andy

To KATHARINE S. WHITE

[Camden, S.C.]
[January 1934]
Tues afternoon, 2 o'clock

Dear Kay:

About ten minutes after I wrote you, the sun broke through the fog, and now it is warm and clear with a west wind. I will not change my plans, however; but will go up to Washington tomorrow night.

It is like old times to see the sun, for without bright hard light and deep shadow the forms and colors of the south lack their authentic laziness. . . . I have just outwitted the management by lunching in my room, on beer and cheese, while finishing a "statement" for the Cornell Sun. I am out of favor with everybody at the Inn except the bellboys, who respect me for the many bottles of beer I order, each with its 10 cent tip. I walked about ten miles this morning (I have been knocking off ten to twenty miles a day regularly, and my calves are as stiff as an old paint brush). It is sweet and sad in my room now, overlooking the garden; I wish you could be here, you would love it with the sun out. My terrier (who seems to reside across the road) has just sneaked out with a dead sparrow. How changeless our lives really are: after several days the sun appears and I have written a poem—and I now recall that when I was here at the age of ten, staying at a private home (the inn being full) we had three grey days, then the sun appeared, and I obliged with a poem which started: "Oh beautiful sun . . ." Much love to you and to Joey—

Andy

To CLARENCE DAY

25 West 45th Street
[March 1934]
Friday

Dear Clarence:

Among the books chosen by the Syracuse Public Library for its shelf marked "Devotional Reading for Lent" is your fine work "God and My Father."

I am noting it in my fine department "Notes & Comment."

Yr fine friend,
E. B. White

• *Although White's brother-in-law Arthur Illian lived most of the time in New York's suburbia, at times he was put in charge of his firm's Florida office. During 1934 the Illians lived in Palm Beach; later, in 1937, they lived in Miami. When the following letter was written, White was visiting the Illians to recover from a bout with the flu, while Katharine and Joel stayed in New York. The nature of Katharine's duties at* The New Yorker *did not permit her to travel as freely as White, who often managed to pull out of the city when he felt like it.*

Carol, the Illians' oldest daughter, the "duck," was now eight, and Noel was four. The third Illian offspring, Sidney, did not come along until 1936.

To KATHARINE S. WHITE

Hotel Vineta
[Palm Beach, Fla.]
[March 26, 1934]
Monday night

Dear Kay—

My scatter-brain letters have probably given you no idea about this place or me or anything else. I've been unable to collect myself—daytimes one can't bear to miss a minute of beach or bike, & night time sleep is overpowering. It's really a gorgeously lazy life. Four blocks away is the sea—a handsome white sand beach, gently sloping, with a pier at one end and the Breakers Hotel at the other. A steady stream of liners passes by, the boats come within a few hundred feet of the beach, keeping well inshore to avoid the north-flowing Gulf Stream. The Illians are always on the beach early, & the children certainly thrive on it. Carol is a duck—never out of the water a second; Noel is as cautious as a kitten, never gets anything but her big toe wet. There are some superb little characters on the sands—a little skinny man who wears a loin cloth & looks like Gandhi, and an elderly lady who appears in a black dress, black hat, black sweater, black shoes & stockings, *black gloves*, & sits under a black umbrella. Yesterday there was much excitement when a girl was stung by a Portuguese man o' war, which is not much fun. She was only a few feet from where Lil and Art and Carol and I were dancing in the breakers, and I heard her yell bloody murder. She kept screaming "My legs! My legs! Oh!" and the fellow who was nearest her grabbed her and pulled her ashore, where the lifeguard removed the long stingers. I saw the man o' war—it's like a jellyfish except it is a beautiful light-blue, and is sort of hollow. I guess the pain is rather intense—although I noticed that the lifeguard and another fellow got stung and didn't cut up. Today there was a strong south-east wind, with undertow & men o' war, so we went to a pleasant pool near the pier and bathed there.

Art leaves tomorrow, so I threw a farewell dinner tonight at Gabrielle's—a little restaurant down the block, very nice. You would really love this place—it's not at all difficult or expensive, as I had feared. The Ritzy folk stick close together & aren't troublesome to the masses at all. Cycling is grand because of the great flatness, & because there are broad paths removed from the motor highway. Many of the houses are

Tuesday afternoon

You are missing something, not seeing me today. Last night in the middle of this letter I began to feel queer in the head (the letter probably shows it) & when I touched my forehead it felt as soft as a piece of putty. I examined it in the mirror & the whole front of my head was swollen like the breast of a pigeon. "Tumor of the brain," I told myself, & collapsed on the bed in one of my panics. The Illians had gone to the movies, so I prepared for the end—wrote a brief note to you, unlocked the door to save the hotel people the trouble of breaking in, and went to bed, full of flatulence, dizziness & fear. This morning, after almost no sleep, I teetered across to Lil's & presented my swollen face. They took me to a doctor and he said it was sunburn. I don't believe him for a minute— I think I was bitten by a spider. However I am alive altho still in a curiously swollen state around the eyes & lips. Trust Daddy to get something the matter with him right away!

Lil checked the sunburn theory with the lifeguard this p.m. & he says occasionally people's eyes swell. But the weakness of the case is that I didn't get badly burned (not anywhere nearly as burned as on Jones Beach or on many other occasions); in fact I have been very cautious about lying around and have stayed under the umbrella most of the time. Don't worry about me—it is just my last attempt to round off a perfect winter in a blaze of foolishness. It makes me mad as the devil because I've been feeling so grand down here, up until last night.

The doctor experience was a honey—the perfect last act in my medical farce. He was an eye, ear, nose & throat man (he would be), studied under Craig, is the darling of the winter colonists because of a perfect throat-side manner; and when I presented my bulb-like face to him he pried my mouth open, peeped at the tonsils & said—"They've got to come out!"

Some winter, heh baby?

I still love you & my dying thoughts last night were of you. Kiss Joe.

Andy

To KATHARINE S. WHITE

The Vineta
Palm Beach, Florida
[March 31, 1934]

Peter Henderson in Florida

From this fat garden, with its slow noon beat,
Its steady shadow and its clinging heat;
From careful palm, from white & blinding wall,
From sleepless lizard & the hot vine's scrawl,
From tropic luxury and southern sweetness
My senses turn (seeking their stern completeness)
To you, my love, & to our northern spring—
Crosby's Egyptian, and the Golden King!

Suggested name for largest
tomato in the world—
M. Ridiculosa

• *The water in the Whites' newly acquired house in North Brooklin came from a well by the barn and was unfit to drink. A "boiling spring" in the woods across the road seemed promising, and White drove to Maine to start work on a new water system, stopping overnight in Boston at 87 Myrtle Street on Beacon Hill, where his wife's sister Rosamond and her husband, John S. Newberry, had a house. The spring was dug out to a depth of six feet, rocked up, curbed, and piped into the house —330 feet distant. It proved to be an unfailing source of water.*

To KATHARINE S. WHITE

[North Brooklin, Me.]
[May 19, 1934]
Saturday night
Borough Hall

Dearest Kay:

A long and lovely day. I sneaked out of 87 Myrtle a little after 6 o'clock, arousing no one. Ros was in Northampton, nurses were just going to work in the Massachusetts General, white shoes and stockings under dark coats. Newburyport was interesting—the shoe factory by the bridge had burned down and the whole town had been up all night. Stopped in Portland & went into the clay tile situation. Decided against them. Tile the size we would need would be too heavy to handle & too expensive. Even the company admitted it. Called at the State House in Augusta but the boys had knocked off. Studied a stuffed moose instead. Very nice. I threw back the Plymouth's top in Augusta and the rest of the ride was sunswept and grand. Pastures were white with spring flowers, and everywhere there was something doing. Took the dirt road to Bluehill—it's perfectly good and much the pleasanter way to arrive. Decided to fix up spring independent of Augusta. In Bluehill (which I reached at about 4 p.m.) I galvanized into action & set wheels going. Mr. Stanley [plumber] promises to get, on Monday, wash bowl ($16.00), toilet ($25.00), & copper pipe (?); Tuesday to install bowl and toilet. Mr. Brooks Westcott [mason] promises to be on hand Monday morning to start operations on the spring.

When I reached home Howard[1] presented me with the State Report. It shows "small amount of dangerous bacteria" and "practically no pollution from sewage or other source." This ambiguous official opinion of our spring did not discourage me. Mr. Westcott, who is one swell guy and who incidentally has been saving old brick for us, came over to call & look the spring over (with Mrs. Westcott) this evening; I showed him the report and showed him the spring & he thinks we are perfectly justified in going ahead. Says the spring looks to him as though it would test all right when it gets cleaned up.

Howard took me on a tour of the estate to show me how hard he had been working. The borders are well groomed, yellow tulips are out, seedlings are showing in the hot frames, bean poles are in place, strawberries are in, & all the vegetables are planted. Two heifers are in the pasture & three more are to come. A Mr. Young wants to buy the hay. Our taxes have gone up. John Allen [a neighbor] has got back his old

1. Howard Pervear, caretaker and gardener for the farm in North Brooklin. He was working on the place when the Whites bought it and stayed with them for many years.

yachting job, & leaves Tuesday for New York much to his delight. He *was* to have helped dig the trench for our copper pipe; but is polishing up his own buttons instead. Haven't seen Percy [Moore] or any of our friends yet. No activity on dock. Lawn has been rolled, our man says.

Am too sleepy to write more. The clock is going, & the peepers. Wish you were here. The house seems lonely.

Love to you and Joe,
Andy

To GUSTAVE S. LOBRANO

25 W. 45th Street
[October? 1934]
Friday

Dear Gus:

I'm sending you under sep cov a copy of "Every Day Is Saturday," a sort of a book. I don't think a great deal of it, but there is an inescapable finality about a book: it represents something done, something finished, a coming-to-a-head of life. And so I'm sending you a copy even though I don't think a great deal of it.

It is almost impossible to write anything decent using the editorial "we," unless you are the Dionne family. Anonymity, plus the "we," gives a writer a cloak of dishonesty, and he finds himself going around, like a masked reveler at a ball, kissing all the pretty girls.

Andy

To ALEXANDER WOOLLCOTT

25 West 45th Street
November [1934?]

Dear Friend and Reader:

Thanks for the ad over the wireless. I have a spaniel that defrocked a nun last week. He took hold of the cord. I had hold of the leash. It was like elephants holding tails.

Imagine me undressing a nun, even second hand.

Yrs,
E. B. White

To CLARENCE DAY

16 East Eighth Street
New York
[November 18, 1934]
Sunday

Dear Clarence:

In that book on advertising which you are going to write, I hope you will do something about the way advertising people are forever trying to identify themselves with the arts. . . .

I have a theory that a great deal of advertising is attributable not to a merchant's ambition for his product but to a copywriter's dream of participation in the world of letters. Self-expression is at the bottom of a lot of stuff which masquerades as industrial promotion.

The fever of creation was strong in the blood of the copywriters I knew at Frank Seaman's agency in the days of my young madness (my cellophane phase). One of them was forever telling me how he would spring out of bed at two o'clock in the morning, with an inspiration for a window shade campaign (waterproof and washable). A moment of sheer genius in the middle of the night.

Yours,
Andy

To HAROLD ROSS

[January? 1935]
[Interoffice memo]

Mr. Ross:

You can have the "Department of Correction" for exclusive use if you want, as I am generous that way. But I don't think that it is the right head for the job—not as good as We Stand Corrected. Department of Correction suggests corrective methods applied to others, not self-correction. Maybe unimportant.

Always happy to do a service to the magazine.

EBW

• *In the spring of 1935, White bought a cruising boat, the thirty-foot double-ended cutter* Astrid. *H. K. (Bun) Rigg was a yacht broker who also wrote a column on yachting for* The New Yorker. *The friendship between Rigg and White ripened when Rigg, together with Edward (Ned) Smith, a friend of Rigg's, helped White sail* Astrid *home to Brooklin. Rigg later became editor of* Skipper *Magazine.*

To KATHARINE S. WHITE

New York Yacht Club
Station No. 6
Newport, R.I.
[June 9, 1935]
Sunday A.M.

Dearest Kay:

Rain, wind, and rain. In spite of five days of adverse conditions, we are right on schedule. Ned and I brought Astrid to Newport yesterday and Bun joined us again. He is writing his column now, and I am considering getting a shave—my beard not having been touched since Tuesday morning. It is long and soft and beautiful. Some of the hairs came in white. I cut my moustache off in Saybrook while waiting for the fog to lift, and am much more comfortable, as the growth was a great collector of odd bits of food, flotsam, etc. Lay right alongside Alastor[1] in New London, and thought of the many good times we had aboard her. She looked shabby.

Astrid is a constant delight; everywhere people speak praises of her, and want to examine her. The first day out was a terror—blowing 25 miles NE, dead ahead. We never set a sail, but motored to Southport, pitching right into it—so rough you couldn't stand up on deck. We passed a schooner under power, overhauling her and leaving her behind as though she were standing still—which she pretty near was. Visited the Scudders in Southport, and next day made Saybrook after dark, against light head winds & foul tide. Fog blew in during the night, and next day we didn't start till about noon, when it seemed to be clearing. Just as we started to enter Fisher's Island Sound, the fog shut down thick, so we put into New London. Bun is a first rate sailor—careful, exact, and conservative. He takes it very seriously and is on the job every minute. Getting into New London was no cinch, and he hit it right on the nose. I'm learning plenty on this cruise—for one thing the importance of always knowing exactly where you are. The stove works great, and we've had good grub & lots of sleep.

Did you see the item about the steamer "Castine," out of Belfast, hitting a rock and dumping a bunch of excursionists into the water? Cheery.

There's a Friendship in the harbor here, bound for Maine. We'll probably shove off together and keep each other company, which will be fun. Right now we're hung up, waiting for the weather to turn around. It can't stay against us forever, and we certainly deserve a break. I miss you and Joe a lot and wish you could be along. Much love to you both.

Andy

To KATHARINE S. WHITE

Wed.—Gloucester [Mass.]
[June 12, 1935]
[Postcard]

Dear Kay—

The wind finally turned around, & we ran yesterday from Newport to the western entrance of the Canal, before a fresh SW breeze. Dinghy

---

1. A yawl White had chartered one summer.

took a sea aboard off Sakonnet & swamped. We never even saw it go. Today was beautiful—light airs, calm sea. Bucked tide through the Canal, & passed our old friend Taormina,[1] of Buck's Harbor. Remember her? Astrid is simply marvelous. We crossed Mass. Bay this P.M. out of sight of land most of way, & hit Gloucester right on the nose.

Much love,

A

• *Gus Lobrano, whose tastes ran more to the literary life than to the business world, left the family travel business in 1935 and took a job at* Town and Country *magazine, where he worked for Joseph Bryan III. He spent most of that summer in the Whites' New York apartment, commuting to Albany on weekends to see his family.*

To GUSTAVE S. LOBRANO

North Brooklin [Me.]

July 15, 1935

Dear Gus:

We snatch eagerly for the paper each day to read the news of the hot wave. It is revitalizing just to know that you are all suffering terribly in town. I have just painted a pair of oars (French gray) and the existence of New York seems questionable. The tides run in and out, clams blow tiny jets of seawater up through the mud, a white line of fog hangs around the outer islands, days tumble along in cool blue succession, and I hate the word September. In Astrid I went deep-sea fishing last week—the first time I had ever done it. We started at six for the three-hour run down the bay and out to the fishing grounds. Thick fog over the sea, and a long slow groundswell, the world blotted out. The fish come in with stupid rapidity—great lumps of things, mostly cod and haddock. The line is as big around as a lampcord. The bait is clams, which soon smell handsomely on the decks. The sheer poundage is fascinating. We filled three washboilers with fish in a morning—well over three hundred pounds. One of the men with us, a housemaster at Lawrenceville, was violently sick—a desolate green morning for him, adding his stench to the clambait. I had a thoroughly good time; but it is the farthest cry from brook trout, with your clean riffle and delicate equipment. I was glad to get a report from 16 E 8, and I send my love to Josephine and all the slipcovers and plants. Did the bat ever show up? Roger really left one there, accidentally. He always has some hideous animal half under control.

---

1. A large sumptuous power yacht owned by tycoon Robert F. Herrick.

I have the greatest difficulty making myself do any work here. Even writing a letter seems an imposition. I get out my weekly stint in a sort of lonely rage—shutting myself in a room and lashing out at people who make the slightest noise about the house. I foolishly agreed to do several articles, and, also, a short book about New York for the Oxford Press. I doubt if any of these things get done, or even started. They simply serve to annoy me, and prevent peace settling down over me.

I've just started National Velvet on your recommendation, and seem about to like it. Wrote some blank verse last week—a sketch for the NYer, called "Much Ado About Plenty," satirizing the pioneer colony in Alaska. I like the first stage direction. It says: "Enter pioneers, and attendants." Are you doing anything besides your T & C stint, or does that sufficiently absorb your attention? My best to Joe, by the way.

Yrs,
Andy

• *E. B. White's father died August 13, 1935, at the family home in Mount Vernon, New York. After the funeral his mother moved to Washington, D.C., where she stayed with her daughter Clara Wyvell.*

To STANLEY HART WHITE

North Brooklin, Me.
20 August 1935

Dear Bun:

I'm anxious to know how Mother is getting on, and also whether she has any plans for the future—I mean with regard to where she is going to live and how. I presume she won't wish to continue living alone at 48 Mersereau, and that will mean either that she'll have to find some other place, or live with the children for a while. Has she talked it over with you, and has she any definite plans?

I thought it would be a good idea for her to come to Maine during the first couple of weeks in September. It would be a lot cooler and healthier than Washington, and I think she would benefit from it—the air is so good. Joe will be remaining here, and perhaps Kay or I or both. If neither Kay nor I stay (and we're not supposed to because of our jobs) we are going to arrange to have a man living in the house. If Mother's bent on getting right to Washington, I won't try to make her change her plans, but I should think it would be lots better for her to come here first for a fortnight.

I wrote Mother to this effect the other day. Let me know how things have been going with you all, and tell me what Mother has said about her future plans. What are you going to do? Are you staying in Mount Vernon, or going to Washington, or what?

Andy

To HAROLD ROSS

[North Brooklin, Me.]
[September 13, 1935]
Friday

Dear Mr. Ross:

Regarding yrs of Sept 10 offering further vacation from comment, would say that I can't really afford same, and will be back in town on Tuesday ready for the frightful grind. . . .

[It is vital] that you and I should come to an agreement about the uses to which the comment bank would be put. It was probably my fault that the St. Anne comment got into the book, because I should have killed it and many other bank comments long ago, but just let it slide. Anyway, seeing it in print gave me quite a turn. In my letter asking for a two weeks vacation, I thought I made it clear that I wanted time off only if the substitute stuff was to be either original new stuff, or the extra comments which I had turned in the week before. If I had known you were going to resurrect my out-dated and oddly inept remark about Catholicism, I would have gladly forsworn any vacation. I regard the bank (as it exists now) as a somewhat expensive concession to my perhaps overdeveloped sense of perfection (or time-liness). Every week I write and turn in more stuff than can be used, so that I can pick what seems best (and what seems to run together best) and stow the rest away to die or to wait. Some of it improves by waiting (as when it becomes timely by circumstance, or becomes apropos a new comment); most of [it] decays and dies. The expense is shared jointly by the magazine and myself. I think the comment page has improved since the bank has been administered this way instead of the old way of having a third party make up the department hit and miss, with the bank as his chief source of supply. The weakness of the system is that, on very infrequent occasions, such as last week, some very ripe paragraph gets into the book.

I think maybe a good idea would be never to set my extra stuff. It could be simply OK'd by you in manuscript and sent back to me, for my folder. This would save the magazine money, would save a lot of Ralph's [Paladino's] time, and might prevent slipups. If you think it necessary always to have a reserve comment supply, in case of acts of God, Ralph could keep the folder. There is really no particular reason why extra comment need be set, anyway. The fact that it has been set makes it harder to kill.

WHITE

• *Nineteen thirty-five was a sad year for the Whites—a death in summer, a miscarriage in early fall. Even the scheduled move from Eighth Street to Forty-eighth Street was tinged with melancholy. They had had six happy years in the Village and felt uneasy about moving uptown into the rented unfurnished house in Turtle Bay—a move brought on by their having exhausted the growth possibilities of the Eighth Street apartment. When the following letter was written, Katharine was in Maine, where she had lingered in the vain hope of avoiding the threatened miscarriage. White had gone to New York to superintend the move uptown. Joel was still in Maine, Nancy and Roger were in New York with their father.*

To KATHARINE S. WHITE

16 East 8th
[September 18, 1935]
Wednesday night

Dear Kay:

Safe home—all pleasant except the last leg from Bedford, where the Roses[1] plied me with a drink which they described as a Scotch highball but which turned out to be straight hemlock. I'm slowly reviving, it being now midnight. Kept Marguerite [the cook] here to administer extreme unction, and she is asleep upstairs. She has apparently been busy— all books, china, etc. seem to be packed, & the place is clean. (She was grieved to hear that you were ill, as were Carl & Dorothy.) I phoned Nancy from there. Roger seemed to be on an extension, listening to [us discuss] the miscarriage. Nancy reported all well & said you were not to worry about R's birthday, as he will understand. He *has* a polo coat.

Hope the mail will bring me good news from you tomorrow. I can't write any more now, as the poison is slowly taking hold. Good luck, & lots of love to you and Joe.

A

To KATHARINE S. WHITE

[New York]
[September 19, 1935]
Thursday noon

Dear Kay:

I've just seen the house and it looks wonderful. Vines are flowering at the bedroom window, and paint is flowering all over the walls and on my coatsleeve. Mr. Brigantine [the painter] and your Mrs. Fay

---

1. Carl Rose, a *New Yorker* artist, and his wife Dorothy.

[the decorator] have been working night and day, and you would be surprised to see how presentable the old manse is. The nasty Italian walls have been smoothed down so they look like any other wall. Final coats of paint go on the front living room and the bedroom today, and I OK'd them, wearing my finest interior expression. Fay has found some of the prettiest curtain material you ever saw for the bedroom, and even my unpractised gaze was enough to know that you will approve of it when it is submitted to you. The house looks 200 degrees lighter than when you saw it, with its fresh light walls, and the garden is heavy with the sounds and sights of September. . . . The bookshelves are 100 inches more capacious at 48th Street than at 8th Street, so I am auctioning off the old family shelves which you and I loved so well. It is probably the first time Mr. Schoen was ever faced with an electrically equipped book-shelf, all wired for fish.[1]

Our telephone instructions from Maine had about as accurate an effect as I anticipated. Marguerite packed the books in the trunk which came up from the cellar. You should see it. If you've never seen "Is Sex Necessary" in the space where the shirts ought to go, you've missed the sights. Have just lunched with McKelway. He and Honey are apartment hunting, and will be unified in October. A good thing, I think. Everybody asks for you, in a worried, loving tone. Miss Terry talks of sending proof. . . .

It is true that Gibbs has a wine cellar. His son is cutting teeth. His moustache is longer than it has ever been before. I am faced with the instant necessity of doing some notes and comment (those little paragraphs in the front of the magazine) so I can't go on with this letter much longer. No one around here has ever heard of infantile paralysis. . . . Jim and Helen are honeymooning at the corner of 8th Street and Fifth Avenue,[2] where the Italian Pistol Club used to be. Jim celebrated Stanley Walker's arrival[3] by entering his office and telling him he couldn't stand him. Stanley apologized, trembling all over. That is all the news I can think of at the moment, except that I wish you were here, miss you very much, and hope and pray that you are all well again.

Love,
Andy

1. Eugene Schoen, an architect, managed the building at 16 E. 8th Street for the Sailors Snug Harbor, owners.
2. James Thurber married Helen Muriel Wismer on June 25, 1935, a month after his divorce from his first wife. Thurber took Helen to Martha's Vineyard, then to the Whites' in North Brooklin. On their return to New York, the couple sublet a furnished apartment at 8 Fifth Avenue.
3. Walker, a long-time city editor of the *Herald Tribune*, had taken a job with *The New Yorker*.

To KATHARINE S. WHITE

[New York]
[September 20, 1935]
Friday night

Dear Kay:

An uneventful day, trying to catch up with work at the office. I still seem to be smothered, but have hopes of pulling out over the weekend. I haven't even taken my suitcase out of the Buick yet—drove right to the garage and left everything aboard. Am going up now to get my typewriter and put in a night of newsbreaks.

Today was a field day for Daise—the office on the brink of moving,[1] and Terry beside herself with the lusty joy of extreme executive ability, taking typewriters right out from under a writer's fingers. Gebert[2] loved it, too.

Paid a visit to the house this afternoon, and it is still very painty, but Mr. B. [the painter] assures me he will be out in time. I had the wonderful idea of getting in touch with Della today. I remembered that in times like this, you always added Della to the scene, so I prodded her into action. She is probably recovering a chair or an old icebox at this very moment.

Books, linen, etc, are all packed, ready to go. I wrote the Friends School and the Steinway Piano Company. Gas is flowing from the stove, and the British have moved into the Mediterranean. Got your note and was sorry not to get better news. Be patient. I'm sure you will pull out of this with flying colors! Lots of love to you & Joe.

Andy

P.S. If by any chance I left three black check books on my desk, will you bring them?

EBW

To STANLEY HART WHITE

245 East 48 Street
17 October 1935

Dear Bun:

The question of the grand piano has come up.[1] It is mine, and I don't quite know what to do about it. Kay has a grand here in town, and

1. In 1935 *The New Yorker* moved from 25 W. 45th Street to 25 W. 43rd Street.
2. William Gebert, the magazine's purchasing agent; described by White as "a man who always had a cigar between his teeth."

1. With his father dead and his mother moved to Washington, White was closing up the house in Mount Vernon.

we have an upright in Maine—which is all we have room for. I don't know what your Piano Situation is, but if you should want this grand in preference to whatever piano you already own, I would be glad to give it to you for the sake of keeping it in the family. At any rate, I won't do anything till I hear from you.

Mother was in town last week, staying with us. We drove out on Saturday to Mount Vernon, so that she could perform a few last pitiful rites over some trifling leftovers such as my sheet music and a few old copies of the *Oracle*. I salvaged some stereopticon pictures—which are really stunning souvenirs of Father's photographic phase, as well as a remarkable record of the early 1900's. Mother gave me the portrait of Grandma Blair and I am having it relined and oiled. James Bridges turned up, having been summoned, and helped empty a few scrap baskets. James is a realtor now (the horse having disappeared) and wears a fine sack suit and carries fountain pens. It was a melancholy pilgrimage—the house quite bare and touched with autumnal chill. Mother, however, looks pretty well and seems in reasonably good spirits. She likes it at Clara's, and enjoys motoring. Clara says she hangs on the postman's arrival, so we all better keep up a steady flow of letters.

Kay has been sick—ending with a miscarriage. Very disquieting and disturbing to both our spirits. She is better now and started work at the office this morning. Note new address, above.

Yrs,
Andy

To HAROLD ROSS

[1935]
[Interoffice memo]

Isn't the trouble with the Boo Department that the word "Boo" has two meanings or uses? One is the "Boo!" which a person cries when springing out at someone, the other is the "Boo" of disapproval at the theatre. I was confused at the Boo Dept.

EBW

To JAMES THURBER

[New York]
[January 1936]

Dear Jamie:

... I had an idea today, which I thought maybe you could use in your inimitable way—sort of a drawing idea. A picture of a patient in a doctor's office, together with the doctor. The patient has obviously been in a wreck of some sort—probably a plane wreck—for one of his legs is completely severed and is lying about three or four feet away on the floor. The doctor has been studying some X-ray pictures. He looks up from these and says: "Good news, Mr. VanHorsen, the X-ray shows that nothing is broken."

Maybe it's a little like your "Touché" picture, but I leave it with you.

Did you know that Weekes[1] was compiling a New Yorker style book which is longer than Gone with the Wind and more complete than Mencken's American Language? In compiling this book, he has come across some rare old Levickiana, including one note (when Levick was managing editor) which says: "*Night club* not to be used any more as symbol of gaiety."[2]

Andy

• *Early in 1936 White was offered the editorship of the* Saturday Review of Literature. *Christopher Morley was then Contributing Editor.*

To CHRISTOPHER MORLEY

In Bed
245 E. 48
[April 27, 1936]

Dear Mr. Morley:

I'm running a slight fever & your letter has not cooled me off any. I am touched, believe me, by your friendly extravagance. My reason for giving you this quick answer is that it may speed up the matter for you. I can't edit the *Sat. Review*, & this is the more painful for me because I like it and believe the things you say of it are true. I am, furthermore, hot for change (for myself)—which doesn't mean disloyalty to the N.Y.'er but more of a kind of super-loyalty to myself. I often feel out on a limb, doing what I'm doing. But not even these considerations can cloud my (minor) poetic vision, & I can give you One Clear No. The trouble with me is I am no editor even with a small E. Understanding this has saved me, & my beloved magazine, much woe. I can't edit the side of a barn. Without wishing to disparage myself, I can assure you that I could sit at the head of any publication you might name & establish a new high for imbecility. At the NYer I am an office boy de-luxe—a happy & profitable arrangement. My function is solely contributive except for one

---

1. Hobart G. Weekes, a copy editor at *The New Yorker*, and the man in charge of last-minute fixes.
2. William Levick, who had done a short trick as managing editor, was now head of the Makeup Department. He was "a man of incomparable irascibility" (according to White).

or two perfunctory chores which I can now do with my left hind foot. I am appalled when I think of taking over the Review. (What a fine, mad bunch of people you must be, anyway, to have cooked up such a notion!) For one thing, I'm a literary defective—I read so slowly & so infrequently that it causes talk even here in my own family; and although it appears to be your intention to seek an editor who is not too deeply covered with book feathers, I am sure you must want one who has heard of a couple of standard English authors & knows their works. Incidentally, although my bronchials are badly clogged, I didn't miss the melancholy implication of your letter: it's all so plain—casting about for someone who wasn't "literary," you thought immediately of ME. I had many a chuckle over that today, and a few honest gulps that were half remorse, half disease.

I have to make this letter short, but I hope not so short that you fail to catch my feeling about the *Review*, & about myself. I love us both too well to be willing to mess things up. My health is always whimsical, and I turn out shockingly little work in the course of a week—much less than I wish I did & far less, I'm sure, than you imagine. Being the head of anything would bust me up in no time. What I do hope for myself is that before long I can rearrange my affairs so that I can devote my limited energy & curious talents to the sort of writing nearest to my heart & pen. If this should turn out to be interesting to the *Sat Review*, that might be another story. Anyway, I have spent the day happily as Your Editor—one delicious day, like those you occasionally read about in the papers: "BOY OF 12 IS MAYOR OF PATERSON, N.J. FOR ONE DAY." It has been a day of unlimited ice cream cones, the sort of day a boy would race home and tell his mother about; and it has been doubly exciting for me because by strange chance it was precipitated by you, Mr. M., who in the old Post days unwittingly supplied 5 o'clock corroboration of my tentative ecstasies (I have always Meant to Tell you This) and infected me with the troublesome gallantry of letters.

Please check my name off with a clear, convincing stroke; this reply is a considered one and is fortified by the extra vision of fever. I have noted the item for my Biographer ("In the early spring of 1936 he was mentioned for Editor of the *Review*"). I thank you all. I will keep the secret, and assure you that when the Last Great Bronchitis comes and a few trusted friends come to my bedside, they will be thoroughly mystified by my delirium, utterly at a loss to account for the weird executive cries of reminiscent authority over imaginary reviewers—cries of "Get in there and get that author!"

Yrs,
E. B. White

To KATHARINE S. WHITE

Wardman Park Hotel
Washington, D.C.
[May 1, 1936]
Friday afternoon

Dear Kay:

The surgeon discovered instantly that there was no possibility of doing anything for Mother. Her liver, gall bladder, & part of colon are cancered. He didn't dare disturb anything, merely sewed her up. She will live a few months, in pain.

Whether this all could have been discovered in time, I don't know. The surgeon says her gall bladder contains five or six stones the size of a hickory nut, which must have been there a long time. I haven't seen her yet, since the operation. I can hardly face the blow of her disappointment when she learns that it was all for nothing. We are not going to tell Mother that it is cancer, but simply that her trouble is caused by the stones. I think perhaps in her case this is the wisest plan. She is very vague about diseases, anyway, and she has never been the sort of person to face facts realistically.

For two or three weeks she will remain in the hospital, then she will have to have special care, probably a nurse. Lill is here, and she is considering taking a summer cottage on one of the beaches near Washington & having Mother with her. Lill and I both feel that Clara will have to be relieved of the problem, because she is embarked on this very extensive venture. I learned to my surprise that it is a full fledged boarding establishment, serving breakfasts & dinners to 35 guests. I haven't seen it yet but it appears to be a high class place, with a monthly income of about $1600. She takes it over June 1, fully equipped with full complement of servants—every room occupied & a waiting list.

If Lill doesn't follow this plan, I shall try to work out some way to have Mother near us in Maine with a nurse, although it is all highly speculative. Mother may not live to see the summer; and the doctor probably won't allow her to travel far. There is a very attractive nursing home near Chevy Chase which we are investigating, as a possibility. All that can be done is to give Mother what small amount of happiness and ease life can still hold. It is not much, I fear. The news came very hard this morning, because our hopes had been high—

Lots of love,
Andy

P.S. Please keep the matter entirely to yourself, as to details, etc.—

To CHRISTOPHER MORLEY

245 East 48 Street
3 May 1936

Dear Mr. M—

I've been in Washington, and have just seen this proof.[1] If I'm late with corrections, no matter.

As for "river-peeper," I was conscious of it. I take it that it is a resemblance, and not a rhyme, and as such is allowable, just as a missing foot is permissible in the last line of the same stanza. However, if you feel strongly (and perhaps rightly) about this, I am quick to accommodate. Make it, if you like:

> Love in the murmurous pond doth ever
> Gird the lips of maid and lad;

I hope I didn't embarrass you over there by sending you this piece, which may well be a pretty flimsy piece of tripe, for all I can tell at this moment. I rose from bronchitis to attend my Mother, who is desperately ill in Washington, and I feel slightly unbalanced about life, deeds, and letters. For heaven's sake, if you feel more like throwing this away than publishing it, do so and I'll be grateful.

E. B. White

To STANLEY HART WHITE

[New York]
Saturday night, May 16 [1936]

Dear Bun:

Mother got steadily weaker, and Wednesday I went to Washington in order to see her for the last time. I got there in the middle of a thunder storm, the air very hot and oppressive, and found her hanging on to life regretfully, aware of the noise and afraid of the lightning. It seemed as though her suffering was more than anybody could bear. But the next day—a clear, cool morning with a fine sparkle—I went in and found her in a curiously exalted state; her pains seemed to be gone, and she talked with a sort of feverish excitement about the experience of death, which she was anxious to make us believe (while she still had strength enough to speak) was beautiful. She was very toxic, and focussed her eyes only with great effort, but she managed to convince us that she had achieved a peaceful conclusion. How much of it was chicanery and how much a merciful truth, I will never know, but she appeared to be enjoying a sort

---

1. Of White's poem "H. L. Mencken Meets a Poet in the West Side Y.M.C.A." The *Saturday Review* ran it, and White later included it in his collection *The Fox of Peapack*.

of spiritual intoxication. I said: "Isn't it beautiful, Mother?" (meaning the weather), and she replied, with astonishing fervor, "Oh, my, oh, my—it's perfectly beautiful" (meaning death). Clara took her hand and said: "Mother, you're perfectly comfortable, aren't you?" And she replied: "Perfectly comfortable." "And you're perfectly happy?" "Perfectly happy." It was an enormous relief after what we had been going through. From the parochial school across the way, Mother could hear the voices of the children singing, and she spoke of that and of how much it had meant to her. Apparently she thoroughly enjoyed the Catholic symbols, and took great comfort in them—liked the big crucifix at the foot of her bed. Occasionally a shudder of pain would make her twitch, and she would murmur, "Oh, oh oh, oh" quickly adding, for our benefit: "That means nothing at all, that means absolutely nothing at all." Her whole mind seemed to be bent on convincing us that all was well with her. She died that night, around ten o'clock; Clara was with her at the time.

Today she received Burr Davis's extreme unction, with the electric organ, the stale lilies, the old colored servants sitting silent and attentive in the little chapel, together with the neighbors from across the street, the doctor who didn't know she had cancer of the liver, and the minister who was sure her soul would go to heaven. Afterwards we drove wearily out to Ferncliff, stopping for the red lights, listening to anecdotes by the interminable Mr. Scholz.[1] I walked down and found Father's stone, which I think is good. We must get another one like it.

This is a very sketchy account of what has been going on these last few days, but I thought you might like to know at least the bare facts. It seems hardly credible that in the course of a single year, Sam and Jessie have gone from this good life.

> Yrs as ever,
> Andy

To STANLEY HART WHITE

> Thursday
> Bert Mosher's.
> Belgrade Lakes, Maine
> [1936?]

Dear Stan:

I returned to Belgrade. Things haven't changed much. There's a train called the Bar Harbor Express, and Portland is foggy early in the morning, and the Pullman blankets are brown and thin and cold. But when you look out of the window in the diner, steam is rising from

---

1. Charles Scholz, executor of the wills of both White's parents.

pastures and the sun is out, and pretty soon the train is skirting a blue lake called Messalonski. Things don't change much. Even the names, you still hear them: names like Caswell, Bartlett, names like Bickford, Walter Gleason, Damren. Gram lives alone in the chowder house, down by the lake, brooding on days before the farm burnt, hanging draperies the Count sends her from abroad. The lake hangs clear and still at dawn, and the sound of a cowbell comes softly from a faraway woodlot. In the shallows along shore the pebbles and driftwood show clear and smooth on bottom, and black water bugs dart, spreading a wake and a shadow. A fish rises quickly in the lily pads with a little plop, and a broad ring widens to eternity. The water in the basin is icy before breakfast, and cuts sharply into your nose and ears and makes your face blue as you wash. But the boards of the dock are already hot in the sun, and there are doughnuts for breakfast and the smell is there, the faintly rancid smell that hangs around Maine kitchens. Sometimes there is little wind all day, and on still hot afternoons the sound of a motorboat comes drifting five miles from the other shore, and the droning lake becomes articulate, like a hot field. A crow calls, fearfully and far. If a night breeze springs up, you are aware of a restless noise along the shore, and for a few minutes before you fall asleep you hear the intimate talk between fresh-water waves and rocks that lie below bending birches. The insides of your camp are hung with pictures cut from magazines, and the camp smells of lumber and damp. Things don't change much. Meadow stream has a beginning in the pickerel weeds. If you push along quietly, a blue heron will rise with a heavy squawk and a flap. The ends of logs that jut out are covered with the dung of little animals that come there to eat fresh mussels and wash their paws at the stream-side. Over at the Mills there's a frog box, sunk half in the water. People come there in boats and buy bait. You buy a drink of Birch Beer at Bean's tackle store. Big bass swim lazily in the deep water at the end of the wharf, well fed. Long lean guide boats kick white water in the stern till they suck under. There are still one cylinder engines that don't go. Maybe it's the needle valve. At twilight, cows come hesitantly down the little woods roads behind the camps to steal a drink in the cove. They belong to a man named Withers. Withers' cows. Pasture bars are cedar, stripped of bark, weathered grey. On rainy days swallows come and dip water, and the camps are cold. When the wind swings into the north, the blow comes. It comes suddenly, and you know a change has come over things, instinctively. Next day you will see a little maple, flaming red, all alone in a bog. It's cold and fearsome by the lake. The wind still holds strong into the second morning, and white caps are as thick as whiskers. When you get back on the road, away from the lake, the road lies warm and yellow, and you hear the wind fussing in the treetops behind you and you don't care. The rocks in the stream behind the Salmon Lake House are colored red and colored green, where the boats have scraped them under water. The clothesline behind Walter Gleason's house is flapping with white wash. . . . There's a house on a hill where a lady lived that used to keep cats. Along the road the apples are little and yellow and sweet. Puddles dry in the sun, and the mud cakes, and yellow butterflies diddle in the new mud. Cow trails lead up slopes through juniper beds and thistles and grey rocks, and below you the lake hangs blue and clear, and you see the islands plain. Sometimes a farm dog barks. Yes, sir, I returned to Belgrade, and things don't change much. I thought somebody ought to know.

En

To HAROLD ROSS

[North Brooklin, Me.]
Tuesday
[August? 1936]

Dear Mr. R.

Two matters for your attention.

I am planning to come to town this Sunday, arriving Monday morning, for a five-day stay. Will be free to take on any commissions which you might like executed, such as Talk rewrite, visits, reporter, etc. Intend to devote the period largely to work, as have not done any to speak of for quite a spell.

Two: is there anybody (his name might possibly be Gibbs) who would want to write two comment departments for the issues of September 12 and 19, myself to receive no pay during the fortnight? I would like to have a respite from this none-too-arduous composition. . . . Anything Mr. Gibbs or Mr. McKelway or Mr. Thurber or (possibly) Mr. F. P. Adams or Mr. G. Hellman might care to write would, I am sure, be acceptable to me—not that it has to be acceptable to me. Maybe Maloney(?).[1] Or perhaps somebody like Mumford. If no one individual wanted to assume the Magnificent Burden, it would probably be quite easy to ask twelve persons each to contribute one paragraph of about 200 words, from which it would [be] simple to make up two departments.

Will you take these things under advisement and let me know

---

1. Russell Maloney had become the chief rewrite man of Talk and was a contributor of satirical and humorous pieces. His "Inflexible Logic" became one of the most famous casuals the magazine ever published.

your wishes, etc. We are having splendid weather and I am building a stone wall. I understand that all literary people, at one time or another, build a stone wall. It's because it is easier than writing.

Yrs,
E. B. White

P.S. Tell your wife we received the beautiful sandalwood butter churn.

To KATHARINE S. WHITE

[New York]
[August? 1936]
Tuesday morning

Dear Kay:

Everything goes well. Train was terrifically hot, but I wrote a casual anyway. Gibbs says nobody writes funny pieces any more; all written by 23 year old Jews, about life. Ross phoned yesterday from his estate, inviting me out, but I declined. Bunny [Rigg] asked me to Fairfield for tonight, also declined. Mr. Knowles[1] would like me for dinner tomorrow night, to see the baby. This is still in the air. Everybody reports a calm summer, and looks well. The office has new paper towels, whiter and softer. Had dinner with Gibbs and Elinor last night at Hapsburg, and they went on to Blake's and to win $45 from an under-salaried Lardner boy.[2] Jim phoned yesterday morning from somewhere in Connecticut, and sounded in good humor, but Gibbs can't stand him any more. Gus is in New Orleans, and Hugh leaves tomorrow for a vacation. Everything is all right at the house except it rained in the bedroom windows, turning the blue to brown; and one night the icebox suddenly let go with a blast of lethal gas, almost killing the two lads.[3] They rushed into the kitchen, fighting their way with eyes streaming and waves of sickness beating them back. Finally got windows open and plug pulled out. Machines are against men, and are simply lying in wait for all of us. I don't know just what to do about the icebox, but I have removed a mouldy melon and am brooding on the whole problem. Mr. Bizantine[4] hasn't showed up yet, but I am working on that, too. Everybody has a key to the house but me. Stanley Walker wants me to do a piece about homing pigeons, and about croquet in Central Park. I have a date with Mr. Chappell at 11 a.m., about Model T. Earl Balch

---

1. Howard Knowles, of the Layout Department.

2. "Blake's" was actually Bleeck's saloon, officially known as the Artist and Writers Restaurant, a popular spot with newspaper men and others who liked to drink and play the match game. John Lardner, son of Ring, was a regular.

3. Gus Lobrano and his brother-in-law Hugh Flick, summertime occupants of the Whites' apartment.

4. The painter "Brigantine." (White never did learn his name.)

is interested in it, I am informed.[5] Yesterday I sent "You Can't Resettle Me" to Berford Lorimer, who is just back from Saratoga and in the mood for anything. I have an even bet of one dollar with Alva Johnston that the Post rejects it.[6] Found a long letter to Joe from Levick at 48th Street, and am forwarding it. It seems to have been written in July and has just been hanging around. Haven't seen Bun yet, but he phoned and says he may still come cruising. I'm going to try and see him today. The McKelways have pretty well abandoned Fire Island, and are back at 51. Mac's mother is in town. Louis & Armand's was full at noon yesterday, with the literary and drinking set, but people seem calm and with a clear light in their eye, and everybody reports a quiet well-behaved summer. Today is cooler, but a hot wave forecast. Miss Terry was seen leaving the office yesterday at 5:20. I have just read all the Spanish news in the Herald Tribune of this date and have decided the H-T is in favor of the rebels and against the Left. Most biased news reporting I have read since I stopped reading the Herald Tribune's political columns.

Build lots of nice fences and defrost your icebox every week. I haven't bought you a tea table underpinning yet, but I have a note on me somewhere that says T T underpinning, and so there is still a chance. Am rewriting a story about a left fielder for the Giants, so had better close. The orange pillows for the garden furniture are unspeakable. Lots of love to all, and tell Roger that most motor accidents are caused by the driver going too fast and not having time to stop.

See you Saturday,

A

• *When the following letters were written, Katharine White was visiting her father and two elderly ailing aunts in Northampton, Massachusetts, while White and Joel stayed in North Brooklin.*

To KATHARINE S. WHITE

[North Brooklin, Me.]
[September 3, 1936]
Thursday night

Dear Kay:

The great stillness has at last descended. Nancy and Roger departed directly after supper, in charge of Bill Schnauzer and Buster. They were headed for the Boston train via the Dirigo Theatre. I believe

---

5. Chappell and Balch were at G. P. Putnam's Sons, which was soon to publish *Farewell to Model T*.
6. White lost the bet—Lorimer bought the piece. It ran in the *Saturday Evening Post* of October 10, 1936.

a bevy, or cluster, of Roger's female friends are expected at the station to see him off. Tunney [Roger's bulldog] is moody, with waves of nausea overcoming him at rather short intervals.

We had a fine, soft rain all last night, steady and wet. Everything was thoroughly drenched at last, including the priming coat on the fence. It still rained this morning, and Joe and I went over to Center Harbor and boarded Astrid to ease the lines. Nance and I sailed her around yesterday morning, lunching aboard and arriving in time for the race.[1] The race, incidentally, turned into quite an affair. There was a flat calm at the start, with the boats unable to drift across the line, all jammed together, panting for a puff. They hung that way for about five minutes, then the wind backed into the south and began to blow hard, rippling the Reach into a lovely sun-flecked turmoil. The Beasts sprang away, and Nance cracked up almost immediately, her rudder-track pulling out. The committee boat towed her in, and then went out to salvage the rest of the fleet. All but three managed to complete one lap, and then turned tail and ran into the harbor. It was a brisk sight; even the harbor was all chopped up with white caps, and in the midst of everything, in ran the Mattie under full press of sail and rounded to off the old steamboat wharf. She looked alarmingly spruced up, and it turns out she has been all re-commissioned and is now a pleasure boat, out of Camden. How are the mighty fallen![2] Nancy was quite disappointed about not finishing her last race of the season, but was sort of glad to be in the harbor. Dick Emery was indignant that the race was called after one lap, and feels that the Haven fleet is growing soft. . . .

Joe is well and is turning over in his mind an invitation to a picnic supper at the Sturtevants on Saturday. Mrs. S. and Peter were by this P.M., and Peter remained for a visit. Ros and John and Jane [Newberry] came to tea, bringing me a book and carrying away three. According to Rosamond, John is very anxious to play tennis. I am invited to South Brooksville with Joe for luncheon on Monday. Fanny laid an egg on Tuesday, and again this morning. She uses the north stall this year, rather than the south. Greater privacy. The cock has disappeared entirely, after an affair with Freddy.[3] I horsewhipped Fred and banished him to the garage, but he seems keen and ready to go.

---

1. Center Harbor Yacht Club fleet's semiweekly race.
2. The *Mattie* was a coasting schooner, built to carry lumber and firewood.
3. A red dachshund. White had brought Fred as a puppy in a Madison Avenue pet shop. His AKC papers, White always thought, had been forged. He was a large, strong-willed, beer-drinking dog about whom much has been written by his master. Katharine White loved dachshunds, but her husband's feelings about the breed were mixed. "For a number of years," he wrote, "I have been agreeably encumbered by a very large and dissolute dachshund named Fred. . . . He even disobeys me when

The woods and sea are beginning to close in already. The blue heron fishes daily at the frogpond. Darkness falls with the meat course. Joe and I have gathered boughs of red swamp maple, to decorate the back porch. Last Tuesday in a strong westerly the Bemis sloop dragged its mooring clear across the harbor and brought up on the mud. Mrs. B. (Chapey) got her off, with some local assistance. No damage. Madeline's food has been very good, with a strong trend to meat balls— or what Joe calls lamb chops.[4] My health has been good, but I don't sleep at night because for some reason I can't breathe when I lie down. Whether this is climate, heart, or an uncured feather pillow, I can't seem to determine.

Joe's latest literary passion is a Camel ad in the funny paper, called "Mysteries of the Undersea World." It is all about a deep sea diver, whose digestive processes are improved by addiction to a Certain Brand of cigarette. I had to read it four times tonight, and then had to play the piano loud after Joe went to bed, so the undersea creatures would swim out of his thoughts. He announced today that he wanted to write letters, but then said that it was impossible to do it without you.

Lots of love from us all, & my best to the Northamptonians.

Andy

To KATHARINE S. WHITE

[North Brooklin, Me.]
[September 1936]
Wed. aft.

Dear Kay:

Just got your train letter, and guess if I post this right away it will catch you before you leave. Everything has been going swimmingly here, and September is a great boon. Things seem immediately better, in applefall. The sweet corn is unspeakably toothsome, and the corners of my mouth ache from the grinding of the salty ears. Joe is still blooming and asks about your return. He screwed up his courage on Saturday and went to Peter's party, half reluctant. When he and I arrived at the Sturdevants', the cottage was seething with slightly older boys, yelling and throwing rubber automobiles. Mr. S. and a bulldog dozed in the maelstrom. Joe clung to my hand and had one of his attacks of the

---

I instruct him in something that he wants to do. And when I answer his peremptory scratch at the door and hold the door open for him to walk through, he stops in the middle to light a cigarette, just to hold me up." Fred died at thirteen, "of his excesses and after a drink of brandy."

4. Madeline Day, a high-school girl, came to the Whites as extra help during her summer vacation. She is now Mrs. Roy Snow, proprietress of a Blue Hill boutique.

shys. But I just deposited him, and soon the party moved down to the shore and from all reports he had a fine time. You should have seen him, on his return, telling me in a half embarrassed, half triumphant way that he had won a prize—for gathering the most firewood.

While he was picnicking, I sailed Astrid around from Center Harbor back to Allen Cove, with Ted, Nan,[1] Lucy, and Ted's sister Marion. . . . Nan brought knitting and rove the yarn through the mainsheet. Ted was all helpfulness, in his strange tutorial way. Lucy steered. I prayed to God nobody would fall overboard, managed to get the anchor on board, wove Astrid through the racing fleet, and finally got squared away. We had a good sail eventually, for we had a grand reach up Bluehill Bay, just strong enough to make it good sailing, without being troublesome. Nan was visited with nausea at the finish. She eats nothing now but Red Astrachans and cake—the Astrachans to make her thin, the cake because she can't resist it. Mr. Keller will be cut for the stone next summer.

I have named our barn Wil-Fan Lodge, in honor of Billy [the cock] and Fanny. There were terrific squawks from the region of the spring the other day, and I ran over with the horsewhip, to find that Bill had got one leg caught in a vine and was yelling his head off while Fred sat nearby, gently worrying him.

On Labor Day the household was up early, dressed in its best. Jean and Madeline went off to the Fair,[2] Joe and I to South Brooksville for luncheon. I believe that the Havenites had their usual chowder race that day, but I have seen none of them, so can't report. Yesterday I staged my own chowder party and picnic on Long Island. It was a success, in [a] feverish way, and ran on into the second day. In fact I am just back from it. It was one of those characteristic picnic days—overcast, ominous, with a good deal of quiet thunder, including the Newberrys. The latter arrived at the crack of dawn, and we got aboard Astrid (with Howard [Pervear]) and started up the Bay to collect the Kellers and Mistress D——, who has long white hairs on her legs that I like to look at. I planned chowder, sweet corn, and cake, and got Madeline to give me explicit directions about the chowder. Two fine haddock lay in Astrid's ice chest, ready to spring, and we had a big pot and onions and potatoes and butter and milk. The first premonitory drops of rain came as the Kellers came aboard at the Slaven stone pier. But there was

---

1. Theodore Keller and his wife, summer visitors to Blue Hill. Ted Keller was master of Dickinson House at Lawrenceville School and head of the school's music department. The Kellers had two daughters, Lucy and Elsa.

2. The Blue Hill Fair—which later was the setting for the Fair in *Charlotte's Web*. Jean was a live-in baby sitter.

blue sky in patches, so we sailed over to the Island and debarked, Astrid's little girl making four trips ashore loaded to her gunwales. It then turned out that Ros had her own system about chowder, and had secreted in her purse some old pork scraps, which she insisted on brewing in my steel frying pan. She dumped this snarling mess into my beautiful chowder. The rain stopped and the heat danced along the beach. Kellers wandered everywhere, with things in their hands, and Miss D—— talked in a high, cute voice about going swimming with no clothes on. John left and did 572 strokes around Astrid, while Ros called "JOHN." I was quietly furious about the pork scraps, and the chowder was fairly nasty, on top of a Manhattan. Nan had made a chocolate marshmallow cake. We left early to play tennis. At two-love the thunder really meant business, and you could hardly serve for the glare from the lightning. At last it struck, in the very saddle of the afternoon, and we all took shelter in the barn, where Herm Gray let us hold the teats of cows and squeeze. Meantime, Astrid lay tied up to the Slaven swimming float, which in turn was tied up to our old mooring. Nan disappeared into the storm to collect Elsa, who was visiting Joe. Ted disappeared to Ellsworth, to say goodbye to a relative. They were both back almost instantly, and there was the question about getting home. Howard brooded about his cows. Rosamond's thoughts turned dimly to South Brooksville, and I said I couldn't leave Astrid, as she was sagging in on the stone pier with the dropping tide. The Newberries said they would return to North Brooklin by car, if they could get anybody to take them— a suggestion which was met with shrieking approval by Miss D——, who whipped out a Ford sedan and was off down the road. I hung around the barn and made a date with Percy Moore, and then went down in the wet to Astrid. Nan and Ted, who knew Miss D—— of old because she had once swung on Ted and broke his glasses at a cocktail party at Nila's, could hardly wait to see whether she would come back for a rendezvous with me aboard Astrid—which by this time was whipping about in a NE storm with her fanny just clearing the stone pier at each bound. I worked for thirty minutes in the downpour rowing a stronger line out to the mooring, after the first line had parted, and then drank a can of tomato soup and lay down, praying for surcease from picnics. Just as I was dozing off, Miss D arrived, true to form, with an apple pie and a Doberman pinscher, who sat outside and wailed. I put her ashore inviolate an hour later, but I'm sure Nan didn't have a wink of sleep, and I acted wise and tired this morning when I showed up at the Kellers' for breakfast. . . .

Lots of love, and see you Sat.

Andy

• *The year 1936 ended with White's locking horns with Alexander Woollcott over the matter of testimonial advertising. Woollcott had sent a lot of letters to friends and acquaintances urging them to give him Seagram's for Christmas, instead of an indestructible gift that he would have to "shove up in the attic." White received one of the letters and dashed off an indignant piece. The New Yorker published it, together with the Woollcott letter, in its December 19 issue, under the heading "Open-Letters Department." White wrote:*

DEAR ALEXANDER WOOLLCOTT: About your request that we give you some Seagram's eight-year-old imported bonded whiskey for Christmas, we're sorry but it's out of the question. Our gift for you is all bought, all wrapped up, ready to go by Western Union messenger to your home on Gracie Square. We have instructed the messenger just to look for a radiance in the sky, and follow it.

Our gift, we are sorry to say, *is* indestructible. It is a tippet, lined with burrs. The tippet we got at Bonwit Teller's, the burrs we picked ourself. It is depressing to us to learn that you eventually will "shove it up in the attic," but many Christmases have inured us to the disappointments of giving and receiving. Many Christmases! How the phrase seems to spell the passing of time! Well, the holidays come and go; yet this Christmas of 1936, thanks to your thoughtful note, has been given an unforgettable flavor, has become a season pervaded with the faint, exquisite perfume of well-rotted holly berries.

God rest ye and Seagram's merry.

EUSTACE TILLEY

Ross, who alternately liked Woollcott and found him annoying, was delighted with the exchange of letters. Woollcott was angry. He recognized the touch behind the pen name "Eustace Tilley" and wrote White a letter defending his participation in endorsement advertising. The communications that follow are White's answer.

To ALEXANDER WOOLLCOTT

[New York]
[December 1936]
[Christmas card]

Dear Woollcott:

Serving the *New Yorker* in my capacity as jackanapes of all trades, I sometimes discover myself in the act of muddying up my friends and acquaintances—as in the case of you and the Seagram letter. I always throw myself into these discourtesies with a will, dreamily hoping to achieve heavenly grace through earthly impartiality. My wife tells me you are convinced that we maintain a Dept. of Animus; but my true belief is we have as little animus as is consistent with good publishing. In your case, my own animus, if any, was against the frantic society to which we all fall victim, in varying measure, and to which you lured my attention at this white season by your open affair with La Seagram. After all, a man's personal excesses are his own business. Privately, I may wish you joy of the lady, but publicly I must give so lewd an alliance a jab, mustn't I?

With best wishes,

E. B. White

To ALEXANDER WOOLLCOTT

25 West 43rd Street
24 December 1936

Dear Woollcott:

I agree that I ought to say why I feel the way I do about endorsements. Even if it makes me sound holier, which I deplore but don't know how to avoid. Please note that I'm not speaking for Eustace Tilley, of which I am merely an arm, a leg, or a groin. I'm speaking for myself.

In your letter you mention honesty and dignity. I don't think endorsements are necessarily dishonest (certainly your letter spoke plainly enough), and I don't give a whoop about dignity. But I am pretty sure of my distaste for the commercial testimonial—find such things offensive, disappointing, disillusioning, on two counts. First, I am convinced that a testimonial, in effect and purpose, is a piece of snobbishness, the implication being that because the testifier is celebrated he is to be aped by the less distinguished citizenry. You will bristle at this, but I'm not accusing you of attempted snobbery: I'm just saying that, once in, you can't help yourself. I once worked long and faithfully in an advertising agency; I know what the boys want, and what they got when they got you. When you, full of an idea, engage to write a piece for a publication, write it, and get paid, you are performing a literary or creative act and are being paid for the results of your talent and labor. When you, again full of an idea, write an advertisement for Seagram on your letterhead, what you are really selling is the name Woollcott, which is valuable to a commercial house because you had previously established yourself as a vivid person who could write and who was interesting and provocative to many people. Now, as one of your readers or as one of your acquaintances, or both, or neither, I object to your addressing me by way of a liquor house in whose debt you are. I feel patronized, and you seem suddenly discredited. When a Mrs. Vanderbilt, with her nails well polished and her hips pulled in, appears in a color page and gives her approval to Lucky Strikes, it reminds me of a Great Lady patting a child on the head and calling it a dear, or of a priest blessing the hounds on their way to the kill. I detest these condescensions and these vanities. Inherent in such an advertisement is the assumption that all shop girls should smoke Luckies and grow up to be a fine lady like Mrs. Vanderbilt. Inherent in your endorsement of Seagram's was, first, the assumption that anyone who receives the letter would, of course, be impressed and honored with a Woollcott letter (if the advertising agency hadn't thought this, they wouldn't have approached you) and, second, that he would wish naturally to be guided by your preferences and predilections. This is the essence of the endorsement idea, and you can't neutralize or destroy it merely by the wording of your letter or your frank admission that you are being corrupted and bribed.

My other reason is the one that everything really hangs on: the importance of a writer's maintaining his amateur standing. I don't give much of a damn whether Mrs. Vanderbilt endorses or not, because I am not particularly engrossed in Mrs. Vanderbilt, what she does, wears, smokes, or thinks. I do, however, give a damn where your interests lie, and what your ties are; it seems important to me; it seems to have a bearing on many other things which are close to my life and my love. I have read you for years. When I heard you plead for civil liberty on the air, I was excited and moved by so eloquent and honest a shot fired toward what I know to be the enemy. When I run across your steady and loyal diligence in behalf of the blind, I feel good that there is still charity and gentleness round and about. I still cling (by my teeth these days) to the notion that writing is a trust, that you were born in Phalanx not as other Phalanxians but with a star over your head and an itch to get going. And that I was likewise, wherever I was born. Then in the midst of your writings comes a letter with a phony salutation and a printed signature, saying that you like Seagram's whiskey. In itself, this document is certain[ly] harmless, guiltless. The harm to me the recipient (or the loss, rather) is that the next time I come across you, in the mail, in print, I feel I must be on my guard, must see what the catch is, may have to read half way through before I can determine whether this is an affiliated utterance or an unaffiliated utterance, and if I discover a paid allegiance, then must make the necessary allowances for the writer's being in the hire of somebody. This, in my opinion, dissipates a man's character, destroys a writer's credit, gradually. When a signature is bought for its own sake, the matter above it becomes suspect.

If your public approval of a trademarked product and your influence can be bought at a price, then, carrying the thing through to an extreme, it is fair for General Motors to try to buy the good will of, say, the Secretary of State, and it is fair for the Secretary to consider selling it. He has a public trust as a servant of the state, you have a public trust as an avowed servant of the Muse or of History or whatever you want to call the thing that you and I do in the world. Our allegiance should be to our constituency, and we shouldn't grind axes as a sideline. That is the nub of my complaint.

As to the New Yorker's manner of handling your letter, I think it was cheesey, and I am the one to blame on that. Several people in the office converged on your letter (they came fluttering in like leaves, the letters did) and seeing how everybody felt and feeling that way myself, I went to work. The result was not so good. My own indignation and sorrow were tinged with bronchitis, which always makes me ugly.

As to the juxtaposition of the whiskey ads, I can't see that it has any bearing on the case. I am paid not by one whiskey house but by many (all of them chattering like monkeys) and I direct your attention to a chemical phenomenon: whiskey houses, in quantities, cancel each other out. The relation of a writer to the capitalistic press is itself a fascinating subject, but I don't see that it is analogous to endorsement advertising. I admit I am in the employ of the Interests, indirectly; but I think you are being a little unfair to imply that ten years of my life can be suddenly undone by a Talon fastener. The New Yorker is something I love very much, and I don't think I am practising self-deception in working for it.

(Incidentally, as a stockholder you may be excited by a piece of news I have just this minute learned: I asked my favorite office boy what he was giving his girl for Christmas. He replied: "A ring set with three small diamonds, and a red velvet dress.")

I am emboldened to write this long, smug-sounding letter, full of how wonderful and right I am and how terrible and wrong you are, first because you asked for it, but more because the persons who have spoken to me about your endorsement have, almost to a man, seemed to feel either offended, shattered, enraged, or just plain startled. I recognize that there are also many other people who do *not* have any such prejudice or feeling about testimonials, but I think many of these used to resent them and gradually got hardened to them from the daily barrage. I certainly hate to be on the opposite side of the wall from Newton D. Baker, whom I admire greatly, but here I am.

Sincerely.
Andy White

•   *White's feelings about New York were mixed: he loved the city (a love he celebrated in many of his writings), but he often felt unfulfilled by urban life. ("The pavements were hard and there weren't any broody hens.") He was tired of working to a weekly deadline, and he yearned for the country. As early as February 1937, while still in town, he was laying plans for a setting of turkey eggs. Springtime without incubation seemed to him incomplete. That same year he tried taking a "year off" from job and family, but missed his wife and son too much and returned to New York after a few weeks. Finally, in 1938 he persuaded Katharine to pull up stakes and try living in North Brooklin all year round.*

For the family, the move to Maine meant some drastic rearranging, both emotional and financial. For Katharine it was particularly difficult. Her roots went deep at the magazine, and it was a wrench for her to give up her well-paying job as fiction editor and alter her close relationship with her stable of writers. Joel, on the other hand, needed no persuading. Even at the age of seven, he was convinced that boats and the sea were the answer to living.

After settling in to their new life in the deep country both Whites managed to maintain close ties with The New Yorker. *Katharine regularly received manuscripts and proofs in the mail, editing them on a part-time basis. She also continued to review children's books. White turned out Newsbreaks every week, contributed Comment off and on, and submitted "casuals," stories, and poems. Shortly before his departure from the city, however, White had formed a new publishing connection. Lee Hartman, editor of* Harper's *magazine, had asked him to write a monthly department from the country. White had agreed to try it, and they had settled on a payment of $300 a month. In July of 1938, White* *hit on the title "One Man's Meat" and turned in the first of the essays he was to write without interruption for the next four and a half years. (On Hartman's death in 1942, Frederick Lewis Allen took over as editor.)*

It is clear in retrospect that this "One Man's Meat" interlude was not merely a change of habitat, it was a change in writing style. White was drifting into the informal essay—a form he gradually mastered. He felt at home in it and became one of its most skillful practitioners. It's also clear that White's love affair with the barn—his close relationship to sheep, hens, geese, pigs, rats, and spiders—was to bloom later in the story of Charlotte's Web, *a book that could never have been written by anyone lacking an emotional involvement in the lives of domestic animals.*

The period 1937–1941, although idyllic in prospect and escapist in nature, proved by no means a time of great contentment or of escape. It was, instead, a time of intense activity and spiritual unease. First the looming disaster in Europe, then the war itself, colored and darkened everyone's life, and the Whites lived continuously in a state of doubt as to the validity and responsibility of life on a farm in times of such gravity. But however uneasy those years were, they were at least fruitful: two more books were published: The Fox of Peapack *(poems) in 1938, and* Quo Vadimus? *(sketches) in 1939. In addition, White and his wife began, in 1940, to collaborate on* A Subtreasury of American Humor, *which was published in 1941 by Coward, McCann and soon found its way overseas, in an Armed Services Edition, to relieve the tedium of war for thousands of soldiers and sailors.*

To **CHRISTOPHER MORLEY**

25 West 43rd Street
12 January [1937]

Dear Chris:

Date of my birth is July 11, 1899. I can't imagine what you're doing with me in Bartlett's, but if it's the spinach joke I hope you quote it right. Only about twice has it been quoted right.[1]

I can't think of a book to review right now but I shall watch the lists closely. Many thanks for the offer.

Sincerely,
E. B. White

1. Morley was co-editor of the eleventh edition of Bartlett's *Familiar Quotations*, and the "spinach joke" was included in the book. It was White's caption for a cartoon by Carl Rose which appeared in *The New Yorker* of December 8, 1928. The caption was one of many that White contributed to the magazine over the years:
"It's broccoli, dear."
"I say it's spinach, and I say the hell with it."

• *White had met Jack Fleming at Professor Bristow Adams' house at Cornell when Fleming was an editor of the* Cornell Countryman. *After he graduated, he went to work with the U.S. Department of Agriculture.*

To JOHN R. FLEMING

[New York]
3 February 1937

Dear Jack:

I am going to set a hen on some turkey eggs this spring to tone myself up and prove that a man can fail at more things than one. Your department got any turkey information that might prove valuable, or disastrous, to me? Don't tell me I have to keep their feet off the ground—my turkey poults are going to have their feet *right on* the ground and like it.

I have a bet with my wife that I can raise our Thanksgiving bird this year, and am anxious to win. My dander is up. Send me your stuff.

Yrs frantically,
Andy

To STANLEY HART WHITE

[New York]
13 March [1937]

Dear Bun:

Thanks for the letter about Christmas. I haven't done anything about Christmas yet because my system is to let it go until I can no longer see the red on a poinsettia and I have discovered that if you trim back a poinsettia to within a couple of inches of the roots soon after New Year's it will bloom again, in fact I have one flowering in the window now. Your study is nothing compared to mine, which is full of live birds. I was in Bloomingdale's one day and happened to discover a hen canary laying an egg—a show of spirit which was too much for an old canary breeder like me, so I took her home ($1.98 including sales tax) and what with the cockbird that belongs to Joe and another hen named Buttercup, the room is little more than an incubator. Birds are all right except you get practically nothing done, as they make everything else seem so unimportant.

Was interested to learn that you, too, are a Tarzan devotee. I have long been a student of Weismuller and his tailor-made jungle, and when I come to make my definitive study of the movies, a whole chapter will be given over to Africa. I am also planning a chapter on "Sound," which will be mostly a description of what film noises are like if you close your eyes and don't look at the picture, and a chapter on "Hollywood trees," which will include the hollow tree, the soft focus tree, the vine (or rope ladder) tree, the all-purpose tree, and the flat crotch tree for Janet Gaynor and one other. It is extremely encouraging to me to realize that, with hundreds of movie critics working like beavers in all the big cities, hardly a word of cinema criticism has yet been written. It's an untouched field, and makes me think there will still be something for me to work out on in my old age. The attempt to combine human speech with animated images has really led to nothing, unless you want to call America's second largest industry something.

We have had what I believe is called a mild winter, although it hasn't seemed mild to me, what with nausea and Nancy's appendectomy and Joe's cut chin and Kay getting a toothbrush bristle stuck in a tonsil divot. Kay was very funny that night—the bristle, securely lodged in her throat, made her vomit up a dollar and a quarter dinner, but the circumstance struck her as so comical that she was in gales of laughter while throwing up, and I had to hold her hair back, which is three feet ten inches long by the most conservative measure, and the whole affair was most grotesque. It was a Doctor West's toothbrush, during the moult. . . .

Bun, there is one matter which has been on my mind, and I can't recall whether I mentioned it to you before. I wish you would let me have the address of the stonecutter who made the marker for Father's grave, together with instructions for having a similar stone made for Mother. (Unless, of course, you have already done something about it.) I haven't been out to Ferncliff this winter, but expect to go soon. I think we should have the two stones the same, and we shouldn't let it go any longer. Will you please let me have the necessary information as soon as possible?

Some time this summer I am quitting the *New Yorker* for at least a year—sort of a delayed sabbatical—and am looking forward to it with some relish. I want to see what it feels like, again, to let a week pass by without having an editorial bowel movement. It is terrible to have to write down one's thoughts before they even get their pin-feathers, and I have been doing that for quite a while. So toward the end of the summer I shall give up my job and devote myself to the miasma of leisure and to the backwash of the spirit. I don't know what I'll live off of, but they say it is called the fat of the land. I can always kill a nice fat canary.

Must get back, now, to my Saturday afternoon inactivity, which this letter has too long interrupted. My best to all

Yrs,
Andy

To KATHARINE S. WHITE

[Miami, Fla.]
[March 31, 1937]
Wednesday

Dear Kay:

Got your letter yesterday, and I can sympathize with you in your Canadian weather with moss hanging all around.[1] It's been cool here, but plenty warm enough for swimming, and it eases us into our sunburns without the usual jolt. Miami is a really handsome atrocity—not even two decades of progress can quite dim its natural splendor—and it has a pleasant, post-season feeling now, with half empty cafes and kids allowed to ride bicycles on the sidewalk, and thinning traffic. Yesterday we had a storm with high seas.

Carol and Noel are in public school, nearby, and don't get any vacation, so they are gone all morning. Joe is in the pink. No schedule and always something to do, and very much on his own. This place is full of little canals, and there is a boat livery which rents little bike-boats, called pedal-paddle boats (Noel calls them piddle-paddles). They seat two, and Joe and I skim all over the canals with the greatest of ease. You will love them.

Sunday we drove to Coconut Grove and watched the Pan-American clippers arrive from South America and the islands, a fabulous spectacle, so big, so well regimented—a handsome terminal building with balconies overhanging the sea where you can sit and sip punch and con the sky for the next ship. It requires a smallboat crew, a dock crew, and an amphibian group to moor the plane—the amphibians being three young men in bathing suits who rush into the sea and fit the plane with wheels so that it can be dragged (by a caterpillar tractor) onto the shore. You'll have to see it when you come down. . . .

Andy

To ST. CLAIR MC KELWAY

3481 Sheridan Avenue
Miami Beach, Florida
3 Apr [1937]

Dear Mac:

It appears I will be doing another dept. from here, so ship along anything you have from the special fellows, God bless them. This is quite

---

1. White was visiting Lillian and Arthur Illian in Miami, while his wife was paying a call on her father in Hibernia, in northern Florida, where for many years he wintered with Katharine's Aunt Caroline.

a dump—a sweet smelling Coney Island, full of pseudo-Venetian canals. . . . I love it, and the sea water is exactly 76° in the sun, which is something. Houses are called "houses" and "pre-hurricane houses," according to how they date. I live in a "house." How is your "apartment"?

See you soon,

Andy

• *White's P. B. Publico piece in the March 6 issue of* The New Yorker *lamenting the disappearance of the "touring car" from the American scene generated a lot of mail from motorcar buffs. J. Thomas Stewart II, an automobile dealer in Omaha, saw the piece and wrote "Publico" that he had a 1930 seven-passenger Lincoln tourer in mint condition. The price was $300. White bought it, sight unseen, and sent an office boy named Wilbur Young to get it. An Omaha paper got wind of the transaction, played it for laughs, and gave Wilbur a sendoff when he rolled out of town at the wheel of the Lincoln. The car proved to be everything Stewart said it was—a dazzling beauty, pearl gray, not a scratch, leather upholstery, a built-in tire pump powered by the engine, and a set of tools alone worth $300.*

To J. T. STEWART

[New York]

May 21, 1937

[Telegram]

WILL BUY THE NINETEEN THIRTY CAR AT YOUR FIGURE BUT WILL NOT GO THROUGH THE LEAD SMELTER STOP HOLD THE CAR FOR ME AND I WILL SEND WILBUR FOR IT STOP WILBUR HOLDS THE RECORD IN QUEENS COUNTY FOR MAKING FIRE BY RUBBING STICKS TOGETHER LOTS OF LOVE TO ALL

E. B. WHITE

• *During his "year off" White hoped to write a long autobiographical poem. His reluctance—evident in the following letter—to discuss the project with his wife stemmed from his having learned the uses of secrecy: when he talked about something, it didn't get written; when he kept it to himself, it stood a better chance.*

Some of the poem did get written, but White soon wearied of it, or fell short of being able to sustain it. When The Second Tree from the Corner *was being assembled, White included a section of the poem under the title "Zoo Revisited."*

To KATHARINE S. WHITE

[New York]
31 May [1937]

My dear Mrs. White:

It has occurred to me that perhaps I should attempt to clarify, for your benefit, the whole subject of my year of grace—or, as I call it, My Year. Whenever the subject has come up, I have noticed an ever so slight chill seize you, as though you felt a draught and wished someone would shut a door. I look upon this delicate spiritual tremor as completely natural, under the circumstances, and suggestive only of affectionate regard, tinged with womanly suspicion. In the world as now constituted, anybody who resigns a paying job is suspect; furthermore, in a well-ordered family, any departure from routine is cause for alarm. Having signified my intention to quit my accustomed ways, I shall do you the service of sketching, roughly, what is in my heart and mind—so that you may know in a general way what to expect of me and what not to expect. It is much easier for me to do this in a letter, typing away, word after word, than to try to tell you over a cup of coffee, when I would only stutter and grow angry at myself for inexactitudes of meanings (and probably at you, too, for misinterpreting my muddy speech).

First, there is the question of *why* I am giving up my job. This is easy to answer. I am quitting partly because I am not satisfied with the use I am making of my talents, such as they are; partly because I am not having fun working at my job—and am in a rut there; partly because I long to recapture something which everyone loses when he agrees to perform certain creative miracles on specified dates for a particular sum. (I don't know whether you know what this thing is, but you'll just have to take my word that it is real. To you it may be just another Loch Ness monster, but to me it is as real as a dachshund.)

Now there comes the question of *what* I am going to do, having given up the job. I suppose this is a fair question—also the question of what I intend to use for money. These matters naturally concern you, and Esposito [grocer], and everybody. Dozens of people have asked: "What are you going to do?" so strong is their faith in the herb activity. I know better what I am *not* going to do. But I won't try to pretend (to you, anyway) that that is the whole story either. In the main, my plan is to have none. But everyone has secret projects, and I am no exception. Writing is a secret vice, like self abuse. A person afflicted with poetic longings of one sort or another searches for a kind of intellectual and spiritual privacy in which to indulge his strange excesses. To achieve this sort of privacy—this aerial suspension of the lyrical spirit—he does not necessarily have to wrench himself away, physically, from everybody and everything in his life (this, I suspect, often defeats him at his own game), but he *does* have to forswear certain easy rituals, such as earning a living and running the world's errands. That is what I intend to "do" in my year. I am quitting my job. In a sense, I am also quitting my family—which is a much more serious matter, and which is why I am taking the trouble to write this letter. For a long time I have been taking notes—sometimes on bits of paper, sometimes on the mind's disordered pad—on a theme which engrosses me. I intend to devote my year to assembling these notes, if I can, and possibly putting them on paper of the standard typewriter size. In short, a simple literary project. I am not particularly hopeful of it, but I am willing to meet it half way. If at the end of the year, I have nothing but a bowlful of cigarette stubs to show for my time, I shall not begrudge a moment of it and I hope you won't. They say a dirigible, after it has been in the air for a while, becomes charged with static electricity, which is not discharged till the landing ropes touch the field and ground it. I have been storing up an inner turbulence, during my long apprenticeship in the weekly gaiety field, and it is time I came down to earth.

I am not telling people, when they ask, that I am proposing to write anything during My Year. As I said above, nothing may come of it, and it is easier to make a simple denial at the start, than to invent excuses and explanations at the end. I wish you would please do the same. Say I am taking a Sabbatical and doing nothing much of anything— which will come perilously near the truth, probably.

When I say I am quitting my family, I do not mean I am not going to be around. I simply mean that I shall invoke Man's ancient privilege of going and coming in a whimsical, rather than a reasonable, manner. I have some pilgrimages to make. To the zoo. To Mount Vernon. To Belgrade, and Bellport,[1] and other places where my spoor is still to be found. I shall probably spend a good deal of time in parks, libraries, and the waiting rooms of railway stations—which is where I hung out before I espoused this more congenial life. My attendance at meals may be a little spotty—for a twelvemonth I shall not adjust my steps to a soufflé. I hope this doesn't sound ungrateful, or like a declaration of independence—I intend it merely to inform you of a new allegiance—to a routine of my own spirit rather than to a fixed household & office routine. I seek the important privilege of not coming home to supper unless I happen to. I plan no absences, I plan no attendances. No plans.

The financial aspect of this escapade does not seem portentous, or ominous. I'm going to have Arty send me the money which comes in from my securities.[2] I'm going to sell the P.A. [Pierce Arrow], which

---

1. Bellport, Long Island. White had spent summers there.
2. Arthur Illian had guided White in investing his savings.

should bring $2,000, of which you get $1500. My taxes are paid, and I have enough money in the bank to continue in the same fifty-fifty arrangement with you in all matters of maintenance, recreation, and love. My luncheons will be 50 centers, instead of the dollar and a quarter number, and I will be riding common carriers, not Sunshine cabs. Instead of keeping a car on service at a garage, I would like your permission to keep the Plymouth nearby at some cheap lodging. I don't anticipate laying in a cellar of wine, or buying any new broadloom carpets. I think if I pull in my ears and you watch your artichokes, we can still stay solvent. I think it is better to do it this way than to try some possibly abortive rearrangement of our way of living, such as letting out the top floor to a Bingo society, or going to France to take advantage of the cheap wines. I notice Joe is already starting to sell his paintings.

Well, this about covers my Year. I urge you not to take it too seriously, or me. I am the same old fellow. I hope I shall give and receive the same old attentions and trifles. I don't want you tiptoeing around the halls telling people not to annoy me—the chances are I won't be doing anything anyway, except changing a bird's water. But I do want you to have some general conception of my internal processes during this odd term of grace. I want you to be able to face my departure for Bellport on a rainy Thursday afternoon with an equanimity of spirit bordering on coma.

Yrs with love and grace,
Mr. White

P.S. This letter is rather long, but I didn't have time to make it shorter, such are the many demands on me these days from so many points of the compass. I realize, too, that the whole plan sounds selfish and not much fun for you; but that's the way art goes. You let yourself in for this, marrying a man who is supposed to write something, even though he never does.

P.P.S. Unnecessary to answer this communication. Would be a drain on your valuable time. Just signify your good will with a package of Beemans—one if by land, two if by sea.

PPPPPS. Will be glad to answer any questions, or argue the whole matter out if it fails to meet with your approval or pleasure. I do not, however, want to discuss the literary nature of the project: for altho you are my b.f. and s.c.,[3] I will just have to do my own writing, as always.

---

3. Best friend and severest critic.

• *Before beginning his "year off" in earnest, White planned a cruise in* Astrid, *to unwind. Charlie Muller was a Cornell friend, a public relations man and the author of books for children. He liked to sail and was a good hand on a boat.*

To **CHARLES G. MULLER**

North Brooklin, Me.

11 July 1937

Dear Charlie:

I was thirty-eight years old today, and spent most of the day trying to build a henyard—which seems an odd milestone. The planks seemed heavy, and I noticed that I quit early and took a drink. We've been here just a week, and I haven't had a sail yet, Astrid having blown the bJesus out of her muffler, or what the boatyard man calls her "maximum silencer." We finally located a new maximum silencer, and she is afloat in the Benjamin River, ready to go. . . .

We've had terrifically hot weather here, and for the first time the swimming has seemed actually alluring. Eight broiling sunny days, with very light wind, if any. The pollen count has been high, and my hay fever has raged quietly all through the customary membranes. It's suicide for me to arrive here on July first, but I do it anyway. I would really rather feel bad in Maine than good anywhere else. Maybe I should warn you what a madhouse you are stepping into here. I have ten turkeys, three dogs, three children, three or four in help at the last count (including the postmaster, who grows wonderful salpiglossis and scabiosa), two water systems, a cesspool, a chimney swift, a moosehead covered with swallow crap, a frogpond, a family of bantams, a Sears Roebuck catalogue, and one hundred and sixty-five chairs. There is also a fine view of Mount Desert. Roger's old bulldog, Tunney, who is twelve and has the worst breath of any dog in Hancock County, is in love again, and goes sobbing all over the house, playing his violin. He located a Scotty bitch down on the shore last summer, and nine weeks later she underwent a Caesarian section, which my wife tells me is no fun. They spayed her while they were at it, but even that doesn't quiet our old bulldog, who apparently lives for his memories. We also have a 7-year-old 7-passenger touring car which I bought by mail this spring from a guy in Omaha, Nebraska. If you would still like to come, I hope you do.

My last stint for the *New Yorker* gets mailed on July 28th, so I'm free any time after that date, but would prefer not to go cruising till about August 1 or 2, as Nancy (Kay's daughter) who is spending this month at the Marine Biological Laboratory in Woods Hole is arriving here the 29th or 30th, and I don't want to disappear with her favorite 30-foot boat too abruptly. I should think if you got here either Saturday or Sunday, whichever day is best for you, it would be O.K. for us. You will probably like to park your tail here for a couple of square meals, to fatten you up against Astrid's diet of beer and stewed periwinkles, and then we can shove off. I have nothing in mind except to poke around this beautiful coast, do a little exploring and plenty of loafing. I don't want to be gone for more than about ten days, on account of the extra load my absence puts on Kay, but ten days ought to give us some sunshine, indolence, and derring do. . . .

Andy

To HAROLD ROSS

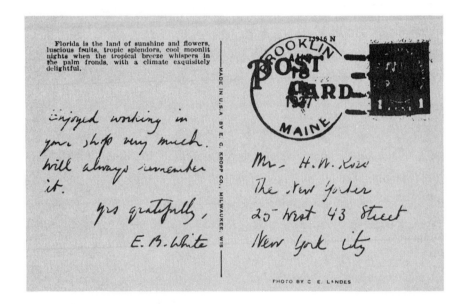

Florida is the land of sunshine and flowers, luscious fruits, tropic splendors, cool moonlit nights when the tropical breeze whispers in the palm fronds, with a climate exquisitely delightful.

Enjoyed working in your shop very much. Will always remember it.

yrs gratefully,
E. B. White

Mr. H. W. Ross
The New Yorker
25 West 43 Street
New York City

PHOTO BY C. E. LANDES

To KATHARINE S. WHITE

[North Brooklin, Me.]
[Early September 1937]
Thursday night

Dear Kay:

I fell asleep after supper and now I have woken up, but not very up. Have just been mackereling with Frank Teagle and Herm Gray, but no mackerel this time. We went to the exact same spot where Fred and I caught all the fish on Sunday, but not a sign of a fish—only a fine sunset, cold, too; and then a run home under power after dropping Herm at the stone dock. It gets dark quickly these nights—almost no twilight. And usually a night wind springs up to stir up the sea. Frank is near-sighted, and thought South Bluehill was Allen Cove. He is a nice kid, although not much of a hand around a boat. Says he's not the outdoor type. He is full of photography, and has taken a couple of dandy pictures of this house—neatly labelled on the back, "E. B. White's house." I'll send them to you. He said his New Yorker scrapbook fell a year behind because of his round the world trip, but that he and another boy recently spent four solid days bringing it up to date. What a pal!

Got your letter this morning, and I think you did perfectly right to give all the money you want to to your aunt. Money is no good anyway except to hand around. You can't take it with you, as Ol' Sage Kaufman pointed out (at considerable profit to himself, I understand). My interest in money is at an extremely low ebb at the moment—I am surrounded by hundreds of bottles of new crabapple jelly, and pears in jars, and ripening cranberries, and turkeys on the hoof, and ducks in the cove, and deer in the alders, and my own mackerel shining in airtight glory. I wouldn't know what to do with a dollar even if I could remember which pants it was in. As for Elsie,[1] I guess everybody has crazy brothers and sisters. I know I have. Stan, by the way, has taken out a patent on an invention of his called "Botanical Bricks," which are simply plant units (like window boxes) capable of being built up to any height, for quick landscape effects, with the vertical surfaces covered with flowering vines, or the like. He thinks that the idea has great possibilities for such things as the World's Fair, etc., where sudden and transient greenery is necessary, also for sidewalk cafes, small city yards, indoor gardens, and many other projects. I think perhaps he has got hold of something, and have written him for more information. He certainly deserves a break.

My days go simply by. I have given up the nine to one schedule, as it was just making me irritable, and when I got thinking about it I remembered that I had never written anything between nine and one anyway. Monday visited John Allen, the smith of Sargentville, to get my pole ax drawed out. Mr. Allen is around and about again after an appendectomy. Been coming on him for twenty years—then all of a sudden she exploded. He had plenty of chance to just lie there and think about things when he was in the Bluehill Hospital, and although he had formerly been opposed to the Automobile, because it had driven out the horses and spoiled a smith's trade, he remembered that it was an auto-

---

1. Elizabeth Shepley Sergeant, Katharine White's sister. She was eleven years older than Katharine, unmarried, and a writer.

mobile that got him to Dr. Bliss in time to save his life. Has changed his mind about motor cars. I pointed out, however, that automobiles were killing people awful fast, too. "By gorry," he said, "I hadn't thought about that. Now I'll have to think it all out again." He said his strength was slow coming back, and this was the first ax he'd upset in a long time. Moses [a Labrador retriever] had a fine visit, eating hoof parings.

Tuesday in the rain set about making an ax handle out of a piece of ash which Howard had, but was getting nowhere with my jack knife, so journeyed to the Slaven barn, where Percy provided me with a wood rasp, a cabinet scraper, and a vise, and built a little fire in the stove, and made a little handle for the wood rasp, and gave me a little box to stand on so the workbench would be more my height. He said not everybody could make an ax handle. . . .

Yesterday was lowery, and I dug clams and ground up my toll bait. Wormed Mose, and got eleven fine roundworms—six inches long each. Thought some of going to the Union Fair, over behind Camden, but the weather was unpleasant. Frank tells me he went and it was great. A much more genuine country fair than the Bluehill one, with lots of horse pulling contests and cattle judging, etc. We must surely go next year.

Howard and I cleaned up the vegetable garden this morning, ready for the plowing tomorrow, if he can get a team. Cut the heads off the sunflowers and made a compost of the bean vines and other leftovers. We're going to take the dock down pretty soon, before the elements do. You can hear it groaning clear up to the house these days, with the wind from the north.

Miss Anderson has a motorbike.

The Burrows girls (whom I still don't believe in) have bicycles but can't ride and are practicing on the back roads. . . .

Newbury Neck has been bought by Seth Parker.[2] (You are now 14 miles from the home of Seth Parker.) No kidding it has.

Daylight Saving Time has been discontinued, and Mr. Pervear arrives at seven and departs at four. . . .

There's a bounty on seals. One dollar.

Mr. Pervear does his nooning indoors these days. . . .

Must climb up now, with my black companion, to the bedchamber, there to doze, rather coldly, till 1:30 a.m., at which hour Moses celebrates his matins. From 1:30 till daybreak, it is anybody's ballgame, with a good deal of heavy-footed fooling around, intestinal gas, revulsion against Freddie's closet lair, and general dawn pageantry. Am thinking

2. Phillips Lord, who played "Seth Parker" in the radio serial.

some of giving up the bedroom for night occupancy, and just curling up on the living room sofa, where the remains of the fire in the Franklin stove spread a certain calm across the night.

Lots of love to you and Joe. Was glad to get the good news about your health. Don't work too hard. It would embarrass me to have you working too hard. We have jelly enough to last us for five years, so take it easy. I have had an entirely new feeling about life ever since making an ax handle.

Yrs,
Andy

P.S. Please send me a pair of long underdrawers from the bottom drawer of my bureau. Get Mr. Hoyt to wrap them up for you, he hasn't anything else to do.[3]

How's Hattie?[4]

To GUSTAVE S. LOBRANO

North Brooklin, Me.
9 September 1937

Dear Gus:

Cranberry and that flyline that goes raspy paspy through the eyelets, getting nicely snarled in the last eyelet, may be all well and good, but our cranberries are getting ripe now, and this looks like a big cranberry year.[1] Every time one of my turkeys looks at a cranberry it flinches; and against the sudden bright red of a maple branch, this is a fine sight, turkeys flinching in the wine-like September air. Moses, the retriever, bit off the left wing of one of the wild birds yesterday—a clean break except for one cartilage which I took care of with my desk scissors. The other two dogs on the premises seized the opportunity to fly at each other's throats, to settle some small difference, and I had to let go the turkey in order to attend the dog fight. After things had quieted down some, I returned and found the bird bleeding to death in a thicket —alders, wild apple, and grapevines. Since it was obvious that I wouldn't be able to catch it, I got my .22 and sat down tediously about six feet away, where I took careful aim and despatched the creature with a shot through the head. In this grotesque situation, with briers tweaking my behind and the memory of the bird as a day-old chick strong in my mind,

---

3. Phil Hoyt worked for a while at the magazine. He had been an Assistant Commissioner in the Traffic Division of the New York Police Department.

4. The Whites' rubber plant.

---

1. The Lobrano family summered at Cranberry Lake in the Adirondacks, where fly fishing for trout was the favorite sport.

I felt that the original Massachusetts settlers would have worried considerably if they could have witnessed this strange degeneracy of man and bird. (As luck would have it, there wasn't an original Massachusetts settler on the place, and I just snuck home and cleaned the gun.)

The picture of the Lobranos, big and little, in the hills of suburbia is indeed enticing. On the chance that you haven't already made your choice, I will tell you what I can about the sweet-smelling Never Never Land. The finest public schools are in Mount Vernon, according to Alice Barrows [Katharine White's cousin], who didn't spend twelve years in them the way I did. Alice works for the Bureau of Education (Washington, D.C.) and says the finest public schools are in Mount Vernon. But I wouldn't advise you to take up residence there. I was born there, but that's another story. Sneden's Landing is a lovely place, still quite countrified (with a dash of Katharine Cornell, Sally Bates, and the Literary Digest) and remarkably close to New York. The rents are not bad in Sneden's—I think you can get a house for around a thousand dollars a year, maybe 800. Most of the year a little ferry makes the trip across to the New York Central R R station at Dobbs Ferry on the eastern shore, and Katharine tells me that it takes just an hour from the Grand Central to Sneden's by train and boat. Sneden's is steeped in Hudson Valley mists and memories—people make their own wine, stamp out their own copperhead snakes, go picking Dutchmen's breeches in the spring. On summer evenings, you can hear the trains across the river, grumbling. There is a good deal of talk about shad.

If you want to be on the Sound, there is a place called Riverside, Conn., which has certain advantages, I believe. Andy Wing of Country Home, who is a good friend of Russ Lord's and mine, would be happy to tell you all about Riverside, I am sure. He lives there, with a wife, three children, and a Toggenburg goat which pees in the davenport. I suggest that you shun such places as Silvermine, Westport, Wilton, Darien, and in through there. Over around Bedford Village, where we used to rent a house, is beautiful country, particularly in fall and spring, but you have to watch out about such technical details as grocery deliveries, milk, ice, and like that. If the distance is too great between where your house is and where your supplies are, the gasoline you use runs into the dough. And the Goldens Bridge Hounds run into your front yard, too. Fairfield, Conn., which is almost to Bridgeport, is fine country. Bunny Rigg has just thrown up a house there, and is raising bantams from my foundation stock. If you want information from him, he is with Linton Rigg & Co., 90 Broad Street. I have a suspicion that commuting from Fairfield is on the expensive side. Long Island is a charming spot, where Walt Whitman took his long walks, endlessly rocking. Christopher Morley lives in Roslyn.

Much as I would like to see you, I suspect that for you to attempt a weekend here would be a hideous mistake. A thousand miles of railroading goes a long way. A couple of people have tried this place for a weekend, with only weird results. Mosher came once, and we had just time to immerse him in the frightful bay and walk him twice along a rather bleak bit of shore in the fog. Then he tore off to the train. Joe Sayre showed up, spent a baleful two hours in the attic writing a column for a Boston paper, and disappeared without speaking. The weekend visitation is a special trick, requiring a fanatical spirit—the sort that takes you to the Helderburgs on those ghostly milk trains. Kay and I manage a couple of weekend trips here during the year, but it is no easy matter to explain to the natives. I can think of nothing that would more surely drain your strength. . . .

As for the Christmas story, I have decided that among the many things I shall not do this year is write for the magazines. A man can always write for the magazines, and this year is a special year, reserved for more fragile, and I hope more abiding joys. I am darned glad, and so is Kay, that your overdue elevation is at hand. I have sometimes wondered whether there was any Harry Bull. In fact I was getting pretty sick of hearing about your raise.[2]

Quite a frost last night.

Yrs,
Andy

To KATHARINE S. WHITE

[North Brooklin, Me.]
[October 8, 1937]
Friday afternoon

Dear Kay:

. . . I think Joe's musical education might be interrupted without cataclysmic results. I really am trying to spend as little as possible this year, in order not to eat too deeply into my savings. I will try to instruct Joey on the piano, if he shows a desire to learn. If, however, you feel strongly about keeping him in the Mannes school, I'll chip in my share. I don't think a half hour lesson once a week is any good—too scattered. And I think I am definitely against a Saturday lesson—more important that he should get some sunshine and outdoor play.

Life goes on here pleasantly, the only sad part being that you can't share these spectacular October days. The maple in the corner of the yard is the most extraordinary red, all over, that I've ever seen on a tree.

---

2. Harry Bull had become editor of *Town and Country* when Joseph Bryan III moved to the *Saturday Evening Post*. Despite the raise, Lobrano was soon to leave *Town and Country* for *The New Yorker*.

Even Howard is impressed. The maple right next to it is still solidly green, for some reason. We've had a couple of warm days this week, but today is cold again, and bright. The northern lights have been putting on a show, too. I spend most of my time working with Howard on the various winding-up processes which I have never before witnessed, and have also been cutting out dead stuff, which gives me a chance to use my ax. Moses is always right at my side, a gay black woodsman, hauling away the little trees that I cut down. He is my bosom friend now, just like a brother, and is much admired by everyone who sees him. This morning I was up at 5:30, for some tide work on the dock and mooring. It was cold and clear, wind NW, a fine morning to be wading around in the sea in your rubber boots. My meal hours have been advancing and advancing. Yesterday I lunched at eleven. The A-frames are all rafted in and piled up, ready for roofing paper; and the walks are stacked in the boathouse. We muffed the mooring today—got it hooked onto the float all right at low tide, but when the tide started to come, the line chafed in two and the rock sank on bottom again. That means I'll be up at 6:30 tomorrow, to catch low water. . . .

Dined at the Frank Teagles' on Wednesday evening, and then took them to Ethel May Shorey, in her drama of the great Northwest. A rainy night, but Frank and Mrs. Teagle and I all sat in the front seat of the Lincoln, and travelled safely. The play, called "Toni," was excellent—a powerful love story, with Miss Shorey as a Sedgwick Tiger Rose, an un-tamed little French Canadian minx in black corduroy breeches and a white pullover sweater—varee, varee fetching—a pudgy 160-pound daughter of the wilds, loved by two airmen who came tumbling in from the storm. Between acts the members of the cast took turns doing musical tricks and telling funny stories. The performance followed a harvest home supper in the hall next door. Bernice, who attended, said it was next to the best supper she had ever had. Chicken pie, the resist-ance piece. I like Mrs. Teagle—thoroughly friendly and spirited. Her life came to a head this summer when a Parker Point cleaning woman fell dead while talking to her. The woman was mad at Mrs. Teagle—held a grudge about something or other; they met on the road in the rain, the woman pulling her umbrella far down over her face so not to have to speak in passing. Mrs. Teagle spoke anyway. The woman raised her umbrella, exchanged a few grim sentences, and fell over dead, of anger. The Teagles attended the funeral services, and said she looked really amiable when laid out—the best she had ever looked.

If there is a grey and green skating cap in my bottom drawer would you send it to me? . . .

You would not feel bad about the state of the world if you could see the state of this part of the world, which is almost more beautiful than the eye can bear. Even the gruelling wars in the East are not without balm, for they have given us Emily Hahn in apotheosis. That Reporter piece was peerless fun, and I think we should have a weekly serial called "At the Front with Emily Hahn," in war or in peace. With Sweetie Pie at Gallipoli. I look forward to Lois Long doing the second coming of Christ, and a feature by Sheila Hibben from the famine areas.

Today there arrived by post a gold medal from the Northeast Harbor Fleet approximately two and one half inches in diameter.[1] On the obverse a map of Mount Desert, overlaid with a triangular pennant, and the inscription, engraved in gold: "Mr. and Mrs. E. B. White." On the reverse, this inscription: "A Token of Appreciation of Your Many Kindnesses to the Northeast Harbor Fleet." It is the first medal I have received since I won the St. Nicholas League gold award, and I am as happy as a boy.

Must go to bed now, this letter having been continued after supper. Mose and I have gone back to sleeping upstairs, since he has taken to resting more easily at night. I just couldn't stand his 2:30 a.m. reveille. In all the time he has been living in the house, he has messed only once, so that's a lot of bunk about the McKelway bitch being better house trained. She isn't better in any particular.

It was in your study.

Lots of love,
Andy

P.S. Am enclosing the last pansy of the year, which bloomed not in any of your pretty borders, but right in the driveway. Also a sample of the maple.

To JAMES THURBER

245 East 48 Street
[October? 1937]
Sunday afternoon

Dear Jim:

Sunday afternoons are about the same as when you left, people walking their dog out, and the dog not doing anything, the sky grey and

---

1. White writes: "The Northeast Harbor fleet, about seventy-five yachts from Mount Desert Island, held an annual racing cruise that often took them to Allen Cove in Blue Hill Bay for the night. The skippers and their crew members used the Whites' float, camped on the Whites' beach, and made themselves at home generally. After several of these visitations, the Club had the medal struck, citing the Whites for tolerance above and beyond the call of duty."

terrible, and the L making the noise that you hear when you are under ether. The middle of the afternoon is the saddest time, because it is neither right after lunch nor right before supper, it is not time to have a drink yet, and if you call someone on the phone, the phone just rings. It is the time little boys come in from the garden and say that there is nothing doing out there. I got back from Maine a week ago, but all this week I have been looking around and wondering why I came away.

I made the drive in an open car with a turkey in the back seat and a retriever in the front. Stopped off at the Coateses' and we ate the bird and freshened up the dog. Els and Bob are all right, and the valley where they live is still full of cowleys and blumes, as always, and the Rehacks' cows and now and then a pheasant. Bob is quitting his job doing *Time* book reviews and has started in doing an art column for the weekly *New Yorker*, where I used to work when I could think of anything to say. He is looking for a furnished apartment in town. Joe Sayre is back from the Vineyard with third act trouble. . . . McKelway is in Ford's with booze gloom. Walter Lippmann and Mrs. Lippmann are getting a divorce. Ruth Fleischmann is now Mrs. Peter Vischer, and (as Ross put it) we now have another little mouth to feed.

I saw the David Garnett piece about you. I can't think how I happened to see it but I did. I doubt if you are the most original writer living, but I doubt whether anybody is. I am the second most inactive writer living, and the third most discouraged. The greatest living writer is Morris Markey,[1] and the greatest living woman is Helen. If you want the names of the other living writers I can probably get Brayshaw to get them for you. And before I forget it, I better tell you what Josephine, who is the most original living North Italian woman, calls my Labrador retriever. She heard us calling him Moses, which is his name, but she apparently didn't quite catch the sound because she invariably addresses the dog as Mosher. "Come, Mosher, come on, naah?" Every once in a while she puts a "Mr." in front of it, and calls him Mr. Mosher. He so hoppy.

I, too, know that the individual plight is the thing. I knew it when I stayed with my mother while she died in a hospital in Georgetown. I knew it day before yesterday when Joe (looking suspiciously like me) stood up in meeting house and recited the 117th psalm before the elementary school. You beget a son when your mind is not on that at all, and seven years later he is there in a clean white shirt, praising the Lord. You spend your days chuckling at the obstinacies of French waiters

---

1. An early contributor to *The New Yorker*'s Reporter at Large Department. Wolcott Gibbs once said of him, "Markey has reached the point where he believes that everything that happens to him is interesting."

and Italian cooks, but always knowing that much of life is insupportable and that no individual play can have a happy ending. If you have the poetic temperament you go on groping toward something which will express all this in a burst of choir music, and your own inarticulateness only hastens the final heart attack. Even when an artist has the ability and the strength to assemble something of the beauty and the consternation which he feels, he is usually so jealous of other artists that he has no time for pure expression. Today with the radio yammering at you and the movies turning all human emotions into cup custard, the going is tough. Or I find it tough.

If you go to Corse, you can either take the little paqueboat from Marseilles or the plane from Antibes. I took the boat one time, stayed up all night on deck to escape the cackaroachies in the bed, and saw Ajaccio just at sunrise. I have never seen anything like that since. There is a good small hotel called Hotel des Etrangers with a pretty garden full of lizards and sweet smelling vines. I suppose there are still vines in the garden of the Hotel and that they still smell sweet. Give my regards to Victor, who will not remember me.

I passed through Litchfield, for the first time in my life, last Saturday, and bought two pairs of boxing gloves in Torrington, junior size, for the wars. It'll be nineteen years come December that I was discharged from the army. Or is it twenty? Litchfield seemed beautiful, and Tony Coates and Joe White liked the boxing gloves. All towns should have a common, sheep or no sheep. George Horace Lorimer and Osgood Perkins are dead. Lots of love to you and Helen from us'ns.

Andy

To JOSEPH BRYAN III

245 East 48 Street
30 November 1937

Dear Joe:

Here it is. I had no idea it was going to come out as long as this, but we Detweilers are wordy folk, and don't know where to stop.[1]

The piece precipitated a minor emotional crisis in my little family, for with inspired timing I showed it to Katharine on the same day that our brand new cook from Nova Scotia told Josephine (the Piedmontese lady who scuffles around the house imitating dogs) that it was a dirty

---

1. The piece was "Memoirs of a Master," in which White, using the pseudonym "Detweiler," recollected all the domestics who had enriched his home. The *Saturday Evening Post* rejected it, and it appeared in *The New Yorker* in 1939 over the signature "M.R.A." It was one of the pieces by White included in *A Subtreasury of American Humor*.

trick to throw garbage into the garbage can until it was properly lined with newspaper. Hell broke loose downstairs and Katharine finished reading the piece in tears, saying that she was no good as a housewife (she said she was no good as a mother either, just for heightened effect) and that she would have to give up her job and make a decent home for me. I told her to get the hell over to the office and win some more bread and stop her blubbering.

If you reject this piece I hope all your pantrymen are typhoid carriers.

Yr lurid old chum,
Andy

• *White took his son Joe, then in the second grade at Friends Seminary School in New York City, to spend a few days in Maine during the Christmas vacation. The Whites' Brooklin house was not winterized, so they stayed at the home of Captain Percy Moore, in Blue Hill.*

To KATHARINE S. WHITE

[Blue Hill, Me.]
[December 31, 1937]
Friday morning

Dear Kay:

I don't know when I've had a better time, sick or well. If you were here it would be perfect. Had a good night's sleep, and this morning am almost whole—no more throat. The snow stopped at nightfall and this morning is bright, clear, cold & gorgeous—the harbor (half frozen over) shining in the sun; the little boys, too, shining in the sun. Joe has friends on the block, is called "Joe" by the larger and more important boys, and his skiing technique has won the respect of everybody. I was feeling too bad to pay any attention to Joe when I first got here, & merely turned him out & told him he could go anywhere in town and do anything he wanted to. He began cautiously, behind the schoolhouse, but by mid-afternoon was zooming down the hill & out onto Main Street, and today he is roistering all over the village with his pals, most of whom seem to have whooping cough but all of whom are alive and happy. In a single day, Joe has become car conscious, and crosses the road with the alertness of a bird. He and I are going over to the Slavens' this afternoon, to superintend cutting a little wood. (Percy always refers to the Slaven place as "the granite"—which has a pleasant note of rockbound eternity, with a touch of Irish.)

As soon as this letter is done I'm going calling—Dr. Bliss, Max Hinckley, etc. Percy said at breakfast he thought maybe Max had begun already to celebrate New Year's Eve. "And by God he enjoys it," he added, with a kind of wistful note. Tomorrow I think I'll take a sandwich lunch & go down to N. Brooklin for the day—& maybe get some skating on the frog pond, which, after all, is as big as Radio City. . . .

This is the last day of 1937, and this letter is full of my love for you and my hopes for the new year. I have had plenty of time for reflection in the last day or two and have decided that you are right about the necessity for planning. A single person can act aimlessly, but where lives mingle and merge there has to be a scheme in advance. Half the fun in life is in anticipation, anyway; & plans are exciting in themselves. A country town on a snowy morning is agreeably deceptive—it leads one to believe there can be no bad in the world—even the dogs feel the extra gaiety and goodness. But deception or not, I feel ready and eager for the new year, and here are my love and hopes and greetings.

Andy

Happy New Year, Mother

Joe

To JAMES THURBER

245 East 48 Street
8 January 1938

Dear Jim:

Katharine and I have just been going over our stack of Christmas cards (we keep them in a big bowl in the hall near the box of hard candies which the Coateses gave Nancy and Roger) and have re-read the stale polite little greetings and thrown most of the cards away. . . .

Sayre, for whom you inquired, is still around town as far as I know. He was last seen at a Christmas entertainment given by the pupils of Friends Seminary, where his daughter, Nora Sayre, is in kindergarten. That particular entertainment established a record of a sort, because one of the angels fainted and had to be carried out by a shepherd and the principal of the school. I wasn't present myself, but heard about it from my lad Joel, who came bursting home with a special radiance all about his head, shouting "Some Christmas! What a mess!" and proceeded to give an imitation of the fallen angel. He was so pleased with this, that he kept giving repeat performances all afternoon, and will still do the angel for you, with any encouragement at all.

You don't have to be in a stalled car near Naples to be out of touch with Joe Sayre, you can be sitting right next to him at Bleeks and get the same remote abandoned feelings. I have encountered him a couple of times at parties, but he just stares at you steadily for a minute and then goes phaaf, like your car, and sits down in a dark corner somewhere to continue brooding. You are precisely right about what playwrighting or playwriting does to people, and I think, also, that Joe waited till pretty late in life to discover that even after you have written a play, it still has to be all done over again by a man named Sig Herzig. You can stand a blow like that when you are 25, but it comes harder after your joints have begun to ankylose and Hollywood has hung rhinestones all over your vest. Plays, as you pointed out, come about as close to literature as a problem in solid geometry. I was looking through a big book which Carl Van Doren got together, called "Great Prose of the World" or some such thing, and suddenly, after emerging from a heaving sea of words which rose and fell with immortal cadences, I fell into the middle of a play by Eugene O'Neill—which I guess Van Doren thought he had to bring in there somehow—and got hung up right away on a Great Prose passage that went "Will you kindly close the door" or words to that effect.

Or maybe we're just jealous.

. . . I have made an unholy mess out of this "year off" business. I haven't produced two cents worth of work, have broken my wife's health, my own spirit, and two or three fine old lampshades by getting my feet tangled in the cord. Kay is restless when I go away, and I am no bargain when I am around, either. Gibbs quit his desk job rather abruptly, and Kay has had a lot of extra work deriving from that. She got grippe before Christmas, and I got it, and we celebrated the 23rd of December by fighting over what Xmas was all about anyway. This left us in a limp beaten state—one of those periods from which one can't escape by merely taking a boat and watching somebody balance a 20-gallon water jar on her head. We're going to have to balance our own jars for a while. I took Joe to Maine last week for his holidays, and stayed in the white, peaceful village of Bluehill, listening to the beat of tire chains against cold mudguards, studying tracks where the deer had pawed the snow under the little apple trees, sliding down hill, and ushering in the new year by going to bed and letting the Baptist church ring twelve clear holy strokes for me. It was a fine trip and we had real winter weather, almost Currier and Ives in its purity. The woods, after a snowstorm, were lovelier than any cathedral, and we went in on a bobsled with some men, and helped jig out some firewood. It was birch. The horse had a bell on.

. . . The lease on this house expires on October 1, and one of the things that is getting us down is trying to decide whether we will renew it (in which case I would have to go back writing my weekly sermon for the NYer) or whether we will chuck the city and go live in Maine maybe. Problems like that, which are easy to solve if you do them quick, or if you have no children, become increasingly intricate and demoralizing if you take to brooding on them and if you have to fit schools and so forth into the picture.

Can't give you much general news of this town, as I don't get around much except to my neighborhood movie to see Dorothy Lamour in "Jungle Princess" which is my favorite picture. . . . Romeyn Berry is back upstate, having been given the sack.[1] Gibbs is commenting. The two happiest people in America are Benchley and Franklin Roosevelt. Benchley's high spirits are those of a retired reformer, who got all his good deeds behind him safely in his twenties. Between 20 and 30 Benchley was worrying about international peace, and fathering two sons. I suppose he still dreams of those days, once in a while. . . . Roosevelt is happy because it has never occurred to him that he really doesn't understand what's wrong with things any more than anybody else does. He is in gales of laughter most of the time. I saw a picture of him going into a church of the living Christ in Washington the other day. He was in stitches. He is happier than Benchley, even; happier than my dachshund who has a new rubber ball. Maybe I could write a piece called "What's So Funny?", in which I ask the president what the hell he is grinning about. But the likelihood is I won't. One of the saddest people of our generation died the other day, Don Marquis. What a kick in the pants life gave that guy! I picked up "The Almost Perfect State" the other day and ran across a passage about what he hoped his old age would be like:

> Between the years of ninety-two and a hundred and two, however, we shall be the ribald, useless, drunken, outcast person we have always wished to be. We shall have a long white beard and long white hair; we shall not walk at all, but recline in a wheel chair and bellow for alcoholic beverages; in the winter we shall sit before the fire with our feet in a bucket of hot water, a decanter of corn whiskey near at hand, and write ribald songs against society; strapped to one arm of our chair will be a forty-five calibre revolver, and we shall shoot out the lights when we want to go to sleep. . . . We look forward to a disreputable, vigorous, unhonoured, and disorderly old age.

What actually happened was, he lost his wife and child, wrote one successful play and two unsuccessful ones, had a stroke, lost his money, lost his second wife, had a couple of other strokes, and finally ended up

---

1. White had suggested Berry, a former graduate manager of athletics at Cornell, as a possible substitute writer of Comment during the "year off." Berry took the job, but the connection was short-lived.

in Kew Gardens or some damn place living with a sister, and even his old friends hated to go see him because it was too embarrassing all round. He wasn't vigorous, or disreputable. There was no shooting out of lights. I guess his sister used to turn them out. He wasn't disorderly, he wasn't even unhonoured—he had more honorary pallbearers than you could shake a bottle of embalming fluid at. Ah, welladay.

You will be pleased to hear that my rubber plant is, in the face of all these things, putting out a new leaf.

Love to Helen, Smessborg, and yourself, from Kay, Joel, Freddie, and yr friend

Andy

P.S. "Memoirs of a Master" is all written, and all rejected—by the Sat Eve Post. I have retired it, along with an empty fish tank, an old can of ski wax, a picture of my grade school graduating class, and a box of unopened carbon paper.

The reason people don't write you oftener, and by "people" I mean me, is you never put your correct mailing address on your letters. This last letter says "Naples, December 22," and contains a tear-jerking paragraph about the American Express, Rome. I am not going to take time to write a full-bodied five-page letter and send it to James Thurber, No Benzina, Italy; or James Thurber, care of Lady Into Fox, England. And this means I will have to put in a phone call to Miss Terry, to find out whether you are Guaranty Trust or American Express, London or Paris. It's easy for *you* to remember this, because you are, in a sense, living it. But my life is a different story. The prospect of calling up Miss Terry is almost enough to keep me from ever starting a letter. Why can't European travelers learn that every letter should contain in addition to the dateline, a line called "Correct Mailing Address"?

I forgot to tell you that my "Memoirs" were rejected by a man named Joseph Bryan III—a coincidence which has done as much as anything to destroy me.

A

• *Early in 1938 Katharine's father, Charles Sergeant, then in his eighties, had fallen ill while in Daytona, Florida. Katharine had gone south to attend him in what was to be his last illness. He died shortly after her return north and was buried in Hibernia, Florida, in the tiny graveyard on the plantation where he had spent many winters. His death, and the chore of settling his affairs, left Katharine tired and depressed, and she and White took off for a Bermuda holiday, where they stayed at "Waterville," a guesthouse run by Ada Trimingham. The Whites had been at Waterville once before—in 1930, shortly after their marriage.*

To GUSTAVE S. LOBRANO

Waterville
Paget East [Bermuda]
[March 1938]
Thursday night

Dear Gus:

The wine dark sea was darker than usual, and pretty gruelling. My stomach held together, but there was a great deal of large scale misery, one broken hip, one smashed face, and several minor abrasions. Kay narrowly missed getting mashed when a writing desk which she had just vacated got wiped out by a heavy leather armchair which went adrift in the public room. We got in hours late and lay at anchor all one extra night outside the channel off St. George's, waiting for daylight. However, here we are. My bicycle is a Raleigh (#187). It is the finest wheel I have ever pushed and gives me the highest satisfaction. The pace of a bike has an almost instant salutary effect on the system—it's a wonder Roosevelt hasn't thought of it in connection with the better life.

Because of the day's delay at sea, our arrival at Trimingham's had, for the other guests, that over-ripe taint which befouls the much-touted guest who simply fails to show up when he is due. Ada had been advertising us for days, and had prepared, for the rare occasion of our First Meal, a roasted turkey with a red rose under its wing. It was eaten by the others, doggedly and in silence. The strain is still apparent. We retire to our room rather early after coffee, leaving the living room free for the bridge players—among them the Pratts from Des Moines, who won a trip to Bermuda in the raffle held at the Junior League ball in Des Moines last November, a bit of good fortune which not even Mr. Pratt's stomach ulcer could stand in the way of fulfilling. Their journey was not without its hazards, however, as it was stipulated that the Eastern Air Line was to waft them on the first leg of this unexpected and ulcerous adventure. Mr. P. still eats nothing but custards and other bland substances. Mrs. P. is excessively gay and open about the ulcer, and drags it into the conversation at all possible moments. Both are keen to talk about Phil Stong. We have, also in our midst, a Miss Dickerman (on the elderly side), who fractured her hip day before yesterday because she thought she could ride through a soft spot (and couldn't). She sells group insurance, and although in obvious pain, was anxious to find out directly how many people the New Yorker employed. She gets around with a cane, and is rubbed frequently by a native rubber. Also a lady golf champion, and mother; and the young couple from Scarsdale; and the unmarried horticulturalist who likes to strip at the beach and take the sun in good earnest. And, of course, others.

We've already had some good swimming and lying about, and are getting used again to the open and shut Bermuda sky—first bright sun, then a five minute shower of rain. The tennis begins on Saturday. Haven't been on the railroad yet but are planning a trip to St. David's. Ada says it was hatred of the railroad that killed Fred [Trimingham]. In memory of him she has never ridden on it, and never will.

I think Bermuda is suffering some from its high pressure sales promotion—they asked for punishment in full page color ads and now they are beginning to get it. But the essential quality of the place is not much changed, and Kay and I are tickled to be here.

My typing is keeping the lady golfer from her sleep, and will affect her score tomorrow, so I better quit. I'll post this air mail, so it will be flown to you at terrific risk of life and limb. (It does seem odd that people should fly here at 250 m.p.h. in order to be able to ride a bicycle.)

Yrs,
Andy

To JAMES THURBER

245 E 48
Apreel 16 [1938?]

Dear Jim:

Before you move out of that Maritime Alp nest of yours maybe I can get in one more letter—making probably two in all. There are a few matters which I want you should know about, including the snatch of conversation which I overheard between two men on the street the other day. Just as I was passing, I heard one man say to the other: "So she had the whole fucking bedroom suite sawed up and put together again." Then there is the matter of the sound effect record which I found in the catalogue of a concern which makes sound effect records. It is a record of a piano being smashed by a man with an ax. I think it costs two dollars, and it seems to me the sort of thing that you ought to have in your home, for rainy days when the mood is on you. I keep thinking quite a lot about this record, and about how much water had to flow over the dam in America before this country was ready for it—first the Pilgrims, with a dead fish in every hill of corn, then the long winter at Valley Forge, then Emerson and the exaltation of those transcendental days when the Peabodys and the Hawthornes and the Hales were founding a pure blood-strain that finally produced Katharine, then bloody Shiloh, and the blizzard of 1888, and the wonderful vital Bull Moose era when you were running your electric backwards to unwind the speedometer and I was playing cops and robbers and wondering why I couldn't pee except when I was alone, then Verdun, and a brave new streamlined airconditioned world crumbling from its own strange malefactions. The recorded sound of a piano being demolished by an ax is the disc we have all been awaiting: the Ultimate Sound, perhaps. The Instrument of the Immortals, getting it in the teeth from a Keen Kutter. . . .

Last weekend we went to Maine to see a man about putting in a furnace. The man arrived by seaplane from Boston. We took everything out of the closets so the workmen could get at the chimneys. Then the blizzard came, and the thermometer dropped to 16, and the waterpipes froze a little bit—just enough so you had to crawl under the porch in the early morning and warm them up with a blowtorch. We sold more than a hundred dollars worth of beds and chairs and tables to one woman over the week-end. Women are suckers for beds, chairs, and tables. I don't know what the hell they do with them. I have made a careful count, and I find that Katharine and I (up until I began to take the situation in hand) owned 21 beds. That's too many beds, Jim. Every one had a spring, a mattress, two sheets, two double or four single blankets, a bedspread, and a comforter. I decided that if we went on accumulating beds, I would end up in the same sort of snarl that Richard Whitney got into. He was just trying to work his way clear of a lot of beds and mirrors and occasional pieces, and now he's in Sing Sing with the other prisoners tipping their caps to him and calling him "Mr. Whitney" respectfully.

Everybody is looking forward to the return of you and Helen. *Stage Magazine* has folded in anticipation of your arrival, and Hanrahan's stock reverts (we hope) to the N Yorker.[1] Ross is hard at work, and I have written a fine parody of *Life's* "The Birth of a Baby," with Irvin illustrations.[2] Gibbs and McKelway are living temperate, clean lives, and Morris Ernst is around defending civil liberties. I have a certain amount of ear trouble, which may be frostbite, but which might just be a touch of mastoid. Nancy has had a job offered her teaching science in the Buffalo Seminary, the Japanese took quite a beating with a loss of 20,000 and Turtle Bay is full of daffodils, English daisies, blooming

1. John Hanrahan, a magazine consultant, had been taken on by Raoul Fleischmann shortly after *The New Yorker* was started, when it was floundering. There was no money available to pay him, so he was paid in stock. It was he who urged Fleischmann to buy *Stage*. When that proved a fiasco, the magazine insisted that Hanrahan return his stock, and he did.
2. "The Birth of an Adult," April 23, 1938.

gallantly among last winter's dachshund turds. I have never known how to spell turd, whether it is turd, or tird. Do you?

. . . I'm planning to move to Maine in the early part of June, taking Joe. Kay will follow shortly, after seeing Nancy graduate from Bryn Mawr and Roger from Pomfret. Terror-struck after a year of not doing anything in the way of earning money to support 21 beds, I have submitted two clipbooks to Harper. One is "The Fox of Peapack," a bunch of ballads, etc. The other is "Quo Vadimus?," a bunch of casuals. I also have a children's book about half done, so I guess I am going into the authoring game again. Do you approve of "Quo Vadimus?" as a title, or should I think of another? If you and Helen want a bed, let me know.

Love,
Andy

McNulty is out of the magazine, which is just as well, as the magazine was not up to him. I knew all along the magazine wasn't up to him.

To KATHARINE S. WHITE

Mrs. Woodward's Boarding House
Bluehill, Me.
April 27, 1938
Wednesday night

Dear Kay—

Santayana, whom I read on the train last night, holds out little hope for our achieving any satisfactory relationship with the Maine people. And the school teachers at supper tonight, when they heard about Joe, stared at me as though I were some kind of madman. I got a cold welcome this trip—Alice Moore turned me down because she was housecleaning, & Mrs. Thurman Gray vetoed me for some reason which I couldn't quite understand over the phone. I began to feel like Joseph and Mary: it would be a joke on the community if I should be delivered of a Messiah tonight, right in this unheated bedroom. Mrs. Woodward (spelling?) has a club foot, & does her own cooking. She used to teach the North Brooklin school, years ago. The district nurse, who sat on my right, invited me to a meeting of the League of Women Voters in Miss Pearson's barn & got me as far as the kitchen door, when I backed out. There was a potter at dinner, too, in a cobalt blue jacket & lemon yellow scarf. Mr. Wilder,[1] passing through town in his sedan, bowed pleasantly.

Our pasture was burned yesterday, & got a good burn. Good progress

---

1. Ray Wilder, owner of the boatyard where White stored his boat.

Family portrait, taken a few months after White's birth in 1899. Top row, left to right: Samuel Tilly White, Jessie Hart White, Elwyn Brooks White, Marion Robertson White. Bottom row: Lillian White, Albert Hunt White, Stanley Hart White, Clara Frances White.

Clara and Elwyn with their mother, in Mount Vernon.

101 Summit Avenue, Mount Vernon, New York.

Lillian and Elwyn, probably taken in Clinton Corners, New York, where the Whites summered at that time.

Beppo, an Irish setter, and Elwyn.

Lillian, Elwyn, and Jessie Hart White at Great Pond, North Belgrade, Maine.

At Great Pond. Clockwise: Jessie, Clara, Stanley, Albert, Lillian, and "En."

High button shoes, about 1910.

Iron lawn animals were high fashion. Elwyn here poses for his father with a dog they discovered.

The Model T, "Hotspur," on the National Parks Highway east of Bismarck, North Dakota, in the summer of 1922. Howard Cushman is in the driver's seat. White wrote on the back of this photograph: "You can run 35 miles an hour through this sand and prairie grass—until you come to a little lake such as the one which shines in the background. Note absence of filling stations and Laxative ads."

In Walker, Minnesota, where White dislocated his right elbow. He had the bones set, rigged a trunk-strap sling, and continued west. The accident, however, posed a driving problem, as Cushman didn't know how to operate the Model T.

A thirty-two mile detour through the sage brush between Forsythe and Billings, Montana.

Between Choteau and Browning, Montana—a road through the Blackfeet Indian Reservation. White took the picture. On the back he wrote: "Picture secured at great personal sacrifice. Note our fine lantern next to the dining room table."

The S.S. *Buford*.

Cushman and White in the fruit harvest, Yakima, Washington.

Katharine Sergeant Angell.
The picture was taken shortly
before her marriage to White.

H. W. Ross, about 1927. The inscription reads: "To Katharine Angell, God bless her, who brought
this on herself."

White and James Thurber,
Sneden's Landing, about 1929.

Thurber and Katharine Angell.

has been made on the house. The new foundation wall has been built for the conservatory, so I guess there's nothing to do but go ahead. . . . Our driveway is a mountain of large rocks. Kitchen chimney gone entirely. Hot water boiler gone. Piano gone. Forsythia out in bantam yard, & it was sunny & springlike today, but with a wind springing up. Howard reports there is no work in town & that Bluehill is dead & is expecting the worst season yet. However, there seemed to be plenty of labor being employed in my yard, & after counting the men I got panicky & rushed to my typewriter & wrote a comment toward defraying the day's damage. This is the only sheet of paper I have, & Fred Kneisel,[2] when he vacated this room, left none: so I will have to quit. Ear is better. Lots of love.

Andy

To HAROLD ROSS

[Blue Hill, Me.]
[May? 1938]

Dear Mr. Ross:

Would stand ready to go back on newsbreaks the first of June, if this meets with your pleasure. I would like to know what quantity of breaks you would be interested in getting, and what you pay. This is important to me although I can see where it might be just a detail in your busy life, otherwise you would have opened up before this and given me the Answer Direct.

My breaks are raised right in the home from hardy vigorous stock, and are guaranteed free from white diarrhoea (pullorum disease). Many of the little "headings" have a long life-span and are used over and over and over again, but I make no extra charge. It's all included in the original price.

White

To GLUYAS WILLIAMS

245 East 48
9 June 1938

Dear Gluyas:

We were delighted to hear that you would be going to Deer Isle after all.[1] The almost total demolition of our nice white house has

2. Son of Franz Kneisel, first violinist of the Kneisel Quartet. Several of the early rusticators in Blue Hill were musicians, among them Wulf Fries, cellist, Bertha J. Tapper, pianist, and Henry Krehbiel, critic. Franz Kneisel owned land and conducted a summer music school, his pupils boarding in the homes of villagers. Concerts were given, and eventually a hall was built on a slope at the foot of the mountain. The school has survived, and one of the pleasures of summertime in Blue Hill is listening to chamber music in "Kneisel Hall."

1. For many years Gluyas Williams and his family had a summer home on Sylvester's Cove, Deer Isle. They and the Whites used to visit back and forth.

pretty well taken the starch out of us, but we will soon be in residence among the ruins, and maybe we can make something of it all. Here in town we are desperately trying to wind up our affairs, dwelling in the sad residue of overstuffed furniture and underdone memories—bare floors, half empty shelves, untouched closets whose doors we dare not open. The paraphernalia of life are really appalling, when you start stirring them up. Kay left for Pomfret this morning to attend Roger's graduation; Nancy finished at Bryn Mawr last week. Joe staged his own celebration with a fever of 103, scaring the daylights out of us, but quickly subsided. In the general turbulence I find I am unable to get any work done of any sort, and spend my time trying to decide whether or not to throw away my biology notebook (Mount Vernon High School), examining the dog for fleas, and running errands. However, the steady disappearance of beds, chairs, mirrors, rugs, drapes, glass, china, and oddments is clearing my blood; we've been holding private sales with considerable success (our prices are right) and in another ten days I hope to be without a pencil to my name, except what's in North Brooklin.

I'll probably leave by car about the 16th, taking Joe, Freddie, Ezekiel (a new puppy), Nick (a bird), Hattie (a rubber plant), and a sack of middlings. Kay will depart a couple of days later, by train, after closing the house and mopping up. (I *must* remember to get that girl a mop.)

My piece "Memoirs of a Master" which you mentioned in your letter wasn't a brilliant success. The Saturday Evening Post canned it, so I retired it to stud. I am an easily discouraged fellow.

See you soon.

Andy

• *White writes: "Ik Shuman was the current 'Jesus' at* The New Yorker. *Ross was always hiring someone to run the magazine—and then not letting him run it."*

To IK SHUMAN

North Brooklin, Maine
[July 1938]
Sunday

Dear Ik:

As to yrs of July 14 regarding my sending some timely comment the weeks of Aug. 27 and Sept. 3, I would say that I believe I can do this all right. If I can't I am not the same old White. Maybe I am not. Lying under a range shelter holding a clinching iron against the roost supports, I sometimes wonder. You didn't say what quantity of this comment, or "guano," you wanted. You mean two whole departments, or what? I would like some comment suggestions to work from in the event that I undertake this writing job. Writing is at best menial work, and I need suggestions, or the "folder."

My black dog got a woodchuck yesterday and ate most of it. Later he was sick.

Yrs,
Andy

To IK SHUMAN

North Brooklin, Maine
[Summer 1938]

Dear Ik:

I thought the check for the answers to hard questions was a fine thing, no complaints. Any money at all that I can get my hands on these days seems like a fine thing, and nobody gets any back talk from me. I am trying to finish a piece about Daniel Webster and the hay fever, which I hope to send to the NYer, for money.[1] Not many people know what a bad time Webster had with his mucous membrane, but he kept writing President Fillmore about it, and I have my hands on most of the evidence. I have just had a very bad time with my own hay fever, but have kept it out of my correspondence, mainly.

My four Bourbon Red poults are doing all right, also my flock of 83 New Hampshires, now in their ninth week. I am a little godsend to the grain company in Ellsworth, as I have never been able to refuse a bird anything. I gratify their slightest whim. The Park & Pollard growing mash rolls in here by the hundred pound bag, in a steady stream. Joe's bantams have increased and I can send you a nice trio at the drop of a foulard tie.

Regards to all,
Andy

•   *Soon after White began contributing his "One Man's Meat" department,* Harper's *magazine placed a display advertisement in* The New

---

1. "Daniel Webster, the Hay Fever, and Me" was published in the July 30, 1938, issue of the magazine. The piece appears in *One Man's Meat* under the title "The Summer Catarrh."

Yorker *announcing the new feature. White was embarrassed and irritated by the ad copy, which implied he had defected from* The New Yorker.

To HAROLD ROSS

North Brooklin, Me.
16 September [1938]

Dear Mr. Ross:

I am sorry and sore about the Harper promotion which Ik phoned me about today. I hadn't anticipated anything like this but I guess I am not an anticipator. Or maybe it was because the publishing side of the Harper organization has always kept so mum about my books: that may have thrown me off. I told Ik that I couldn't very well tell Harper's they couldn't insert an ad about me in the NYer, but that I would object strenuously if there was any implication that I had quit the NYer. I was just trying to be fair to all parties in this unattractive matter. I also sent a wire to Lee Hartman asking him please not to use my photograph in a NYer ad, but to use a caricature instead if he insisted on stressing the pictorial side of me.

I find it very disturbing to be advertised, as I have noticed that it is the advertised authors that stink. I am pretty sure I am going to stink from now on, and it might just as well be in Harper's as anywhere, I suppose. A writer is like a beanplant—he has his little day, and then gets stringy. I gather from your letter that you don't see why I should be writing 2500 words a month for Harper's rather than the same amount for the NYer. There are a couple of reasons for this. One is, in a department like N & C there are certain limitations in subject matter and in manner of expressing yourself which, after ten years, become formidable and sometimes oppressive. With a signed department, using "I" instead of "we," I can cover new ground, which is necessary at this stage. The other is, a monthly department gives me about three weeks of off time, which I can devote to a sustained project, like shingling a barn or sandpapering an old idea. I want this interval during which I don't have to produce anything for publication. I can't get it with Notes & C. because they come along every Friday, rain or shine. Those are the reasons I grabbed off a job with a quality monthly. (See Time for an account of how Harper's is giving up quality and taking me instead.)

It is not all velvet, this monthly life. I think on the whole they worry more about it than I do—anyway they keep writing me letters, telling me how to go about everything. It seems that the big trick is to fill exactly four pages without any white space on P. 4. This goal is arrived at by a bit of wizardry which I haven't yet mastered but which I study every night before retiring. The deadline they have given me is the tenth of the month for the second month following. Fancy me in a

Christmas mood by Columbus Day. I stuck a turkey in my November department and it was greeted with a roar of approval because it was the right bird. Luckily I happened to *have* a turkey on hand that I could stick in.

Answering your question about my doing some Comment, my intentions have been to do some provided it didn't interfere too much with this 3-week lull that I spoke about above. I have not been getting many comment ideas here on my own hook, and probably won't until I take to reading the papers again. I expect to start reading the papers again when I get back from the Cornell-Harvard game in Cambridge (Cornell 12—Harvard 0). I will pick up the paper and read about the game, and the first thing you know my eye will rove over to Berchtesgaden and away we'll go. I don't dare read the papers for my Harper's column because I would get a mild dysentery worrying about what fifty days lapse was going to do to my stuff. Fifty days is almost three years, pal.

Yrs,
White

To GLUYAS WILLIAMS

North Brooklin, Maine
[mid-September 1938]

Dear Gluyas:

Some of the time we sit dolefully around the radio listening to Czechoslovakia and hurricane victims, but most of the time I am on the barn roof, shingling. The roof, on blue days, commands an unsurpassed view of sea, sky, and mountains—with a patch of yellow pumpkins in the left foreground and a bough of red apples practically in your lap. I am even contemplating a cupola (or what Al Townsend calls a cubalo) as a proper base for a golden arrow weather vane. It is wonderful, how completely a man can occupy himself with a cupola, with Europe hanging in the balance and tidal waves washing decent people out to sea. I trust you and yours were not washed out to sea, as it would make us feel very sad and smug.

Joe has completed two weeks in the Brooklin school without incident. Mackereling has been unusually good—Astrid took 104 aboard last Sunday afternoon in the rain, off Long Island. Kay is knitting mittens—a clumsy miracle on a par with wireless telegraphy, synchro-mesh transmission, and the McCormick reaper. Our furnace (steam) is half in, half not in. Radiators sitting around, in approximately (but not quite) the right position. I have done two departments for *Harper's Magazine*, but still don't feel that it is anything but a sort of dream—and haven't the slightest conviction that I can do another. Wednesday we go to the Union Fair, to watch the horse pulling, then on to Belgrade for a night.

And the week after that we trek to Boston for the Cornell-Harvard game —our sop to civilization for the autumn term.

Yesterday we motored (by high-powered motor car) to Bah Hahba [Bar Harbor], for Kay's periodical hair washing at the Frances Fox Institute. Dressed nattily in tweeds, we patronized the leading hardware store where we had a very funny time, being waited on by an extremely tony proprietor (in mouse-grey vest and silver handled cane) who doggedly complied with our requests for one large garbage pail with pedal attachment, one agate tureen for scraps to be saved for the pig, two 8-quart galvanized pails (for watering the pullets), a chromium toilet paper holder for the cook's john, twelve sheets of brown wrapping paper, and a ball of twine. He stood it as long as he could, and then asked: "Have you just arrived?" We said no we'd been here for ages. With that as a parting crack we shouldered our foul containers and marched out.

One thing I like about the country is the way everything moves indoors with you, come fall. Spiders, flies, hornets, dogs, crickets, bantams, lice, mice, everything. I don't see how we can be lonely with this company. And to top it all, the Portland Press Herald printed a list of Who's Who in Maine. There were only nine of us.

Yrs,
Andy

To AMY FLASHNER

North Brooklin, Maine
30 September [1938]

Dear Miss Flashner:

I am listing my choice of titles in the order of which I approve of them. You may take any one.

1. Quo Vadimus?
2. Parables and Prophecies
3. Dr. Vinton and other matters
4. The Wings of Orville
5. Dusk in Fierce Pajamas

I'm sorry I have been so long sending you a title, but I haven't been able to think of very bright things to call a book.

The copies of "The Fox of Peapack" have arrived and I think they look fine. Now that the dove hangs over Middle Europe, America ought to be right in the mood for a little book of topical ballads, nicely rhymed and essentially cheerful in tone. Throwing modesty to the winds I sat down and wrote the enclosed suggestion for an advertisement which I would like you to insert in all morning and evening papers in the United States at a cost of only three million dollars. I think it will whet people's curiosity in great shape. You needn't sit there and scoff, either: I used to be in the advertising business and was doing very well when something snapped and I began writing ballads. Naturally I don't believe all those nice things I have said about myself in the ad, but we poets have to get along somehow. I really wrote it because I have always wanted to put William Randolph Hearst next to a concrete septic tank.

Tell your boss Mr. Saxton that I finally quit thinking about book titles when I arrived at one called "The Pop-Up Book for Sit-Down People."

Yrs. rhythmically,
E. B. White

To JAMES THURBER

[North Brooklin, Me.]
[mid-October 1938]

Dear Jim:

I opened up the Sat Review and got into one of my wincing moods, ready for a good old-fashioned wince, but I'm damned if I didn't come through in good shape.[1] Why I hardly got even so much as a little teeny squirm out of your piece. I am much obliged (yes terribly much obliged) to you for your warm, courteous, and ept treatment of a rather weak, skinny subject. Only here and there were you far off. I do not sail a 30 foot boat expertly. I sail one courageously—a different matter. And the strange dreamlike quality of my interview with Robert Nathan in the reception room will probably never be caught except in my own version called "Journey's Dead End," to be published with other matters come spring (Harper & Brothers, h'ya boy?). Of course, all that guff about my shrinking, quiet disposition is a curious hangover from a legend started, I believe, by Alexander Woollcott about ten years ago and perpetuated doggedly ever since. Hell, I was just as hale a fellow, just as well-met, as anybody else who worked around the place; only I passed up a Sunday breakfast invitation one time at the Woollcott home, and since I was the only little-known person who hadn't shown up promptly, Woollcott had to invent a cock-and-bull story to save his reputation as a salon holder without peer. So he spread it around that I was shy. I doubt if I am shy. I am more on the pushy side, like you. The only reason I am not recognized as I strut through the Algonquin is because, among all the thousands of people around New York whom I have met, not one of them can remember a single thing I have ever said that was either amusing or

---

1. A piece about White by James Thurber appeared in the *Saturday Review*, October 15, 1938.

informing. I am a dull man, personally. Nobody ever seeks me out, not even people who like me or approve of me; because after you have sought me out, you haven't got anything but a prose writer. I can't imitate birds, or dogs; I can't even remember what happened last night. . . .

However, I think your piece is fine, and I appreciate your doing it. (After all, I know what a selfless and sacrificial mood you have to get into, in order to do anything for the Sat Review. Last spring in Bermuda I put in 53 hours doing a book review for them, and got nine dollars, or 17¢ an hour. That's small pay even for a Cornell man.)

Thanks, pal. If you see me in the Algonquin, I want you to smile and nod.

Lots of love to you and Helen,
Andy

To MORRIS BISHOP

North Brooklin, Maine
30 October [1938]

Dear Morris:

I feel that "gay" is not quite the word for what we are in Maine. Alert, perhaps. Busy certainly. But our mood ranges from bewilderment to a well-disciplined New England rapture. This is not the "gay" phase. I was gay at seven, again at twenty-three, and expect to achieve gaiety once more at eighty, just before the final distemper.

Your note was encouraging, and I appreciate your bothering to write me about my somewhat desperate little affair with Harper's. Reading over my first couple of departments, I am not at all sure that I can make out with this sort of monthly encyclical—I sound like Thomas Mann on the Concord and Merrimac. Now that my pullets are laying well, I have an almost overpowering urge to let pure thought go by the board and write nothing but rather sharp notes to my grain dealer.

This set-to with the soil, or "earth," which Katharine and I are engaged in, is a manifestation well worth exploring; whole carloads of creative, impractical people are sprinkling the land of their forebears— or at any rate the land of *somebody's* forebears. We examine, with the simple wonderment of a child, the elementary processes of nature, over-emphasizing (I dare say) the ignoble properties of the city and the town, emulating the competence of genuine countrymen, and acting often in a thoroughly comical manner. There is something quite funny about the rediscovery of America, if I could just get it down. I suppose it was going on a hundred years ago, in transcendental days, and was just as amusing then as now; but today we have the added absurdities which arise from the attempt to live simple lives with General Electric appliances. The cellar of this old farmhouse is perilously like the boiler room of the Queen Mary: you can hardly see the McIntosh and the Northern Spy for the pressure gauges.

I trust that you are enjoying, as I am, the barbarous pleasures which surround a winning football team, and that we will meet in the not too impossible future. Kay and I send our best to Alison,[1] you, and the small Bishop.

Sincerely,

Andy

• *Cass Canfield first worked with White on* Quo Vadimus? *When Eugene Saxton died in 1942, Canfield became White's editor at Harper & Brothers.*

To CASS CANFIELD

[North Brooklin, Me.]

November 3, 1938

[Telegram]

WHY NOT USE TITLE QUO VADIMUS PLUS SUB TITLE QUOTE OR THE CASE FOR THE BICYCLE UNQUOTE TITLE YOU ARE GOING AHEAD WITH IS OBVIOUSLY MISLEADING SINCE YOU TOOK IT TO MEAN BEWILDERMENT IF YOU ARE SCARED OF A LATIN TITLE REMEMBER THAT A BOOK CALLED QUO VADIS USED TO RUN NECK AND NECK WITH THE BIBLE AND THE BOY SCOUTS HANDBOOK WHAT IS SO TERRIBLE ABOUT LATIN? ESPECIALLY IF YOU HAVE A SUB TITLE WHICH REMOVES ALL DOUBT

E B WHITE

To JAMES THURBER

North Brooklin, Maine

18 November 1938

Dear Jim:

Thanksgiving won't seem like Thanksgiving to us away from the Thurber house, but we didn't see how we could make it. It turns out Elsie [Sergeant] is coming here for a week's visit, and anyway Woodbury isn't within our weekend range, even with me at the wheel. There are something like 452 miles separating you and yours from us and ourn. I am getting to be more realistic about mileage than I used to be: even to go to the movies we must drive 28 miles there and 28 miles back. Joe goes 2.5 miles to school—partly on the hoof, partly motor-driven. Kay goes 46.6 to get her hair washed—and is lucky even at that. We go 51 miles to

---

1. Morris Bishop had married the painter and muralist Alison Mason Kingsbury. Their daughter was also called Alison.

meet trains, 28 miles to buy a bottle of Amontillado, 9 miles to a package of Kleenex, 13.6 miles to a cord of slabwood; and even to harvest the two dozen eggs which my pullets lay daily (at no prearranged signal from me) I have to walk 100 feet. My pullets are laying fools, but they have a strange thing the matter with them which causes them to shake their heads. I have looked this up in my pamphlets, but I can't find out much. It's like a dog biting himself viciously in the pocket under his hind leg—you can't tell much about it, whether it's worms or fleas or eczema. These birds of mine never stop shaking their heads and it is beginning to get to me. Sometimes I stand there and get thinking that maybe they are shaking their heads over *me*. "Poor old White," they say, shaking their heads. I asked Lennie Candage what it meant when they started shaking their heads. (Lennie was over here building a new foundation wall under the north end of the barn so it wouldn't be too cold for the pig in the barn cellar: and there is a story in that, too, it's what always happens to me—I get a pig so that we won't have to buy hams, and then I rebuild my barn around the pig at an expense of perhaps a thousand hams, or more than you and I could eat (with mustard) during the rest of our natural lives, if you can call mine a natural life.) End parenthesis. Anyway, Lennie was here, his old felt hat a mass of spider webs where he'd been walking around in cellars doing foundation work, and when I put it right up to him about my pullets shaking their heads he said, "God, I dunno nuthin' 'bout chickens. I just feed 'em, and if they do good I take the money; if they sicken, I dump 'em. That's all I know 'bout chickens." Just the same, I wish they'd stop shaking their heads.[1]

On the whole we are getting along here pretty well and liking it. There is something in me that keeps making me want to do things I am not very good at, and of course the country is the ideal place for that. I have made things about as hard for myself as anybody conceivably could, I guess, what with installing a coal furnace that has to be hand-fired (by me), and acquiring a lot of miscellaneous live animals that have to be fed, watered, nursed, wormed, bedded, scolded, and worried about. This place teems with trouble, of one sort and another. I am up every morning at twenty past six, trouble shooting. The community here is a very strange box of bon bons, with a surprise in every layer. In summer time it is impossible to find out much about what goes on but in winter you begin to get to know people.

(Later, Sat. the 26) We had a light fall of snow for Thanksgiving Day, and yesterday we awoke to a N.E. blizzard, a gale of wind and plenty of what the sportswriter on the Bangor News calls the fine white

1. It was Candage who gave White his most prized bit of agricultural advice: "The time to cut hay is in hayin' time."

particles. The wind was blowing so hard the snow never hit the ground at all, just went along till it brought up against something. When Kay learned that no milk had come and that the power lines were down, she was just like Mrs. Peterkin on the famous morning when the Peterkins arose to find a white world and no butcher. I spent most of the morning applying hot towels to frozen pipes in the woodshed, rescuing small animals and birds from strange unsuitable locations, stoking fires, and battening down barn doors. We soon were without water, the power being off, and this suggested a trip to the spring—which is across the road in an alder thicket, about three hundred and fifty feet away. I remembered that I had equipped the spring with a concrete cover, and that in my zeal I had fitted this cover with a large, cheap padlock—the sort of elaborate, fussy gesture which a city man makes when he first comes to the country and begins tampering with fundamental matters, like water. It is an exciting moment, when you renew your acquaintance with a spring (a locked spring) during a driving snowstorm. Joe and I and the hired man fought our way through drifts groin high, dragging our buckets. Things were a little quieter in the woods, and we scraped the snow off the spring top and Joe applied oil to the lock. I had brought a hack saw along. It seemed an odd thing to approach a pure spring of water with, a hack saw. To my surprise the lock gradually loosened up and admitted us to my water, which we scooped out in enamel pails and lugged back through the blizzard to the house. It wasn't that anybody particularly wanted any water, either. Nobody wanted any water. Six hours later the power came on again, and with it the full pipe, the pure-flowing tap.

Yesterday was the day, too, when Ethelbert ("Mighty Lak a Rose") Nevin's daughter Doris had invited us to dinner to meet Mary Ellen Chase. But not even as idyllic a literary occasion as that could take place in such a great storm: the snowplow hadn't come through, and there was just no getting authors together. We've got another storm in our lap, but are taking it quietly—we have laid down our hack saws and will beat them into plowshares come spring.

We are very lucky in our "help" this fall, our dinners being cooked for us by Miss Milly Gray, a kindly white-haired lady . . . [who] is full of prophecy and lore of all kinds. She looks under the lid of the stove for signs of milder weather. She has a humorous regard for a set of deities called "they." Her references to these spirits are always made with a half deprecatory manner, as though they were a rather troublesome, quirky, ill-tempered group of gods. "I was thinkin' one snowstorm might be enough for one week," she said this morning, "but they didn't think that way." Or, commenting on my Labrador retriever, "They didn't skimp any, when they made that one, did they?" She keeps up a running stream of conversation with herself, alone in the kitchen, and has a lively interest in wild flowers.

Life is just about alarming as it ever was, it seems to me. I worry some about my brothers and sisters, most of whom are in one sort of trouble or another. The piano business has folded, leaving Albert clean. My Washington sister [Clara Wyvell] is giving up her boarding house and going to a small town in upstate New York to live with a sister-in-law. Art Illian has moved from Chicago to Kew Gardens—which somehow sounds unpropitious. And my brother Stanley, while still teaching landscape architecture at the University of Illinois, is fooling with a patent on something called Botanical Bricks. My book of poems has brought me a handful of letters, from people like Ada Trimingham and the man I bought the touring car from. But it is apparent from reviews and sales that I will have to write something a whole lot better than that if I am to continue in this game. I don't know which is more discouraging, literature or chickens. Roup, favus, thrush, range paralysis, the spiral stomach worm, the incessant shaking of the head—these specters take their place alongside rejected newsbreaks, teeny books of poems, and the exhaustion which comes with the fortieth birthday. Incidentally, my fear of mold, which you mentioned in your piece, is still strong; and I am delighted to learn in my poultry bulletin that my birds and I may be called away together. There are several poultry diseases caused by fungi (molds), the most common being Aspergillosis. The causative agents are the common green mold, *Aspergillus fumigatus*, and the black mold, *A. niger*, which grow on vegetables and other kinds of matter. The affected birds mope, separate themselves from the remainder of the flock, or remain in a sitting posture. The difficulty of breathing increases rapidly; they gasp for breath and make movements of the head and neck as if choking; there are fever, diarrhea, drooping wings, great depression, a tendency to sleep, and finally suffocation and death. Thrush is another fungi trouble. In bad thrush cases, you have to flush out the crop with a 2-percent boric acid solution. I haven't yet met the chicken which would let me flush out its crop, but a man never knows.

You and Helen must pay us a call soon. It is bleak here for visitors, and uninteresting, but we expect them to come just the same. I will try to have my ice boats made by the time you arrive. An ice boat is a good way to get away from mold—except, of course, the sail. The sail gets moldy, and you have to watch it.

Lots of love, and thanks for the invitation to Thanksgiving.

Yrs,
Andy

To DAISE TERRY

North Brooklin, Maine
14 December [1938]

Dear Miss Terry:

Would you have your office order me a copy of "Last Poems" by A. E. Housman? I want to give it to Roger for Christmas. He asked for Housman poems, a bottle of Amontillado, and a top hat. I can only assume that he is going to sit around in the hat, drinking the sherry, reading the poems, and dreaming the long long dreams of youth.

Yr distant friend,
E. B. White

To FRANK SULLIVAN

North Brooklin, Maine
20 December 1938

Dear Frank:

I got your letter (October 19, 1938) and your clipbook[1] ("Oyster of Great Price") and will now sit down and thank you for them. It is great to *be* sitting down. There is not enough of that done here on my place— in fact, the turbulence of country life is a disillusioning, or at any rate, an unexpected factor in this change of residence. I had looked forward to long cozy evenings around the blazing birch fire, with my dog dozing at my feet and in my hands a good book ("How to Raise an Oyster," by Frank Sullivan) but the fact is we spend most of the 24 hours on a quick scamper and my room is clogged with unopened copies of the *New York Times*, probably full of rather nasty news. I'm up about six every morning, and immediately after breakfast I take a mild sedative to keep from getting too damn stirred up over the events of the day, the heady rhythm of earth, the intoxicating wine-dark sea which laps my pasture, the thousand and one exciting little necessities which spring from a 12-room steam-heated house standing all alone in a big world. There is a strong likelihood that the country will be my undoing, as I like it too well and take it too seriously. I have taken these 40 acres to be my bride, and of course that can be exhausting. I dance attendance on my attractive holdings, all day long. Kay and I are both drawing closer and closer to an electric water pump, farther and farther from the world of books ("With Pearls in Arabia"). I don't even have my dog dozing at my feet in the evening because we've got it figured out that if he is going to sleep in the cold barn after we go to bed, he ought not lay around in the living room getting overheated. So we put the poor

---

1. *A Pearl in Every Oyster.*

bastard out right after supper, to shiver in his straw pile twelve hours instead of only eight. All kinds of odd complications like that about Maine life. This afternoon I ought to do newsbreaks, but instead of that I have to make a motor trip of 54 miles to buy some tiny cardboard boxes in which the members of the Parent-Teacher Association will place the popcorn and candy for the children of Brooklin. In New York I never indulged in any charitable nonsense like that, but in this town we are at the moment the No. 1 glamour family, the family to which the leading citizens instinctively turn in any crisis. In NY I never attended a PTA meeting, figuring that a parent went through enough hell right in his own home—and besides, there was always some other place you could go, like to a professional hockey game; but I wouldn't miss the PTA meetings here. It was at the last meeting that they voted to raise the salary of the librarian in the Brooklin library. She now gets $13 a year. I believe it's to be almost doubled. They're even talking of putting lights in the library, so people can see to read after dark. (It gets dark here at ten past three in the afternoon.)

The trouble with Maine is it has too distinguished a past. Every day the Bangor *Daily News* runs a long feature piece on Maine lore or history, usually an interview with an octogenarian who still thinks of himself as returning from the China Seas with a sandalwood box for his bride—or a bride for his sandalwood box. Or he is in a clipper ship in a gale off the Horn. I think this kind of reading makes the present generation restless and unhappy, and they are always looking for something bold to do. We had a blizzard on Thanksgiving, and somebody suddenly remembered that there were a lot of deer hunters in the woods, so the state cops rounded up a squadron of snowplows (which were badly needed right where they stood) and went bursting through a woods road on a rescue expedition which would have been a lifesaver for a cliché expert dying of exposure. Giant planes roared from the Bangor airport and swooped down to drop bundles of food and first aid supplies to stormbound hunters. The Field Artillery horned in on the fun, and as near as I can make out held up the operations considerably by insisting on establishing short wave radio communication between the tractor plows and the Artillery base in Bangor. (I have often wondered what an artilleryman says to a driver of a snowplow, but apparently he has a message.) The story made great reading and got better and better, until, toward the end of the fifth column on Page 2, it turned out that quite a few of the hunters wanted to stay in the woods "until later in the week." The hunting was just getting good, and all the hunters from around here have enough rye in camp to keep them till spring anyway.

On the whole we are getting along fine, miss our friends some, but not too much; we have pork chops hanging by strings in the garage, apples in the attic, jams and thermostats in the root cellar, and a spruce tree waiting for me to chop it. I also have an instep waiting for the first merry axblow. We were tickled to get your book, and your Hollywood visit piece (which I had never read) wowed me. Would like to be in the pool with you now, treading champagne. K sends love.

Merry Christmas,
Andy

To EUGENE SAXTON and CASS CANFIELD

North Brooklin, Maine
18 January 1939

Dear Messrs. Saxton and Canfield:

I am deeply grateful for the pretty books you sent me at Christmas time, which I have already woven into a song.

> Said Garamond to Tomlinson,
> Said Caslon to Millay,
> We feel we are the very type
> You need on Christmas day.

I had never read "Illusion: 1915" and was much amused and instructed. Sometimes the imminence of war, long drawn out, such as we have been fretting under, seems as illusory and incredible as war itself—and I expect a French colonel wearing a hunting horn to break into the scene. At any rate, the past year has seemed dreamlike to me, and I am waiting for someone to take me aside and tell me that it isn't true about Austria. But nobody does. Part of the illusion is the perfectly true fact that my wife has an old aunt living in Tokyo, who gives garden parties for the Japanese wounded.[1] I just go out and mix up another hot mash for my hens. I can't even drink very much (which would help out) as liquor has taken to going straight to my nose, cutting off my breath. It used to just go to my stomach—but that was before the pogroms.

Our immediate household, now in the eighth month of its confinement, is thriving, on the whole. We are beginning to get things in hand: the fires burn with steadier heat and less popping and sparkling; the

---

1. Annie Barrows Shepley, sister of Katharine White's mother. She was the "Aunt Poo" about whom White wrote in the "One Man's Meat" essay dated June 1942. In middle life, she had surprised her New England family by marrying a young Japanese student, Hyozo Omori, whom she had hired as a cook at her home in Woodstock, Connecticut. Although Poo's roots were in Maine, in 1907 she and her aristocratic young husband went to live in Tokyo, where he founded Japan's first settlement house, Yurin En. Mr. Omori died in 1912, but Poo continued to live on in her adopted Japan. During the Second World War, with Japan our enemy, the Whites were uneasy about her health and her safety; but when word came of her death, all indications were that she had been showered with honors and that she had died of natural causes.

dogs have reached a working agreement with the black-and-white kitten; and when I want a hammer I can find a hammer, not a brad awl. There is some slight advantage in living as a recluse, in that one makes one's own crises, instead of getting them out of the newspaper. Tomorrow we will have the cat altered. That takes care of another day.

We are probably coming to town for a few weeks along about March, and shall hope to see you then. Again thanks for the good books.

Yrs,
Andy White

•   *Anne Carroll Moore was the New York Public Library's first librarian for children's books and a power in the children's book world. An admirer of White's prose, she was delighted at the rumor that he was writing a book for young readers. The book was* Stuart Little. *(Although in the following letter White says he started the book "about two years ago," he was not being accurate. The first two or three chapters were written in the early 1930s.)*

To ANNE CARROLL MOORE

North Brooklin, Maine
15 February 1939

Dear Miss Moore:

It was good of you to write me about the piece in Harper's and I'm glad if it gave you any pleasure. I started to write a book for children about two years ago, and have it about half done. Perhaps with your encouragement I will get round to working some more on it. I really only go at it when I am laid up in bed, sick, and lately I have been enjoying fine health. My fears about writing for children are great—one can so easily slip into a cheap sort of whimsy or cuteness. I don't trust myself in this treacherous field unless I am running a degree of fever.

Our house is a little more orderly, now; we gave away most of the review copies at Christmas, and can now make our way about the rooms. We gave quite a few to a small library in this village, where they were much appreciated, I think.[1]

Thanks again for your letter. I will try to get to work on the book. Meantime, please save shelf space in your library, public though it may

1. When the Whites moved to Maine, Katharine was the children's book reviewer for *The New Yorker*. She continued in the job, writing from North Brooklin. Review copies littered the house, and from time to time Katharine passed them on to the Friend Memorial Library in Brooklin—an institution to which she became deeply devoted and which she helped to revive from an almost moribund condition.

be, for a copy of "Quo Vadimus? or The Case for the Bicycle," to be published in a couple of weeks by Harper. (Advt.)

Sincerely,
E. B. White

TO EUGENE SAXTON

Hotel Gramercy Park
New York
1 March [1939]

Dear Gene:

Herewith an unfinished MS of a book called *Stuart Little*. It would seem to be for children, but I'm not fussy who reads it. You said you wanted to look at this, so I am presenting it thus in its incomplete state. There are about ten or twelve thousand words so far, roughly.

You will be shocked and grieved to discover that the principal character in the story has somewhat the attributes and appearance of a mouse. This does not mean that I am either challenging or denying Mr. Disney's genius. At the risk of seeming a very whimsical fellow indeed, I will have to break down and confess to you that Stuart Little appeared to me in dream, all complete, with his hat, his cane, and his brisk manner. Since he was the only fictional figure ever to honor and disturb my sleep, I was deeply touched, and felt that I was not free to change him into a grasshopper or a wallaby. Luckily he bears no resemblance, either physically or temperamentally, to Mickey. I guess that's a break for all of us.

Stop in here for a drink some fine afternoon. We are enjoying room service and would like to see you.

Andy White

• *After White had declined the editorship of the* Saturday Review, *Bernard DeVoto, who had declined the post before it was offered to White, changed his mind and took the job. The following memo was written one afternoon after White had returned to* The New Yorker *office from lunching at the Seymour Hotel.*

TO KATHARINE S. WHITE

[Interoffice memo]
[March? 1939]

Dear Mrs. White ("Tootsie"):

Lunching alone at the Seymour (Manhattan cocktail, cream of tomato, turkey club sandwich with fried sweets, meringue glacé, and coffee) who do I see but a party of ten, Miss Loveman[1] in charge, arrang-

---

1. Amy Loveman, an editor of the *Saturday Review of Literature*.

ing, introducing, making all go well, with the Editor of the Review at elbow's point with the beautiful Martha Gellhorn, so blonde, so young, selling so well, and on the other side the Booky Monthy man with the dandruff, and other authors, critics, writers, full of anecdote and the #3 luncheon, the #5 luncheon; as literary a sight as you could find all along 45th St., and sitting there alone, with last night's cigar still smouldering in my viscera and today's glacé untouched in the hard light, I looked at the happy intellectual gathering and said, "There, but for the grace of DeVoto, sit I."

Ah welladay.
Mr. White

To EUGENE SAXTON

North Brooklin, Maine
11 April 1939

Dear Gene:

I will do my best to make some progress with Stuart Little. I can't make any promises, as the effect on me of forced labor is sometimes rather dreadful. My wife is nagging me about Stuart, too; in fact today I told her she would have to stop—that she was driving me too hard. I think it made quite an impression on her.

All I can truthfully say about Stuart is that I will keep fall publication in mind as a goal, but that everything depends on whether the finished product turns out pleasing to mine eye. I would rather wait a year than publish a bad children's book, as I have too much respect for children.

One of the problems, of course, would be to find a satisfactory illustrator, and I wonder if you have any ideas on this subject. It would have to be somebody who likes mice and men, and who knows a little of their hopes, joys, disappointments, etc.

I will keep you informed as to progress, if any, of the book. Right this minute I am wet nurse to 250 small red chicks, and God help my publisher and my readers—all ten of them. . . .

Yrs,
Andy

To STANLEY HART WHITE

North Brooklin, Me.
19 April 1939

Dear Bun:

I am hiding, too. It's hard though. I feel sure that Italy, Germany, and Japan all know where I am, as well as a lot of people who will drop in about suppertime in summer when the roads are open. Snow keeps a lot of them away at this season. . . .

We have had a nice time here, and I like living in Maine the year round. It gets me pleasantly out of touch with all the things that are well worth being out of touch with. Also it gives me a chance, at last, to play with tools uninterrupted. I never realized how strong this desire is in me: probably inherited from my paternal great-grandfather. Practically the most satisfying thing on earth (specially after fifteen years of trying to put English sentences together against time) is to be able to square off a board of dry white pine, saw to the line (allowing for the thickness of the pencil point) and have the thing fit perfectly. It is best in the late afternoon, when the shop is warm from the brooder stove and the sun comes in the windows and lies along the bench among the curly shavings.

Am going to New York next week for the opening of the World's Fair, as the NY'er wants me to do a piece on it for them, and are paying my way.[1] Putting the World's Fair into two thousand words ought to tone me up.

Yrs,
Andy

To FRANK SULLIVAN

North Brooklin, Maine
26 May 1939

Dear Frank:

Thanks for the potassium. I believe that the commercial fertilizer I am using on the vegetable garden contains quite a lot of potassium, and so I've been stealing a few mouthfuls now and then. Katharine has been taking some sort of powder in water before breakfast every morning for a year, and *that*, it turns out, contains potassium. That's marriage, Frank—the man has the sensitivity, the woman gets the potassium.

I have been trying to get round to writing you in regards to a book of humor, yes humor, which K. and I have agreed to get together for Coward, McCann. Inasmuch as you will some day receive a check for $3.61 representing your share in the royalties of this book, I have no compunctions about asking your advice and help. Can you give us any suggestions about what to include? Name one funny thing you ever read (by an American). We are going to include some verse, but I think

1. "They Come with Joyous Song" appeared in *The New Yorker*, May 13, 1939. The piece was later reprinted in *One Man's Meat* under the title "The World of Tomorrow."

the book will be preponderantly prose. What we hope to be able to do is to get together, in one big volume, not just the standard chestnuts of Dooley, Twain, Sullivan and the like, but those lost jewels which lie tarnished in old newspaper files and scrapbooks. (Incidentally, have you any clips of your newspaper pieces that didn't get into book form and that should be studied by us serious students of humor?) Can you recall, offhand, any outstandingly funny piece of drama criticism, or baseball reporting, or such like by the Wits of the Old World? (I don't suppose we can include Pete Vischer's music criticisms, however hilarious. You boys tried hard, but with Pete writing the music reviews you were licked before you started.[1])

This book is going to take a lot out of us before the year is up, and my colon is tense in anticipation. I think if we succeed in rounding up the sort of stuff we have our mind on, it ought to be a good book and a handy one. The slightest tipping and hunching we can get from our friends will be of great value, because it is damn hard to remember the pieces that ought to get remembered. I happen to have a peculiarly bad memory, anyway, and things go in one sinus and out the other. . . .

Lots of love,
Andy

To HAROLD ROSS

North Brooklin, Maine
15 June 1939

Dear Ross:

This is in answer to a letter you wrote on a Thursday. I got the stock and wish to thank you very much. You were right in assuming I had forgotten about the agreement.[1] I had. But I remember it now, and wonder if I lived up to my end of it. The wording is pretty vague—I mean that part about my contributing "occasional comment." Mine was so occasional you could count it on the fingers of a millworker. If I didn't earn my stock let me know.

I approve of your idea of dropping the comment page from the book. Our attempts to draw a line of distinction between page one and the pages which follow has always confused readers (when they heard about it), and I have seen a startled look come into the eyes of persons

---

1. White thought Vischer's attempts at music criticism in the *World* wildly funny.

---

1. In its early years *The New Yorker* occasionally gave its writers a bonus payment of stock. The magazine was unable to pay contributors and staffers a high rate, and this troubled Ross. Stock was one way to take up the slack. It was also a bait to encourage greater production—in this case more Comment from White.

to whom the news suddenly got broken. I never approved of the idea of illustrating comment, because for one thing the illustrator usually got all the mechanical breaks and for another thing if a comment is any good it not only doesn't need illustration but often is incapable of being illustrated in the mood in which it was written.

The more people you have writing comment, the better, in my opinion. The more elastic the page (mechanically), the better. The less you think about the structure and problems of the comment page, the better. The more you think about its possible contents, the better. In short, the better.

If I were in your shoes I would forget there ever had been a comment page, a White, a Berry, or even a Hyde or a Gibbs. Just go ahead and do your stuff and let it start and end where and when it naturally does. You will always get comment and you will always run comment, but it shouldn't be so god damn structural and (as to size and shape) premeditated. A Malman spot is fine. A caricature or a cartoon is fine. And they ease the whole situation instantly.

On Page 2 of your letter you ask whether you could expect of me occasional or frequent comment, or maybe thirty a year. I should say that you could expect thirty. I shall set for myself a goal of one comment a week, a shining goal. Coolidge did it, why can't I? Incidentally, I think I have devised a way by which I could be hunched from the office without any particular expense or trouble on either side. Whoever receives the stuff in the office known as "comment suggestions" always has a batch of it left over each week. This batch consists partly of material which has to be returned to the owner, partly of press agent stuff. Let Miss Terry send me the press releases, and I can use them and throw them away. If the volume seems too much, she could throw half away, send me half.

As to filling in for Gibbs for a month this summer, I can't do it. I will start sending in some comments, but I can't write four departments, complete with commas and funny remarks, this summer.

I don't want to make any change in my Harper arrangements at present. In some ways I don't get the fun out of it that I would get out of the equivalent amount of work for the New Yorker, and I also find it rather difficult. I dislike writing an article of a specified length—just as I disliked writing a comment page of a specified length for you. But on the other hand I think it was a good thing for me to have done, and a year is too soon to quit—except for some quite definite reason. My situation in writing for Harper's may, as you suggest, be psychological; but it is also cushy. It keeps me in fairly good health and gives me enough to live on. If I had no responsibilities or obligations of a domestic sort, I would most certainly arrange my life so that I was not obliged to write anything at any specified time for anybody. I admire people who have the guts to do this. What I am trying to do is to approximate that condition without actually achieving it fully.

There is, then, no immediate likelihood that I will drop the Harper's department and make a deal with you to do a piece a month. I have no agreement, either written or verbal, with Harper's, but they merely permitted me to go ahead until further notice and I said I would. I don't know what they think about the whole thing, and suspect that they are a little surprised that the stuff hasn't turned out to be in a comment vein. I'm not sure they are entirely delighted with me as a contributor. In some ways I feel a lot more at home in the New Yorker, and get into a stride quicker; also it is a better magazine. More comical and interesting.

Thanks for all your interest in my work and the opportunities which you offer.

Yrs,
White

• *White holds unorthodox views about the system of payment by anthologists. Often reprinted himself, he feels that the flat fees dreamed up by anthologists are mystical sums and that writers with big names usually get paid more than lesser known writers. White believes in profit sharing, or royalty sharing; he knows that a book is a gamble, and he feels that the contributors should be in on the gamble. When he and Katharine White put together their* Subtreasury of American Humor, *he insisted that the contributors receive a percentage of the royalties. His publishers—who saw a lot of intricate bookkeeping ahead—reluctantly complied.*

To MORRIS BISHOP

North Brooklin, Maine
23 June 1939

Dear Morris:

I have been corresponding with one Raymond F. Howes on the subject of using a piece of mine[1] in a book to be called "Our Cornell." I have not, however, found out from him what I want to know; his letters have a friendly ambiguity which has begun to disturb me. I turn to you for enlightenment.

If by donating my article I would be serving my Alma Mater (that

---

1. "I'd Send My Son to Cornell," which had appeared in *University*.

girl!), I would be happy to do so. If, on the other hand, I would simply be helping another anthologist over the rocky road of life, I would just as lief get paid. That is all I want to know—what sort of book this is. Can you tell me?

In Howes' last letter he said: "Rym Berry and Morris Bishop, for instance, would, I think, feel very uncomfortable if, at this stage of the game, I went to them with an offer to pay them for their contributions." He then suggests (for me) a lump sum of $25. The implication that you and Rym can be uncomfortable in the presence of money, while I can maintain my famous calm, is what finally got me down. Am I Cornell's son or ain't I?

Of course, I brought this all on by answering Howes' first letter with a request for a statement of what sort of book it was and who was going to get the dough. I am notoriously stern with anthologists, and intend to continue being stern, as I have found, on the whole, that they are a cagey lot (I'm not referring to Howes) and seldom work out their program with fairness to their stable of authors. I am not interested in horse trading and it makes me howl with rage when Mr. Howes extols your loyalty and Rym's and in the same breath slips me twenty-five bucks. What the hell goes on here, anyway? . . .

Yrs,
Andy

To HAROLD ROSS

[North Brooklin, Me.]
[September 28, 1939]
[Telegram]

SORRY CANNOT SEND ANYTHING TRY RAYMOND GRAM SWING

WHITE

To GUSTAVE S. LOBRANO

[North Brooklin, Me.]
[November 27, 1939]
Monday

Dear Gus:

A recent communication from the *New Yorker* stated that you were in the market for scenes and stories of "high life." I instantly was reminded of my own dead past, and of my former life which was at one time so high that I suffered from dizziness.

At any rate, I searched through my files and extracted "Memoirs of a Master," which I wrote while living in high style on 48th Street. I submitted it, *at that time*, to the *Saturday Evening Post*, but it was rejected. I didn't want to submit it to the *New Yorker*, because I was afraid that the persons then in my employ would read it and perhaps feel hurt. Possibly that danger is now past, and your magazine would like to publish it. It would have to be in two parts; and it would have to be anonymous. Even published anonymously, I feel that there is some question about certain parts of it. But I leave that to you to judge.

Andy

The butt joint where the two caps met at the corner came out perfectly—smooth, clean, and hard. Tomorrow I shall be hanging the gate. The snow is still with us. Joe, with another boy, is constructing a shanty of poles under a big spruce down on the shore, where they plan to work the clam flats and become independently wealthy.

To CLARA WHITE WYVELL

North Brooklin, Maine
14 Jan. [1940?]

Dear Tar:

You can bring anybody except you better not bring that cattle man, as I have sheep here and there is a continual feud between us sheep raisers and those cattle men. Let me know when you are coming and I will send you some road information that ought to be very useful to you, as I am an authority on New England highway pitfalls.

We have had a good winter so far, nobody has broken his neck, and the weather has been cold and clear. The snow we got before New Year's is still with us, although it is beginning to peter out now. It will be wonderful to see you again, as it seems to me it has been a long while. The place we live in is twenty-five miles from a movie, but I will take you every night just the same. During the daytime you can collect eggs, or you can hunt for gloves. We spend most of our time hunting for gloves, as I have a dachshund puppy who hides them on us. If you have any gloves, don't bring them, as you will never see them again.

Our guest rooms are all on the north side. Nobody lasts long in them. Don't forget to put some anti-freeze mixture in your car radiator and drink some yourself. I don't know whether you own any woolen underdrawers, because it is none of my business, but they are the only kind that do any good. I have never worn an overcoat since coming here to live. It is all done with woolen underdrawers. Remember my warning never to visit me between the first and the tenth of any month!

EBW

TO CHARLES G. MULLER

North Brooklin, Maine
[January 18, 1940]

Dear Charlie:

It's a little bit sharp here today (3° below), and is a nice time for answering letters dated December 7 and like that. All in all we have had a mighty good winter so far, with only one thaw that amounted to anything. The Old Farmer's Almanac hit it right on the button, too.

This morning the cove is skimmed over with ice, and if we get snow within the next couple of days, there is a good chance that the bay will freeze clear across, much to the distress of the scallop draggers and the smelt fishermen. Even now the C.G. cutter Kickapoo is breaking ice at the entrance to Patten Bay, over in Surry, so the smelt colony won't be left holding a dead fishline.

(Later) I was interrupted by the necessity of transporting our two dachshunds to Bluehill, for an appointment with their doctor. We have two dachshunds, now. One wasn't enough trouble. They both have ear mites—which are invisible parasites, forerunners of ear canker. Quite a lot of my time goes into transporting things here. I drive Joe to school every morn at eight, and return with a loaf of cracked wheat bread and a package of Brillo. I transport the cook to the movies, and the sow to boar. I carry dry shavings by the truckload (I now own a truck), cordwood from the woodyard, rugs to the dry cleaner, and old cedar fence-rails for building yoke fences. I am always carrying something—a burdensome life, but kind of soothing. My sheep are soothing, too. They come up out of the pasture at this time of year and stand around in the barn, and that is very soothing to me, to see sheep standing around, waiting. Quite a few of my ewes look as though they would have early lambs, and all are thrifty. I have begun graining them—feeding out a mixture of five parts oats, three parts whole corn, one part bran, and one part linseed oil meal. I am as fussy with a mixture like that as with a mixture of gin and French vermouth. My poultry operations have expanded considerably since you were here: I have a large laying house and a flock of would-be layers that turned and bit me in mid season. It was the most stinging defeat of my life, for I put a good deal of my energy into the project, raised the birds by hand from infancy, ranged them on green range, groomed them for the battle, designed and built the house, and saw them go into production in early September looking like a million dollars and shelling out in great shape. All of a sudden some little thing went wrong and they began coming apart, the way pullets do when the vitamins don't add up right, or when a couple of them get going to the bathroom too often. From forty dozen eggs a week I slid off to about fourteen dozen, and cannibalism began taking its ugly toll. Ah welladay! A man learns a lot in a year, if he hangs around animals.

Well, I cannot keep my eyes open any longer, as it is 10:05, five minutes past my bedtime. If I don't get my sleep here, I am sunk. When a man's whole year's work with hens goes wrong, there's only thing for it—plenty of sleep.

Andy

To JOEL WHITE

The Grosvenor
35 Fifth Avenue
New York
[June 23, 1940]
Sunday

Dear Joe:

From my hotel window I can see the apartment building on Eighth Street where we used to live when you were a baby. I can also see the trees of Washington Square, and the backyards of the houses on Ninth Street with their little gardens of potted plants and trellises. The Sixth Avenue Elevated is gone, and New York looks very different on that account. People still like to come out in their sun-suits on Sunday morning and sun themselves in their roof gardens, and they still spend a good deal of time taking dogs out for a walk, not realizing how lucky they are that there are no porcupines. Everybody that I talk to is very gloomy about the war and about the defeat of France, but that is true everywhere today. In Radio City, where we used to skate, there is an open-air restaurant, with people sitting at little tables under big green umbrellas. The fountain is going and makes a great noise.

How has everything been going in Maine? I miss you a lot and wish I could be there right now, although my hay fever bothers me less in the city than in the country. Is Barney[1] coming to cut the hay? I hope so. And did you get any Barred Rock chicks from Mr. Sylvester?[2] Tell me all about these things, and whether you have caught any fish.

There is a church right opposite the hotel, and every afternoon the chimes ring at about five o'clock when people are coming home from

1. "Barney Steele," writes White, "was a Joel White hero who had a team of work horses and who sometimes let a boy take the reins."
2. Leon F. Sylvester, poultryman and storekeeper of South Blue Hill.

work. It reminds me of being a student at Cornell, where the chimes in the library tower used to ring every afternoon toward the end of day. I suppose right now the bell in the church in Brooklin is ringing, too, five hundred miles from here.

Tell Mother that everything is going along all right, and that I'll try to get a good deal of work done in the next few days so that I'll be able to be back in Maine soon. I'm still hoping that you and I can take a little camping trip this summer, so you better keep your ax sharpened up and your boots oiled. I hope you'll help Mother as much as you can while I'm away. Give my love to her and to everybody, and write me if you get time.

Affectionately,
Dad

To IK SHUMAN

North Brooklin
[August 3, 1940]
Saturday

Dear Ik:

I think it would be very nice if I could have my two weeks vacation starting the 12 of August. What does my vacation mean? Does it mean somebody else does the newsbreaks, or does it mean I let them accumulate for two weeks to give myself the sensation of a vacation without really getting one? With the exception of two weeks one September when somebody else did comment, I never had a vacation from the *New Yorker* in the whole time I worked there. I used to hear about this vacation, but it never happened to hit me. But I like the idea.

Yrs,
Andy

To FRANK SULLIVAN

North Brooklin
9 August 1940

Dear Frank:

We mailed those scrapbooks back the other day, and are grateful to you for the trouble you took (and for the scrapbooks you sent). We are going to use the piece about the deckhand that fell in the East River and cried "Ahoy," and that famous answering cry came: "Ahoy awhere?" We also have you booked for the Vand't Convention, and Weekend at Lady Astor's. So we are working you gradually into our book, and consider you very deserving. I got a nice fit of nostalgia reading your scrapbooks. The world was concerned about such odd little matters in that halcyon decade—it's like reading fairy tales. Not a Messerschmitt in the whole lot.

We're still in possession of a couple of books of yours but haven't forgotten them, and will be returning them presently when another wave of doing-things-up overtakes us. Getting together an anthology is a test of strength and twine. It takes a heap o' wrappin' paper to get out an anthology. Our progress is still pretty slow, partly because my wife is a conscientious gal who can't decide on anything till she has read everything, and partly because I keep sheep.

Up until about a week ago our summer was a miasma of sickness and despair. Joe got a sinus infection, K got intestinal grippe or summer complaint, and I got my annual hay fever only in a new big improved package. We are emerging into the light this week and looking around. The only thing that brightened life for us during the bad spell was an exchange of diplomatic notes between me and the Columbia Broadcasting System on the question of using my long poem (July Harper's) on the Columbia Workshop hour together with a poem of Steve Benét's. My messages began coming from a man whom the Western Union operator at this end described as Max Whlye. I was pleased as punch to be in communication with a Mr. Whlye, and the whole affair improved steadily, because it turned out that Columbia was objecting to the word "Spry" in the poem (Spry is a vegetable shortening and a Columbia client) and they felt that it was an improper theme for a poet. I countered. They counter countered. Finally I gave them the word Crisp, which delighted them. The upshot was that they finally gave the hour over to Black Jack Pershing, an upstart bard who wants us to lend some destroyers to England. Benét and I and Crisp were shelved for a week, and will appear (I hope) this Sunday at 8 pm advt.[1]

Katharine sends her love to you, and we both do for that matter, and thanks again for the help.

Yrs,
Andy

To EUGENE SAXTON

North Brooklin, Maine
19 August 1940

Dear Gene:

About the suggestion that pieces of Meat be published in book form, I am by no means against this idea and hope I didn't give that

---

1. On August 11, White's poem "Radio in the Rain" was broadcast with "Nightmare at Noon" by Stephen Benét.

impression. I doubt that there is enough material to pick from, at this date, however. So far I've written only 25 departments and of these I should imagine that less than half would be suitable for book publication. When the autumnal calm settles over North Brooklin, if it ever does, I will glance through the files and be better able to judge.

There is one objection to the project which is on my mind and which perhaps made me sound unenthusiastic: my last two books have been clipbooks, and I have been hoping that before publishing another such I could produce an Original Work. This would do a great deal for my spirits, even if it did nothing very much for the American public. Although I fell down on my face in attempting an Original Work last June, I still have hopes of regaining my poise and my stride; so if I seem apathetic about One Man's Meat it is only because it would mean just another clipbook. . . .

Andy

To KATHARINE S. WHITE

North Brooklin
[August 26, 1940]
Monday

Dear K:

Pleasant callers today were Dr. Edmund Devol and the Bishop, in a sport coupe.[1] They had just had lunch with Fritz Kreisler and were on their way to Dr. Moorehead. They looked well and sleek and were sorry not to have seen you. The Bishop has just come into some money ($52,000). He beat Joe two games of croquet. I offered them drinks but they abstained. The Doctor was enchanted with our house, and poked around among all the bedrooms, punching the springs and looking behind things. They leave Bar Harbor shortly for a spell at Newport, and then back to the diocese and the enema.

No mackerel last night, after a hard try under perfect conditions. Apparently nobody's getting them and they just aren't in the bay this summer. I may try Orcutt's harbor as a last desperate chance.

. . . Had a nice letter from Frank Sullivan this morning, all about the difficulties of being a Roosevelt supporter among the tycoons of Saratoga-in-August. He is confident that England can't be licked.

Mrs. Milliken phoned, inviting you and me to lunch on Thursday

---

1. Edmund Devol, M.D., and his friend Bishop Samuel Trexler were New York acquaintances of the Whites', summering in Bar Harbor. Devol was a fashionable physician—a high irrigationist. He had at one time attended Harold Ross.

when the N.E. cruise comes in. She said she thought perhaps we would like to see the fleet "from a different viewpoint." I refrained from explaining that not seeing the fleet at all was a big shift in viewpoint, and, from our position, practically perfect. I told her you were in New York and that I couldn't come. If the radio has anything to say about it, the cruise is going to get rained on. All signs point to wet weather.

Didn't get much done on comment today, what with the callers and so forth, but hope to progress tomorrow. Pre-blasting operations were being carried on, drilling the rocks preparatory for the charges of dynamite. Howard thinks we should take out the small clump of trees in the field—not the peninsula but the island. I am now in favor of this, although I wasn't at first. Have studied the matter carefully today and believe it will improve rather than detract from beauty of field, besides making great advance agriculturally. Would appreciate immediate wire from you on this important matter, as I don't want to do anything without your permission, but time is at hand to strike. Howard says a good farmer wouldn't hesitate a minute. These are days for high courage.

Everybody is fine here, Joe is asleep, Roger reading breaks for me, Myra just returned from the day's outing, Fred and Min[2] curled together on one cushion. I must quit now to get back to work on comment. Don't get all razzled out in the city, and come back fresh and ready for a Fair day.

Lots of love from all,
A

To KATHARINE S. WHITE

[North Brooklin, Me.]
[August 27, 1940]
Tuesday night

Dear K:

No appreciable progress on comment, and it has to be mailed tomorrow morning, so this will have to be a quick note. The rain didn't materialize—instead we had a beautiful day, too good for you to have missed. Dynamiting started early—the men as happy about it as the little boys. Everyone danced and shouted and waved red flags. Not much damage to the rocks, but great good to everyone. This afternoon I worked with Howard digging out rocks, and am dead tired, like a chump. Walter Pierce [a neighbor] has noticed that cars slow up as they pass our place, and has been studying over it. This afternoon he an-

---

2. Minnie, a black dachshund bitch.

nounced that he at last knew the reason. It is because our field is the biggest plowed piece in this part of the county, he says. . . . Joe is fine— was host to large numbers of itinerant croquet players this afternoon— and tonight sat by the radio listening to a sob ballad about a little boy named Joe who was everything to his mother. He was visibly affected. It's quite cold tonight, and I have a fire. Frost is predicted for some sections. We miss you and will be looking for you back.

Love,
Andy

To KATHARINE S. WHITE

[North Brooklin, Me.]
[October 14, 1940]
Monday night

Dear K:

We had a beautiful drive home, with Joe scarcely able to sit it out, for thinking about his eel traps. We stopped last night at Concord and made an early start this morning. . . .

Lawrence was here to welcome Joe back, with the sensational news that all the eels except two had escaped from the car. It's either sabotage or a faulty car. The grim work of catching them all over again has begun.[1]

I have a letter from Fred Allen (Hartman is in Atlantic City again, where his roots seem to be—I think he must model in sand on the side) saying that he cut two sentences out of my piece about automobile design, because they "seem to me to be libelous on their face" and be- cause "they would probably make it impossible for us ever to get a line of automobile advertising again."[2] It seems odd to me that it is "libel" when I say that it is hard to back an automobile without running over your own dog or child. I am just back from a thousand-mile drive, and the only trouble with my piece is that it is an understatement. Twice on the trip I had to send Joe out of the car, to wig-wag instructions to me during commonplace maneuvers.

I'll send you some mail in the morning, and will attend to the grape harvest.

Lots of love,
Andy

PS. Am being very courteous to Fred during your absence, out of respect.

—————————

1. A "car" is a floating wooden crate for holding live lobsters—or, in this case, live eels. Lawrence Matthews was Joel White's best friend at this time.

2. Frederick Lewis Allen edited White's "One Man's Meat" pieces when Lee Hartman was absent. In this case, White thought he overstepped.

To BERNARD DEVOTO

North Brooklin, Maine
18 October 1940

Dear Mr. DeVoto:

This must mean you. Apparently this reader begins at the beginning of my department and goes through to the end of yours without catching his breath at your by-line.[1] What do you say to union now?

Yrs,
E. B. White

To FREDERICK LEWIS ALLEN

North Brooklin, Me.
[October 20?, 1940]

Dear Fred:

I am a fairly good natured guy but not about modern automobiles. The modern car is not only an atrocious piece of designing, it symbolizes the degeneracy that the magazine boys are yapping about. It is dishonest (all this nutty emphasis on streamlining is so much bilge) and it is deadly. My 1939 Plymouth, bought in the summer of 1938, had three dented fenders before the dawn of the year in which the car was supposed to have been made. These busted fenders were contributed by my wife, a careful woman 5 feet 2 inches high. She dented the fenders because she has to guess where she is in relation to the tangible world, and her guesswork is not always one hundred percent accurate. My own guesswork is a good deal better than hers because I have been driving ever since I was taken off the breast and put on solids; but the fact that driving becomes increasingly a matter of guesswork makes me very, very mad. I am just back from a 900 mile drive, and twice during that drive I had to let my son out of the car so that he could direct me, by hand signals, into or out of a narrow spot. Only a man of rather childish faith dares back a modern car without a stooge to give him the All Clear.

I have just read the New Yorker's motor show department, and it is a lot of crap. The fact is, cars are less good looking than they were in 1926. They look like a badly laid egg, or a torpedo that didn't quite jell. They are a mass of unrelated chromium bands and miscellaneous ellipses. Mechanically they are practically perfect (except that they haven't enough clearance and get badly injured the minute they leave the tar) but what good is a mechanically perfect thing if the operator is victimized by it?

Greyhound buses, and some trucks, have seen the light and are

1. DeVoto's column "The Easy Chair" followed "One Man's Meat" in the layout of *Harper's*.

putting the driver in a forward position where he can have a look around. But I can't afford a Greyhound bus. My automobile doesn't allow me a view of the road, and my magazine doesn't allow me to get sore about it. As Bert Lahr used to say, I'm in a quarry.

Andy

As punishment for your removing two sentences that were not libelous and that you were scared to print on account of hurting advertisers' feelings, I am enclosing some extra homework for you.

To GLUYAS WILLIAMS

North Brooklin, Maine
[December 25, 1940]
Christmas night

Dear Gluyas:

Have just been through "Fellow Citizens" (by Gluyas Williams, Doubleday, Doran) and I am impressed and felt I should tell you so, even at the tag end of this feast day. Probably a million American males have known the child in the seat ahead, but you were the guy that got it down on paper. Benchley certainly did a nice clean cut job in the introduction and to it we would like to add our amen. May the Lord give you strength forever!

We've had quite a nice Christmas (I spent mine mostly with animals, which is a help); a complete attendance and a white countryside, with enough snow on the roads for sleigh riding behind an old horse named Fanny—not without reason. Many rather simple people presented us with many rather simple gifts, which pleased us inordinately (Kay has just this minute opened a box containing a venison pie and 2 cactus blossoms, from the lady who does our washing), and if it weren't for the generally diseased condition of the world, we would feel that our cup runneth over. Ate our own goose and drank some American "burgundy."

Lots of luck to your book and a happy new year to all,

Yrs,
Andy

To KATHARINE S. WHITE

North Brooklin, Maine
[Spring 1941]
Tues morning

Dear K:

This is one of those mornings, the decibels working up to a crescendo, with many visiting boys all of them named Hawless. Dogs bark, sheep cry, domestics chatter, Howard and I stand three feet apart and yell directions at each other, the water pump and the coffee grinder run incessantly, and the young crows cry for the old life they once knew. You don't know about the crows, I guess. We have crows, now. Joe located a nest (in the tallest spruce in the county), ascended, and brought back two babies, one for himself and one for Lawrence. He immediately sat down and wrote Lawrence the triumphal news. The crows live in the woodshed, in a crow's nest. Fred knows about it.

Your letter just came, and I'll be in Ellsworth at 8:40 on Saturday. I sent off what mail there was for you yesterday, and today there seems to be nothing of any consequence. I'm keeping right after the anthology work, and so far have eliminated a lot of stuff but haven't turned up much of any value. I have out practically every bound volume in the place, and am working on them day times, and the smaller lighter books at night, when I can't hold such heavy weights. . . .

Everything is fine here and will be finer when we get you back again. My neck is gradually solidifying [from arthritis], and I look forward (but not much) to a life of looking straight ahead.

The crows have pale blue eyes.

My goodness, the boys are now cutting the lawn.

Lots of love,
Andy

To GEOFFREY HELLMAN

North Brooklin, Maine
24 June 1941

Dear Hellman:

Maybe we haven't mentioned that we (my wife and I) are getting together a fine large book of American humor. Anyway, we are. We'd like to use the first half of your profile of Dr. Chapman, the bullfinch man, ending with the sentence "He had decided to become a full time birdman." Also your casual about the lost Taft alumni. Will you permit us to?

The payment is like New Yorker scrapbook and album payment— royalties being divvied up among the contributors. This is (I think) to be a three dollar book, with fifteen percent royalty. Editors get half, writers get half. It ought to make you very very rich and happy. It is, conservatively speaking, driving us nuts. But even so, I think maybe it will turn out to be a good book. Title: *A Subtreasury of American Humor*.

You will probably soon receive the customary permission request from Coward-McCann, but I am writing you direct to put the old personal squeeze on you. In a sense you have us in a corner, as I would not con-

sider issuing a book of humor which did not contain Dr. Chapman occupying the nests of some of the larger birds himself.

White

To HAROLD ROSS

North Brooklin
25 June [1941?]

Dear Mr. Ross:

Thanks for offering me the chance to write the foreword for the
soldier drawing book, but I think somebody else better do it. I feel out
of touch with the drawing situation and with soldiers, too.

Your other letter received, about my covering the war for N&C. I
have been turning this over for two or three days, hoping I might see
some way it could be managed but I don't. In one respect I would like
to do it, because quite often in the last three years I have wished for a
more immediate outlet than a monthly column; when I get steamed up
about something I don't like to wait five weeks, or is it seven. Seven. On
the other hand I find it very difficult to write comment from here. Most
of the stuff I have written for Harper's has not been commentary—it has
been description or narration or specialized criticism. Based on what is
happening to me where I am.

But there are other reasons why the thing seems impossible. I think
the comment page, as presently managed, is discouraging for a writer.
(I have thought this for a long time, maybe ten years.) I believe that
an editorial page should be one of two things: either a signed page, for
which one man would take the responsibility, or an unsigned page
designed to express a sort of group opinion and which would be considered sufficiently important to warrant the managerial staff's meeting
and discussing it each week, to give aid and counsel and ideas, and
where opinions would generalize in group fashion. For a while in the
early days, this was done. But then when the magazine got into long
pants, Comment was just handed over to somebody (eventually me)
and except for a perfunctory clipping service no other aid or stimulus
was provided. After a while it got to be a curiously demoralizing literary
exercise, because it was impossible to tell who was talking. When I write
something I like to be out in the open—either as an individual or as
the interpreter for an articulate group. But comment gave me a cloudy
feeling all the time, and still does when I try it. A comment paragraph
seems about 90 percent me, and 10 percent Santa Claus or something.
I feel like an overcoat with a velvet collar.

I'm sure I've gone over this ground with you before, but still feel
the same and am repeating because your letter seems to call for an

answer. For my own part, I don't see any solution. I am, I guess, a one-paper man. When I was doing Comment for you, I put everything into it and wrote nothing for any other paper. Now I'm doing this Harper column, and am putting my stuff into that. I'm no good at spreading myself around. Very concentrated fellow.

Lately I haven't felt sympathetic enough toward the NYer to make me hot to produce anything. Sometimes it says things that annoy me—usually not because of what they are but because of the way they are said. And other times it fails to say things that seem to need saying. The war is so damn near that it is no longer possible to use printer's ink in place of blood in a man's circulatory system, and Tilley's hat and butterfly return to plague us all. I couldn't bounce off a paragraph a week on the subject of the war, full of "we's" and "us's," when I wasn't sure what key we were all trying to play in.

Writing anything at all is a hell of a chore for me, closely related to acid indigestion, and I take it seriously enough so that I don't want to maneuver myself into any literary stance which is as indistinct and badly defined as comment-writing, because I know it would make me quite sick, and probably my readers, too. Harper's isn't as much fun, and I sometimes feel like a stranger and lonely, but at least I seem to know who is writing and it isn't Jack Frost.

Thanks again for the offer, which I set store by.

White

To HAROLD ROSS

[North Brooklin, Me.]
[June 26? 1941]
Thursday night

Dear Ross:

I think I will come Sunday night, getting to New York on Monday morning. I won't be able to do a great deal of work on comment, but maybe can help out. Primarily I have to finish up the book we are working on and will be putting in practically all my time on that.

Got your letter. As far as New Yorker policy goes, I am as bewildered as anybody else. I believe in certain principles of life and thought, and in times like these all I can do is reaffirm this belief insofar as it seems to bear on the news, or the news on it. Sometimes this "moral" frame seems incompatible, or inconsistent, with skepticism. A skeptic doesn't like to believe anything, for fear it will ruin his intelligence (or his backhand drive), and on the other hand, a believer can't be too skeptical or it affects his faith. That is why everybody is all mixed up.

The way to do, if I write any comment, is to print what you believe in and throw the rest to hell. It is the American system and I like it.

White

P.S. I will be domiciled in town, not in country. I might, however, like to take a quick browse through your library of humor, if such exists.

To KATHARINE S. WHITE

Hotel New Weston
New York
[July 1, 1941]
Tuesday night

Dear K:

Things are progressing—I have my Harper piece half done and hope to finish it tomorrow. If I do it will be the first time in history it has been completed before the fateful 10th.

The heat is tremendous, extremely moist and oppressive and thundery, but I haven't minded it much, just sitting around the hotel room in a pair of drawers. There is a cross draft, like a sirocco (or is it a simoon?) through the areaway. The air-cooled places are almost untenable, the difference is so great.

Had dinner with Ik last night and Ross is taking me tomorrow. He invited me to the country but I declined. He wants me to write some comment for them this week, but it is early closing and I don't see how I'm going to do any. . . .

Saw Gus today and he tells me that the *New Yorker* had a cancellation yesterday—too pro-British and too pro-war. My! However, in the newsreel I observed that the audience hissed the German troops and clapped the British tanks. Dr. Flick[1] reports (from Hyde Park) that the President looks quite ill. . . .

Ik has bought a food freezer (sort of a home Birdseye unit) and he and Betty are solidifying their peas and beans and chickens, sub zero, instead of canning them. All right until the electricity goes off some balmy spring evening, and botulism sets in. Ik has offered me a job on the New Yorker Magazine, which I thought was white of him. Made me feel like a boy again.

Lots of love to you and Joe, and I'll be looking for you next week.

Andy

---

1. Alexander Flick, Lobrano's father-in-law, New York State Historian.

To KATHARINE S. WHITE

Hotel New Weston
New York
[July 5, 1941]
Saturday

Dear K:

. . . Don't fret about the hay, and if Joe's crow is disturbing every-body, it should be got rid of. You sounded so harassed and turbulent this morning over the phone, I worry about you.

After the broadcast ["Information Please"] last night, Ross took me along with Gunther, Fadiman, Duranty, Pringle, Pringle's Miss Emery, the other Surry girl, and a Mr. Balderston, author of Berkeley Square. Fadiman was simply swell, and while everybody else was shouting and arguing, he quietly gave me dozens of tips for the anthology, which I carefully noted down with a pencil borrowed from Duranty who was on pins and needles for fear he wasn't going to get it (the pencil) back. He's a fussy little man. He and Gunther are not pessimistic about the war, but differ widely as to strategy and aims.

Love,
Andy

• White often had an urge to revisit places he had known at an earlier time. In the summer of 1941 he went back to the Belgrade Lakes, taking with him his young son. It was after this visit that White wrote "Once More to the Lake," for his column in Harper's (October, 1941). The piece has been one of the most widely reprinted of White's essays.

To KATHARINE S. WHITE

Bear Spring Camps
[July 24, 1941]
Thurs. afternoon

Dear K:

Very hot here today, and everyone is in the lake, lying around in the shallows like so many frogs. Joe has been in for more than an hour without showing the slightest tendency to come out. He is a devotee of fresh water swimming at the moment, and it really does seem good to have warm bathing for a change. Very relaxing.

Got your letter this morning, and it was nice to hear from home. If Joe has any head lice, they are a waterlogged lot at the moment. But if the crow is a nuisance, I would like you to get rid of him. There is no point in harboring anything that just gives people trouble. Get Howard to take the crow away and turn it loose.

Joe and I went fishing last night after supper and caught 5 white perch. We have been eating fish steadily—of our own catching. We now have a perfectly enormous outboard motor on our rowboat, which I am unable to start, except semi-occasionally. This is deeply disappointing to Joe. When the motor does choose to start, it leaps into a frightful speed, usually knocking us both down in the boat. Negotiations are under way to exchange it for a smaller pet. I must say I miss the old one-cylinder gas engine of yesteryear which made a fine peaceful sound across the water. This is too much like living on the edge of an airfield.

I haven't started on the preface [to *A Subtreasury of American Humor*] yet, but will soon. I'm not going to read your notes until I've written something, as it is easier for me that way.

This place is as American as a drink of Coca Cola. The white collar family having its annual liberty. I must say it seems sort of good. Raymond Duncan is here in a brown smock, and Dorothy Lamour, and Eddie Cantor and the Peterkins. Everybody you've ever seen on Main Street or on Elm Avenue is here. Gebert is here.[1] He just came in with 5 bass and his little girl carrying the landing net.

News is now being spread all through the camp that it is 106° in Bangor. Bangor is a great comfort to Maine people in hot weather.

Lots of love from us both. Please relax and take life easy. This is vacation time in the U.S.

Andy

To KATHARINE S. WHITE
[North Brooklin, Me.]
[Summer 1941]
Monday night

Dear K

Here it is, and if my bones weren't proliferating it would be better, but it is the best I can do in this summer of 1941. Get right after it and give it the works. I trust you absolutely to doctor it any way you think it should be doctored. There are probably parts which should come out and things that should go in, so pull them out and put them in. My only request is this: that if you have any additions that could as well go

---

1. Actually, a camper who resembled *The New Yorker*'s William Gebert—big cigar, wise look.

into a sectional preface as into this general preface, you save them for the sections.[1]

The most important thing, of course, is that you bring a ruthlessly critical mind to my facts and my theories in this preface. I haven't had much time to think things over and I am probably all wet on a lot of things in here. If a lot of this stuff seems wrong or foolish or childish, just take it out. I would much prefer that the preface be short and contain one or two incontestable facts and a sound observation or two, than that it run along at some length and just be a lot of twaddle. In my present state of mind, I can't tell how much of this is sound or true.

I had a somewhat longer and more elaborate ending to the piece, but took it off, and I think it is better this way. . . .

I decided that the way to handle Irvin Cobb was with a deep silence, like the grave. I didn't even get the word "genial" in anywhere, although I fully intended to, and perhaps can yet.

I'll send along the short prefaces as soon as I can knock them out, which ought to be tomorrow morning. Things are OK here, although I had a nightmare last night which did me in—all about a rat that wouldn't go away from me because it wasn't afraid of me. I awoke with a wrench and a start and a terrible buzzing in the head, and for a while I thought perhaps the Chair of Belgrade had really got in its work.[2] But the buzzing left before morning. Min and the pups are fine. I weighed them today. Both girls weigh 16 ounces. Boy weighs 18. They are just one week old. Min eats well, ate all her own supper tonight and hooked part of Raffles'.[3] Walter Pierce mowed the field today and it looks like a golf green tonight. The rain has helped it a lot and it is going to come out better than I had hoped. Even the upper piece has begun to catch on. Joe is fine and is crazy about "The Yearling." Gives it highest praise. He already wants to sleep in the woods again, and he and Lawrence were bug-proofing their igloo today. I told him he would have to wait till you get back, as I think he needs a few more nights sleep before another bender.

Lots of love,
Andy

1. White had completed the first draft of the Preface to *A Subtreasury of American Humor*. The "sectional" prefaces in the book describe different kinds of humor.

2. White's stay in Belgrade had been interrupted by an accident. He was watching an evening movie in the recreation hall when a pile of heavy benches came loose and fell down. One of the benches struck him on the back of the neck, stunning him. He and Joel left the next morning for home.

3. A wire-haired fox terrier White had won on a 25-cent ticket in a raffle. He took the puppy home in his pocket and gave him to Joel.

• *Harry Lyford's friendship with White dated from 1918, when Lyford was a private and White a corporal in the Student Army Training Corps at Cornell, where the soldiers were housed in fraternity houses converted to barracks. After Pearl Harbor, Lyford wrote his corporal, suggesting that they again stand firm against the enemy.*

To **HARRY LYFORD**

North Brooklin, Maine
28 December 1941

Private Lyford, step forward and take that cheese out of your mouth. At ease, men, this is another war (and another Lyford)—oh the same distant sound of carnage, the same revelry in the canteens, but still, another war. What a day it was for me, Lyford, when you went Deke, my rear rank pillaged, robbed of its punch. They were always tricking me that way: I would develop a Lyford from raw stuff, groom him, sharpen his nerves, toughen him so his spine crackled from the rigidity of every occasion—and then poof, he would be hustled across the street to another Greek letter society. That was my war. I presume it was your war, too. So you liked old L Company better, did you? Well, I did time in the Chi Psi house, too, although I'm darned if I can remember what letter of the alphabet it was. All I remember was the palatial privies, and the enormous responsibility of being NCOICQ among those endless urinals. The war was made of porcelain, in those days.

I don't know quite what it is made of today and am trying to find out, as I take it you are too. My wife and boy and I have been living in this little village in Maine for the past four years. We used to come here in summer, and got more and more negligent about returning to town in the fall, until one year we just never did go back. My wife quit her *New Yorker* job, retaining only a sort of half time long range connection, and I quit mine except for the newsbreaks, or justifiers, which come in by the thousands and which I have always edited. *Harper's* gave me a department in their dignified rag, and I have been making my living by describing my antics with sheep and poultry to an audience which appears to be half envious, half contemptuous. Our farm is a salt water one, the pasture ends in clam flats. Across the bay are the high peaks of Mount Desert Island, where rich folks rusticate in summertime in their yachting caps and their memories of Victorian pomp. Here on this side of the bay are lobstermen and scallop fishermen and farmers, a rather down-at-the-heel place which we are very fond of. The pastures are rocky and poor, and there is none of Wisconsin's lush and fertile beauty. (I sometimes wish there were about three acres of it mixed in with my fifty acre place.)

I'm in a quandary about the war—or, as Bert Lahr says, I'm in a quarry. Maine suddenly seems too remote to satisfy my nervous desire to help in a bad situation. My reason tells me that I can contribute most effectively by staying right here and continuing to produce large quantities of hens' eggs and to write my stuff every month; but the human system seems to demand something which has more of the air of bustle and confusion. I may try for a job in Washington, in the high realms of propaganda. Or the draft board, locally, may settle the whole matter for me with one quick swoop. I'm only 42, and most of my teeth still show through the gooms. Here, anybody with natural teeth is taken for the army. There are only three or four of us in the whole county. My wife being an earning girl, gives me no deferment, and I expect none. The corporal may indeed rise again. I pray God you will be standing behind me. Wearing a white plume. A bold white plume, my Cyrano!

It was swell to hear from you.

Corporal White

●   *The war brought the Whites back to New York to a series of furnished apartments, and to* The New Yorker, *whose editorial staff had been decimated by the mobilization. In the spring of 1943, White notified Frederick Lewis Allen that he was quitting the column "One Man's Meat." He had had almost five years of it, had lived continuously in Maine during that period, and some of the essays were out in book form.*

The family was growing up. Nancy had married Louis Stableford in 1941 and followed him from one military base to another. Kitty (Katharine S.) Stableford, the first grandchild, was born in Topeka. Roger married Evelyn Baker, a Boston girl, in 1942 and after a stretch at Lowry Field in Denver disappeared overseas—to Hickam Field in Hawaii, where he became an editor of the Air Force magazine, Brief. *Joel enrolled in Exeter in the fall of 1943.*

*During the war White began experimenting with short editorials on world government. The New Yorker ran most of them, although Ross regarded White's position as Utopian and impractical. "As for me," White says, "I also regarded world government as a Utopian idea, but it struck me that absolute national sovereignty was about as impractical as anything that could be dreamed up, and I still think so." One of the Comments, which ran in the December 25, 1943, issue of the magazine, became the title essay of a collection—*The Wild Flag—*put together in 1946 by Houghton Mifflin.*

It was during the war years, too, that White finally completed the first of his books for children, Stuart Little, *which was published in 1945.*

TO EUGENE SAXTON

North Brooklin, Maine
28 January 1942

Dear Gene:

I'm coming to town with my book under my arm next week and hope to see you. Am pleased with the way the thing has shaped up, after some preliminary confusion and discouragement.

As it now stands, the book is made up of about a 75% selection from my total *Harper's Magazine* output, plus two pieces from the *New Yorker* which seemed to fit into the scheme, namely a piece about Daniel Webster and the Hay Fever, and a piece about the opening of the World of Tomorrow in Flushing. Both pieces were written within the period of my *Harper* department, and both are written in the first person singular.

Thus the book shapes up as a sort of informal journal of the three years before the war. It is arranged chronologically. Each piece will have a date and a title. The length, roughly estimated, is around 75,000 words. I have written a total of about 100,000 words for the Meat department and, as I say, this selection will use about three-fourths of the whole amount.

I have some ideas concerning this book which I want to discuss with you. For one thing, although the majority of the pieces were written from my home in Maine, I think it would be a mistake to put the book out as another one of those Adventures in Contentment, or as an Escape from the City, or How to Farm with a Portable Corona. This is a book of essays on a wide variety of subjects, both urban and rural; it is not a tract on subsistence farming, and it is not a handbook of retreat. It is, as you know, intensely personal, but not designed to prove anything. It is colored by my New England surroundings, but it is not dedicated to them. In short, it is a book about me-and-life, and should not be tagged with a country label. (You may wish to differ, of course, but I think when you go over the manuscript you'll see what I mean.)

Is there any chance of spring publication, rather than waiting till fall? It might be a better plan if it were physically possible. I seem to recall that you said fall, but this is a timely book.

My title, so far, is "One Man's Meat," but I am trying others in hopes of improving it. Am against prettying the book up with wood cuts, but think probably a wood block jacket of some sort would be right.

I have to be in Washington this Saturday and Sunday on a government job I am doing, but expect to be in New York the first of the week and will probably stay for perhaps ten days. Haven't thanked you yet for your very generous gift of books at Christmas, but haven't written any thank-you letters yet this year. We farmers are always behind, you know. If we lived to be a hundred we'd never catch up.

Yrs,
Andy

P.S. Erratum: there are 3 New Yorker pieces, not 2.

• *After Pearl Harbor the government decided to get out a pamphlet on the Four Freedoms enunciated by President Roosevelt in his State of the Union speech of January 1941. The pamphlet was to be widely distributed and to be translated into many languages. White was invited to Washington to help with the project, along with Malcolm Cowley, Reinhold Niebuhr, and Max Lerner. Archibald MacLeish, then Librarian of Congress, was "ringmaster."*

White was recruited to write the Freedom of Speech section; subsequently he was relieved of that task and put to work doing a rewrite job on the whole thing. Two of his friends, Henry Pringle and Jack Fleming, were at work with the Office of Facts and Figures in Washington, and it was they who advised MacLeish to give White the rewrite assignment.

To KATHARINE S. WHITE

Carlton Hotel, Wash.
[January 31?, 1942]
Saturday night

Dear K:

This has been quite a day and I still don't know what to think about our emergency government, which seems at first glimpse frightening and wasteful and ineffective. The four freedoms showed up on time, in the persons of Max Lerner and Reinhold Niebuhr (who is some customer) and Malcolm and me. I could see that the others had been through the mill before—they seemed to know their way around the Office of Facts and Figures. Malcolm greeted me, deafer than ever, wearing an ear instrument. Henry Pringle was sitting at one of the desks, passing things to a stenographer. The place is vast and windy, like a terminal. I was taken around and introduced to dozens of research workers and borrowed writers, including the Miss Wolf (now Mrs. Kuhn) who worked at the *New Yorker* in the Ingersoll era. Malcolm had an enormous folder, crammed with freedom stuff. At eleven we went into a conference room, vast and terrible, which turned out also to be MacLeish's office. We sat about a table and the others talked about the project, in vague terms as far as the job went, but in the most awful intellectual detail, all of it over my head. . . . Behind me, Mac-Leish was sending messages through an automatic speaker to a secretary beyond a glass partition, but the speaker didn't work and the secretary would keep coming in. The pamphlet which we were supposed to be preparing was, as far as I could make out, intended to give popular form to the President's war aims, that is, the four freedoms which he mentioned in his speech on the state of the nation; but if the people understand it, they are better than I am. I couldn't understand anything, and wished I was home. They seemed to wait for me to say something about freedom of speech, but I kept quiet, not knowing anything to say, except I asked about how many words it was supposed to be and when it would have to be in, but nobody knew. Then it turned out we were all going to MacLeish's house for luncheon. They talked about assigning me some research people to prepare whatever I wanted prepared, so I finally told Jack Fleming that I was probably out of my class, as I wouldn't know what to ask a research person to look up. He said not to pay any attention to the others. He introduced me to Marty Summers, who is a friend of Joe Sayre's, and whom I liked. Then we all drove out to Georgetown to the MacLeish house—Fleming, Summers, the 4 freedoms, and our host. MacLeish looks a little like Doctor Devol, and he is some smooth poet. We had sherry and then went in to lunch—a very special noodle dish with sour cream and grated cheese, then ham and mushrooms and Schoonmaker red wine. MacLeish has a very disarming manner, a blend of friendliness and aloofness, guaranteed to set you at ease. He took charge immediately of the conversation and stated the project before ever the first spoonful was spooned up. He made the gathering seem as though history was being written there in that room and that upon our shoulders had fallen the task of translating the greatest document of all time. His most adroit feat of the meal was the way he relieved me, almost imperceptibly, of the job of writing the section on freedom of speech. All of a sudden, it turned out that I had been relieved. It was so painless I hardly knew it was being done myself. He simply turned it over to Lerner, as he ticked off the various parts of the pamphlet. It was, he said, obviously the easiest of the four assignments and Lerner had written it so many times he could turn it out in half an hour. My duties were to go over all four freedoms with an eye to improving the form of the writing.

We withdrew for coffee and more conversation. I couldn't see any reason why I had come to Washington, and still can't. I asked Marty Summers afterward why he thought they had taken freedom of speech away from me, and he said he thought it was because Fleming had whispered to MacLeish that I couldn't get mixed up in any research department.

After coffee we sat around and suggested people who should be "called in" to review the manuscript, people from as far as California were suggested and solemnly noted down. The "methodology" of the preparation of the pamphlet was discussed. It was decided to meet in Washington again in two weeks. (A mere 750 miles, each way, for me.)

At 5:30, Henry Pringle came to the hotel here for a drink, bringing with him Mr. Hamburger of the *New Yorker* (now of Facts and Figures) and another F&F man whose name I didn't get. I gather that they are all $8,000 men, and are doing various informational jobs. Henry flashed a transportation pass book, good for any amount of travel at government expense, which he said was the fifth freedom—freedom of egress.

I am bewildered, as I said, about the trip here. It is always sobering to encounter the intellectual idealists at work, for they seem to live in a realm of their own, making their plans for the world in much the same way that any common tyrant does. The conversation today reminded me a little of the early New Deal period when Wallace was talking about one God and one king—and it all seems so far removed from the people, who are all full of tiny faults and virtues and whose name is Schmalz and Henderson. It is really kind of funny: the President, in a time of extreme gravity, draws in skeleton form a wholly Utopian picture and now it is up to the writers to state it more in detail without either embarrassing the government or being so specific as to make it controversial. (This is particularly true of Freedom from Want—which is a nice freedom if you can get it.)

Although the extravagance and the homely pomp of today's performance has jarred me, it is not a wholly discouraging scene. The President's technique of surrounding himself with his severest critics has a certain democratic healthiness to it.

[No signature]

To KATHARINE S. WHITE

Hotel New Weston
[New York]
[February 4, 1942]
Wednesday

Dear K:

Just had an idea. You remember the water colors Henry Poor had left over from Ethan Frome—I know he sent us one as a Christmas card, but weren't there others too? Just occurred to me there might be a jacket there for my book, if there were no conflict as to publishers, etc., and if Henry approved the idea, and if the picture seemed to fit the book. Anyway, if you happen to know where those pictures are, how about digging them out and having a look.[1] I am going to see Gene Saxton tomorrow for lunch, or shall we say for "claret." Last night I worked all evening finishing up the titling and the arranging and numbering, etc. So it is all ready to turn in.

Your two letters have come, and I'm dreadfully sorry to hear about all the pains and colds and everything, it is so discouraging. I had plenty of trouble, too, over the weekend, as you have probably gathered from the nasty little note I managed to get off to you yesterday. The thing would be funny if it were a slightly less responsible sort of job (maybe it is funny anyway), but I am now left with thousands of un-transcribed notes—the kind of thing you scribble on your program in a dark theatre—and the burden of collecting these into a document which will suit the President and the Supreme Court Justices and Mr. Churchill and Aunt Poo, and which will explain to a great many young men why they are about to get stuck in the stomach, and which will reconcile Max Lerner with Felix Frankfurter and myself with God. This is a very sobering assignment and only once in a while do I think it is funny. It is dangerous to get playing with words on the very highest of planes, because they become (unless you are careful) like checkers men and eventually take charge. But I am determined that there will be no pretty writing, and an absolute minimum of statements which I do not fully understand myself. Just how I can interpret the concept of freedom from want, when economics are so mysterious to me, is something I have hardly dared think about. But I've been brooding some about it, and it seems to me that the promise which was made to the world by the Four Freedoms statement was justified (at least in the "want" clause) by the new feeling of responsibility which is evident in government. The awful tangle of bureaus and offices in Washington is depressing and discouraging, but as you become involved in it you begin to feel encouraged when you see what a sustained and determined attempt is being made to solve the old riddles. However clumsy and messy it is, the sheer decency of the program is inescapable, and sometimes impressive.

One of the people called in to offer suggestions was Hamilton Fish Armstrong, whom I liked. I talked to him only rather briefly but he seemed like a person I would get on with, and I'm thinking of looking him up here in New York for a criticism of the manuscript when I get something on paper. Of course, what I fear will happen to this writing

---

1. Henry Varnum Poor had done the illustrations for the Limited Editions Club edition of *Ethan Frome*. Nothing came of the idea of using one of the leftover illustrations on the jacket of *One Man's Meat*.

job is what always happens to anything that I don't get going on right away, but let hang around to cool for a week or two. I never have been able to revive anything. But I haven't written a word on this, largely because of the way MacLeish arranged the whole thing. I always write a thing first and think about it afterward, which is not a bad procedure, because the easiest way to have consecutive thoughts is to start putting them down. But with this project there have been mountains and oceans of talk, and dozens of people and shades of opinion. The manuscripts turned in by the experts are pretty forbidding and dreary, and more are coming. I finally piped up, on Sunday morning when our brilliant company was gathered in the leather and mahogany sanctuary of the Librarian of Congress, and suggested that Malcolm Cowley's piece be copied and circulated to everybody, and that everyone should turn in a brief comment or criticism of it which would be a help to the man who had to do the writing on "want." This seemed like a bright idea to the rewrite man in me, as I was hoping to get other people into my own predicament, the necessity of saying the words on paper. It is being done, but I guess it was regarded as a tactless or presumptuous suggestion. Poor Malcolm is taking quite a beating, anyway, with the Dies boys after him and Pegler sniping at him. I'm sorry for him.

Two or three times during these proceedings I was tempted to ask why, if the pamphlet was to be an extension and an interpretation of the President's formula, we shouldn't just go and ask him what he meant. But I shut up about that. My own position through all these conferences was really awfully embarrassing—all these bigwigs who had given up their time and taken long rail journeys, to talk about abstract matters, and they kept glancing at me to be sure that I was getting the full significance of what they had gone to so much trouble to contribute. A lot of it was just nonsense. I mean, I don't think there is much sense in calling a meeting of super-intellects on a Sunday morning in the Library of Congress to discuss freedom of speech for a pamphlet which is to instruct and inspire filling station helpers and manicurists mostly. It struck me that it was simply MacLeish investing his own job with some velvet trappings. Freedom of speech is old stuff and the record is pretty clear and available. It was rather disheartening (at that particular session) to see how much acrimony could be developed over fine and delicate points among men who were, presumably, all striving for the same good end. I'm afraid the word Supreme has been a very unfortunate thing in Frankfurter's life—although I never knew him before, and don't really now. He was very anxious to get off the phrase: "steering between vapidity and indiscretion." But I felt he had been working on it for quite some time.

Well, I love my country and I like to live free, and so I haven't given up the job yet. But the nervous strain of the preliminary rounds was too much for my stomach, and all the old dizziness and vapors returned to plague me. Living at the Riggs' was a little difficult because they had only just moved in and had no furniture or cook. But Mrs. Rigg is terribly nice, and I was glad to be there.[2] Whenever Bun needs money, he gives a pint of blood and gets 25 dollars. Then he eats apricots to make more blood. . . .

I think the person for MacLeish on this job is Gypsy Rose Lee. She could handle it better than I'll be able to. Lots of love to you and Joey.

Andy

To JOHN R. FLEMING

Hotel New Weston
New York, N.Y.
[February 5?, 1942]
Thursday

Dear Jack:

Got your stuff today, and thanks. That issue of the *Land Policy Review* has bucked me up enormously because of a little filler at the bottom of page 24, where it says:

> The keeping of sheep has made
> characters so strong, so brave,
> manly, and true that they have
> changed the history of the world.

That gave me courage to go ahead. After all, I still have three weeks before the lambs begin to come, and the history of the world (if tonight's *World-Telegram* can be believed) badly needs changing.

Lots of love,
Andy

To KATHARINE S. WHITE

Hotel New Weston
[February 8, 1942]
Sunday morning

Dear K

Whatever else comes of this job, I certainly don't want you and Joe to delay coming to town. I'm more anxious about Joe's health[1] than I

---

2. During his stay in Washington, White had been a house guest in the Georgetown home of his friend H. K. Rigg's mother.

1. Joel had a serious sinus condition for which surgery had been recommended. Eventually the Whites decided against an operation, and the condition cured itself.

am about Batavia, and more eager to see you than to save the world. (The chances are better, too.) As far as disturbing a writer at his work, this hotel bedroom might just as well have been filled with howling monkeys this past week, for all the work I've been able to get done. . . .

Jim has kept phoning me (I guess he keeps phoning everybody these days) and I finally went up to his house last night, where there were an English major and a DeGaullist and their wives and we had a long international discussion, from which Jamie left the world in smouldering ruins as usual. . . . Jim is very grey, but is lively and in pretty good spirits. Helen gave him a mandolin for Christmas, and I pleased him by being able to play it, tremolo and all.

I shall finish up my *Harper* piece today, turn it in tomorrow and get started on the other job. Had lunch with Mike Galbreath the other day and they are expecting a baby next month.

Lots of love and please don't put off coming, as it is a ridiculous idea. Unsound.

Love,
Andy

To KATHARINE S. WHITE

Hotel New Weston
New York, N.Y.
[February 9, 1942]
Monday

Dear K

We are invited to the Saxtons for Monday evening, which I am recording so that I won't forget.

Gene says my book is eligible for the Harper prize. From the tone of his voice, I should say that its chances are something less than good, or terrible.

At his house last night I described in great detail the rejuvenation of the Brooklin Library (by you) and everybody was much interested and enthusiastic about Miss Dollard.[1] Also Nathaniel Peffer was much interested in Aunt Poo, as well he might be.[2]

Love,
Andy

---

1. "Miss Annie Dollard," White relates, "was in charge of the library when we came to live in Brooklin. She was a tiny spinster with firm convictions about which books were fit to read. The library had acquired *The Grapes of Wrath*, but Annie took it off the shelf and placed it on her chair and sat on it. That solved that."

2. Nathaniel Peffer, professor at Columbia, was an expert on the Orient.

To JOHN R. FLEMING

25 W 43
NYC
[February 21?, 1942]
Saturday

Dear Jack:

Report to the nation—

The piece is pretty near done, and I think Washington's Birthday will see it completed. I don't believe Washington himself ever faced greater odds than I have faced in trying to pull so many shades of opinion into a harmonious design. I would rather try to throw a dollar across the Potomac. Make it two dollars.

After the piece is done, it will have to go through my typewriter again, to take off some rough edges, introduce a little grammar, and destroy the last trace of pretty writing. That will mean another couple of days. I think, then, that I can send you something by about the 24th or 25th of this month. I had hoped to get it written more promptly, but for a solid week I was too sick to work, and the rest of the time I've been worrying about my boy, who is now here with me in New York for treatment.

You might pass this word along to Marty [Summers], or to Archie, or to whoever is doing most of the wondering where some results are.

See you soon,
Andy

To JOHN R. FLEMING

The New Yorker
25 West 43rd Street
New York
2 March 1942

Dear Jack:

I sent off the draft by mail to Henry Pringle on Sunday and trust that it has arrived in your office by this time and has sent everybody into gales of laughter.

I expect to be in New York for another ten days or until the doctor gets through doing what he wants to do with Joe. So if I am wanted in Washington to do any more work on the four freedoms, will you let me know as soon as you can. I presume that from now on it will be a matter of undoing White and pinning freedom's pants up again—for which work my services will be far from needed.

The job was pretty tough going, partly because of my ignorance and partly because (from the evidence contained in my notes) the experts managed to cancel each other out and the net result was nobody wanted to say anything on the subject. This left me holding a very odd bag indeed and my attempt to make Milo Perkins and Ham Fish Armstrong into bedfellows using Malcolm's bed will probably take its place alongside those countless other desperate sorties which honest patriots are making these days in their zeal to keep the faith.

Yrs,
Andy

PS. You asked in your letter about expense money. I turned in some railroad receipts to your man, but have not heard anything yet. My application form may have been unsatisfactory, as I failed to fill in the part about having been in jail. Figured it would be bad publicity for your office.

To JOHN R. FLEMING

The New Yorker
25 West 43rd Street
New York
15 April [1942]

Dear Jack:

Thanks for the kind words.

Can't tell you much about what happened to the four freedoms. I saw one of them on 44th Street the other day. Undressed her with my eyes and found her beautiful.

Yrs,
Andy

To HARRY LYFORD

North Brooklin, Maine
19 April 1942

Dear Private:

. . . Your life as small town editor sounds fine—the sort of thing I once thought maybe I would be doing (until I fell in with city slickers and other evil characters in Gotham). You spoke of the "upward grope of the community." Do communities grope upward? I've often wondered. Much of the time they seem just to grope. I am in a little town that is, in a sense, dying on its feet. Last year, one child was born (there are about 700 inhabitants, scattered over quite a large area). One baby. (There were two, as a matter of fact, but only one with proper credentials.) All the young men seem to feel that if they are to amount to anything, they must get out, go somewhere else. That seems wrong, somehow. Every community ought to offer a promising life to its new generation, it seems to me. I am a decentralist, at heart;

I think the business of making the earth produce and bear fruit should be participated in by almost everybody—a much more even distribution of the population.

Heavy snow here today, but it is disappearing fast. I sowed some seed in the field across the road, sowing it on top of "the last snow"—a traditional practice hereabouts. How anybody knows which is the last snow, I have never found out. Last spring it was still spitting snow in May.

We all send loud thanks for the cheese. I can see now why you married a Swiss.

Yrs,
Andy

To EUGENE SAXTON

North Brooklin, Maine
25 April 1942

Dear Gene:

Here is the stuff for the front jacket flap, or flip, or whatever. It is slightly reworded here and there. I guess it'll do very nicely now, if it's OK with you.

That crack about my being "one of our leading essayists" was put in by my wife, who was whistling to keep her courage up. For "one of our leading" read "only remaining." She's just scared.

I hope I didn't gum up everything by wiring you to kill the foreword. I don't really care, one way or another, whether there is a foreword or not—I just didn't want *that* one. I think the book should not be held up too long and will send you another foreword in a day or two. This time I promise it will stay sent.

Sincerely,
Andy

Very balmy here today, lambs jumping, daffodils springing, and a warm summer breeze.

To H. K. RIGG

North Brooklin, Maine
21 May [1942]

Dear Bun:

Glad to hear you're fighting the war in the Marine Division.[1] I'm fighting it with brown hens' eggs, and waiting—a bit nervously—to be drafted. We've been having practice raids here, and I dash

1. Rigg was a lieutenant in the Coast Guard.

around the roads at night blowing a horn and feeling kind of silly. Am also learning to shear sheep. The sheep look as though they'd been through the siege of Corregidor when I get through with them. But wool brings a good price this year.

Haven't had time to miss Astrid yet but that will come later.[2] Incidentally, ask Linton if he won't send me the balance so we can wind up the deal. He wrote me in April saying he would, but I haven't received it.

Roger graduates from Harvard (we hope) this year, so I guess we'll be entraining for Cambridge and class day very shortly. My Washington trips are over for the time being.

Regards to all, yrs,
Andy

To EUGENE SAXTON

North Brooklin, Maine
28 May 1942

Dear Gene:

The author's copies arrived this morning, along with some edible soy bean seeds, and I am dashing this off to tell you that I am delighted with the appearance of the book and think Harper's has done very nicely by me. It looks like the kind of book I might like to read—although I wouldn't know about that without skimming it through.

So well satisfied am I with this book that I wish to place an order for 12 copies, to be sent to me at this address, and at the author's discount. Send bill and I will send check.

Am enclosing, for your amusement, a cutting from Page One of the Ellsworth *American*, to whom you sent a review copy. We don't go in for criticism or subtle nonsense here; when a man has something to sell, we just say so, and in no uncertain terms.

I see that Amy Loveman gave me a nice notice in the B of the MC News.

Sorry you can't be here for the dipping tomorrow. Am using an English dip (Cooper's) which I like partly because it doesn't stain the fleeces and mostly because the instructions on the package contain the word "whilst."

Yrs as ever,
Andy

---

2. *Astrid* had been sold.

To HAROLD ROSS

North Brooklin, Maine
20 September 1942

Dear Mr. R.

Thank you for your friendly and courteous letter, in regard to one thing and another. I am with you about the Underwood. My wife presented me with a brand new Underwood some months ago—one of the handsomest gestures she ever made—but to date I have not been able to make it spell out a single god damn word. I have worked over it, and under it, for hours at a time, but it is listless and impotent. I finally sent it to Bangor—or rather I took it there when I went up to see Lamour.

As I wrote Shawn, I will try to do a little comment each week. I would like to do a great deal of comment, as it appears to be the way I am best fitted to earn a living, but it is almost impossible to write in my present situation. However, I will continue to devote some time to it. It should be very carefully watched, from your end, because I do not keep abreast of affairs, here, and am quite likely to say something which might sound very odd indeed in the light of what has been going on. Also, the war tends to make me (and everybody) lose my perspective, or grip. Writing any sort of editorial stuff about this universal jam that everyone is in, is for me a gruelling and rather frightening job, and I know what Gibbs means about the way he feels.

I have been thinking about your suggestion that married men be given a chance to take an army examination, to relieve their mind. Of course it is what we would all *like* to have, but I doubt if we can expect the army to be that obliging. I guess the doctors are pretty busy just doing what they are doing. Also, the army naturally wants to examine a man at the time he is up for induction, not just any old time, and they wouldn't want to do it twice. I'll ponder this some more, but I suspect you are asking too much.

One thing that continually amazes me about this regimented wartime life is the matter of strikes. We take it for granted that no man's life is his own, any more—that is, the army can give him the nod and he has to leave home and family and put on a uniform and try to get ashore on the Solomons. He has no say-so about any of this. But another guy, in an airplane factory, can lay down his tools for a day or a week and thumb his nose at the whole war in the name of organized labor. This seems to me completely inconsistent. Our whole industrial life has, in a sense, been drafted, yet we still go on babying the unions. Maybe I better ask Pegler about this.

K just got a phone message from Roger's girl (in Boston) that she and Roger are going to get married next week in Denver, where he is in the army. His commanding officer told him he would give him every night off for two weeks—a rather touching concession to l'amour on the part of our armed forces. I have a feeling the army is at bottom very sentimental. It's going to be a slow war, but we'll probably win it— with our girls at our sides.

Yrs,
EBW

To EUGENE SAXTON

North Brooklin, Maine
20 September [1942]

Dear Gene:

I was glad to hear about the book. If it would just keep going for a little while, it would be a help.

We are having our equinoctial storm tonight and I ought to be down on the dark and rain-swept shore, watching my boats come adrift from their moorings and pile up on the rocks at the head of the cove. So far, this month, we have had mostly fog and heat—very unseasonable for Maine. My pullets are housed and in production, going strong, and this week I am going to get a cow, a purebred Guernsey one of whose hips has slipped. I never realized that sometimes a cow's hip drops down out of place, but it seems to be the case. Doesn't seem to affect the cow's spirits any. I don't know yet how it will affect mine.

We still get just about enough gas to keep us on wheels for what we regard as essential errands, and so far I haven't blown a tire. Joe has been made a patrolman at school, and is so moved by his new sense of authority that he wears his white belt and silver badge even when he is at home, off duty. He had a good summer at camp and came home looking well. . . .

Love to you and Martha from us all,
Andy

To KATHARINE S. WHITE

North Brooklin, Maine
[Sept. 29, 1942]
Tuesday morning

Dear K:

. . . Bill Henderson is here this morning, and a new plank floor is under construction for Sukey [the cow] who has been eating little apples and may not live to see the new home. At the moment, however, she seems robust, and no nearer fresh than when you left. I am on easier terms with her, now, and we go out together on the same rope with some familiarity. The kitten is fine and gets along all right until Fred and Raffles act jointly, when there is hell to pay.

Saw Frank Hamilton this morning and he is working on the problem of changing our watch—or says he is. We had frost last night but not a killing one, and the flowers are still lovely. I moved your plants into the plantroom from the barn because it seemed cool enough indoors for anybody or thing. Told Bill Henderson this morning that you were on your way to Denver[1] and he said: "That would be hard work for me, I despise to go anywhere. I'd rather dig a ditch than go to Ellsworth."

We had the mobilization last night and for all I know everything went off all right, and very snappy—it was all over within an hour. Joe and I had supper at 5 o'clock and were all ready when the call came. There was an incident in front of Gott's store, which seemed to involve Jean Redmond and Hollis Gray, and the public health nurse showed up from Bluehill. Ken [Parson] says he is going to keep all incidents in the center of town, to save rubber. I trust our enemies will do the same.

Joe is well, and has been shorn. He has set out to complete his war stamp book and is in a financial mood, with overtones of shack-building. He seems to have plans to do some clamming with Lawrence, riding the crest of the 16¢ market. Your pullets set a new high yesterday, with 158. One Barred Rock went down and never got up, and two birds from the big house failed to survive a purge.

I haven't been able to get my piece started, but will get after it soon. It's very unfortunate that Bill Henderson waited until Harper-time to put in an appearance, as it is almost impossible for me to write and remodel at the same time.

Wish Joe and I could be with you all on Saturday and I hope you will take things easy and try to get a vacation and a rest while you're away. Give Roger and Evelyn my very best and tell them how sorry I am to miss their wedding. I'm sure Evelyn will be the prettiest bride Pike's Peak has ever looked down upon.

Lots of love to all from us both,

A

To STANLEY HART WHITE

North Brooklin, Maine
26 December 1942

Dear Bun:

We had a nice Christmas. There was plenty of snow, and the first gift to be opened was 5 lbs of pigeon grain which Joe's Uncle Art Illian had sent him, and the package had developed a lovely leak—so we had a fine covering of snow outdoors and a beautiful drift of grain in the living room. And Nancy's puppy ate quite a good deal of both snow and grain, because of the excitement and all, and then had one of its pukin'

---

1. To attend Roger's wedding.

spells in K's study under the piano. We spent Christmas morning at the spotting post watching for enemy planes but didn't see any, and for dinner we had one of my young geese. The goose had disappeared last week during the cold snap (we had ten below zero for four days straight) and had spent several nights away from home. But we thawed him out and warmed him up and he tasted fine. Last night it began to snow again, and today we've got it for fair, with a NE wind piling it into drifts. We got your fine present, which Joe took care of right away. He decided to convert the stamp into four 25 centers and left it in an ashtray in the kitchen cabinet for safekeeping, where Nancy found it when she was putting out a cigarette on it. It is still in nice shape.

I haven't figured out yet what Paul V. McNutt [Chairman, War Manpower Commission] wants to do with me in this war, but am going ahead farming and writing for the present. K and I have both taken back some of the *New Yorker* work which we chucked when we came here, because the staff has been so depleted and the magazine is very short handed and they keep pestering us to do the work! This is all right except the days aren't long enough for everything. It takes practically a whole day, every day, to figure out how to get certain things done without using any gas.

I should think it would be fun teaching camouflage, but I will be glad when a ship can look like a ship again. Nancy's husband got a commission the other day and is learning how to teach fliers high altitude physiology—so they will put their oxygen masks on without complaining. It's a damned weird war, with you trying to make things invisible and me with a big signboard in my lane, signed by General Hugh Drum, warning me to stay off my own property.[1] And my hens being waked at four A.M. when the electric light goes on, and violating the dim-out until breakfast time.

Well, it's sundown and I have a date with a cow. You will never know what a cow is like until you have lived with one. . . .

Yrs,
Andy

To MILDRED B. WHITE

North Brooklin, Maine
[January 1, 1943]
New Year's Day

Dear Mil—

Our family seems to be starting the year 1943 on the spotting post in West Brooklin, where we scan the skies and catch up on correspondence. Even Joe is here with us today. We are letting him stay home from school because the road is iced up, and he decided he would become an

---

1. As a wartime security device, signs were posted to keep people out of byways and lonely roads.

observer for the day. The view from this post is grand—an arm of the sea called Eggemoggin Reach stretches out in front of us with a Northwest wind blowing the caps of the waves, and beyond the Reach are the white fields and dark woods of Deer Isle, and clear over in the west beyond Penobscot Bay are the Camden hills. The same wood stove which used to heat the scholars, when this was used as a schoolhouse, is burning cheerfully this morning, flinging its heat around in the same irresponsible way. Joe and I have just been conducting some experiments with a thermometer placed at different levels in the room, and have discovered that there is a difference of nineteen degrees between the temperature at one inch above the floor and the temperature at five feet above the floor. So that a man's toes are nineteen degrees cooler than his nose. Then there is another drop of sixty-two degrees from schoolroom to backhouse seat, and a change in wind direction from NW to straight up.

We had a rough month of December with many storms, much cold, and lots of darkness, but Christmas was a good day and we all had a nice time of it. The woolen gloves you sent me are coming in handy already and you were a peach to give me such a good present. Did you knit them yourself? I ought to send you some yarn from my black sheep, sometime, so you could make Bill [White] a sweater like the one Joe has on today. It's a wonderful garment—still smells like a sheep, and sheds rain like one. Tell Al I was going to send him some firewater for Christmas but never got my order off. I guess he'll have to wait for his birthday instead. We all send greetings & hope that 1943 will bring good news and good health for all.

Lots of love,
Andy

• *When the following was written, Katharine White was in Mt. Sinai Hospital in New York for surgery, brought on by a fall on the ice while in Maine. White's sister Clara came to Maine to stay with young Joel so White could be with his wife in the city.*

To KATHARINE S. WHITE

North Brooklin, Maine
[February 25, 1943]
Thursday

Dear K:

The mild weather ended in the night, and it is cold and clear today —and beautiful. Clara is due to arrive in Bluehill this afternoon just before supper and Joe is staying there today to save gas.

Here's a report on the rationing yesterday afternoon with Miss Ada Herrick and Mrs. Harding at the Corner School. They snipped all the coffee stamps out of Joe's book, he being under coffee age and that being their instructions. (They did that with all children's books, I made sure of that.) I declared 7 lbs. coffee and they took four tickets from my sugar book and three from yours, or vice versa; and I declared one can catsup and they took that from my new ration book Number 2. So I think everything is all in order.

Mrs. Gray and Howard and I went into a huddle about the smoked meat in the attic and decided that it had better be moved to the woodshed, so we did that. Howard says he keeps his meat in his garage right through the coldest weather. The attic was getting pretty warm in that mild spell.

Four hundred and thirty-seven persons had registered for Ration Book Number Two at the close of rationing yesterday afternoon. Owen Flye was still unaccounted for, but they were expecting him. That gives you a pretty close indication of the population of the town and how it has dwindled. A couple of years ago I think it was around seven hundred.

Mrs. Idella Love sent her greetings and sympathy to you and warned me that we would be approached shortly on the subject of the Red Cross (I believe it was). Miss Herrick also sent her best to you. She seems to be quite deaf.

Town meeting is Monday and I will be there to look after the interests of the Friend Memorial Public Library in your absence. The town report has arrived and you are featured as usual; I will send or bring it as soon as meeting is over. . . .

Joe is fine. He took over the little weak lamb yesterday and began pumping skim milk into it at frequent intervals. It was a beautiful little thing, lying in a carton on the kitchen shelf. I knew it would die but I didn't tell him that and he nursed it with great care all afternoon and evening and then set his alarm clock for 2 A.M. so that he could give it a feeding. The clock failed to go off, but the lamb never knew the difference. It was dead this morning.

The house looks fine with its new paint job and waxed floors. I have been straightening things up as best I can. Min and Fred and Raffles are in excellent fettle and gave us a big welcome yesterday. If you were here, everything would be great.

I have all my work and all Howard's to do.

Love,
Andy

To FREDERICK LEWIS ALLEN

North Brooklin, Maine
13 March [1943]

Dear Fred:

For some months I have been trying to figure out what I had better do about my life, since it is apparent that I am trying to do too many things. I have talked this over with myself, back and forth, and am reluctantly reporting that I must quit "One Man's Meat." This must seem rather odd and sudden to you, but the truth is I have had great difficulty, all along, writing essays of this sort, as they do not seem to come naturally to me and I have to go through the devil to get them written. Several times I have sent off a department which did not satisfy me and which I sent only because it was to fulfill a promise, or continuing obligation, or whatever you call a monthly deadline. So the only thing for me to do is to quit.

I feel a peculiar disappointment, almost a defeat, in this, and hope *Harper's* will feel mildly disappointed too. It ought to be the most congenial job in the world for me, and the fault is entirely mine if it isn't. Certainly I have had nothing from Lee [Hartman] or from you but the nicest treatment in all matters.

If it is all right with you I would like the piece I turned in Thursday to be my last piece. But if you feel that I owe you more notice than this, I am willing to try to do one or two more. I haven't figured out just what I will use for money from now on, and I trust I may occasionally be able to sell *Harper's* something or other. For the present, I have farm work and editorial work enough to keep me busy if not solvent, and I am hoping that my health (which has been rather sketchy lately) will improve by my cutting out this regular chore.

I would have talked this over with you before leaving New York but I had not at that time arrived at a clear decision in my own mind, and there would have been no point in bothering you prematurely. It seemed wiser to break the news to myself before breaking it to you.

Sincerely,
Andy

PS. If you contemplate running anything in the Personal column by way of explaining my absence, I'd appreciate the chance to see it before it gets into print.

To FREDERICK LEWIS ALLEN

North Brooklin, Maine
20 March 1943

Dear Fred:

I'm very grateful for your letter and naturally I'm glad if my stuff has given satisfaction. My mind is made up, however, and although I may be doing a foolish thing, or taking a wrong turn, all anybody can do is follow his nose in these woods.

The desire is very strong in me to rid myself of any writing commitment. It is not simply that I want a vacation or a rest (although almost everyone would welcome such a pause in this period of history) but rather that I want to change my state of mind, and there is no other way to do it. I want to write when and if I feel like it. A department hanging over a man's head is, as you say, very good discipline—but at the moment discipline is not the sort of medicine I need.

You mentioned in your letter that you wondered whether I might be sore, or miffed, about anything. There is nothing to this. If there were, I would tell you fast. (When I get annoyed, I grow loud and windy and put myself right down on paper.) I told you what I thought about the *New Yorker* piece, and its appearance at this time is the merest coincidence, so don't give it a second thought.[1]

You asked for one more MEAT. I hate to say no and I hate to say yes. I feel incapable of writing one and am afraid that if I were to try, the result would be deplorable. I would much rather end up with the Central Park piece, which I think is up to snuff or better. I think Harper readers will prefer it to anything I could whip up in the next couple of weeks, so I hope you'll think this over.

Again I want to say thanks for your letter and for the generous spirit of it. Running a column in your paper has been a lot of fun, not to say a privilege, and I'd like nothing better than to feel that I was able to go right on doing it. But I don't, and I know that nothing can change that. My plans are nebulous. I may have to walk out on farming, too, unless I can find out what makes me feel so lifeless all the time. No punch any more. My doctor is feeding me strychnine, which is what I always thought they fed dogs when they didn't want the dogs.

Sincerely,
Andy

---

1. The reference is to "Harold Ross and *The New Yorker*" by Dale Kramer and George R. Clark, which ran in the April 1943 issue of *Harper's Magazine*.

To GUSTAVE S. LOBRANO

North Brooklin, Maine
[March? 1943]
Tuesday

Dear Gus:

Why don't you come on down here for a few days of trouting and smelting? The ice is leaving the brooks and things are pretty nice here now. One of the boys in the elementary school caught an 11½ inch trout day before yesterday on a fly that Joe tied, and what man has done man can do. . . .

My sow is pigging on the 28th, goslings are due to hatch next Monday, and the tides will shortly be coming right for bringing the smelt in after supper. We have had a lousy stretch of weather for the past fortnight, but I look for it to break. It is the eternal optimist in me. In spite of the weather I have managed to get my fields burnt off, lambs cut, chicks started, ration books renewed, cow sold, pigs engaged, hair cut, dog plucked, seedlings thinned, shed built, letters acknowledged, furniture recovered. As soon as I resigned from *Harper's*, things began to move smoothly. There is apparently something about being a *Harper* [Magazine] author which unfits a man for routine accomplishment. It is like trying to tend the furnace in a dinner jacket. The woodcock are mating this week and you can see them sky-dancing above the pasture in the early part of the evening. Joe has been able to get within ten feet of one. The male always alights on the same spot from which he took off, and by creeping toward the place during his dance you can get very close. You better visit us before they start rationing travel, which is in the cards, I am told.

My year's supply of wood (12 cord) was sawed yesterday by a Model T engine. Such vigor and stamina as you never saw.

Lots of love from us all,
Andy

To HAROLD ROSS

N. Brooklin, Me.
12 April [1943?]

Dear Mr. Ross:

. . . I am at work on a comment on the curious relationship between General Douglas MacArthur and screen star Dorothy Lamour. I just found out yesterday that General MacArthur's first wife's daughter was Miss Lamour's second husband's first wife, or I would have acted sooner.

Yrs sincerely,
White

To HAROLD ROSS

[North Brooklin, Me.]
[April? 1943]
Monday

Dear Mr R

It seems to me time I answered your letters—I would have done so sooner only have been under certain pressures of a local nature, here. I quit the Harper job for no particular reason, other than what seemed to me an inability to write any more pieces of that nature and that length. Feeling the way I did about the matter, I thought it better to drop out. I never did like the long dreary Harper interval of two months between conception and parturition—although at that it's shorter than a hog, which is 114 days.

As for writing for the NYer, I certainly aim to. But I see no reason for changing the present understanding, which is that I should turn in some comment each week and get paid for what is accepted. You spoke of my becoming the "principal contributor," but I would think that the principal contributor should be the one who turns in the most acceptable stuff, whether it happens to be me or somebody else. I can give more time to writing comment now, but I don't want to make any weekly income arrangement. Such an arrangement is sensible if a person is doing the whole department, and accepts that as his weekly responsibility, as I used to; but now that I'm on a piecework basis, I should like to continue getting paid for exactly what I do. You asked if I wanted to agree to do a certain minimum number of words weekly for a certain minimum number of weeks. I don't want to sign myself up for a specified amount of comment as long as I am living 500 miles from first base, because it is too difficult, sometimes, to turn out anything at all, much less a specified amount. In New York I could always dig up a department, by looking around in an old folder or a new barroom, but here the situation is different.

I ought to be able to do a little better on comment from now on because, for one thing, I have just convinced the gas ration board that I should receive enough gas so that I can make one trip a week to the Bluehill post office, to mail my stuff. Hitherto, I have had to catch the mailtruck that passes our door early in the afternoon on the same day that I receive the comment stuff from your office (Wednesday). Gave me very little time to turn around.

Am very much obliged for your kind offers but think there is no point in trying to apply a lot of mystical arithmetic to my simple job, as though we were a couple of actuaries. Hell, I was delighted to learn that you still felt you could make a commentator out of me. I have no illusions, though, about what I can do now that I'm somewhat out of touch. If I should ever return to living in town for all, or at least more, of the year, I might easily want to renew, or increase, my NYer work if you were of that mind. Right now, I simply want to do as much as possible on a straight contributing basis, no guarantees and no bonuses.

White

To HAROLD ROSS

North Brooklin, Maine
3 May 1943

Dear Mr. Ross:

Thanks for your letter. I regard N&C highly, and the *New Yorker* seems to be the only magazine I maintain any relationship with, of a passionate nature. [DeWitt] Wallace has been sort of fidgeting around, but I guess it's just a literary correspondence, like the last time. He keeps mentioning Woollcott's name and a hush falls over the typewritten page. Last week he sent me a great thick hunk of dough and a small proofsheet of a *Harper's* paragraph he said he had scheduled for his next issue, but I found where his digestive staff had lopped off one of my sentences and frigged around in their curious manner, so I sent everything back and said that unlike a vanilla bean I did not wish to be extracted. Hell, some day I may toss off a really good sentence or two, and wouldn't want a hair of its head touched. The truth about the [*Reader's*] *Digest* is that they approach every manuscript with the hope of gaining a line of type before reaching the middle of the third sentence. That is no way to approach a manuscript.

(The way to approach a manuscript is on all fours, in utter amazement.)

White

To H. K. RIGG

North Brooklin, Maine
June 4, 1943

Dear Bun:

K and I got a big wallop out of hearing from you, and we had you placed on the wrong hemisphere, for one thing. I am still farming it and guess I will be for the duration, although we plan to spend next winter in New York catching up on sleep and drinks. Joe just graduated from grammar school and will probably be going off to boarding school in the fall if we can comb the sheep-shit out of his hair and get him into some clean clothes. This has been quite a year for us. K fell on the ice in February, just as we were leaving for a week in the city, and when we got there she had to be rushed to the hospital for a major operation. She's all right now but it was hell while it lasted. Came right in lambing time, too. The winter hung on long past its time and when spring finally came the rains came with it and we had nothing but rain, with the garden plots under six inches of water. However, I produced 14 lambs, 5 pigs, and 272 chicks and 5 goslings in spite of the weather and they are all doing well. A neighbor of mine had a sow which had 21 pigs, an almost unheard of number. I was over there when she started in having them, about eight in the evening, and I hung around till she'd had half a dozen, then I went home to bed and next morning I went back and she was still discharging pigs. Four of them were born dead and when I asked the owner what had caused that, he said: "I dunno, but there was an awful lot goin' on all around 'em and they probly died from the excitement." . . . K and Joe send their best.

Andy

To FREDERICK LEWIS ALLEN

North Brooklin, Maine
2 July 1943

Dear Fred:

Thanks ever so much for sending me the letters. That crack about [Louis] Bromfield being a *real* farmer roused my sporting blood and I will gladly take him on at any time, he to choose the weapons—anything from dung forks to post-hole diggers or 2-ounce syringes for worming sheep.

I read about Gene's [Saxton's] death in the *Times*, two or three days late, and it was an awful shock although I knew he was in poor health. I was very fond of him and will miss him like the devil. It does seem strange that he and Lee [Hartman], who were so close, should wind up their affairs within such a short space of time.

Sincerely,
Andy

To CASS CANFIELD

North Brooklin, Maine
13 August 1943

Dear Mr. Canfield:

Thanks very much for your letter.

I would like to discuss my publishing life with you some time, as there are some things on my mind. There is no rush about it, however, as I have no book ready to go.

One thing I'd like your opinion on is whether you think a new edition of "One Man's Meat," which would include some of the later pieces that came out after the book did, would be a sensible idea. I don't know what I think about it, but it occurred to me—or rather, it occurred to my wife, who is the person in this family to whom things occur.

Sincerely,
E. B. White

To HAROLD ROSS

North Brooklin, Maine
22 August 1943

Dear Ross:

Roger Angell's journalistic experience has been a short one, because he went right from college into the Army Air Force. He had a summer working at Simon & Schuster's reading manuscripts, submitting opinions, and doing general chores. He was, I am quite sure, well thought of around there. Simon gave him a very strong letter recommending him for O.C.S. (He's a corporal at the moment, teaching power turrets at Lowry.)

He also worked one summer at *Country Life,* as editorial office boy and handyman. He has a Harvard degree. In his prep school, he edited the school paper.

My belief is that he has a rather sharp editorial talent which these meager jobs do not indicate. When my wife was editing the *New Yorker Short Story Book,* Roger turned out to have a pretty sound knowledge of that kind of stuff and helped her with opinions and recommendations, practically all of which made a good deal of sense. He did some reading and general work for us when we were getting together the *Subtreasury of American Humor,* and again his opinions were pretty darn good and he seemed informed as well as critical.

I invariably use him as a first reader of newsbreaks whenever he is around the house, as he is air tight and is, in fact, one of the few living authorities on *New Yorker* newsbreaks. He actually remembers them. It's uncanny.

Although he is a member of the family I have little hesitancy in recommending him for a shot at editorial work. He lacks practical experience but he has the goods.

Much obliged for your interest & all,
White

P.S. Since my first letter to you, he has been picked, with one other soldier, to write a history of Lowry Field for the Air Corps. My God.

To **HAROLD ROSS**

[North Brooklin, Me.]
20 Sept [1943]

Dear Mr. R.:

Thanks for the letter. Am not trying to convince anybody that there won't be wars, as I don't believe it myself. Am merely asserting devotion to, and some faith in, an idea for which wars have been fought before and will be again. Thing that got me going was the constant implication that the idea had better be adjusted to fit the requirements of the winning side. I think it is a non-adjustable idea, like a non-adjustable wrench, and you got to take it or leave it. I am also aware that Nature governs Man and regards many of these questions as academic. The disappearance of the eel grass is easily as disturbing as the concentration of troops along the Channel. I am composting rockweed with sheep manure and producing a complete fertilizer without chemicals.

EBW

• *White asked Daise Terry to mail two identical letters to him, one by air mail, the other by regular mail, to see whether air was quicker.*

To **DAISE TERRY**

[North Brooklin, Me.]
[September 25, 1943]
[Postcard]

White calling. The two letters arrived together, same mail, same bag, same morning. I enjoyed them both very much. See you soon.

(I have always known that the airplane was essentially a slow poke. Fusses around too much at the start and finish. Flashy, but impractical.)

• *In the fall of 1943, White, who had been having "head trouble," ended up in a hospital in Cambridge, where he underwent an operation on his nose—a turbinectomy. This gave him no relief but was, as he says, "the fashionable nose operation of the time." His stay in the hospital resulted in the piece "A Weekend with the Angels," published in* The New Yorker, *January 22, 1944, and later reprinted in his collection* The Second Tree From the Corner.

To GUSTAVE S. LOBRANO

[Boston]
[October 1943]
Sunday
Zone of Quiet

Dear Gus:

They couldn't think of anything else to do with me, so they removed a small bone from my head—just on the chance. I rather enjoyed it, on the whole. It's steadying to have a little surgery when you're feeling keyed up: Keeps your mind focussed on a single spot instead of all over the place. They got at the bone through my right nostril, which I consider very resourceful, and the morphine was just what I had been needing all along. Nothing more relaxing than a good cutting by a man who knows one end of a knife from the other.

Hospitals are fun now because all the competent people have gone off to the fighting fronts, leaving the place in charge of a wonderfully high-spirited group of schoolgirls to whom sickness is the greatest lark of the century. They pop in your room at 3 a.m. looking perfectly beautiful and wanting to rub your back simply because they have been taught the back-rub. I am writing a casual about them which I'll finish if it doesn't key me up too much.

Am leaving for Maine Tuesday night, arriving Wednesday morning. Am looking for you to arrive any time thereafter and stay a long while.

Love to all the boys and girls on 43rd Street.

Andy

The only change this operation will make in our sheep catching plans will be that *you* will do *all* the rough physical work instead of only nine tenths of it.

To HARRY LYFORD

North Brooklin, Maine
28 October 1943

Dear Harry:

. . . Your sod-soaker hit here about three weeks ago and liked it so well it has been here ever since. Nobody has ever seen such a dirty wet fall, and my sheep are still on the island and my house is rapidly becoming an island, too.

I'm recovering from a nervous crack-up which visited me last summer and which has given me a merry chase. I never realized nerves were so odd, but they are. They are the oddest part of the body, no exceptions. Doctors weren't much help, but I found that old phonograph records are miraculous. If you ever bust up from nerves, take frequent shower baths, drink dry sherry in small amounts, spend most of your time with hand tools at a bench, and play old records till there is no wax left in the grooves.

We're leaving Maine tonight for Boston, New York, Boise, Denver, and then New York for the winter if we can get an apartment. We'll be working for *The New Yorker* as usual. My theory about myself and the war is that I can contribute most from my old editorial perch, where my screams and flappings are not supervised by any agency. One thing the end of the war will mean for me is that I can get another of those cheeses. We still talk about it.

Yrs,
Andy

To HAROLD ROSS

[New York]
[December 1943]

Mr. Ross:

I agree (and always have agreed) to do newsbreaks for The New Yorker (and for no other publication). I agree cheerfully to this. And since I agree to perform this service for The New Yorker—and am very glad to get the work—there is no reason to pay me a large sum of money. I would regard such a payment as a gift, or a stunt, or a device, and I do not want any gift, or any part in any stunt or device.

As for the proposed raise in the weekly salary payment, I would be glad to get a raise any time it is permissible to give me one. I understand that it is *not* now permissible.

I long ago made an agreement with myself not to sign agreements with publications. This has worked out well, and I have no reason for changing my way of living and working.

E. B. White

To STANLEY HART WHITE

25 West 43 Street
[mid-January 1944]
Monday night

Dear Bun:

I spent the weekend wishing that you weren't sick, and wondering whether there was anything I could do for you. Mildred called me up and said that you were in a hospital in Chicago, for a going-over.[1]

Is there anything you would like, such as a pony and pony-cart? I

---

1. Stanley had a malignant tumor near his heart and was being treated with deep X ray at the Illinois Research and Educational Hospital. The doctors were not optimistic, but the treatment worked and he recovered.

would be glad to send you a pony. I always wanted one, and figured that my only chance of getting one would be if I was laid up in a hospital.

If you want me to come out to Chicago and manage your doctors for you, let me know, as I have just had a great deal of experience managing doctors. I had a nose operation in Boston last fall, which didn't amount to a damn, and which really turned out to be a godsend, because I wrote a piece for *The New Yorker* about being in a hospital and got paid more than the doctor charged me for the operation, which I considered a very unusual feat, as well as a clearcut victory over the medical fraternity. You will find the piece in last week's issue if you want to know about my hospitalization.

Joe returned to Exeter last week after his vacation, most of which he spent in bed chewing sulfa pills. I had a letter from him this morning saying that he was way behind on Latin but had been admitted to a riflery class—which is going to present a problem to the academy because he is left-handed and likes to sneak up on his target from behind. I have always wished that you could know Joe better so that you could teach him all the things you taught me. I started to make a list, the other day, of the things you taught me between the ages of four and fourteen, and it is quite an interesting list. I will show it to you sometime. You have probably forgotten. Once a teacher, always a teacher.

Roger and Evelyn (his wife) were here on furlough last week, and Nancy was here with her baby. I am a grandfather by proxy, which is the most convenient way to be one.

Don't forget to let me know if there is anything I can do for you.

Yrs,
En

To KATHARINE S. WHITE

Stevens Hotel—Chicago
[January 30, 1944]
Saturday night

Dear K:

After a day here I don't know what to make of the situation but am glad I came. I had a talk with Blanche this morning, then Janice joined us for lunch, then we all took the "L" out to the hospital. Stan was in bed, didn't look as bad as I expected he would, and seemed tremendously glad to see me. His face is swollen, but less so than it has been. Both arms are greatly swollen, to about twice normal size; his hands are puffy, and his left arm is tender. But he was rather lively & talkative and high spirited. Whatever he is going through, he is meeting it with an amazing show of energy. His great size gives him a sort of majestic appearance. He hasn't been in a hospital since he was a boy, and the whole thing seems to amuse him. I had no chance to be alone with him & the conversation was general. Tomorrow I shall try to see him alone, and shall also try to see the doctor—which may be rather a trick because it is a very queer place. It is a State Institution and nobody pays anything. Ordinary hospital routine is not observed. It is rather dirty, gloomy, and depressing, with none of the esprit de corps of a hospital. Patients wait on themselves and on each other. Stan has the run of the place and spends part of his time helping internes run tests on other people. He can walk about as he pleases. At night he sleeps under an oxygen tent, which he operates himself. Every second day he receives X-ray treatment, which is followed by a mood of depression. . . .

Janice is wonderful. She is as cute as a cricket, & is a life saver for me. She has a good job in the designing dept. of the Lakeside Press (R. R. Donnelly), and seems to be coming along. She is unsophisticated, for 26, but is very attractive and intelligent. One of the things that seems to be most on Stan's mind is that Janice and I get acquainted —which is understandable under the circumstances. He was much more anxious that she and I go to the zoo tomorrow than that I visit him, and made me promise to take her.

Saw Clara in Washington. She thought it might be better if she waited and came out later. As I say, the picture is confusing & I don't know just what to do for Stan.

Lots of love,
Andy

To KATHARINE S. WHITE

[February 1944]
[Interoffice memo]

Mrs. White

I have just been amusing myself computing what it cost me in money to write the Classics Club poem.[1] My refusal of the book club judgeship last summer was because I suspected I might want to write something, some time, about a book club, and I presume this poem is it. Figuring the judgeship at approx. $30,000 (over a period of say ten years, which is just a guess), and subtracting the $175 I got for writing the poem, I make the cost only $29,825. Probably the most expensive poem I ever wrote.

EBW

---

1. "A Classic Waits for Me," published in *The New Yorker*, February 19, 1944, and later in *The Second Tree From the Corner*.

• *Harold Ross felt the way White did about the "digesting" of articles and stories, and in December 1943 he notified the* Reader's Digest *that they could no longer reprint* New Yorker *material. A little later it became apparent that DeWitt Wallace was planting articles in periodicals in order to be able to reprint them later in the* Digest, *and that he was paying large sums to both writers and magazines. Ross and White felt that the* Digest, *in generating the contents of other publications, was exercising an unhealthy amount of editorial control over the magazine field. In February 1944, at Ross's request, White wrote a letter, "To Our Contributors," for* The New Yorker *in which he criticized the practice. It was signed "The Editors."* The New York Times *picked it up, and some fur flew in the publishing world.*

To STANLEY HART WHITE

115 East 35 Street
2 March 1944

Dear Bun:

I've been so messed up with one thing and another I haven't had any time for letter writing. *The New Yorker* is a worse madhouse than ever now, on account of the departure of everybody for the wars, leaving only the senile, the psychoneurotic, the maimed, the halt, and the goofy to get out the magazine. There is hardly a hormone left in the place. . . .

The *Reader's Digest* bust-up has reverberated all over the map, and slews of letters have come in to us from readers and writers, tipping their hats. There has been quite a lot of publicity about it in newspapers and magazines, with editorial comment, and today I learned that the *New Republic* is going to cut loose, too. The tough news is that our reporter, [John] Bainbridge, who is working on a comprehensive story about the *Digest*, has just been reclassified 1-A and will probably soon disappear, like everybody else.

Have about decided to go to a doctor about my head, as there seems to be a kite caught in the branches somewhere. But it'll probably be six months before I get around to going. We got our seed order off yesterday, splitting it between Peter Henderson and Joseph Harris. It always steadies me to buy seeds, even though I don't know what to do with them when they arrive. Luckily K does. We're going back to Maine the 17th of this month, two weeks from tomorrow, and Joe will be with us for his spring holidays.

My book [*One Man's Meat*] is going to be republished this June with some new stuff, none of it very hot. My publishers regard this as a rather pale venture and I guess they are right. Well, another month or six weeks and the smelt will be running in the brooks—and for the same old reason.

En

To STANLEY HART WHITE

North Brooklin, Maine
[March 1944]
Sunday

Dear Bun:

This has been a wonderful week for us here, with plenty of lambing and smelting and all kinds of weather. There was a snow squall the first night, and next morning it came off cold—one above. Season's first lamb arrived that afternoon, while Joe and I were sawing some firewood into short lengths to fit into a smelt-tent stove. We had the ewe in a horse stall right next to us and the sound of our bucksaw and her labor pains were all one sound. Next morning we got up at five-thirty and started for Surry Bay with a sack of wood and a bottle of clam worms. It was snowing hard and continued to snow all day. We had never fished for smelt through the ice before, and we were warned that if we wanted to try it we'd have to go right away because the ice was expected to leave the Bay that week on the big tides which, with the softening weather, cause the bust-up. Smelt tents are little houses framed with light sticks and covered with grain sacks that have been stretched tight. A normal size tent is four feet by five feet, with a height at the ridge of a few inches less than standing room. There were about three dozen tents in the middle ground on Surry Bay, making a sort of little village. The tents are painted all colors of the rainbow—whatever paint a man happens to find left over from some other job. You would think that spending a day sitting on an ice cake in a snowstorm you would be in danger of being cold, but the reverse is the case. With the stove going, you are apt to get overdone. The fish hole is a foot wide and the full width of the tent, and gets skimmed over every night so you have to break it out with an ax before you start fishing. The lines are made fast to pegs on a stick which is suspended by flexible wooden arms directly over the hole. My tent had five lines. You sit on a box or keg. Directly in front of you are the lines—like a rather primitive harp. At your left is a tiny shelf for your worms, with a small hole through which light can enter so you can see to bait your hooks. Just beyond the fish hole sits the stove, about as big as a rich man's stomach. Next to it is your tiny pile of stovewood, each stick about eight inches long. Everything in a smelt tent is in miniature, and even the smelt are miniature fish. It is a lonely existence, alone all day in a smelt tent, but you are pretty busy. Things move fast. When you haul in a smelt, you simply slap it at the strike-box and toss the hook right back down the hole. The bait usually remains. Smelt fishermen arrive all together and depart all together, and there is an unwritten law that nobody can go tromping over the ice during the fishing period—which is a couple of hours before low water and a couple of hours of the flood. The people in smelt tents talk back and forth when the fishing is dull, but when the smelt are taking hold you don't hear anything except the occasional slap of a fish against a strike-box, and the purring of your stove, and the flutter of snow outside. We made a good catch, and had a fine day of it. Two days later the ice left, so we were just in time. This has been an unusually good winter for the smelt fishermen—the price has been up to 45 and 50 cents a pound, and fellows around here have made as much as a thousand dollars smelting.

A little later in the spring the smelt will be running up the brooks at night to spawn, and you go out when the tide is coming and haul smelt out with your fingers.

This letter seems to be about smelt.

My head has been pretty good since my return to Maine. I am encouraged, and think maybe it will come around all right. Joe has had a great time this week. This is really home to him, and he hasn't been here, much, since last July when he started summer school at Exeter.

My old black sheep had twin lambs night before last, but she has been failing for the last couple of years, and I doubt if she gets through the spring. She has lung trouble, and it is beginning to get her. My prettiest lamb so far came yesterday morning about three o'clock, a very neat parcel, and everything shipshape. Shepherding is nice work if you like it, and I like it. Everything about a sheep smells good, except the infected scrotum of a castrated lamb. (I usually have a couple of such cases each spring, because the fellow that cuts my buck lambs for me is loyal to his grandfather's method and to his grandfather's memory. I usually have to perform a second operation a couple of days later myself, with a safety razor blade, to let the pus out. I also do all the docking of tails myself, with a dull ax.) One farmer near here always saves the nuts of his little pigs, when they are cut. They are about the size of almonds. I have held so many pigs, for a castration, that I am now in demand around here as a holder. Not everybody holds a pig just right when it is being cut, but I do. It is a good idea in the country to be able to do one thing well, and that seems to be my thing. Never would have thought it.

We're returning to New York tomorrow night for a couple of weeks, and Joe goes back to school for the spring term. I've been glad to hear from your letters that you are improving, and I trust they will soon kick you out. Give my best to Blanche and Janice, and tell Janice my barnyard has the Chicago zoo backed off the map, at the moment.

Andy

To **HAROLD ROSS**

North Brooklin, Maine
15 May 1944

Dear Mr. Ross:

I was glad to hear in this morning's mail that you were probably not going to skip any issues.[1] My reasons for being glad are dull and I will let them go. Am writing to say that if there is anything I can do to help during the lean period when other people are on vacation, let me know. My head doesn't knock so much as it did last fall.

The more I thought about it, the more it seemed to me that it would be generally regarded as a sissy thing for the NYer to go dead on a couple of issues, particularly this summer. I would hate to have to phrase an explanatory announcement telling the public how exhausting it is to publish a magazine. The public's response to any such announcement would be nuts. I am sure that this would be a very bad time to pull our exhaustion on our readers, a lot of whom are pretty well pooped out themselves for one reason or another. However, I have not wanted to say much about this matter, as I am not exactly in a position to.

White

To **HAROLD ROSS**

North Brooklin, Maine
[June 1944]

Dear Mr. Ross:

Would you be good enough to sign this, in the role of my employer? I am applying for gas to enable me to drive to the Post Office to mail comment.

Sign where the red check mark is. Please recommend 72 miles, where it says "recommended mileage." The finished product would look something like this:

H. W. ROSS	72	The New Yorker Magazine

Please return this promptly, like a good employer. And as a reward I will try to write you a casual called "About Myself," beginning "I am a man of medium height." The piece would then go on to tell other things about me, taken directly from forms such as the enclosed. It would be a fascinating record.[1]

Thank you.
E. B. White

1. Because the magazine was so short-handed, Ross had seriously considered making it a biweekly.

1. White did write a piece called "About Myself," beginning "I am a man of medium height"—a line he stole from a monologue by Charles Butterworth. *The*

To STANLEY HART WHITE

[North Brooklin, Me.]
June [1944]
Friday

Dear Bun:

Any time you feel in the mood for it, I hope you will come on to Maine for a visit. We have a table seating six, and I noted yesterday that there were only five people at it. The only time K and I expect to be away from home this summer is the first two weeks in August, when we are going into retirement north of here. I don't know whether you would find anything to do on this place, but you would be very welcome, and there is a quality of insanity about the whole thing not unlike the Polk Street joint [Illinois Research and Educational Hospital]. . . . The latest addition to the group is a horse, a comic prop if ever there was one. It is a young mare who saw through me the first time she laid eyes on me. I see no good coming out of this relationship.

I was very glad to hear that your health is improved and hope that you can hold the gain. My head has spells of being pretty good, and then it starts knocking again. I am not sure but that it is the result of a lifetime of thumbing my nose at my allergy. What used to be spasmodic hay fever, limited to a certain season of the year, now seems to have gone into a chronic disease of the mucous membranes (the Bronx Concourse of the head) and this seems to cause a deterioration of all surrounding nerves, fibers, and other pieces of string. I meet this dismal situation by bringing a horse into the picture—horses having always been the most active and violent stimulus or aggravation. I got the horse to cut the hay that feeds the horse. (That cuts the hay.) Grass is indeed, as Whitman so well knew, the very heart of life, and although my sensitivity to grass will be the death of me, I wouldn't trade it for anything there is. Hay fever is like a love affair with a destructive but irresistible woman—there is the quality of fatality about it, as insistent as a June afternoon.

Did you see in the *Times* the other day that my book [*One Man's Meat*] was one of several that have been banned by the Army and Navy and disallowed for the Armed Services Edition? The Adjutant General of the Army found that it contained certain "political implications." This has given me more pleasure than anything that has happened in a long time, although it costs me 90,000 copies at approximately nothing per copy. At least the soldier vote is now safe, and the boys can pick up their presidential preferences from the comic strips and other

---

New Yorker bought the piece and ran it in the issue of February 10, 1945. It was included in *The Second Tree From the Corner.*

reliable American sources. I am beginning to feel a little more like an author now that I have had a book banned. The literary life, in this country, begins in jail. . . .[1]

Yrs,

En

To HAROLD ROSS

[North Brooklin, Me.]
8/1/44

Mr. Ross:

Could you put a little notice on the bulletin board asking people *not* to use a stapling machine on newsbreaks? I have to unstaple them with my finger nails. I bleed quite freely, and it all runs into time, too. There is no way of preventing contributors from using staples, but you ought to be able to stop paid employees from doing it.

No staples, please.

EBW

To HAROLD ROSS

[North Brooklin, Me.]
13 Aug. [1944]
[Postcard]

Dear Ross:

Hope you can handle the stapling threat, but I wouldn't be too optimistic. Once machines get going, once people feel the throb and the excitement of the metallic clinch, there is little likelihood that you can call them off. I suspect that more and more things are going to be stapled together in the world. I think stapling machines are going to get bigger, and quicker. It is going to be very hard, from now on, to do newsbreaks, because the clipping is going to be inseparable from the letter. I am bloody but uncowed. No staples.

E. B. White

To HAROLD ROSS

North Brooklin, Maine
18 Aug. [1944]

Dear Ross:

The unstapling machine arrived yesterday and has given me new courage to go on. So far, the only thing I have had to unstaple is the

1. The Army later had second thoughts about *One Man's Meat* and lifted the ban. The book appeared in an Armed Services Edition, and its author received many letters from homesick servicemen overseas.

card marked "Mr. H. W. Ross," which was attached by staple. Anyway, it gave me a nice workout, although in order to hold the box properly, I had to cover the instructions with my hand, which made it necessary for me to memorize the instructions, instead of reading them as I went along. The "Mr." in front of your name sounds like a phony, by the way. Sounds like the "Prince" in front of Romanoff. I suspect you are an impostor—have all along.

If they can invent a thing to remove staples, it is conceivable that they can eventually find something to emasculate a rocket bomb. Anything is possible today, as you know.

This is just to thank you for the Ace Staple Remover.

Brig. Gen. White

To HAROLD ROSS

[North Brooklin, Me.]
[August 28, 1944]

Mr. Ross:

Thanks for the Harper advt. from your valued magazine. I would have seen it anyway, but was glad to get it hot from your stapling department. The firm of Harper, I have discovered over a period of years which might roughly be described as too long, is feeble-minded, but it is the sort of feeble-mindedness which holds a man in thrall. For instance, lots of publishers' ads are feeble-minded, but very few of them can work as much incompetence into a single column space as this ad does. You will notice that in presenting the new Harper quartet of essayists (Rebecca West, Adams, Ferril, and Martin) the firm carefully pointed out, a little lower down in the column, that "Mr. White is our finest essayist, perhaps our only one." This should not only be pretty discouraging to a prospective Harper reader, but should give Rebecca West a great lift in preparing her copy. Harper is the only firm I know of that deliberately pays out good money to cut their own throats. Not to speak of the throats of their authors. I have had my throat cut by Harper's for so many years I hardly notice the blood any more. Just a thin trickle that scarcely stains a man's shirt.

I would have changed publishers fifteen years ago, only I don't know how you change publishers. The first half of my life I didn't know how babies came, and now, in my declining years, I don't know how you change publishers. I guess I will always be in some sort of quandary.

White

P.S. The de-stapling machine works better than I would have believed possible.

To STANLEY HART WHITE

North Brooklin
Friday, Sept. 1 [1944]

Dear Stan:

I had just gone out when you phoned last night, and Aunt Caroline took the call. She is slightly deaf, and probably had to make up all the answers. The reason nobody else was in the house was that we were all out returning a visiting pig to its owner. When the owner came along the road to meet us, he looked accusingly at the pig and said: "Hell, everything I own is adrift tonight."

We are darn glad you are coming. I wrote you yesterday, pointing out that the railroad might offer you an easier journey. I am a firm believer in the rails. They lie solid and purposeful, and they cut right through the country as though they owned it. I am a great rail man—do not like planes or buses but am fond of the cars. In fact, I am hoping this fall to ride on a railroad I have always intended to try—the Belfast and Moosehead, so called because it starts at Belfast and doesn't go anywhere near Moosehead. The whole run is only forty miles, from the beginning of the line to the end, which is just a nice distance. One of the cars, I am told, has had its seats removed and kitchen chairs installed, as more practical. I will show you the timetable when you are here.

Evelyn leaves for Boston tomorrow, to go job hunting, so there is no problem about a bed. Her St. Bernard left last week, and the departure of a St. Bernard from a home is one of the finest things that can happen to the home.[1] . . . I imagine you will be here in time to dig a few potatoes. We always start digging potatoes right after Labor Day around here. The hired man does the digging, and the rest of us sit around and talk about it, sometimes picking up a spud or two and looking for rot or sunburn or net necrosis. There is a nice view of the bay from the potato patch.

Unless I hear from you to the contrary, I will meet your bus in Ellsworth on Wednesday night. If you decide on a different system for getting here, you better send me a wire.

Yrs,
En

P.S. (Sunday) Have just discovered this beautiful letter, written two days ago, under a pile of beautiful junk on my desk. Yet I seem to recall addressing an envelope to you and putting it in the mail bag. Now I wonder what was in *that*? . . .

---

1. After Roger Angell was transferred to Hickam Field, in Hawaii, his wife Evelyn spent several weeks with the Whites in Maine with her dog Chloe—according to White, an insane St. Bernard who had running fits, and who insisted on rescuing swimmers who were not in need of rescue.

• *Harold Ross read the following letter and returned it with this comment:*

> Lobrano: Noted. That Maine fishing is a racket, hocus pocus. There is undoubtedly a motor road within one-eighth of a mile to where White wound up, but that was concealed by the natives, who make things difficult and mysterious, and expensive.
>
> I wish his health would improve. Damn it.

To GUSTAVE S. LOBRANO

North Brooklin
25 September [1944]

Dear Gus:

I aimed to write you a letter when I was encamped on Lower Joe Mary lake tangling with the pickerel, but I am late with my correspondence. There were several mornings when I was late with the pickerel, too, on account of the very great heat we encountered. I never knew the woods to be hotter than on those first days of August. I never knew myself to be any hotter, either.

The proprietor of the Camps, one Leon Potter, is a testy man with bowel trouble. I came to like him after the first shock of his disapproval was over. He liked me better when he discovered that I didn't pretend to know about canoes. "By Jesus," he told me, "I been running this place twenty-nine years and I can stand anything except somebody who knows about canoes." He could see a deer at distances that would make Zeiss tremble to think of. The Camps are on a little point of land in a beautiful stand of Norway pines, and are well removed from what used to be called civilization in happier days. First you take the railroad to Millinocket, then you take a car to the landing at Ambejijus, then you cross Ambejijus and Pemadumcook in a motorboat to the mouth of Joe Mary stream, then you transfer to a 20-foot canoe (and you better God damn well not know anything about it, either) and ascend the stream till you get to the quickwater, then you take a trail through the woods to the landing at Lower Joe Mary and wait there until Mr. Potter poles the canoe through, then you take a smaller motorboat and tow the canoe to camp four miles down the lake. Katahdin glowers down at you during this entire trip, the loons complain at every lake, and when you finally arrive about noon and slip into your swimming trunks, Mr. Potter tosses out the ugly hint that dinner is in five minutes and no nonsense about ten minutes. It takes a day or two before you get treated with any civility by Mr. Potter. I think he was probably more amiable before his bowels started to go wrong, but not much. I think in two years he will be dead, and is using the time to good advantage. . . .

My bad health is now more than a year old, and alternately angers and frightens me. I long ago got reconciled to not feeling good, but am still not reconciled to turning in a bad performance all the time, or no performance—it seems to be mostly that. My nerves are better than when you trundled me to Boston last fall, but something seems to have hold of me by the top of the spine and is giving me the double twist. The details are boring and unconvincing.

Terry is on the phone, trying to sell my wife a house in Turtle Bay, from the sound of things. They are yelling at each other—the loudest real estate transaction I have ever heard. It seems Dorothy Thompson owns the house and there's not a stick of furniture in it, not a stick. What the house needs, obviously, is a stick of furniture. Well, it was 1937 that I began fighting my way out of Turtle Bay, and it looks like I've lost. We'll be back if Terry's voice holds out and the gas furnace in the cellar really works. Remind me to get hold of a stick of furniture.

The title of Sid's [Perelman's] piece "So Little Time Marches On" is the funniest thing I have read in the magazine for a long time, and the piece was funny, too. Haven't got round to "The Weeds" yet but am saving it for a lull. Last night we had a frost, and today is quiet and cold with very clear air and the brilliant sting of end-of-summer. My ram was found dead by me last week. Either he ate a little piece of fence wire or he was kicked by a horse. He leaves my next spring's lambs un-fathered. Joe is back in Exeter, settled in a room with a Bostonian for a roommate. Everything seems to be going all right except his soccer shoes were taken during the summer, and also his Oklahoma album.

If you want to shoot a duck, this is a good place to shoot a duck from.

Love from us all,
Andy

To STANLEY HART WHITE

North Brooklin
8 October the Red [1944]

Dear Bun:

K and I are just back from New York and Boston, respectively. K signed us up for the last remaining furnished apartment in Manhattan at a monthly rent that ought to take the Kremlin. Address 37 West 11 after Election Day. I went to a doctor in Boston who turned up the news that I have too many red cells. I don't know what that means except that I have too many red cells. I also have more pumpkins than I am going to need this winter. The two things together probably have produced my head condition.

While we were away one of the chimneys caught fire. No damage, except to the cook's nerves. Also while we were away one of the maples got red all over and is a pretty sight when the fog lifts and lets you get a look at it. I went out to Exeter from Boston and saw Joe at school. He has a room-mate who is a rather neat, tidy kid and likes to have things just so—pictures straight, books in an orderly row on shelf, desk clean. Joe has met this situation by starting construction on a model airplane about the size of a Liberator. The room when I saw it looked like a place the Germans had just withdrawn from in a hurry. I asked Joe how he was doing in English and he said "All right except that every theme comes back with every sentence marked 'colloquial.' "

Minnie is in heat and Fred is trying to adjust the demands of passion to the limitations of arthritis. He starts toward her bearing a bouquet of American Beauty roses, and falls on his pan before he gets there. It is wonderful to see his old misshapen frame aglow with Love's deathless fire. It is also lucky that he hasn't far to fall.

I got your letters (one from Polk Street and one from Urbana) and was glad to get the news. Will write again soon, enclosing some spare red cells. Or you can have a pumpkin if you'd rather have a pumpkin.

Yrs,
En

To HAROLD ROSS

North Brooklin, Maine
Saturday (Oct. 21, 1944)

Dear Mr. Ross:

Thanks for note about comment. . . . I am sometimes amazed that I should be writing these things and that you should be publishing them. I have written literally dozens of such pages and thrown them away, because of self doubts. But on the whole I think it is a good idea to present this sort of argument, if only to sharpen the distinction between diplomacy (which is simply a poker game on a big scale) and government, where the cards are always on the table. A hell of a lot of people have never discerned any essential difference between these two forms of human activity. Already you can see the beginnings of the big post-war poker game, for trade, for air routes and airfields, for insular possessions, and for all the rest of it. I hate to see millions of kids getting their guts blown out because all these things are made the prizes of nationality. Science is universal, music is universal, sex is universal, chow is universal, and by God government better be, too.

Dewey has been hollering about "secret diplomacy." But secrecy is the stuff any diplomacy is made of. Hitler is the only honest writer on this subject. He admits in cold type that there are no rules, no laws, and that a nation writes its own ticket. The so-called laws which will go into effect with a security league are not really laws at all, as long as the sovereignty remains in the separate nations and not in the people themselves. Agreements, it seems to me, are not capable of being enforced by police power because the God's truth is, every nation goes into a league with fingers crossed and with the knowledge that, ultimately, in a pinch, it will have to act independently.

Federation has the advantage of setting up a true, instead of a phony, government, and still permitting the individual states to have a sort of life of their own. Whether it would work on a global scale, knows God. I conceive it to be my duty at least to throw out the idea and define the words. You will, I am sure, receive some letters bawling you out for publishing stuff which is the work of a dreamy-eyed schoolboy, but I am not much embarrassed by these charges, because it is impossible for anybody to be dreamy-eyed, by comparison with the Jules Verne stuff that is taking place every day in the war.

EBW

To HAROLD ROSS

[New York]
3 January 45
[Interoffice memo]

Mr. Ross:

Have talked it over with Mrs. W. and our unusual expenses attributable to wartime work for NYer would be $100 per month rent, $25 per month service, or a total of $125 per month for an eight-month period. If the magazine feels inclined to pay our expenses to that amount, we accept with thanks. Payment should go half to KSW, half to EBW, to keep the records straight.

White

To STANLEY HART WHITE

[New York]
[January 1945]
Sunday

Dear Bun:

Don't worry about my health—I am a lot better and plenty good enough for my purposes. I had two things the matter with me—mice in the subconscious and spurs in the cervical spine. Of the two the spine trouble was less bothersome. It took me eighteen months to find out how you get rid of mice and if you ever need to know I'll be glad to give you the instructions. The whole key to the neurotic life is simple; in fact the simplicity of it is the greatest hurdle, because it tends to make it impossible or unacceptable to highly complex natures, who insist on meeting their troubles with suitably devious devices and cures. Anyway, here I am, in the clear again and damned thankful to be there. I can work without falling all apart, and can sleep—which is quite refreshing after a year and a half.

Joe has been here for the holidays and has enjoyed going out around the city on his own. He disapproves of cities, on the whole, however, and is almost too fiercely addicted to the Maine coast. One day I went up to the Bronx Zoo with him. We viewed tigers from Bengal, bears from the Pole, gaudy birds from tropical forests, and a whole assortment of strange and wonderful snakes. Joe didn't say much about any of them—but we finally wound up at the sea-lion pond where a keeper was throwing fish to the sea-lions. Overhead were half a dozen sea gulls which had turned up on the chance of a fish. One of the gulls let out a scream, and Joe looked up in sudden recognition and said: "Oh boy!" (Successful trip.)

Christmas was quiet but we had a good time. Thanks for the stamps which you sent—they were much appreciated. Lil, Arty, Noel and Sid were here for dinner the other night—I was amazed to see how the girls had grown. Art has gout, but Lil looked exceedingly well. K sends her best and with lots of love to Blanche & Janice. I was delighted to learn that you are so much better.

En

To WILLIAM SHAWN

[February 1945]
[Interoffice memo]

Shawn:

In the comment on *Life*'s storage wall, I wrote: ". . . a pretty good case can be made out for setting fire to it and starting fresh." Some studious person, alone with his God in the deep of night, came upon the word "fresh" and saw how easily it could be changed to the word "afresh," a simple matter of affixing an "a." So the phrase became "starting afresh" and acquired refinement, and a sort of grammatical excellence.

I still think people say "start fresh." I shall continue to write "start fresh," to say "start fresh," and, in circumstances which require a restart, I shall actually *start* fresh. I don't ever intend to start *a*fresh. Anybody who prefers to start *a*fresh is at liberty to do so, but I don't recommend it.

An afresh starter is likely to be a person who wants to get agoing. He doesn't just want to get going, he wants to get *a*going. An afresh starter is also likely to be a person who feels acold when he steps out of the tub.

Some of my best friends lie abed and run amuck, but they do *not* start afresh. Never do. However, if there is to be a growing tendency in the *New Yorker* office to improve words by affixing an "a," I shall try to adjust myself to this amusing situation. Characters in my stories will henceforth go afishing, and they will read Afield & Astream. They will not be typical people, they will all be atypical. Some of them, perhaps all of them, will be asexual, even amoral.

Amen.
E. B. White

• *In the spring of 1945* The New Yorker *sent White to San Francisco to report on the founding of the United Nations. His assignment was to write a Reporter-at-Large piece and also file timely Comment.*

To HAROLD ROSS

North Brooklin, Maine
[March 30, 1945]
Friday

Dear Mr. Ross:

Thanks for your note. You don't need to do anything about getting me a bed in San Francisco, since all accredited correspondents will be assigned a room at the Palace Hotel—according to your Mr. [Harding] Mason.

I hear Russia is going to be represented at the conference by one of the office boys.

Yrs,
EBW

To HAROLD ROSS

Roomette 5—Car N63
Overland Limited
[April 21, 1945]
Saturday

Dear Mr. Ross:

In order to ride facing forward, I have to sit on the toilet. Three nights and two days on the toilet is a record, for me.

Untrue about having to put your clothes on the floor. You put your clothes in a closet. Anyone putting his clothes on the floor in this roomette would be out of his mind or fond of treading on things.

Otherwise am very comfortable. Have never travelled more elegantly except at my own expense. There are a couple of delegates aboard but they are busy trying to learn English from pocket dictionaries, so I haven't disturbed them.

Yrs for a just peace,
White

To GUSTAVE S. LOBRANO

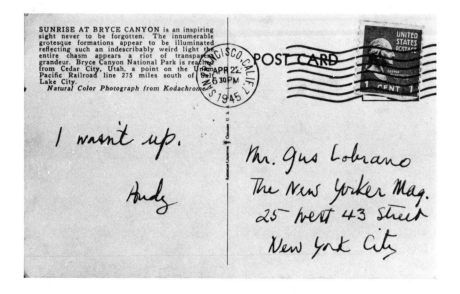

To HAROLD ROSS

San Francisco, Calif.
May 3, 1945
[Telegram]

REPORTER PIECE IS TURNING INTO CALENDAR OF EVENTS WORTH WHILE IN FOUR FOOT IAMBIC VERSE PERIOD IF IT DEVELOPS FAST I WILL WIRE YOU PERIOD OTHERWISE NOTHING THIS WEEK BUT COMMENT HAS ANYBODY EVER WIRED A POEM QUESTION MARK

E B WHITE

To **HAROLD ROSS**

San Francisco, Calif.
May 4, 1945
[Telegram]

FORECAST REPORTER PIECE TODAY SAME LENGTH AS OTHER AND EVERY
BIT AS UNINTERESTING PERIOD NO POEM

E B WHITE

• *Stuart Little was in production at Harper & Brothers. White and Ursula Nordstrom, head of the Department of Books for Boys and Girls at Harper's, were corresponding about the Garth Williams illustrations.*

To **URSULA NORDSTROM**

North Brooklin, Maine
29 May 1945

Dear Miss Nordstrom:

I'm returning the picture under separate cover. I like Stuart's crawl stroke very much, but I agree with you that Harriet isn't right. Her hair should be smoother and neater, also her legs should look more attractive (Harriet has beautiful legs), and her skirt should be fuller. I am enclosing a clipping from a Sears Roebuck catalogue showing a girl that looks like Harriet. Also Montgomery Ward's No. 21, which I suspect is the same girl. I hope Mr. Williams can save the Stuart part of this drawing and insert a new Harriet without having to redraw the whole thing. . . .

Sincerely,
EBWhite

To **URSULA NORDSTROM**

North Brooklin, Maine
7 July 1945

Dear Miss Nordstrom:

Dr. Carey looks a lot like President Truman.

Sincerely,
EBW

To **HAROLD ROSS**

[North Brooklin, Me.]
10 July 1945

Dear Mr. Ross:

You and your checking department and your proofroom have tangled with the wrong man in the matter of pigeons. I know about pigeons not from ornithologists but from the birds themselves—that is, from observing them, raising them, tending them, and living closely with them. A squab is fully grown when it is about four weeks old. At that age, it is fully feathered, is still being mouth-fed by the parent birds, and is ready to leave the nest. If mouth-feeding were to cease after ten days, as your ornithologist so glibly informs you, the squab would certainly die, as it is incapable of leaving the nest at 10 days, and is therefore incapable of getting any food for itself. The squab which I saw from the hotel room in NY was full-grown. It had left the nest and was being fed by one of the parent birds. It was a blue Homer. It was fully feathered. It was approximately four and a half weeks old. It was not "new born," for two reasons. The first reason is that, like all fea-thered creatures, it had never been born, it had been hatched. If you understood birds, birth, and such matters, you would know that chicks and squabs are not born. Eggs (in a manner of speaking) are born, but not chicks. Chicks, squabs, etc. are incubated and hatched. The second reason is that it was about four and a half weeks old, and was a full grown squab.

As for the "her"-"hen" typo, I guessed that it was a typo and that it would be caught, but from this distance and at this phase of the New Yorker's development, there was no telling whether it was a typo or a correction. Ten years ago I would have been reasonably sure it was a typo. Today, with pigeon-checking at the pitch it has reached, I can't be so sure. You may not realize it, not being a writer and con-tributor, but the impression the magazine now gives anyone turning stuff in, is that the material will first be completely dismantled, then as-sembled again in the assembling plant. During the process, a full grown squab will be reborn.

A writer loses confidence in himself. I am not as sure of myself as I used to be, and write rather timidly, staring at each word as it comes out, and wondering what is wrong with *it*. I don't know about editing, but my guess is that if the NYer ever reaches that degree of perfection toward which it is tending, when each word will have been taken aside and re-plated with silver, there won't be much left. I should not live 500 miles away and write about pigeons. It is too far away, and I know too much about pigeons.

White

• *Toward the end of the following letter to his brother, White men-tions that Anne Carroll Moore, doyenne of the children's book world, was trying to discourage the publication of* Stuart Little. *Miss Moore had just retired from her job as children's librarian at the New York Public Li-brary, and still had a great deal of influence at the library and among publishers. After reading the galley proofs of* Stuart Little, *she wrote a friend saying, "I was never so disappointed in a book in my life" and told Ursula Nordstrom that the book "mustn't be published." She also wrote a fourteen-page letter to Katharine White strongly urging her to persuade White to withdraw the book.*

In her reply to Miss Moore's letter, Katharine said:

> I'm of course very sorry that you do not like *Stuart Little* and thank you for writing that letter which I realize must have been very hard for you to do. My husband and I both appreciate the interest which made you write it. I can only hope that you are mistaken of course. Andy likes Stuart and so do I, and his publishers have never before been so enthusiastic over any of his other books as they are over *Stuart Little*. . . .

> You are right, of course, that Stuart gets out of hand and it's true, too, that the story follows none of the conventional patterns for fantasy. But I can't help feeling that the unpredictable quality of both Stuart, the character, and *Stuart*, the book, is one of the book's merits. Didn't you think it even *funny*? I can still laugh, reading the proofs, and Ed Aswell of Harper's reported that he and his eight-year-old son laughed out loud all the way when he read it aloud, though not necessarily always at the same places. So what I hope is that children of all ages *may* happen to like *Stuart* for its humor while their elders read it for its satirical and philosophical overtones. Actually, I myself have never known whether this book was a juvenile or a novel. It's a *dream*—quite literally—just as *Alice* is supposed to have been. Just recently the notes Andy made after he had that dream (more than twelve years ago) turned up, and I was surprised to find how clearly the story had followed them. . . . I am honestly not at all afraid of its hurting E.B.W. to have it published, or Harper's either, whether or not it is a financial or literary success.

To STANLEY HART WHITE

North Brooklin
11 July [1945]

Dear Bun:

I bet you didn't know that I have a friend (John McNulty) who is writing a song called "Keep Your Dreams Within Reason." I saw McNulty for one night in Hollywood when I was on my way home from San Francisco, and he was very depressed about conditions in movieland, and was trying to find relief by writing a new kind of dream song, "Keep Your Dreams Within Reason." I think you would like McNulty. He used to play the piano in a moving picture theatre in Andover, Mass., during the silent screen days, and can still do "hurry" and "fire" and "mother love" and the others.

We are having a plague of arthritis and tent caterpillars, also thunder storms. Things look pretty good, though, after all the rains of the spring. Joe has an infected finger and hand, but it doesn't seem to slow him up any. He sets an alarm for 5 a.m. every night—so he won't lose any of the summer by oversleeping. It seems that the only time you can pull a lobster trap is between five and seven in the morning, before the fog has lifted.

I was 46 today, and celebrated the occasion by hanging around a sawmill.

21 July

This letter got laid (or pushed) aside. I think I started shingling a building instead. We have been having a fog mull for the past week— the kind of dampness which puts out a cigarette after the third puff, the kind where you leave a pair of sneaks beside your bed at night, and in the morning you have to dump them before putting them on. I have just finished a letter to a professor in West Virginia University, who sent me a reprint of an essay of his on Thoreau, and in the course of writing the letter I remembered something (probably the oddest comment on Thoreau ever made) that a Cornell prof told me twenty-five years ago. He said that Thoreau was "all right, but I wish he had more get-up-and-go." I treasure that remark, and when the pain in my neck is bad I comfort myself with it, and go around muttering "The god damn son of a bitch had no get-up-and-go."

Tell Janice she got out of a lot of work by not getting the job of illustrating my book. It turns out that it is to have between 80 and 90 drawings. The former head of the Children's Book division of the NY Public Library managed to get hold of some galley proofs, and has written my wife a 14-page letter telling her how lousy it is. K refused to show me her reply, but I suspect it set a new world's record for poisoned courtesy.

The thing that has given me the most pleasure here this summer is a Shirley poppy that slipped its mooring and drifted forty feet to a spot in the gravel driveway, where it has bloomed profusely and alone, a brilliant testimonial to my courageous stand against edging. An edger came with the place, but I held out against it, and for years the place had a neat lawn, a neat flower border, and a ragged edge to the drive. With gas rationing the lawn began to encroach on the gravel drive, and the clover came in surprisingly fast, but the thing still looked inconsistent until the poppy turned up one morning. It has been a sensation.

K and I are taking a vacation from *New Yorker* work during September. We shall probably stay right here and spear a few flounders. So long, and keep your dreams within reason.

Yrs,
En

To JOHN R. FLEMING

North Brooklin, Maine
15 September [1945]

Dear Jack:

I dispatched your contribution to the magazine and you will shortly hear from them or me or both. Am surprised that MacArthur sits between Washington and Lincoln, as I had always pictured him between Christ and Daniel Boone.

In submitting stuff to the *New Yorker*, send factual stuff to William Shawn, and fictional stuff to G. S. Lobrano. The trouble with sending it to me, aside from the fact that I don't read anything anyway, is that I am usually in Maine and the trans-mailing delay is scandalous.

Was surprised to hear that you are leaving the government, and not the way you found it, either. It has often given me a feeling of stability to know that, no matter what sort of shuffling was going on, Fleming was in there looking out for my interests. It will not seem like the same government with you gone. But I hope you like the new job [at *U.S. News and World Report*] and that Luce doesn't get you.

I have discovered, rather too late in life, that there is nothing so much fun as building a boat. The best thing about boat building is that it allows absolutely no time for writing; there isn't a minute to spare.

Yrs,
Andy

To DAISE TERRY

North Brooklin, Maine
[October? 1945]

Dear Miss Terry:

I know you will be interested to hear that I left New York, by mistake, one day sooner than I intended to. Meant to go Friday, got on the train Thursday in error. Pullman seat was for Friday. I just stood up.

Yrs in error,
EBW

To URSULA NORDSTROM

North Brooklin, Maine
21 October [1945]

Dear Miss Nordstrom:

. . . Yesterday I dispatched [an autographed] copy of Stuart Little to Stuart Little, an eerie business. The latter, I am glad to say, appears to be an amiable man. It's just as well.

Sincerely,
EBW

To URSULA NORDSTROM

25 West 43rd Street
14 November [1945]

Dear Miss Nordstrom:

One or two of the Harper ads referred to Stuart as a "mouse." This is inaccurate and probably better be abandoned. Nowhere in the book (I think I am right about this) is Stuart described as a mouse. He is a small guy who *looks* very much like a mouse, but he obviously is not a mouse. He is a second son.

There are a great many words that your advertising department can summon for this strange emergency: being, creature, party, customer, fellow, person.

(I am wrong, Stuart *is* called a mouse on Page 36—I just found it. He should not have been.)

Anyway, you see what I mean.

Yrs,
E. B. White

• *On November 23, 1945, Leonard Lyons wrote in "The Lyons Den," his column in the* New York Post, *"There will be a to-do about the New York Public Library's reluctance to accept* Stuart Little, *the children's book by E. B. White." On reading this, White, who has a low regard for gossip writers because of the way they toss innuendos around, dispatched the following letter to the children's librarian who had succeeded Anne Carroll Moore.*

To FRANCES CLARKE SAYERS

North Brooklin, Maine
24 November 1945

Dear Mrs. Sayers:

You have probably seen by this time the Leonard Lyons column in the *Post* in which he predicts a "to-do" because of the "reluctance" of the Library to put "Stuart Little" on the shelves.

. . . I thought I had better write and let you know that I am not one of the to-doers—if indeed such there be. Mr. Lyons seems to suggest . . . dark and terrible goings on in the world of juvenile letters. As for me, I don't believe it and shall continue to support the system by which librarians and book committees are free to select books without pressure from interested parties. I have a little something to do with a small library in North Brooklin, Maine, and it seems to me that libraries are subjected to a steady (and very healthy) pressure from readers themselves, whose wants and whims in the long run have to be satisfied. That is the only sort of pressure I believe in; and I hope you will understand that if there has been any other sort of pressure in behalf of my book, it has been outside of my knowledge and against my wishes.

Sincerely,
E. B. White

P.S. To the best of my knowledge, Harper & Brothers feel in this matter as I do, and I am sure they had nothing to do with the Lyons item.

To STANLEY HART WHITE

239 East 48 Street
25 November [1945]

Dear Bun:

This is one of those Sundays when the Times and Tribune lie dead on the floor, and we make it an indoor carnival of loose ends, half buried correspondence, and diseased houseplants. This morning I stacked firewood in a neat pile on the balcony outside the living room, building up tiers of dirty kindling with the same rigid artistry that a Maine farmer lavishes on his spruce and birch. I ought to bathe a dog today—it's that kind of a day.

We had Clara here for dinner last Wednesday. She is a governess in a family named Sloan on Central Park West—takes care of a two year old girl and has Wednesdays off. She looks and feels fine and likes the job. The world is still mysterious to Tar, and she is ageless.

Katharine and I still go to work at *The New Yorker* every day, but we probably just make it all the harder for them to get out a magazine. There are vast quantities of employees, filling endless corridors and cubbyholes. Nobody knows the name or occupation of the others—just as in Grand Central. It's fun to be there—more like travel than like work.

We're planning to go to Maine for Christmas—big attendance this year, including Nancy and her husband and two children, [and] Evelyn, and Joe. We hoped Roger would make it from Hawaii, but it looks bad.

I had a letter from a producer who wants to put Stuart Little on the stage. Am holding the title role for you.

Yrs,
En

VIII

A PARTY OF ONE

1946–1949

• *During the years following World War II, the Whites continued at* The New Yorker, *where Katharine was one of the fiction editors. Fed up by the annual frustration of trying to find a furnished apartment in housing-short New York, they rented and remodeled a duplex apartment on Turtle Bay Garden, at 229 East 48th Street.*

White, like many other sensitive writers, began early on to feel the threat of McCarthyism and the loyalty check system and wrote many Comments which spoke out against that form of domestic tyranny. In 1949 Here Is New York *was published. A short book, it had been written the year before at the request of* Holiday *editor Ted Patrick and published in* Holiday *magazine.*

To CHRISTINE WESTON

[New York]
17 January [1946]

Dear Christine:

I have a stuffy habit of putting aside books I think I am going to like, waiting for a chance to read under decent conditions. Yesterday was Bhimsa Day in Fhorty Ehieghth Shtreet.¹ I have a nice little fever of 99 —the flu kissed me as delicately as a frightened girl, and I lay in bed feeling really quite well. It is a luxury to me to read in the morning, because usually I haven't the strength of character for that, and I went unerringly to Bhimsa and had such a wonderful time that I can't not

---

1. Christine Weston's book for children, *Bhimsa, the Dancing Bear,* had been published in December, and she had sent a copy to White.

tell you about it, the way I carried on with the drums and the cymbals (I get reading aloud when I am feverish in the morning) and sniffing the aromatic old sheets and blankets under which I was hiding in my bullock cart. The robber dance contest stirred me up so that I was dubbity dubbing myself right out onto the floor, and I think I was heard through the walls, because someone in the next house shouted: "Bears?" Anyway, it seems not to have done me any harm—today I am normal again. Furthermore, I want a bear. I wish the next time Robert finds a cub in the woods, he would let me have it, and meantime I will try to pick up a drum second hand, and a couple of clashers. One wonderful thing about your book is the feeling it gives that if you just have a bear nothing will get you—a reversal of the old childhood fancy that something is *going* to get you and that in all probability it will *be* a bear.

I suppose now that you are running with twentienth century foxes, you are a little snooty about other animals, and perhaps brush off your old friends with a nhod. But I LOVE BHIMSA!!

Andy Dubbity White

To **DOROTHY NIELSEN**

[New York]
April 5, 1946

Dear Mrs. Nielsen:

There is no sequel to "Stuart Little." A lot of children seem to want one but there isn't any. I think many readers find the end inconclusive but I have always found life inconclusive, and I guess it shows up in my work.

Thanks very much for your letter. I am glad that your children liked the book.

Sincerely yours,
E. B. White

To **HAROLD ROSS**

5/2/46
[Interoffice memo]

Mr. Ross:

This seems like the outline of a good piece, but too involved for me to take on. When three or more facts have to be marshalled, I get upset.

EBW

To STANLEY HART WHITE

[North Brooklin, Me.]
23 June 1946

Dear Bun:

The number of people who haven't heard much from me since Christmas is mounting every day. Still, I feel bad about not having written you. As a matter of fact I did write you a letter a couple of months ago, just as I was leaving town for Sarasota, but when I read it over it did not seem to make any sense on any subject, so I allowed it to fall lightly into the scrapbasket.

I have heard from Lil that Al has been given an extension until July 1st.[1] I don't know what his plans are or whether he has found a suitable apartment. I can't think of anything you can do to help, unless you know of a place they can get. It seems to me that they may have to make some sort of temporary arrangement, placing their furniture in storage and living in a summer rental until the housing shortage eases up a little. A lot of their trouble has been the bewilderment and confusion that afflicts people when they are suddenly confronted with their own impedimenta, and the contents of the attic is debouched on the living room floor. Life's accumulation is more discouraging than life itself, when stirred up.

K and I had a winter of virtually unrelieved trouble and corruption. We are now somewhat relaxed, K relaxing with arthritis, I with hay fever. We drove to Exeter last week and reclaimed Joe, and he looks pretty well. Our household seems small, by comparison to recent summers. Most of my sheep lived through the winter, and I have a few good lambs—at which passing motorists cast hungry glances, as they drool by. I was interested to learn that you're planning to visit Seattle. You can send me a postcard of Mount Rainier—which you won't ever see because of the smoke. I worked in Seattle from Sept. 1922 to July 1923, and I think the mountain was visible about three times during that period. The thing to do in Seattle is to ride around on street cars—only they are probably buses now, and that's no fun. The old Yesler Way car was pretty good, in its way. It ended [its run at] Lake Washington. Rhododendron time in Seattle is fairly spectacular, only I can't think when rhododendrons are in bloom. I spent most of my time going to weekly luncheons of the Owls, the Moose, the Eagles (biggest eyrie in the U. S.), the Realtors Association, the Young Men's Business Club, the Kiwanians,

1. Albert White and his family had occupied the Mount Vernon house at 48 Mersereau after the death of White's parents. However, the house, by the terms of the will, was owned by all six heirs and, with the estate now being settled, the Albert Whites had to find another place.

the Rotary Club, and lots more. Seattle is a very young city (or was in 1922) and everybody was under the impression that something wonderful was about to happen to the Northwest—like making a lot of money. Nothing ever came of it. My high point as a reporter was when I was assigned to fly low over Lake Washington in a seaplane and look for a body. The Times was an enterprising paper and always made a commotion about whatever they did. I never found the body, but it turned up a few days later in a local morgue. I imagine Banff will look the way it does in the promotional literature. I skipped Banff but spent a very instructive week in the jungle just outside MacLeod, Alberta. Anyway, I hope you have a fine time.

Your complaint about agriculture not having got around to my writings is unfounded. The latest USDA bulletin for bee keepers used my poem ["Song of the Queen Bee"] as a sort of obbligato.

My best to Janice and Blanche,
En

To HOWARD CUSHMAN

North Brooklin, Me.
14 August [1946]

Hum:

"Bold son," please, not "Proud son." Don't misquote me, even at this late date. I have checked to make sure. Kentucky's Greatest Newspaper (*Louisville Herald*) for Sunday May 14, 1922 is at hand, and the word is "bold." Attendance at the track was 70,000—or, as the Herald wittily put it, "70,000 strong." The great and the near great were there, and notables attended "from afar" to watch the gallant Morvich. An entry in my journal (Beta House, Cincinnati, Mon., May 15) records that the managing editor of the *Herald* was a Mr. Montgomery, and that he asked me whether I did that sort of thing "for glory or for money." I replied for money. Ah, kingly sport! Ah, Beta Theta Pi! Ah, Cushman and Kentucky in the May! . . .

Riding a strong wave of insanity (and luck) my own bride and I have taken an unfrnshd apt at 229 E. 48 and are being frnshd by a decorator—which is the same as being clipped in a joint, only it's legal. I expect to attend the housewarming in my bare feet. Hope to see you there.

Joe will be ready for college in one (1) year. Doesn't look at the moment as though any college will be ready for him, but that's another matter. Is Nancy married?

Yrs 'sever,
Ho

• *About the following letter, White writes: "I spent hundreds of hours (it became almost an obsession with me) observing the United Nations —first at Hunter College (a subway trip), then at Lake Success (train and bus), then in Turtle Bay (an easy walk). Considering the amount of time I put in, I wrote very few pieces."*

To HAROLD ROSS

[North Brooklin, Me.]
19 Aug [1946]

Dear Mr. R,

I have received from the United Nations (Nations Unies) an application for accreditation (Demande d'Admission). I mean they sent me the blank, to fill in. The letter accompanying it says that in anticipation of the General Assembly, a new system of accreditation for the Press will be put into effect on Sept. 1.

I don't know whether you want me to apply or not, and am writing to ask. If The New Yorker is to have only one accredited reporter, for instance, it probably ought to be a more reliable journalist (less spotty) than me. If, on the other hand, the NYer is allowed more than one man, maybe I should apply. Kindly let me know your wishes in this matter.

Yrs for a united world,
EB White
Division de la Presse

To STANLEY HART WHITE

North Brooklin
12 September [1946]

Dear Bun:

I have done no work and written no letters this summer, and it has felt pretty good—except that I kept doing a lot of other equally nerve-bouncing things, such as deciding whether Joe could or couldn't take the car out each evening. (The State of Maine lets 15-year-olds have driver's licenses, probably on the theory that the younger they are the softer their bones.) It is hard on the parents, who sit home in a brittle condition hoping that the oil reserves of earth will soon peter out. The summer reached a sort of peak the day we went to the Blue Hill Fair and K tried to take a leak in the bushes just as the trap-shoot started. She came out with only a minor flesh wound, but she might as well have been through Anzio. We all thought it was very comical, and one shooter (I heard later) got 25 pigeons out of a possible 25.

The next night Joe took a thirteen-year-old girl to the Fair, and she got sick on the swings, vomiting with centrifugal force.

We are starting for Boston tomorrow morning early, to attend a wedding in Louisburg Square and to put Joe back in school. It always amazes me that the idea of weddings has persisted the way it has. Considering the amount of disturbance and trouble a wedding causes, as well as the expense and the danger of everybody getting poisoned on chicken salad that has been eked out by adding five pounds of bad veal, you wonder anybody has the guts to stage it. I think weddings would die in no time at all, if it weren't for women, who seem to get some inner (and probably shabby) excitement out of the occasion.

Boston

14 September

We got into a taxicab on Charles Street a few minutes ago, and discovered that it was driven by a grey-haired woman and a dog. The woman shifted and made change and the dog steered. Boston is perennially surprising and enjoyable. Mayor Curley's name is part of a flower arrangement in the Public Garden—welcoming the Veterans of Foreign Wars. And the ducks still follow the swan boat around the lake, picking up a living from the first class passengers.

K and I are planning to go back to Maine for a couple of weeks and then to New York for the winter. We have taken an apartment at 229 E. 48 Street. I have a book coming out this fall called "The Wild Flag"—a collection of New Yorker paragraphs on tremendous themes. In it I make my debut as a THINKER, which in these days is like stepping up on the guillotine platform wearing a faint smile.

Our health is neither very good nor very bad. I was delighted to learn that you had a good trip to the West. News of the family has been rather sparse this summer, but I'll be seeing some of them soon I hope.

Best to Blanche & Janice,

En

• Ursula Nordstrom had written White that sales of Stuart Little had reached 100,000 copies. White responded with this note and a gift of caviar—"guaranteed to contain 100,000 sturgeon eggs." By 1975 the book had sold over half a million copies, not counting paperback editions.

To URSULA NORDSTROM

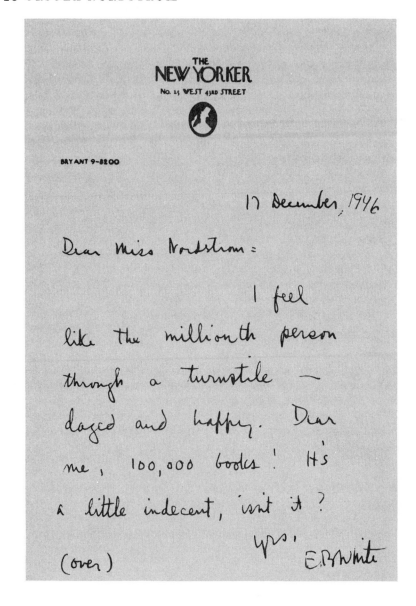

THE
NEW YORKER
No. 25 WEST 43RD STREET

BRYANT 9-8200

17 December, 1946

Dear Miss Nordstrom=

I feel like the millionth person through a turnstile — dazed and happy. Dear me, 100,000 books! It's a little indecent, isn't it?

yrs. E B White

(over)

When I recover from my
100,000th head cold, which
is now upon me, I'd like
to take you to a Milestone
Luncheon at some fashionable
restaurant, in celebration.
You can eat 100,000 stalks
of celery, and I'll swallow
100,000 olives. It will be
the E B White - Ursula Nordstrom
Book and Olive Luncheon.

EBW

To HENRY S. CANBY

[New York]
December 21, 1946
[Telegram]

VERY GRATEFUL FOR YOUR INVITATION[1] BUT FEEL IT IS TOO EARLY IN LIFE TO JOIN AN INSTITUTE OF LETTERS AS IN MY PRESENT CONDITION I CAN BARELY KEEP UP WITH LETTERS THEMSELVES. THIS IS IN KEEPING WITH MY DISINCLINATION TO BELONG TO CLUBS AND SOCIETIES, EVEN INCLUDING THOSE FOR WHICH I HAVE THE HIGHEST REGARD. WITH MANY THANKS,

E. B. WHITE

To HENRY S. CANBY

[New York]
22 December 1946

Dear Dr. Canby:

I sent you a wire yesterday, to which I feel I should add a few words by way of amplification. I do not decline invitations for the sheer fun of declining them, or because it seems a brisk and cocky thing to do. The fact is, I have no membership in any society or organization, and this non-joining comes naturally to me. I sometimes suspect that I go a little out of my way to stay clear, and that this has the look of attitudinizing.

I am extremely grateful for your invitation to become a member of the National Institute. But I realized, when I got thinking about it, that the only legitimate reason for joining anything at all is an intention of participating in the work of it. And I long ago discovered that I had neither the energy nor the inclination nor the special talents that belong to membership in a group, whether literary or social.

That's the whole of it, and I ask your indulgence and send my thanks.

Sincerely,
E. B. White

To STANLEY HART WHITE

25 West 43
[January 1947]
Friday

Dear Bun:

I'm glad to report that even now, at this late day, a blank sheet of paper holds the greatest excitement there is for me—more promising

---

1. To become a member of the National Institute of Arts and Letters, of which Canby was Secretary. White later had a change of heart and accepted a subsequent invitation.

than a silver cloud, prettier than a little red wagon. It holds all the hope there is, all fears. I can remember, really quite distinctly, looking a sheet of paper square in the eyes when I was seven or eight years old and thinking "This is where I belong, this is it." Having dirtied up probably a quarter of a million of them and sent them down drains and through presses, I am exhausted but not done, faithful in my fashion, and fearful only that I will die before one comes out right— as though I had deflowered a quarter of a million virgins and was still expecting the perfect child. What *is* this terrible infatuation, anyway? Some mild nervous disorder, probably, that compels a man to leave a fiery tail in his wake, like a ten-cent comet, or smell up a pissing post so that the next dog will know who's been along. I have moments when I wish that I could either take a sheet of paper or leave it alone, and sometimes, in despair and vengeance, I just fold them into air-planes and sail them out of high windows, hoping to get rid of them that way, only to have an updraft (or, a change of temper) bring them back in again. As for your gift of so many sheets of white bond, with rag content, I accept them in the spirit with which they were sent and shall write you a book. It will be the Greatest Book that has Ever Been Written. They all are, in the early wonderful stage before the first word gets slid into place.

Happy New Year!

En

To STANLEY HART WHITE

[New York]

1 March 1947

Dear Bun:

Your description of K's bodyless appearance in the American liter-ary scene amused her very much,[1] and you are quite right that she has been lenient about the whole thing. I would be scared to give her more than one dimension, however, for fear she would take six or eight—she is so much brighter and better educated than I am that if I were to let her out of the box she'd give me away in no time. A man who skates on thin ice shouldn't carry bundles. As a matter of record, I have been brooding for a long time on the possibilities of writing a biography of my wife, based on the amazing assorted-chocolate facts which a husband is bound to pick up about a woman's past in the course of a marriage. We were in Boston last week, and K looked out

1. As an editor Katharine White is a behind-the-scenes person. She has in-fluenced and guided many prominent authors but seldom sees her name in lights.

of the hotel room at the tower of the Custom House. "When Cousin Mary Perley saw that tower for the first time," said my wife, "she snorted and said, 'Humpf. Sticks up like a sore thumb.'" Later we went to Mechanics Hall to the dog show, and K said: "The last time I was in this place I was a child, and some men in canoes were shooting the rapids." It has occurred to me that if I collected a couple of thousand such items, I would have a biography of a Boston girl.

My favorite anecdote about K is of a visit she paid to Aunt Poo in Woodstock, Conn. Somewhere she had heard of a flower called "Traveler's Joy," and the name and function of this posy excited her so much that she got hold of some seed and went out into a roadside which already teemed with enough wild flowers to make a traveler drunk with ecstasy, and scattered the seeds carefully along the way, to bring joy to travelers.

I go out a couple times a week to the Security Council meetings in Lake Success (near Great Neck) which are held in a gyroscope plant. Gyroscopes are still being made there—just in case. For relaxation I am reading "Life on the Mississippi," and Kilvert's Diary.

En

To JOHN B. WENTWORTH

[New York]
March 10, 1947

Dear Mr. Wentworth:

I still think the American press informs the people, not completely and not without bias, but informs them. I was simply comparing it with a truly kept press where nobody gets any information at all.

I think that it is not so much the relationship between business office and editorial office that should worry people in a democracy as it is the dwindling of ownership of the press. As [long as] there are a lot of papers and a lot of owners I think the news gets out, even news such as you complain about. . . .

Sincerely,
E. B. White

To RUTH CHAPMAN

[New York]
April 10, 1947

Dear Miss Chapman:

Thanks for suggesting that I be photographed, but I shall have to decline the invitation. Had all my teeth photographed the other day, and nothing good came of it.

Sincerely,
E. B. White

To STANLEY HART WHITE

229 East 48
19 April [1947]
Saturday

Dear Bun:

When Lil was here the other night, she told me she had not written you about Arthur's death. He died suddenly on March 26. I was in Florida and Lil didn't notify me, either. She let Marion and Clara know right away, and Marion and Arthur [Brittingham] were at the funeral services.

Art had gone to work, felt sick at the office, and at the end of the morning had started for home. Luckily he had taken a business friend along with him. They got as far as the Penn Station, where Arty collapsed—a perfect conclusion for a true railroad fan. Lil is OK, and so are the girls. Their financial situation is not too hot, but adequate, I think. Carol is working in a travel bureau in Garden City, lives home, and will contribute. Art left some insurance and some securities, and Lil has applied for a federal pension, I believe, as Art was in the First War.

Art's father is still alive. He has a sort of office-boy job in Wall Street, and lives in Manhattan.

I'm just dashing this off to you as I'm not sure you even know about the matter, and I'm sure you will want to. I was very fond of Arty—he was always occupied in doing favors for other people. He died intestate, but there was a case of beer on its way to me at the very moment.

Yrs,
En

•   *The following note was occasioned by the smallpox scare of 1947, when many adults, including Lobrano and White, were vaccinated against the disease. Myrtle Powers and her sister Etta Sawyer, widows, of West Brooklin, Maine, were with the Whites as cook and housekeeper.*

To GUSTAVE S. LOBRANO

229 East 48
[April? 1947]
Tuesday

Dear Gus:

It is now quite generally known that you have smallpox and it seems to me ill-advised (and rather immature) to keep up this pretense. I went for vaccination yesterday morning, taking Mrs. Powers and Mrs.

Sawyer along; and on the way back from the doctor's office, in the cab, Mrs. Powers told me the story of her first immunization, some sixty-two years ago, when she was a little girl in West Brooklin, Maine. She reached into a flour barrel one day and managed to tear her upper arm, near the shoulder, on a protruding nail. The thing healed but left a distinct scar. Some weeks later all the children in the village were marched in to old Doctor Herrick's office (three and a half miles, afoot), to get vaccinated against the pox. Mrs. Powers says that she was frightened at the idea, and that when her turn came she boldly told Dr. Herrick that she "had already been vaccinated."

"Have you?" he said.

"Yes," she replied, rolling up her sleeve.

"Why, so you have," said the good man. And that was all there was to that. Medicine has seen its best days.

Turtle Bay Garden is in its first mad blush of spring, and as soon as you are no longer contagious, you must come here for a stroll in our leafy setting—or what Bowden Broadwater [a co-worker]calls "this decadent close." . . .

Andy

To STANLEY HART WHITE

North Brooklin, Maine
[July 1947]
Saturday

Dear Bun:

Got your letter about coming east and was glad to hear the news. My getting to Boston isn't very likely unless something comes up that would take me to New York. But why don't you take a little jaunt down here to see us? . . .

Joe finished Exeter this June and has been admitted to Cornell, but thinks he'll wait one year before entering. At the moment he is absorbed in boats and girls and sometimes a combination of the two. I haven't been doing much of anything—just tinkering with a strawberry patch, watching phoebes through binoculars, and mixing drinks. A doctor last spring told me that I would be all right if I quit writing. He said most writers were neurotics—if they weren't neurotic they wouldn't go to the trouble, the enormous trouble. I find that Not Writing is very soothing, but haven't figured out yet what I will use for money.

Lunch is ready.

Yrs,
En

• *In an editorial published on November 27, 1947, the* Herald Tribune, *though somewhat grudgingly, supported the right of the movie industry to blacklist the "Hollywood Ten" and any others who refused to answer questions before J. Parnell Thomas's House Un-American Activities Committee. The following letter, White's reaction to the editorial, was published in the* Tribune *on December 2.*

To the NEW YORK HERALD TRIBUNE

New York, New York
November 29, 1947

To the New York Herald Tribune:

I am a member of a party of one, and I live in an age of fear. Nothing lately has unsettled my party and raised my fears so much as your editorial, on Thanksgiving Day, suggesting that employees should be required to state their beliefs in order to hold their jobs. The idea is inconsistent with our Constitutional theory and has been stubbornly opposed by watchful men since the early days of the Republic. It's hard for me to believe that the Herald Tribune is backing away from the fight, and I can only assume that your editorial writer, in a hurry to get home for Thanksgiving, tripped over the First Amendment and thought it was the office cat.

The investigation of alleged Communists by the Thomas committee has been a confusing spectacle for all of us. I believe its implications are widely misunderstood and that the outcome is grave beyond exaggerating. The essence of our political theory in this country is that a man's conscience shall be a private, not a public affair, and that only his deeds and words shall be open to survey, censure and to punishment. The idea is a decent one, and it works. It is an idea that cannot safely be compromised with, lest it be utterly destroyed. It cannot be modified even under circumstances where, for security reasons, the temptation to modify it is great.

I think security in critical times takes care of itself if the people and the institutions take care of themselves. First in line is the press. Security, for me, took a tumble not when I read that there were Communists in Hollywood but when I read your editorial in praise of loyalty testing and thought control. If a man is in health, he doesn't need to take anybody else's temperature to know where he is going. If a newspaper or a motion picture company is in health, it can get rid of Communists and spies simply by reading proof and by watching previews.

I hold that it would be improper for any committee or any employer to examine my conscience. They wouldn't know how to get into it, they wouldn't know what to do when they got in there, and I wouldn't let them in anyway. Like other Americans, my acts and my words are open to inspection—not my thoughts or my political affiliation. (As I pointed out, I am a member of a party of one.) Your editorialist said he hoped the companies in checking for loyalty would use their powers sparingly and wisely. That is a wistful idea. One need only watch totalitarians at work to see that once men gain power over other men's minds, that power is never used sparingly and wisely, but lavishly and brutally and with unspeakable results. If I must declare today that I am not a Communist, tomorrow I shall have to testify that I am not a Unitarian. And the day after, that I never belonged to a dahlia club.

It is not a crime to believe anything at all in America. To date it has not been declared illegal to belong to the Communist party. Yet ten men have been convicted not of wrongdoing but of wrong believing. That is news in this country, and if I have not misread history, it is bad news.

E. B. White

• *On the same page on the same day that White's November 29 letter was published in the* Tribune, *another editorial appeared entitled "The Party of One." It said that people like Mr. White "have been with us since the dawn of civilization. They have always been highly valuable elements in our civilization and nearly always as destructive as they have been valuable." Members of the party of one were also characterized as "probably the most dangerous single elements in our confused and complicated society."*

White's reply to the "Party of One" editorial appeared on December 9 under the heading "Mr. White Believes Us Needlessly Unkind."

To the NEW YORK HERALD TRIBUNE

New York
Dec. 4, 1947

To the New York Herald Tribune:

The editorial that you wrote about me illustrated what I meant about the loyalty check system and about what would happen if it got going in the industrial world. My letter, expressing a dissenting opinion, was a letter that any conscientious reader might write to his newspaper, and you answered it by saying I belonged to "probably the most dangerous element in our society." Thus a difference of opinion became suddenly a mark of infamy. A man who disagreed with a Tribune editorial used to be called plucky—now he's called dangerous. By your own definition I already belong among the unemployables.

You said that in these times we need "new concepts and new principles" to combat subversion. It seems to me the loyalty check in industry is not a new principle at all. It is like the "new look," which is really the old, old look, slightly tinkered up. The principle of demanding an expression of political conformity as the price of a job is the principle of hundred percentism. It is not new and it is blood brother of witch burning.

I don't know why I should be bawling out the Herald Tribune or why the Herald Tribune should be bawling out me. I read those Bert Andrews pieces and got a new breath of fresh air. Then I turned in a dissenting opinion about an editorial and got hit over the head with a stick of wood. These times are too edgy. It is obvious to everyone that the fuss about loyalty arises from fear of war with Russia, and from the natural feeling that we should clear our decks of doubtful characters. Well, I happen to believe that we can achieve reasonably clear decks if we continue to apply our civil rights and duties equally to all citizens, even to citizens of opposite belief. That may be a dangerous and false idea, but my holding it does not necessarily make me a dangerous and false man, and I wish that the Herald Tribune next time it sits down to write a piece about me and my party would be good enough to make the distinction. Right now it's a pretty important distinction to make.

E. B. White

[*Determined to have the last word, the* Tribune *printed a parenthetical editorial comment right underneath White's letter. The comment began* "Perhaps we were over-emphatic in our disagreement with Mr. White, but since the same editorial which suggested that he belonged to a 'dangerous element' also said that it was a 'highly valuable' element, he can scarcely hold that we were attaching any badge of 'infamy' to him." *The editor went on to express the* Tribune's *regard for White, to deny that its editors were the slightest bit afraid of war with Russia, and to state that they continued to feel that Communism was* "exploiting toleration in order to destroy toleration." *The comment concluded that* "We may be misguided in our attempts to deal with it, but it seems to us that Mr. White fails to deal with it at all."]

To FELIX FRANKFURTER

[New York]
December 12, 1947

Dear Justice Frankfurter:

There are more devils than angels around here at the moment, but I shall continue to give tongue.[1] Your letter was most encouraging. My

---

1. Frankfurter's congratulatory letter to White about his exchange with the *Tribune* had contained the phrase "speak with the tongues of angels."

Tribune excursion into the realm of civil liberties covered me with a surprising lot of goat feathers, and I could hardly get my breath and needed a letter like yours.

Many thanks.

Very sincerely yours,
E. B. White

To MAURICE ZOLOTOW

[New York]
December 15, 1947

Dear Mr. Zolotow:

Thanks for the letter—I'm a little late answering. It's true that I am not well informed on Communist Party maneuvers, but that's not the point. The point is whether we want the government to step into communications industries and start hiring and firing the employees. I'm against it, because I know where it leads. My editorial[1] was not a commentary on the character, motives, or ability of the Hollywood men, it was a warning against industry surrendering its prerogatives to government, and allowing itself to decline to the point where it is incapable of running its own show.

I am firmly on your side about Communism, but I believe that in order to keep it in check, we must not stir the deep fears and hatreds of the American people and make suspects out of millions of innocent citizens. That is just exactly what the Communists are hoping we *will* do, if my guess is any good.

Sincerely,
E. B. White

• *The essay "Death of a Pig" was published in the January 1948 issue of the* Atlantic Monthly. *On January 7, an article about the piece appeared in the* Ellsworth (Maine) American. *It implied that White, an outlander, had written unfairly about his veterinarian, E. J. McDonald.*

To E. J. MC DONALD

[New York]
January 14, 1948

Dear Doc:

You probably saw that piece in the *Ellsworth American* calling me down for the pig story. I'm not sure I understand the more cryptic

---

1. Notes and Comment in the December 6, 1947, issue of *The New Yorker*, a blast at the Hollywood producers who had fired ten writers in a loyalty purge.

passages, but the last couple of paragraphs seem to indicate that I was deliberately using people's names with intent to humiliate them. And that disturbs me, because although I am often an inept writer (and pigman) I don't think of myself as malicious, and I certainly hope I didn't hurt your feelings or those of your wife. If I did, I am deeply sorry and want to apologize to you and to her in no uncertain terms.

Thirty years of being a writer have convinced me that people are always trying to read something into a man's motives, and are finding hidden meanings that exist only in the eye of the beholder. I had no ulterior motive for writing that story (unless you want to call a desire to earn a living an ulterior motive), and I was merely attempting to describe as accurately and factually as possible, a curious interlude in my life when comedy and tragedy seemed to cohere.

If the comedy turned out to seem not so funny to you, when you saw yourselves in print, I am truly sorry and am sore at myself. I started out using fictitious names, instead of real ones, but my experience with the use of fictitious names in connection with real events is that the populace manages to hang the wrong name on the wrong character, and that, too, makes for bad feelings and misunderstanding.

One thing I wonder about was whether people thought I was trying to take a quick punch at veterinary medicine in Hancock County. If so, that, too, is just somebody's imagination at work. I think I made it clear in the story that veterinary medicine was in a healthy condition even though the pig wasn't.

If you can enlighten me about the "consultation" that the *Ellsworth American* writer says he knows all about, I'd appreciate it. After you . . . left I took another drink and consulted only with God. Even He didn't seem to be able to loosen up that pig, and he died before the medicine arrived in the mail.

At any rate, I don't mind being attacked in the papers—that happens to me almost every week of my life, and I am not even punch-drunk. I *do* mind, though, if I caused you any embarrassment merely to satisfy my own literary whims. A writer has his problems, the same as a doctor. Sometimes I get so discouraged by writing that I think seriously of giving up the life, and changing to a nice clean line of work, like bailing out cesspools or painting the under side of boats.

Anyway, I wish you and Mrs. McDonald a happy New Year, and a long and fruitful life. And if I got you off to a queer start by rushing you into the public prints via my pighouse, I hope you'll forgive me.

Sincerely,
E. B. White

To STANLEY HART WHITE

229 East 48 Street
24 January 1948
Saturday

Dear Bun:

Many thanks to you and Blanche for the *Countryman's Companion*. It seems to be a good collection. . . .

I have had a rather wild fall and winter so far, thanks to my incurable habit of putting practically anything that comes into my head down on paper and getting it published in newspapers and magazines. It is a lousy habit and I would be better off if I were a confirmed drunkard. I got into a little argument with the *Herald Tribune* on the subject of loyalty-checking, during which they ran an editorial about me saying that I belonged to the most dangerous element in society. I was delighted, as I had not known my own strength up till then. It seems that all you have to do to be tagged "dangerous" nowadays is to stand up for the First Amendment to the Constitution. Then I wrote an editorial in *The New Yorker* on the subject of the Hollywood purge and the Un-American Activities Committee, and I was soon getting courted by all the Communist front organizations. My desk got so deep in Red literature that I had to fumigate myself every night before going home. It was worse than athlete's foot. Then a piece of mine came out in the *Atlantic Monthly*, a simple rustic tale about the death of a pig, and the *Ellsworth* (Maine) *American* attacked it as malicious. You can't even come out against constipation in America any more.

However, things in general are all right, and my head feels rather better than it did a year ago. There's not much news to report. Roger and Evelyn had a baby girl a couple of weeks ago,[1] and Roger is supporting it by working for a magazine called *Holiday*, a travel publication based on the perfectly sound idea that everybody in the United States would like to be somewhere else. Joe is working for a construction company, helping remodel the *Times* Annex.[2] K still works like ten horses at *The New Yorker*, but her spine is on the blink and gives her a lot of bad trouble. I was interested in your review of the Fifth Edition of Webster's. I own a copy inscribed "To Stuart Little" from Robert C. Munroe, the president of G. & C. Merriam Company.

Zoe mou, sas agapo.
En

---

1. Their first, Caroline S. Angell, called Callie.
2. After graduating from Exeter, Joel White waited a year before entering Cornell, and took an interim job in New York.

To BRISTOW and LUELLA ADAMS

229 East 48th Street
16 February 1948

Dear BA and Ma:

If I had Bristow's stamina and muscle tone, I could write a good letter of appreciation and appraisal, but I am too pooped by the day's developments for that, and shall have to confine myself to a few withering lines. K and I had a long session with her doctor this afternoon and we are both convinced that he is right in prescribing a fusion operation on her spine. Not a bright prospect but brighter, on the whole, than the one she faced of being always restricted and always in pain.

Under separate cover I am despatching the following articles: (1) a copy of "Stuart Little," (2) a copy of "The Wild Flag," (3) a typed copy of the poem of the lovelorn advertising man.[1] The last, by the way, is not only a bum poem but included in one of the rarest volumes of poetry in America, called "The Lady Is Cold," of which Bristow claims to be possessed.

The Lehigh Valley Railroad did pretty well by us and got us back to town only about an hour late, and Joe made a quick change into work shoes and funny pants and disappeared in the direction of the N. Y. Times Building, to resume work on the construction job. We both had a wonderful weekend. I don't know how to thank you enough for letting us into your house. It means a lot to me that Joe's first impressions of Ithaca and of Cornell should have been colored by the atmospheric quality of 202 Fall Creek Drive. If he doesn't like the place now, he can go climb a tree. I haven't yet had much of a chance to talk with him, but I gather that Cornell was everything and more than he had imagined. (Note: never use everything and more in the same sentence—it leads to destruction.)

Wandering around the place, I was myself seized with the terrible desire to be a freshman again. There is something about those mild hills and that cradled valley that never stops working in the blood.

It was tantalizing to sit again in the Navajo-Balinese-walrus room among the cherry paddles and pictures painted in sand, drugged with milk punch and memories. And I enjoyed every minute of the Saturday night blizzard on Alumni Field, with the lap robes flying under the spinning wheel, all doors frozen tight, and the steady shifting of the gears. It seemed to me that Cornell, in twenty-seven years, hadn't changed in any vital way. A little more alcohol, perhaps, a little less cocoa; a good

---

1. "A Young Advertising Man, After a Hard Day at the Office, Writes to the Girl He Loves."

many more automobiles, a little more holding of the hands between the sexes. . . .

Don't forget that we have a spare bed at 229 East 48. It has your name embroidered on the spread.

Love from all,
Andy

• *Charles and Sadie Henderson were neighbors and close friends of the Whites in Maine. The two families saw a good deal of each other and were in constant communication—some of it by hand-cranked telephone on a party line. Charles Henderson was a lobsterman and also kept sheep and geese.*

To SADIE HENDERSON

[New York]
April 19, 1948

Dear Mrs. Henderson:

The operation took place Thursday morning and Mrs. White stood it very well. The doctors seem to think that they have found the real trouble and fixed it. They cut a piece of bone out of her pelvis and spliced it into her spine with a couple of lag screws. This will give her the support which she needs and should eliminate the pain which she has been having for so long.

A letter came this morning from North Brooklin which I think is in your handwriting and I am taking it up to the hospital this afternoon and I think it will raise the patient's spirits immensely. These last couple of days have been very difficult for her in bed because it is hard for her to get even halfway comfortable and the doctors have to keep her heavily doped. But things are looking up and every day sees some improvement. This is just a brief note to let you know that all is well and you will hear more from us soon. . . .

Lots of love from us both,
E. B. White

To WALTER MAGNES TELLER

25 West 43rd Street
May 24, 1948

Dear Mr. Teller:

I don't know what quoting "pretty extensively" means in this case. I'm withholding permission, generally speaking, on the reprinting of the

Malabar review,[1] because for one thing I plan to include it in a book of verse, and I think I ought to have first crack at it on account of my being the author.

If you want to quote from it, you'll have to do so pretty sparingly, rather than pretty extensively. I think the law allows you to swipe a little of it, but not much—like taking a single grape as you pass the fruit bowl on the sideboard.

Sincerely,
E. B. White

• *When he was writing* Comment *for* The New Yorker, *and therefore speaking for the magazine, White felt that it was inappropriate for him to supply publishers with blurbs on books. The galleys in this letter were of William Maxwell's novel* Time Will Darken It.

To CASS CANFIELD

[New York]
June 11, 1948

Dear Cass:

Thanks for the Maxwell galleys. About fifty unborn books a year arrive in the mail for me, accompanied by letters similar to yours of June 4th asking me for comment. I thought perhaps it's only fair to let you know that I have a long record of silence, or muteness, and don't give out statements about books in advance of publication, for the bland reason that I don't like to. So a publisher is presumably wasting money to keep me on his list.

I'm just telling you this as a routine intelligence service, and because you are my severest friend and best publisher.

Yours,
Andy

To KATHARINE S. WHITE

North Brooklin
[June 1948]
Tuesday afternoon

Dear K:

Your letter came this morning, and I read Mrs. Dow hers from you, as she said she was too busy to read it herself and if I read it to her she

---

1. A rhymed review of Louis Bromfield's *Malabar Farm*. It appeared in the May 8, 1948, issue of *The New Yorker* and later was included in *The Second Tree From the Corner*.

could keep right on cleaning the living room during the reading. So I stood in the center of the room, turning and twisting so as always to be facing her as she darted and dipped around, flicking dust out of bookshelves and dabbing Dutch Cleanser onto door frames. I sometimes think that the only way I could ever bring Josie [Mrs. Dow] and Howard [Pervear] to a standstill is with a shotgun—and I'm not even sure I could *hit* Josie, as she is quicker than a woodcock.

The day started with Joe taking a long showerbath to wash his hair, and the water leaking down through the kitchen ceiling onto the counter. Just at 7 a.m., through the awful cloud of my sleeping potion hangover, I heard Howard's voice yelling for me. I presumed we were burning up, and jumped out of bed in a terrible daze—to find that Joe's hairwash was dripping into the kitchen. Howard's hullabaloo was out of all proportion to his curiosity about the cause of, and location of, the drip. He just wanted to make sure nobody was in bed during a flood. Joe and I later removed the panel, exposed the pipes, found the place where the water was getting through, and the seam will be puttied tomorrow when things dry out. . . .

Mrs. Dow has just entered this room bearing fresh dotted Swiss curtains, and the sight of them going up at the window took me swiftly back to the early fall ritual in 101 Summit Avenue when the dotted Swiss suddenly appeared, after summer emptiness, and the rooms seemed to this child richly cozy and full of home cheer and protection.

The Hanover ordeal was both good and bad, but I came through it all right and am no worse for the wear. It ended happily enough, but I had a frightful night Saturday night at the Inn, caused partly by my natural uneasiness and fear of platforms and partly by Dartmouth's over-conscientious system of providing each honorary candidate with an Escort. Mine was named Bill Pulley, a very nice boy from Ohio, who got me on the phone the minute I arrived, weary, in my bedroom, and who insisted on escorting me every second. He would have escorted me to the bathroom if I had let him, and would have brushed my teeth. He was presumably acting under orders, and his orders were to see that I was walked here and there and shown things. The upshot was that instead of my having a rest after the journey, and a leisurely dinner, I had Bill Pulley. The dining room was crowded and the service slow, and twice during the meal I was informed, by special runner, that Pulley was waiting outside. So I bolted the chicken, filled up immediately with gas and apprehension, made a quick tour of the murals and the band concert, and then was escorted to a play at the Hall, sicker than a coot. I had also received phone messages and notes from President Dickey, wanting me to come to his house after the show. Just as the show ended, it began to pour rain, and my escort produced a raincoat for me, and Joe and I ran back across the quadrangle to the Inn. I was due at the Dickeys' house but by that time (about 11:30 pm) I was not only sick but was wet, too. So I just got into bed and didn't even have the strength to phone the President's house. After a while the phone rang and the Secretary of the College was on the line, wanting to know whether I wasn't coming over. I told him I couldn't, and would see him in the morning. . . . I couldn't take anything to eat, couldn't take liquor, couldn't stand up, couldn't lie down, couldn't stand it with the light on, or with the light off, and was virtually a total casualty. Poor Joe was left holding the bag, and did it very well; but I was pretty sure that I was cooked, as far as ever showing up for my graduation exercises next morning. I debated whether to swallow a knock-out capsule, and was hesitant about doing so because I thought that with my insides completely solidified that way, it might be better to be awake than asleep. However, I finally took the dose, and slept. Sunday morning I felt hardly any better but I decided that it would be even harder to get *out* of the ceremony than get in it.

At ten, we honorary characters assembled, were introduced, met the President, were fitted with gowns and caps, were temporarily hooded for the benefit of photographers, and then for a long while stood around on one foot waiting for the President and the Dean and a little man out at the airport to decide what the hell to do about the fact that it was drizzling out of doors. I had been able to take into my stomach only a tablespoonful of orange juice and about three ounces of oatmeal. So the old emptiness and dizziness and vapors seized hold of me and I had to pretend to carry on a literary conversation with Ben Ames Williams, a large hearty writer, while the flashbulbs popped. Nobody who has never suffered my peculiar kind of disability can understand the sheer hell of such moments—but there they are. Anyway, we all lined up after a bit, and outside the senior class lined up on the quadrangle in two straight rows making an aisle, and then after a long, long wait with no chance to sit down, we started out, led by the President, and marched (or shuffled) through the human aisle, while the seniors gave us the eye. The only thing good about it, from my point of view, was that if I had started to fall down, there would certainly have been a man there to catch me. I fell not, and the procession continued for about an eighth of a mile to the Bema, a mild declivity well suited to flatulence as there were no echoes. There the seniors filed up to the platform and took their diplomas. It didn't last long. Then we all beat it over to Webster Hall, a small auditorium.

When my name was called I managed to get my hat on and stand up, leaving my program on the chair. (I had been sitting on my program, because I realized that I would need two hands to manage the hat adjustment.) I teetered over to where the President was standing, and was followed by a couple of friars bearing the white hood. The hood was white, quite big, and shaped like a loose-fitting horse collar. The President cited me for literary bravery (he little knew), the hood was slipped over my head, the diploma was slipped into my hand, there was some clapping and a couple of boos, and I walked back to sit down. I guess it must have been when I reached over to pick the program off the chair that my hood got hung up on Ben Ames Williams. Anyway, when I got seated the thing was up over my face, as in falconry. I truly lived up to the *New Yorker*'s reputation for waggishness and clowning, as I sat there feebly pulling at the hood—a fully masked Doctor of Letters, a headless poet. I gave the boys their money's worth and I didn't mind it, particularly, as I wasn't really sure that anything much was wrong. Some learned man in the row behind me finally reached forward and rearranged me into some semblance of academic dignity.

Hoods have a tiny loop that you are supposed to pass around a button on your vest, to give them a downhaul. But I forgot to do it. I guess I am the type that would forget to pull the ripcord.

After a Martini at the President's luncheon party, I felt revived. Joe and I ate with Former President Hopkins and wife, at a little table. Quite a number of people at the party turned out to be relatives of yours, but I'm not sure I can identify them. . . . I was asked to autograph things. Then Joe and I left and scooted for Maine—a beautiful drive north up the Connecticut Valley and over the mountains to Bethel.

If this is to get into the mail I'll have to quit. Did any honest passerby return the brand new fishing rod that Joe and I left on 48th Street leaning up against the iron fence as we drove off?

> Loads of love and loads of regret
> that you weren't with me in Hanover to
> share my honorable hour. I can do the
> hood act for you, as I own the hood.
>
> A

To BEN AMES WILLIAMS

[New York]
[June 1948]

Dear Ben:

At New Haven they have caps with stiff underbodies—you can put them on one-handed.[1] I encountered another sort of trap, however. I was standing with a lot of others in the President's office, and a

---

1. White got three honorary degrees during the spring of 1948: from Dartmouth, Yale, and the University of Maine.

stranger tugged my sleeve and said: "Mr. White, I'd like you to meet Dean Acheson." "How do you do, Dean Acheson," I replied, courteously.
Everywhere, traps.

Sincerely,
Andy White

• *Harold Ross and E. B. White were against noise. They were particularly against it when the audience was captive. At this time music and ads were being broadcast very loudly in New York's Grand Central Station and on buses in Washington, D.C., and White's Comments opposing the practice had been appearing in* The New Yorker. *Justice Felix Frankfurter, who had read the Comments, sent White a copy of an antinoise opinion he had written, inscribed "For E. B. White, whose judicial opinions are the envy of Felix Frankfurter."*

To FELIX FRANKFURTER

June 29, 1948

Dear Justice Frankfurter:

I was very glad to get the copy of the opinion in the sound truck case, and I prize your inscription and thank you for it. I had read some of the dissent in the papers. Certainly nothing has come along lately with such lovely nuances as this amplification business. At the rate we're going, in the world of noise, we may shortly be faced with Supreme Court decisions recorded, amplified, and shouted down from low-flying planes—and find even Justice itself getting to be a public nuisance.

Very quietly yours,
E. B. White

• *When White happened to witness the birth of twin fawns in the deer park of the Bronx Zoo—"a scene of rare sylvan splendor in one of our five favorite boroughs"—he wrote a Comment about it for* The New Yorker. *He received many letters, one of them from John Tee-Van, the zoo's director. The piece appears in* The Second Tree From the Corner.

To JOHN TEE-VAN

25 West 43rd Street
New York
June 29, 1948

Dear Mr. Tee-Van:

There is no question about my returning to the Bronx Zoo, as long as I have the use of my legs. I've been a visitor since about 1908. At that time I lived in Mount Vernon, and my father sometimes broke the awful spell of Sunday afternoon by a trolley trip to the Bronx—always after a heavy dinner, and with many difficult transfer arrangements. For years I saw the Zoo only on the Sabbath, and it never occurred to me that there were people there on weekdays.

. . . One thing that impressed me that morning at the deer park was how weak are the powers of observation of zoo visitors. I suppose a dozen persons, in all, wandered past while the doe was getting her lambs going, and none noticed the incident of birth. In Maine, most schoolboys would give their right arm to be in the woods and witness an event like that.

The cow moose came along with her calf soon after the second fawn was up, and I was amused to see that the doe didn't seem to mind the moose (probably an old bridge partner) but she drove the calf away.

Sincerely,
E. B. White

To DAISE TERRY

North Brooklin, Maine
14 July [1948]

Dear Miss T:

I'm going to be in New York from July 28 to August 4 as I am very homesick for the heat and stench and tensions of the city. Could you get me a hotel room for the above period? The Algonquin is OK, or any other public house you think suitable.

Also need a berth (lower or upper) on a train called the Bar Harbor Express for the night of August 4. If you have any difficulty with this railroad business, perhaps Mr. Norman can help, as he seems to be thick with the railroad crowd.

Sorry to inject these matters into your day, but I understand you thrive on confusion, complexity, and near-defeat. There is an LCT (Landing Craft Tank) in our cove this morning. It is here to pick up a load of pulpwood for Lightweight Harry Luce, who owns a paper mill in Bucksport. I watched the LCT take the beach on the flood tide last night. It nosed into the shore, lowered its ramp, and instead of disgorging a few tanks it just waited quietly until a truck appeared bearing pulpwood. The truck mounted the ramp, turned around, backed up, and dumped its load. Then went back for more. Thus rolls the course of the Luce empire, riding the throbbing engines of old dead wars. Some day it will crush us all, and you and I will go down together—you clutching a reprint permission request, I an amorphous comment suggestion.

Till then, and *even* then, I am yrs,
EBW

To WILLIAM SHAWN

[North Brooklin, Me.]
[July 15?, 1948]
Thursday

Dear Bill:

Sorry about that pulpwood. I never would have wired it, only I missed the mail and thought maybe you might want to fill a hole with some sort of fiddle faddle. Almost all the pulp around here goes to the mill at Bucksport, which was bought recently by Time-Life. But after I got back from the telegraph office I got wondering about it, and decided I had better check. So I rowed across to where the LCT was beached (unquestionably the longest single-scull saltwater journey ever made by a New Yorker reporter for checking purposes—2 miles in moderate sea) and learned that the god damn boat was not going to the Harry Luce mill, but was going to pass right by it and continue up the Penobscot River to a mill in Brewer, Me.—probably some rival outfit supplying paper to us or Mademoiselle.

Where *do* we get our paper, anyway? Or do we just use old paper towels from the men's room?

Yrs,
Andy

Send me the proof (if you set the piece) and maybe I can get something out of it. It seems kind of interesting that our ex-landing craft are still finding work to do on beaches.[1]

To KATHARINE S. WHITE

[New York]
[Summer 1948]
Thursday noon

Dear K:

Just finished comment for Comment Day, and now start for lunch with Gus and for dentistry with Jack Miller—to replace small divot removed by the oral hygienist at an earlier sitting for which I paid ten dollars. It was terrifically hot here last night and I writhed at the bottom of one of those Algonquin air shafts, thrashing about and alternately taking off and putting on my pajama top. On the whole, though, my physical condition is good enough, and the city is cooler this morning. Lunched with Ross yesterday, but he said only one funny thing. He

---

1. *The New Yorker* ran the piece (September 4, 1948) and solved the problem neatly by inserting the word "presumably" in front of "headed for the paper mill at Bucksport."

said "When Hawley[1] and Shawn try to go through a door together, *nobody* gets through." I guess we better save that one for the book.

Everybody has asked most solicitously for you and I spend quite a lot of time describing your Condition. The Algonquin people (I mean the staff people) apparently think about nobody much but you. They just wander around carrying napkins and things, thinking about you. . . .

Later – post dentistry

I am not to eat anything sticky in the left side of my mouth from now till Tuesday. Inasmuch as everything in New York is sticky, I should come out of this in a peculiarly emaciated condition. Dr. Miller keeps apologizing, as he drills. . . .

Ross has just been in here to tell me that his daughter Patty is sailing for England at midnight tonight with her Mother on the Queen Mary. Patty just had Ross on the phone to ask him about his taking her to dinner, and she said: "Are we going to dinner alone?" Ross said yes, they were. "Oh, goody!" replied Patty. This now has Ross worried—to know why his daughter wants to dine with him alone. He sees something sinister or baffling in the arrangement. Apparently the last time Patty sailed, Ross presented her with some advance proofs of the Rebecca West Greenville piece, as a bon voyage present. This time she is demanding flowers. A wonderful family, the Rosses.

I am debating whether to ask Ross to take me along to the sailing of the Mary, thinking maybe I could get something for the *Holiday* piece, but I guess I'll just stick my head out the window at twelve and listen to the horn.

New York seems to me less relaxed in summertime than it used to be. The place is full of tourists and hasn't thinned out as much as I expected. Most of the air-conditioning is on the brutal side—just a few degrees different from the Ellsworth freeze locker. But I haven't really had a chance to take anything in yet.

Hope you and Joe are making out well and that you won't try to do anything too spectacular in my absence. It seemed sad to be leaving Maine, even for these few days. Lots of love,

Andy

P.S. I'm going to try Air Mail on this, to see if it makes a difference. I have an idea that when it gets to Old Town, it proceeds by canoe down river.

---

1. R. Hawley Truax. An old friend of Ross's, his adviser on business matters, and a director of the company from *The New Yorker's* early days, he became treasurer in 1943.

To KATHARINE S. WHITE

[New York]
[Summer 1948]
Sat morn in Old Algonquin
reservation

Dear K:

Had dinner with Rog and Evelyn last night and they start for Snedens [Landing] this morning. They seemed well but heat-drunk, as was everybody yesterday—a real killer. Cally wore a simple loin cloth and a ribbon in her hair, and sat bolt upright on the floor looking very cute and taking part in everything. . . .

I am about to start for the Brooklyn Bridge, which I understand commands a view of the lower city. There were five people here for breakfast this morning in the dining room, all out of towners except me, none of them able to understand the language spoken by New York waiters. . . .

Attended a Goldman Band Concert last evening on my way home from the Angell apartment, and I must say there is nothing in all the world like Central Park on a summer night. Missed you. . . . I trust you are reading every word of the Bentley spy hearing, as there is nothing much funnier, to my mind, than Russian spy activity, with eager girls laboriously copying everything out of Walter Lippmann's files, instead of just buying a Tribune and reading it all in the paper next day; and the spies all getting together at Schraffts 46th Street for one of those Colonial Luncheons; and Senator Wherry remarking that he thinks it is a very serious thing indeed that a young lady of Miss Bentley's background should have been interested in Socialism. . . .

I will now proceed to the Bklyn Bridge and think of you from there.

Andy

To MRS. FRANK ELLERSIECK

[New York]
October 18, 1948

Dear Mrs. Ellersieck:

Thanks for the letter, and I'm glad you and your son liked the book. There is not much likelihood that there'll be another Stuart book, as this one caused me trouble enough for one lifetime. I just signed a contract for translation into the Malayan, and I feel as though this mouse was slipping away from me.

Sincerely,
E. B. White

To MRS. CHARLES CARY COLT

[New York]
November 16, 1948

Dear Mrs. Colt:

It was good to hear from you again after so long a time. I'm answering, rather than Katharine, because she is at the moment finishing up her annual children's book review for *The New Yorker*, and it is a most time-consuming job.

We are, both of us, sympathetic with the spirit and aims of A.D.A., but neither of us feels free to engage in political action, although often tempted. The reason is simply that being an editor and being an editorial writer of The New Yorker imposes an obligation of political detachment. I feel, as an opinionated writer, that I can function more effectively and honestly if I don't join a group and accept a group program, however sympathetic to it I may feel. Katharine feels the same way about her work as editor, in which she must deal with many writers and many manuscripts.

We're particularly sorry to decline in this case, and it was very good of you to ask us.

Sincerely,
E. B. White

To WILLIAM MAXWELL

[New York]
16 November [1948]

Dear Bill:

Katharine says you have had some experience with your books going into foreign language publication. "Stuart Little" seems to be going abroad in a big way, and so far I am far from happy with the results but don't know what I am doing wrong. K says that you yourself arranged for the translation of one of your books, instead of leaving the matter to the publisher. I've been simply signing contracts tossed at me by an agent named Horch, and although the contracts call for a "faithful translation," I sometimes wonder how much of a beating Stuart and I are taking from this fidelity. I have just received a copy of a book called "Rikki, Die abenteuerliche Geschichte einer kleinen Maus" which I recognize as the Viennese version of Stuart. There is also a book called "Peter Lille," one called "Tom Trikkelbout," and another called "Stuart Mus." There is a contract now waiting my signature for Japanese-Korean rights, and God knows what name, or alias, he will travel under in the east. I wonder whether you have any ideas on all this. I'm not enough of a linguist to know whether a Dutch

Stuart Little should be called Stuart Little or Tom Trikkelbout. But it is beginning to dawn on me that I damn well better find out, and I don't know just how to go about it. Lawyers and agents are certainly no help.

Incidentally, I read your Elm Street novel [*Time Will Darken It*] with great joy and satisfaction and envy, and found two mistakes, which I painstakingly copied down on a piece of paper and then lost the paper. One was on (I think) p. 57, when you meant to say surrey and said cart or vice versa—anyway, you had somebody getting into the wrong vehicle. The other escapes me at the moment.

Yrs,
Andy

To CHARLES COLE

25 W. 43 Street
New York
December 13, 1948

Dear Mr. Cole:

I don't know how to "reveal any aspect" of myself deliberately. Everything a person does or says is, of course, revealing. But *you're* going to write that term paper, not me.

Note the grammatical error in the preceding sentence. Very revealing.

Good luck and I hope you pass the course.

Sincerely,
E. B. White

To HAROLD ROSS

[North Brooklin, Me.]
[1948?]

Mr. Ross:

I promised you a list of people who generate comments. Here it is.

Gibbs
Hellman
Hamburger
McNulty
Bishop
Jacobi
Kinkead
Mangold
Coates

Hyman
Bliven
White
Gill
Cotler
Newhouse
Liebling
Ross, H
Hofeller

E. B. White

P.S. I received your note about signalling you in advance when I write a comment. I shall endeavor to do same. Last week I wrote a comment unexpectedly and turned it in, with misgivings. My feeling is that Gibbs, or whoever is carrying the load on comment, should get clear priority whenever there is the slightest conflict, or duplication. By this I mean that a timely conflict that comes in at the last minute and tends to muss up something Gibbs has done ought to be tossed out without question. Writing comment is bad enough without having a last-minute-Johnnie in your hair.

I don't think this problem is going to come up much, as I don't anticipate that I am going to submit much comment, being occupied with other work these days. But I would like to feel free to submit comment along with the other comment submitters, and can feel that way only if I am sure I'm not getting the Special Treatment.

To STANLEY HART WHITE

229 East 48 Street
2 January 1949

Dear Bun:

I haven't read the book yet, as we gave a New Year's Eve party for 100 people and I'm too busy counting empty bottles and removing stains from the carpet. But I thank you and Blanche for sending me the book and hope you had a good Christmas. I am starting 1949 in a somewhat relaxed and benign condition as the result of a decision to give up the responsibility of the New Yorker's editorial page.[1] I intend to apply myself to more irregular and peaceable pursuits for a while,

1. Although he liked to write Comment and found the short paragraph a congenial form of expression, White didn't like the responsibility of producing the first page of *The New Yorker* week after week. The magazine paid him well to do it, but he found it a strain. For the second time in his life, he decided to quit the job. He continued, however, to contribute to the page.

to work patiently instead of rapidly, and to improve the nick of time. I may even try for a job on that platform which the Army hopes to establish 200,000 miles up, beyond the pull of gravity; it is conceivable that a person who no longer feels a gravitational pull might find himself no longer obedient to the pull of conscience and the pull of nationality—which would be a great joke on the Army, having gone to such trouble.

Joe returns by train to Ithaca tonight after his holidays. He likes Cornell much better than he liked Exeter. He likes soccer better than history, and he likes naval architecture better than soccer. He has a Zippo cigarette lighter, and when he pulls at a cigarette he looks to be tasting life to the very lees. His sweater is white, with red numerals 1952. Last week he registered for the draft and acquired an entirely different number.

My old dog Fred, whom you probably remember, died on Dec. 31 at the age of thirteen years and four months. With the exception of a brief spell during puppyhood when he suffered from an inflammation of the bowels, I think he never missed a meal in all those years, something of a record. Actually, he managed even to double his own record, because of a system he worked out for getting the cat's meal, too. It was a complicated system, involving accurate timing and the mastery of certain doors and stairs. In his later years, suffering from hard arteries, it cost him a lot of pain, but he never completely abandoned it.

Happy New Year to all,
En

To J. T. STEWART
[New York]
April 6, 1949

Dear Grandpa:

Sorry I missed your call. I was in Maine, tending to business. Do not upbraid me for not answering letters. I gave up corresponding in the middle thirties when it became apparent that there was a conspiracy in this country directed against me, in which thousands of strangers banded together and sent me things in the mail. Whenever anybody in the United States finds something on his desk that he doesn't know what to do with, like a newspaper clipping or a copy of his high school paper, he puts it in an envelope and addresses it to me. So I quit answering letters. But I make an exception once in a while in your case, as my sympathies get the better of me when I think of you out there among those smelters and eviscerators.

You are right that the pieces in the *New Yorker* are too long, but you must remember that they are written by tired old men who no longer have the strength to write short. My *Holiday* piece ["Here Is New York"] ran 7,000 words—the ramblings of a garrulous old fool.

Sincerely,
White

To KATHARINE S. WHITE

[New York]
[early May 1949]
Sunday aft

Dearest K:

Min and I are holding the fort this afternoon, with La Jenkins out sporting. The awful hot spell broke last night and today is clear and beautiful, with a new bird in the Garden, let us call it a Willow Pitkin. Across the street, the entire janitorial family has blossomed out in pink carnations, which Agnes says is for Mother's Day and is a sign that the Mother is alive (for those who have "passed on" the carnation is always white). Ergo: the Mother is alive, but has been "put away somewhere, in an institution." I am glad to have these matters resolved for me.

Have been having quite a bout of work since you left, and am a third of the way through my final draft of The Piece ["The Morning of the Day They Did It"]. Have reached the stage where I am suspicious that it is perhaps the lousiest concoction I have dreamed up to date, but am going doggedly ahead and will let others decide. Visited the Planetarium on Friday night (my first visit) to bone up on Space, and bought a book there on rockets. It is most helpful. Yesterday afternoon paid a call on my tailor, J. Bastian, for a fitting. He said many people, mostly females, had exclaimed at the great beauty of the fabric from which my jacket is being made. I am getting quite fond of J. Bastian . . . and I may develop (from this connection) into something of a dandy. Was greatly drawn toward a blue material on his table, and he explained that it was being made into a suit for Raymond Fosdick ($160). Imagine old Fosdick shelling out a hundred and sixty bucks for a suit. Mr. Bastian confided that Fosdick's wife wants to get him into some sporty clothes, broad stripes and bright checks, but that he won't budge.

Hawley and Alethea [Truax] had me to cocktails last night at Number 17½, and there were quite a few guests—Paul Nevin and his wife the timber cruiser, Ann Nevin Chamberlin and husband, Mrs. Frederick Lewis Allen (unaccompanied), Mary Petty, Alan Dunn, Whitney Darrow and Middy, and a lady who said she was a classmate of yours at Bryn Mawr but that she never graduated—hated the place. Can't recall her name. It was the first time I had had the opportunity of watching Hawley tending bar. He does it with the same gruelling intensity that goes into his other types of work, and with the same unearthly glee. His hand, gripping the big Martini mixer, his other hand stirring, his eyes held within a few inches of the swirling ice, on his lips a tiny smile—truly a dedicated man. . . .

I have spent part of today judging the Herald Tribune Fresh Air essay contest. Nothing of any literary merit in the lot, but they made rather fascinating reading nonetheless—what happens to people when they take strange kids into their homes. I have rendered my judgment, which wasn't too hard. . . .

Found a note in my typewriter (from Ross) on Friday, simply saying: "Ginger Rogers is in town." But have not acted. Minnie peed on the dining room rug from drinking excessive amounts of water due to the heat. I applied Dogtex and the stain is not noticeable. Have heard nothing from Joe, nothing from Atkin,[1] nothing, in fact, from anybody. . . .

There is no news of any consequence and I am writing this mostly to send my love. I have tickets to take you to see the Gi'nts play baseball next Sunday afternoon, a week from this day. I can't tell you who their opponents will be, as I am not well informed along those lines. An office boy is selecting our site in the stands and is taking the assignment *very* seriously. I believe he rather leans toward first base. Terry told me *she* always sat between first and second. That I'd like to see.

Love to all the Newberrys and to
Aunt Crull, and to YOU

Andy

• *White was not satisfied with "The Morning of the Day They Did It" and, after selling it to* The New Yorker, *withdrew it in the following letter to Ross. Ross eventually talked him into allowing it to be published. It appeared in the February 25, 1950, issue of the magazine and, later, in* The Second Tree From the Corner.

To HAROLD ROSS

North Brooklin, Maine
20 May 1949

Dear Ross:

I've read my piece over in proof, don't like it, and don't want it published. What I suggest is that, if you are willing, you credit me with

---

1. William Atkin, naval architect, who was drawing plans for a cruising boat for White. (The boat never got built.)

the amount paid me, and I will turn in other casuals (shorter) against it and work it off that way. If you don't want to do it that way, I'll refund the money.

My trouble with that piece was that I turned it in in too much of a hurry (was trying to clean things up) and never really took time to read it. (I took time to write it, but not to read it—which is always a big mistake.) I think I must have been impressed by the mere fact that it was finished—in other words I assumed that because it was completed it was meritorious, a preposterous assumption.

Please don't try to argue me out of this. Have given the matter careful consideration. A writer should have the privilege of withdrawing a piece as well as the privilege of submitting one, and I just don't happen to like this piece.

Yrs,
White

To CASS CANFIELD

North Brooklin, Maine
3 July 1949

Dear Cass:

With regard to the dollar book, I think the title *Here Is New York* is all right. I am sending for a clipping of my piece, to see whether the text needs any tinkering. I don't think it does, but I shall write you definitely as soon as I can get my hands on a copy.

I am satisfied with the terms you suggest in your letter, that is, 10% on retail to 5000 copies and 15% thereafter.

I'll leave it to you to find the sort of photograph you think is appropriate for the jacket. I didn't think the *Holiday* photography was any ball of fire. As for the tailpiece, I am asking my secretary, Miss Terry, to send you a clipping from a recent *Herald Tribune*, showing the Turtle Bay Garden willow. I should think an artist could work from that very easily, but if the artist wants to get into the Garden he can simply go to Number 230 East 49 Street, which is the office, and explain his errand.

I'm writing Jim Thurber about *Is Sex Necessary?* If it is all right with him, I guess we can dream up something new in the way of an introduction.[1] If memory serves, that book will soon celebrate its twentieth birthday 11/7/49. It's already older than most dogs.

I read somewhere, the other day, that sex was going out.

Yrs faithfully,
Andy

---

1. The "Coming of Age" edition of *Is Sex Necessary?*, with White's new introduction, was published in celebration of the book's twenty-first birthday.

To STANLEY HART WHITE

North Brooklin
15 July 1949

Dear Bun:

. . . This is the summer of the grandchildren. Nancy and her three kids[1] are in a cottage about a mile from here, and we are inundated. They all came over this morning to help us prepare peas for the freezer, and it was like the finale of a tumbling act. While Kay and Nancy shelled, Kitty and Jonny threw the empty pods at each other, and I stood in a corner sealing the cellophane liners with an electric curling iron. The peas are now safe in a steel drawer 24 miles from here, held at a steady temperature of 5 degrees below zero. Our ancestors never had fun like that.

There has been a certain amount of violence around here this spring, not counting Nancy's children. Our chimney got hit by lightning in April, and I blew the furnace up in May. It was time for it to blow up, I guess. Anyway, it proved easy work. All I had to do was chuck in a piece of an old plank, on top of a wood fire, and away she went. Made a dandy noise. I guess there was a little dynamite or something buried in the plank. I still have some of the same plank left, and the next time I use it on the fire I am going to stand further away. The insurance adjuster was down from Bangor to case the joint, and he seemed impressed by the infinite variety of my disasters. The chimney looked like an act of God, but the furnace looked exactly like an act that I would be likely to put on, judging from my appearance. After a little talk, he had me pretty well convinced that I had no business chucking stuff into my own furnace, and I got the impression that he felt God was rather cheeky, too, fooling around with a brick chimney that was out of his territory. . . .

Joe has a job this summer, in a camp on Deer Isle. He teaches kids how to sail. Right now, he and three other guys are bringing a schooner from Rhode Island down to Maine, and from the radio weather reports they have had nothing but fog and easterlies. It wouldn't surprise me if they ended up in the Caribbean. . . .

En

To JAMES THURBER

North Brooklin, Maine
27 July 1949

Dear Jim:

I heard from Terry about Rosy's accident,[1] and your letter just came with reassuring news. How the human frame extricates itself from the

---

1. Katharine (Kitty), Jonathan (Jon), and Sarah Stableford.

1. Thurber's daughter had been in a car accident.

entanglements of this gasoline nightmare that we live in, is sheer magic. I am so glad that Rosy got through without a bad emotional shock, and without her good looks being all jarred to pieces. Katharine and I will send her some sort of greeting to the hospital. Incidentally, if there should ever develop any complication about a pelvic bone, please bear in mind that we are good friends (and patients) of Dr. Frank Stinchfield at the Medical Center. He did the wonderfully successful spinal fusion for K, and is considered tops in bone surgery. K, with her patched spine, is now swimming every day, rowing boats, and gardening. A Stinchfield triumph.

One detail that escaped you about the accident is that July 11 was my birthday. I won't try to make anything of it. . . .

Joe has a job at a camp on Deer Isle, near here, and is on the water practically the entire time, so we are having a summer in which our nights are made restless not by the screech of tires in the back part of the mind, but by the sound of wind in the branches of the trees, and the fear of fog in the hollow of the stomach. Joe's job is to take kids cruising and instruct them in sailing. On a SE wind, we can hear the fog signal ten miles down the bay, off the ledges. He came over to see us the other day, stayed for supper, and left just as dark was coming on, in a 15-foot sloop, disappearing toward the east as the thunderheads gathered. I think that if I had known that Rosy was lying in a nice, steady hospital bed that night, with no fog in the corridor, I would have swapped parenthood with you, sight unseen. But any way you look at it, it's a gruelling course.

I'll see what I can do about a preface for Cass. If you know anything about sex, let me know. Maybe the preface should just be a factual story of our parenthoods, with the mists swirling around a pelvic ring, and the fog signal moaning down the bay. . . .

Andy

To DAISE TERRY

[North Brooklin, Me.]
1 August (rabbit, rabbit) [1949]

Dear Miss Terry:

Would you kindly buy one dozen red cardboard portfolios, size 10 x 15 inches, at the stationery store down in the lobby, and bill me, and send to me? Size everything, dear. Ten by fifteen. Not some other crazy dimension.

Brooklin is exhausted after a three-day centennial celebration, held in the middle of the tropic heat wave. I put in about 75 hours building a float for the procession of floats and decorated bicycles, and won first prize ($15). The Governor crowned Miss Brooklin 1949, the ball team won its two games, a lady sang "America the Beautiful" standing in front of the Baptist Church in the pouring sun while I knelt in the cemetery across the street next to the grave of a friend of mine who was shot for a deer in 1939, and the town exploded five hundred dollars' worth of fireworks from Chatto Island on Saturday night in competition with a thunderstorm. Everyone in town commented on the very popular fact that when the next centennial rolled around, he wouldn't be here.

The principal character in our winning float was our neighbor Mrs. Charles Henderson, dressed in my wife's grandmother's dress. There was a very nice picture of her in yesterday's *Portland Sunday Telegram*, on the same page with a picture of another friend of mine, Ginger Rogers. The latter is separating from her husband, of whom she once said: "He is everything I ever dreamed of." I met him once, and he was everything I ever dreamed of, too.

Rgds to Greenstein[1] & the mesdames.

White

To JOHN MC NULTY

21 August 1949—Sun night
North Brooklin, so named because
the boundary on one side follows
the line of the brook

Dear John:

Regarding Colinus virginianus virginianus (or Bob White) I am glad you are keeping your ears open. No use sitting around the smallest state in the Union not listening. When I got your letter I turned right to Forbush ("Birds of Massachusetts and Other New England States," 3 volumes). This is the set of books my wife once gave fifty bucks for. I was impressed. Most of the females I know, they get fifty dollars together it don't go to no set of bird books. Anyway, Forbush backs you to the hilt in regards the Bob White.

> "VOICE.—Common call, an interrogative whistle *wha-whoi?* or *wha-wha-whoi?* the last note with a rising inflection. Usually translated as *Bob-white, ah Bob-white* or *buck-wheat-ripe, more-wet* or *some-more-wet,* head thrown upward and backward on the final interrogative note; the gathering cry, *ka-loi-kee?*; the reply, *whoil-kee Ryall* (apparently at this point the bird is working up to saying *er-George-Ryall*[1]); etc., etc."

---

1. Milton Greenstein, a lawyer who came to *The New Yorker* in 1945. He has proved invaluable to the magazine and to White. "Everybody, including me, consults Milton about everything," White says. "He always has the answers."

---

1. Race-track columnist for *The New Yorker*.

In the nineteen years I have been coming to this part of Maine I have heard a Bob White only once. According to Forbush, the greatest danger these birds face in winter is getting stuck under a hard crust of snow. They form coveys and let themselves get snowed under, on purpose, but then a rain comes, followed by a freeze, and they are licked. I am just showing off, now.

The thing I like best in Forbush is the way he ends up each section with a plug for the bird. He heads this "Economic Status," and it usually consists of a detailed account of the contents of an individual's stomach, showing how he befriends the farmer by destroying harmful insects. Forbush struggles to be strictly impartial in his "Economic Status" windup, but his passion for birds is so great that it is always a losing battle. When he got around to defending the Belted Kingfisher, he just had to put his head down and throw punches in all directions. But his conscience got the best of him finally, and he ended up: "The mice and grass-eating insects on which it feeds surely count in its favor, and the bird probably deserves protection by law, *except about fish hatcheries.*" The italics are mine.

The only work I have done this summer is write an introduction to a new edition of "archy and mehitabel," which I guess will just about put a new sole on my sneakers. I have lost the knack of earning money by putting one word after another. For a little while, there, I was catching some 3 pound flounders (toward the end of July), and money seemed silly. Now the flounders have left and I don't know—maybe money is the thing. I blow hot and cold about it all the time. I understand Ross is on his way to New Brunswick, to fish. Ross fishing is one thing I have always wanted to see. Can you imagine how he would rile up a stream?

Yrs,
Andy

To MORRIS BISHOP

25 West 43
Columbus Day and the drum's
ugly sound in the sidestreet
[1949]

Dear Morris:

I would have got this back quicker only you caught me in transit, driving a green sedan through yellow valleys, with no appreciable effect on the poetic midform. I am delighted, not to say touched, by your interesting (and I trust perceptive) estimate of little old me.[1] I have inserted

1. In the Introduction Bishop had written for the Harper's Modern Classics edition of *One Man's Meat*, published in February 1950.

Times after *Seattle,* changed four years in Maine to five years, which I believe to be the correct number. (I doubt that Joe could have got to Exeter in four years from Brooklin's third grade, and I sometimes wonder how he managed to do it in five.) I have inserted the words "part of" on Page 6, as being a more moderate and more truthful statement of the case. The last couple of chapters of "Stuart Little" were no dream, they were a nightmare: I wrote them doggedly and while under the impression that I was at death's door and should catch up on loose ends.

I had no idea you were at work on a study of White, in fact I thought Irwin Edman had been tapped for it. But maybe that is another edition. At any rate, I hope the pain was not unbearable and that the pay was decent. I like your piece very much and feel slightly stripped, or shucked —pleasantly so, as I imagine a plain girl might feel (in dream, of course) when she gets undressed and everything goes all right. I have dared transpose pholgiston. (My first time, too.)

I had a feeling, when I read on Page 7 "He has made bourgeois idealism respectable" that the word "respectable" was unfortunate. This is your business, not mine. But isn't your word there some word like "tenable," or "plausible"? The word "respectable" would be all right in its pure sense (assuming that I have indeed done anything to bourgeois idealism) but "respectable" has become a tainted word, thanks to the nature of respectability. End suggestion.

Jumping to the bourgeois game of football (Columbia at Ithaca, Oct. 29), there is some talk of it. The beating we gave you last time, when we arrived afoot and minus one spinal column, still lingers in our minds if not in yours. If we try a repeat on you, it will at least not be afoot, it will be aDeSoto.

Many, many thanks for "An Introduction."

Yrs proudly,
Andy

P. S. I think there should be an aside, somewhere, by the subject himself, to the effect that he first gazed upon the midform of poetry when he looked upon Bishop's Incomplete Works.

To CASS CANFIELD

25 West 43rd Street
19 October [1949]

Dear Cass:

Glad to hear that the book can come out in December, thus alleviating my wife's holiday distress. She had it ticked off against a lot of names. As for me, not being a bookclub man, I didn't catch on to what "dual selection" meant and had to have it explained out to me by a literary character.[1] I thought you were talking about one of those "dividends" of which I had heard. Am of course glad to have been selected, although I don't see why they waited till I wrote such a teensy book. However, I guess that is their business, since I'm not one of the judges, having turned down a judgeship years ago in favor of grading eggs—which turned out to be more fun.

After the book has made its first little splash and has been devoured by the club-members, I think you might try placing it in Greyhound Bus Stations and next to the ashtray in motels.

My next book *is* in sight. I look at it every day. I keep it in a carton, as you would a kitten.

Andy

To HAROLD ROSS

[October 27, 1949]
[Interoffice memo]

Mr. Ross:

Regarding your query of the "which" in the sentence: "He had to be clutching a solitary buck, which he had wheedled from his budget by going without butter."

I think this is an instance where "which" is the right word, "which" being non-defining. The purpose of the clause is not to define the buck, but to make a further observation about the man.

EBW

[*Ross wrote this reply on White's memo and returned it to him. "White: I was cockeyed. Weekes also told me. I read 20,000 wds on Thursday, or anyhow 10,000."*]

• *Ross had received a letter from a relative of Katharine White's accusing him of firing an employee for being a Communist, and White drafted the following reply. In the end it was Ross, and not White, who answered the accusation, so White's letter was not sent.*

Richard Boyer was a regular contributor to The New Yorker, *on a drawing account. He was forthright about his connection with the Communist party, and the editors always picked subjects for him that were*

---

1. *Here Is New York* was one book of a dual selection of the Book-of-the-Month Club.

nonpolitical. Ross discovered, however, that Boyer was using New Yorker *stationery to write personal letters that were essentially political documents. After that, Boyer was not given any more assignments.*

To ———

229 East 48 Street
New York City
20 November 1949
[Unsent letter]

Dear ——— :

You say Boyer has been fired, but I doubt that you know what you are talking about. I'm just as interested as you in the relationship between an independent magazine and a Communist writer. It is a fascinating relationship and, in these times, an important one. But I don't believe you know anywhere near as much about the duties and difficulties involved as I do, or as Ross does. *The New Yorker* disagrees with practically everything Boyer believes in (and when I say *The New Yorker* it includes me). Nevertheless, it has given Boyer a fair shake, and Boyer (who has always professed his beliefs) has given *The New Yorker* a fair shake. The only thing that could interrupt this relationship is the nature of the Communist Party itself, which has a much too cozy feeling about its flock and which is always trying to twine itself in a magazine's hair. In this respect it differs from other political parties.

The New Yorker has never fired a man for his politics. It has never, to my knowledge, tried to tell any contributor what to think or any critic what to feel. It has never tried to "convert" Boyer, or obstruct Boyer, or do anything else with Boyer except buy his stuff when we liked it, and let it lay when we didn't. *The New Yorker* is a damned fine magazine and an honest one, and you are a lucky lady to be in a position to buy it and read it (20 cents) along with other journals of varying or opposite opinion. *The New Yorker* is primarily concerned with putting out a good sheet dissociated from any party or group; and as soon as a party shows signs of wanting to exploit an individual's connection with the magazine, *The New Yorker* begins to freeze up, rightly. It is my belief that Boyer has talked these matters over with Ross and is under no misapprehension about how the management looks at life. Furthermore, no contributor is immune from operations of the merit system. When Boyer wrote (for the *Daily Worker*) some reportorial articles that experienced editors like Bill Shawn and Harold Ross regarded as thoroughly non-objective, it didn't raise his stock any with the magazine. If there is one thing The New Yorker takes a dim view of, it's a reporter playing footsy with his facts.

316 /   LETTERS OF E. B. WHITE

I once wrote a paragraph sniping at Boyer because he sounded off, at the Waldorf, about what a lousy thing the press is in this country. I love the press in this country. For all its faults and deficiencies, for all its Peglers and Winchells, and for all its Whites and Boyers, I don't think you can beat it anywhere. At any rate, Boyer's remarks were duly reported in the papers and got read. Mine, too, were published and got read. And that, in short, is what I like about the press.

An independent journal can't maintain its independence if it ever allows itself to be maneuvered into the position of seeming to accept, or approve, the opinions of an individual with whom it disagrees. That's all *The New Yorker* is concerned about in relation to Boyer. We're not *primarily* interested in the fate of any individual, although we are emotionally and temperamentally interested in the fate of all writers and artists. We just want to put out what we think is a good magazine. To that end you couldn't ask for a better man than H. W. Ross. For you to have written him such a frantic letter seems to me typical of the hysteria you were hollering so loud about.

Sincerely,
Andy

To ANN GRAVELY

[New York]
December 8, 1949

Dear Miss Gravely:

I don't know where to begin. I am five feet eight inches tall—but that's an odd place to begin. I am fifty years old—but that's a dreadful place to begin. I ate too much for lunch—but nobody would want to begin *there*. As for my work, the only thing I can tell you about it is that a lot of it has been published, all of it was hard, and some of it was fun. Haven't got a photograph. Maine, incidentally, is not my native state: I was born in New York State, but now live much of the time in Maine.

Sincerely yours,
E. B. White

IX

TURTLE BAY

1950–1951

•   *Life at* The New Yorker *was harried during the early fifties. Harold Ross was ill, no longer able to work at his usual pace. On December 6, 1951, he died, suddenly, during surgery for lung cancer.*

White wrote, in the issue of December 15: " . . . Ross regarded every sentence as the enemy, and believed that if a man watched closely enough, he would discover the vulnerable spot, the essential weakness. He devoted his life to making the weak strong—a rather specialized form of blood transfusion, to be sure, but one that he believed in with such a consuming passion that his spirit infected others and inspired them, and lifted them. Whatever it was, this contagion, this vapor in these marshes, it spread. None escaped it. Nor is it likely to be dissipated in a hurry.

"His ambition was to publish one good magazine, not a string of successful ones, and he thought of The New Yorker *as a sort of movement. He came equipped with not much knowledge and only two books —Webster's* Dictionary *and Fowler's* Modern English Usage. *These books were his history, his geography, his literature, his art, his music, his everything. Some people found Ross's scholastic deficiencies quite appalling, and were not sure they had met the right man. But he was the right man, and the only question was whether the other fellow was capable of being tuned to Ross's vibrations. Ross had a thing that is at least as good as, and sometimes better than, knowledge: he had a sort of natural drive in the right direction, plus a complete respect for the work and ideas and opinions of others. It took a little while to get on to the fact that Ross, more violently than almost anybody, was proceeding in a good direction, and carrying others along with him, under torrential conditions. He was like a boat being driven at the mercy of some*

internal squall, a disturbance he himself only half understood, and of which he was at times suspicious.

"In a way he was a lucky man. For a monument he has the magazine to date—one thousand three hundred and ninety-nine issues, born in the toil and pain that can be appreciated only by those who helped in the delivery room. These are his. They stand, unchangeable and open for inspection. We are, of course, not in a position to estimate the monument, even if we were in the mood to. But we are able to state one thing unequivocally: Ross set up a great target and pounded himself to pieces trying to hit it square in the middle. His dream was a simple dream; it was pure and had no frills: he wanted the magazine to be good, to be funny, and to be fair. . . .

"When you took leave of Ross after a calm or stormy meeting, he always ended with the phrase that has become as much a part of the office as the paint on the walls. He would wave his limp hand, gesturing you away. 'All right,' he would say. 'God bless you.' Considering Ross's temperament and habits, this was a rather odd expression. He usually took God's name in vain if he took it at all. But when he sent you away with this benediction, which he uttered briskly and affectionately, and in which he and God seemed all scrambled together, it carried a warmth and sincerity that never failed to carry over. The words are so familiar to his helpers and friends here that they provide the only possible way to conclude this hasty notice and to take our leave. We cannot convey his manner. But with much love in our heart, we say, for everybody, 'All right, Ross, God bless you!'"

• *Changing the design of New York taxicabs was a crusade of White's for many years. Ross encouraged him by passing along anything he came across on the subject.*

To **HAROLD ROSS**

[January? 1950]
[Interoffice memo]

Mr. Ross:

I've read this, and thanks. The controversy is muddied up by a lot of irrelevant factors, plus politics. The thing that would benefit New York, or any other city, would be a cab that is properly designed to fulfill the special function it has to perform. These cabs are not so designed. They are simply slight modifications of pleasure cars—and a pleasure car is about the poorest object you could get, as a model. Taxicabs are long and low because for thirty years automobile manufacturers have been boasting of long, low cars. I have personally measured the opening (vertical distance) of a cab door. It is roughly 38 inches. A taxicab is the only thing I know of that expects its patron to enter and leave by an opening 38 inches high. If you had to enter your apartment, your subway, your saloon, your bank vault, or your hall closet through a 38 inch opening, you would be infuriated, and would rebel. Thirty-eight inches is about one-half the height of a man. It makes sense as the entrance to an igloo because of the temperature factor involved; and it makes sense as the entrance to a small cabin cruiser because a high superstructure has disadvantages at sea. A high roof to a New York taxicab has no disadvantage, it has every advantage. New York cabs should be approximately 16 inches higher, should have a hood approximately 12 inches shorter (slightly smaller motor), and should get shed of all the crap they have inherited in the way of flowing fenders.

Did you know that I had been asked to speak on this subject, and allied subjects, at a symposium on automobile design at the Museum of Modern Art? It is beginning to dawn on people that they are being had.

P.S. I'm not going to speak.

Yrs,
E. B. White

Right

Wrong

To HENRY SCHUMAN

[New York]
January 23, 1950

Dear Mr. Schuman:

It wouldn't do any good to send me galleys of a book, because I don't comment on books—except to my wife under cover of darkness.

With many thanks,
E. B. White

To DOUGLAS M. FOUQUET

April 19, 1950
[New York]
[Collect telegram]

DOUGLAS M. FOUQUET
HARVARD CRIMSON
CAMBRIDGE, MASSACHUSETTS
SORRY CANNOT SPEAK DO NOT KNOW HOW MANY THANKS

E. B. WHITE

To EDWIN WAY TEALE

[New York]
May 3, 1950

Dear Mr. Teale:

Yes, I remember the passage in the [Thoreau] journals, and was amused to read it again. I'm afraid it doesn't quite fit our "Fascinating News Story" department but thanks for sending it.

Saw a brown thrasher in my backyard in 48th Street this morning, between Second and Third Avenue. Each year I see about a dozen migrants in this small green enclosure—robin, jay, scarlet tanager, hermit or olive backed thrush, towhee, thrasher, white-throat (he was here three days ago) and a few warblers. They arrive like traveling salesmen, spend a night or two, and then depart, and I always wonder whether I'm looking at the same individual that I saw a year ago. Am I?

Sincerely,
E. B. White

To JAMES THURBER

North Brooklin, Maine
6 June 1950

Dear Jim:

I think "The Thirteen Clocks" is indeed a wondrous tale and very musical and melancholy. I'm sorry to be a bit late in getting this letter off to you but have been laboring over a few local todals and thrins of a Maine springtime, with black snappers gnawing the chard and black bitches only half defending their honor.

I've read the story twice and think its only fault, if it is a fault at all, is that it is so concentrated a diet, with new characters and events and twists appearing in almost every sentence. This, plus the similarity of names—Mark, Mock, Hark—makes it occasionally hard to follow in a narrative sense, and I found myself working at it as I would at a double crostic. Doubtless this is your intent, or at any rate it is perhaps necessary to the nature and manner of the narrative.

In several places your system of not paragraphing to indicate conversational shifts makes tough reading, for this reason: when you follow a quote with "said the Prince" and then begin another quote within the same paragraph, the reader in most instances has no positive way of knowing whether the new quote is a continuation of the Prince's remarks or the beginning of some other person's remarks.

Being a poetical work essentially, the tale has to be concentrated. I wonder, though, whether in its main moments you haven't sacrificed the simple fluency of tale telling in order to add another ounce of fantasy or fun. I think the final winning of Saralinda might well be stated with greater ease and simplicity and clarity, and I'm also not sure that you have made Saralinda say or do anything that convinces the reader that she is as hot as you say she is.

I have a minor suggestion about the foreword. The first part of it sounds as though you were on the defensive—as though you were prematurely sore because the wrong people were reading your book or the right people weren't. And the second part, where you explain what the book is and what it isn't, is to my mind a questionable tactic, and I think you are just sticking out your zatch, and many a tosspan and strutfart will run you through.

Lots of love, and a happy hooding at Kenyon.

Yrs,
Andy

To H. K. RIGG

[New York]
[June? 1950]
Wednesday

Dear Bun:

Good to hear from you and am enclosing the description of a dachshund descending the stairs. Also a photograph that somebody sent me, to illustrate. Would like the picture back, eventually. My advice, if you have a dachshund puppy, is to subscribe to the *New York Times*, and instead of reading it just distribute it liberally all over the house. In my opinion it is impossible to housebreak a puppy three months old. When they get so they lift their leg, they begin to like the great outdoors. Up until then, it's largely wasted effort. Fred, who died last year at the age of 13, was so tough and lascivious that I never hesitated to beat the tar out of him for his crimes of one sort and another. Minnie, who is now pushing eleven, is so sensitive and considerate that I don't dare speak a hard word to her, for fear it will bring on a spell of diarrhea. You have to watch out about dachshunds—some of them are as delicately balanced as a watch. . . .

Best regards,
Andy

P.S. That business about stairs is no joke. We have a flight of rather steep back stairs in Maine, and Fred nosed over twice. After that he refused the stairs, and always went around and used the front stairs (which were much flatter) even when he was in a hell of a hurry.

[*White liked the photograph mentioned in this letter so much that he later made a sketch and used it as a Christmas card. See p. 323.*]

• *Dale Kramer was writing* Ross and The New Yorker, *published by Doubleday in 1951. Ross himself did not cooperate with Kramer but told members of his staff to do as they pleased.*

To **DALE KRAMER**

North Brooklin, Maine
25 August 1950

Dear Mr. Kramer:

I don't expect to be in New York for quite a while—maybe the middle of October. I guess it's true that *The New Yorker* has had more of an effect on American letters than some other magazines, but opinions differ widely whether the effect has been good. You can find a couple of very scholarly treatises in the quarterlies showing that the whole business is largely degenerative.

Thurber can write you an informative letter about American letters and trends in same, but I can't, as letters have never been my interest, only my fate. I read farm journals and boating magazines and my favorite authors are people nobody has ever heard of. I can't very well say whether I brought anything to the early *New Yorker*, except a certain eagerness (which was characteristic of many of the early employees

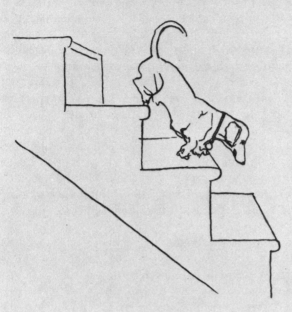

When you come down on Christmas morn
Propelled by gravity and mirth,
We hope you find a world reborn,
Smelling of fir...and peace on earth.

KATHARINE and ANDY WHITE

in that shop) and a certain naiveté, which was particularly characteristic of me as I was late in developing, was ill at ease, and probably
fairly perceptive about the city. I was unhappy and unproductive in the
jobs I held after getting out of college—I didn't like advertising, or
publicity, and although I liked newspapers and reporting I couldn't
qualify on newspapers or press associations (although I tried hard),
as I wasn't quick enough and wise enough, and was scared of them.
So when the *New Yorker* came along, it proved a more promising re-
ceptacle. The piece you mentioned in your letter, "Child's Play," is one
I haven't reread in many years, but I recall the incident clearly. A waitress in a Childs restaurant spilled a glass of buttermilk all over me, and
I had no difficulty writing a piece about it and selling it to the NYer,
and the experience was illuminating and greatly heartening to me, as
I felt a sudden burst of confidence and of wellbeing. Writing about the
thing had come naturally, and I realized that I had unconsciously
stylized the action, and I felt that at last I had produced something that
made sense journalistically.

I think *The New Yorker* was bound to happen, just as another
magazine is bound to come along sooner or later to overshadow it. Ross
wasn't so much seeking a formula as he was trying to shake off the
formulae of *Life, Judge, Puck, Harper's*, and all the rest. Jokes were
mostly he-and-she, essays were tweedy, feature writing was at low ebb,
humor was barber shop. The NYer took a fresh grip on the bat and
swung at everything, unabashed. Ross was as enthusiastic as he was
wide-eyed; and his uncompromising nature attracted a lot of good, if
inexperienced, people to his side. That's about all I know about the contribution to letters, except that it was a lot of fun. And a lot of work.

Sincerely,
E. B. White

P.S. My wife, whom you mentioned in your letter, was not primarily
concerned with casuals and fiction in the early stage of the magazine.
She was messed up with the whole works—as was every editor at that
time. For the first ten years, fact and fiction lived together in sin. They
became departmentalized gradually. Katharine, over the years, has had
a lot to do with fiction people and poets; but in my opinion (and I think
in Ross's opinion) her major contribution was in getting out a funny
paper that was also a sound and good paper. She was heavily engaged
with the artists in the years before the magazine had anybody in the
office whose job was art. She edited Flanner, Pringle, Alva Johnston
and a lot of others before it ever occurred to anybody to label their stuff
Fact. She was deep in the dingles of humor, and she was a whiz. No two

people in the world could be more different than she and Ross, but they met at one point (they both thought the same things were funny), and the collision at this point sent up sparks.

To GUSTAVE S. LOBRANO

North Brooklin, Maine
5 September 1950

Dear Gus:

Herewith a poem—a sort of brief agricultural history of our times.[1]

For your information, domestic rye grass is widely used as a cover crop on gardens and fields, so that they won't lie bare during the winter. Seeding rye grass is a standard practice nowadays, for conservation and soil building.

Super is superphosphate. Everybody in the country calls it super— the way you call the telephone the phone.

If you like the poem and are wondering about scheduling, it should either run soon or a year from now, as rye grass is sown from midsummer to early fall.* . . .

Andy

*A year from now fills me with deep gloom.

To EARLE DAVIS

[New York]
October 27, 1950

Dear Mr. Davis:

I've had a number of requests to reprint "The Morning of the Day They Did It," and have said no to them all.

Got my reasons. One reason is that I am not sure it's a public service to describe the end of the world, even in a spirit of satire. People are jumpy, right now, and I see no reason to explode paper bags.

Sincerely,
E. B. White

To JAMES THURBER

[New York]
2 November [1950]

Dear Jim:

Ross asked me to pass this along to you after I'd read it. This guy accuses you and me of setting sex back a hundred years. Ross pondered

1. "Thoughts While Sowing Five Pounds of Domestic Rye Grass at 40 Cents the Pound," published in *The New Yorker*, September 23, 1950.

that a few moments, in his inquiring way, and then said: "Facts don't bear the son of a bitch out. Population figures have increased."

Professor Clark's personal gods seem to be Freud, Marx, and Mabel Dodge Luhan. He really gets going at the end, when he lauds the "merry maleness of Alexander Woollcott."

Andy

To STANLEY HART WHITE

25 West 43 Street
12 November [1950]

Dear Bun:

Thanks for the letter (23 September) about the magazine. I guess the *New Yorker* hangs on, but it is a hell of a different magazine from the one I went to work for in the twenties. Ross worries about this constantly but always ends with the remark: "Ah Jesus Christ it's still worth 20 cents."

Lil was here for dinner the other night and we were talking about you. Lil looks fine and seems happy. Her hair has lost most of its red, but she looks young and gay. Last summer she put Sidney in a girls' camp in Belgrade. Lil dropped in at the rebuilt Gleason farmhouse and saw Millard and Mae [Gleason]. She said Millard is obviously a sick man and won't be around long. . . .

K and I are both pretty well, if a bit punchy. Both K and Joe had virus pneumonia in September, so the summer ended on a note of terramycin. Joe, after two years at Cornell, is now in M.I.T. where he seems to belong. They work the pants off him but he is liking it and doing well. Is taking naval architecture. Tech has a fleet of sailing dinghies right in front of the joint, in the Charles River. This is Joe's idea of a proper university: step out of a classroom into a boat. No nonsense about dry land. . . .

Yrs,
En

To HARLAND W. HOISINGTON, JR.

[New York]
December 15, 1950

Dear Mr. Hoisington:

I agree with you that world federation is the final answer to war. I disagree, however, with your idea that a single legal system can serve free nations and authoritarians. I think such "law" would be unenforceable by its nature, and that the authoritarians would themselves *be* the law, as they always manage to be. You may be right, but so may I. At any rate, I'm against any proposal that suggests a compromise arrangement, and am in favor only of that type of world government that specifically subscribes to a bill of rights, and denies dictators.

The fact that I am now eating some of the words in "The Wild Flag" doesn't bother me any, as long as I manage to say exactly what I think at this moment.

Sincerely,
E. B. White

To MRS. M. R. RUSSELL

[New York]
December 21, 1950

Dear Mrs. Russell:

Millicent is an imaginary girl that the poet took a walk with.[1] It's just a poem about a young man and a girl taking a walk and enjoying the world in each other's company. Happens all the time.

Sincerely,
E. B. White

To LAWRENCE LANGNER

December 29, 1950

Dear Mr. Langner:

Thanks for your letter about a musical play.[1]

I do not have any material of my own that would be suitable—or at least nothing comes to mind. Of course there are dozens of legends and stories kicking around that have a Maine coast background, but I'm sure Frank Hatch knows them better than I do.[2] One of the spectacular things that happened in Maine was the shipwreck, many years ago, of a vessel carrying a small circus. Elephants, monkeys, ponies, and people were washed ashore and must have greatly added to the life of the fishing village, while they lasted. A children's book based on that incident was published some years back, I believe. If you want to look at it, I can dig up the title.

Sincerely,
E. B. White

1. In a poem called "Sunday" in White's first book, *The Lady Is Cold.*

1. Langner, a director of the Theatre Guild, proposed that White collaborate in writing a musical. White was mildly interested, but nothing came of the idea.
2. Francis Hatch, of Castine and Boston, was a collector of stories and legends about Maine. He also aspired to the theater.

To KATHARINE S. WHITE

[1950?]
[Interoffice memo]

Mrs White:

Levick used to carry rocks in his pockets to throw at taxis and buses that failed to stop for him. Got this from D. Terry, at lunch.

EBW

To LAWRENCE LANGNER

[New York]
January 5, 1951

Dear Mr. Langner:

The book you asked about was "The Circus Boat" by John Hooper, published by the Steven Daye Press in 1939. It is out of print. The Library may have it in the juvenile department.

There are, of course, original sources that might prove more instructive than the book itself. A friend of mine is librarian of the Bangor Public Library and I'll write and find out whether he has anything on the circus wreck.

As to my collaborating on a musical play, it would depend somewhat on when the work would have to be done. I am loaded with work at the moment, and there is a possibility that I may go to work on a documentary motion picture, here in New York, in the spring or early summer.[1] On the other hand, I hate to stand up an elephant.

Sincerely,
E. B. White

To MR. and MRS. ALFRED Z——

[New York]
January 9, 1951

Dear Mr. and Mrs. Z——

The story "Zwarte Piet" was published because we liked it, and for no other reason. I think that people who look for signs of race discrimination in the New Yorker with a magnifying glass will always find those signs, but more often than not the discrimination is in the eye of the beholder. The New Yorker publishes whatever it considers sound and good, and theoretically we include Negroes in the contemporary scene along with whites. In practice, Negroes enjoy a certain immunity to the shafts of satirists and cartoonists. Every week we publish drawings depicting the frailties and idiosyncrasies of the human race, as our artists

---

1. The documentary, of *Here Is New York*, was never filmed. Six years later, however, Andrew Rooney adapted the piece for a television show.

see them. But we do not feel entirely free to include colored people in comic situations, for the reason that the public is as yet incapable of looking at a Negro as an individual, and persists in looking at him as a symbol.

When we publish a drawing like the Halloween cover, showing a colored woman about to encounter a spook, it immediately draws letters of complaint from high-minded but edgy white people who accuse us of holding Negroes up to ridicule. Our attitude is that the highest respect we can pay the colored race is to hold it up to exactly the same type of spoofing to which we subject the white race and all other races, since this is evidence that we regard people as individuals and all men as equals in the sight of artists as well as of God.

Sincerely yours,
E. B. White

To DALE KRAMER

25 West 43rd Street
February 8, 1951

Dear Mr. Kramer:

I don't know anything about American humor that is fit to print, but if you want to see me about the matter I am at your service after I get rid of this cold, which will be Friday.

Sincerely,
E. B. White

• *Ann Kenyon, who knew White's friend John McNulty, was a sheep breeder in Rhode Island and a reader of White's books. She had sent him a clipping from the New England* Homestead *containing the words "rive," "froe," "shake," and "knurl." A correspondence developed, and White actually did, as proposed in this letter, trade a boat for some bred ewes. He also later bought a ram lamb from Kenyon stock.*

To ANN KENYON

New York
11 February [1951]

Dear Miss Kenyon:

To rive a shake, it is a good idea to turn it over, face down, and rive it that way. My froe has two small knurls just below the clevis pin which give it a surface elegance. But I always say that in the long run it's breeding that counts.

As for McNulty, I can never picture him at sea, and the only body of water that I think he might feel at home on is the East River—which commands a view of Second Avenue. Yesterday afternoon he won $167, and was surprised and pleased.

What kind of sheep do you have? I have a 12½ foot Dyer Dhow fully equipped for sailing that I will trade for some bred ewes.

Sincerely,
E. B. White

P.S. A froe is a cleaving tool, and to rive is to split. As for shake, it may be a typo for stake or it may be a crack in timber. All three words are in Webster. My subscription to the Homestead expired a few years ago, and this ad tempts me to renew.

To ANN KENYON

[New York]
24 February 1951

Dear Miss Kenyon:

Never look into a sheep's past, it is almost always a dark chapter. This projected trade of ours sounds even more involved than most country matters, and the fact that a trout has somehow got into the thing (along with a barren ewe, pronounced "yo" as in yo-yo) gives it an air of real fantasy. The perfect arrangement would be for you to load your dhow with the sheep and start rowing along the coast in an easterly direction, and I rig my dhow and start beating up to the westward. When we met, you could step into my boat and I into yours, and I would try and have a string of trout along to make it all seem legal, and to counterbalance the shoats, the sprinkler, and the Bantams. The sprinkler, incidentally, might well be powered and rigged as a bilge pump.

To get back to Suffolk ewes, from which I rarely stray very far, my ambition is to buy two or three that are not infested with dhows. I know how to cope with worms, but I cannot take on a ewe with a dhow —simply haven't the facilities or the patience. I am convinced from a careful study of your letter that the sensible thing for me to do is *not* interrupt any sheep's springtime but bide my time till fall, then buy unencumbered stock from you—pregnant, perhaps, but roughly unencumbered. The fact that I now know somebody who has Suffolks has lifted my spirits enormously. I've never been much for the woolly faces, preferring the smooth and open countenance whether in man or beast.

Sincerely,
E. B. White

To URSULA NORDSTROM

25 West 43rd Street
March 1, 1951

Dear Miss Nordstrom:

Thanks for the report . . .

I've recently finished another children's book, but have put it away for a while to ripen (let the body heat go out of it). It doesn't satisfy me the way it is and I think eventually I shall rewrite it pretty much, in order to shift the emphasis and make other reforms.[1]

Sincerely,
E. B. White

• *The Whites' tax returns were prepared by the New York firm of Greenbaum, Wolff & Ernst—the "Ernst" being their friend Morris Ernst. Because they were residents of Maine and moved back and forth between city and country, working and earning in both locales, there was often a question of how much, if anything, the Whites owed New York State in taxes. Ernst usually supervised, but delegated the details to junior members of the firm, of whom Arthur Strasburger was one.*

To MORRIS L. ERNST

[New York]
March 1, 1951

Dear Morris:

Your letter is clear on all points and thanks for it. We gave Mr. Strasburger our dates of arrival in and departure from New York during 1950, and although I didn't compute it, I take it that we are within the limit of seven months.

I think Katharine's work would almost exactly fit the formula of $\frac{7}{12}$ths. My own is less easy to figure, but I see no way to do it except by the same formula; if it satisfies the State, it satisfies me. A writer's life and his production are so haphazard, so unpredictable, and so divided between periods of pregnancy and deliverance, that there can never be any sharp means of reckoning his time and his fruits. These days he is lucky to be fruity at all, and the State ought to be glad to learn that he's still alive.

Yours,
E. B. White

---

1. The book was *Charlotte's Web*. White did put it aside for about a year. He then rewrote it extensively, introducing Fern, who was not in the early drafts.

To MARGARET RAUSCH

[New York]
March 6, 1951

Dear Miss Rausch:

Thanks for your letter of February 28. I don't want the piece reprinted in a textbook.[1] It was written in 1943, and China, in that innocent year, was not a Communist land. I used the Chinese delegate as a symbol of wisdom. I'm afraid that the school-children of 1951 might mistake him for a symbol of Communism. Such are the ravages of time.

Sincerely,
E. B. White

• *The poem referred to in this letter is "I Paint What I See." White writes: "Miss Lausch was not the only reader who thought I was siding with Rivera, who was a Communist, and against Rockefeller, who wasn't. In the course of my long literary life I've learned that some readers just can't believe that a writer can ever be objective: they read something deep or symbolic or sinister or political into every work."*

To GRETCHEN E. LAUSCH

[New York]
April 10, 1951

Dear Miss Lausch:

Years ago, a mural was painted by the artist Rivera on the walls of a building in Rockefeller Center. It was attacked by critics on the score that it was leftwing propaganda. And it was removed, after a controversy between the Rockefellers and the artist.

My poem simply reported the event, in ballad form. I'm a minnesinger from away back.

Sincerely,
E. B. White

To LEWIS REYNOLDS

[New York]
April 24, 1951

Dear Mr. Reynolds:

I'm very grateful for your note of condolence. Fred has been gone more than two years, but I can't see that he has slipped any. He's on my mind a good deal, and I'm not entirely sure that all his bills are paid—he charged everything.

Sincerely,
E. B. White

---

1. Miss Rausch, an editor at Scott Foresman, wanted permission to reprint White's Comment in *The New Yorker* about the wild flag.

To CAROLINE B. SERGEANT

229 East 48th Street
New York City
27 April 1951

Dear Aunt Crully:

I hope this letter will reach you on your birthday, to bring you my warmest greetings. May it be a happy day for you! I can hardly believe that you are celebrating your 89th—when last seen by me, only a couple of months ago, you gave no indication of any such piling up of years. Unless I can discover some loss of animation and wit, I shall not take any stock in these stories circulating round about your age.

Spring, which has been reluctant this year, has arrived at last, and Turtle Bay Garden is bright with tulips, hyacinths, daffodils, and even apple blossoms. Yesterday we were visited by a brown thrush, this morning by a white-throated sparrow. These wonderful renewals and visitations luckily proceed without regard to world events, and without them I don't know how we would manage to hang on. One of the world events that has been least to my liking was the recent triumphal procession of General MacArthur, whose interpretation of our course of action I find hard to take. However, one incident of the General's homecoming amused me very much: I found your niece (my wife) seated at her desk before breakfast, calmly writing a letter to the President of the United States. I felt that this single act of a steady and responsible citizen rather cancelled out the hysterical parade that followed later in the day.

When we were in Maine a few weeks ago, I took a few pictures of the barnyard and of the geese. I'm enclosing some prints for your amusement. You can see by the lilac bush that spring had not advanced much at that date; but from the look in the eye of the geese you can see that it was expected.

Again I wish you a joyful day and many happy returns. And my best to Ros and John.

With lots of love,
Andy

To MIRIAM L. RICHMOND

[New York]
May 1, 1951

Dear Miss Richmond:

I'm enclosing a couple of copies of the poem ["Song of the Queen Bee"]. Can't send you a clipping from the magazine, as that particular issue got used up and none is available.

Sorry to report that the situation among bees has changed since

I wrote the poem. The scientists won, and queens have been inseminated artificially. The drone not only isn't in the air, he's not even conscious—they knock him out with CO_2. Ah, progress!

Sincerely,
E. B. White

To CARRIE A. WILSON

[New York]
May 1, 1951

Dear Mrs. Wilson:

I find the world very perplexing, just as you do, although I don't think our armies are simply serving Standard Oil. That is too thin a story of so great an effort.

If the vexatious world of people were the whole world, I would not enjoy it at all. But it is only a small, though noisy, part of the whole; and I find the natural world as engaging and as innocent as it ever was. When I get sick of what men do, I have only to walk a few steps in another direction to see what spiders do. Or what the weather does. This sustains me very well indeed, and I have no complaints.

Many thanks for your very kind and encouraging letter.

Sincerely,
E. B. White

• *Alexander Lindey was another of the lawyers at Greenbaum, Wolff & Ernst who worked on the Whites' tax affairs. Later he went in business for himself and represented White when he was negotiating the sale of the motion picture rights to* Charlotte's Web.

To ALEXANDER LINDEY

[New York]
May 2, 1951

Dear Mr. Lindey:

Thanks for the progress report. I have abandoned the notion that the State, or the Federal Government, will ever understand writers, and am content with a denominator of 250 if that is the denominator that appeals to them. There is considerable evidence to support the theory that writers are not worth understanding, anyway. It is certainly true that they spend 90 per cent of their time in questionable and often gaudy pursuits that seem irrelevant to the business of creation. I think they can be likened to a prestidigitator, one of whose hands is extremely active, attracting the eye of the beholder, while the other hand, unnoticed, is doing the real work of stuffing a handkerchief into a false pocket. I don't fully understand writers myself, and never fail to be surprised and pleased when I manage to produce a handkerchief.

Sincerely,
E. B. White

• *Asked to tell more about the "incident" in the following letter, White had this to say:*

"It all happened a long time ago. As I recall it, some wag had stolen the sign in front of John S. Sumner's Society for the Suppression of Vice, carried it home to his Village apartment, and put it to use as a cocktail tray. The New Yorker learned of this and ran a short piece about it in Talk. Sumner was sore as the dickens and tried to pry the name of the thief from the editors—without success. As a peace offering, the magazine suggested that it provide the Society with a fine new sign, and Sumner accepted the offer. At this point, master minds around the office got to work and dreamed up an elaborate scheme to further embarrass the Society and the foul world of Anti-Vice. Ralph Ingersoll and I hired a carpenter to build a sign with a false front—that is, it had a panel that could be slid out, exposing a quite different scene. We persuaded an artist (I think it was Arno) to paint a picture of Sumner in which his hat was being kicked off by an almost naked chorus girl. The plan was to present the sign and, after it was hung, visit the place some dark night and remove the panel, leaving Mr. Sumner fully exposed with his high-kicking cutie. I was elected to perform this act of thievery and actually did pull it off, with the help of my friend Ted Pratt. I can't imagine The New Yorker *up to any tricks like that nowadays."*

To **THEODORE PRATT**

[New York]
May 16, 1951

Dear Ted:

The incident of the sign seems to stay alive, garnished and changed with the dimming of memories. Hutchens called me about it and I filled him in as best I could.[1] I don't think Woollcott had any share in the plot— you must have been thinking of Ralph Ingersoll. He was the master mind, but was noticeably absent when it came to climbing a ladder. Anyway, it is all going to be revived in a dismal book by Dale Kramer

---

1. John Hutchens was writing on *Ross and The New Yorker* in the *Herald Tribune*.

called "Ross and The New Yorker," advance sheets of which I have seen.

And what petty thieveries are you up to these grim days, sweet my ladder man?

Yours,
E. B. White

To JAMES THURBER

North Brooklin, Maine
14 June 1951

Dear Jim:

I feel like a louse, or tick, for not having written sooner in answer to your nice letters, but have been having my spring orgy in the barn, settling arguments among the geese, taking temperatures, replacing young robins fallen from nests, stepping on the edges of hoes and rakes, challenging black flies to fifteen rounds without even attempting to make the weight, and constructing jury-rig incubators that would make Rube Goldberg blush. My life as a gooseherd the past three weeks would be worth setting down, if I had a moment, but there are no moments available around here at this season. I raised three young geese and a gander last year, and this spring they thought they would take a whirl at sex and reproduction. In March the gander decided that an ordinary 10-quart galvanized pail would do for a mating pond (his exact words were, "I'm ready if you girls are") and when I got back here in May the three geese were all sitting on eggs in three nests that I had lined up in the barn. When the first egg hatched and the goose saw the result of her labors, she jumped off, grabbed the gosling by the neck, and threw it high and wide. The gander and the other two geese cheered the play loudly. I heard this rally, retrieved the gosling, placed it in a small carton at the back of the kitchen stove, and raised it by hand. Meantime the other two geese lost track, in the confusion, of which nest belonged to which goose, and I think they changed places—which resulted in giving one of them a total incubation tour of seven weeks before she was through. A day or two later, the other one quit sitting, leaving the eggs for me to sit on. I discovered that one egg was already making a noise like a gosling, and being sympathetic with claustrophobes, I placed this egg in a small box of sawdust, got a hand-drill and a pair of my wife's scissors, took a large draft of Old Newburyport rum, and went to work. I drilled through the shell in what I thought was a likely spot, inflicting only a slight wound in the right shoulder. After an hour's digging, I produced a gosling—somewhat premature, as it still had the yolk hanging to its ass. I rigged up an incubator, using an infra-red lamp and many other accessories I found in the attic. For 24 hours, life fluttered. I had no sleep, as the bedroom was too full of stuff for me to lie down and I didn't feel sleepy anyway. The child lived, but I discovered it had a plugged touch-hole, due to my surgery. A goose that can't shit is a travesty on nature (I hope your secretary isn't reading this to you, if she is give her my love) and I felt so guilty that I spent the next three days getting the plug out. It sounds implausible, but this gosling is today not only alive but devoted to me—screams when I am out of her sight, and wants to sit in my shirt pocket for warmth and companionship. The more I see of geese, the more I think they know what they are doing.

You said in your April letter that you thought I had the wrong idea about humor in our time. I haven't got any idea about humor except that I seldom think of anything funny to write, which is why our time doesn't get more humor by Old "Our Time" White. Ross never gives me any encouragement, anyway, as he broods a lot about the comment page, as he has been doing for 26 years, and keeps muttering "Chrissake, I never did know how to lead off the magazine."

We have given up our earlier idea of going somewhere for the month of July and are going to stay right spang here, where we like to be and where the food is good. Joe was here for a few days, and then returned to M.I.T. for summer school, to try to catch up with himself before the Army catches up with him. He has had his induction notice but is deferred until August 20, by reason of having taken the student exam.

I tore a fine, big gash in my skull just before leaving New York—the sort of skull wound I have often dreamed of. Did it on the hard underbelly of an awning bracket. For several days I couldn't comb my hair, as it was impractical, and acquired a very jaunty little new hairdo that made me look quite like a belted kingfisher. Milt Greenstein drove with me to Maine, as K was ordered to travel by train, and I was scared to drive alone, as I was under the impression that there was a large piece of the awning bracket just under the first layer of grey matter.

I'm sending this letter to the NYer rather than Bermuda as I fear you may be in transit or in Connecticut. Haven't done anything yet with Mr. E. Linden Binden Bouillon, but I don't think that there is anything stopping me except a good night's rest without a gosling in my pajama pocket.

Love,
Andy

To JAMES THURBER

North Brooklin, Maine
15 June 1951

Dear Jim:

Your letter got here a few hours after I mailed mine to you, addressed to the New Yorker. I don't think you need have any qualms about the Charles L. Thurber piece, as there isn't a word in it that isn't affectionately written, and even if Robert queried every line, you still have every right to paint a portrait as it appears to your eye.[1] Probably it is natural that members of a family should get lathered up when one of them sets out to explain an ancestor, and there is a kind of jealousy involved in it, and that, too, is natural. But as you say, it is distressing.

About the Kramer book, I don't think the NYer is trying to stop it off, merely protesting certain things about it. I think Kramer was not quite forthright when he approached some of us. He wrote me a year ago and said he was writing a book on "American humor," and that naturally there would be stuff in it about the New Yorker. He asked if he could see me and I said sure. I was in Maine at the time, and he didn't get to see me till fall, and when he turned up, the book had somehow acquired the title "Ross and The New Yorker." However, despite this somewhat cagey approach, I sat around for a couple of hours trying to give him what assistance I could. I also spent a whole day going over his mimeographed sheets, pencilling in stuff. My only out-and-out gripe was that he had dug up several extracts from a youthful diary of mine, which I think he had no right to do and which didn't make any sense anyway. The way he worked it, it certainly sounded as though I had handed him the stuff—or at any rate it would have seemed that way to anybody who hadn't read "One Man's Meat," and the world is full of such people. I agree with you that The New Yorker can't expect to publish profiles, or anything else, unless it is willing to have the tables turned. I don't think Kramer has written much of a book, but that's beside the point.

Yrs,
Andy

To DAISE TERRY

[North Brooklin, Me.]
1 August [1951]

Dear Daise:

Here's something to go back to the Boys' Room, or Capote Hall.[1] Hope you are well. On second thought, you are always well, so I can relax. We are through the worst of the summer—the "vacation" part, and are now back at work. Breath is coming regularly again, but the extreme exhaustion has taken its toll. I have never figured out why we spend July in this place—it is like a children's party at which Olsen and Johnson drop in. Among other records shattered in July here was the

---

1. The piece, "Gentleman from Indiana," was about Thurber's father, one of several family portraits in *The Thurber Album*. Robert Thurber, Jim's younger brother, was furious about it, and the two brothers became estranged.

---

1. Truman Capote had once been an office boy at *The New Yorker*.

record for rainfall and thunder. We not only went through all the usual routine of haying and berrying and transplanting and baby sitting and canning and freezing and Picnicking, but we did it with the water up around our knees and the lightning playing up and down our shinbones. If you want any hay, let me know. How are all those little girls that surround you in that enchanted circle? I suppose you have a whole new set of faces for me to memorize. Tell Milton [Greenstein] there is enough driftwood on my beach, after the last southeaster, to provide him with a hundred thousand lamp bases—all of them gnarled and curious. Did you know Milton was a sucker for driftwood? It was the only thing on this place that really stirred his fancy. *Holiday Magazine* wants me to tour America for them next month, so I better get the names of some of those motels from you. Am really too weak to tour America, except in an ambulance.

Yrs,
EBW

• Holiday *asked White to drive coast to coast, as he had done in 1922, and write some pieces about America. He accepted, but got only as far as Galeton, Pennsylvania. "I discovered that I was traveling so fast I might as well be home in bed, and I didn't see any way to slow down, so I gave up the idea . . ." he wrote his brother Stanley at the time. The assignment was passed on to John Steinbeck, who made the trip and wrote* Travels with Charley. *When Howard Cushman heard about White's prospective trip he sent him some notes on their 1922 journey.*

To HOWARD CUSHMAN

North Brooklin
29 October [1951]

Dear Cush:

Your notes, thank God, were just where I thought they were, and they are now herewith enclosed—with thanks again for having gone to all that bother.

Here are a few remarks, page by page, for what they're worth and with no warranty of their accuracy.

Page 1. According to my journal, we left Mount Vernon at 3:30 of a Thursday afternoon. The date was March 9, and we were in Poughkeepsie by nightfall—a fine, brisk run. So that meal at the Smith Brothers restaurant must have been supper, not lunch. We holed up in a hotel, where you promptly composed the first triolet of the excursion.

> She holds me in Poughkeepsie,
>   I cannot get away;
> She thinks I ain't a gypsy—
> She holds me in Poughkeepsie,

Until with her I'm tipsy:
I guess I'm stuck for aye.
She holds me in Poughkeepsie,
I cannot get away.

(We weren't wasting any time, and those lyric forms from France rode with us all the way.) We spent the next night (no triolets) in Schenectady, at, I guess, the Beta house. In case it has slipped your mind, you carried a tobacco called Serene Mixture, and I found this appropriate, since serenity was to be our keynote. In East Aurora, the waltzes were Schubert. I can still play one of them, but not well.

Page 3. The Phi Gam at Elyria was George Calvert, but I would imagine that his name is infinitely irrelevant, and I don't remember whether it was toilet bowls or what. Repairs to the Ford at this juncture were seventy-five cents—50 cents for a busted radiator and 25 cents for a fan belt. Relevant indeed. . . .

Page 13. The limerick last-line contest netted us $25, much better pay than sonneteering in Louisville. The 25 bucks was awarded to "E. B. White, Beta Theta Pi house, 1625 University Avenue SE, Minneapolis." Honorable mention went to Stephen H. Brown, O. A. Glasow, Minnie R. Long, V. M. Arbogast, and M. D. Rudolph. Just in case you've forgotten.

In Minneapolis, I peddled roach powder for a day or two, but it was not a success. I was a lousy peddler, and the powder itself may have been inferior. I don't know.

Page 14. I did not spend a night in the hospital. The doctor gave me ether (on top of a quick slug of corn whiskey that I drank while being carried in to the sanitarium by a kind fellow with an automobile) and he re-set my arm in the afternoon. I came out of the moonshine-ether treatment with the highest jag I ever had, and the most articulate. There is a nurse in that hospital, if she is still alive, who has heard everything, about everything. I left out nothing. But they sprung me, and you and I went back to the soil, and I slept on the ground that night, waking at about four A.M. with an intolerable pain in my arm, caused by the swelling of same inside the tight bandage or cast. I handed you my hunting knife and instructed you to cut me adrift, which you did, muttering and grumbling the whole way, being deprived of your sleep at an unholy hour.

I think it was you, not me, that landed the great Hotel Room Card job, with the friendly printer. I was knocked out with the arm, and I think you met up with the printer and started the wheels turning. I've always been very thankful that I once saw a Tom show. Unique.

"Monday we made fifteen dollars. Cush had been talking with the editor of the Cass County Pioneer—a typical country weekly. The editor put him next to some dope—so the editor said. Anyway, it worked. A new hotel had recently been erected on Leech Lake. Cush went to the manager and told him that he (Cush) would supply the room cards, containing rules and regulations, free of charge if the manager would let him solicit small ads for the margins. So we drew up a dummy, and out of about thirty business men in Walker (you ought to see a Walker business man) we sold fifteen. That netted $26.50 and the printing bill was $11.00. The whole thing consumed less than twenty-four hours, and we shook the dust of Walker Tuesday noon." (And a little later in my journal) "Every curve in the road brought forth a new lake to view, shining blue and peaceful and unmolested. It was a day of very white clouds, and very blue skies, and very dark green spruces behind their lighter hardwoods. Wild roses lined the road timidly all of the way."

Page 16. Can't recall the reason for our going down to Hardin from Billings. It was in Hardin that I played the piano for two (I think) nights in a cafe, for meals. This, in retrospect, seems really quite wonderful to me. Can a fellow still wander in to a small town cafe in America, with 'merely the ability to knock out a couple of tunes on a piano, and persuade the management to set him up to a few meals? Seems to me unlikely. We must have hit America at a particularly vulnerable time.

Page 20. Beg to correct you here. Hotspur's rear end collapsed when we were *boarding* the ferry. The incline was very steep, and I'll never forget the feeling when Hotspur suddenly lost his bowels, and we slid back down. The ferryman suggested that we "pull the son of a bitch up onto the boat" and he would help us fix her while going back and forth on the river. This we did. I think the money we lost while taking a cooling swim in the Columbia River was on the eastern (Kennewick) shore, and I think it was two silver dollars. It was *not* a five dollar bill, because you wouldn't be diving for a five dollar bill, and I remember diving over and over again. It was silver. And the ferryman took pity on us, and produced a couple bucks from his own pocket, pretending that somebody had come up with them. He was a real guy, that ferryman. Hotspur's ailment, incidentally, was a broken pinion gear in the rear end—a fairly costly little item.

Item. The cafe in Hardin was Becker's Cafe. You were a hay hand in the fields, according to my record. We slept in an oat bin on the ranch where you worked. (I recall that oat bin. Clean place to sleep, though a little hard and unyielding.)

Item. In Cody, I sold my Corona for twenty dollars. We were that far down hill.

Page 21. I never worked for the *Seattle Star*. Helm got me a job with the *Times*, which was the rich Blethen paper. I did a short stint for the *Post-Intelligencer* (Hearst) after my discharge from the *Times*.

Andy

• *When Cornell's new president, Deane W. Malott, delivered his maiden speech, part of it was word-for-word from a piece by Harold Taylor, president of Sarah Lawrence College, which had been printed in the Spring 1949 issue of* Harvard Educational Review. *Somebody spotted this, and White, in the line of duty, turned it in to the magazine for the Funny Coincidence Department (November 10, 1951).*

To HAROLD ROSS

[New York]
[October? 1951]
[Interoffice memo]

Mr. Ross:

Here's a college president lifting from another college president, for his maiden speech. Seems incredible, but there it is. Like most Funny Coincidences, it worries me, as to its fairness, because of the implication that the plagiarism is deliberate. In this case, my bet is that Malott (who is an ex-businessman—he used to grow pineapples) assigned a lieutenant in his office to help him get up a speech. And this is what developed. He even uses quotes, in one place, but no mention of what he is quoting from. I guess it's a public service to publish these things, but there is no question about this being very damaging to Malott. We once flirted, if you recall, with the idea that we could somehow take the accusatory note out of Funny Coincidence, but I have never doped out any way to do it. Just running the stuff, in parallel, is per se accusatory, I guess. Short of a diagrammatic subhead saying that, well, we realize that these things sometimes just happen innocently, I can't see how to manage it.

EBW

To IRITA VAN DOREN

[New York]
November 13, 1951

Dear Mrs. Van Doren:

About that annual request for the names of three books, I wish I might be taken off your list of readers.[1] I'm not sure just what it is about

---

1. Once a year, Mrs. Van Doren, editor of the *New York Herald Tribune* literary supplement, wrote to a list of well-known people, asking each to name the three books he or she had enjoyed most in the past year.

naming three books that disquiets me, but there is something. I might prefer to describe three baths I have taken in 1951, or to name three muffins that have satisfied me. Books, no.

Many of my friends are the writers of books, and I find it ruffling to hunt around book titles for a balance (sometimes extremely delicate) between delight and friendship. I could settle for three books every one of them in my circle of friends, or I could starkly rule out all such suspect selections and name three books by total strangers. Or I could get cute, and name the book I happen to be reading and liking (by G. A. Henty). But I prefer merely to keep quiet about my book life.

I do not mean this in any sense as a criticism of the *Tribune* feature —merely wish to save the *Tribune* the price of a telegram by establishing myself on your records as a non-book namer. It takes all kinds to make a world.

Very sincerely yours,
E. B. White

To STANLEY HART WHITE

[229 East 48 Street]
[November 30, 1951]
Friday

Dear Bun:

I had a fine time with your daughter after I finally found her. The telephone proved almost completely ineffectual, as I kept calling Mabel when Mabel wasn't there. However, she showed up on Wednesday noon at the office, looking very much on the ball, and K and I took her to lunch. After lunch, Jan said she wanted to check out of the Barbizon to escape paying another day's freight, so she and I went up there and then to my apartment with her suitcase and dunnage (she had begun to acquire paper bags with stuff in them). I asked her when her train departed—after issuing an invitation to stay over for Thanksgiving— and she said: "Some time between five o'clock and six thirty." I thought that one over for a minute, as it seemed to contain a whole new approach to railroading, investing it with the sort of geniality that it ought to have in these trying times. Not convinced that the railroads had really achieved this relaxed state, I examined her ticket and then we called Grand Central and after a chatty time we concluded that the train went at 6:30. That gave Janice and me a little time for window shopping, and also for a cocktail at the apartment with K before the departure. I took her over to Grand Central to put her on board, and the terminal, with its pre-holiday smash crowd, looked as though everybody had rushed onto the field to pull down the goal posts. Janice led me over to some steel lockers about three-quarters of a mile beyond the train gate, and produced some more paper bags—a real squirrel. I was beginning to wonder whether we would ever manage to work the kind of deception play that would enable us to get back through the crowd to the train gate, when Jan began plucking at one of the packages. "You've simply *got* to see this fabric," she murmured, as a new wave of 50,000 people swept out of the shuttle and went by us on the double. I was having a wonderful time, as I had never looked over drapery material in Grand Central on Thanksgiving Eve and am always ripe for any new experience. So we set everything down and Jan held one corner of the thing and I held the other. If we had had a couple of tent poles and some spikes we could have camped right there. It was certainly a beautiful fabric and was generally admired. . . .

We had a big Thanksgiving party yesterday, with perfect attendance. Nancy and her gang drove from Easton, Pa., Roger and his came from Sneden's Landing, and Joe came from Boston. Total of twelve. We had snappers, funny hats, pin-the-tail-on-the-donkey (which is now called stick-the-nose-on-Rudolph) and potato races, and it sounded like fight night at the Garden.

Yrs,
En

To JOHN R. FLEMING

[New York]
4 December 1951

Dear Jack:

Thanks for the pipeline stuff from Ithaca. I had been wondering what, if anything, was happening. A kid who works here, lately graduated from Cornell, told me that there had been a considerable disturbance, but he didn't know any details.

In the same mail with your letter, I received a copy of last Friday's *Sun*, which had it spread all over P.1. (It is known locally as "the *New Yorker* incident.") The most recent issue of the *Alumni News* appears to be sitting on it.

Plagiarism is not a simple phenomenon, and the business of being the Funny Coincidence man for this socialite magazine has sometimes given me pause. There are, I believe, roughly three kinds of plagiarists. There is, first, the thief, who, either because he is emotionally unstable or in desperate need, just goes out and swipes something. Then there is the dope, who is a little vague about the printed word and regards anything in the way of printed matter as mildly miraculous and common property. And the third plagiarist is the total recall guy, who can read something or hear something and later regurgitate it, practically word for word, not knowing he is doing it. This last customer is, of course, an innocent man, and that is why the Funny Coincidence department is an uneasy spot, for although the title doesn't charge anybody with malfeasance, there is always the implication that somebody is either a bum or a crook. In Malott's case, my guess is that he is just not very bright. His statement published in the *Sun* makes no sense, or rather it fails to vindicate him. He says he got his material from "some educational handout or filler paragraph in a weekly newspaper which was printed with no reference to source or authority." Well, the president of a university ought to know that everything, no matter what, originates somewhere. It has an author, however obscure, however ghostly, and you can't knock him off, even though it is a convenience and saves work.

I'm mildly depressed by "the *New Yorker* incident" because I love Cornell and wish that the president's chair was occupied by a scholar—that is, a man who is serene and magnanimous and doesn't have to fiddle around among educational handouts and filler paragraphs to supply himself. I've never met Malott. Saw Bristow last summer and he told me that he was favorably impressed with the new prexy.

I didn't know you had a son on the *Sun* staff. My boy went to Cornell for two years, got fed with trying to be an Arts student, and switched to M.I.T. and naval architecture.

Yrs,
Andy

To ELIZABETH S——

[New York]
December 10, 1951

Dear Miss S——

I'm sorry to be so late answering your letter, but the editor of this magazine died a few days ago, and I'm behind in my work.

I'm not sure, from your letter, what the nature of your unhappiness is, but you sound unhappy. The atmosphere of a college often seems unbearably frivolous and meaningless. And I suppose it sometimes seems unpromising for an incipient writer—if that is what you are. But no matter what environment you are in, you are learning to write if you really care deeply about writing. I cannot think of an *un*interesting environment.

Lately I've felt a little disturbed about college education—the way it is going, I mean. Scholarship, in the old-fashioned sense, is at low ebb. Science is in the ascendent, and it is veiled in secrecy, much of it. All this makes me uneasy, but I know it is, more than anything, merely a reflection of the times. And you students not only have to take the reflected glare, but you have to *be* the times and set up a light of your own.

I don't at all agree with you about frivolity. I should not try to learn to write without learning first to be frivolous. Get yourself a pair of pedal pushers as a start. Also a Webster's Collegiate dictionary, so that you need never again misspell "apparel." And remember that writing is translation, and the opus to be translated is yourself.

And lots of luck—we all need that!

Sincerely,
E. B. White

To H. K. RIGG

[New York]
11 December 1951

Dear Bunny:

Ross died last week and we have been in something of a scramble here, as well as feeling quite shot. K and I were both awfully fond of him, and we have the sensation of being disembowelled, as he was very much a part of our lives and our work.

Was swell to get your letter in the middle of everything. I had been wondering where you were. Am also greatly tempted to take you up on that idea of coming down to the islands, as I've never seen them and everybody says the climate is perfect.

If you've got a piece about Nassau under your hat, bring it out and let's have a look. *The New Yorker* runs *regular* letters from big cities like Paris, London, and Washington. It also runs occasional stuff (usually not called a Letter) from anywhere at all. There is, for instance, in the current issue (Dec. 15) a piece by [Richard] Rovere from Key West, which you might like to look at. It runs under the heading "Our Far-Flung Correspondents." Your piece sounds as if it might belong under that head.

K and I are going to try to get to Maine for a little while in January, during Joe's midterm vacation. Joe is still naval architecting at M.I.T. He designs dinghies for *Rudder* readers with one hand, and studies the midsection of the Europa with the other. He is also deep in the middle of love, love, love, and is going to bust out of college if he doesn't come up for air. He has also bought a lobster boat and built a lot of traps in order to make his fortune next summer so he can marry the girl. He also appears in December *Rudder* with a design he did for his old man, who was about to go to a watery grave in a 12½-foot Dyer dhow and had the presence of mind to get into something a bit quieter. I had the little boat built by an old guy in SW Harbor last spring, and it worked out fine for me—steady as a church, and with a lug rig that goes up and down like an old umbrella. Another one of Joe's designs is being built by a dry cleaner named Krushwitz, but Joe hasn't seen the boat as he fears Krushwitz thinks the designer is a much older man, and doesn't dare go near him.

Sorry you didn't get to Allen Cove last summer. We had nothing but rain, though, for most of the time. The fall was nice.

Yrs,
Andy

To ELMER DAVIS

25 West 43rd Street
16 December 1951

Dear Mr. Davis:

It was an odd telegram even before Western Union got to work on it.[1] I have an idea your name was on a preferred list to get an invitation to the funeral (it was an invitation affair on account of the small parlor), but then something went wrong, and the telegram was an attempt at rectification. A lot of strange and wonderful things happened that weekend. Ross managed to play his last scene in a mortuary chapel that had been sold out years in advance—it held only 350 people and the staff alone pretty nearly filled it. The scene, incidentally, was quite moving—such a bunch of normally noisy and disorderly people sitting so quietly, so respectfully, and so completely forlorn.

While I have you at my mercy, I want to thank you for your emanations from my radio. You couldn't come at a worse hour, as we are just sitting down to supper. But I am grateful anyway.

Sincerely,
E. B. White

To J. D. SALINGER

[New York]
December 17, 1951

Dear Mr. Salinger:

It was good of you to write that note, and I thank you for what you said. I felt worried, as well as sick, attempting to say anything about Ross in his own magazine. A letter like yours helps relieve the worry.

Sincerely,
E. B. White

---

1. The telegram informing Elmer Davis—author, journalist, and news analyst for ABC—of Ross's death had been garbled in transmission.

To FRANK SULLIVAN

229 East 48
[December 17?, 1951]
Sunday morn

Dear Frank:

I was damned glad to get your letter as my "beautiful" piece about Ross didn't seem beautiful at all to me after the third reading and I was quite properly worried about it. It was the kind of piece he would have tagged right away as writer-conscious—an adjective I believe he invented. So your O.K. was very important to me, and I send my thanks.

I felt just the way you did about the funeral. I'm perfectly sure that I never saw such a bunch of fine but essentially disorderly people sitting together in so tranquil and quiet a state of mutual anguish. I've been reflecting lately on my own rather curious relationship with Ross. The things that matter a great deal to me, most of them, were of not much interest or importance to Ross, and vice versa, and we really only met at a rather special level and at one place—like a couple of trolley cars hitched together by a small coupling. The thing I thank God for is that that connection proved flawless and was never even strained, not even in the middle of Ross's towering rages. His rage, actually, was one of the sustaining things at the magazine because it was usually a sort of cosmic rage directed not at the person he was shouting at but at the enemy. Ross's private enemy is a study in itself. In retrospect I am beginning to think of him as an Atlas who lacked muscle tone but who God damn well decided he was going to hold the world up *anyway*.

I liked your piece this morning on humorists and dearth of same, and am making plans to move this week to the Petroleum V. Nasby Home, where I would like to sit on a bench with you and play slapjack.

Hawley came over to our apartment the Saturday after Ross died and told us about the last months of Ross's life, medically. I don't know how much you know, and I guess I'm not at liberty at the moment to tell anything. But I can tell you, in case you're not sure, that in addition to everything else he did, Ross ended up in a blaze of extraordinary personal courage and devotion to certain people and things. I don't like to think of the noble Ross but I fear his last days were exactly that and when you add it to everything else . . . well *you* add it.

Yrs,
Andy

P.S. I can't answer your question about why you opened the book to Aes Triplex because I've never read Aes Triplex. One thing Ross and I *did* have in common—neither of us had ever read anything.

• *When he received a letter from a vice-president of Con Ed telling him that his refrigerator might be discharging poisonous gas and that he should leave a window open, White lost no time in getting to his type-writer.*

To J. H. AIKEN

[New York]
December 21, 1951

Dear Mr. Aiken:

I am a stockholder in the Consolidated Edison Company, and I rent an apartment at 229 East 48 Street in which there is a gas re-frigerator. So I have a double interest in your letter of December 19. It seems to me a very odd letter indeed.

You say that my refrigerator, even if it seems to be operating properly, may be producing poison gas, and you suggest that I open a window. I do not want to open a window. It would be a very unpopular move with the cook. Furthermore, I haven't the slightest intention of living under the same roof with a machine that discharges poison gas. Your recommendation is that I get plenty of fresh air—enough to coun-teract the effect of the gas. But I cannot believe that you are serious.

Will you be good enough to let me know what sort of poison gas is generated by a Servel gas refrigerator, and in what quantity, and how discharged. I know that there is a vent at the top of the machine and that some sort of warm air flows from the vent. I have always assumed it was hot air. Is it something else?

I also know that a gas refrigerator poses a carbon problem, and I ask the landlord to remove the carbon about once a year, which he does. But your letter makes me think that the matter is not so simple and I am anxious to be enlightened.

If gas refrigerators are, as your letter suggests, discharging poison gases into people's homes I don't want to own a gas refrigerator and I shall certainly sell my stock.

Sincerely,
E. B. White

To KENNETH BIRD

[New York]
December 28, 1951

Dear Mr. Bird:

I wish I might say yes to your offer of a regular job of writing for *Punch*. I would like very much indeed to be a contributor, but I cannot at this time take on an assignment such as you suggest.

My literary output is small, and right now I don't feel that I should dispatch any of it overseas, however much I believe in the exchange of ideas. I must devote myself to getting at a few long-overdue projects and to finishing up some that are in various stages of completion. This will leave me no time for additional work.

You were very good to consider me and I hope you will be able to find someone to produce the sort of thing you have in mind. Thank you for your sympathetic remarks about Ross. The thought of a magazine without him is a very hard thing for us all to live with.

Sincerely,
E. B. White

To MARILYN BOYER

[New York]
December 31, 1951

Dear Miss Boyer:

The essay ["Once More to the Lake"] is about a man who feels a sense of identity with his son—a fairly common feeling. But the sense of identity is all mixed up with a feeling of being separated by the years. A child, by his very existence, makes a parent feel older, nearer death. So when the little boy in the essay puts on a cold, wet bathing suit, the man feels the chill, as though *he* were experiencing it. Only for him it is a truly chilling experience, because it suddenly seems to foreshadow death.

At your age this is perhaps hard to understand. It will become clearer to you later on. Meantime, be thankful that a wet bathing suit is just a wet bathing suit.

Sincerely,
E. B. White

• *During the late forties and early fifties White had been at work on another book for children, inspired this time by daily life in the barn on his Brooklin farm.* Charlotte's Web *was published in 1952. Although disturbing at first to some adults—White's publishers tried to persuade him to change the ending—the book continues to be treasured by countless readers. By 1976 its sales in hardcover and paperback were more than one and a half million. In 1954 Harper & Brothers also published* The Second Tree From the Corner, *a clipbook of pieces primarily from* The New Yorker.

To **LARRY EISENBERG**

[New York]
February 25, 1952

Dear Mr. Eisenberg:

Thanks for the letter, the critique, and the gripe.[1] In 1951, the magazine bought stuff from 63 new writers (fiction and verse—I don't know about fact). That's about one new face a week. It doesn't satisfy our dream, which is to publish about a dozen new people a week, but it's better than most magazines manage. If you don't believe me, try keeping books on it.

All manuscripts get read—always by two editors, sometimes by four, as a check. Rejection slips are not attached mechanically, they are attached mournfully and prayerfully. The thing *The New Yorker* is most

---

1. Mr. Eisenberg, a reader, had complained about *The New Yorker*—always the same stable of writers, too many reminiscences. It wasn't White's job to answer letters of this sort, but once in a while he did it anyway.

eager to get is good stuff from new writers. But nobody gets in except on performance, or what the editors regard as performance, which is conceivably something you might not agree with.

As for the large number of reminiscent pieces, nobody is more aware of it than we are. The trouble is, a very large proportion of everything submitted is reminiscence. I guess it's because the world today is intolerable to sensitive minds, so they escape into the past. You fix up the world and we'll run fewer reminiscences.

Sincerely,
E. B. White

To H. K. RIGG

[New York]
13 March 1952

Dear Bun:

Bill Shawn is the new editor, not me. Don't know where that rumor got started, but I know I'm damn glad I'm not the editor of this whizz bang sheet. Too much work in it and I don't like the hours. Also, I don't know how to edit.

Your piece is enclosed, as it didn't get by. I am sorry that it got held here so long, and I tender the official apologies of the magazine for not acting quicker. This business of sitting on pieces while the author chews his fingers is something that has got to be remedied, and I am sure it will be, just as soon as we get some more manpower around here. You were the victim of the acute shortage of editors, caused partly by Ross's death, partly by the fact that one of our guys has been on jury duty for about three months. The pressure has been bad on Shawn, but I'm damned sorry that your piece got caught in a basket.

We're finally getting a whiff of spring weather. K and I are taking off for another short trip to Maine next week, and ought to just about hit mudtime. I think I'd rather be sailing for a warm island like Nassau, but one of the penalties of having a joint like our house in Maine is that whenever we get a breather we always head straight for there. I've got chicks coming and lambs coming, not to mention an oil burner for the furnace and some setting geese. If you're thinking of raising geese I can set you up in business.

Yrs,
Andy

• *When he signed the contract with Harper for* Charlotte's Web, *White availed himself of a "maximum payment" clause: in order to spread his tax obligation over a period of years, he set the sum of $7500 as the limit he was to receive from the book in any one year. His estimate of the book's earning capacity, however, proved far too low. Instead of petering out,* Charlotte's *sales began a steady climb, and the book earns a lot more than $7500 every year. "The rest of the money," White says, "is held for me by Harper—probably in a sock somewhere."*

To URSULA NORDSTROM

North Brooklin, Maine
27 March 1952

Dear Miss Nordstrom:

I sent a copy of the agreement to Milton Greenstein at the *New Yorker*, who will look it over for me. I suggested that he call you if he had any questions.

I think a limitation of $7500 would be a good idea, and I will ask Greenstein about this. It sounds like an extravagant dream to me, as I never believe that any book is going to sell.

I meant to ask you, and forgot, whether you had ever encountered any story plot like "Charlotte's Web"—that is, any case in fiction of a spider writing words in its web. I'm not well read in juvenile literature, or any other kind, and am always fearful that I have unwittingly created something that has already been done by somebody else. If you know of anything even remotely like this, will you tell me what it is?

Wish you could be here today to see my characters in the flesh. Had a lamb arrive yesterday morning at breakfast time—a boy. He is already out in the barnyard, playing in a snowdrift. Two of my geese are nesting—one of them right in the sheepshed, the other atop a manure pile. Charlotte's children are due shortly. It's quite a day here today.

Sincerely,
E. B. White

• *Garth Williams, who had done such a notable job of illustrating* Stuart Little, *was now at work on* Charlotte's Web. *He early ran into trouble in his attempt to create a satisfactory Charlotte. The preliminary drawings showed a spider with a woman's face. White was leery of this and tried to help Williams by sending him spider books. In the end, after many sketches had been submitted and rejected, White said, "You better just draw a spider and forget about a countenance." And that's what Williams did.*

To URSULA NORDSTROM

North Brooklin, Maine
28 March [1952]

Dear Ursula:

I am too exhausted to call you Miss Nordstrom any longer. Too much typing for a man of my years.

Under sep cov I am sending you "American Spiders" by Willis J. Gertsch, of the Natural History Museum staff. Will you be kind enough to pass it along to Garth Williams for his amusement. Aranea Cavatica is not shown in this book, but there is a spider in Plate 23 called Neoscona that looks like Charlotte, pretty much. Charlotte, however, has a rather nice little design, or engraving, on top of her abdomen—sort of like a keystone.

There is a very funny picture in this book that I think Garth should see. It is "A" on the unnumbered page preceding P. 85. The eyes and hair are quite fetching.

Plate 1 shows an orb web covered with dew.

Am also enclosing a N.Y. Public Library slip giving name and class mark of the McCook work on spiders. This is in three volumes, containing hundreds and hundreds of pictures. Garth might find it helpful to thumb through these majestic tomes. He'd better watch out, though—once a man gets interested in spiders, there's no time left for art.

Yrs,
Andy

To CASS CANFIELD

North Brooklin, Maine
29 March 1952

Dear Cass:

Your note was very encouraging and you were good to write it. After I get through with a book it always seems terrible—for a while, anyway. I'm glad I rewrote "Charlotte's Web," even though it took me an unconscionable time to do it, as it gained in the process, I think. Whether children will find anything amusing in it, only time will tell. No doubt they would like it better if my barn cellar were loaded into a space ship and exploded in the general direction of Mars. . . .

Yrs,
Andy

To JAMES THURBER

25 West 43 Street
6 April 1952

Dear Jim:

I'm just back from North Brooklin, where I ate a scallop stew and attended a lamb's birth. It was a good stew and an easy birth. Before leaving, I chopped the lamb's tail off with an ax just to show who was boss. You've got to keep these little creatures in their place, even if you are the Dog's Best Friend for 1952. . . .

You should have hung around these shores one more day and taken in our party.[1] A hundred and thirty-one people showed up. Stanley Hyman was the first man through the door, at 9:02. Peter Arno was the last man at the piano, a sweet player. He followed Shawn, who is hot and who performs with the same spirit of dedication as when editing a five-part profile. There was dancing of a sort, and I think the whole affair, with its contrapuntal literary and emotional atmosphere, excited Brendan Gill more than any similar cotillion he had ever attended. He found overtones in every glass. . . . We wrapped the party up at 4:45, but it had a couple of hours of early morning enchantment—the kind of goings on that made you feel that the door would presently open and in would walk Scott and Zelda. Arno, much to my surprise, came early and went the whole route. He drank gin and ginger ale, and did not get drunk. Gluyas Williams came early, took one drink, and all the blood left his head and he had to be helped up to the men's coatroom, and then back to the Harvard Club. My theory about blood leaving a man's head is that it suddenly leaves when he finds himself saying things he only half wants to say, to somebody whose name he has not quite caught, in a room where nobody remembered to open a window. The evening ended for MacKelway with his going to the wrong room for his coat, and finding the cook in bed. MacKelway was enchanted. "Who are you?" he asked. The cook invited him out. "That's all right," said Mac, indulgently, "but I just want to know, *who* are *you*?"

I see I have been misspelling McKelway. I guess this is the time of life where I start misspelling the names of people I have known since the Coolidge administration. Maybe I am misspelling Coolidge—which will be the next phase.

Not much news around here. I finally finished my children's book and turned it in to Harper. Garth Williams is going to illustrate it.

Spring is making little sashays about coming to town, but it has been a fairly unconvincing demonstration so far. It's what Maine people call "crow weather." I still think Maine speech is about the most satis-

1. Given by the Whites to honor William Shawn on his being named editor of *The New Yorker*. There were 140 invited guests.

factory. I asked a guy the other day where he was cutting wood. "I'm cutting on my father-in-law," he replied. (You are the only artist to illustrate that.)

Love to you both,
Andy

To MARION WHITE BRITTINGHAM

25 West 43
[April 1952]
Tuesday

Dear Marion:

Congratulations to you and Arthur on your fiftieth anniversary! I guess I am a little closer to the right date than when I tried to greet you on your birthday a year ago. I seem to remember that I missed that one by about a month.

K and I wired you a pot of tulips last week as a sort of combination Easter and Golden Wedding remembrance, but I see by your letter that you were in Doylestown and I'm afraid the florist shop may have got discouraged. K and I are still recovering from our own Easter—we had all five grandchildren hunting eggs in the living room, and 12 for dinner. Johnny Stableford, age 7, arrived last Friday all alone on the train from Easton,[1] and was our weekend guest, and we were very busy showing him the town.

How does it feel to be a golden bride? I'm not going to be able to make the party at the hotel on Sunday, but I'd like to drive out some day this week, maybe Friday, and pay you a little call in honor of the occasion. I'll call up in advance to make sure you're home.

If you were married in 1902, I must have been almost three years old; and unless I am much mistaken, your wedding is just about my earliest memory. I distinctly recall our parlor being roped off to form an aisle. And you must have been the gal who walked it. How the years do roll, and wouldn't it be nice if we could slow them up a bit!

K joins me in sending love to you both,

Andy

To CAROLINE B. SERGEANT

229 East 48th Street
New York, N.Y.
26 April 1952

Dearest Aunt Crully:

Congratulations on this momentous occasion—your 90th birthday! I wish I could be there to see you and greet you, but that is not to be, and

---

1. Where his father, Louis Stableford, is Professor of Biology at Lafayette College.

the best I can do is to send you my love and a small gift by mail. It is a pink sweater, and I hope it will be useful and give you a bit of pleasure now and then—to keep you safe from those icy Florida breezes. If you would prefer another color, or another material, the sweater can be exchanged I am sure.

If you could hear Katharine speak of you, as I so often do, with such grateful affection, I am sure you would be proud and happy, at 90, to look back on a life so useful and so rich in the unselfish gifts you have made to those around you. My own feeling and admiration is of comparatively recent vintage, but even to me—a rank newcomer in your circle of influence—you have given the kind of sober happiness that comes from knowing and loving a Lady of Quality. And you cannot imagine what fun it has been for me to see how young you are in everything but years. You are my dream girl in that respect. Forgive this praise—it is the penalty, your just penalty, for reaching ninety in top form! I am enclosing a clipping from the *Ellsworth American*, telling of a trio of your contemporaries. If they seem excessively active, it is probably because in so cold a climate they don't dare sit down. . . .

K, you will be glad to know, is in good health save for a minor skin affliction, and looks even more beautiful than usual. We are both busy getting ready to take off for Maine a week from Thursday. Turtle Bay Garden is at its loveliest right now—full of tulips and blossoming shrubs, as well as a small but distinguished company of white-throated sparrows and hermit thrushes—transient visitors whose presence here seems miraculous. I have just finished a book and will send you a copy when it comes out.

I must close this inadequate report. It carries my warmest love and best wishes for the happiest of days on April 30th.

With deep affection, as ever,
Andy

To JANICE WHITE

229 East 48th
27 April 1952

Dear Jan:

Nice to get your letter, and forgive me for not answering sooner. I don't advise you to try to federate this world over the next weekend, because I don't think it would work. Most of the stuff in "The Wild Flag" is all right as far as it goes, but it was written prior to 1945. In 1945 it became apparent, in San Francisco, that the dream of coming out of a world war into a more orderly state of affairs was being knocked into a cocked hat. I was on the premises myself, and saw the show. The notion that the Soviet Union was a pleasant ally, and was looking for the same rainbow that we were, turned out to be just a wistful idea. So we are now in the situation of trying to save something worth federating. You can't federate a tyrannical social order with a popular government type of social order, any more than you can federate oil and water. Since the end of the war, the nationalist spirit has been in the ascendant, largely because the tension in the world failed to relax when it was discovered that the Soviet leaders were engaged in their broadscale scheme to move into other lands, convert everybody to their religion, and, wherever expedient, to snitch the local government and annex a piece of territory. They are so convinced of the rightness of their philosophy that they are able to make a good deal of headway, being not handicapped by the same code of conduct, the same ground rules, that our society imposes. Anyway, the immediate task of people who believe in the free spirit, in the free conscience, and in government by the consent of the governed, is to nourish and sustain these lovely institutions and ideas wherever they are present in large or small degree. I think that the World Federalists (and I am one of them, although not an organization man) are currently stuck with a rather rigid program and a much too cozy blueprint. I think that the problem is not to "sell people" on federation, or "establish world law"—the problem is to hang on grimly through this hurricane that we are now encountering, and gradually to reestablish contact and communication with the vast populations with whom we are out of touch at the moment, thanks to the Iron Curtain. I think that the most precious thing in the world is not the concept of federation but the concept of justice—that is, justice as it has been developed in the western world. The only sort of One-World that I would settle for, is a One-World firmly based on that type of justice.

One of the curious paradoxes of this mirthful and mournful century is that the very process of struggling through the cold war against communist expansion tends to make us lose our grip on our own democratic techniques. We grow tyrannical fighting tyranny. This is bad. I think the most alarming spectacle today is not the spectacle of the atomic bomb in an unfederated world, it is the spectacle of Americans beginning to accept the device of loyalty oaths and witchhunts, beginning to call anybody they don't like a communist. I think the most depressing thing that has happened in my lifetime is that an official blacklist of actors and radio artists, called "Red Channels," has actually become a handbook to which radio and television directors turn, before hiring an actor. This has changed the whole climate of our country. It has introduced a contagion that can sweep into every home and office, changing the world we now know into an entirely different world. I think it is terribly important that we don't permit that change to take place.

The only light I see is that there is now some hope of a relaxation of tension; and I believe that until the present tension *does* relax, very little headway can be made toward the world that federalists dream of. This being a presidential year, there isn't going to be any noticeable diminution of tension till after Election Day, but I'm hoping that there will be a healthier atmosphere then. There is very little question in my mind that eventually—maybe this century, maybe next—the world will become politically unified. There is no other sensible conclusion. It may be the unity of disaster, when we all go up in a jolly burst of fissionable fuss, or, if we can hang tight awhile, it may be a more comfortable unity, when we knock some sense into each other's heads, quit calling each other "foreigners," and get down to business.

I would say, offhand, that the duty of a young federalist in this decade is to quit worrying about federation, and worry about communication. Millions of Slavs, millions of Chinese, millions of Indians are out of touch with us. Their problem is not federation (of which most of them have never heard), their problem is rice and their problem is justice. Our State Department is tackling this business with the so-called Point Four program, but is greatly handicapped by lack of money (among other things), most of the money being diverted to the military defense program.

Anyway, I admonish you to put first things first. You can't sell world law to anybody unless you can get him on the phone, and unless he has experienced the kind of law you mean. The reason the U.N. committee on human rights can't come up with anything in the way of human rights is because they are trying to draft a code of conduct that fits both the communist system and the capitalist system, and it can't be done.

Sorry to interpose a vexatious intermediate step on the road to world order, but I'm afraid it's there, and I don't advise that anyone underestimate it.

Love,
Andy

• *Richard de Rochemont wanted to make a film of* Here Is New York *and had submitted a treatment by Lois Jacoby. White had also outlined a way in which the film might be constructed—his idea was to introduce a character who wasn't real, thus turning the thing into a fantasy. Like many of White's other flirtations with the theatrical world, nothing came of this one. Except for his children's stories, the bulk of White's writing is ill-suited for dramatic adaptation. Nevertheless, he has often been approached by hopeful producers and other dreamers of stage and screen.*

To RICHARD DE ROCHEMONT

[New York]
April 28, 1952

Dear Mr. de Rochemont:

I've read the Lois Jacoby treatment and feel that you and I should get together soon for a talk. I'm leaving for Maine pretty quick and would like to see you one day this week. It might be a good idea if I were to come to your office at a convenient time, instead of our slugging this out at the luncheon table.

I am worried about the Jacoby treatment and feel that no good can come of it. It seems to me the city gets sunk without a trace and that whatever of merit there was in my book gets pretty well lost in the attempt to build a story on the old trite triangle theme. I think the proposed movie must be, essentially, a photographic tour de force, in which the city is the central thing—not love, love, love. (I'm not against love, but it wasn't what my book was about.)

Having no experience at all with the movies, except as a spectator, I feel shaky and ineffectual in this dilemma. I think the weakness of Miss Jacoby's script is that she started to build a story but kept pulling back in favor of "Here Is New York," so she wound up with neither fish nor fowl. I think the same weakness is inherent in my own brief outline of a treatment. At any rate I have tried, in my mind, to develop my outline, and I don't see it clearly at all—don't know whether it's a sound idea to have the words of the book uttered by a character in the film.

I've re-read my book in line of duty and the only virtue it has, that I can see, is that it tries to give the city an extra dimension. The problem is how to catch that on the screen—how to do for Manhattan what Flaherty did for Aran Island. I don't think this can be done by having a guy involved with a hard-boiled actress and another girl, and I also think that Miss Jacoby's thesis that a person to survive in New York must be tough in the right way is much too pat and is just as true of Chillicothe as of New York.

Anyway, let's get together. If we could get started in the right direction, I think I could be of considerable help as a writer. At this point, I realize I am practically no help at all.

Sincerely,
E. B. White

To KATHERINE B. FAULKNER

[New York]
May 6, 1952

Dear Miss Faulkner:

I don't want to lend my name to sponsor a political candidate because I occasionally contribute editorials to *The New Yorker*. The only
sensible way for an editorial writer to live is to limit his political activities to the interior of the voting booth—that wonderful, wonderful place.

Sincerely,
E. B. White

To CASS CANFIELD

[North Brooklin, Me.]
20 May 1952

Dear Cass:

Thanks for the encouraging letter. I'm awfully glad that my spider
has been well received locally—or shall I say internally? Am worried,
though, at not having seen the Garth Williams picture that Ursula said
was being put in the works for use in the catalogue. I would like to see
the picture, because I feel that the book must at all odds have a beguiling Charlotte. The solution, I am quite sure, is for the artist to depict
attitudes and postures, rather than facial expression. Spiders don't have
much of any face—in fact they hardly have any head, or at least the
head is relatively inconspicuous. But they have eight wonderfully articu-
lated legs (arms), which offer a great chance for ballet treatment. Garth
is such a wonderful artist that I am sure he will succeed; but for a while
there he was bogged down in an attempt to produce a face.

As for my collecting some poems, or some prose, or both—I have
it in mind and hope to get at it soon. Will be in New York for about
a week in June—10th to 16th. Hope to see you.

Best regards,
Andy

To URSULA NORDSTROM

North Brooklin, Maine
24 May 1952

Dear Ursula:

Thanks for the dummy cuts and the jacket design. I like everything.
The group on the jacket is charming. My only complaint is that the
goose looks, for some reason, a bit snakelike. Perhaps this is because its
beak is open, or perhaps because the eye is round like a snake's. You
sound so rushed that I presume you don't want to make any revisions,

and I would be satisfied to have the jacket go as is, if it seems right to you. But no goose-lover in this house is satisfied.

The web effect is OK for the purposes of jacket design, but that type of rather mussy Charles Addams attic web is not right for the illustrations. I'm sure that Garth realizes that. Charlotte weaves quite an orderly, symmetrical web, and Garth has it right in the picture of Charlotte thinking—which, incidentally, I like. Smooth legs and smooth abdomen are correct. (Actually, Charlotte's legs are equipped with fine hairs, and these are mentioned in the book, but the overall effect is of smooth, silk-stocking legs.)

I think Fern is delightful in both pictures, and I couldn't be happier about her. Wilbur, also, is perfect on the jacket—very beguiling. In the dummy picture, where he is lying flat, weeping, I got a momentary shock because when I first glanced at the picture, it looked as though his right front foot were his snout. If there is time, I think it would be helpful simply to remove that foot entirely, leaving his snout nicely outlined against the straw. (I've tried this, by blocking it out with my fingernail, and it looks fine with just one front leg showing.) And by the way, I think Harper & Brothers should take Charlotte's advice: Never hurry and never worry. What's all this rosh, rosh, rosh?

On the whole I am very pleased with developments, and have complete confidence that Garth will handle everything beautifully. If this letter isn't helpful or doesn't answer what is necessary to know, call me up. Our number here is Sedgwick (Me.) 106.

Sincerely,
Andy

To URSULA NORDSTROM

North Brooklin, Maine
23 July 1952

Dear Ursula:

The corrected drawings are fine and I am very grateful to Garth for his trouble. I don't think it is necessary to do anything about Mrs. Arable in #3. She looks all right.

Thanks for the tall tales of Robert the Bruce.[1] Spiders expect to have their webs busted, and they take it in their stride. One of Charlotte's daughters placed her web in the tie-ups, right behind my bull calf,

---

1. Worried that his spider story might resemble other spiders in literature or in life, White had questioned Miss Nordstrom about it, and she had come up with the story about the Scottish king Robert the Bruce. Robert, while in prison, watched a spider make several attempts to spin a web. The persistence of the spider inspired him to break jail and return to the wars.

and I kept forgetting about it and would bust one of her foundation lines on my trips to and from the trapdoor where I push the manure into the cellar. After several days of this, during which she had to rebuild the entire web each evening, she solved the matter neatly by changing the angle of the web so that the foundation line no longer crossed my path. Her ingenuity has impressed me, and I am now teaching her to write SOME BOOK, and will let Brentano have her for their window.

My wife has a virus infection of the liver, called hepatitus—probably spelled wrong but certainly no fun any way you spell it. She is yellow all over and can't eat, and is supposed to be enjoying her vacation of three weeks from the *New Yorker* editing job.

Sincerely,
Andy

To GUSTAVE S. LOBRANO

North Brooklin, Maine
29 July 1952

Dear Gus:

I've been slack about writing you about my hepatitis victim, but have been largely engaged motoring betwixt here and Bangor to view the patient. I tried to phone you last week and just missed you at the lunch hour. K is considerably more cheerful, and more comfortable, than she was on Thursday morning last, when I converted my DeSoto Non-Firedome Eight into an ambulance and rolled north up the mighty Penobscot, to Ward S. I have no doubt that you have already heard directly from the Ward, for she keeps needling me for letter paper and stamps. She is a beautiful shade of yellow, with blue polka dot design— where the student nurses try their skill at hypodermics. They are robust, carefree girls, wildly aiming. My talks with the doctor lead me to believe that hepatitis is a virus infection of the liver, that it can be caused by a fly bite or by eating a small snack of contaminated food at a modern sanitary air-conditioned drugstore counter, or even in the home. Jaundice (or what hereabouts is called the janders) is an associated phenomenon. A funny coincidence in this case is that K's doctor is himself recently recovered from hepatitis; and there is a strong local suspicion that she contracted the disease from him—a just punishment for the crime of consorting with an Ellsworth medico instead of a Blue Hill man. I have within the last two days greatly complicated the already confused business by coming down with a rotten cold—which leaves K thoroughly stranded. I can't even phone her, as the telephone hasn't struck Bangor yet.

Both of the doctors in this case have tipped me off to one thing, namely that the convalescence is apt to be a long drawn out affair, and that rest and relaxation are the only cure. I pass along this tip, so that you can bear it in mind in planning ahead for fiction department operation. My prediction is that she will soon be calling for work; and my advice is to accede to her demands rather reluctantly, in the Stevenson manner. It will, I think, pay to short-change her for a while.

Our summer, as you can imagine, has been a rather sick thing—an afternoon snooze from which one wakes feeling depressed and queasy. The heat and the drought persist; fields and lawns are like badly laid cement floors; crops languish. All during June and early July I was seized with the worst hay fever in years. K started to get vague pains about July 4, and I think carried the disease around with her for quite a spell before it leapt at her throat, and at her liver. I slept through most of the political conventions, but had a wonderful stroke of luck at the end. I was awakened at about 2 one morning, because I had inadvertently left the sprinkler running, had pumped (by so doing) my spring dry, and had filled the water pipes, toilets, heaters, etc. with noisy air. I merely turned all valves and master switches and was about to fall back into bed when Joe informed me that the balloting was over and that Stevenson would be on in a minute. So I sat down at the radio and heard the acceptance speech. It seemed a wonderfully healing sound after the razzle dazzle.

Hope you are well, strong, happy, fit, and convinced that all is for the best. Well, almost all.

Love,
Andy

To URSULA NORDSTROM

North Brooklin, Maine
29 Sept [1952]

Dear Ursula:

Thanks for your dandy letter and for the book. If I ever get time I'm going to read the book. I think it looks very nice and I agree with you that the endpaper is too bright. But on the other hand, I'm not sure that anybody thinks about endpaper except publishers, and probably not more than 1800 people in the United States have ever heard the word "endpaper," and they are all Stevenson people.

Enclosed are some remarks that I hope will satisfy your Publicity Department.

Sorry to learn that Dr. [Henry] Canby is revolted by spiders. Probably he doesn't meet the right spiders. . . .

Yrs,
Andy

To URSULA NORDSTROM

25 West 43rd Street
22 October 1952

Dear Ursula:

Thank you for your letters of the 14th, 15th, 16th, and 21st, with their newsy enclosures. I have been meaning to call you up, and in fact did call you up, but your operator said you were talking and I am not a man to interrupt a lady when she is talking.

So far, "Charlotte's Web" seems to have been read largely by adults with a literary turn of mind. I have had only a sprinkling of childhood reaction to the book—those vital and difficult precincts—and will not know for a little while how it sits with the young. I have a step grand-child named Caroline Angell who is a quiet little girl of about five. She listened attentively to the reading of the book by her father, and said: "I think there was an easier way to save Wilbur, without all that trouble. Charlotte should have told him not to eat, then he wouldn't have been killed because he would have been too thin."

Trust an author to go to a lot of unnecessary trouble.

Yrs,
Andy

To URSULA NORDSTROM

25 West 43rd Street
October 28, 1952

Dear Ursula:

Don't stop writing me so many letters.

Have been out of town buying sheep. Was gone three days, and bought four sheep, which is better than a sheep a day. Covered five states and saw Adlai Stevenson in the flesh. He is not as pretty as one of the sheep, but he seemed in good order.

Yours,
Andy

P.S. My first fan mail on Charlotte was a long letter from a California vegetarian, who feels that my book shows that I am ripe to take the veil and live on grain, fruit, and nuts. I guess I'll never lack for nuts, anyway.

To PHILIP M. JOHNSON, M.D.

[New York]
November 14, 1952

Dear Dr. Johnson:

The New Yorker has never argued that there are any areas of government that are sacrosanct and beyond criticism. And after the last four months I don't think you need worry about whether the minority can take a swing at the party in power. Our complaint was that the Republicans, when they were on the subject of Korea, seldom let a chance go by to play on the strings of parenthood—the tears of mothers, the anxieties of fathers—and whenever this happened we called it a low punch. As a person, I am as jumpy about Korea as the next man, as I have a son who is about to go into the service, but I try not to let my jumpiness get in the way of my judgment about what is happening there and why. Korea is, I believe, the first example of military action undertaken on the basis of a charter agreement among member states of a world organization. Nobody knows whether it will prove out, and I'm not optimistic about the efficacy of "collective security" as a device; but I certainly think it is unique and different. The term "police action" carries with it no implication that it is less bloody than it is, and I don't think the Administration has ever so implied. Certainly *The New Yorker* didn't in its comment.

Sincerely,
E. B. White

To MRS. DAMON BOYNTON

[New York]
November 20, 1952

Dear Mrs. Boynton:

I didn't know there was a Democrat in Trumansburg [New York] but it's nice to hear from one. And when I recall that I once walked two-thirds of the way across the Fall Creek bridge on the handrail, and that you might have been playing down below, it terrifies me.[1]

Many thanks for writing.

Sincerely,
E. B. White

To URSULA NORDSTROM

25 West 43rd Street
December 5, 1952

Dear Ursula:

I am relieved to learn that the first printing [50,000 copies] wasn't too ambitious and that there will be a second. My wife is buying a great many copies and has, I believe, managed to exhaust the first printing

---

1. When he was a student at Cornell, White once attempted to cross Fall Creek gorge by walking the handrail of the Stewart Avenue bridge—an aerial challenge that would have been perfect for the Wallendas.

almost singlehanded. I'm not sure there is any profit for the author in this sort of arrangement, but I shall not attempt to work it out on paper.

Would it be all right if I sent the librarians some candles for Christmas, for use in their candlelight meeting? I mean the kind that explode.[1]

Sincerely,
Andy

To GRADE 5-B, LARCHMONT, NEW YORK

25 W. 43
New York, N.Y.
26 December 1952

Dear Pupils of 5-B:

I was delighted to get your letters telling me what you thought about "Charlotte's Web." It must be fine to have a teacher who is a bookworm like Mrs. Bard.

It is true that I have a farm. It is on the sea. My barn is big and old, and I have ten sheep, eighteen hens, a goose, a gander, a bull calf, a rat, a chipmunk, and many spiders. In the woods near the barn are red squirrels, crows, thrushes, owls, porcupines, woodchucks, foxes, rabbits, and deer. In the pasture pond are frogs, polliwogs, and salamanders. Sometimes a Great Blue Heron comes to the pond and catches frogs. At the shore of the sea are sandpipers, gulls, plovers, and kingfishers. In the mud at low tide are clams. Seven seals live on nearby rocks and in the sea, and they swim close to my boat when I row. Barn swallows nest in the barn, and I have a skunk that lives under the garage.

I didn't like spiders at first, but then I began watching one of them, and soon saw what a wonderful creature she was and what a skillful weaver. I named her Charlotte, and now I like spiders along with everything else in nature.

I'm glad you enjoyed the book, and I thank you for the interesting letters.

Sincerely,
E. B. White

• *In its Christmas roundup of books, December 15, 1952, Newsweek gave* Charlotte's Web *a blurb that read: "Charmingly sentimental tale*

---

1. After the cool reception the New York Public Library had given *Stuart Little,* White was not above taking a poke at librarians. His wife had regaled him with tales of the candlelight meetings she had attended at the Library when she was reviewing books for *The New Yorker.*

for children and adults about a spider and a pig, written with many a fearful glance backward for fear of horse laughs from the left." White found this blurb cryptic and dashed off a letter to Robert Cantwell, book editor for Newsweek, *but never sent it. Instead, he mailed the letter to Cass Canfield, who fired a blast at* Newsweek *and received an "explanation" from Cantwell—which he showed White.*

To CASS CANFIELD

25 West 43rd Street
December 29, 1952

Dear Cass:

The Cantwell letter is certainly a masterpiece of Fuller Explanation, and I'm glad to have the offending clause dissected so painstakingly. I didn't know that while writing "Charlotte's Web" I was sitting behind a psychological barrier created by child psychologists, but one lives and learns.

The only unfavorable criticism I've had, of my children's books, has been from a couple of librarians, notably Anne Carroll Moore, who read "Stuart" in galleys and wrote me a long letter against it and who doesn't like "Charlotte" either.[1] I suppose librarians regard themselves as child psychologists, and I'm sure they'll be surprised to learn that this places them squarely on the left. And so it goes.

Pamela Travers[2] said, in a review in an English paper, that anyone who writes for children successfully is probably writing for one child—namely, the child that is himself. I think this comes close to the truth, and if any "barrier" operates it is the internal barrier that separates the child from the man.

It's impossible to know, of course, whether Cantwell, in that queer blurb, was trying to dunk a liberal-democrat in the red pot, or whether he was trying—as his letter suggests—to express a complicated piece of critical analysis in half a dozen words. I thought the funniest sentence in his letter was the one denying you the *right* to state that his review lacked clarity. I hereby give you back that right on a platter.

Yours,
Andy

---

1. Miss Moore, writing in the *Horn Book* for December 1952, said: "Fern, the real center of the book, is never developed. The animals never talk. They speculate. As to Charlotte, her magic and mystery require a different technique to create that lasting interest in spiders which controls the childish impulse to do away with them." (The letter Miss Moore wrote about *Stuart Little* was not addressed to White but to his wife.)

2. British poet and the author of *Mary Poppins* and its sequels.

Joel White in Washington Mews, when the Whites were living at 16 East 8th Street.

Joel White at the shore in Maine, about 1939. The small building in the background is where White works. From it have come *Charlotte's Web, The Trumpet of the Swan*, dozens of essays, hundreds of Comment paragraphs, and thousands of Newsbreaks. It now boasts a chimney and a schoolhouse stove.

Katharine White and her three children, Joel White and Nancy
and Roger Angell.

The Whites' farm.

The cutter *Astrid* in Tenant's Harbor, Maine.

Joel White, about 1940.

Fred, in his prime.

White and Katharine at work on *A Subtreasury of American Humor*.

White in his *New Yorker* office. The dog is Minnie.

Katharine White, Wilbur, and friends.

Joel and Allene White shortly after their marriage in 1953.

William Strunk, Jr., author of *The Elements of Style*.

White defending the plate with his granddaughter, Martha.

Joel White, about 1970

White with his
youngest grandson,
John Henry Angell.

Photograph © 1976 Jill Krementz

Katharine and E. B. White with Susy.

• *The managing editor of the* Ford Times *had asked White for a piece on the Model T and the early days of motoring. "From Sea to Shining Sea" ran in the July 1953 issue.*

To EDMUND WARE SMITH

[New York]
December 29, 1952

Dear Mr. Smith:

Thanks for the prompt check and the friendly greetings. I'm very glad you are satisfied with the piece.

I'm returning the original and the copy, with a pencilled addition in the copy—to explain the dictionary. It's O.K. with me to delete the word "Ford" twice on Page One if you can't stand four-letter words, but to my ear the first sentence reads better if the word "Ford" stays in. However, suit yourself—I realize you have a special problem.

For a title I suggest: "From Sea to Shining Sea," with (if you use subtitles) a subtitle such as "A memoir of Model T and the days of Blue Book touring." I don't like "Hail, My Lovely!" because it evokes my earlier piece, which strikes me as a dubious procedure. Of the other listed titles, my preference would be for Number 5, but I think "From Sea to Shining Sea" is better.

Best wishes for 1953.

Sincerely,
E. B. White

To KATHARINE S. WHITE

[1952?]
[Interoffice memo]

Mrs. White:

The effect of drugs on people is entirely "mental"—just their imaginations at work. Got this from D. Terry, at lunch. Alan Dunn and Mary Petty lie on their beds and hang their hands overboard to relax them and this cures everything. Dunn has never done such good work as since he has hung his hands overboard.

EBW

To STANLEY HART WHITE

229 East 48
11 January 1953

Dear Bun:

Our thanks to you and Blanche for the circular candy arrangement. It exactly suited our requirements, as we now have roving bands of small children passing through the apartment, some of them lineal descendants, some of them scouts from neighboring backyards who have discovered how to get into this building and which floor to come to. The candy was much admired and quickly dispatched, and I even managed to pinch a limedrop for myself, by quick footwork. . . .

Louis de Rochemont wants to buy the motion picture rights of "Charlotte's Web" offen me for a full-length animated film, but I am being coy about it, so far.[1] In an attempt to soften me up, he threw a small, heavily-loaded luncheon party for me the other day in the Cloud Club, which is at the top of the Chrysler Building just beneath the needle, and when I arrived there it looked faintly familiar, and I remembered that I had reached that floor twenty-three years ago by climbing the wooden ladder of a 2-inch pipe scaffolding. "Jesus," I thought to myself, "I'm getting ahead." The earlier visit was on the whole more fun, and more windswept.[2]

That girl I used to skate with was Mildred Hesse, and she turned up, in a completely unrecognizable form, at Noel Illian's wedding last June which I attended. She had been briefed about my presence, but I hadn't been briefed about hers, and I had a 5-minute conversation with her in which she knew who I was and I didn't know who she was except that she was a Mrs. Smith. It was a hot afternoon, no ice on the pond. . . .

En

To ALEXANDER L. CROSBY

[New York]
January 22, 1953

Dear Mr. Crosby:

The paragraph [in Comment] that bothered you was not meant to be either blustery or threatening. What we were trying to say is rather hopeful—that the consequences of using modern weapons are so grave as to be a real deterrent to anyone's starting a war—on either side.

As far as the cockroach is concerned, he is definitely a contender and will bear watching. It is an odd thing about humans that they as-

---

1. Louis de Rochemont is Richard de Rochemont's brother. While Richard continued his efforts to make a movie out of *Here Is New York*, Louis was after *Charlotte*. Nothing came of either pursuit.

2. In the early days at *The New Yorker*, when White was a reporter for The Talk of the Town, Managing Editor Ralph Ingersoll discovered that White didn't mind heights and sent him aloft at every opportunity. On the occasion referred to here, White had discovered, after making the ascent by elevator and ladder to the top of the unfinished Chrysler Building, that the base of the needle, where he was standing, was only about eight feet square.

sume a sort of natural dominance, or ascendancy. Yet they are new-comers, relatively speaking, and are not as well adjusted to their environment (from present indications) as many older forms. I think it's quite all right to point out, once in a while, that man's ingenuity may be his worst enemy. And I certainly agree with you that we've got to live in peace if we're going to live at all.

Sincerely yours,
E. B. White

• *Colson Henry Allen, a Brooklin neighbor and a man of many talents, came to work for the Whites as caretaker in August 1952. He had applied for the job some years earlier and been turned down—a decision White now regards as the craziest mistake he ever made in his life. Allen is still with the Whites—a long and happy association.*

To HENRY ALLEN

[New York]
[February 1953]
Monday

Dear Henry:

I don't know yet whether I'm coming. . . . In case I don't get there, here are some suggestions that may help you in setting up the brooder pen for the chicks. The shipping date is March 1—which probably means that they will land in Ellsworth at the express office on Monday or Tuesday. At any rate, you'd better have your brooder pen ready by Saturday afternoon.

Sweep out the room, install the roosts (if they are not already there) and hook the roosting frame up against the east wall, where it's out of the way. The parts to the brooder stove are in a carton in the attic of the house, I am pretty sure. The carton contains the motor, the red cap to the motor, the thermometer, the wafer for the thermostat, the curtains, the legs, and a couple of bulbs. Install the legs and curtains first. You can do this best with the stove suspended in air. The legs want to be in the first position, so the curtain will just about touch the floor when the stove is lowered. Don't ever lower the stove *without* its legs, or you'll bust the little switch underneath.

Bolt the thermometer to its bracket. Screw the wafer onto the spindle. Put a white bulb in the socket in the top of the stove, and a red bulb in the socket underneath—for an attraction light. (I'm not sure there is a red bulb that works, but if there isn't, it doesn't make much difference—you don't have to have an attraction light.) To install the motor, lower the stove to the floor, remove the metal strap that covers the motor hole, set the motor in place, and bolt the strap on again. Test the motor and give it a couple drops of thin oil in two places. The stove can now be hoisted out of the way.

Spread litter, preferably Servall. I would make the litter fairly deep. Get all the lumps out of the litter and rake it till it is smooth and level. Then spread a lot of newspapers underneath where the stove will be, covering all the area shown by the ring on my sketch. In the attic of the garage I think you will find a roll of hardware cloth about 18 inches wide, tied with a string. This is the guard wire, to be put around the stove to control the chicks for the first few days. I staple this wire to the north wall as shown, and let it come around the stove so there is just enough room for you to get by on the south side, where you can look into the peek-hole in the stove and read the thermometer. The thermometer wants to be adjusted so it is about an inch from the floor and so you can see it by looking through the hole. I always keep a flashlight on the window-sill to enable me to read the temperature of the stove.

The motor is simply a blower, to carry air downward into the stove. It can be left plugged in for the entire period of brooding. Once a week give it a shot of thin oil.

To adjust the temperature of the stove, simply back the spindle off so that the wafer doesn't touch the switch, and let the stove heat up. Keep watch of it, and when it reaches 95°, set the spindle up till it touches the switch-point and breaks the contact. You can tell when this has happened because the white light will go off. In very cold weather, it may take quite a while before you can get your stove up to 95°. In case of extreme weather—below zero—you may even have to light a fire in the drum stove to warm the building up. The only real trouble with an electric brooder stove is that it doesn't have what it takes in extreme weather—but it is wonderful in normal weather. Usually, I have not ordered my chicks till April 1, and the stove has done the business all right. I hope it will be all right in March weather, too, but you'll have to watch it for a few days, and give it a lift with the drum stove if necessary.

The thermometer has marks on it, showing proper temperatures for first week, second week, third week, etc. Follow the markings and you'll be all right. I think a drop of about five degrees per week during the brooding period is O.K. The way to cool off the stove is to set up on the spindle.

I put four little wooden half-inch blocks in the litter for the four legs of the stove to rest on, but you can suit yourself. Anyway, the curtain wants to almost touch the litter during the first few days. Then, as the chicks grow, you raise the legs.

I guess you are sick of this letter by this time, so I won't make it much longer. I know that you know how to brood chicks as well or better than I do, and I have only written this because I thought, with a new stove and all, it might be a help. You will find chick waterers in the garage, up overhead. Also, I think you will find cardboard feeders either in the garage or in the house attic, that are useful for the first few days. I feed chick feed (fine grain) for the first couple of days, to prevent their pasting up; and then go right onto starter mash. My experience with chicks is that if you have everything fixed up pretty good to begin with, they take hardly any effort and you have good luck. And if you *don't* have things fixed good, they cause plenty of trouble.

Newspapers are useful only for the first two or three days. The guard wire can be eliminated as soon as the chicks know their way to the stove.

EBW

To JOHN DETMOLD

25 West 43rd Street
February 10, 1953

Dear John:

I shall of course sign the book for your mother, and will deliver it to Peter for presentation on February 20.[1]

As to your notion of an allegory, there is none. "Charlotte's Web" is a tale of the animals in my barn, not of the people in my life. When you read it, just relax. Any attempt to find allegorical meanings is bound to end disastrously, for no meanings are in there. I ought to know.

Sincerely,
Andy White

To RICHARD DE ROCHEMONT

[New York]
March 19, 1953

Dear Mr. de Rochemont:

I was glad to get your letter and learn that you're still thinking about the picture. I don't know Zeckendorf,[1] but know enough about his energy and his dreams to be worried. I think that if he should

---

1. John Detmold's mother managed the houses on Turtle Bay Garden. Peter was John's younger brother.

---

1. De Rochemont's efforts to make a movie of *Here Is New York* had led him to William Zeckendorf, the real estate developer.

seem inclined to put up the money, we'd have to find out how much he would insist on throwing his weight around. He weighs 250, and I'm only 140 with my adjectives on.

Money is money, and it is what we need to make a picture. But I naturally don't want to get involved (and I don't believe you do either) with a situation that would turn the springtime of 1953 into a carnival of real estate values. I think that to make the New York piece into a decent, and even a profitable movie, we would have to stick to the literary and pictorial values inherent in it, if any, and not get ourselves in telephone connection with Bill Zeckendorf's publicity department, alert though it may be to the vision of the future metropolis.

I'm willing to try writing the script, although I'm scared of it, simply because I've never attempted scene-writing and am likely to prove a washout. I think I can handle the dialogue all right, but will need a certain amount of help from you or from somebody in the business of devising the sequence of events and the events themselves. I think basically the treatment I submitted is a sound setup for the New York piece, but I'm very sure that it will not be an easy thing to get on celluloid. In a way it offers the sort of challenge that Mr. Zeckendorf is said to relish, and maybe he's just our man. Whatever he is, he's the author of one of my favorite remarks: he said that every business man can add two and two and get four, but damned few of them can add two million and two million and get four million, because they get scared. That is a profound observation and shows intellect of high order.

Sincerely,
E. B. White

• *White had been a patient of Dr. Carl Binger, a psychiatrist, for a brief period. It was following one of his visits to Binger that White wrote his short story "The Second Tree From the Corner."*

To CARL BINGER

[New York]
March 25, 1953

Dear Carl:

I sound about as good in German as I feel in English. But there isn't anything the matter with me that a guillotine couldn't cure. My only trouble is in my head, and even that is improving. By the time I'm 90 I'll be as sound as a dollar, and the dollar will be completely gone to pieces.

Sincerely,
Andy

• *When White went to Alaska in 1923 as a member of the crew of the S. S. Buford, his bunkmate was a saloonsman named J. Wilbur Wolf. Wolf, like White, was a college graduate knocking about the world. He appears, seasick, in White's essay "The Years of Wonder," being tended by White in their quarters in the ship's brig.*

To J. WILBUR WOLF

[New York]
March 25, 1953

Dear Wilbur:

Your description of Valentine's Day in Nebraska, with your receiving a book from a retired professional librarian, is wonderful. And of course I'd be delighted to sign the book.

The Wilbur of the book was named not after you but after a pig I used to have named Wilbur. It's that simple. So help me, I used to have a pig named Wilbur, and he was a fine pig, too. I can't say whether the name is beautiful or not, but I'm sure Fern thought so, and that is all that matters.

As for your having the keys to the pantry in the Buford, the plain fact is that it was I who had the virility and the stamina to *reach* the pantry during the storm, and thus save lives. You were so flat you couldn't have reached the door of the brig. Worst pukin' spell I ever saw. But I had one almost as bad myself this winter, earlier, in Maine, when I got the flu and had to be revived with an infusion. I thought of you.

Sincerely,
Andy

To MRS. B. J. KASTON

[New York]
April 10, 1953

Dear Mrs. Kaston:

Thanks for the letter and the picture of Charlotte's cousin, which is very pretty.

The idea of the writing in Charlotte's Web came to me one day when I was on my way down through the orchard carrying a pail of slops to my pig. I had made up my mind to write a children's book about animals, and I needed a way to save a pig's life, and I had been watching a large spider in the backhouse, and what with one thing and another, the idea came to me.

Sincerely,
E. B. White

To JAMES THURBER

[New York]
19 April 1953

Dear Jim:

This is the latest vista opening up for "Is Sex Necessary?" but I'm beginning to get suspicious that these vistas are just peepholes and that the book is being peddled in foreign countries as spicy reading. I think that if this is the case, it can eventually hurt our other books. Maybe I underestimate the capacity of Argentinians and Japanese to appreciate American satire of the 1920's, and I certainly have nothing tangible to base my feeling on. It's just a hunch. At any rate, I've talked it over with Milton Greenstein and with Katharine, and they are inclined to agree that the old sex book, in translation, is beginning to look sour.

Then Mr. Smith who signs this letter says he is in touch with "a good Argentine publisher." I don't know just what that means, either. I suppose a "good" publisher is one who doesn't talk back to Mr. Peron. And the letter ends: "Considering the importance of this subject to Latin Americans I am sure you will be eager to bring them the benefits of your research." This sounds either awfully cute or awfully naïve, and I tend to think it is cute. Anyway, it doesn't fill me with a desire to cooperate. If we decline this invitation, we each stand to lose about seventy-five bucks, but I have an idea it is money well lost. I just don't want you and me to be introduced to the Patagonians as the Chick Sales of the pampas, and I don't trust publishers out of my sight. It is hard enough to trust them when they are plainly visible. Let me know.

Andy

To MARGARET HALSEY

[New York]
23 April [1953]

Dear Miss Halsey:

I had just read your piece in the ALA Bulletin about taking your daughter to the public library, where she liked "the little chairs and the books about fierce things," when your letter arrived protesting the editorial in the April 18th issue about human rights. Since I am the author of the offending remarks, it is up to me to answer your complaints.

The New Yorker isn't against freedom from want and didn't attack it or minimize it as a goal. But we're against associating freedom from want (which is an economic goal) with freedom of speech (which is an exact political principle). There is, I believe, a very real and discernible danger, to a country like ours, in an international covenant that equates human rights with human desires, and that attempts to satisfy, in a single document, governments and philosophies that are essentially irreconcilable. I do not think it safe or wise to confuse, or combine, the principle of freedom of religion or the principle of freedom of the press with any economic goal whatsoever, because of the likelihood that in guaranteeing the goal, you abandon the principle. This has happened over and over again. Eva Peron was a great freedom-from-want girl (specially at Christmas time), but it also happened that *La Prensa* died and the Argentinians were left with nothing to read but government handouts.

If you were to pack croquet balls and eggs in a single container, and take them travelling, you would probably end your journey with some broken eggs. I believe that if you put a free press into the same bill with a full belly, you will likely end the journey with a controlled press.

In your letter you doubt whether the man who wrote the editorial had given much thought to the matter. Well, I've been thinking about human rights for about twenty years, and I was even asked, one time during the war, to rewrite the government pamphlet on the Four Freedoms—which is when I began to realize what strange bedfellows they were. A right is a responsibility in reverse; therefore, a constitutional government of free people should not award any "rights" that it is not in a position to accept full responsibility for. The social conscience and the economic technique of the United States are gaining strength, and each year sees us getting closer to freedom from want. But I'm awfully glad that the "right to work"[1] is not stated in our bill of rights, and I hope the government never signs a covenant in which it appears.

My regards to your daughter, who (human rights or no human rights) is my favorite commentator on the subject of public libraries.

Sincerely,

E. B. White

To **DOROTHY LOBRANO**

229 East 48
16 May [1953]

Dear Dottie:

I've just finished "A Fair Wind Home" and it gave me a fine time. Thanks for sending it and for the other Ruth Moore book. She is certainly a natural story teller and when she gets her hooks in you, there is no escape. I think one reason she's so good is that she has such affection for the people she's writing about: there is just no substitute for that kind of emotion. Of course, like all historical novelists, she occasionally gives my credulity an awful shaking up. When Frank Carnavon throws Lizabeth into the sea from the deck of the *Turkey Feather*, climbs down a rope ladder, cuts the skiff free, and then finds Lizabeth

---

1. Right of everyone to a job.

dog-paddling her way to the boat, I began to tremble with the violent intensity of disbelief. I even started to do a little quiet arithmetic on the side. The *Turkey Feather* was running before a gale, which means that she was probably doing about nine knots—but we will call it eight to be conservative. Eight knots is roughly 48,000 feet per hour, or 800 feet per minute. I figure that Frank Carnavon, a heavy man, must have taken at least a minute to scramble down the ladder and cut himself adrift, but we will give Miss Moore the benefit of the doubt and say that he was able to manage it in 45 seconds—a very credible performance in a gale. That means that when the skiff dropped free of the ship, Lizabeth was left approximately 600 feet behind, or more than six times the distance between third base and home. "God help all," thought Carnavon, and I echoed his thought. The woman had all her clothes on, presumably didn't know much about swimming, and was surrounded by cresting waves. Carnavon describes her as "a good, sweet woman, honest as the day," but I think she was far more than that, if she made it to the skiff. She was practically Esther Williams.

K and I had a flashy trip to Maine last week, carrying a dachshund puppy in a rented car. Now we are chewing our fingernails waiting to get back on June 1.

Lots of love,
Andy

To JOHN R. FLEMING

North Brooklin, Maine
23 May 1953

Dear Jack:

Thanks for the good word. I'm afraid my poem[1] isn't as nicely written as "Paradise Lost," but anyway, it's shorter. I'm appalled at the goings on in my country, and surprised, too, as I thought that the election of Eisenhower would suffuse the populace with confidence and dispel the vapors, but it seems to have worked just the other way. In the same mail with your letter came one from a lady in San Antonio, saying that the city manager is proposing that all communistic books be taken from the public library and burned. The Library Board protested, and the manager has promised to fire the protestants.

Stiff upper lip, Mr. Fleming. Hot afternoons have been in Montana, and we've ridden them out before. I'll turn your John Hersey suggestion over to my boss. Many thanks, and I hope we meet sometime soon—these intervals are getting perilously long.

Yrs,
Andy

---

1. "The ABC of Security," published in *The New Yorker*, May 9, 1953.

To CASS CANFIELD

North Brooklin, Maine
28 May 1953

Dear Cass:

I've made no progress at all on the proposed collection, but Katharine and I are coming to New York to spend the month of July in the delicious quietude of our 48th Street apartment, far from pollen and grandchildren and unresolved problems in agronomy; and whilst in these happy surroundings, we shall devote ourselves almost exclusively to putting together a book (with an occasional afternoon off to support the Giants), and I am hoping that by August 1, or shall we be liberal and say August 15, I will have a manuscript for your consideration. If this scheme should pan out, would I be in time for spring publication, 1954?

Yrs,
Andy

To ROBERT W. WHITE

June 11, 1953

Dear Mr. White:

Thanks for the letter about my visit to the pond.[1] I *thought* I recognized you on the station platform. Thanks, too, for the clipping about Thoreau Heights, or depths. I read through it with snakelike abandon and enjoyed it. I doubt, however, that the development will be cleared by the Loyalty Review Board; after all, Thoreau was a fairly irregular fellow and did a great deal of trespassing on other people's property, which is un-American.

Sincerely,
E. B. White

• *Brooks Beck and his wife Wendy had lived for a while in an apartment above the Whites at 229 East 48th Street.*

To BROOKS BECK

[New York]
June 12, 1953

Dear Brooks:

Many thanks for the kind words. You ask what is a Republican to do. The answer is, of course, simple—vote democratic.

---

1. "Visitors to the Pond" (*The New Yorker*, May 23, 1953) was an imaginary visit to Concord and Walden, poking Senator McCarthy in the ribs.

Your revelations about the works of Marx being in the Adams House and the Longfellow House touch me closely. Years ago, a friend of mine named John Mosher, who was a cutup, presented all his friends at Christmas with a copy of *Das Kapital*, because (he said) the red jacket was so Christmassy. I still have it on my shelf in Maine, and I suppose it has been dusted time and time again by our housekeeper. I'm beginning to get uneasy about it. The only reason I don't take it out and burn it is because I haven't yet got around to reading it, and I hate to burn anything I haven't at least skimmed through. Also, it reminds me of Mosher.

My best to Wendy.

Sincerely,
Andy

To JAMES THURBER

[New York]
[July 6, 1953]
Monday

Dear Jim:

Do you like the title: "The E. B. White Papers"? Would appreciate your opinion. It occurs to me that there are a hell of a lot of writers named White, and that one of them may have already worked this gag.

I flew a kite without a tail around the year 1912. It was not called a jet kite, it was called a tailless kite, and the crossarm had to be bent bow-shaped and held in a curved shape by tying the ends of the crossarm together with a piece of string. Tailless kites flew all right once you got the adjustment on them, but they were as high spirited as a fox terrier and you had to watch them.

We came to New York in July because it seemed like a quiet, serene place to be. Katharine and I were right in our seats on the first base line at the Polo Grounds yesterday and saw the Giants beat the Dodgers 20-6. It was like watching Bowden Broadwater knock out Dempsey in the second. My only trouble in New York now is that I am beginning to get a closed-in feeling in the subway—the threshold of claustrophobia. I am at that bad age when I can't afford to ride to the Polo Grounds in a taxicab but am too shaky to enjoy the underground. I figure that after I have published seven more books I will be able to go to the Polo Grounds in a cab but will not be able to make out the figures on the scoreboard.

Andy

To CASS CANFIELD

25 West 43rd Street
20 July 1953

Dear Cass:

Sorry to be a little late with the enclosed information. Maybe it's the heat.

I estimate that the book will be roughly 50,000 words. I haven't got a title yet, but am referring to it—somewhat glibly—as "The E. B. White Papers," which would be fine if my name were Somerset Maugham. I will try to come up with a title in the next few days. . . .

I'll be leaving for Maine on the 29th. At this writing, I don't know whether I'll deliver the manuscript before I go, or take it along with me for another few days of polishing up and removal of bugs. It's going to be a queer book—a sort of dog's breakfast—but I think it will contain some good things and will be arranged in an amusing way (by my wife, who is good at arrangement). If you are to be in town before the 29th, let's get together.

Yrs,
Andy

To URSULA NORDSTROM

North Brooklin, Maine
4 August 1953

Dear Ursula:

I am perfectly free to go to Cleveland on November 1st, and I would do anything to satisfy Arbuthnot the Radiant,[1] but the plain fact is I have nothing to say to parents beyond what is in the book and I therefore cannot put on any such show. My feeling about the world of books is fairly simple: I will engage to write a book but I will not engage to promote one—no matter who the author is. I know that the reading public has an unhealthy curiosity about authors-in-the-flesh, and I think that nothing really sensible ever comes of it. I have a sort of vague curiosity about Dorothy Lamour, but I'm sure that the place for me is in the second row mezzanine, in nearly total darkness, on a paid admission. The same goes for parents, Arbuthnot or no Arbuthnot. If I ever got face to face with a parent, I would probably insult him. Or her. It would not be safe to turn me loose in a Book Fair—it might take Harpers ten years to live it down.

The gift box of books arrived, and Katharine, I am sure, is writing

---

1. May Hill Arbuthnot, librarian and authority on children's literature.

you in appreciation. It is a lovely gift and I wish you could see the Brooklin Library, where the books will live.

Yrs,
Andy

To MILTON GREENSTEIN

[North Brooklin, Me.]
11 Aug [1953]

Dear Milt:

I have a section in my forthcoming book called *Answers to Hard Questions* and am wondering whether it's all right to include the following one:

Q.: I took out a marriage license in Camden and we lived together for 15 years. Then he left me. Another man wants to marry me. I remember now that some way we forgot to get married. Do I need a divorce? M.F.—Philadelphia Record.

No, honey. Some way you just won't need a divorce.

What think?
Andy

To DAISE TERRY

[North Brooklin, Me.]
[September 1953]
Tuesday

Dear Miss Terrific:

Do you know whether or not I am obligated to buy any of those Bachrach views, over and above the prints you ordered for Harper? I can't see any reason for buying any. I intended to give my wife a birthday present of some pictures, but she does not like any of these views of me, as they do not seem to correspond to her image of me—which I am now beginning to wonder about.

If you would like one of these pictures for your Very Own, I would be charmed to give you one on St. Patrick's Day. You can call your shot. Also, I want to be in a position, photographically speaking, to satisfy any and all demands from editors and publishers who occasionally call up and want a picture. How do I do that?

I was host, yesterday, at a small select picnic on Hog Island in the heat of the day. It was unmarred by any untoward event except that the Sterling Professor of International Relations at Yale fell on a slippery rock and broke, I believe, two ribs. Oh, and there was that nail I ran into my heel, I almost forgot. The squall coming home wasn't nearly as bad as some I have been through.

Yrs,
EBW

To DAISE TERRY

North Brooklin, Maine

7 October 1953

Dear Miss T:

It is raining today, creating the perfect setting for a return to the dark Bachrachian theme. . . . And by the way, did I ever tell you that the son of Mrs. H—, our cook, often wears the cast-off suits and coats of Mr. Fabian Bachrach? Just how this comes about I can never remember, but it seems to be a fact. All you really have to know is that our cook's son wears Fabian Bachrach's old things.

Anyway, sitting here in the rain, dressed in my own trousers such as they are, and they aren't much, and with my poor head swimming with the old dizziness that afflicts me every so often, I would like to accept your suggestion that I place an order for glossies. I think 12 is a pretty number, and 8 x 10 is the sweetest little size in the world, and $18.75 is an absolutely perfect price to pay. I couldn't be happier. The view I want is the view that shows the head without the belly—not the one that shows me clear down to the waist. I am too modest an author to let the public see me clear down to the waist—unless, of course, you can wangle one of Fabian's old suits for me to wear.

So will you order the god damn glossy prints, please, and then let's both consider the incident closed. It was an unhappy period in my life, but there have been many.

Today is the day my beautiful wife and I had chosen for starting on a 3-day motor trip through the golden fall, and to take in the Fryeburg Fair, and to revisit Hayford's-in-the-Field at Chocorua, enjoying a respite from our labors, and viewing western Maine at its lovely time of color. And what happened? First my head falls apart, then the rain comes. So here we sit, staring at the red Timely tags, and the paper clips, and the unanswered letters, and the undone things. Oh, another thing that happened was that the car no longer steers properly—but what the hell, neither do I.

I don't know whether the defeat of the Brooklyn Dodgers by that other team had anything to do with my failing health or not, but I seem not to have been the same since Furillo banged that homer all for nothing. I understand that Ruth Flint[1] is trying to establish the theory that Eisenhower voters were Yankee fans. Tell her the man I want her to interview on that is Kinsey. He would be the key figure in any inquiry of the sort, it seems to me.

Yrs,

EBW

---

1. Reader of final page proof at *The New Yorker*.

To FRANK SULLIVAN

North Brooklin, Maine
Columbus Day [1953]

Dear Frank:

Of the Important Fall Authors pictured in my last Tribune, I thought you were perhaps the least lovely. (I am thinking particularly of Nadine Gordimer.) But no, I guess Christopher La Farge is less lovely than you, and there is not really enough of Lin Yutang showing. He looks like the Theodore Pratt of the Far East, except he is never there. My wife keeps writing to Nadine Gordimer—always about matters of syntax if you can tie that. Anyway, it was a nice issue of the paper and was also a painful reminder that I hadn't yet thanked you for "The Night."[1] You were not only an Important Summer Author for me, I might almost say you were my only summer author. I love "The Night" and I love your inscription in the front, and I love you. Your sword— which you call little and wooden—is the best sword there is, and the only one I have any confidence in, and you are the one that can swing it the way I like to see it swung.

I felt my age here and there in your book—I couldn't remember, for instance, which [Conning] Tower contributor it was who said, "All work and no play makes jack." I guess I must have known once. But it isn't as funny as "An apple a day is the evil thereof." I am extremely fond of that one, and it stays with me as I walk in my orchard on these golden afternoons, testing the leaves for scab, rarely eating a piece of fruit. Apples have never agreed with me, and that makes it perfect. As for front porches, my wife, Katharine, if grilled, will tell you that she once lived in a house in Marion, Mass., that had a front porch with a Dutchman's Pipe vine on it. My house, 101 Summit Avenue, Mount Vernon, N.Y., had a front porch that rambled around onto the north side, next to Billy Denman's yard, and part of the porch was screened and was covered with a honeysuckle vine so that we could pinch the butt end of the honeysuckle blossoms and pull the pistil through, with its one drop of nectar, and drink the nectar. The screened portion of my front porch was called "the Togo," named for Admiral Togo. This was before Pearl Harbor. We children never called the porch anything but "the Togo," and our playmates, who at first thought we were crazy, got used to it after a while. July nights in the Togo were the best of all, with the mosquitoes buzzing outside, and school all over with for the year, and the smell of honeysuckle.

I expect to be an Important Winter Author, and if I live that long I will send you a book to get back at you for sending me "The Night." If

1. Sullivan's book of collected pieces entitled *The Night the Old Nostalgia Burned Down.*

I don't live, I will go straight to heaven and will wait for you there.

What was in that glass on your bedside table, in the picture? The captions never tell things like that.

Yrs thankfully,
Andy

P. S. Katharine is preparing to read "The Night." I did not allow her to read it during the summer, as I did not want it moved here and there and everywhere all over the house, the way she does, and my place lost. I keep the upper hand here. Give a woman an inch and she'll take an ell that hath no fury.

• *When the Book-of-the-Month Club offered a guarantee of $20,000 for* The Second Tree From the Corner *on condition that the publication of the book be delayed for six months, White balked. His refusal surprised Harper's—offers from BOM are almost never declined.*

To CASS CANFIELD

North Brooklin, Maine
18 October 1953

Dear Cass:

About the offer from the Book-of-the-Month, I feel disinclined to put off the publication of the book for a half year—which is about what it amounts to if they are talking about August 1 as a possible date. I can understand their desire to have a flexible book, but I think they should recognize an author's predicament in the matter of topical pieces. I can think of a lot of events that would necessitate my yanking things out of the book, if the events were to occur. The book is ready to go now, and by its nature it ought to go with reasonable promptness, not sit around for six months waiting for history to catch up with me. I have already had to eliminate some stuff from the book because of the passage of time—stuff I hated to take out. It strikes me that the BOM people are probably not nearly as well aware of the character of the material, in its relationship to time, as I am, and that if the matter is pointed out to them they might be willing to step up their date, if indeed they want the book as is. My pregnancy is something like a sheep's— when my time is come, I drop the lamb, even though it's snowing outside. And I am now ready (after a 20-year gestation period) to produce. I don't want to wait around to suit a book club's fancy. Hell, I've already had to revise my book club poem, and remove my arm from the shoulder of Hendrik Van Loon, because the poor fellow is dead.

Yrs,
Andy

To CASS CANFIELD

North Brooklin, Maine
28 October 1953

Dear Cass:

After mulling over the Book-of-the-Distant-Month Club proposal, I've decided not to accept it. If they want to publish me by May, I'm willing to wait that long, but I don't want to agree to August.

Am sorry about this but am trusting to my instinct in the matter, rather than to any reasoning. I feel we should go ahead and publish the book in January, and let book clubs catch us if they can. My books never seem quite to meet the needs of BOM, and I am always some sort of "dual" or "dividend" man, never a bride. But I always feel like a bride when I have a book, and I cannot let a book club make all the arrangements for the wedding. I plan to set the date myself, and maybe mix the punch. This, I know, is expensive for Harper (not to mention me),[1] but I count heavily on you in these pinches, and you have never failed me.

I think The Second Tree will do all right without club sponsorship, and that there will be pleasure and profit in it for both of us. There are other things in life besides twenty thousand dollars—although not many.

Yrs,
Andy

• *In his junior year at M.I.T., Joel White met and married Allene Messer, a New Hampshire girl who was living and working in Boston. When the following letter was written, Joel was a senior, he and his wife and week-old son were occupying an apartment in Charles Street, and his father had traveled to Boston to have a look at his new grandson, Joel Steven White.*

To KATHARINE S. WHITE

The Ritz-Carlton
Boston
[December 1953]
Wednesday night

Dear K:

I've just come from dinner at 81 Charles, and it was a very fine occasion. Steve is a charmer—quite big for his age, very friendly and responsive, contented with life, and obviously well cared for by Allene,

---

1. The division of the income from BOM on *The Second Tree From the Corner* would have been 50 percent to White, 50 percent to Harper's.

who looked pretty and happy. The baby is full of smiles and good humor, and seems to love people. He looks a good deal the way Joe looked in some of his baby pictures, but is quieter. Joe is very proud of him and produced a weight chart showing his progress carefully recorded on graph paper. All in all a grandchild that should make you happy. Allene has a device that enables the baby to take his bottle unassisted—they simply put him down on the floor and he feeds himself, the bottle being encased in a sort of pin-cushion affair that he is able to hold on to.

Joe hasn't heard yet from Newport News but he expects to shortly.[1] He showed me pictures of the place and it is enormous—the biggest in the country, I believe.

Met Ursula Nordstrom on the train—she on her way to visit the Editor of the Horn Book. She told me that my turning down the B of the M Club was the breeziest thing that had happened to Harpers in her time, and had people standing out on the fire escapes talking it over. . . .

Love,
Andy

To **ROBERTA STRAUSS**

[New York]
January 21, 1954

Dear Miss Strauss:

Sorry to have taken so long, getting an answer to you.

Your proposal is certainly challenging enough for anybody. It had never occurred to me that the life of Christ could be a subject for a comic book—probably because it doesn't seem funny. Now that I have adjusted to the idea, I still don't want to undertake it, as it is primarily a labor of adaptation, rather than of creation, and I'm not a very adaptable man.

Thanks very much for giving me the chance.

Sincerely,
E. B. White

To **ELIZABETH AMES**

[New York]
January 25, 1954

Dear Mrs. Ames:

It was kind of you to bring up the possibility of my working at Yaddo.[1]

If ever I arrive at the point where I sit down to do some writing, I

---

1. He had applied for a job with the Newport News Shipbuilding Corporation.

---

1. Mrs. Ames was Executive Director of Yaddo, in Saratoga Springs.

shall remember your invitation, but I'm still writing standing up. In fact, I sometimes think that the only conditions that make me write at all are the familiar and well-loved annoyances of home, of office, and of headlines, and that a setting of planned quietude and the hush of undisturbed creative effort would merely unnerve me. Even at home in Maine, where I have a "study" of my own, I seldom use it for writing, but instead work in the middle of the living room where the household tides run strongest.

But I'm grateful to you for the idea.

Sincerely,
E. B. White

To STANLEY HART WHITE

229 East 48 Street
11 March 1954

Dear Bun:

I broke a toe on Monday and have been slowed up in writing to thank you for "Samuel Tilly White," which is quite a piece about quite a man. It took me completely by surprise, and that was half the fun. I can hardly believe that tomorrow marks the century.[1] You mentioned in your memorial essay that there was a likeness discernible in the *Times* photograph. Baby, you should have seen me this week—carrying a cane. I not only looked a little like Father, I felt like Father. A cane is what does it, in the end. It gives dignity, direction, restraint, and a general sense of owning whatever you set the point of the cane down on. A broken toe isn't bad, and I rather recommend it—specially if you are troubled (as I often am) by the Notself.[2] The minute I broke my toe, my head felt wonderful. Everything was concentrated conveniently into a small, distant member, and I had no other troubles or doubts for a couple of days. They are beginning to crowd back on me now, as the pain recedes, and I am having to wave the cane at them, as at a small noisy dog.

I thought your tribute was as happy (and felicitous) as it was unexpected. Pop was a golden man living in a golden age, doing it well, and barely realizing that he was dumping six kids into an age of terror and destruction. I think at the end he worried a bit about this, and he did not underestimate either the meaning or the damage of the First War; but I'm glad he died before the real carnage began—not because he wouldn't have had the character to stand up to it but because it would

1. Samuel Tilly White was born March 12, 1854.
2. "The Notself," says White, "lives in the dark subbasement of the psyche. He helps the janitor."

have destroyed the pattern that you and I like to remember, and that he fitted so beautifully.

It is hard to know, precisely, what a parent transmits to a child, and I have often wondered—not only about what I received from Father but about what I handed along to Joe. Pop was not only conservative (in a rather sensible and large-spirited way) but he was tidy in large and small ways, and I think those are the traits that found their way into the second generation. I can see it in my work. I don't always like it, but I can usually see it. I don't know whether a passionate love of the natural world can be transmitted or not, but like the love of beauty it is a thing one likes to associate with the scheme of inheritance. Anyway, I want to say thanks for your lovely and successful attempt to recapture something that is very dear to all.

K and I have had a long-drawn-out succession of melancholy and dreary events, since about the first of December when I got sick to my gut. After Christmas, K got the intestinal flu, then I got it, then K received word that her sister Rosamond in Sarasota was hospitalized for an operation, then the sudden news of Rosamond's death. K had to take off immediately for Sarasota, because her 92-year-old aunt was being evicted from the house. I couldn't go along, as I wasn't well enough, so Nancy went—leaving her little family of half-grown children in Easton, Pa. While K was away, I tried to take on some extra work for *The New Yorker* and pounded myself so hard that I developed shingles. K got back to town and two days later came down with mumps. (I'm not making this up.) Minnie, our dachshund, observing that everybody else was swinging it, came down with the tapeworm, and she is so old (fifteen) that her doctor decided she would not be able to survive the regular tape treatment, and would have to have the "B" treatment—far more complicated. K's mumps were horrible, and the penicillin shot that the doctor gave her backfired. One night the refrigerator got into the act by expelling carbon fumes, or something, and we sat up all night in our overcoats with the windows wide open to ward off asphyxiation. And so the days wore on. Monday, having nothing better to do, I broke my toe rather sullenly against a door.

Our real problem, of course, is Aunt Crully. To Katharine she is like her own mother, as she brought the girls up. We leave by train on Saturday for Sarasota to get her settled temporarily, with nurse attending, and then later on we will probably bring her to Maine and settle her into the house. She was with us there for quite a spell when we were living there the year round. Well, it's been quite a winter and I hope it's over. So far I haven't developed mumps.

Love,
En

To URSULA NORDSTROM

25 West 43rd Street
March 12, 1954

Dear Ursula:

The beautiful copy of "Charlotte's Web" arrived and is being much admired.[1] I show it around as though I had bound it myself. I haven't inscribed it to myself yet, as I haven't been able to think what to write on that page that tells all about how it sold so many copies, but I am looking forward to the autographing, from me to me—a wonderfully narcissistic occasion. I'm going to do it while leaning over a pool.

Anyway, this is my most beautiful book. I shall treasure it always, treasure you always, treasure Harpers always, and try not to lay up my treasure on earth but take it with me. . . . Katharine is just over mumps, I am just over shingles, Minnie is just over tapeworm, and I have just broken the third toe of my right foot. How are you?

And thanks again.
Andy

To BRISTOW ADAMS

25 West 43 Street
29 March 1954

Dear BA:

I was delighted to get the tear-sheet from that unrecognizable Sun-paper, and I wish I could have heard your fifteen minute commentary. I can't seem to recall whether the Sun ran book reviews in my day, but at least it placed the masthead at the top of the column. What do they call it now—the maststep?

I'm glad you like Mr. Volente.[1] I wrote it a long time ago for Harper's and they didn't want to run it and tried to talk me out of it. Frederick Lewis Allen had just become editor, and I never did make out just what he had against the piece except I think he didn't like the word vomit. Apparently *Harper* readers never throw up. Anyway, I just hung around in his office looking sheepish and not saying much in my own defense, and finally I went away and the piece appeared.

I am a grandfather. And on top of that, we are soon to be joined by Katharine's 92-year-old Aunt Caroline, better known as Aunt Crully.

---

1. A leather-bound copy of *Charlotte's Web* was presented to White when 100,-000 copies of the book had been printed.

---

1. Mr. Volente is the man in White's piece called "The Hotel of the Total Stranger," which appeared in the "One Man's Meat" department of *Harper's* magazine and later in the book *The Second Tree From the Corner*.

She tips the scales at an even 80 lbs., and likes sherry . . . She's quite deaf but I can make her hear after we've both had a couple of rounds.

Love to Louella.

Ever thine,
Andy

To SHIRLEY WILEY

[New York]
March 30, 1954

Dear Miss Wiley:

My wife is helpful to me in my writing, but she does not write. She is an editor. An editor is a person who knows more about writing than writers do but who has escaped the terrible desire to write. I have been writing since 1906 and it is high time I got over it. A writer, however, writes as long as he lives. It is the same as breathing except that it is bad for one's health. Some of my writings have won prizes but awards of that sort are not very much fun or satisfaction and I would rather have a nice drink of ginger ale, usually. Writing does have its rewards but they do not come in packages.

Hope I've answered all your questions.

Sincerely,
E. B. White

To DAISE TERRY

N. Brooklin
Apr. 4, 1954
Sunday morn

Dear Miss T:

Enclosed are a few items for distribution among my friends. Blowing a living gale here from the NW, and the temperature this morning early was 10°. All water pails frozen solid, pasture pond solid, all doors resisting all attempts at ingress and egress, frost-proof valve on outside water line frozen, master of house all alone and frozen, barnyard sunny and full of little black-faced lambs and their mammas. I have spent most of my time, since getting here, keeping the kitchen stove hooked up to fever pitch. Coldest 4th of April since 1879. Am living on a straight diet of rye whiskey and Franco-American spaghetti. The first night I was here, though, I boiled a potato and it was quite an experience. We have a shelf of cookbooks in the kitchen here, and I finally found one of them that told how to boil a potato, and I followed directions to the letter and it came out fine. I am sitting here right now planning my Sunday dinner menu and it has just come to me—rye whiskey and Franco-American spaghetti. Luckily we had a wonderful spaghetti crop last summer, and it keeps well. I find it the most convenient of all foods because while it is warming in the saucepan I keep tasting it to see whether it is warm enough, and by the time it is warm enough to eat, it is all eaten, so that means there are no dishes to wash—all I have to do is rinse the empty saucepan and hang it up on its nail over the stove. If everybody knew my secret it would revolutionize domestic life in America.

If you encounter my wife you might tell her that I am alive, as she will be wondering about that.

Yrs,
EBW

To GROUCHO MARX

[North Brooklin, Me.]
April 12, 1954

Dear Mr. Marx:

Before our correspondence attains the intensity of the Shaw-Terry Letters, I want to explain my suspension in the spirit world—which is sometimes misinterpreted.[1] Ross had a theory that if he could throw me with a better class of people, I might be more productive. (Ross entertained some incredibly unsound ideas and at great cost to himself.)

At any rate, once in a while he would pry me loose, and on the whole they were miserable experiences for the persons who got involved. I think of an evening when he attempted to throw me with Ginger Rogers and we all went down to Chinatown for a debauch that should live forever in Miss Rogers' memory as an example of midnight stagnation. (Another Ross illusion was that he understood Chinese food.)

It is nice here in the spirit world and if you get here I would like to buy you a drink. Garbo is here. We maintain separate residences, for appearances' sake.

Sincerely,
E. B. White

---

1. In a letter, Marx had accused White of adopting the mantle of Garbo. The letter ended, " . . . to me you are just a wraithlike figure who lives in a spirit world."

• *Mrs. P. M. Crawford had read "Afternoon of an American Boy"
in* The Second Tree From the Corner. *She wrote to White about her own
memories of growing up in Mount Vernon.*

To MRS. P. M. CRAWFORD

[North Brooklin, Me.]
April 14, 1954

Dear Mrs. Crawford:

I did not go to Wilson's Woods to pick violets, I went to catch
lizards. I saw the place the other day and you couldn't see the violets
(or lizards) for the TV antennae.

Mrs. Schuyler may have been "the angry one" but she was also the
one I was secretly in love with. She played the piano for assembly, too.
I can remember the way Frank Wilcox used to hook his thumbs in his
belt, in some of those western strong man parts, to make himself look
rugged. My father, I believe, was rather keen on Ina Hammer. But I
preferred a girl in one of the musical shows, who wore tights and said
nothing.

I danced at the Alcazar, but only under protest and in white gloves.
Haven't thought of Molly Messiter in many a year, but it is a name that
never dies in memory.

I was not called "Eddie," I was called "En." And I did not mind
being on the Fulton Avenue bridge when a train passed under. Once,
knowing that I was to pass under myself, en route to Belgrade Lakes,
Me., I stationed two of my pals—Freddy Schuler and Billy Denman—on
the bridge at the proper hour, so that they could wave goodbye to me as
I stood triumphantly on the rear platform.

Had a letter recently from Miss Hackett of P.S. 2. She is in her
eighties, is well, and spends part of the time in Washington, part upstate
somewhere. The Prospect Avenue Hill was good coasting, but there were
some winters when Sidney was even better, because it had an S turn in
it. And it carried you through the very heart of The Dell. Our house,
where I was born, stood right at the top of the hill, where the coasters
gathered; and many times, on winter nights, I would have to go to bed
and lie there listening enviously to the sounds of the late revellers with
their Flexible Fliers and their bobs.

I can't seem to place you in the scene, but I was not strong for red
hair. Too much of it in my own family, I guess. Three cases—Marion,
Stanley, and Lillian.

Sincerely,
E. B. White

To URSULA NORDSTROM

North Brooklin, Maine
14 May 1954

Dear Ursula:

The BOM plan for tying Stuart and Charlotte together, which I have named the "H-BOM" plan, is all right by me, and I look forward with pleasure to $1975, all the more so because by a curious coincidence I have just spent $1975 trying to build a small terrace on the north side of the house, and not succeeding. I couldn't make out from your letter whether Harper was waiting on me for approval of the thing, but my recollection was that I told Cass over the phone, from Boston, that it was O.K. to go ahead.

I keep dreaming at night that I am on the witness stand and somebody is asking, "Are you now or have you ever been a member of the Book of the Month Club?" Actually, books are not safe to read—yesterday I lay down for a half hour after lunch, with a book, and while lying there quietly was stung under the right eye by a tremendous wasp that came along and wanted to put me out of my pain, and almost did.

Yrs,
Andy

To JOHN BRUSH

[North Brooklin, Me.]
1 July 1954

Dear John:

It was good of you to send your felicitations on my degree.[1] Colby, which I think is your alma mater, gave me one a couple of weeks ago, so I am really loaded. I was amused at the skyline of Mayflower Hill— neo-Colonial surmounted by TV antennae.

Thanks for your propaganda leaflets, which I studied with much interest and I hope profit. Nothing is too orthodox for me, as I'm not very well equipped with faith and find the lack of it a darn nuisance and very hard on one's health. I suppose I have something in me that roughly corresponds to religious feelings, but like the earth before the Lord got after it, it is without form and void.

I hope this letter reaches you before your departure for Europe. Katharine and I have been trying to depart for Europe for about eight years, now, and every time we book passage some sort of calamity overtakes us. We've reached the point of not daring to buy tickets, for fear of

---

1. From Harvard. White's cousin, a Baptist minister and Colby College alumnus, had also sent him some church literature.

precipitating a crisis. We now have, between us, six grandchildren. Many of them are nearby, and they manage to give the illusion of a trip abroad, so we are not badly off.

Sincerely,
Andy

To GUSTAVE S. LOBRANO

North Brooklin, Maine
9 July 1954

Dear Gus:

I did a little haying yesterday—the greatest form of debauchery my body knows, with the possible exception of McNulty—and as a result I am spending today indoors paying the tab, making small, indecisive movements here and there among the quiet rooms, trying a drug now and then. This letter will be my major thing of the day. It could easily be the last thing I ever write, from the feel of it. It seems rather pat to send it to a fellow in a hospital but you're going to get it whether you like it or not.[1] I learn from the grapevine that you passed all your tests, so I presume you are now suffering from a black case of post-barium letdown. That is, I think, almost a disease in itself and should be recognized as such. So many times, on the southbound express of the Independent Subway, returning from the Medical Center after going through my annual checkup and receiving the nod from the doctor, I have felt the frightening waves of disappointment beating on my brainshore. I hope you are not having them. I don't know any relief from them—although I usually go straight from the subway to a saloon and build a temporary breakwater. You ought to be in a saloon, not a hospital, if my diagnosis is any good. Tell the nurse this; it is sure to amuse her.

I told Atchley about post-barium letdown one time, and he listened with the greatest attention.[2] A year later, when I passed my exam, I thought he was going to walk right out and see that I got to the subway, without mishap. (No comma, sorry.)

In two days I will be fifty-five. Next paragraph.

I don't mind being fifty-five except that I seem to be in such a hurry all the time, instead of the other way round. K is suffering today from post Thurber casual letdown, which is a lower level disease not to be compared with our high distress. The sun is out, the airs are gentle,

---

1. Lobrano, who had been plagued by bad health, had gone into a hospital for tests. Nothing turned up, and he was released, still not feeling well. A year and a half later he died of cancer.

2. Dr. Dana W. Atchley of Columbia Presbyterian Hospital was for a number of years White's New York physician.

the Boston plane is overhead bound for Boston and piloted by a man named Shorty, the hay is tumbling up into the hay-wagon unassisted by me thank the good God, the tide is coming, the mail truck is coming, the sheep are being bitten to pieces by the flies (although the sun is slowing the flies up, too), and we have people coming for dinner. Whenever I feel particularly bad we have people coming for dinner. They plan it that way.

Aside from haying and entertaining my grandchildren, I am spending the month of July in retirement, writing a memorial essay for the Yale Review celebrating the hundredth anniversary of the publication of *Walden*.[3] I can't think of anything to say about this event except that Thoreau preferred the sound of a cowbell to the sound of a bell in a belfry. It is hard to build an essay on that, but I take on hard stuff like that all the time. Hell, I am just through writing some bird captions for the Ford Times—which turns out to be a bird magazine. If I had known what the last days of a writer were going to be like, I would have watched my step, years ago.

The barnyard fence that you and I built in the late fall, one year, still stands in a slightly rebuilt form, and needs painting; so if you ever want to paint a fence, come down and bring your own brush. One of the queer things that's happened here lately is that, in the middle of everything, we built a terrace. It all started from a very simple desire to set up a windbreak on the north side of the house. But before we were through we had torn out a whole wall, rebuilt a room, dug trenches to run cement for a brick wall surrounding the "terrace," brought brick from Penobscot and flagstones from Boston, ordered a cedar windbreak (when I have any amount of cedar right on the place here), and paid a local contractor two and a half million dollars for demolishing the homestead. We got into the terrace operation before we knew that Rosamond was going to die and K was going to get mumps and I was going to get shingles and intercostal neuralgia and the lambs were going to be ripped open by a barn owl. So we were stuck with it and we are still stuck with it. But my optimism and strength know no bounds and right in the midst of all the construction I moved the roses right into the terrace borders, so the workmen could smell the delicious scent of roses while they laid bricks. The roses lived, and gradually the workmen stole away, and given another twenty years or so, it'll be a mighty pretty little terrace. I started with one architect, but we now have two, and they don't get on.

As I said before, the mail truck is coming. Write and let me know

---

3. The piece, "Walden—1954," was published in the September issue of the *Yale Review*. White later included it in *The Points of My Compass* under the title "A Slight Sound at Evening."

how you are. Sorry to inflict this lousy letter on you but I've been wanting to write and my days don't come out right. I do hope you're feeling
better.

Yrs,
Andy

• *Right next to the Brooklin Library was a house called the "Earl
Firth" house. It was unoccupied, it belonged to the Library, and it was
an eyesore and fire hazard. Katharine White, who feared for the Library,
itched to get rid of the house. With the following letter, White gave her
a check to cover the demolition costs.*

To **KATHARINE S. WHITE**

[North Brooklin, Me.]
18 July [1954?]

K:

So many times I have felt that I wanted to present you with a fine
ruby, or we'll say a perfect sapphire, or a couple of matched pearls that
step along together, yet in the presence of rubies, sapphires, pearls or
in almost any jeweled atmosphere whatsoever I have turned away
empty, blinded by the glitter probably. This impotence in my relationship
with precious stones has left me a rich man, and you are my precious
stone, all the more so because you don't glitter. So I now have the strong
desire to make you a gift in lieu of rubies, and it seemed to me the
other night that the thing you most wanted was to tear down Earl
Firth's house—so I am giving you that, my love my own. Hit it hard
and true!

EBW

To **DAISE TERRY**

[North Brooklin, Me.]
[July 28, 1954]
Monday

Dear Miss T:

I have, in times gone by (and Baby how they've gone by!), written
comments on the subject of Thoreau's *Walden*. I would like clip-
sheets, or copies, of any of these comments that Miss J.[1] can put her
rubber finger on without straining.

Have just written a piece for the *Yale Review* on the subject of

----

1. Ebba Jonsson, the *New Yorker*'s librarian.

Walden and am having nightmares from the fear that I have plagiarized myself. At my age, Miss T., a writer repeats like an onion.

Thanking you in advance for your courtesy, and thanking Miss J. for hers, I remain,

EBW

To STANLEY HART WHITE

North Brooklin, Me.
22 September 1954

Dear Bun:

I learned from Al that you have been in the hospital ever since I saw you, or almost. He didn't give me your address so I'll send this via Blanche. The way you were sailing Martinis through the air at Locke-Ober, I didn't think there was anything wrong with your health and I am very sorry to hear that they are pointing Geiger counters at you. However, I can report a very startling thyroid cure, thanks to the atom age—a young girl, daughter of Ted Cook who used to write the syndicated column called Cook-Coos. They hung a few atoms on her, and she bounced back like a rubber ball. Thurber also had the atomic cocktail— and if I know Jim he immediately asked for a re-fill and talked everybody under the table. Anyway, he's still around and doing fine and I owe him a letter, come to think of it.

My days are as tattered as ever—I got myself embroiled with a documentary film man named Arthur Zegart, to write the script or narration for a TV film on lobstering.[1] He is completely disarming and completely exhausting—has flown here three times from New York to get things "lined up". . . . Not a single foot of the film has been exposed yet, but we now have a fisherman lined up, and if I can ever quiet Arthur down long enough to get a camera turning, maybe something wonderful will happen. I will let you know the date, so you can get your TV screen hooked up to the proper channel, or ditch.

Otherwise I am all right. K is punchy from trying to get Aunt Crully settled somewhere for the winter so we can pull out of here and get back to work. We had two hurricanes hit us right in the teeth, one of which you can read about in the current *New Yorker* if you can find the place. It's called "Our Windswept Correspondents" and I am they.

Let me know your address and your progress, and let me know if I can do anything to help you in whatever situation you now find yourself

---

1. Robert Saudek, executive producer of the CBS "Omnibus" program, had persuaded White to write a short TV documentary on lobstering and had sent a young director, Arthur Zegart, to see the Whites, scout the coast, and shoot the picture. Together White and Zegart put together a film showing a Deer Isle fisherman, Eugene Eaton, hauling his traps on a rough day in Jericho Bay. The film was broadcast on December 5, 1954.

in. One thing I have always intended doing is to re-design the Hospital Bed, which is almost as badly conceived as the Modern Car. (I know just how to do it, too—you have to have three small mattresses instead of one big one, so that when the bed is cranked up or down, it can break squarely into the proper angles, instead of curving like a new moon and breaking every vertebra in your spine. I just need the time, that's all.)

With love,

En

To CASS CANFIELD

North Brooklin, Maine

4 October 1954

Dear Cass:

About the Bennett Cerf inquiry, I have no interest at the moment in collecting my "early work." Most of it is in collected form already, a lot of the rest of it isn't worth collecting, and I'm not in a collecting mood, nor do I want a Modern Library man to start picking around in my spotty past.

And as you say, anything of that sort would be for Harper anyway.

I'm not even sure I'm a writer any more—a TV director of documentaries has been here, and I am sinking in coils. I have a grandson in one room, a 92-year-old aunt in another, a son headed for the Army in another (sharing it with his wife, who will have her second baby in December), and the camera and sound crew strung wildly all over the county, shooting in all directions and waiting for me to write a narrative. So you see I am not collecting early works—I am barely able to swallow my own spit.

Bennett Cerf has been reading the Sunday book sections, that's what's the matter with him.

Yrs as ever,

Andy

•   *Paul Brooks, editor-in-chief at Houghton Mifflin, had published* The Wild Flag. *The "Walden piece" in the following letter is "Walden— 1954."*

To PAUL BROOKS

[New York]

November 26, 1954

Dear Paul:

Thanks a lot for the kind words about my Walden piece. The *Yale Review* is a surprising medium. I have had reactions to the piece from exactly four readers (including you). One was from a young woman two doors down the hall, another from a young woman in the Transvaal, and a third from a Philadelphia lady. You are the only living male to speak of it, and I am perfectly sure the South African woman would not have mentioned it had not my wife sent her a marked copy. The Philadelphia lady didn't like my putting direct quotes into the mouths of moderns, and said so in no uncertain terms.

Yrs,
Andy

To HELEN MARGOLIS

[New York]
December 22, 1954

Dear Miss Margolis:

You ask what happened.[1] Nothing much happened. (Which is so often the case.) The man was not cured, I would say. But he experienced, as one sometimes does, a sort of temporary miracle during which courage returned to him with a rush, a sudden influx of earthly beauty—in this case a mere tree as it appeared bathed in light.

As for my remark about sanity in the introduction, I agree with you that it could be misleading, and, as I look it over, on your insistence, I feel rather sorry I dropped it in there at all. I also agree that the story is too short; I was trying to wrap up a complicated thing too hastily. But the story "The Second Tree From the Corner" is not about a man who is insane or about to lose his sanity. It is about a garden variety neurotic who merely *feels* as though he is going nuts—a common sensation in this century. I think I must have made that prefatory remark because I myself no longer take sanity as seriously as I used to—and have felt a whole lot better since dropping it for the hot potato it is.

I cannot tell from your letter whether you are simply taking a fling in literary curiosity, or whether you are troubled, so I am trying to answer your query with care. Ordinarily I do not feel under any obligation to explain my writings, since they are presumed to be self-explanatory—or at least open to any interpretation anybody wants to put on them. But I do get uneasy when I find that something I have written causes a reader any pain or apprehension. One trouble, of course, in explaining my stuff is that I'm not at all sure I understand it myself. If the "Second Tree" means anything, it merely means that courage (or reassurance) often comes very unexpectedly, and from a surprising source. For which we should all be, I guess, profoundly grateful.

Sincerely,
E. B. White

---

1. Miss Margolis, a reader, had asked White the meaning of his piece "The Second Tree From the Corner" from the book of the same name.

XI

WILL STRUNK'S LITTLE BOOK

1955–1959

•   *The Whites were still at* The New Yorker, *where Katharine again became head of the Fiction Department after the death of Gus Lobrano in 1956. But the biannual migration was beginning to take its toll, and White yearned for the continuity of life on the Maine farm. Katharine, too, after fulfilling her responsibilities to the Fiction Department —she had promised William Shawn two years—was beginning to think about at least partial retirement. In 1957 she took the step, and the Whites vacated the apartment in Turtle Bay and returned to Brooklin.*

Early in 1957, H. A. Stevenson, editor of the Cornell Alumni News, *and a long-time friend of White's, sent him a gift out of their common past: a copy of Professor William Strunk's little textbook on usage and style. On seeing the book again, White was inspired to write an affectionate piece about the late Professor Strunk for* The New Yorker (A Letter from the East, *in the issue of July 27). J. G. Case, editor at Macmillan Company, spotted the piece and wrote asking White whether he would be interested in reviving the book. His original proposition was simply to use White's essay as an Introduction, but the project expanded and White ended up revising the text as well.* The Elements of Style *by William Strunk, Jr., and E. B. White was published in 1959.*

To L. M. REUVERS

[New York]
January 7, 1955

Dear Mr. Reuvers:

I feel very lucky to have such a letter, and I am grateful to you for writing. The ghostly presence in the world of people who are, in a sense, friends even though they have the good sense not to materialize, is a great comfort to a writer. Of course, a realistic man, although allowing himself to be warmed by invisible friendships, is careful not to set too much store by them, for he knows that he can neither justify nor solidify them: the man-on-paper is always a more admirable character than his creator, who is a miserable creature of nose colds, minor compromises, and sudden flights into nobility. (Even so, I am grateful.) I suppose readers who feel friendly toward someone whose work they like seldom realize that they are drawn more toward a set of aspirations than toward a human being. Nevertheless, I am grateful, and I thank you again.

Sincerely,
E. B. White

To CASS CANFIELD

25 West 43rd Street
20 January 1955

Dear Cass:

There is a short passage in "One Man's Meat" that cries out to be fixed or dropped. It is the sentence on Page 17 that ends ". . . to remind us daily of dead Christians and living Jews." How I ever managed to give birth to that one I will never know, but anyway I did, and I keep receiving letters about it—mostly from students, who are very anxious to know what I had in mind. I can't say I blame them.

Is there any way of making a correction, for subsequent printings if any?

Yrs,
Andy

P.S. I was referring, of course, to the prisoners who were enduring a living death in concentration camps, and to dead soldiers. But the wording is not only infelicitous, it is just plain crazy.[1]

To FIFTH-GRADERS IN CLEVELAND HEIGHTS

[New York]
January 21, 1955

Dear Members of the Fifth Grade:

When I wrote Mrs. Stevenson the other day, I had not had time to read all your letters, but now I have done so, and they are a fine lot of letters. Thank you for letting me know what you thought about "Charlotte's Web."

1. The offending passage was changed. It now reads, " . . . to remind us daily of wounded soldiers and tortured Jews."

You asked whether I had kept any animals on a farm. I have raised a good many young pigs, lambs, chicks, and goslings in my barn. I will tell you something that happened to the young geese last winter. There is a small pond down in the pasture and the geese use it for a swimming pool. They start from the barnyard, walking slowly; then as they get nearer the water, they break into a run; and then they spread their wings, take to the air, and land on the pond with a splash. But one night, early last winter, the pond froze during the night. The young geese had never seen ice, and knew nothing about it. They started for the pond, sailed into the air, and when they came down for a landing, their feet struck the ice and they skidded the whole length of the pond and crashed into the opposite bank. That's how they learned about ice.

Thanks again for your letters.

Sincerely,
E. B. White

To STANLEY HART WHITE

229 East 48 Street
6 February 55

Dear Bun:

. . . I'm going into the hospital in about a week for a hernia operation, as I seem to have blown a muscle. Every countryman gets a ruptured gut eventually. I got mine from lifting too many glasses. Also, I think they are congenital. Pop got one when he was about my age, and he never lifted anything heavier than a receipted bill. They say the operation isn't much, and that the latest technique is to reinforce the wall with wire mesh—probably a Reynolds aluminum product. My only fear is that when they open me up they're going to find shad roe. It's just the season.

My new granddaughter is a cutey, name of Martha. She and her Ma and her brother Steven are now living in a small place at 59 River Street, Boston. Joe has about a month more at Dix and then will presumably be shipped away somewhere. If K and I can hold together this spring, we're planning to ship ourselves to England in the Mauretania for a few weeks. Have booked passage, but I won't believe it till I see the docking lines being dropped off.

I studied the list of symptoms you sent me, indicating a thyroid condition, and I have every one of them but am disinclined to do anything about it. My tremor is so bad I can't write longhand any more, but it is not necessary in my line of work. Saw Marion and Art Brittingham not long ago when they dropped in for a short visit between trains.

Marion is a bit stiff in the joints but looks fine, and Arthur hasn't changed in 40 years. Still wears a bow tie and can answer any question right on the button. He is building a greenhouse.

The New Yorker will be thirty next week.

Yrs,

En

• *The following letter was written from White's hospital bed on the eve of surgery. The Misses Forbes, Fox, Robinson, and Cullinan were young secretaries in Miss Terry's secretarial pool at* The New Yorker.

To **DAISE TERRY**

[Harkness Pavilion]
[February 1955]

Song to Be Sung by Daise Terry and Chorus of Maidens—*Greenstein* on the *Recorder*

Lying here at the zero hour,
My thoughts return to Terry's bower—
Oh, pulsing room! Unstately hall!
Oh, Daisy and her maidens all!
I count you over, one by one,
Miss Forbes, Miss Fox, Miss Robinson,
Miss Cullinan, and Mistress T.
My rosary! My rosary!

Tomorrow when I'm carved to shreds
I'll see in dream your bobbing heads,
And when they stitch me up with laces
I'll think of all your pleasing faces,
And as I heal by slow degrees
I'll hear the clatter of your keys—
And if the gods are not too stern
Why, like MacArthur, *I'll return.*

E B W

TO ROBERT W. PATTERSON, JR.

[New York]
March 8, 1955

Dear Robert:

I doubt that I'm going to be much help to you in your dilemma, but I'll do what I can.[1]

The "primary characteristic" of my writing is something you'll have to figure out for yourself by reading it. I tend to write about myself, I seldom use a word or phrase from any language except English (because I don't know any other language), and I don't make any attempt to please the reader.

Basic likes and dislikes? Strong feelings for or against things? Well, it's all in the books, and if you have read them you must have picked up a few hints. Every writer likes to think that he's on the side of the angels and that he tilts against injustice, but you have to form your own opinion. I like inboard motors better than outboard motors—you can say that if you like. And I like sail better than power. I dearly love the natural world.

You can always find out a few things about authors from biographical notes on book jackets, from prefaces, and from reference volumes in the Noble & Greenough library, but the best way is to read their works—they always give themselves away sooner or later. I cannot outline my life briefly unless you pay me an enormous fee—it would take me months. I was born in 1899 and expect to live forever, searching for beauty and raising hell in general.

Please give my best to your father when you see him.

Sincerely,
E. B. White

• *The following is White's reply to a letter that began, "Dear Mr. White: I am a confused senior at Newton High School."*

TO ARTHUR HUDSON

[New York]
April 1, 1955

Dear Mr. Hudson:

I am a confused writer at 25 West 43 Street, and one of the reasons for my confusion is that students want me to explain myself.

---

1. Patterson, the schoolboy son of a friend of White's who lived on Mount Desert, was struggling with an English assignment, and had asked White to outline his life briefly.

I can't explain myself. Everything about me is mysterious to me and I do not make any very strong effort to solve the puzzle. If you are engaged in writing a theme about my works, I think your best bet is to read them and say what you think about them.

The question of "style" is a vexing one, always. No sensible writer sets out deliberately to develop a style, but all writers do have distinguishing qualities, and they become very evident when you read the words. Take Hemingway and Willa Cather—two well known American novelists. The first is extremely self-conscious and puts himself into every sentence and every situation, the second is largely self-effacing and loses herself completely in the lives of her characters.

Sorry not to give you more assistance but you can appreciate my predicament.

Sincerely,
E. B. White

To ROBERT L. SMOCK

[New York]
April 18, 1955

Dear Mr. Smock:

Thanks for your letter and the suggestions.

Quite a number of children have written me to ask about Stuart. They want to know whether he got back home and whether he found Margalo. They are good questions but I did not answer them in the book because, in a way, Stuart's journey symbolizes the continuing journey that everybody takes—in search of what is perfect and unattainable. This is perhaps too elusive an idea to put into a book for children, but I put it in anyway.

I appreciate your taking the trouble to write, and my best to Peggy and Polly.

Sincerely,
E. B. White

To HOWARD CUSHMAN

Chagford
Devon [England]
15 June 1955

Dear Cush:

They say *down* in Maine for a very good reason. Sailing boats used to be the principal means of getting to and from Boston, and since the prevailing winds along the coast are SW, Maine was a down wind sleighride, while Boston and New York were uphill all the way for the mariner. Next question.

Your letter reached me in London, where I was not smelling any dung or compost but was trying to dodge in and out of a Mayfair hotel without being seen by any of the innumerable employees. Finally we beat it for here, rail strike and all. The only employee at this hotel is named Valerie, and she sneaks in at 8 a.m. with coffee and bacon and leaves me at peace with my whisky and Schweppes water the rest of the day. I have become a walker, except I have no brogues, no stick, no pack, and no cap. I do carry a Mac, though, rolled neatly, for the little downpours between the bright intervals.

Chagford has the distinction of having once used the same body of water for its drinking supply and its drainage system—as neat an arrangement as I've ever heard of. A poet was murdered here, but not recently. The inn was built in the 15th century, and you can sit on a can named "the Improved Vesta" and gaze out at a thatched roof. The countryside is incredibly beautiful—if I were a sheep I wouldn't live anywhere else. Day starts at 5, with the chorus of ring doves and cuckoos outside the window. Sunset about 9:30.

We may visit the Cotswolds but we are fairly immobile, because I'm scared to drive a car here and it's too costly to have a driver. Also we may fly to Frankfort to see Joe, who is a PFC in the Army at Geln-hausen.

. . . One of my memories of departure from New York is that smell of demolishment. One nice thing about England is, nobody has knocked anything down in nine hundred years—except the Germans.

Yrs,
Andy

To HOWARD CUSHMAN

North Brooklin, Me.
11 August [1955]

Dear Cush:

I don't think I ever thanked you for the Omsk poem, which reached me when I was dizzy from travel (England) and heat (New York) and when—come to think of it—I was sitting in nothing but my trunsk. I made an effort to bring your poem to the attention of the editors of the New Yorker, but I think they were barely conscious and it did not get taken. Willie Strunk would have liked it, though; but Willie is dated, alas, and so are the days when poems had hearts that were young and gay and were written by extroverts and drunsk. Nowadays they are written by the late Dylan Thomas, who drank more than any of us but wasn't relaxed enough.

I have two grandchildren living in the top floor of a farmhouse in a small village in Germany. This seems to me absolutely incredible, and every time I think about it I give myself a sharp rap on the side of the head to test whether I can still pick up routine sensations. It seems odd enough that you and I are grandfathers, but I be god damned if I can get used to this particular circumstance. Joe's wife wrote me that Steven (my grandson) wears *lederhosen*, sticks his hands in his pockets like a Bavarian hotel keeper, and plays cricket with the little German boy in the next house.

K and I are sitting here waiting quietly for the two hurricanes that are promised us, and on the whole we are enjoying a peaceful interlude. Hope you, too, are at peace and in good health.

Yrs,
Andy

To HOWARD CUSHMAN

[North Brooklin, Me.]

[Summer, 1955]

HINDSIGHT THROUGH GUNSIGHT PASS
Or, Anybody With Half an Eye in Yakima Could Have
Foreseen What Is in Germany and Maine[1] Today

Was Cush his time investing
Simply to make some westing?
What sought they thus afar
In their small trembling car?
  Was White inviting
  His soul for writing?
Don't be ridiculous!
Like migrant birds questing
They sought grounds for nesting.
Cushman and White
Were in spring flight,
Scrawling in youth and happiness
The prelude to grandpappiness.

Andy

---

1. Where Cushman's daughter Nancy (Mrs. Martin Dibner) was living.

To GLUYAS WILLIAMS

[New York]

4 November 1955

Dear Gluyas:

Another of our sharp-eyed New England contributors sent us the *Boston Globe* clipping about the panic at the Myopia Hunt, and it got into the works before yours arrived. You have to be frightfully quick with the scissors to win. But thanks anyway.

You asked what kind of time Katharine and I had in England. A rather odd time, on the whole. We left America in such a hurry (following the sudden death of Aunt Caroline in Maine) that we never got around to planning an itinerary or booking ourselves in England's inns and transport systems. We said to each other that we'd just go to England and loaf around from place to place; we would hire a car and I would drive gravely through the merrie countryside. The only reservation we made was at the Connaught Hotel in Mayfair, which turned out to be the most fashionable joint in London and probably the most expensive. (I thought it was going to be a sort of British Algonquin.) Well, when the Mauretania docked at Southampton and we went ashore with our trunk and ten pieces of "hand" luggage, the British railways were on strike because of their disaffected footplatemen. So we hired a Southampton taxi to carry us up to London, a wild and weird journey on highways jammed with lorries. One thing that happened on the journey was that I lost my courage about driving a car on the lefthand side of the road in England. Teatime found us still taxiing and when the driver cried: "Do you wish to stop for tea or shall we press on, sir?" I answered "Press on!"—a phrase I had never used in my life but which was just the forerunner of a whole series of idiotic attempts to speak English to the English.

My week in London was just a mild and uncomfortable excursion into ineptitude, during which I felt at all times unsuitably dressed and unable to speak properly. I refused to answer the phone when it rang because I couldn't make out what the person at the other end was saying. Rebecca West's husband phoned to ask us to Henley and he might just as well have been a solicitor of some sort. After one attempt to patronize the bar in the Connaught I gave up, from fright, although I badly needed a drink the entire time. I guess my high (or low) point was the day I approached a liveried doorman on the street and said: "Good morning. Could you direct me to the office of Thomas Cook?" Half way through this polite sentence I glanced at the man's cap and read the words "Thomas Cook & Son." I was standing directly in front of the place. The whole visit in London was like that. I got so I hated London and felt trapped. It was just too big for me, and it was cold and dark. Perhaps a more lucid account of the period could be given by my valet at the Connaught.

From London we traveled by chauffeur-driven car to a small inn in Chagford, Devonshire, where we stayed a week recuperating and having a fine time among the hedgerows and along the banks of the river Teign. By this time there was a dock strike and a strike of Cunard stewards, and we spent the rest of our stay figuring out a way of getting back to New York. We landed in New York on Sunday, July 3, to find that all eight million residents had gone away to the beaches in 90 degree heat. K and I didn't even attempt to get into our apartment, we just went to the Algonquin and lay down. Except for the manager, we were the only ones there. The dining room was closed.

Some day, after a lapse of two or three years, I think I'll write an account of my trip abroad.

We had intended to fly to Frankfort for a couple of days to see Joe and his family, who are stationed nearby, but we had to abandon that idea when we found that our time had run out.

Kenneth Bird asked for you.

Yrs,
Andy

• *The piece discussed in the letter that follows was the first of the "Letter" pieces that White was to write during the next few years. "Letter from the East" was dated December 10, 1955, and* The New Yorker *ran it in its issue of December 24.*

To **WILLIAM SHAWN**

North Brooklin, Maine
Friday 9 Dec [1955]

Dear Bill:

This piece is timely, on account of the stuff about Christmas trees, etc., and I may be springing it on you too late. It is also a sensationally slight piece, and if you don't care for it, or if it means a lot of rearranging of the book, the thing to do is send it back and I can probably salvage quite a bit for a possible later Letter.

I tried various heads and now lean to Letter from the East. Seems to me that if I can latch on to the four points of the compass, I can manage anything. A letter from Nome or from 110th Street would be Letter from the North. A letter from Third Avenue would be from the East. And so on. I tried such words as Letter from Hereabouts, but didn't come up with anything I liked.

Am also enclosing some source stuff that might be of use to checking.

Best regards,
Andy

To PAUL BROOKS

[New York]
January 12, 1956

Dear Paul:

I have no objection to that quote. I guess I said it all right, although I don't recall the circumstances.

I had forgotten *Weeskaijohn.* I did read your piece, though, when it came out in the *Atlantic,* and enjoyed it. David Thompson's description of the whisky-jack is so close to a description of me as to be acutely embarrassing: ". . . is easily taken by a snare, and, brought into the room, seems directly at home, when spirits is offered, it directly drinks, is soon drunk and fastens itself anywhere till sober."[1]

The Canada Jays mentioned in my "Letter" were the first I had ever seen around our place in Maine. I spotted another bird last summer that thoroughly baffled me. It belonged, I'm pretty sure, to the family of jaegers, skuas, fulmars, etc., and it used to take a bath in the fresh-water pond in my pasture. Its wings were somewhat more dagger-like than a gull's and in the air it ranged about very rapidly. I never identified it to my own or anybody else's satisfaction, but I thought fondly of it the other day when a fulmar showed up in New York and the *Times* reported the intense disappointment of the museum authorities on having to release it. Seems they hoped it would die so they could stuff it.

Best regards,
Andy

---

1. In his piece, "A Canoe on the Border Lakes," Brooks had explained the derivation of "whisky-jack"—a common name for the Canada jay—from the Indian *weeskaijohn* ("he who comes to the fire") and had quoted nineteenth-century explorer and geographer David Thompson's description of the bird.

To GUSTAVE S. LOBRANO

229 East 48
[January 14?, 1956]
Saturday

Dear Gus:

My latest missive from Mike [Galbreath], received this morning, ended "Give Gus my best"—so I hasten to pass the greeting along. The word PERGE also appeared on the postcard, so I pass that along too. What we all need is a lot more, and better, perge.

I am just winding up a four-week spell of New York stomach, but I think I'm coming out on top. Passed my annual physical exam at the Medical Center this week, but didn't enjoy it as much as a year ago, when the electrocardiogram operator (a female) asked me my age and whether I had had any drugs that morning. And I replied "Fifty-five, and I've had nothing but a little opium." My heart reacts with increasing irritability to the EK machine as the years roll on. But I don't mean to dwell on my own health at any length, as yours is so much more perti-nent. How are you? I get reports here and there, mostly in the vicinity of the water cooler. I was saddened to learn of the return of phlebitis and all those lousy injections, and I hope you'll soon be released from *that*, and that we can all converge on Hawley's [Truax's] gall bladder, which is certainly the gayest of them all and has, in my imagination, almost the quality of a May pole.

There is not much news that I can bring you from the Outside World because I don't get to the Outside World as often as I used to, and sometimes days slip by without my picking up any informa-tion at all. But I hope you heard the Sevareid broadcast last night, when he described how most of the members of the Cabinet had stabbed themselves in the back with their own pen, starting with Dulles and ending with Benson's remarkable communication in Har-per's.[1] His description of the Republican stalwarts with sharp quills sticking out of their flesh was quite funny. Anyway, I am cheered up when I see our political giants discovering that the lil ole writ-ing game isn't quite the sleighride they like to think it is. After the events of the last couple weeks, I think the entire Cabinet wishes it had never heard of the printed word. What will probably result from these pratfalls will be a great speedup in the investigation of MAG-AZINES.

Well, good old 1956! Whatever it brings to our frail bodies, it's going to bring a lot of wonderful TV and radio listening to our tired old

1. Both Benson and Dulles were claiming not to have read pieces published with their imprimatur—Benson a letter in *Harper's*, Dulles the "brink of war" article in *Life*.

ears. I dearly love a presidential year. What capers! What laughs and spills! And—at the end of the line—a real, live President. And the people's choice at that.

Get well. These are great times.

Love,
Andy

Perge!

To STANLEY HART WHITE

229 East 48 Street
21 January 1956

Dear Bun:

Except for waves of nausea that glide through me on their little cat feet, I'm fine. We greatly enjoyed the plant you and Blanche sent us and it served as our table piece for many days, flanked by a couple of candles that arrived from Germany, where all my direct descendants seem to have drifted. The two gifts combined beautifully and your plant bloomed with great ferocity and shed many a glow—and of the right color for the diningroom. We had our Christmas dinner out at Roger's house, a few miles north of here on the Hudson, where there is always plenty of food and drink and action and cats and dogs and grand-daughters. I really enjoy Christmas best when I can just sit back and drink and let somebody else work it out, which is the case when I go to Roger's. The news from Joe is pretty good. He gradually maneuvered the Army into a seven to five job as company clerk—which wasn't too hard, as he seems to be the only person in his company who can read and write. So he is able to be with his wife and children quite regularly, with time out for occasional field trips. We received quite a batch of good snapshots the other day, and now know in a general way what Steven and Martha look like. Steve talks and thinks almost entirely in German and acts as interpreter (at the age of two) for his Pa and Ma, who still think in English when they think at all. . . .

Do you expect to come east in 1956? Somebody told me you were going (or had gone) to California for a while on a teaching job. But I hear all kinds of things. I am looking forward to 1956 because I love political oratory and rallies and suspense. My prediction is that the right man will win. I don't know how he'll manage it, but he will.

Yrs,
En

P.S. I saw a very old single-cylinder Palmer engine recently and it started me thinking about the Jessie. I would like to know the true story. Did you and Al frame and plank the boat? And where did you get the molds? Did you install the engine? I was pretty young and remember only that there was a fuss out there in the barn, and also I recall the day the motor was given a dry run. Didn't some professional boatbuilder show up to perform the finishing touches? And how in hell did Father ever get the Jessie to Great Pond from Summit Avenue? I used to love to steer the boat, but was disappointed that there was no way to sit directly behind the wheel—always must sit either on one side or the other. This meant sighting along a deck seam, which I didn't care for. I wanted to sight straight across the prow.

To DODY GOODMAN

[New York]
January 24, 1956

Dear Miss Goodman:

The "Queen Bee" is available for the kind of use you have in mind.[1] The only catch is, I have to be convinced that it would be presented with good taste. I don't know just how that can be accomplished, but maybe you can suggest a way. The poem obviously lends itself to being loused up if somebody happens to want to play it dirty. I didn't write it as a plug for insemination, I wrote it as an appreciation of the upper air. And I don't want it brought down to earth by being given the wrong emphasis.

The only sort of deal I would be willing to make would be on a licensing basis—that is, no outright sale. But that part is less of a problem than the matter of taste.

So far as I know, the only person who has performed the Queen Bee in this country (it has been done on BBC) is Helen Taft Manning, the daughter of President Taft, who does it with great regularity—and, I hear, great effect—at Bryn Mawr to edify the young ladies. I have never seen her interpretation but have always wanted to.

Sincerely yours,
E. B. White

To TED PATRICK

[New York]
February 8, 1956

Dear Ted:

I don't want to try a piece on Downtown New York. It is a foreign land to me, and if I'm going to wander around a foreign land in the near future for any gainful purpose it'll damn well have to be some long pink

1. Miss Goodman, a professional entertainer and comedienne, had requested permission to perform White's poem "Song of the Queen Bee."

subtropical paradise where I can lie down between drinks. I'm bushed. The only place in lower New York where they lie down between drinks is the sidewalks of the Bowery, and that's too hard a bed for me now.

Your lazy, tired, grateful friend,

Andy

To **WARREN M. DAVISON**

[New York]

February 17, 1956

Dear Mr. Davison:

Thanks for your invitation to take part in the Forum program on humor.[1] I can't do it, because I am incapable of making a speech.

I have known about this deficiency all my life but just this week I discovered, through X-ray examination, the true cause of it. There is a small exit called the "pylorus" leading from the stomach, and in me it closes tight at the slightest hint of trouble ahead—such as a speech, a platform, an audience, or a panel discussion. It closes and it stays closed, awaiting a turn of events that suggests smoother going. A man with a tightly shut pylorus is in real trouble and should be in a hospital, not a forum.

So I must beg off, as I always do when it comes to speech making. But I am grateful to you for the chance and I am sorry I have to miss the occasion.

Sincerely yours,

E. B. White

• *En route to Sarasota, the Whites were visiting Dr. and Mrs. Joseph T. Wearn at their Castle Hill Plantation. The Wearns were old friends and summer neighbors in Maine; Katharine White and Susan (Tue) Wearn had attended Miss Winsor's together. The piece referred to in this letter was the "Letter from the East" published in* The New Yorker, *February 18, 1956. It was later included in the collected essays,* The Points of My Compass, *entitled "Bedfellows."*

To **JAMES THURBER**

Yemassee, S. C.

24 February 1956

Dear Jim:

Thanks for the kind words about my piece, and also for the instructions on how to spot a Communist. . . . There is a wonderful pond on this plantation, and among its inhabitants are alligators and otter. I thought

---

1. Davison was Program Coordinator for the Harvard Law School Forum.

of the picture you painted on the side of the boathouse at Camp Otter. Remember? Of course nobody ever saw an otter on Otter Lake, and I haven't seen one here yet, but I encountered an otter once in a lake in Nova Scotia and it is the only animal in the world that really looks as though it had been designed by you. You thought you were drawing a Thurber otter, but by God you were drawing an otter.

K and I pull out of here on Monday and head for Sarasota for a drink of sun tan oil. Love to all.

Andy

To FRANK SULLIVAN

Siesta Key
Sarasota, Fla.
3 March [1956]
Saturday

Dear Frank:

Your name came up on my last visit with Gus and I thought you might like to hear what he said. I went out to Chappaqua on a Saturday afternoon—it was two weeks ago today—and sat with him for about an hour, in short takes. He was a surprising sight, terribly thin of course, and with a Lincolnian beard. The bones of his face, accentuated, plus the chin beard, actually made him *look* like Lincoln and I got quite a jolt. I had known for only a few days that he was a dying man—the secret had been rather closely held. Gus gave a little cry of recognition when I was brought into the room by Jean and presented. I sat down and began dropping a few names by way of making a stab at conversation. He kept fading in and out, with the drug, and when he was in he was pretty close to being on the ball. I said that we'd heard from you, and that you'd been visiting Governor Harriman of all people. Gus stared at me a second and then pursed his lips behind the whiskers, smiled faintly, and said: "Now wouldn't you think a man in his position . . ." Then he faded. It was pretty obvious that the sentence would have ended, ". . . could avoid the company of low clowns." Or words to that effect. Or you can write your own ending. I am sure it was leading up to a little old joke of some sort.

Did I ever tell you about the day I walked Gus through Boston to show him a few sights—this was a few years ago. We started up Beacon Hill and turned into Louisburg Square. "This," I announced, "is Louisburg Square." Gus gazed quietly at the cozy scene. "Is it all right to smoke?" he asked.

K and I are here until about the 26th, and we both send our love.

Yrs,
Andy

To ALISON MARKS

[New York]
April 20, 1956

Dear Miss Marks:

I'm very grateful for your letter. My theory of communication is different from yours. I think there is only one frequency and that the whole problem is to establish communication with one's self, and, that being done, everyone else is tuned in. In other words, if a writer succeeds in communicating with a reader, I think it is simply because he has been trying (with some success) to get in touch with himself—to clarify the reception. . . .

Sincerely,
E. B. White

•   *Dorothy Wirth had written the G. & C. Merriam Company complaining that the biographical section of Webster's New Collegiate Dictionary failed to list E. B. White, although it listed P. G. Wodehouse, Orson Welles, Dorothy Parker, John Kieran, William Saroyan, and others.*

To DOROTHY WIRTH

[New York]
April 23, 1956

Dear Mrs. Wirth:

Very sporting of you to cross swords with the G. & C. Merriam Company in defense of my honor. I loved the answer you got. It has always seemed to me that when there are more candidates for a biographical list than there is space to publish their names, some sort of field trial should be held, in which persons of equal "importance" could vie with one another by running twice around a track, or doing a back flip off a diving board. *I* can stand on my head, and might easily have Orson Welles at a disadvantage in this respect.

But don't let the matter worry you. It doesn't bother me any.

Sincerely,
E. B. White

To LORLYN L. THATCHER

[New York]
April 23, 1956

Dear Miss Thatcher:

I see that *The New Yorker* addressed you as "Mr." Thatcher in a recent communication. My apologies.

The interpretation of my "Letter from the East"[1] by one of your

1. Of February 18, 1956.

pupils is quite staggering. But you can tell her that I probably wouldn't be able to do any better myself. You can also say that there are no symbols in the piece, to my knowledge. Why does everyone search so diligently for symbols these days? It is a great vogue. Fred symbolizing "the government as a whole" is such a terrifying idea that I am still shaking all over from fright—the way he used to shake from the excitement of anticipation. I'm afraid your pupil (perhaps because my wording wasn't clear) got the idea that Fred was afraid of a red squirrel. Fred wasn't afraid of a cage of polar bears laced with rattlesnakes and studded with porcupines. The only time a wave of terror would overtake him would be when he would discover that he wasn't able to emerge backwards from situations (or holes) that he had entered frontwards. He suffered from claustrophobia at this point, and was really in fright. Twice I had to take up the floorboards of buildings under which he had pursued a skunk, because even though he had managed to kill the skunk and stink everything up, he was then too exhausted and sick to his stomach to back out the way he had come in.

Please give my regards to your pupil and suggest that some day, when she's in a relaxed mood, she read the thing again, this time without symbols. Or she might try my "Letter from the South" (April 7th issue), which has no politics in it and might give her more pleasure.

Sincerely,
E. B. White

To J. JOSEPH LEONARD

[New York]
April 30, 1956

Dear Mr. Leonard:

I admire your pluck, but I don't want you to try to adapt "The Door" for a TV show.[1] I am a fellow who likes to leave well enough alone, and I am not even convinced that "The Door" is well enough. Anyway, I'm going to leave it alone.

Thanks for asking.

Sincerely,
E. B. White

To EDMUND WARE SMITH

[New York]
May 21, 1956

Dear Mr. Smith:

I haven't been to Maine in so long I have forgotten what it feels like, almost. My wife is held close to New York nowadays by her job, and I

1. Leonard was a producer at Channel KETC in St. Louis, Missouri.

stick around and watch the Giants on TV. I was interested in the size of your wife's vegetable garden. My wife's plot is the same (200,000 acres) but there is an annex called "the asparagus patch." This adds about a third again.

I have run through the kodachromes without encountering a single bird that I am acquainted with, and I see no point in writing about what I don't know about at first hand. I can't blame you for wanting to introduce western birds, but I think you'd better get a western bird man to write the captions. I really don't want to attempt it. Incidentally, if you ever need a caption on the European bullfinch, I am your man. I purchased one two weeks ago (found him in Queens across from a cemetery —"ring twice" the sign said over the doorbell), and he is sitting on my foot as I write this. He has a little song that goes: "The hell you say." A very pleasant bird to have around. Wears a black hood, like the Sandeman sherry character.

Sorry I can't take on your assignment. Am returning the koda-chromes herewith.

Sincerely,
E. B. White

To STANLEY HART WHITE

[New York]
19 July 1956

Dear Bun:

Did you know that in Charleston, S. C., there is an old French Protestant Huguenot church that bears the following notation cut in the stone of the stairway to the entrance:

Built 1681   Rebuilt 1845
E. B. White, Architect

Joe and his family got back from Germany last week and landed in Brooklyn, by military transport, early in the morning of my fifty-seventh birthday. My grandson immediately propositioned me and said he would like to go spazieren.

En

To FRANK SULLIVAN

25 West Etcetera
20 July [1956]

Dear Sul:

You wrote me a letter on my birthday although in your bumbling way you made no mention of that, but I was just as pleased to get it as though you had realized that I was born July 11, 1899, a fact you could easily have verified by turning to any standard reference volume that gives little known facts about little known people. On your suggestion I am having the passage from my last piece[1] carved in stone feldspar. The expense is considerable so I am sending the bill to you, as I think of you as a "good fellow." My birthday was unusually nice this year. A military transport named the Upshur, which my secretary calls the Upstart, docked at 8 a.m. at 58th Street, Brooklyn, carrying Sp-3 Joel White US 51331642 and his unnumbered wife and two children. You don't get to 58th Street, Brooklyn, at eight in the morning without a bit of dawn busting, but my wife Kate and I were fit and ready and out on the streets that day before the Daily News. The scene on the dock was the kind of emotional binge you forget keeps happening two or three times a week even in these relatively peaceable days—about twelve hundred wonderful looking foot soldiers, with their wonderful faces, staggering and lurching down a gangplank under the crushing load of an immense duffle bag, to set foot again in the land of the Big PX, and, about one in every twenty, to collapse into the arms of hungry mothers, fathers, wives, and sweethearts. I got so excited by the moving scene and the earliness of the day that I had to be led away to a stable bench by my stable wife, to set for a few minutes. My two grandchildren's faces were visible on deck for about an hour before the Army managed to disgorge the little group onto the dock, but we finally made it. Joe got in a bus for Fort Hamilton and the rest of us got in a cab for Turtle Bay, where we lived violently and happily ever afterward.

If you moved around in the right circles, the way I do, you wouldn't have to recognize Foster Dulles from photographs. In the late Roosevelt or early Truman era I managed to spend an evening in Dulles's company, or presence, at the apartment of F. Eberstadt,[2] who is well off otherwise. What I chiefly remember is my arrival on the arm of my child bride, Katharine S. White. We stepped off an elevator into what I supposed would be a public hallway in the apartment building, and I careened off the car in the middle of a loud sentence about the general plushiness of the surroundings—the kind of phrenetic remark an editor of the *Daily Worker* might make about the Guaranty Trust Company if he stopped in to cash a check. Well, the hallway turned out to be strictly private, with a butler and the hostess waiting under my sour little pop-up to make the catch. And to top everything off, there just beyond the coffee table stood J - - n F-st-r D- - - -s, ready to explain everything. I remember he had shoes on.

---

1. A "Letter from the East" in *The New Yorker*, June 30, 1956, entitled "Coon Tree."

2. Ferdinand Eberstadt, an investment banker, husband of Katharine White's friend Mary Tongue Eberstadt.

Sometime when you come to Maine to visit us, we will let you sleep in the whippoorwill room (usually called Nancy's room) so you can get the full treatment. A whippoorwill is a bird of darkness and he is also improved by a little distance. I heard my first whippoorwills in 1922 when I was camped on a hillside in Kentucky. Below, in the valley, the birds started to call, at dusk, and it was an incredibly beautiful orchestra, just as yours in the Adirondacks must have been. But when a whippoorwill sits on your doorstone at 4 a.m., he can lead you right to the edge of madness. Some country people still think the bird sucks milk from the udders of goats—hence "goatsucker," which is another name for the bird. (Stick around with me, Sul, and you'll learn the most fascinating facts.)

Have just returned from New York's air raid drill and am pretty tired, so will close. (Air raids in this building are celebrated by having everybody go to the tenth floor—a number somebody thought of.) I just wanted to thank you for your birthday letter. K. gave me "Ring Lardner" for my birthday and I finished it last night and it made me unutterably sad, along toward the end.

Yrs with love,
Andy

P. S. One reader who pondered about my head being in traction advised me to give up the pulleys and weights and just tie on a cluster of balloons, which, he said, would give me more freedom to move about. I like this idea a lot, but am counting on you to shoot me down if I overplay it.

• *John McNulty died in July 1956 of a heart ailment, leaving his wife Faith and a small son, Johnny.*

To FAITH MC NULTY

North Brooklin, Maine
31 July 1956

Dear Faith:

I'm sending this to the NYer because I don't have your Rhode Island address, and I guess it doesn't make much difference when you get it anyway. The letter I'm really late on is the one I failed to write John when I knew he was sick and miserable. When K phoned me yesterday morning and told me that he was dead it was a double blow— I felt not just old and sad and lonely but guilty too. I used to envy John his ability to get off a letter. A lot of the ones he wrote me seem to have been written just as he stepped out of bed in the morning and before the rest of the world was conscious. I have most of those letters, as I seldom throw letters away, and they are sort of in a class by themselves as they were almost always the kind of communication that required no answer. I hate letters that have to be answered (don't answer this one) and John's always left the recipient perfectly free to enjoy himself, no obligation. I don't know who I'm going to lounge around the streets with any more. He was the only deliberate walker of my acquaintance (I was never sure how much his gait owed to his bad heart and how much to his temperament, but it didn't really matter). I'm afraid this is already beginning to sound like a letter of condolence and I want to nip that in the bud. You know I loved John and I don't have to give reasons but just want to send my love to you. The papers haven't got here yet (they make the last few miles to Brooklin by oxcart) so I have not seen the notices. Katharine is getting here tomorrow morning on the sleeper and will probably have them with her.

I think an awful lot of John's stuff is going to stand the nasty test of time. His ear was so wonderful—better than anybody's I can think of, better than Lardner, O'Hara, or any of those contenders. And when I think of all the recent dead ones whose names still mean something but whose works are lost in the files, the Brouns and the Woollcotts and the rest of them, it makes me feel good that McNulty is going to be more durable in black and white. I guess I told you about the automobile ride with John and Johnny which ended with a bedtime story, designed to soothe and regale the little boy—a long, detailed and beautifully spoken recital of morningtime in the home of a horseplayer. It was both funny and touching and although I would not be able to repeat any of it with any accuracy, I haven't forgotten any of it, either.

Much love from
Andy

• *Eugene Kinkead, a* New Yorker *editor and contributor, had written a profile of the great spider authority, Dr. Alexander Petrunkevitch. White intended to pass along any useful information to Arthur Zegart, who hoped to film* Charlotte's Web.

To EUGENE KINKEAD

North Brooklin, Maine
13 August 1956

Dear Gene:

Thinking of spiders with a cameraman's problems in mind, do you know how much they are good for under studio conditions? I mean, is an orb weaver likely to spin and repair her web in confinement, as in a terrarium?

I am trying to advise and assist a man who aspires to make a naturalistic movie (no animation) of "Charlotte's Web." He will need all sorts of spider shots—construction of web, repair, fly in web, wrapping up of fly, spinning egg case, laying eggs, emergence of young spiders, maybe even ballooning if it is possible to photograph. I am trying to figure out the best way to go about it. If you have any ideas, from your Petrunkevitch association or your easy-going personal relationship with spiders themselves, would appreciate your word on the subject. I have already worked out the problem of getting a word spun in the middle of the web: I intend to get Daise Terry to spin it.

As you have perhaps noticed, I am always in some kind of trouble.

Yrs in Arachne's toils,
Elwyn

To KATHARINE S. WHITE

North Brooklin
[September 15?, 1956]
Saturday morn

Dear K:

. . . Joe and Allene moved into their place yesterday afternoon, taking me somewhat by surprise. I didn't know, when you phoned yesterday morning, that they planned to leave. They just sort of glided away taking the two children and not much else. Everything seems to be going—stove, refrigerator, brand new Maytag washing machine, lights, and water. I stopped by for a few minutes at the end of the afternoon to make a gift of eggs and beer and found Joe and Allene seated in apparent tranquillity in the kitchen. Steve was in the bathroom brushing his teeth. Wash was hanging on the line. That house has tide in front of it and Tide in back of it. When Steve came out of the bathroom his hair was sopping wet—his idea of brushing his teeth was to turn a glass of water over the top of his head, for thoroughness. . . .

The weather has suddenly turned very fallish and the outlook is clearly end-of-season—front door of the yacht club locked, three or four rowboats still hanging to the float half full of water with the oars sloshing around in the bottom. I think Joe and Tue [Wearn] leave today. I haven't decided about my own departure yet. I feel pretty good, although tired from the labors of the summer, and there are a few things I want to get done. . . .

Mrs. T and Mrs. F[1] are fine and everything is good here except that

1. Claribel Tainter, housekeeper, and Mrs. Arlene Freethy, the cook.

you are not here, and when you are not here the place has a hole right down through it from attic to cellar. I still mourn my goose, and I miss you every hour.

Love,
A

To STANLEY HART WHITE

[New York]
[September 27, 1956]
Thursday

Dear Bun:

This is the way to put your head in traction.

You need a weight of about fifteen pounds, and in your case I have shown an electric iron. I plugged it in just to give the whole experience an extra dimension. In Maine, I use a boat anchor because I happen to have a boat anchor. You have to buy the head halter—at one of those surgical appliance places that have a window display featuring bedpans and artificial legs. It might be a sensible idea to pick up an artificial leg while you are in there buying the halter, to have in reserve. Head traction is quite pleasant once you get the hang of it. All it does, I think, is to exercise the big neck muscles that have lain idle since we all came down out of trees. The dose is ten minutes of traction, two or three times a day. I usually follow it with two or three highballs, but I follow almost everything with that. The thing I like best about traction is that it takes place in the barn. I never use it in New York because it would seem inappropriate. I climb trees instead.

We are going to Maine by train tomorrow night to spend about a week, and will then return to town. Joe is working in a small boatyard in Brooklin and has rented a house in the village.[1] A partially blown-out hurricane seems to be coming up the coast just in time to make our journey a memorable one, and the rain and the wind have already arrived in Manhattan.

Haven't any particular news at the moment but just wanted to be sure you got into traction smoothly. If you added a table and got the adjustment just right, it is conceivable that you could take your pants off and have Blanche iron them *while* traction was going on. I never tried it, but I use a boat anchor.

Yrs,
En

To J. DONALD ADAMS

[New York]
September 28th, 1956

Dear Mr. Adams:

Thanks for your letter inviting me to join the Committee of the Arts and Sciences for Eisenhower.

I must decline, for secret reasons.

Sincerely,
E. B. White

To KATHARINE S. WHITE

[North Brooklin, Me.]
1 November (bang bang!) [1956]

Dear K:

The latest *Reader's Digest* says people should actually *express* their love for one another, otherwise it withers. So I will just mention that I love you. I always do everything the *Digest* tells me to do.

Have had a perfect trip so far. Fern went into the shallow muddy water Tuesday morning, with workmen actually at work on deck while

---

1. Joel White, on completing his military service, returned to Brooklin and found a job with Arno Day, owner of the boatyard in Center Harbor. Day was a good builder of wooden boats and Joel, with a degree in naval architecture, was eager to learn the practical side of construction.

she was being launched.[1] I watched, saying a little prayer for her and chuckling at the same time—the way you acted at Nancy's wedding. It was very comical and exciting to me. And then the mast was stepped, then Aage came whirling out from Boston and leapt into action, and we rigged her with odds and ends of string and twine and anything we could find, and bent the sails on. Before you could catch your breath, Aage had hoisted the sails, and I jumped aboard in my shirt sleeves— a perfect Indian summer day—and Aage backed the jib, and we were off, narrowly clearing a mud bank and headed for a nearby causeway. Variable winds swept us back and forth, dodging boats, moorings, mud banks, government markers, and flotsam with here and there a little jetsam. Fern whistled along with hardly any air in her sails, and left the smoothest wake I ever saw behind me—you would think nothing at all had been through the water. With Aage at the tiller we ran hard up on an invisible mudbank. "Do you suppose you could run that little engine?" he asked, drawing hard on his pipe. "Certainly," I said. I pressed the starter, there was a cry of response from the Palmer, and I threw her into reverse, and we backed off the mud and glided away under sail again. It was a wonderful day. Fern is almost unbearably beautiful, and easy to manage. And comfortable. And roomy. You would hardly know there was an engine in her, so nicely is the engine concealed. When Aage and I got back to Boston, on your father's elevated railway, I invited him to the Lincolnshire lounge for a drink and we lifted our glasses to the boat. Also I had a nice talk with him about naval architecture in general, and he opened up, about Joe and everything. He said nobody should design boats for a living unless he truly loves to create something and is willing to stand the ups and downs of a luxury business. And he said yard work, such as Joe is doing, is very important.

Yesterday I started to fly to Maine, got to the airport, asked for my flight and was told that my plane was "overhead." "Overhead?" I said. "Oh, yes," the man said. "They can't get down now on account of this ground fog." So I went away from there and found a nice Boston & Maine train that was not overhead, and had a beautiful quiet trip on the little old ground, through the nice woods and fields.

Today am hunting steer calves while every other man in Maine is hunting bucks and does. Men regard me as a real daft one, and I guess I am a daft one all right. But I have a pretty boat and a pretty wife and I will find a couple of calves, and I will get along some how. I heard the

1. *Fern* was a 20-foot sloop, a double-ender, built for White in Denmark from a design by Aage Nielsen. The launching took place from a shipyard a few miles south of Boston.

President on the air last night and thought he did all right, but we are certainly on one of Mr. Dulles's well-loved brinks. Apparently the Labor party in England is going to make it tough for Eden.

I am booked on the State of Maine for Saturday night, so will see you Sunday for breakfast.

Much love,
A

To ROBERT N. S. WHITELAW

[North Brooklin, Me.]
January 2, 1957

Dear Mr. Whitelaw:

Very pleasant to hear from you again, and thanks for your kind wishes.

Here on the nearby parkways we now have wayside coffee shrines, where motorists who suspect themselves of driving too recklessly can stop to pray and sip. I see a tremendous future for the railroads, which resolutely resist change, even though the Pullman Company now calls the toilet room the "annex." I set out for Maine by train on the night of December 20th (Bedroom B, Car 1240) and reached Bangor just sixteen hours later, in the middle of the following afternoon, having made good exactly thirty miles an hour. I was much impressed by the railroad's feeling for tradition, and its unwillingness to throw out more than one mail sack at a time, in the days of the intercontinental missile. Put your money, if you have any, in the railroads.

Sincerely,
E. B. White

To FAITH MC NULTY MARTIN

North Brooklin
2 Jan [1957]

Dear Faith:

What do you mean you want to "let us know that you've gotten married"—don't you think I have my own sources of information and that I keep track of you day and night? I would have written sooner but I got a Christmas tree ornament stuck in my pancreas, and it kept winking on and off, and I was too distracted to write letters. As for giving you my blessing, anybody who can combine marriage and Christmas is a proper genius and you not only have my blessing but I am lost in admiration. As far as that goes, I have always been lost in admiration— which was obviously Martin's condition, too—and any blessing I could bestow on you would be relatively useless as it would be tinged with envy for this Martin. But if it's my blessing you have set your little heart on, then by God my blessing you shall have, useless though it may be around the place and probably a great dust-catcher, too. Your letter sounded as though you and Johnny were fine and happy, and that made me feel fine and happy, and in addition to these crazy blessings of mine I send you all my love and best wishes for this wonderful occasion. I can't stand people being unmarried, it just makes me edgy, and besides that I was worried about you and was hoping that your life would get straightened around again and in the best possible and practically only way. Which has happened and which makes me delighted.

That Christmas greeting you mentioned in your letter was one of the damndest offbeat literary snarls I ever got myself embroiled in.[1] Sullivan can pick and choose and when a name comes up that works he can include it and when a name doesn't work, he can just pitch it out. But not old White. The personnel sheet (actually 4 sheets, single spaced) was what I set out to go by, and little did I know what was ahead. . . . A couple of times I gave up and saw Katharine quietly reach for the supply of personal greeting cards which would have to be dispatched if I failed my loony mission. Then I would go back and pick up the beat again, between visits from the doctor and the laying on of his hands. Some higher power, plus my great love for the staff of *The New Yorker*, kept me at it, and I finally got it in the mail—with only one name misspelled—and a non-staff member at that, Vincent Sheean.

My pain departed on the 24th, so I set to work drinking and laughing and had a fine Christmas.

Please give my warmest greetings and felicitations to Mr. Richard Martin and tell him I received a table saw with a tilting arbor for Christmas and he can make use of it any time he can get down this way. Best to Johnny and lots of love from

Yrs,
Andy

To **ROBERT M. HUTCHINS**

[New York]
January 4, 1957

Dear Mr. Hutchins:

My ideas about civil liberties are pretty much limited to what I know intimately, which is the press.[1] At the moment I'm not in good

---

1. For Christmas in 1956, White wrote a rhymed greeting that included the name of everyone on *The New Yorker's* personnel sheet.

---

1. Hutchins, president of the Fund for the Republic, had asked White to comment on a prospectus Hutchins had written setting forth the Fund's program on civil liberties.

health and for that reason, if for no other, cannot offer you much in the way of constructive criticism. Your outline certainly seems comprehensive and good.

Under the press, I presume the Fund will examine the tendency of newspapers to die or merge, leaving a city like Bangor, Maine, without an opposition press. Under television I should think the Fund might notice the fact that performers of all kinds (newscasters, actors, singers, entertainers, commentators) have been persuaded to speak the commercial. The sound of news and the sound of soap are a blur in the ear —an unhealthy condition essentially, I think. Under privacy, the captive audience is a field worth study. The New Yorker, as you may recall, did a bit of spade work in this area.

I don't know how much teaching the Fund's program calls for, in proportion to study. Studies tend to get over-subtilized, sometimes. Teaching, I think, can well stand great simplification and can begin with the primary grade sort of instruction, since the majority of people have a rather shaky conception of the anatomy of liberty. There is nothing much to be "taught" about equality—you either believe it or you don't. But there is much that can be taught about rights and about liberty, including the basic stuff: that a right derives from a responsibleness, and that men become free as they become willing to accept restrictions on their acts. These are elementary concepts, of course, but an awful lot of youngsters seem to emerge from high school and even from college without acquiring them. Until they *are* acquired, the more subtle, intricate, and delicate problems of civil rights and freedom of speech are largely incomprehensible.

Sincerely,
E. B. White

To ALICE SHERMAN

[New York]
January 9, 1957

Dear Alice:

Thanks for the letter. I don't believe I can write a book about a horse because I don't know any horse.

Sincerely,
E. B. White

• *Odette Arnaud, a French literary agent, represented White in negotiations with the French publisher Hachette, which was bringing out a new edition of* Charlotte's Web *with new illustrations. The first French edition had appeared in 1954 with the original Garth Williams drawings.*

To ODETTE ARNAUD

[New York]
January 25, 1957

Dear Miss Arnaud:

Thank you for submitting the illustrations for "Charlotte's Web" (Les Aventures de Narcisse).

I would like to make one suggestion which Hachette's artist may find helpful. A spider's legs are attached to the thorax, which is the section between the head and the abdomen. None of the legs originates in the abdomen. It is a very common mistake, in spider drawings, to have the legs misplaced in this way.

With best regards, I am

Yours sincerely,
E. B. White

• *Sol Linowitz, a lawyer, had submitted an "Amplification" letter to* The New Yorker *taking issue with some of White's arguments in the "Letter from the East" in the December 15, 1956, issue. The magazine had not published Linowitz's letter, which prompted him to write another.*

To SOL M. LINOWITZ

[New York]
[February 1957]

Dear Mr. Linowitz:

I do not participate in making editorial judgments, but devote myself to writing and contributing, so the question of whether your letter was to be used was out of my realm. I can say, in general, that while the New Yorker occasionally publishes "amplifications" they are usually on questions of fact, not opinion.

At any rate, I want to thank you for your letter. I think you have me wrong when you say that I argued that the dangers of war could be dispelled if the words of the Charter were different. I don't think peace is that simple. Nor was I arguing for perfection—merely for clarity and for certain prerequisites of membership being included in the Charter. I quite agree with you that constant use is what makes charters and constitutions come alive and take on meaning: but to begin with, they must not be full of ambiguities and deliberate loopholes, and I think the United Nations Charter is, to some degree.

Sincerely,
E. B. White

• *The following letter was written on White's arrival in New York after an eventful journey that had begun with a flat tire on the way to the railroad station in Bangor. White had transferred to a taxi, leaving Henry Allen struggling with a faulty jack.*

To HENRY ALLEN

[New York]
22 February 1957

Dear Henry:

I hated to drive off and leave you lying in the ditch with all your troubles. I figure the wear and tear on your good trousers will set you back at least five dollars and the wear and tear on your nervous system another five, so I am enclosing ten, in the hope of making partial reparation for the damages. The thing I really worried about was that you were going to get bumped off by some passing motorist. Hope you will drop me a line and let me know how you made out.

My departure from Bangor was sensational. The taxi driver had to slow down to 25 miles an hour all the way through Brewer, and then we hit a traffic snarl at the intersection near the new bridge, and the car ahead of us seemed incapable of making a left turn. My watch said 6:30 as we got through the green light. Crossing the bridge, the telephone in the taxi started squawking, and the dispatcher began chatting with the driver, asking him where he was and how he was getting along. "We're all right," said the driver. "We're on the bridge." I looked at my watch again and it said 6:31. We screamed into the station yard, jumped out, and the engineer saw us coming and I guess he took pity on me. They had the train all locked up, ready to go, the bell was ringing for the start. The taxi driver grabbed my bags and whirled down the platform, and I trotted behind, carrying my fish pole and the Freethy lunch box. The trainman saw this strange apparition appearing, and he opened up the coach door. I plunged on board and the driver threw the bags on, and away we went. I had no ticket, no Pullman receipt for my room, just a fish pole. For the next hour or two, I was known all through the train as "that man." But the porter got interested in my case, the way porters do, and he stuck me in the only empty bedroom and told me to sit there till we got to Waterville. The conductor stopped by, every few minutes, to needle me, and between visits I would close the door and eat a sandwich and mix myself a whiskey-and-milk, in an attempt to recuperate from my ordeal. At Waterville the conductor charged in and said: "Put on your hat and follow me!" Then he dashed away, with me after him. He jumped off the train and disappeared into the darkness. When I located him in the waiting room he looked sternly at me and said: "Are you the man?"

"I'm the man," I replied.

"Well," he said, "go back and sit in the room. It looks as though Bangor didn't sell it. But we'll know at Portland."

So I sat in the room some more and had another drink. At Portland, the porter said: "Get something on and follow me!" He dashed away and I ran after him. He beat me to the station by twenty yards, but I caught up with him at the Pullman desk, where the conductor and the Pullman conductor sat side-by-side, reviewing my case. It was a little like a court martial, but I kept forking out the money, and the porter swiped a pencil and drew a line in the chart opposite Bedroom B. And finally the case was dismissed, and they handed me a receipt, and I found my room again on the train—which had meantime been switched onto another track, just for the hell of it. Anyway, I made it to New York, and had a good night's sleep into the bargain, once I got the railroad people quieted down. I guess the next time you and I start for Bangor, it better be at 4:30, and with a jack that fits under the car.

Yrs,
EBW

To BRISTOW ADAMS

229 East 48 Street
23 February [1957]

Dear B. A.:

For a man who has been cut down by about 50 per cent, you write a mighty fine letter, and I was awfully pleased to get it; I realize what it cost you in labor. I am sending you, under separate cover, a bee, to stir up the air in your room.[1] He is not a real bee but has a pleasant personality, and comes from Denmark. If you have to lie in bed all day, looking up, then you need something to stare at, and I guess a bee is as good as anything. I hope he will provide a slight link with the outside world which you love so well.

I am just back from Maine, where I spent five or six days admiring the winter scene and visiting with my son and my two grandchildren. Previous to that, I was in the hospital here for a short tussle with the

---

1. White's teacher and friend was in a nursing home near Ithaca.

doctors, but I escaped, and not much the worse for the experience.[2] They gave me a general anesthetic, and under the influence of it I started to write again, and have been writing ever since—it was sodium pentothal, which is said to be the truth drug. I don't know which makes me more miserable: writing, or being unable to write. Both are bad. My doctor flew to the Virgin Islands last night for a change of scene.

The city is quite warm and springlike on this February afternoon, and it seems to be full of out-of-towners who have drifted in for the Washington's Birthday weekend. It is pleasant, but Maine was more fun. My neighbor's sheep barn was full of new lambs, the cove was still partly frozen over, there was snow in woods and pasture, and the delicate footprints of the fox on his way across the pond. I hope all goes as well with you as can reasonably be expected, and I'm looking forward to the next "Plantations."[3]

Love,
Andy

TO NAN HART

[New York]
February 25, 1957

Dear Nan:

I am quite late in answering your letter, but I had a short bout in the hospital, and then went to Maine for a while. I'm distressed to hear about your failing eyesight, but I must say that you seem to be taking it in your stride, and your handwriting is practically as good as ever. I had no trouble at all with your letter.

My friend James Thurber is almost completely blind—he lost an eye when he was a child, and the other eye gradually went bad. For a blind man, he leads an amazingly active life, both professionally and socially. He turns out twice as much writing as I do, who can see. And he gets about and goes wherever he feels like going.

You asked whether any of my stuff had been included in the Talking Books. The most recently published book of mine, called "The Second Tree from the Corner," was recorded, and I presume it is obtainable from the Library of Congress or wherever you get those books. It is a collection of miscellaneous stories, poems, essays, and comments. Some of them might amuse you. And it includes "Farewell, My Lovely," the piece about the Model T Ford in which I arrived at Dot S Dot in the

---

2. A bronchoscopy, to find the cause of some trouble White was having with his throat.

3. *The Cornell Plantations*, a quarterly which Professor Adams had edited before his illness.

wonderful summer of 1922. Do you remember how you applied horse liniment to my dislocated elbow and succeeded in straightening it out? Another thing I remember well are those breakfasts that started with stewed rhubarb covered with heavy cream. But I mustn't harp on my ambrosial past.

Tell Harry that he and I are at last in the same business. I acquired two white-faced calves last fall, on my place in Maine. One is a heifer, one is a steer. They are growing well, and although we have had a very cold winter in Maine, and they have access to hay in the barn, they seem to spend a great deal of time down in the wooded pasture, browsing like deer. They haven't cost me, in feed, anything like what I imagined they would. If the heifer develops well, I may breed her, although she is a cross between a Hereford and a milking shorthorn.

I still continue to work for *The New Yorker*, but not as hard as I used to, and Katharine still holds down her job and works harder than ever. We both own about three shares of stock in the Northern Pacific Railroad—which should be a good excuse to ride out to Montana and take another look at the Crazies.

Yrs affectionately,
Andy

To **H. A. STEVENSON**

25 West 43
2 April 1957

Dear Steve:

I was overwhelmed to get the little book, filched from the library, and I hope I deserve it. Last night I went through it, seeing Will in every word and phrase and line—in Charles's friend, in Burns's poems, in the comma after each term except the last. What a book, what a man! Will so loved the clear, the brief, the bold—and his book is clear, brief, bold.

It may be that I'll try to do a piece on "The Elements of Style" for *The New Yorker*. Perhaps you can fill me in on a few matters on which I am vague or uninformed (My memory is poor and needs jolting). Do you recall the name of the course known as English 20?[1] Was it called "English usage and style"? Was the "little book" on sale at bookstores in Ithaca, and were students in English 20 asked to buy the book? The title page says "Privately Printed, Ithaca, N. Y., 1918" and overleaf there is the mark of the "Press of W.P. Humphrey, Geneva, N. Y." Would this mean that Will paid the bill for getting out the book, or would the University have picked up the tab? I am, as you see, ignorant on such matters. Do you know whether the book was used in colleges

---

1. The course was English 8, not English 20.

and universities other than Cornell? I take it no use is made of it by the English Department in this day and age; it would be considered too arbitrary, too cocky, too short. ("Omit needless words. Vigorous writing is concise.") Did you come out of English 20 owning a copy of the little book? Do you still have your copy? For some reason that escapes me, I think I never had a copy of the book, even when I was a student in the course. I could be wrong about this, but I seem to remember being somewhat baffled (at first) by frequent references to "the little book," not knowing what the "little book" was. Even now, I am not certain whether these pages come back to me as pages that I studied, or whether I simply remember the contents as they were reproduced in class by Will himself, who must have followed the book pretty closely. ("Make definite assertions.")

If you can answer, and feel like answering, any of these tedious questions, I would be delighted to hear from you.[2] Hell, I would be delighted to hear from you anyway. ("The lefthand version gives the impression that the writer is undecided or timid; he seems unable or afraid to choose one form of expression and hold to it.") . . .

Thanks again, Steve, for this gift. This is a late day (I almost said a "very" late day, but Will hated "very") for me to meet up with "The Elements of Style" by William Strunk, Jr. I shall treasure the book as long as there are any elements of life in my bones. Hope you and Mildred will get to Maine again. If you do, you will get fed, not merely ginned; and I will put you in my 18-foot sloop and whirl you round and round. ("Place the emphatic words of a sentence at the end.")

Yrs gratefully,
Andy

To FRANK SULLIVAN

229 East 48
[April 20, 1957]
Saturday

Dear Frank:

Tomorrow will be a grim Easter Day for you, with no Kate to share it with you,[1] and by the time this tardy letter reaches you, it will be another day. I would have written you before this, but have been sick abed with a cold (partially induced by standing in the draughty night while a

---

2. Stevenson replied but didn't have all the answers. The Macmillan Company later discovered that the book—first privately printed by Strunk in 1918—had subsequently undergone some transformations. It had been revised and circulated for many years before White got his hands on it, but was still, in 1957, unheard of outside the academic world.

1. Kate was Sullivan's sister, of whom he was very fond and with whom he lived when he retired to Saratoga Springs.

Japanese exploded two tons of fireworks over the North River),[2] and am still languishing. K and I dispatched a flowering plant, or a pot of flowers, or some such thing, to you this week, for installation at 135, in the hope of making Easter a trifle less cheerless. I hope the gift arrived in time.

I, of course, feel cheated in that I never met Kate. For a woman who was unmet, she had a remarkably strong personality. Ross and Gus used to tell me of her, and the rest I picked up from your own affectionate chronicles of life on Lincoln Avenue. But personality or no, I have been aware of how much a part of you she was, and so have been thinking very much of you this week, since K brought me the news of your great loss. To stand alone must be the greatest jolt and the greatest challenge of all, and my only reason for writing this letter, aside from sending my love, is in the hope of assuring you (as so many others will be doing) that you stand in quite a crowd—of those who cherish you in friendship undiminished by distance and by time. I can't say this very well but I feel it very strongly.

I pray that your immediate sorrow will be, in the long run, therapeutic, and that the awful anxieties that went with Kate's illness now being over, you will be able to recapture your spirits and even start tangling with a typewriter—which is sometimes the best therapy of all. (I am not one to talk, as I haven't been able to look mine in the face for quite a while—but I still think it's true.)

Please forgive the inadequacies of this letter, and remember that K and I have you ever in our minds.

Love,
Andy

P.S. It is also necessary at this season to establish firm emotional connections with a major league ball club, to share in the agonies of their defeats and the ecstasies of their triumphs. Without these simple marriages, none of us could survive.

• *Under the heading "Answers to Hard Questions," White wrote a piece on city pigeons, which appeared in* The New Yorker *for May 4, 1957. It elicited from Margaret Lieb, a biology professor at Brandeis University, a poem about the untidiness of pigeons, ending with the stanza:*

> This is the reason for the lack of love
> Twixt man and pigeons: while he likes the symbol
> Of grace and peace, man, painting his own picture,
> Resents all contributions from above.

---

2. To celebrate the U.S. World Trade Fair.

To MARGARET LIEB

[New York]
May 13, 1957

Dear Miss Lieb:

Mens sana in corpore sano
Can always stand a pinch of guano.

Sincerely,
E. B. White

To GERARD W. SPEYER

[New York]
May 13, 1957

Dear Mr. Speyer:

I don't feel that I know the answer to your question. My own disinclination to allow anything of mine to be published in Curtain countries arises partly from bewilderment, partly from a natural caution. Further, I am monolingual and have no way of knowing whether a translation is faithful to the original, short of hiring someone to determine the matter for me.

In theory, I favor the widest possible circulation of literary material that has merit, and this would include the crossing of national borders and curtains. But I am well enough acquainted with Communist zeal to know that the Communists are eager to get hold of the work of non-Communist writers, whenever they see a way to turn such work to their own uses and advantage. So I have been reluctant to give them a crack at mine. I've had several books published in foreign countries (England, France, Norway, Japan, and so on) and my experience is that when a book goes into another language and another country, it seems to swim out of my ken, and I never know what in hell is going on, assuming anything is. If this is true of England and France, I figure that it would be even more the case in Hungary or Russia.

But I say, I don't know the answer. There are arguments for a course of action opposite to mine. Maybe it's partly a matter of temperament. I think perhaps my attitude is simply: "You take down that curtain, you stop jamming that radio, and you can have my books."

Sincerely,
E. B. White

P.S. An example of the way the Communist press grabs something and gives it a twist is the case of a Chas. Addams cartoon which the Hungarian press got hold of. It was a typical Addams picture—two monstrous little children playing with a toy guillotine. In Hungary, this was, I am told, published to illustrate the way children in America are brought up.

To AARON HARDY ULM

[New York]
May 16, 1957

Dear Dr. Ulm:

The pigeon stands somewhere between the swan, which is fiercely monogamous, and the domestic rooster, to whom one dame is like another. Pigeons pair off, two and two, and in his fashion the male pigeon is faithful to his Cynara.

By and large, after a male has succeeded in dazzling the little hen of his choice, he steadies down and is thereafter concerned with her alone, and with the nest that they build and tend together. This is *usually* the case, but as in most communities, there are some sports, some divergent personalities. I kept pigeons when I was a boy, and my recollection is that sometimes a cock pigeon would gather to himself two wives, and I'm not sure but that the reverse is true, too.

To answer your question: The male pigeon knows perfectly well whose eggs he is sitting on—he is sitting on the ones to which he has himself imparted vigor.

Sincerely,
E. B. White

To C. J. BROWN

[New York]
May 17, 1957

Dear Dr. Brown:

I am the lad who wrote ". . . the first faint flush of yellow jaundice" and I had quite a time getting it into the magazine over the objections of the copy desk. The cry of "redundant" was raised against me, and against it.

But while there are no other shades of jaundice than yellow, it is also true that the phrase "the yellow jaundice" is a common expression—one I have heard many a time. I think I heard it first when I was a child, living in a suburb, and I have heard it many times among country people in country circumstances. It is a little like "a red, red rose," or "a little small dog." Anyway, it wasn't an "error" in that it was written deliberately.

Thank you for your watchfulness. You say you have an advantage, in that you are a doctor. But I have an advantage, too, in that I am not. I just listen to what people say, and sometimes, when a colloquialism serves my purpose (or seems to), I use it.

Yrs for healthy livers,
E. B. White

• *Martin Dibner, Howard Cushman's son-in-law, invited White to accompany him on a canoe trip, one hundred years after Thoreau's last venture into the Maine woods.*

To MARTIN DIBNER

[New York]
May 29, 1957

Dear Mr. Dibner:

I, too, think with some longing of the Allagash and the East Branch. My longing is tempered with uneasiness, however. If I were only as old as Thoreau was when he and that Indian set out, your invitation would be irresistible. Thoreau was just a youngster—a man in his forties, a man whose paddle had never dipped into a martini. I am no longer in the same boat, or canoe. My Allagash is a river almost without current, almost without mosquitoes. In short, I am a dead voyageur, and you have burdened your canoe with a corpse.

But thanks for the try.

Sincerely,
E. B. White

To ROBERT MOULTHROP

[New York]
May 31, 1957

Dear Mr. Moulthrop:

Thanks for your letter. I'm very glad to know that Stuart and Charlotte can take some of the pressure off an adolescent. I haven't been an adolescent for a number of years but I can remember that the pressure was fierce.

Sincerely,
E. B. White

To KATHARINE S. WHITE

[North Brooklin, Me.]
[June 1957]
Tuesday after lunch

Dear K:

I have time for just a quick note B. F. (before Forrest).[1] My rail journey was fine—they changed me into a room and I slept all night. But Bangor gave me a belly ache (beef in casserole at the Penobscot Exchange) and in Brewer, entering an upholstery shop in search of slip-covers for the car, I slipped in a mudhole and darn near pulled my insides out of me. So when I arrived home, in rain and cold and wind, I collapsed in coils and am just beginning to emerge. Today is

---

1. For many years Forrest Allen delivered the mail.

lovely, with a warm sun. August [a dachshund puppy] is thriving—slept all night in the plant room without disturbing anyone. He is big, bouncy, and very able. Another Fred, I would say, but without such a heavy charge of original sin. This morning I visited Allene and the children on their sunny doorstep, which is one of the pleasantest places in town for sitting. Martha is really something to see now, with her pony tail, her healthy color, and her vast affection and good will. Steve looks very fine in a new, close haircut. Allene was in the shirt you sent from Sarasota and appeared happy and healthy. Have not seen Joe yet but have talked with him on the phone, and they are coming to dinner soon. Some asparagus has been put in the freeze already. The house is in a welter of curtaining. Our crab apple tree has never had so many blossoms. A borrowed hen is on 12 bantam eggs in a horse stall, and I have a broody of my own, which I shall set tonight on 5 goose eggs. Yesterday there were wild ducks on the pond, swollen (the pond) by recent rains. Everything is green and enticing, but the weather has been on the cold side, and I don't think lilacs and apple blossoms are appreciably ahead of normal years—which is a break for you. Have not heard from Arthur yet, but imagine he will call tonight. Wearns due here Thursday, I am told, for a brief spell, so I guess I may see them.

Must go now, must arise and go on my many errands. I plan to start for New York in the car on Friday, arriving Saturday.

Love,

A

• *Thurber and White were approached by Twentieth Century–Fox about the possibility of filming* Is Sex Necessary? *Both men were wary.*

To JAMES THURBER

25 West 43rd Street
1 July [1957]

Dear Jim:

You got any idea what sort of monkeyshines 20th Century Fox has in mind? I presume Cary Grant would play Dr. Zaner and Sophia Loren would be Early Woman. The script would be by Tennessee Schmalhausen, and you and I would stand outside in the lobby making fudge, as a diversionary device.

The one thing that's completely clear in Klinger's letter is the phrase "at a low figure." It is like Hollywood to expect to get the only complete survey of the entire sexual scene at a low figure.

Yrs suspiciously,
Andy

To **RICHARD L. STROUT**

[New York]
July 10, 1957

Dear Dick:

Greetings. Your letter to that poor fellow who is trying to diagnose my prose style was very generous. You had one fact wrong, though. The original MS, which you said was destroyed "many, many years ago," is on my desk.[1] Just out of curiosity I walked into our library a few minutes ago and asked the girl if it existed and she said, "Oh, sure. It's right here." And she reached over somewhere under a couple of boxes and handed it to me. It is MS #2442. Attached to it are a dozen or so "opinion sheets"—one editor talking to another. Also your letter to Ross, dated Mar. 21, 1936.

I asked the girl where *my* original typescript was, and she said, "Well that's a different matter. Yours would be in the cellar, and it's out of my jurisdiction."

Just thought you'd like to know how we handle things around here. I'm a cellar boy. You're right on deck.

Yours faithfully,
Andy

To **FRANK SULLIVAN**

[New York]
16 July [1957]

Dear Francis:

Everything worked out just as you planned.[1] It was wonderful. The years fell away from my shoulders (along with a little dandruff), the cares and miseries vanished (along with a couple of gin-tonics), and I became excessively beautiful and dangerous to women—attractive, badly informed, overdressed, the whole works. You forgot just one thing—you forgot to get rid of the mosquitoes for me. Turtle Bay in July is the mosquito's nursery and I am the mosquito's baby. The truth is I came perilously close to missing attaining age 58 by the narrow squeak of just one night. I had perfected the technique of killing mosquitoes with a face towel, and on the night of July 10, spurred by many a small triumph, I climbed up on Katharine's swivel desk chair, holding the towel in my right, hanging carefully to a nearby bookshelf with my left. I went into my windup, delivered, and I was wide and outside. As

---

1. The "original manuscript" was a piece about the Model T which Strout had submitted to *The New Yorker*. It was the piece from which "Farewell, My Lovely" by "Lee Strout White" grew.

---

1. Sullivan had sent White a birthday letter, cataloguing the good things he wished for him.

the mosquito passed me overhead, flying fast, I instinctively took another swing at him, and this time I forgot to hold on to the bookshelf. The swivel chair—which must be the pride of the Timken Roller Bearing Company—did a full turn, and I began a descent that came so near impaling me on the point of a bridge lamp that I am still shaking all over. On July 11, I was still alive, but badly bitten and badly shaken.

Anyway, your letter carrying birthday greetings was wonderful to get, and I can't expect you to think of everything. I was truly amazed that you had thought of my birthday at all. My wife remembered it and took me to a play about a man who arrived on earth from a planet where the people had given up sex. (She's such a card.)

For us the rather melancholy business of breaking up our 48th Street apartment has begun. We walk by a chair and put the finger on it. We glance at a shelf of books and without a word from either of us, some book bites the dust but doesn't know it yet. In the fall, all survivors will be loaded into a van and will start for Maine. And there, at the other end, the work will begin of changing "Joe's room" into a "television room," and other transformations of a doubtful sort. Where the piano will end up I don't know, unless in the henpen. There is certainly no room in the house for it.

Thank you, thank you, sweet my Frank, for your lovely letter. And Happy Social Security to both of us, you a little sooner than I, perhaps, but no less social, no less secure.

Love from lucky old
Andy

To J. G. CASE

25 West 43rd Street
New York
July 29, 1957

Dear Mr. Case:

Thanks for your letter.

I'm enclosing my copy of "The Elements of Style." You can see at a glance that Professor Strunk omitted needless words. Whether the book has other virtues that would recommend it to teachers of English, I don't feel qualified to say. Some of its charm and value for me unquestionably derives from my memory of the man himself—his peculiar delivery of these rules of usage and the importance with which he managed to invest the subject. Sometimes the book, like the man, seems needlessly compressed, and it is undeniably notional. On the other hand, it contains several short essays that are gems; they still tickle me. My guess is that Will Strunk had a particular reason for writing this handbook: I think he felt the need of a labor-saving device in correcting papers. With the "little book" in the hands of his students, he could simply write in the margin of a theme: "See Rule 2."

Should you decide that you want to re-issue the book, I would feel justified in giving Macmillan permission to use my piece only if I was satisfied that the Strunk heirs were happy about the project. Professor Strunk's widow is alive, I believe—living at 380 Crown Street, Meriden, Conn. There is a son Oliver Strunk who is on the Princeton faculty, 80 College Avenue. And there is another son, Edwin, with the Chrysler Corporation. He lives at 1594 Penistone Road, Birmingham, Mich. Whether the copyright is in effect or not, I would expect you to get permission from the estate and pay royalties to the estate.

As for me, I think I should receive a share of the royalties, and I'd like your suggestion as to what sort of division you would think fair to all concerned.[1] The *New Yorker*, incidentally, doesn't enter the picture —it does not take any reprint money. Never has. The contributor gets all. (It's a very lovable old weekly.) See Page 40 of the little book—use of the word "very."

As for my essay, I'm quite willing to fix the first sentence (burn fewer books). I am also willing to do whatever I can to make the piece useful and suitable as an introduction. I may even have a bit more to say on the subject of rhetoric, now that I am suddenly faced with this unexpected audience.

I'm leaving for Maine on Wednesday night. My address there is North Brooklin. Please take good care of "The Elements of Style."

Sincerely,
E. B. White

To **WAYNE MORSE**

[New York]
September 17, 1957

Dear Senator Morse:

Thanks for your letter and the copy of your remarks on fallout. I'm glad you plan to open up the subject in the Senate in January.

It seems to me people in all countries, with the possible exception of Japan, accept without challenge the authority of anybody at all to contaminate sea, air, and earth. This is a "right" that is as dubious as it is catastrophic. If national security results at last in general unwholesomeness, surely none of us will be secure. We will simply all be sick.

Sincerely yours,
E. B. White

---

1. Royalties are divided equally between White and the Strunk estate.

• *In September 1957, Dr. Frank Barron, director of the Creative Writing Project at the University of California Institute of Personality Assessment and Research, wrote White asking him to come to Berkeley, along with twenty-nine other individuals, and be studied, as part of a research program funded by the Carnegie Corporation. Dr. Barron, in describing the project, wrote: " . . . we have conducted research on such topics as these : independence of judgment and resistance to conformity pressures, social responsibility, motivation towards professional achievement, personal soundness, recovery from neurosis, complexity in personality structure, and esthetic and ethical sensitivity."*

To FRANK BARRON

[New York]
September 18, 1957

Dear Doctor Barron:

Thanks for your kind and unexpected invitation to come to California and be investigated. I shall have to decline, although the trip sounds exciting.

I don't suppose I should feel any deep disinclination to be studied, but the fact is I do. Even if you were to find that I had made no recovery from my neurosis, and that my personality was complex (which it may well be), and that I was sound, sensitive, and well motivated, I still don't know that anything would have been added to the field of knowledge. As a guinea pig I would be unreliable and shifty. My tendency would be to get drunk, to escape the embarrassment of being watched, and this unsavory episode would have to go in the record, to be studied for hidden meanings that weren't really there. In short, I feel that my best bet as a writer is to sit still and write. As my time gets shorter and shorter, I feel that more and more.

But I do thank you for the chance.

Sincerely,
E. B. White

To EDWARD W. WEIMAR

[New York]
November 11, 1957

Dear Mr. Weimar:

Thanks for your letters and the [Ambrose] Bierce blacklist.[1] I had never seen it. I'm sorry to be so late in acknowledging your gift—am right in the middle of dispersing the contents of our city apartment, preparatory to moving to Maine, and I am covered with dust and distraction.

---

1. Of literary faults.

I don't know anything about baseball, and wrote the Giants piece[2] because I spent July watching my wife watch television. It was hot and I like to write when it's hot. You could count the times I've been inside the Polo Grounds on the fingers of Mays's glove. My wife, by the way, is the former Mrs. Angell who you say helped you with John McEntee Bowman.[3] She is a truly gifted writer-helper, and I have had to do my own work in secret for twenty-eight years in order to maintain any feeling of personal accomplishment. We are planning a trip to San Francisco, come spring, to see if we can pick up second base in the fog.

Sincerely,
E. B. White

To LUELLA ADAMS

North Brooklin, Maine
24 November 1957

Dear Mrs. Adams:

When I was young and full of beans I used to keep a diary, only I called it a "journal" to make it sound more impressive. I wrote in it so steadily and over so many years that it is eight inches thick and contains probably the world's finest collection of callow and insipid remarks. Anyway, I have been thumbing through it this morning. An entry dated "January 26, 1920—10:00 P.M.—Monday" includes the report that "Last night I sat in Bristow Adams' den before an open fire, with Peter Vischer, Lee A. White, Mr. Church, Russ Lord, Russ Peters, and Stevenson, and talked until about two o'clock. We discussed a great many things from the ethics of newspaper work to the oppression of Korea by the Japanese. We smoked pipe upon pipe, drank coffee, and had a very enjoyable time."

And a month later (February 24, 1920—12:20 A.M.) I wrote: "I have spent the evening at Professor Bristow Adams' house where several students gather every Monday evening to smoke and talk. I admire B. A. a great deal for his good humor and his sincerity and I value him as a friend. He is hospitable, tolerant, just, and jovial. He considers it part of his duty to entertain undergraduates. Sympathetic, kindly, and apparently without a care in the world, he is a fine balm for a frenzied spirit. I hope that our friendship will not be interrupted."

Well, our friendship is at last interrupted. But B. A. has such a secure place in my affections that even the Great Interrupter is not going to do a very good job. Those first years at Cornell were lonely ones for me—the pages of my diary are full of homesickness and

---

2. "The Seven Steps to Heaven," which ran in *The New Yorker* of September 7, 1957.

3. Subject of a Profile in *The New Yorker*.

other sorrows. But at your house I found relief, and in that upstairs sitting room B. A. dispensed a good deal more than entertainment and coffee. I guess it was his knack of treating a young man as a companion rather than an oddity that made all the difference. I remember so well how good it was for the ego, the spirit, and even the intellect. I used to walk back across the bridge at midnight feeling all smoothed out and peaceful. Oh those nights at the Adamses! The nearest I get to that kind of tranquillity these days is to go out to the barn and pay a call on some of the characters out there, who are also peaceable and good conversationalists.

I feel very bad that I haven't written you of late. It takes a full charge of dynamite to get me to the point of starting a letter. But I've often thought of you, in your long sorrowful vigil, and I hope that these months have not worn you down. I'm sorry, too, that I did not see Bristow once more before he died, and yet in a way I am content not to have seen him flat on his back—he was essentially an upright man and I want to remember him that way.

Katharine and I are recuperating from the business of dispersing the contents of our apartment in New York. We are here in Maine for keeps now, I hope, and K has at last given up her full-time job at the magazine and is working part time and at long distance. Our house is in a hooroar, with the back kitchen all ripped to pieces for a face-lifting job, and we can't even find our way to the refrigerator without a compass. But I guess the dust will settle eventually.

Please give my love to all the children of your house and tell them that I loved their father, which they know anyway. There should be more teachers on more campuses like Professor Bristow Adams, and more wives just like you. But that would be impossible.

As ever yrs, and with
much love,
Andy

• *Gardner Botsford is Senior Editor of the Fact Department at* The New Yorker.

To GARDNER BOTSFORD

North Brooklin, Maine
6 December 1957

Dear Gardner:

The next time you are loitering at the corner of Third and 48th, looking at the girls in their winter dresses and wondering whether to drop in at the Emerald Café for a dram of Seagram's Old Hemlock, I wish you would kindly deliver a message for me to my friend Joe

Vitello, who vends papers and rubs used orange juice on shoes at that intersection. I would like Joe to be told that I misinformed him about the date of the "Here Is New York" television show. He is watching for this show because he is in it, and he naturally wants to see himself in the pitchers. The correct date is Sunday afternoon, December 15. I hope you can see your way clear to deliver this simple, heartfelt message to Joe. I would drop him a line, saving you the trouble, but I have no confidence in the resourcefulness of the Postmaster General. For all I know he is at Cape Canaveral blowing on the fuse.

If this letter sounds peremptory or bossy it is because I have just dined on wild meat. My son dropped us off a haunch of venison the other day, and we pounced on it tonight, claw and fang. When our cook, Mrs. Freethy, appeared with the platter, she had a funny look on her face and before she left the room she said, "You won't give any of this deer meat to Augie, will you?" (Augie is our dachshund puppy who is bursting with the most revolting kind of health.) I replied that I hadn't planned slipping any of the venison to Augie, but why did she ask. "Well," she said, "I gave a tiny piece of deer meat to Tiny once, and Tiny almost died. She had to be rushed to the vet. It happens to dogs all the time, all over the county." Katharine and I, needless to say, settled down to our doe steak with enormous relish, and with tall over-flowing glasses of replenished Scotch.

I hope you and Tassie are the same or better. Come here any time you feel like it, you will never return. And don't fail to deliver the message.

Yrs as follows,
A

To DAISE TERRY

North Brooklin, Maine
2 January 1958

Dear Daise Daise:

You were a daisy to send us such pears and I am just about to surround another one. We bring them to the stage of ripeness where they not only flow easily down the throat but they run down your chin, too. It's called runoff by us farmers. Well, they are lovely pears, really loverly. Another good thing you did for me was to clear up my desk paste problem, which is often my number one professional problem. With this dispenser and this quart jar of Cico I feel that I can look ahead to the next fifty thousand newsbreaks with equanimity, by which time I will be dead and somebody else can sit around getting his fingers sticky and thinking of those funny little taglines. . . .

We had a nice Christmas, all in all. I had been sick for about two weeks but got feeling pretty good on the 24th and started out in a whirl to do my last minute shopping. I figured the stores were all out, so I went down into the woods for stuff and made out all right. Christmas Day was a very pretty day, and we had a mail delivery, and people called up, and I did my usual amount of drinking and cutting up, and we ate some fish eggs and smoked ham. Then I went out while there was still light enough to see by and shut the geese up and gave them a pail of water to play with, and grained the bantams and shut them up, grained and watered the hens, picked up the eggs, carried the eggs to the cellar, pitched down some hay for the heifers and mixed them some grain in the proportions Stanley Walker told me about, filled the woodbox in the kitchen, emptied the garbage and rinsed the pail and dried it and installed a wax paper Sanette filler, closed the garage doors, shut off the outside water line, and plugged in the Christmas tree. I always like Christmas here because there is a barn attached to the house and it makes the whole thing a lot more real than when you just see it on television.

Thanks again, Daise, for everything, and stay strong and fit in 1958.

Yrs with love,
Buster

To MRS. BARD and FIFTH-GRADERS

North Brooklin, Maine
3 January 1958

Dear Mrs. Bard and 5th Graders:

Thanks for all those letters. I'm afraid I am very late with this answer, and if I don't hurry up you will all be promoted into another grade and won't have Mrs. Bard any more.

It is quite cold in the barn tonight—the thermometer says 14°. The water pails are frozen and the windows are frosted up. Down in the barn cellar where the sheep used to be are two big Hereford cows. They weigh about a thousand pounds each and they have big white faces and long horns. When I go down there to pitch hay to them, the geese always talk the matter over as I go by. I haven't seen Templeton in a long time—I don't think he's around, these days. A good many of Charlotte's descendants still live in the barn, and when the warm days of spring arrive there will be lots of tiny spiders emerging into the world. And each of the cows will have a little white-faced calf and will take the calf down the lane into the pasture to drink at the pond and to browse around in the woods. And the goose will fix herself a nest in the barn and she will sit on her eggs for four weeks and then the goslings will arrive. So I am looking forward to spring.

I enjoyed all your letters and am glad you had a good time reading my book. I don't know where you got the idea I was retiring. I don't intend ever to do that. But if I don't stop answering letters I'll never get another book written.

> Sincerely,
> E. B. White

TO ARTHUR MAC GILLIVRAY, S.J.

> 25 West 43 Street
> 2 February [1958]

Dear Father MacGillivray:

Thanks for the post card showing one of my favorite bodies of water, and the towers it reflects. You ask if some of my writings haunt me; they sure do. At my age I am haunted by the feeling that everything I write I've written before, only better.

> Sincerely,
> E. B. White

TO CASS CANFIELD

> North Brooklin, Maine
> 30 April 1958

Dear Cass:

I'd much rather not be interviewed for the Writers at Work series. For one thing, they would have to call it "Writers NOT at Work." Or "Sick Men."

I realize that I have done very little for Harpers in the nature of promotional work, but you will just have to put it down to my poor disposition. Incidentally, did I ever thank you for the Hemingway interview? The one that explained that he always wrote standing on the skin of a Lesser Kudu. (I always write sitting on my arse, except when I have piles.)

> Yrs,
> Andy

• *The following letter is to White's oldest nephew and his wife. Brittingham had retired from the Army with the rank of colonel and had gone to live in Florida.*

TO ELEANOR and ARTHUR BRITTINGHAM, JR.

> North Brooklin, Maine
> 4 May 1958

Dear Eleanor and Art:

This is a fine time to be answering your letter, but I've been in such a foul mood lately I haven't dared write letters for fear they would sound like a countdown. I don't know what kind of pneumonia I had, but it ran around inside me like a dervish. Actually, I think I had a new disease, just discovered this winter, called Pulmonary Alveolar Proteinosis. You get it from inhaling modern products, like detergents, insecticides, plastics, and therapeutic drugs. For all I know to the contrary you can get it from watching television. Anyway, it leaves its victims either dead or wishing they were.

I liked your disquisition on hospital design. I spent some of my time in hospital writing a piece on automobile design, and it was published and I have received hundreds of letters about it from disgruntled car owners. I am also an old student of hospital nuttiness. When I start for a hospital, the first things I pack in my overnight case (ahead of pajamas and bathrobe) are (1) a piece of strong cord about six feet long, (2) a jackknife, and (3) a pint of whiskey. I immediately on arriving tie one end of the cord to that crazy bed-spanning table, and the other end to the headboard. Then when a nurse comes in the room and pushes the table out of reach, I can recapture it by pulling the string.

You are right about the beds—they should go up and down hydraulically, like any sensible barber chair. I always got out of bed, the last thing at night after the nurse had fixed everything to suit herself, and tucked the sheets and blankets in around myself so I wouldn't fall out while asleep. It would have been like falling off the Chrysler Building. One thing I learned years ago about hospitals is, you should *never* stay in bed. I've never yet used a bedpan. Always leap back and forth to the bathroom. Two years ago I had a hernia operation one morning, and went to the bathroom under my own steam in the afternoon, to prevent them from pulling a catheter on me. I managed to start the old bladder going by dashing cold water from the tap all over my frontside. Damn near fainted, but made it back to bed before anybody discovered me.

Another thing I discovered, that time, was that there is a gadget in every hospital setup called a "colon lavage," and it is exactly the right size and shape for cooling splits of champagne. I always notify a rich friend the minute I get into a hospital and ask for a few splits. Then I swipe ice from the bedside water pitcher, fill the colon lavage, and keep a split cooling. You have to know these things, otherwise you die.

Spring has come at last—the town road crew removed the snow fence last week, officially ending winter. Barn swallows arrived right on schedule, May 1. We had a spit of snow yesterday but it always snows here in May just to prove it can do it. My goose is setting on twelve eggs which I believe to be infertile because of a queer situation in the barnyard. I have one goose and two ganders, and from my observations I would say that the ganders are pansies—they were inseparable all spring, and the goose kept her distance. However, I'll know for sure on the 23rd.

Thanks again for your letter and forgive me for being so late with a reply. K was sick this winter, too, and had to have some painful treatments, and she still doesn't feel right. We're going to New York for a few days, the end of this week, for another short bout with the doctors. Hope all goes well with you in Lake Worth.

Yrs with love,
Andy

To STANLEY HART WHITE

North Brooklin, Maine
10 September [1958]

Dear Bun:

I guess I owe you three or four letters. Have been uncommunicative lately, and lagging in life's race. We wanted to get you and Blanche here for a visit while you were in the East, but we were so much on the move ourselves, with visits to medical clowns in Bangor and New York, that it seemed impractical. Marion whirled in here one afternoon, with Jessie at the wheel and a friend of Jessie's in the back seat, hell bent to get back to Bridgeport the following afternoon. Marion is rather brittle and unsteady on rough ground, doesn't attack stairs, but otherwise well and happy and enjoying her dynamic grandmotherhood, by land and sea and air. I popped her over to Joe's house and gave her a quick tussle with Steven and Martha White, Martha wearing an eye patch and looking like an advertisement for Hathaway shirts. Had a very funny letter yesterday from Marion, describing the arrival at 3 A.M. of Clara and Janet bearing the ashes of the late Mr. Gilbert.[1] They had got turned around on the highway and had lost their bearings. Next day they glided off to the cemetery where Father and Mother lie, and Clara kidded the management into letting Mr. Gilbert in, too. We are a wonderful family of lovable rakehells, when you put everything together. . . .

I failed to thank you for your memorial vignette of Mother. It was fine of you to send it around, and I loved the part about how she simply sat down and thought out what Father would have done under the circumstances. I find myself almost daily trying the same device, and against what odds.

---

1. Husband of Janet Wyvell.

Our health has picked up a bit, but K has to take periodic treat-ments . . . and for these she goes to New York, usually by train and usually accompanied by me. I go along to pick up the hairpins that keep springing from her back hair. Here at home, she works what she calls "third time" for *The New Yorker's* fiction department, except when our letter carrier (who makes his rounds with a fox cub in the front seat with him) forgets to drop off her work envelope. She spends a lot of time worrying about flowers, and I let her. As for me, I am re-plank-ing the little scow I built about twenty years ago when Joe was needing his first boat. This should take me about three years to accomplish, by which time Joe's son will be big enough to mess around with it. The only writing I do these days is obituary notices of my friends at *The New Yorker* who keep fading away, the latest being Wolcott Gibbs. I don't know who will knock out my obituary when I die, but I think they have three or four youngsters in training for it—on a special diet of bread and tears.

I'm interested in your plans for moving to Denver and will put Denver down in my travel folder as a place to go. I had intended to go to San Francisco this fall to watch the Giants but they goofed out on me. I don't understand baseball, really, so it's probably just as well.

Yrs,
En
Elwyn Hwit*

*This is original spelling from a Scotch dictionary of names.

•   *James Thurber, at work on* The Years with Ross, *sent White a copy of a letter Harold Ross had written to Henry Luce after the two men had had a stormy meeting about Wolcott Gibbs's Profile of Luce, which was written in the style of* Time *magazine and published in* The New Yorker *of November 28, 1936. Thurber did not publish the letter.*

To WILLIAM SHAWN

North Brooklin, Maine
20 Oct 1958

Dear Bill:

I'm enclosing the document I received from Jim. He says, in his letter to me, that it is "one of two copies" he has had made, and that he got it from "a young lady I don't know." This young lady, he says, sent it to him "with the wonderful and hilarious statement that it has been used for years in journalism courses throughout the United States." Amen.

My recollection of this affair is that the NYer allowed Luce to see proofs of the Gibbs piece, partly because *Fortune* through Ingersoll had sent proofs of their NYer piece over to our place. I think they went to Fleischmann, not to Ross, but anyway, they got around. When Luce read the Gibbs parody, he not only checked facts (which weren't even facts, being parody) but he got sore and began complaining about the tone and everything else. The famous meeting took place, and this letter got written.

It seems to me that this letter is *New Yorker* property, not Ross property, but I don't know the legal side of it. Anyway, both K and I wrote Jim and advised him against using it, on the score that Ross wouldn't want it published.

Yrs,
Andy

To J. G. CASE

[New York]
November 3, 1958

Dear Mr. Case:

For the guidance of your catalogue writer, here is the way the book stands.

I have tinkered the Strunk text—have added a bit, subtracted a bit, rearranged it in a few places, and in general have made small alterations that seemed useful and in the spirit of Strunk. The first two sections of the "Composition" chapter sustained the heaviest attack; I felt that they were narrow and bewildering. (In their new form they are merely bewildering.)

I have added a number of entries in the "Words and Expressions Commonly Misused" chapter, and as a result that chapter will run longer. In the main, though, the "little book" will end up very nearly the same size as the original: it will still be small, concise, opinionated, non-comprehensive—a squeaky voice from the past.

My *New Yorker* piece, I think, should go unchanged (except for the lead sentence) as a preface. I shall write a short note, or foreword, explaining the circumstances that brought the book back into print and telling roughly what has taken place.

I am dropping Chapter VI, "Words Often Misspelled." In its place will appear a chapter by me, called (tentatively) "An Approach to Style." Here I drop a few cautionary, and I fear paternalistic hints; I discuss style in its broader meaning—not style in the sense of what is correct but style in the sense of what is distinguished and distinguishing. The foreword will make clear that this chapter is my work, not Strunk's, and that my professor might, if alive, heartily disapprove of every word of it.

This essay on Style—Chapter VI in the book—runs around 3500

words, I would guess. I have been letting it stand, to see if some of the lumps and other impurities would settle, and I hope to improve it before I have done. In writing it, I deliberately departed from the strict rhetorical face of style, in an attempt to give the little book an extra dimension, which, considering what is taking place, it can probably use. In short, I shall have a word or two to say about attitudes in writing: the why, the how, the beartraps, the power, and the glory.

I am in New York this week and will be returning home to Maine on the 11th if my wife is able to travel by then. I'm taking the book back with me for the final go-around and to give it the inestimable advantage of coming under her editorial eye. She is a better grammarian, organizer, teacher, editor, and mother than I am, and has saved an untold number of lives.

Yours sincerely,
E. B. White

To J. G. CASE

North Brooklin, Maine
17 December 1958

Dear Mr. Case:

I have removed "Introductory" and the book now has five chapters, not six. Instead of quoting Strunk's remarks in my "Note," as you suggested, I paraphrased them, which seemed quicker and less fussy.

The *Vanity Fair* quote is gone, and I was delighted to see it go. In its place are a few opening sentences from *Northanger Abbey*; there is nothing loose about them, and they are funny. I like this better than Mr. Gibson's *Howard's End* quote, which, out of context, seemed not to pull together. But before Gibson's notes arrived I had been reading Forster, and I have a quote from *Two Cheers for Democracy* that I like that you might prefer to the Jane Austen. I will send it along.

I was busy working a lot of your and Miss N's suggestions into the text, wherever we were in agreement, when your letter came along (December 12th date) and stopped me cold. Do you remember that wonderful moment in the McCarthy hearings when Mr. Welch turned to Mr. Cohn and in his high, friendly voice asked, "And now, Mr. Cohn, when you found that one-third of the photograph was missing, were you saddened?" (Such a wonderful verb for little Mr. Cohn.) Anyway, I was saddened by your letter—the flagging spirit, the moistened finger in the wind, the examination of entrails, and the fear of little men. I don't know whether Macmillan is running scared or not, but I do know that this book is the work of a dead precisionist and a half-dead disciple of his, and that it has got to stay that way. I have been sympathetic all along with your qualms about "The Elements of Style," but I know that I cannot, and will-shall not, attempt to adjust the unadjustable Mr. Strunk to the modern liberal of the English Department, the anything-goes fellow. Your letter expresses contempt for this fellow, but on the other hand you seem to want his vote. I am against him, temperamentally and because I have seen the work of *his* disciples, and I say the hell with him. If the White-Strunk opus has any virtue, any hope of circulation, it lies in our keeping its edges sharp and clear, not in rounding them off cleverly.

In your letter you are asking me to soften up just a bit, in the hope of picking up some support from the Happiness Boys, or, as you call them, the descriptivists. (I can write you an essay on *like-as*, and maybe that is the answer to all this; but softness is not.) I am used to being edited, I like being edited, and I have had the good luck and the pleasure of being edited by some of the best of them; but I have never been edited for wind direction, and will not be now. Either Macmillan takes Strunk and me in our bare skins, or I want out. I feel a terrible responsibility in this project, and it is making me jumpy. And if I have misread or misconstrued your letter, I ask your forgiveness and your indulgence.

The above, written by the below, are, of course, fighting words, and will, I am sure, bring you out of your corner swinging. But I think it is best that I get them down on paper. I want to get back to work, make progress, and make a good book; and until we get this basic thing straightened out, there isn't much chance. It is ghostly work, at best; and surrounded as I have been lately by a corps of helpers, all of them trying to set me on the right path, it is unnerving work.[1] Your letter did unsettle me on a number of counts.

All this leads inevitably to *like-as*, *different than*, and the others. I will let them lay for the moment, sufficient unto this day being the etc. My single purpose is to be faithful to Strunk as of 1958, reliable, holding the line, and maybe even selling some copies to English Departments that collect oddities and curios. To me no cause is lost, no level the right level, no smooth ride as valuable as a rough ride, no *like* interchangeable with *as*, and no ball game anything but chaotic if it lacks a mound, a box, bases, and foul lines. That's what Strunk was about, that's what I am about, and that (I hope) is what the book is about. Any attempt to tamper with this prickly design will get nobody nowhere fast.

Another thing that has disturbed me has nothing to do with you or

---

1. Case had commissioned three or four grammarians well versed in the textbook field to submit suggestions to White.

Macmillan—it is that when I reread my piece on style, it left me with a cold feeling of having failed. I am reasonably well satisfied with the gist of it—that is, the advice, the reminders; but the introductory section not only failed to invigorate me but left me wondering whether a lot of it shouldn't just come out of there. I would welcome your advice. I started the thing quite differently, in earlier drafts, and arrived much sooner at the main body of the piece.

Sincerely,

E. B. White

P.S. When I said, above, that Macmillan would have to take me in my bare skin, I really meant my bare *as*.

• *The chapter White wrote in* The Elements of Style *called "An Approach to Style" contains some remarks on the question of when to omit "that" from a sentence. White advises students to be guided by their ear, and he had originally invented a sentence to illustrate his point: "He felt that the girl had not played fair." Here, said White, is an instance where one's ear is a help. "Omit the* that *and you have, 'He felt the girl . . .' "*

Jack Case found this too racy for classroom use and asked White to substitute something else. White did, but not without entering a plea for "that girl on P. 81."

To J. G. CASE

[North Brooklin, Me.]
[December 1958]
Thursday

Dear Mr. Case:

Here is Chapter V, with the fixes, giving each Reminder a heading. I had to do a bit of rewriting here and there. . . .

As for the controversial matter of that girl on P. 81, I am in favor of leaving her in. She illustrates the embarrassments of prose, and she will be missed if you dismiss her. But I'll not make a fuss about it if you are sure you want to make the cut. I thought of two sentences that would make a substitute:

He felt the fur was too costly.

He saw the light was off.

They are pale by comparison to my girl, whom I am beginning to admire for her pluck, but you may have them if you want them. They won't create a disturbance in class. (That may be one trouble with classrooms nowadays—no disturbance, all down the line.) My reason for believing that this girl is in good taste and would not be an embarrassment is that she is *presented* as an embarrassment. And anything that is presented as an embarrassment is not likely to prove embarrassing, just as anything that is presented as *funny* or *interesting* is not likely to be f. or i.

This girl should have me for her lawyer.

Yrs for the iron word and the
felt girl,
E. B. White

To STANLEY HART WHITE

North Brooklin, Maine
15 January [1959?]

Dear Bun:

Your man Vrest Orton,[1] who will probably end up in a vrest home, came through again at Christmas, and we have had some nice pancakes and other tasties, thanks to you and Blanche. I think the space age version of the country store, with its crackerbarrel literature and old horehound candy decor, is one of the finest manifestations of this sad day of wistfulness and remembrance of things past. And I guess old Vresty is lining his pockets pretty nicely, too. We occasionally send him an order for deerskin gloves and a bag or two of stone-ground meal. I don't know what he has for a stone, there, but you can probably grind meal satisractorily with an enormous plastic cylinder studded with rhinestones, if you go about it right. And I have an idea Vresty Orton goes about things right.

The spiders in your basement may have thinned out because of bug spray, but I doubt it. Spiders are tough, and nothing much bothers them (except an occasional writer), but I have discovered that the spider population in my barn cellar and my outbuildings varies greatly from year to year. I don't know why, but my guess is weather conditions at the time of hatching. Like almost every other creature in the arachnid and insect world, they throw a lot of eggs around, and just hope.

Marion went into the Bridgeport hospital last week for tests, following a spell of jaundice, and the latest report is that she may have an operation. I am in touch with Jessie, who is standing by.

I do not want a child's crib in good, or bad, condition. Two children (Joe's) are going to be staying with us next week, but both of them would laugh a crib out of business.

Yrs,
En

---

1. Keeper of the Vermont Country Store mail order operation.

To J. G. CASE

North Brooklin, Maine
19 January 1959

Dear Mr. Case:

I have marked one copy of your report, and my marks will answer your questions, I think, except for the ones I have left for this letter. . . .

Page 39, first sentence. Your fix is acceptable to me, but I have suggested another way that may be better.

Page 45. I still like my horse, and see no harm in him—he neither bites nor kicks, being clever.[1] But I shall not stand in your way if you will kill a horse. I merely warn you that animals, somehow or other, creep into my work—animals and occasionally girls—and if you eliminate them, you are running the risk of being left with nothing of any substance. . . .

Pages 80-81. Take this fine girl away and bring on Queen Elizabeth. I am now madly in love with the girl, and will do everything I can to protect her—which starts with keeping her out of a textbook.

Page 88, line 2-4. If you object to cinch, change it to "easy matter" or something of that sort.[2] But I don't think there is anything confusing about the passage. I doubt that one person in a thousand would read "no cinch" and think of a horse's girdle. You've read this piece so many times you are seeing horses. And I've read it so many times I'm seeing Death Valley.

Thanks again for the pleasant lunch at Booth's Hall last week, and my best to Cloudman.[3] Hope this letter and the enclosed report answers everything—I have been writing it while surrounded by grandchildren wielding Tinker Toy structural elements. They've got even more questions than you have. Shouldn't a skyscraper have a windshield wiper? I had a quick answer for that one.

Yrs,
E. B. White

To STANLEY HART WHITE

N. Brooklin
[January 25, 1959]
Sunday

Dear Bun:

What year did I first go to Belgrade—do you know? I'm doing a railroad piece, or trying to.[1] Seems to me it was 1904 or 1905. You and

1. Under "Clever" in his word list, White wrote: "Note also that the word means one thing when applied to men, another when applied to horses. A clever horse is a good-natured one, not an ingenious one."

2. "Case balked," White says, "at 'Writing good standard English is no cinch.' He said it sounded like a horse's girdle."

3. Harry Cloudman, a Macmillan executive.

1. The piece was written, and *The New Yorker* ran it as a "Letter from the East" in the issue of January 28, 1960. It was included in *The Points of My Compass*, under the title "The Railroad."

Al, as I recall it, had been the first of the family to visit Great Pond (as guests of somebody?) and Father got wondering about you, and followed along, didn't he? I seem to remember that it all started with you and Al on the opposite shore of the lake, and that Father fell in love with the place, rented a camp (Happy Days?) and took all the family either that same summer or the following summer.

Do you remember the approximate running time of the Bar Harbor Express? My recollection is that it left Grand Central at 8 p.m. and arrived in Belgrade Station next morning at about 9 or 9:30. I can probably dig this information out from old time tables, if I get desperate. My hunch is that the New York–Belgrade run was about a thirteen hour trip in 1905, and now, half a century later, it is still about a thirteen hour trip.

Yrs in haste (am running for a
train that no longer exists),
En

To **HOWARD CUSHMAN**

[Sarasota, Fla.]
[February 1959?]

Dear Cush:

Thanks for the New Statesman clip. I liked that clause "for ruin almost always begins in the home." But I guess it's also true that salvation almost always begins just as the umbilical cord is cut, and we are what we are. Neither my mother nor my father read the comics (except Hans and Fritz) but they didn't read anything else, either (except my father used to read the published sermons of Henry Ward Beecher), and although I was once exposed to "Alice in Wonderland" (and didn't care for it), for the most part I was exposed to nothing at all in the home—that is, in the way of good reading. Curiously enough, I see in my own grandchildren—and even more in my proxy grandchildren —a far greater exposure to the good books and the good words, but no real preoccupation with them, no tender, loving care, such as you and I felt. It's a proper mystery.

K and I are trying to find the same old sun on the same old Florida key where her sister used to have a house. So far, we have had cold winds and rain, but even so it's a nice place to be, what with the mourning doves at morn, and the redbird saying "Portugee, Portugee," and the little cold snake in the pump house waiting (as are we) for things to warm up.

Andy

To JANICE WHITE

[North Brooklin, Me.]
June 16, 1959

Dear Jan:

Before I mark up the books (which have not arrived yet) I thought I'd better find out for sure what you wanted. Do you want me just to write my name, or should I indicate that the books are a memorial to Fran, presented by you?[1] I want to be sure that I am properly carrying out your wishes. So will you drop me a note.

I had a fine letter from Stan not long ago and am delighted that he and Blanche have plumped for Denver, as it sounds as though it would agree with them fine. The business of stopping work, after almost a lifetime of it, is tough on many people, but I think Stan is going to feel it less than these old chairmen of the board—some of whom go into a state of shock when they no longer have any papers to ruffle about in the morning.

We are awaiting, breathlessly, an influx of grandchildren of assorted sizes. Joe's wife is about to have her third, by Caesarian section in the Ellsworth hospital, and while she is out of the running we are taking Steven and Martha (age 5 and 4) into our house for a couple of weeks roistering with tinker-toys and space ships. And on top of that, we are also taking our oldest grandchild, Kitty Stableford, a blonde starlet age 15, who plans to attend a French school in the morning (2½ miles away by bicycle) and clean up the space ships and bathe the space-tots in the afternoon. The piano is out of tune, my wife and one of my cows have diarrhea, the temperature outdoors is 48, the milk supply is contaminated with strontium 90 from fallout, rain has been falling ever since Memorial Day, our neighbor's boy just held up the Sunday night Bible class with a .22 automatic pistol and abducted one of the girls in the minister's automobile, the asparagus is growing *down* into the ground instead of up into the air, the lilacs look as though they will still be blooming right through the Fourth of July, and I have lost both pairs of glasses. Hope you are not the same.

Love,
Andy

P.S. Tell Stan I have a textbook out, on English usage and style, and will send him a copy. It explains everything.

1. Frances White Earl, Albert's daughter, had just died, leaving three little girls.

To **DOROTHY LOBRANO**

North Brooklin, Maine
4 September 1959

Dear Dotty:

I'm delighted to add an albatross to the birds around here, and I look forward very much to reading Admiral Jameson's book [*Wandering Albatross*]. Our house is groaning with fog-bound grandchildren at the moment, so I have got no further than a study of the courtship photographs. What wonderful pictures! The albatross appears to be second only to the Brooklin (Me.) square dancers in style, ecstasy, and movement.

Are you coming to Maine this year? This has been the summer of the great discontent and widespread confusion, weatherwise, healthwise, and otherwisewise. June gave us 27 days of fog and rain, three days of sun, and a new grandson named John Shepley White. It also gave me a stomach ache that lasted nine weeks, reduced me to 129 lbs. of plucky skin and bones, and landed me finally in Harkness (in the enema and witchcraft department). They photographed me from many bizarre angles, gave me a money-raising brochure to edit between waves of nausea, and sent me away on the morning of the ninth day. Am feeling better—why, I do not know. But am.

Joe is now a partner in the boat yard where he has been working. He looks great and loves the life, which is a fine blend of manual dexterity and cerebral dream. His oldest boy, Steven, begins school next week—an experience he is approaching with resolution and fortitude. The bus is bright yellow. When Joe started school here about 22 years ago, the bus was nonexistent and he took the 2½ mile walk in his stride, which was firm.

K is pretty well but has to take periodic treatments (of a non-serious sort) at the Medical Center, so we come to town every six or eight weeks. We've been using the railroad, but the executives of the Maine Central plan to put a stop to *that* bit of nonsense. They have announced that railroading in Maine is at the threshold of a golden age, and that this age will begin just as quick as they can get rid of the last passenger—which they hope to do by mid-October. The last passenger, although they failed to mention this, is going to be me. And I am going to be put off the train kicking, screaming, and hurling oaths and stones. Golden age yet! I've had a bellyful of golden ages in this backsliding century. . . .

Love,
Andy

To LOUIS LEVY

[North Brooklin, Me.]
September 10, 1959

Dear Mr. Levy:

Thank you for your letter about "The Elements of Style." I am glad you find it a good guidebook.

I think the expression "dress up" is a useful—certainly a familiar—colloquialism. Little girls dress *up* when they go to a party, perhaps because their thoughts go upward. A man dresses for dinner; his thoughts are presumed to be under control, like his studs. If you place a hat, or a garland, on a horse, you dress the horse *up*. A sergeant, on the other hand, dresses a private down. These words *up* and *down* are amusing in themselves. Do you slow up, or do you slow down? Robert M. Coates once wrote a piece on this subject for The New Yorker, many years ago. I think your instructor in English at the University of Oklahoma was quite within his rights to advise you not to dress *up* anything. But I have granddaughters, and every once in a while I notice that they are dressing *up*. Way up.

Sincerely,
E. B. White

To VIRGINIA BAILEY

[North Brooklin, Me.]
September 16, 1959

Dear Miss Bailey:

The dash didn't get into the book, but it seems to get into my writing now and then—the way things do. As for three dots . . .

Everybody is confused about "I were," but if I were you, I wouldn't let it worry me. It belongs to the subjunctive mood.

I say *eether*, rather than *eyether*. But you can say anything that comes into your head, never forget that.

Sincerely,
E. B. White

To STANLEY HART WHITE

North Brooklin, Me.
22 October 1959

Dear Bun:

Marion died in the middle of the morning last Friday the sixteenth, and we received the news (as I presume you did) at the end of the day. I decided to go on to Bridgeport; I have never found funeral services rewarding in any way, but nevertheless felt a compulsion to go and sit with the others. K went along and we got to the Barnum Hotel on Sunday afternoon before dark, and a few minutes later Lil showed up. It was a beautiful day—windy and bright, the foliage fading, and downtown Bridgeport deserted, the streets drafty and mean, and the hotel empty. Al and Bill had arranged to meet Lil for supper, after calling at 3 Sedan Terrace, so K and I changed our clothes and got back in the car and started to drive out to the house. It was dark by now, and I was so exhausted from our long drive that I got within two blocks of the place before realizing that I hadn't switched my lights on. It didn't seem to make much difference.

At the house we found Arthur, Jessie, Frank, Elsie (Frank's wife) and their two youngest—Patty and Keith. Also a Mrs. Carr, who had once been courted by Arthur Jr., and her husband Mr. Carr. The house looked about as always, no plant or sailboat or ingenious fixture having been removed in the past thirty years or so. The big round dining room table completely filled the dining room, and the centerpiece was a little Confidence rose—one of Marion's favorites, shell pink. A neighbor had brought in a ham, and there was coffee and tea for the hungry, and we all kissed each other in that queer tentative way, full of emotion but a little wide of the mark. Arthur immediately started to demonstrate an infra-red heat lamp to me, and little Patty embraced me and showed me a new collection that Arthur had prepared for her—a lobster claw with an elastic band around it to make it snap, a piece of asbestos, a lump of coal, and an Indian scraping tool. The three alligators that had lived for so many years down cellar had been disposed of. Arthur looked pretty well—much better than when I visited the hospital a month ago. Occasionally, he would bring Marion into the conversation, and end up crying. On the whole, he has stood the strain quite well (he spent a very great deal of time standing watch at the hospital, and there were sixteen days of coma at the end, during which he worried about whether she was in pain). He is, I think, 82, and looks twenty years younger. Jessie, who really managed everything, was thoroughly exhausted.

The service was held at 8 o'clock, at Stear's Funeral Home, on Fairfield Avenue. Marion lay in a gray casket, which was closed; and many of her friends gathered. We of the family sat across the hall in another room, Bill with a heavy cold, Al looking thin and tired, all of us solemn, while a pleasant red-faced minister from White Plains read scripture. I think his name was Checker—a friend. The room was terribly hot, and I had drunk two cups of tea and became dizzy with emotion, heat, a palpitation spell, and the general distaste for ritual of any kind, but I managed not to keel over. In Marion's death, which in a way symbolizes the death of all of us children, I guess we feel a special twinge, which is more than sorrow, and more nearly fright—an involvement that is inescapable. I kept wishing you were there, but of course did not expect to see you, because of the great distance. Clara was missing, too.

Marion was buried on Tuesday morning in Arlington National Cemetery. Just how or why this came about, I do not know. Arthur is a veteran of some war or other, and two of his sons are professionals, and patriotism has held his life together like a bright thread. So I guess he had long looked toward Arlington. Whether Marion knew where she was headed, I do not know, but separation from Arthur in life or death would have been unthinkable. She is in good company, as she was followed into the cemetery that same day by General George Catlett Marshall, attended by President Eisenhower and Harry Truman. A military guard of honor was present for Marion, and she was attended by Clara, Arthur, Frank, Manton, Conrad, and Conrad's wife.

I miss Marion very much. In our upstairs hall we have the family picture hanging, and it seems temporarily to have lost its tone.

Yrs,
En

To HOWARD CUSHMAN

North Brooklin, Maine
26 October 1959

Dear Cush:

Being equipped with extra-sensory perception, I knew you had left West 4th Street, but I didn't know it was Philadelphia until your letter arrived. I had a weekend in your city about a year ago, memorable for a stomach virus and the inability to order a drink on Sunday. I can't say I am wild for the Rittenhouse Square Sabbath, but there is always the Schuylkill and those boat clubs. I advise you to learn to scull a single-oar shell, or maybe you and Jit[1] could manage a longer one. (You could stroke her. Hup!) Am sending you three copies of the little book— the two you sent me and the one I was *going* to send you except I knew you had left West 4th Street. Every veteran of English 8 gets a copy for free.

Life as a textbook editor is not the rosy dream you laymen think it is. I get the gaa damndest letters every day from outraged precisionists and comma snatchers, complaining every inch of the way. They are out to get my colon, just the way your doctor was. I shall soon turn on these hungry hordes and let 'em have it. Still and all, I am glad I revived the little book, and so is Emilie Strunk, widow of Will, now in her 80's and living alone in Meriden, Conn. It is a 50-50 deal, on royalties, but I

---

1. Howard Cushman's second wife, Jeannette.

gather that some of my sniveling Cornellians are under the impression that I am pocketing the entire loot. Emilie writes me comical little letters that are on the border between senility and agility. Have also heard from Willie's brother in Cincinnati, and from Oliver. My favorite review, so far, was by a bearded columnist in Peterboro, Ontario, who offered the opinion that everything I write sounds as though I were just going to bed with a hard cold. I snapped a post card right back, saying, "Hard cold nothing. This is cholera."

K and I were interested in your remarks about the Ross book,[2] as the book has been the cause of much sorrow and pain around the shop. The first couple chapters are pretty good—Jim could always reproduce Ross's mannerisms and general demeanor, and vividly. But most of the book seems to me, and to K, a sly exercise in denigration, beautifully concealed in words of sweetness and love. As soon as Jim got famous and successful—which was very soon—he began brooding about the low pay he had received for his early casuals. And then he remembered that some of his pieces had been rejected, and this was an insult to genius. Curiously enough, it was in England, where Jim has been lionized in a big way, that the sharpest reviews appeared. To see England fallen so low threw Jim into a deep depression, from which he has just begun to recover.

I liked the Muggeridge review, by and large. (I had seen it, but thanks, anyway.) Muggeridge had the great advantage of having once edited an adult comic weekly and also of having known Ross.

I gave birth to a fine new grandson (John Shepley White) last June. Except for this pleasant event, my summer was a dud. . . . Have lost ten pounds in the melee, and you wouldn't know me, or want to. Am pale, wan, and ugly, and I don't want you to remind me that digestion is the better part of pallor, either.

The really sad news about the sad, sad summer is that my oldest sister Marion was hospitalized with cancer. She died about ten days ago, in Bridgeport, and is the first of the six of us to depart these shores. I think likely you never met her (Mrs. Arthur Brittingham). She was a red head, and a fine, gentle woman.

I'm probably going to be in town for the first couple weeks in November, staying at the Algonk. If you get over, drop into my 43 St digs or the hotel and we'll lift one to Gunsight Pass. (On an empty stomach, natch.)

Yrs,
Andy

---

2. *The Years with Ross*, by James Thurber.

XII

LETTERS FROM THE EAST

1960–1965

• *The years from 1960 through 1965 were difficult ones for the Whites. Katharine was ill for much of the time, first with a carotid block, which required surgery, then with another arterial condition for which she barely managed to avoid surgery, "by strength of character," as White puts it. She then contracted a rare skin disease, which put her in the hospital for long stretches, and the treatment for which—massive doses of cortisone—left her a semi-invalid.*

White continued to write, primarily Letters from the East for The New Yorker. *He also collected a number of his "Letter" pieces in* The Points of My Compass, *which Harper's published in 1962. An E. B. White Reader, edited with commentary and questions by William W. Watt and Robert W. Bradford of Lafayette College, was put together by Harper's College Department.*

To **JOHN KIERAN**

[North Brooklin, Me.]
14 January 1960

Dear Mr. Kieran:

I've been sick and during this time your book on the natural history of New York has been a great resource and pleasure to me and I want to thank you for it. I am no naturalist, and you had me on the ropes most of the way, but I enjoyed it. In a general sort of way I am pro nature and pro New York, and you mingled them so beautifully. I have seldom seen a semi-popular book with such an array of classical and scientific information in such good order. Even with your great knowledge of birds and beasts and flowers, it is obvious that you did your home-work, not to mention your proofreading.

You come through very clear, poking a warbler's nest and having a mouse jump out, catching a snapping turtle in the act while boys poke her with sticks, hearing the thud of a flying squirrel while sitting on a verandah. I think I made only one visit to the little swamp next to the lake in Van Cortlandt, but its wildness lingers in my mind—the dampness of the world, the redwing, the wren, the turtle, the cattail (or, as we say in Maine, cacktail). I despair of a society that is trying to drain all swamps and make them into airfields, but maybe I am in a despairing mood.

Today we had a delegation of Evening Grosbeaks, along with regular customers—the Black Capped Chickadees (there is a brown cap offbeat chickadee around the place but I haven't seen him yet). Last week, I had the great pleasure of a visit from the Whiskey Jack, who hung around the back porch for almost an hour, looking for a handout. And two Sundays ago, the Pileated came to the big Balm o' Gilead tree in front of the house and spent a couple of hours remodelling it according to ideas of its own. This tree is as hollow as a soil-pipe, and every spring a raccoon female ascends 30 feet and has her kittens in a big hole. The Pileated didn't like this hole—wrong dimensions. But the hole has two vents, higher up, on the north side, and the woodpecker, in his red toboggan cap, spent the morning enlarging the topmost hole—probably to make a convenient roosting spot in bad weather—then took fright and has not been seen since.

I don't know whether you have ever seen Turtle Bay Garden—a friend of mine once described it as "that decadent close." I was lucky enough to have a bedroom overlooking it for many years. It is between the Emerald Saloon and the United Nations, and it attracts birds because it has running water and good cover. Every spring and fall, I found the chewink, the brown thrasher, the hermit thrush, the white-throat, the robin, and several warblers. And twice I saw the ruby-crowned kinglet, vying with the Emerald. How wonderful it is. And excuse this letter. And don't answer.

E. B. White

To ROBERT S. BABCOCK

[North Brooklin, Me.]
February 5, 1960

Dear Governor Babcock:

It's always fun finding out what happens to readers, and I am glad one of them recovered sufficiently to become lieutenant governor of a very pretty state [Vermont]. Morris Bishop was right, I do get discouraged, but letters like yours cheer me on. Am very grateful to you for taking the trouble to write and for the things you said.

I'd rather have a political man interested in the wild flag than any other kind of man, because it is, after all, essentially a political matter. I fear that some of my early remarks on the subject were more feverish than wise, and when I reread them, I am appalled at my youthful assurance. That flag won't wave during my lifetime, but I guess it's made of good material and will at some future time catch the rays of the sun, assuming we don't put out the sun meantime by bouncing things off it.

Thanks again for your encouraging letter. I am proud to have it.

Sincerely,
E. B. White

To FAITH MC NULTY MARTIN

Sarasota, Florida
Wash Birth [1960]

Dear Faith:

Am sitting here with the Gulf of Mexico lapping at my entrails, doing newsbreaks. This one made me laugh but I am sending it back to Rhode Island. If Hoyland Bettinger is a real man who went off a real cliff, we shouldn't use the break. If, on the other hand, Emil White and Patricia Roberts are a couple of beatniks working the humor beat, I still don't want it. How sad that I cannot use this break from you, Faith McNulty, sender of some of the best newsbreaks!

I have one nice break in this batch, though, and will tell you about it.

"A French horse player, he appeared with the orchestra at its recent Carnegie Hall Concert."

Tagline: But his thoughts were far away.

Love,
Andy

To STANLEY HART WHITE

Siesta Key, Sarasota, Fla.
5 March 1960

Dear Bun:

I haven't thanked you for your letter, complete with map of Long Pond, Great Pond, and the depot at Belgrade. Shades of Messalonskee! My railroad piece got me a slew of letters from old buffs and other disconsolate ex-passengers, some of them quite funny. I hit the Bar Harbor Express schedule (1905) right on the button—left Grand Central 8 p.m., got to Belgrade at 9:30.

We missed one summer at the pond because Mother decided Lillian wasn't having a classy enough social life among the Hudnuts, the Gallaghers, the Kelseys, the Pinckneys, the McCartens, and other strays. That was the year we (Father, Mother, Lil, and I) went to Bellport and stayed at the Wyandotte Hotel. In my journal I find a report of Lil's first Saturday night at the Wyandotte. A dance was held, and Lil had to sit it out—no takers. It was one of those American crises, with the Great South Bay unmoved in the background.

K and I are back here on Fiddlers Bayou for a few weeks, and at the moment are as cold as only Florida can make you. The snakes and lizards haven't started to crawl, and until that happens I'd rather be in Perth Amboy. Florida real estate is just as delirious as ever—the city planners have hit on a way of making every piece of property a "water front" piece. They simply dig a straight, narrow ditch every few yards, leading them in from the numerous bayous, and holding the banks with concrete retaining walls. It's as practical as the Paris sewers and just about as pleasing to the eye. But by God every man has a water front, with dock and outboard motorboat at the ready. In Florida you may not be able to lead a horse to water, but you can always lead the water to the horse. Speaking of water, we're drinking one of Father's favorite brews—Poland Water. . . .

My love to Blanche and Jan.

Yrs,
En

To CASS CANFIELD

North Brooklin, Maine
14 June [1960]

Dear Cass:

Thanks for your friendly note about my gold medal.[1] It's too big to wear and too small to roll like a hoop.

One of these days, if I can escape long enough from the barium sulphate crowd, I'd like to bundle a few of my essays up and send them to you to make a book. Be patient, and be on the watch.

Yrs faithfully,
Andy

P.S. Shame on you for letting John Updike get away from you. That shook my confidence in Harper, publishers since 1817 and old enough to know better.

---

1. In 1960 the National Institute of Arts and Letters awarded White the Gold Medal for Essays and Criticism of the American Academy of Arts and Letters.

To DOROTHY LOBRANO

North Brooklin, Maine
June 14 [1960]

Dear Dotty:

I'm terribly late in thanking you for the very funny letter about that Ceremonial.[1] I was in town last week, and planned to call instead of writing, but *that* got loused up, too—as I spent all my time posing in the nude for the Harkness X-ray crowd and couldn't seem to muster strength to lift the receiver at day's end.

Anyway, it was fine of you to give me such a good report of the litry doings on West 155th Street. It's just as well I wasn't on hand for the occasion, as Mailer would undoubtedly have scored a direct hit and it would have got in the papers.[2] MEDALIST STOPS GLASS HURLED BY MALCONTENT. Incidentally, where does a man keep a gold medal? This one just makes me uneasy. I tried it in a bottom drawer and it seemed needlessly obscure. I tried it on the table in the hall and it seemed ostentatious. Maybe I'll have to build a trophy room, like the ones you see on "Person to Person," but that would mean throwing out a wing and I'd have to melt down the gold to pay for the addition. I see no solution to medals and don't really enjoy them. Medals should be edible, so you could get it over with and have a moment of enjoyment. I will gladly give you this medal if you need something round and yellow. After all, you're my godchild and so far I've not given you so much as a licorice drop, which is the kind of godfather I've turned out to be. But I love you. . . .

K has reduced her job at the magazine to a six-months-a-year stint—which I will believe when I see it. (My hunch is she will work twelve months as usual, and get paid for six.) Her flower gardening life is at fever pitch now, and our perennial borders are works of art—cars slow down as they go by, to see the wonders Katharine has wrought. We used to employ one man on the place, but now that K has learned the Latin names of plants, it takes three. But it's a nice way to go broke, surrounded by such beauty. Joe is now a partner in the firm of Day and White—the Brooklin Boat Shop. They have acquired the property where the boatyard is, and in doing so also acquired a fish factory. They haven't decided what to do with the fish factory, but I imagine you can just own a fish factory, the way you own

---

1. At the American Academy of Arts and Letters. White's medal was awarded him *in absentia*.

2. During the party following the proceedings a cocktail glass came crashing down into the courtyard. The assumption was that it had been tossed by Norman Mailer.

a cocker spaniel. Joe's wife is president of the PTA in Brooklin and is the mother of three—Steven 6, Martha 5, and John 1. They all put to sea in a boat Joe built, every chance they get, and I am the kind of grandfather who doesn't dare ask whether the kids wear life jackets or not, and haven't dared look.

Thanks again for the letter, Dotty, and I'm awfully sorry I didn't get a chance to get in touch with you last week. Please give my love to Jean and Sandy when you see them.

Yrs,
Andy

To **DAISE TERRY**

[North Brooklin, Me.]
[June 1960]
By the sea
Tuesday

Dear Miss Terry:

Now that you've joined the gay crowd on the 20th floor, I've decided that my small residual affairs at the magazine should be concentrated all in one heap, in order to simplify matters. This can best be done, I think, by having everything—phone calls, mail, breaks, etc.—go to K's secretary, Miss Nosher. She is in almost daily touch with Katharine, and this is an advantage to me because I can slip in a request or answer a question without having to write a letter or make a separate long distance call. Also, her whole job is to be a secretary, whereas your whole job is just a little short of God's, only you work longer hours than God and do better work. I have talked this over with K and with Milton and I would have gone into a huddle with you about it while I was in New York, but so help me every time I tried to do it, something came up, like Jap Gude—who took me to a puppet studio on Barrow Street where I rode up in an elevator that had sleighbells in it. As Ross would say, that's my life. (Incidentally, I wish you would get Fleischmann to put sleighbells in those new elevators of ours, right in front of the electric eye.) . . .

Things are hopping here this morning by the sea, and I wish you were here to take charge—a new disease on the raspberries caused by the wrong mulch, sonic booms rattling the henhouse windows and throwing the ovulation out of whack, no beauty parlor appointment available until next Monday, rats in the cesspool, mealy bugs in the begonias, worms in the radishes, and a fine blue sky over all, wind northeast and gentle. This is the place to be if you can take it. When you come to visit, remind me to show you a warbler's nest made of fox hair. And other interesting sights. I have now had four (4) barium enemas, and the score is even—two positive, two negative. The doctors are fighting it out among themselves, and they can have it.

Yr overexposed friend,
EBW

To PATRICIA NOSHER

[North Brooklin, Me.]
[November 1960]
Friday

Dear Pat:

... Thanks for that [Herblock] cartoon showing the way I looked on Election Night. The only thing wrong in it is the coffee pot. I went off coffee and onto Scotch when Kennedy's early lead began to dwindle. Then around 2:30, I went off Scotch onto milk. Then back to Scotch at bedtime (ten minutes of four). I think there was a short, early interval of brandy and Benedictine, as a gesture to that little town in New Hampshire that knows its own mind and went 9-0 for Nixon. Anyway, I hope you got through the night better than I did. The next presidential race will have to have a Gabor sister as one contender, to keep me up after 11:00.

Yrs,
EBW

• *The Whites' interest in John Updike developed early in his writing career, when Katharine saw in him a promising new talent. This letter was occasioned by a fan letter from Mr. Humphrey Fry, a reader who had written to White on the mistaken assumption that he was the author of a* New Yorker *Comment written by Updike.*

To JOHN UPDIKE

[New York]
28 November [1960]

Dear John:

An aging novelist is going to send you his novel. I liked that comment, too. Its being written by a young sprig, instead of by me, merely aggravates my own need for encouragement.

Other things by you I have greatly enjoyed lately are the Marquand comment and the Ted Williams piece. Have not read "Rabbit" and doubt if I will. Your writing shakes me too much and I have not yet recovered from "The Poorhouse Fair," which I read while occupying a beach cottage in Florida during violent floods and winds, and which made me shake all over the whole time.

There are a few comforts of age: *you're* going to have to write to Mr. Humphrey Fry, not me. I take comfort in that.

Yrs,
Andy White

P.S.   The Algonquin Hotel is on fire as I write this. I left my room there a few moments ago and found the fire department outside on the street. The Algonquin met this crisis as it meets all other problems of hotel management—with resourcefulness bordering on the eccentric. Instead of phoning in the alarm, it sent Mrs. Bodne (wife of the owner) and her daughter Barbara around the corner, to break the news to the firemen at the firehouse.

To MORRIS BISHOP

North Brooklin, Maine
[January 2, 1961]

Dear Morris:

A pleasure to get your fine letter and the pretty view of Penn Yan.[1] I am surprised that Mr. Keast found my reply equivocal—I thought I was just declining his cordial invitation[2] in a charming but positive way. Which doesn't, of course, mean that I have no wish to revisit Ithaca. Those motorcycles of yours make it seem much closer and dearer somehow, and Katharine and I are counting on them when we come your way. She twisted her knee this morning while frying bacon, the only woman of my acquaintance ever to sustain this interesting accident, and a very lucky woman, too, as I managed to catch her as she was going down, and caught the bacon, too.

By the way, if young Alison[3] wants more than forty bats, I wish she would come here and remove the ones that cling to our kitchen chimney between the attic insulation and the roof. There is a metal filing cabinet just beneath them where our old bank statements are stored; it is getting hard to find the Morgan Guaranty Trust Company for the guano. I keep thinking the bats are rabid, too. A man has to have thoughts that he can turn over in his mind if he is to get through the days in this rather isolated region.

---

1. Bishop collected old postcards and showered them on his friends.
2. To speak at Book and Bowl, the undergraduate literary society at Cornell. Rae Keast was professor of English.
3. Alison Bishop Jolly, anthropologist, daughter of Morris.

We thank you and Old Alison for your delicious invitation. Today, for the first time in thirty-five years, K starts the year free of editorial duties—a Retired Person. I must say she looks a little as though she were entering Leavenworth. Although I've always been ready to bleed and die for the magazine, her own attachment to it has been much more solid, steadier than mine, and I think the breakup will be unsettling for a while.

Otherwise we are well. I have my sinking spells and my panics, and for the most part fritter away my time with inconsequential matters and pails of water. But I [am] up and around, and thankful to be here still, and not Gone.

Love and good cheer from us both.

Andy

• *Dr. Edward Teller, of the Lawrence Radiation Laboratory, Berkeley, California, had read White's "Letter from the West," dated June 4, in* The New Yorker, *and wrote White expressing his strong agreement with White's views on the futility of disarmament and the critical need for a federation of free states.*

To EDWARD TELLER

[North Brooklin, Me.]
January 2, 1961

Dear Dr. Teller:

I'm glad you liked my piece and I'm very pleased to have your letter. I would have answered sooner, but my grandchildren take Christmas seriously and I have been on trial.

When I discussed weapons testing in the piece, I was thinking of tests in the atmosphere, and should have so stated. Like all laymen, I am always out of date when it comes to the devices of science. My argument for a test ban was based on the assumption that tests are made in the air and are large and dirty, which, of course, is no longer a good assumption. At any rate, I'm for keeping our military strength at peak capacity consistent with decent air to breathe, and if testing is necessary, I'm for testing.

As for shelters, I used the hole-in-the-ground more as an illustration of negative, defensive thinking than as an undesirable thing in itself. I suppose a hole in the ground is indicated at this point, although temperamentally I am more inclined to take my last stand on the barn roof, where I can have a look around. Perhaps that's because I have never been in combat, and so indulge myself in a spurious cockiness. Perhaps it's because at my age I'd rather go out with a bang than a whimper. But I'd just as leave have some holes in the ground in America provided Americans don't get the idea that that's *all* we need, and that, once equipped, we can relax in peace. People tend to become preoccupied with anything that is tangible, immediate, and local—like a hole in the ground—and because of being preoccupied they lose sight of the main issue—the critical need for a political structure that embodies the perquisites of free government and that is supranational not just in intent but in design.

Thanks again for your instructive and congenial letter.

Sincerely,

E. B. White

To STANLEY HART WHITE

North Brooklin

27 January [1961]

Dear Bun:

Haven't thanked you yet for the Voltaire, but have been using it daily—or nightly. It's a little like sipping absinthe, which I tried once when I was young and could sip. (Now I just swallow gin and fall asleep.)

I still remember with pleasure the contemptuous look on your face when I explained to you, a year ago in the barn cellar, that cow manure was beneficial to the soil. These things stay with me. We've had sub-zero nights lately, and the manure pile is like a volcano getting ready to erupt—steam rises from the tip, moistening the cobwebs above, which then freeze in beautiful lacework. Enchanting place, loaded with intimations of pneumonia.

K has been ill since Christmas with a new disorder, as yet unexplained. She will enter the hospital on Feb. 4 (if I can find a way to get to New York over these roads) and will presumably have neurological tests. We've taken a house in Sarasota and bought rail tickets and made a lot of incidental arrangements, but these plans will blow up unless the doctor gives K the signal. Right now, life is about as disorderly as it can get; we've just had the grandchildren visiting us for a week, while Joe and Allene were away; and in the middle of that, I was hit with the flu and so was Henry, leaving no one to do the chores. We had a blinding blizzard on Inauguration Day, and the next morning the children remembered that they had left a large inflated rubber frog (with a beautiful yellow belly) down in the boathouse at the shore last summer. Grandfather and Steven were the ones to work their way down through the drifted snow and make the rescue. When we finally reached the boathouse, it looked like the wheelhouse of a dragger that has been at sea in the winter storm; the whole front of the building was iced up, and we had to chisel the doors out to free them. The horse's name is Whitey and the frog's name is Greeno, and they were glad to be carried up to the warm house. All subsequent parcheesi games were played on horseback, and Martha slept with Greeno.

Despite her troubles, K is trying to write a garden piece for *The New Yorker* while packing a trunk. It is almost impossible to move from one room to another in the house because of the accumulation of seed catalogues. Spring, if it ever comes, will be quite acceptable to me.

Yrs,
En

To KELLOGG SMITH

[North Brooklin, Me.]
February 3, 1961

Dear Mr. Smith:

I doubt that a Society is what is needed to preserve the language. The Society might easily become rigid, arbitrary, and generally objection-able—like the movie's Board of Morals, which encourages the most degrading and immoral films. Language is a matter of taste, and I think what is lacking today is discipline—in the home, the kindergarten, the college, the studios, everywhere.

I have no idea how one encourages a return to taste and discipline. Sorry I can't give you more support. A bureau of weights and measures is useful because it deals with something that is exact and static. A Society of Correct Language seems to me unpromising, the language being fluid and the servant of whim and fancy.

Sincerely,
E. B. White

To PATRICIA NOSHER

[North Brooklin, Me.]
[Early Spring, 1961]
Wednesday

Dear Pat:

. . . We had six inches of rain here last Saturday, and the coon hole began taking water. The coon declared it a disaster area at about 8 o'clock in the morning. She moved her four kittens, one by one, down the tree and across the road, stowing them under the floor of Art Waldron's workshop. (He's a potter, and a very noisy one.) Monday morning, tiring of life under a ceramist, the coon moved her babies back again, against fantastic odds. On each trip, from the time she left the tree to her return with a kitten in her mouth, her elapsed time was eight minutes.

Yrs,
EBW

• *White's reminiscences about his trip to Alaska aboard the S.S. Buford in 1923 appeared in the March 25, 1961, issue of* The New Yorker, *under the heading "Letter (Delayed) from the North." White heard from several readers who also remembered the* Buford.

To MRS. CHAFFEE E. HALL, JR.

[New York]
April 17, 1961

Dear Mrs. Hall:

If your parental home in Kodiak was where Captain Lane was that night, the hospitality must have been warm, because he didn't get back till all hours. I was much interested to read your long reminiscent account of your Alaska days, and I'm glad you found some old friends among the characters in my own memoir. I did not know that Louis Lane ended as a bay pilot, or that he died while deer-hunting. (I think he would have preferred to die hunting the polar bear.)

My only regret about the Buford trip is that it gave me no real experience of Alaska itself. I do retain a very strong recollection of Kodiak—the night was rainy and cold and foggy, the kind of cold that really penetrates. I remember a skiff coming alongside, with some ragged, half naked children standing in it. They seemed perfectly impervious to the cold and the wet, as though this might be one of the balmiest nights of the year, which, for all I know, it was. . . .

Sincerely,
E. B. White

To DORCY COLE STEVENS

[New York]
April 17, 1961

Dear Miss Stevens:

I keep learning new things about the *Buford,* and your letter was very informative. It doesn't surprise me at all that the cook went berserk and jumped overboard—the smell of the main galley made death seem wonderfully desirable.

As for bathing, I think I must have taken a bath or two during my elegant stage, the first six days. But I never remember bathing after that, and probably decided that since the men I was serving were dirty, a certain amount of personal encrustation was the thing.

Thanks for writing—I'm glad you enjoyed the piece.

Sincerely,
E. B. White

To B. W. HUEBSCH

25 West 43rd Street
April 17, 1961

Dear Mr. Huebsch:

Thanks for your letter about the *Buford*. Several people have written in, reminding me that I was preceded on board by Emma Goldman and Alexander Berkman, but although I love anarchists I doubt that I shall try to write anything about that earlier voyage.[1] One reason I like anarchists so much is that Ross once lent me Emma's autobiography— a fabulously funny book. Do you remember how they tunneled day after day, from a secret place outside the walls of a Pennsylvania jail, to release one of their boys (it might have been Berkman himself), and when they finally surfaced, they were right in the middle of the prison yard? Anarchists have a true simplicity of mind: a low-powered bomb planted in a room with a high-powered capitalist, and poof!—the good society. I wish I owned the book. (But it was in two volumes, and even Ross didn't own it—probably belonged to Charles MacArthur.)

I'll pass your suggestion along, in case *The New Yorker* might want to revive the deportations story. Many thanks for writing.

Sincerely,
E. B. White

To MRS. DOROTHY W. SANBORN

[New York]
April 18, 1961

Dear Mrs. Sanborn:

The ending of "Stuart Little" has plagued me, not because I think there is anything wrong with it but because children seem to insist on having life neatly packaged. The final chapters were written many years after the early chapters and I think this did affect the narrative to some extent. I was sick and was under the impression that I had only a short time to live, and so I may have brought the story to a more abrupt close than I would have under different circumstances.

---

1. The *Buford* had at one time been owned by the U.S. government. When Goldman and Berkman were deported, it was the *Buford* that carried them away.

My reason (if indeed I had any) for leaving Stuart in the midst of his quest was to indicate that questing is more important than finding, and a journey is more important than the mere arrival at a destination. This is too large an idea for young children to grasp, but I threw it to them anyway. They'll catch up with it eventually. Margalo, I suppose, represents what we all search for, all our days, and never quite find.

Sincerely,
E. B. White

• *Late in March, White had written a letter to a little girl named Cathy Durham, in answer to one from her asking why he hadn't produced another book for children. His letter said: "Dear Cathy, I would like to write another book for children but I spend all my spare time just answering the letters I get from children about the books I have already written. So it looks like a hopeless situation unless you can start a movement in America called 'Don't write to E. B. White until he produces another book.' " This letter apparently offended Cathy Durham's librarian, who returned it to White with a note taking him to task for cruelty. His reply follows.*

Eventually, letters from children arrived in such numbers that White found it impossible to keep abreast of his mail. His wife, with the help of a part-time secretary, now fields most of it, and his publisher cooperates by supplying a printed folder containing a "letter from the author" that is sent to every child who writes.

To MISS B——

North Brooklin, Maine
May 7, 1961

Dear Miss B——

I'm sorry this letter has been put off so long, but there has been serious illness in my family and I have let things slide in consequence.

I was surprised when my letter to Cathy Durham was returned to me by you. Of the thousands of letters I have written to children, it's the only one that has bounced, and I don't feel quite sure what happened. I assume you were disinclined to exhibit it, but I think the letter belongs to Cathy and if you'll send me her address I'll return it —she might like to have it about twenty years from now when she can fully understand what it is all about.

Cathy, as I recall it, asked me why I had not written another book for children, so I told her. (I don't always tell the exact, whole truth to children, but my tendency is to do just that.) Then I made what I considered was a little joke: I suggested a movement in America called "Don't write to E. B. White until he produces another book." In all this I see nothing ungracious or cruel. I do see that I raised a question that should be of interest to librarians and school teachers, namely, should they, in their zeal to put children in touch with books, also attempt to put them in touch with the authors?

The practice of having youngsters write to authors is now widespread. It is an innocent, and perhaps laudable, diversion; but it has arithmetical consequences that teachers and librarians seem unaware of. The author is hopelessly outnumbered. You, as a librarian, tend to think of your exhibit as an isolated case, but it is one of thousands. The result is the author is swamped with mail. Letters now come to me faster than I can answer them. Many of the letters contain requests— for an autograph, for a dust jacket, for an explanation, for a photograph. This to me presents a real problem. I have no secretary here at home, and if I am to deal with my mail I must do it myself; if I am to mail a book I must find the wrapping paper, the string, the energy, the right amount of stamps, and take the parcel to the post office up the road. This can occupy a whole morning, and often does.

I haven't solved this problem and don't really know what I shall do. I may give up answering letters, or, as some writers do, throw them back on the publisher—which seems to me evasive and unsatisfying.

About four years ago, I had an idea for a story for children. It seemed like such a pleasant idea that I spent my spare time for several weeks doing research and making notes—the raw material of a book. I put everything in a folder and there it still lies, awaiting a spell when I feel enough caught up with life to tackle the writing. Every once in a while I take this folder out and examine it, hungrily. But then I look at my desk where the unanswered letters and the undone things lie in accusing piles, and I stick the folder back in its corner.

When I was a child, I liked books, but an author to me was a mythical being. I never dreamed of getting in touch with one, and no teacher ever suggested that I do so. The book was the thing, not the man behind the book. I'm not at all sure that this separation of author and reader isn't a sound idea, although there are plenty of teachers and plenty of writers who would disagree. It is somewhat a matter of temperament, I guess. A lot of writers thrive on a rich diet of adulation and inquiry and contact; they like to read from their works, sign their name on flyleafs, and take tea. Other writers are very anxious to do anything that will promote the sale of their book, and they spend much time and energy fanning any spark of public interest. As for me, as soon as I get a book out of my system, I like to forget about it and get on with something else. So in the long run, although I'm not immune to praise and to friendliness, I get impatient with the morning mail, because it is, in a sense, my enemy—the thing that stands between me and a final burst of creative effort. (I'm sixty-one and am working against time.)

Margaret Mitchell once remarked: "It is a full-time job to be the author of 'Gone With the Wind.'" This remark greatly impressed me, as being an admission of defeat, American style. (Miss Mitchell, incidentally, was not overstating the matter—she never produced another book.) I don't want being the author of "Charlotte's Web" to be a full-time job or even a part-time job. It seems to me that *being an author* is a silly way to spend one's day.

If I caused Cathy any uneasiness by telling her a literary truth that is perhaps beyond her immediate comprehension, I am indeed sorry. But the letter, I think, properly belonged in your exhibit and you should have boldly stuck it on the wall, where it might have stirred the interest of visitors concerned with school and library practice.

Sincerely,
E. B. White

• *Arthur Zegart's efforts to promote the production of a live movie version of* Charlotte *had come to naught, and Louis de Rochemont had revived his proposal for an animated version.*

To LOUIS DE ROCHEMONT

[North Brooklin, Me.]
28 June 1961

Dear Mr. de Rochemont:

Here is the letter I threatened to write. I'll try to keep it from turning into a trilogy.

While animation is a perfect device for satire, *Charlotte's Web* is not really a satire. It has a thread of fantasy, but essentially it is a hymn to the barn. It is pastoral, seasonal, and is concerned with ordinary people in, for the most part, ordinary situations. The heroine dies, the summer ends, and when the story comes to a close the girl, Fern, is a different girl—she has matured a little. Her interest has shifted from the barnyard animals to a boy who gives her a ride on the Ferris wheel.

Because of this, it has occurred to me that the book, if handled with imagination, might make a motion picture in live action—real girl, real barn, real creatures. A good deal of the action in the book would present no problem whatever to the camera. . . . And then there are the parts that are out of the question for the camera and that would need an assist from the drawing board. The critical problem would be to arrive at a smooth transition between live scenes and animated scenes. If this problem can be solved at all, I believe the key lies in narration—in particular, narration by Fern herself.

Fern, in the story, often runs home and tells her mother about the goings-on in the barn cellar. Her mother is uneasy about the whole business and she presses Fern for details. In a film, this happy accident could be greatly useful. Fern could even turn out to be something of a sketch artist, and, when grilled, could draw pictures for her mother showing what the barn cellar crowd looks like—the spider, the rat, the pig. These rough sketches of hers would be the germ of the animated characters, and the action could then go quickly from narration to dramatic animation. The most difficult scenes in the book would thus be presented in retrospect and in animation—as recaptured by the little girl. . . . The thing that would make the real spider interchangeable with the drawing-board spider, the real pig with the drawing-board pig, would be the voice—always the same, and unmistakable. . . .

I also think a small amount of general narrative would be useful —a narrator speaking directly to the audience, using words from the book. Children rather like to be told something in plain words, and although the movie maker usually regards narration as an admission of defeat or a sign of weakness, I think in the case of "Charlotte's Web" it might be appropriate. It could be the intimate, relaxed kind of scene-setting that Thornton Wilder's narrator did so effectively in "Our Town."

An experience I had with the problem of illustrating the book is perhaps what gives me the courage to propose this live-action method of filming. When Garth Williams tried to dream up a spider that had human characteristics, the results were awful. He tried and tried, but we ended up with a Charlotte that was practically right out of a natural history book, or, more precisely, out of my own brain. And I pulled no punches in the story: the spider in the book is not prettified in any way, she is merely endowed with more talent than usual. This natural Charlotte was accepted at face value, and I came out ahead because of not trying to patronize an arachnid. I think a film maker might have the same good results by sticking with nature and with the barn. . . . I saw a spider spin the egg sac described in the story, and I wouldn't trade the sight for all the animated chipmunks in filmland. I watched the goslings hatch every spring, and I feel the same about that.

Anyway, I hope I've given you the gist of this idea. It could easily be a very sour idea, but it has stuck in my head for a long while, and I'd love to know whether you think it has any merit.

Sincerely,
E. B. White

To HARRY LYFORD

25 W. 43
September 14 [1961]

Dear Harry:

I hope you're not joining the ranks of those who scoop everything off their desk, put it in an envelope, and mail it to ME. Your recent communication shows an alarming trend. But thanks, old soldier. I didn't know Thomas Wolfe was having a come-back. When last seen by me he was climbing a vine on the rear wall of Max Perkins's apartment, drunk as a weasel and very noisy. He was in his climbing phase. . . .

May your declining years be busy ones!
Andy

To RUSSELL LANE

[New York]
September 25, 1961

Dear Dr. Lane:

I'm enclosing two checks, to cover the two bills.[1] Will you kindly return Katharine's bill, receipted, in the enclosed envelope?

She has had a grim time of tests, ending with the arteriogram a week ago. This showed no tumor, but disclosed a block in the right carotid artery. The doctors believe this to be the cause of her troubles, and they have instructed us to go to Rochester, N.Y., for surgery. The surgeon's name is Rob, and he has done a number of these operations with success. We're planning to leave New York on Saturday on the day train, and K will enter Strong Memorial Hospital that night.

She was all prepared for a brain tumor and was bewildered and upset at the news of the arterial block. But Dr. Atchley assures me that it is a less serious procedure, and with a much shorter recovery period. . . .

Three or four nights ago, at the hotel, she had the worst seizure she has ever had, and it lasted many hours and scared her and me. But on the whole she has survived this whole period wonderfully and she now realizes that she must relax, as the slightest excitement seems to

1. Dr. Lane was an internist at the Blue Hill Hospital.

bring on an attack. Nancy Stableford, my stepdaughter, will go along with us on the train—which will be a big help—and she will probably remain in Rochester for the operation.

Hope you managed to carve out a pleasant vacation for yourself these last couple of weeks. We both want to thank you again for your steady attendance at the house these past months. We're looking forward to getting home, and I hope we can head straight to Maine from Rochester, leaving New York to take care of itself.

Sincerely,

E. B. White

•   *In the early sixties White began donating his attic-full of manuscripts and correspondence to the Cornell Library. George H. Healey was curator of rare books.*

To GEORGE H. HEALEY

[New York]

September 27, 1961

Dear Mr. Healey:

A letter of mine presumably flashed by yours of 18 September, so here is a further attempt to communicate. . . . "Charlotte's Web" is all ready to go now, but it is in Maine and will have to await my return home. The book has gone into ten or a dozen foreign editions, and I'll be glad to send you a copy of each of them, if you'd like. Also any correspondence that might be amusing. . . .

After the first of the year, I shall set to work rounding up all the rest of my literary material. When I have it under control, I will send it to you and you can then invite the appraiser to Ithaca for a tour of inspection.

The New Yorker has saved all the original material that went into its issues as far back as 1934. (The stuff from 1925 to 1934 was presented to the Paper Drive during the Second War by a patriotic, if slightly insane, member of our advertising department.) Among this vast collection are many things by me. (I recently poked around in just one envelope representing just one issue, and my pugmarks were all over the place.) I can exhume this dusty material if it is of interest to Cornell. It probably reveals, more clearly than any other item in my mixed-up literary life, the early zeal that beset me. It also contains some of Ross's pencil editing, which should hold countless generations of inquisitive freshmen in thrall and convince them that there must be an easier way of making a living. . . .

Sincerely,

E. B. White

To MRS. N. J. SHOPLAND

[New York]
September 28, 1961

Dear Mrs. Shopland:

. . . The characters in "Charlotte's Web" were not presented as hicks; today's farmer is anything but. Neither were they presented as intellectuals who use the language with precision. Very few people in any walk of life speak and write precisely and correctly, and I don't myself. Your two letters, for example, contained mistakes—in the first letter you spelled grammar "grammer," and in the second letter you used the word "forbearers" when you meant "forebears."

I know the Zuckermans and the Arables quite well, and although I am not a farmer, many of my good friends are. I agree with you that the modern farmer is often a man of considerable education. But I think you are under a misapprehension about the nature of writing and the duties of a writer. I do not write books to raise any group's cultural level, I simply put down on paper the things I see and hear. I report speech as I hear it, not as it appears in books of rhetoric. If you ever take up writing, I advise you to keep your ears open, and never mind about culture.

Sincerely,
E. B. White

To WILLIAM S. MC CANN

Rochester, New York
11 October 1961

Dear Dr. McCann:

On the eve of departure I want to thank you for offering shelter to a couple of wanderers.[1] Thank you for the loan of this typewriter. Thank you for the early reassurance you gave us about the operation, and for your support during same. Thank you for directing my nose into a paper bag[2] (I am using a green one from the drug store at the moment and it is working well). Thank you for coming over here to the motel when I was scared—I am not inclined to apologize for my anxieties, because I have lived with them long enough to respect them, but I am always grateful to anyone who takes them at face value. And thanks . . . for the afternoon in the country, with the dace and the grape. They were wonderful.

What I am most grateful for is that you have given Katharine

---

1. Dr. McCann, now in partial retirement, was for many years physician-in-chief of the Strong Memorial Hospital in Rochester.

2. People who tend to "overventilate" during periods of stress sometimes breathe into a paper bag for relief, thus getting a charge of carbon dioxide.

such a good feeling about Rochester and the hospital and Dr. Rob and the operation. It was not easy to come here cold, the way we did, and we both loved the way you warmed the whole business up for us. I am sorry we can't linger for a few days, to repay our debts, but I guess we must start along. I am leaving a bottle of Jack Daniels as a last desperate attempt to say thank you, but it falls far short of our true feelings for your great kindness to us. I'll try to get a picture of Katharine being hoist by my boat anchor, so that you can see your physiotherapy in action in my barn. Please visit us when you come to Maine.

Sincerely,

E. B. White

To DOROTHY LOBRANO

North Brooklin, Maine
2 November 1961

Dear Dotty:

According to a tremor on my grapevine, you have landed a job with the magazine. This is the nicest bit of news I've heard in many a day.

I don't know when you are scheduled to begin work. Physically, the *New Yorker* is forbidding to the newcomer; it is like a rather badly arranged house of detention—little cells everywhere, and the long, grim corridors where people pass each other with no sign of recognition and as though sleep-walking. Do not permit this structural queerness to depress your spirits. Underneath everything is a strong tidal current, sweeping inmates onward and upward—a fine bloodstream and a great heart pumping away. My metaphor is already overwhelming, and I'll just leave you with my blessing and hope to see you in the corridors soon.

Love,

Andy

• *An editorial on the death of James Thurber in the* Washington Post *on November 6, 1961, gave White a great deal of credit for Thurber's meteoric rise to fame. It elicited from White the following disclaimer, which the* Post *ran on November 17.*

To THE EDITOR OF THE WASHINGTON POST

North Brooklin, Maine
[November 16, 1961]

To the Editor:

In 30 years the facts about anything at all seem to shake down into a sort of innocent distortion, and this is true of the facts about

James Thurber and me. The piece on Thurber in your Nov. 6 issue sounded as though he and his work would have lain unnoticed if I hadn't come along. This, as far as I'm concerned, is a pleasant theory, but it is a preposterous one. I did nothing to get Thurber appointed to the staff of the New Yorker except drop his name one day when Ross was casting about for names. I dropped it, and I let it lay, because I knew nothing about Thurber at that time. I had met him at the apartment of a friend (who, incidentally, was about as "Bohemian" as Herbert Hoover) and I thought he was a funny guy.

I did not "help him become an international celebrity"—he became one because he had what it takes. Nothing in the world could have stopped him. Even my much-touted admiration for his early drawings, although real enough, was touched less with perspicacity than with desperation. He and I needed some drawings to illustrate a book manuscript ("Is Sex Necessary?"). We thought we would stand a better chance with the publisher if there were some drawings. So we scooped up a few that were lying around in our office, and Jim drew others to fit the text. Harper & Brothers were bewildered, but they were game; they published the book not knowing they were launching a great artist. I didn't realize what was happening either.

Thurber's gateway was not me, it was *The New Yorker* itself. As soon as Ross saw Thurber's writing, he knew he had a humorist on the premises. I am writing this disclaimer because, although I would like to take credit for all the things you said, the facts don't stand up, and I think it must irritate Thurber's friends and relatives, who know a great deal about the matter, to hear me spoken of in this extravagant way. But thanks for the piece anyway—every man likes to be a king maker, if only for a day.

E. B. White

To CASS CANFIELD

North Brooklin, Me.
November 24, 1961

Dear Cass:

I have no objection to your using my words on the dust jacket of "The Last Flower" and I'm glad you plan to re-issue the book. Too bad it can't come out in a more attractive form—the original one never seemed right to me. Jim didn't think much of it, either, apparently, for the inscription in my copy reads: "For Andy and Katharine, With love and thanks for their help, without which Harpers would have ruined this more than they already have (2 blank pages, 5 reversed cuts). If you're going into the theatre, stay in the theatre; otherwise stay in town and keep your eye on Harpers, the playboys of the Western World. Jim."

The book would have gained, I think, if it had been smaller. Jim had switched from using a pencil to using a pen, and his pen strokes were seldom as sure and clean as his pencil strokes. Many of them showed tremor, and this became exaggerated by reproducing them so large. You might want to consider issuing a really beautiful book, smaller in size, and using good paper.

I think the color frame on each page works out well, but I should imagine that buff would be better than baby blue. The frames should be wider, and the drawings proportionately smaller. As you see, I'm still keeping my eye on Harpers.

Yours,
E. B. White

To RICHARD T. GORE

[North Brooklin, Me.]
November 27, 1961

Dear Mr. Gore:

Thanks for your letter and for the church calendar. The item is funny, but it would be ineffective without the proper names, and to use the names would be in bad taste, I fear. So I am reluctantly returning it.

I'm pleased to know somebody who has swum half way across [Walden] pond. Thoreau used to bathe on arising, and I've often wondered whether he wore some sort of swim suit or went in transcendentally.

Sincerely,
E. B. White

To ALEXANDER B. TOTH

[North Brooklin, Me.]
November 29, 1961

Dear Mr. Toth:

You are right that no humorist has ever won the Pulitzer prize—there is something not quite first rate about funny men. However, I won the silver badge and the gold badge of the St. Nicholas League when I was a child, and I've not felt the need of any prize since then.

I believe Thurber left his literary papers and his manuscripts to Yale.[1] I'm sure the Yale Library will treasure them, and they will con-

---

1. Yale did get many of the Thurber papers, but the larger part went to Ohio State University.

stitute the living memorial you plead for. Of course, somebody might put a statue of a Thurber dog in Central Park, next to Balto.

Sincerely,
E. B. White

To PAUL BROOKS

[North Brooklin, Me.]
December 13, 1961

Dear Paul:

I hope I didn't cause you a lot of trouble about the "Wild Flag" manuscript. It will probably turn up in my attic when the dust settles, if it ever does.

I was about to write you when your letter came. This, too, concerns "The Wild Flag." Not long ago I learned that the United World Federalist organization sells the book for fifty cents a copy. I presume this means that they buy the books from Houghton Mifflin in quantity and resell them, absorbing part of the cost as an organizational expense. I'm asking about this because I find it unsettling to have my book peddled as a sort of handbook by this organization, many of whose political panaceas I sharply disagree with. It is an odd situation for an author. "The Wild Flag" was written about sixteen years ago and has grown whiskers, and although I have no quarrel with its basic idea, I am greatly embarrassed to find myself being used by a political action group whose interpretation of the world government theme strikes me as fallacious and dangerous. Could you enlighten me as to what the situation is, exactly? That is, do you have any special arrangement with UWF? Did you print a supply of the books for them? It has occurred to me that the book might be out of print by this time, except for this one outlet. At any rate, I'd like to know what the facts are.

I think it's fine that you are taking over the record program of Cornell's ornithologists. I own the "Bird Song" record, and it is a favorite of our dachshund, who expressed his enthusiasm for it by clawing the fabric off the front of our old Magnavox. Oh, he loves boids. (He once caught a barn swallow on the wing—which isn't bad for a low-posted dog.)

And my congratulations on getting Rachel Carson on contamination. It is a book I have known was in the making and one I await with impatience and general gloom.

Yrs,
Andy

To PAUL BROOKS

[North Brooklin, Me.]
January 5, 1962

Dear Paul:

Many thanks for your explanatory letter. Sorry my book has fallen on such hard times; those 843 copies that you are stuck with should really be sent back to me, the way Ticknor and Fields once tossed one of H.D.T.'s works back to the author. Then I could say, with Thoreau, "I now have a library of twelve hundred books, 843 of which I wrote myself."

When the world finally gets a government (which it must surely have some day), I think you and I should be given a small government post in recognition of our services and our sacrifices. Meantime, the best of luck to you in today's chaos.

Sincerely,
Andy

To JOHN UPDIKE

North Brooklin, Maine
12 January [1962]

Dear John:

I would rather read an unwritten novel by you than a written one by almost anybody else. The piece in this issue[1] is wonderfully moving, moved me wonderfully, is almost unbelievably good, except I believe it. I went right from the O'Hara story into your grandmother and it was like entering a garden through a little gate. I keep trying to discover what it is (what mysterious thing) that elevates writing to the level where combustion takes place, and I guess it is simply that in writing there has to be an escape of gases or vapors from the center— Core Gas, that is. And even this explanation is unreliable, because God knows there was always gas escaping from Hemingway but a lot of the time it reminded me of the farting of an old horse. This mystery is not going to get solved in a hurry. Meantime, thanks for the shining thimble of your grandmother.

Yrs,
Andy

---

1. "The Blessed Man of Boston, My Grandmother's Thimble, and Fanning Island," in *The New Yorker* of January 13, 1962.

To STANLEY HART WHITE

N. Brooklin
Jan 21 [1962]

Dear Bun:

I called Carol yesterday to find out about Lil, and she told me that Lil had had a mild heart attack—so mild, apparently, that she didn't even know she was having it. The doctor put her in a hospital for two weeks, then she came out and stayed for a while with Carol and Tom,[1] and now she is back home. Lil had not written me a darn thing, and all I knew was what turned up in letters from Arthur Brittingham and Mildred, which wasn't very clear. Anyway, Carol reports that she is feeling quite chipper now, and that Noel and Sid are helping her with cooking and housework.

At the very end of Christmas afternoon, I washed my hands with Pears Soap, and was comforted. The day started with a blizzard and with me leaning too hard on a shovel at 6:30 in the morning. The phone went out for 24 hours, the truck that usually plows me out broke down, and my youngest grandson John stirred up a bit of private confusion by removing most of the tags from the gifts under the tree. All in all it was quite a day, but the Pears Soap was relaxing after so much turmoil. I took the bar of Sapolio into the kitchen, where it was greeted with amazement and with cheers, and we all stood around talking about Spotless Town and the peaceful era before television detergency, when nobody had heard of "dirt backwash" and things went along very nicely anyway. I hadn't realized that Vrest Orton had Pears Soap and Sapolio up his sleeve, and K and I were pleased with your gift. . . .

Joe's partner in the Brooklin Boat Yard decided to pull out of the business. . . . Joe last week bought the partner's share and is now sole owner and operator, up to his ears in reorganization and general commotion. In this climate, a boatyard man's Number One riddle is how to paint 40 boats in three days of good weather that you usually get in a Maine springtime.

Hope all goes well in Denver. Wish I could get out there on the rails some time. Love to Blanche and Janice.

Yrs,
En

---

1. Tom Baker, Carol Illian's husband.

• *Harriet Walden, who has served* The New Yorker *in various secretarial and supervisory capacities for many years, took over the Whites'
affairs from Daise Terry. Miss Terry remained on the staff for several
more years in a less demanding job, then retired.*

To HARRIET WALDEN

[North Brooklin, Me.]
March 1, 1962

Dear Harriet:

The missing portfolio has been found. I had carefully packed everything in a mailing envelope before leaving home, with instructions to
send it to me when I asked for it. Then I forgot to ask for it. That's
me. In a space capsule, I would forget to yaw.

You asked about opening my mail. Go ahead and open everything
except the ones from Bardot.

Yrs,
EBW

To J. G. CASE

Fiddler Bayou
30 March [1962]

Dear Jack:

The next grammar book I bring out I want to tell how to end a
sentence with five prepositions. A father of a little boy goes upstairs after
supper to read to his son, but he brings the wrong book. The boy says,
"What did you bring that book that I don't want to be read to out of up
for?"

And how are YOU?

Yrs,
Andy

To URSULA NORDSTROM

[Sarasota, Fla.]
31 March 1962

Dear Ursula:

I am sorry if I puzzled you with my arithmetic. Anybody who
receives seventy-five hundred dollars a year from an old book shouldn't
go around mystifying his benefactors. All I meant in my letter to you
was that when Charlotte goes up over the ceiling (which is where a
spider belongs anyway) there is not a penny in it for me. There is
presumably a penny in it for my grandchildren, though, and that is
good enough for me. Their names are Steven, Martha, and John. John,
who is now three, has invented a small friend who lives in an empty

peanut butter jar and is called Deedee Ham-O. This little fellow (according to John's mother) does everything John would like to do—never has hair cuts or gets his face washed.

I never intended to get you tangled up with the Royalty Department over my queer affairs. I was the boy who set $7500 as the maximum amount. Ross once said that a New York cop was incapable of thinking of any sum over fifteen hundred dollars—a remark that still strikes me as very funny. Well, I am a little like Ross's cops—I am incapable of thinking of any sum over seventy-five hundred dollars. To me that's all the money there is in the world, and it's more than enough.

Yrs,
Andy

• *Beulah Hagen had been Assistant to Cass Canfield for many years, although she had not worked with White before* The Points of My Compass *was in preparation.*

To BEULAH HAGEN

North Brooklin, Maine
7 May 1962

Dear Beulah:

We're so near the end of these negotiations I am going to call you Beulah and you can call me Whitey or Butch or Andy. . . .

The manuscript is almost ready, and I plan to put it in the mail on May 15 and drive right from the post office to the liquor store, and you can receive it on May 17 and drive right to Sarasota without reading it.

I must leave you now to build a support for an espaliered apple tree with the wind NW at 30 miles per hour. Everything around this place depends on me for support—it is disgusting.

Yrs,
Andy

To J. G. CASE

North Brooklin, Maine
July 13, 1962

Dear Jack:

You chose a real whiz ("Whizzer White," they call me) when you picked me for your grammarian. A man named Betz, in Riverside, Connecticut, has turned up the best boo boo yet. Look on P. 52, first paragraph. "There is no . . ."

There *is* no inflexible rules, all righty!

Some day I shall make a trip to the attic, examine the original manuscript, and find out whether I really wrote that. Meantime, I plan to burn my typewriter and scatter the ashes over Lower Fifth Avenue.

Yrs,
Andy

To CASS CANFIELD

North Brooklin, Maine
18 September 1962

Dear Cass:

A copy of my book arrived yesterday and I hasten to say that I am pleased with its appearance. The text is a little weak, but physically it's a fine book, and I thank you one and all.

You even managed to get it here on Katharine's birthday, which was a help to me, as I had no gift for her and palmed this off on her.

I wish I looked like Niccolò Tucci. Have you seen his picture on the jacket?[1] That's the way an author should look. Now compare it with the picture of me. I appear to be digging a piece of wax out of my left ear.

Yrs,
Andy

To STANLEY HART WHITE

Fiddler Bayou—which
the post office calls
4444 Ocean Boulevard
Sarasota, Florida
St. Valentine's Day [1963]

Dear Bun:

This letter has been a long time in the making, but I've been spending most of my time with doctors and radiologists and their girls in nylon uniforms. I think the X-ray parlor down here will soon be fully automated, and you will just hear the command, "Hold your breath, please; stop breathing!" from a wall outlet, like Muzak in a restaurant. Sarasota's doctors are overworked, because everybody comes down here to die, and they want a physical checkup first. I stepped off the Silver Meteor of the Seaboard Railway (remember how Father loved that railroad when it was called the Seaboard Air Line?) with a duodenal ulcer, only I didn't know it. By the time the ulcer was discovered, it was no longer bothering me much, and I laced my bland diet with generous dollops of gin, on my private theory that ulcers are caused by anxiety

---

1. Of *Before My Time*.

and the way to avoid anxiety is to drink. But meantime I developed a truly spectacular array of ailments and miseries extending all the way from gout to an ulcerated tooth. I lost my voice and I lost my nerve. The climax came when a dentist sent me to the office of an extractionist who would be a worthy opponent for Cassius Marcellus Clay, the lyrical pug, and whose receptionist knocked me out with a long draught of paregoric and other sedatives while I was still in the waiting room. The tooth never came out, and I drove back to Fiddler Bayou having opium dreams at the wheel.

I am quieter now, and can form simple words and mix martinis. But it was a bad old time for a while. We wouldn't be here at all had our doctor in Maine not urged us strongly to try the warmer climate as the best control for K's arterial trouble. She does feel some better, and is able to take short walks, and perhaps can avoid surgery. But I put her over the jumps last month, with my total collapse, and she's now busy trying to recover from ME. No small assignment.

I think I'm going to like *Landscape,* and thanks for the gift of it. The Luten article filled me with a warm glow of sympathetic passion. I'm sitting right in the middle of one of the better population explosions, and I have green memories of what this delectable sandbar was like before the fuse was touched off. The city fathers of Sarasota regard themselves as visionaries if they look as far ahead as, say, nineteen days. Anything beyond that is too far in the future to be worth monkeying with. And there have been some wonderful boomerangs and a truly scorched landscape. One of the Ringlings, years ago, owned a key near town called Bird Key and his deed included the right to fill. When a promoter finally got possession of Bird Key, he went right to work with a scoop, and scooped up about half of the bottom of Sarasota Bay, substantially increasing the size of his holdings by just spreading sand in all directions. A side result of this brilliant real estate operation was that the tidal current in Big Pass jumped from something like 3 knots to something like 7 knots, and this created quite a scooping operation in itself, washing away the beaches all the way from the mouth of the Pass half way into town and causing a real beaut of an erosion problem. All the property owners along the Pass had to build groins, so that what was once a lovely little stretch of natural beach, complete with dunes, sea grape, and Australian pine, now looks like a broken-down docking facility.

On top of the population explosion we have, this year, the aftermath of the Great Freeze—which occurred in December. Of all dreary sights, a dead palm tree is one of the dreariest, with those loud brown fronds scraping together in the cold wind. As near as I can make out, the coconut palms and the Royal palms are goners, but not the cabbage palm and the palmetto. The Australian pines, lofty feathery trees which are some-times also used as hedges, are brown and will probably not come back. The sea grape is brown, but shows signs of latent vigor. The punk trees, which I love, were hard hit. Our landlady sawed hers off about half way, and thinks they will revive: but even if they do revive, I doubt that they can recapture their original handsome shape. The hibiscus is shot. So are the enormous banyans—their corpses are heartbreaking to look at. Even the mangroves got nipped pretty hard, but I don't think you can stop a mangrove—or even get one of their roots with child.

Our weather has been chilly, but we have been reasonably com-fortable. If life smoothens out with the coming of spring, we will be glad we're here. K and I both stagger under a galloping frustration: her head swims and prevents her from doing another garden piece, which she dearly wants to do: and I've not been able to write a damn thing in two years. But I am taking daily shock treatments by bumping my head accidentally on the bottom of a rowboat that is suspended in the car-port, right where I step out of the car. This may bring me round eventually.

Love to you both from both of us.

En

To DAVID E. LILIENTHAL

[Sarasota, Fla.]
February 26, 1963

Dear Mr. Lilienthal:

Thanks for sending me the copies of your Stafford Little Lectures. I am reading them with a good deal of interest and agreement.

To be against disarmament, these days, is like being in favor of influenza—people don't seem to grasp what you're talking about. I think the popular acceptance of weapons control, or weapons reduction, as the road to peace is easily as alarming as the power of the accumu-lated weapons themselves. You've done a great service in your attempt to dispel these fantasies of life.

Sincerely yours,
E. B. White

To FAITH MC NULTY MARTIN

Sarasota, Florida
11 March [1963?]

Dear Faith:

Johnny is right, you can be stuck with your private monsters. I never thought of it that way until I read his piece, and as you say, he has been reading around in The Works.[1] But he is right about your own private monsters.

I've got a leafy jungle down here, in case you want an adventure, but the weather has been so lousy nobody would even settle for an adventure. Luckily, my real estate man, who weighs 230 pounds and is a friend of Ted Williams, lent me a rod and reel and a fast boat—he did this in desperation—and I have been having good fishing, for me.

Tell Johnny to read Santayana for a little while, it will improve his sentence structure.

Yrs,
Andy

To ROBERT M. COATES

Fiddler Bayou
[Sarasota, Fla.]
11 March [1963]

Dear Bob:

At the end of a day of sickness I stumbled on "Special Care" in what I believe is called "working proof" and read it and felt better right away.[1] It is a wonderful piece. Coates in his stride, life-giving as death so often is. Of course I bridled when I got to "from his own vantage point of twenty-eight." You fiction writers! As an elderly essayist who ages on paper, year by year, just as he ages in the mirror in the bathroom, I resent this literary license that enables a lovesick old recovery case to lop thirty years off his hide at the stroke of a typewriter and with the lovely Mrs. DeCasiris, an older woman, dying in the next bed. I felt that she suffered an undeserved hardship in a hard time. But these are mere quips and quibbles; the thing is, it's such a fine piece. Gives me courage to go on, in the mournful sixties. Shows what man can do, with what he remembers. And one of the best parts, I thought, was the part about time becoming fluid in a hospital, and the way you float in it. Last summer I spent seven days in Harkness, floating. Nobody came to see me, nothing happened, I didn't eat or drink, I didn't read, it was a private room, my doctor left town, the nurses disappeared one by one into the heat of summer and vacations, and I was alone, truly afloat in time, more alone than I have ever been in my life.

We've been here in Sarasota since early January, enjoying indiffer-

---

1. Young Johnny McNulty had been reading his father's writings and had sent White a story he himself had written.

1. Coates had been hospitalized for a throat ailment and had written a story that he called "Special Care." It ran in the May 25, 1963, issue of *The New Yorker* under the title "The Captive."

ent health and the scraping sound of dead palms. I have an ulcer, K has a blocked artery, and we sit around waiting for a change in weather and in luck. The water in the Gulf, despite the severe winter, has warmed to a tolerable 62° and I stumble into it every morning from a convenient little strip of sand at the mouth of the bayou, within stroking distance of dolphins. I have abandoned writing after two sterile years, and good riddance. But then there come these uneasy days, when I pick up a "Special Care" and feel a return of the old special itch.

The throat, as you discovered the hard way, is unquestionably the seat of the emotions. In January, on this unheated sandbar, I developed about ten ailments all within a week, and as a result went into what in happier days we used to call a "nervous breakdown." The thing I remember with the greatest chill is the way my throat closed up on me, my vocal cords got rough, and I couldn't swallow pills. Fortunately I was able to swallow whiskey, from long practice, and continued to do so. And recovered after a fashion.

Hope you and Boo[2] are wintering well, and congratulations to you, Robert M. Coates, for doing it again.

Love from us both,
Andy

To CAROL ILLIAN BAKER

Sarasota, Florida
15 March 1963

Dear Cally:

It was so nice to get your letter. . . . I think the biggest trouble with the best-seller list is its title, because the word "best" has a sneaky way of attaching itself to the books themselves. Time Magazine publishes two lists—the first is called "Best Reading" and the second "Best Selling," which is a step forward.

As an author of books, I like to study the best-seller list; it lets me know how I'm doing in the marts of trade. I have never run a bookstore, but I can see that a list such as your boss suggests would be helpful. One of the reasons people consult the best-seller list when selecting a book is simple fear—they're scared they will be caught in a social group without having read what other people have read.

It's my belief that the publishers, rather than the book reviewers and the compilers of lists, are the real jokers in the litry world today. Twenty or thirty years ago, a good house like Harper or Scribner had good editors, whose mind was on their work and who were interested in finding and developing promising writers. At Harper's there was

---

2. Astrid Peters, Coates's second wife, herself a *New Yorker* short story writer.

Eugene Saxton. At Scribner's there was Maxwell Perkins. And there were others. Nowadays most of the publishing houses are operated like a garment business—someone tries to find out what the public wants and then someone is delegated to produce it. This results in non-books, or near-books. Considering the low state of the publishing business we are lucky to get as many creditable books as we do. . . .

Haven't seen the albino dolphin but have been swimming with porpoises who like this tiny strip of beach.

Love,
Andy

To ROGER ANGELL

[Sarasota, Fla.]
5 April [1963]

Dear Rog:

Now that the grapefruit days are over, I can report that your man Al Weis looks good. Lopez has used him a lot, both at short and at second, and he has been all you could ask for, defensively, but hasn't done much with his bat. For my money he is a more capable shortstop than Hansen—but you would have to get that confirmed by Lopez, I guess. They've been saving Fox, on account of his Great Age, and Weis has filled his shoes nicely, although his feet don't turn out the way Nellie's do.

Baseball was a life saver for us this winter—the one thing K was able to manage in the way of relaxation. She was able to attend most of the games, walked to and from the car without much pain, and generally enjoyed herself. Nothing else down here has given her any pleasure this season and she has been very depressed because of her disabilities and very disappointed at her lack of progress. . . .

Both of us, of course, are suffering from the onset of professional inactivity, or inadequacy, or both, and in her case it is greatly aggravated by her almost-lost dream of writing another garden piece or two, so as to put a book together. She came down here with a foot-locker loaded with catalogues and garden books, and she has hardly been able to touch it. She hasn't quite given up but her spirit is badly cracked, and it is the saddest thing I have ever had to live with, to see her this way, after having done so much for so many, and now unable to do a small thing for herself. I sometimes think I would give everything I own for one garden piece, one book, and one restored lady.

Your letters have been a big help, as she feels she is really in touch with the way things are. . . . We've had a month of consistently good weather, but Florida usually manages to mess things up somehow or other—this year a "red tide" has been hanging off the coast, and we were visited with a beach-full of dead fish. It *can* be dreadful—in 1947 they were using bulldozers to clean up the fish piles, two people died of respiratory troubles, and many had to leave the Key. About ten days ago, cormorants, raccoons, manatees, and sea turtles began dying from paralysis—unexplained. We had a sick shag in the Bayou, and a general uneasiness because nobody could get anything analyzed in a lab. People have been knocked over from eating oysters and clams, and so it goes. This may not have been the winter of Kennedy's discontent but it has been the winter of mine.

Love,
Andy

To MARK VAN DOREN

[New York]
April 29, 1963

Dear Mark:

Sorry I can't sign the letter. I'm for a test ban treaty, as I think it is worth the risk involved. But I don't think coexistence with a nation whose territorial ambitions are, by its own admission, unlimited, is or can be peaceful. And I am flatly against disarmament, which I believe to be a delusion—a harmful and costly one. The best statement I've seen on this was in David Lilienthal's series of Princeton lectures recently.

Sincerely,
E. B. White

To CHARLES MORTON

Hotel Algonquin
New York
6 May 1963

Dear Charley:

I take up my ballpoint to thank you for your three fine pieces,[1] the last of which I just finished, having returned to the hotel after a session (my first) with a periodontist, who proposes to remove a small section of my gum, or goom, tomorrow noon, thus detaining me another day in this city of shadows and memories. To a large extent my memories of the early *New Yorker* agree with yours more than with those of the other memoirists who have tackled that difficult subject and those elusive years. And I thought that you, more than the others, recaptured the amiable spirit and wondrous intent of the magazine and its hopeful editor. Too much has been written, I think, by people who nursed a particular grudge, like some drowsy sailor nursing his last beer at

---

1. In the *Atlantic Monthly*—reminiscences of *The New Yorker* in the thirties, when Morton had worked briefly for the magazine.

the end of the bar—people who failed to see the sandstorm for the grain of sand in their eye. So I found your genial and comical account extremely refreshing and gratifying, for those were, by & large, good days for all of us, dead or alive. Your description of the depression was quite enchanting, and also disturbing to me, because I have lived all my life with a guilty feeling about the depressed years. *The New Yorker* was, of course, a child of the depression and when everybody else was foundering we were running free, and I still feel that I escaped the hard times undeservedly and will always go unacquainted with the facts of life.

I still do newsbreaks for the magazine but am otherwise disengaged, and for the last two years have been unable to write. They have been bad years for the Whites, with Katharine continuously ill. . . . We have been in Florida this winter (it helps relax the arteries but otherwise makes one rather tense) and are trying, against odds, to get home to North Brooklin. . . . Miss Terry is still at work but in an easier job. I lunched with Shawn today; he had a banana on Special K, I had a 3-minute egg on white toast. Thanks again for the memories.

Sincerely,
Andy White

P.S. Forgive this cautionary postscript: this letter is for your eyes, not for the readers of the *Atlantic*. EBW

To JOAN LARKIN

[New York]
May 7, 1963

Dear Miss Larkin:

To answer your letter of inquiry, my essay "Walden," written in 1939, is a factual report of a visit to Concord and the pond.[1] In the early parts of the essay, the reader is reminded that the world changes very little, basically, and that Thoreau's account is "a document of increasing pertinency." Thoreau was a prophetic man—many of his observations seem truer today than when they were written. The complexity of life, which he deplored and which he warned against, increases year by year.

There is no satirical intent in the essay: I simply reported on what the modern visitor to the Pond sees—the popcorn wrapper, the DuBarry pattern sheet, littering the place, but along with them, the immemorial frog note, bridging the years and tying us all together. The boys singing "America" were there on the pond, skylarking, having a fine time, making

---

1. The piece appeared in the "One Man's Meat" department of the July 1939 issue of *Harper's Magazine*.

what was once a quiet place into a rather noisy one. There was nothing derogatory in this report—I loved the boys and I love America, popcorn wrappers and all. I also love to think back on an earlier Walden Pond, before it had been taken over by civilization, and when its principal visitors were fishermen, trappers, and philosophers.

The final paragraph is a commentary on Thoreau's bachelor state— to remind the reader that his ideas on "economy" were those of an ascetic, a celibate, and not all of them are realistic when applied to a young married man (which is what I was at the time) whose thoughts were on taking home a baseball glove to his small son.

Usually, I don't explain my writings at length, but your letter with its suggestion that the piece was derogatory of our society showed that you were reading things into the essay that are wholly false. So I am taking this chance to straighten you out. You might like to look up another piece on "Walden" that I wrote on the 100th anniversary of the book's publication. It appears in my collection called "The Points of My Compass," which you can probably find in your public library if you are so minded.

Sincerely,
E. B. White

To BEULAH HAGEN

North Brooklin, Maine
1 June 1963

Dear Beulah:

Thanks for all the things you have been sending me—the citation, the original drawings, the Delta paperbacks, and the nifty copy of my latest book in blue and gold. Now what I need is YOU, to file all these fine gifts in their proper places, which, in this house, means a trip to the attic. I've made one big improvement in the attic since my return home: I gave the cream separator away, to a neighbor who has a cow that has recently freshened, and in its place built bookshelves all around the base of one chimney, to hold bound volumes of *The New Yorker*. We have a complete set of the *New Yorker* bound volumes; starts in 1925, and you can imagine what that does to an old house that has many windows and no wall space.

We're right in the middle of apple blossoms, lilacs, and hay fever, and are coming to the end of tulips, daffodils, and fritillaries. Next thing that's going to happen is my birthday, then the total eclipse of the sun.

Yrs,
Andy

To CASS CANFIELD

[North Brooklin, Me.]
7 June 1963

Dear Cass:

Thanks for sending me the ad in the *New Statesman*. The British reviewers have been very kind to my book, and I hope it will mean that a few Englishmen will take a chance on buying the book, if only to keep Jamie [Hamish] Hamilton's courage up.

The sales here have exceeded my early guesses and I'm pleased that I was able to get up over 50,000. Not bad for a clipbook.

The other day I read a letter Thoreau had written his mother and it had a reference to you in it. He had been visiting publishing houses to see if he could earn some money. "Among others I conversed with the Harpers—to see if they might find me useful to them—but they say that they are making fifty thousand dollars annually and their motto is to let well alone." I thought you might be amused by this.

Yrs,
Andy

• *Howard Cushman sent White a telegram to congratulate him on being named by President Kennedy to receive the Presidential Medal of Freedom. The wire read:*

This morning's tidings make me glad.
Congratulations, Freedom's lad.

To HOWARD CUSHMAN

North Brooklin
July 9 [1963]

Dear Cush:

Your merry telegram pleased both me and the Western Union gal in Ellsworth, who had to deliver it over the phone and who was relieved not to be interrupted in the middle of it, an experience she had had a couple of days before when she began reading Kennedy's wire to my skeptical wife. The President was a bit long-winded, and after K had dutifully scribbled the first thirty or forty words on a scratch pad, she said to the girl, "Is this a practical joke?" (There's a wife for you!) "No," said the girl a little stiffly, "Western Union is not allowed to transmit practical jokes." And where was I while this embarrassing exchange was going on? Why, in the tub, of course, where Freedom's lad should be, soaking the gurry out of me armpits.

Anyway, it was good of you to start warming up the wires. Most of my distant friends were much too heavily engaged celebrating the Fourth, and the local crowd maintained a decent silence—anything Kennedy does to you, in these parts, is considered no worse than a bad cold. . . . For a couple of days I sneaked around the house in a hangdog fashion, but am gradually recovering my natural poise. . . .

Love,
Andy

To CASS CANFIELD

[New York]
July 19, 1963

Dear Cass:

I'm very much pleased that my book has been chosen to be part of the International White House Libraries. Thanks for letting me know about it. I had not heard of the program but am delighted to be associated with it through *The Points of My Compass*.

We are in New York for a few days. Katharine came out of the hospital this morning, after taking some tests. There will probably be surgery, but the doctors think we can wait until fall, when the nights are cooler and the surgeons are not fly fishing.

Best regards,
E. B. White

To DAVID BRADLEY

[New York]
July 22, 1963

Dear Mr. Bradley:

My apologies for being so late in replying to your letter. It was a most satisfying letter to receive, and I am always astonished to discover that my haphazard literary popsicles have found takers in places like Helsinki.[1] High school students in America are something else again— once in a great while I get a really wonderful blast from one of them, taking me apart at the seams, which I love. Got one this winter from a young man in Miami who said that my Florida Key piece (written before he was born) showed a complete misconception of Florida and an utter disregard of simple facts.

Many thanks for your report, and best regards.

Sincerely,
E. B. White

1. Bradley, author of *No Place to Hide*, had taught English in Helsinki for two years. He had written White that *One Man's Meat* occupied a "unique place in the hearts and minds" of his students there.

•   *"The Door," probably the most widely reprinted of White's pieces, ran in* The New Yorker, *March 25, 1939. Some twenty years later, William R. Steinhoff, chairman of freshman English at the University of Michigan, decided to track down, if he could, White's sources for the queer omelette he had put together: the experiments with the rats, the washable house, the poet (deceased), the man out in Jersey who began taking his house down brick by brick, the prefrontal lobotomy. Steinhoff succeeded in tracing everything to real events and people. He reported this detective work in an article about "The Door," published in* College English, *December 1961. "It is good to remember," he wrote, "that as a work of art Mr. White's story has its own sort of victory, art's recurrent though never final conquest of the seemingly irrelevant and disorderly flux of human experience."*

For several years after its publication, White felt disinclined to have the piece reprinted. Eventually, requests became frequent and he overcame his reluctance. The story has appeared in dozens of textbooks and anthologies, baffling many a freshman and cheering many a neurotic.

To **ROBERT L. DE LONG, JR.**

[New York]
July 22, 1963

Dear Mr. DeLong:

I'm very far behind in my correspondence and am not even sure whether your letter got an answer or not.

If there is any specific symbolism in "The Door" I am not aware of it. Religion was not in my mind when I wrote it, and you are quite wrong when you interpret the piece to mean that religion "does not answer the big questions of existence."

Few readers seem to realize that "The Door" is a somewhat factual piece. *The New Yorker* had sent me to write a report of an exhibit in Rockefeller Center—some sort of house that had unusual materials and features. I was feeling bad and I had a fever. When I came back to the office, instead of writing a straight piece, I wrote a dizzy one. You asked what the last paragraph meant. I think it mentions stepping out onto the street and the street comes up to meet the man's foot. That's what happened to me.

The rats in the piece had appeared in an article in *Life*, and I happened to have it—among many other odd items—on my desk at the time. A lot of things got thrown in as I went along.

Sincerely,
E. B. White

To FRANK SULLIVAN

North Brooklin
28 Aug. 1963

Dear Frank:

. . . K and I were sorry to hear about your pneumonia, but applauded your decision to stay home. In a hospital you would just get salmonella from the eggs, or staph from the insanitary condition of the pantry. I'm damn glad you didn't have the real honest-to-God pneumonia, which I was visited with about ten years ago. It took me one afternoon between four and five o'clock. My doctor fed me a few terramycin pills and said he didn't think it could be pneumonia because I wasn't weak enough for that. Just before I died, they put me on a train for New York (we still had trains in those gaudy days) and I spent the night in an upper, swigging aspirin and White Rock. There was no room at the inn when I reached Harkness, so I was bundled over to Neurological, across the way. I didn't much care where I was because I was dying anyway, but I remember feeling sorry for myself about dying, as I dearly love life, and I started to cry. Next day they ordered me out of bed and into my clothes, and they loaded me into a wheel chair and stuck my felt hat on my head and wrapped a grey blanket around me and at the last moment the nurse grabbed up the one bunch of flowers that had arrived and placed these carefully on my chest, and an orderly appeared and we began the long hot, lonely underground journey through the tunnel under Fort Washington Avenue. This tunnel follows the same route as the steam pipes, and the temperature down there was even higher than my own, which was around 104. I steadied the flowers so they didn't fall off, but I felt pretty wispy just the same. In Harkness, they switched me from terramycin to acromycin, gave me a blonde nurse who complained that I didn't shave my armpits, and here I am. . . .

Right now we have Roger and his two teen-age daughters visiting us, which, to put it mildly, enlivens the scene. For scene read bathroom. Roger and his wife were divorced a few weeks ago, and this has been an added touch of gloom for K. The girls are old enough to feel the breakup very deeply, and on that account they have not been easy visitors, albeit merry by times.

Much love from us both,
Andy

P.S. I had a very fine dream last night. A friend flew over in a small plane and seeing me on the lawn reached out and shook hands, the plane being still airborne. Then he said he guessed he'd hop out and stay awhile and that the plane would go home by itself and his wife would fly it back later. I took him in the house for drinks, but found General Eisenhower occupying an upstairs room, where he was having a prostate operation by a local physician. The General was not anesthetized and was directing every move himself. Can't tell you whether that nifty little plane got back because I soon left the land of Nod. Hope your dreams are happy ones like mine.

• *John Updike's dedication of his volume of poems,* Telephone Poles, *to Katharine and E. B. White inspired the following letter.*

To JOHN UPDIKE

3 Sept. 1963 Parked outside
Blue Hill Hospital, waiting for
KSW to emerge

Dear Updike (John)

In youth, when I was the creator,
I was a lusty dedicator;
But now, the blood all drained from me,
At last I rise a dedicatee
(All thanks to thee.)

Katharine and I were surprised and very pleased to turn up at the head of your telephone poles. It was kind of you to admit us to this fine book, and I've been reading and re-reading the poems with an extra pleasure and satisfaction. I particularly love "The Great Scarf of Birds," "Mosquito," and the Castro-Hemingway. Our bird scarf here is formed of cowbirds—those wicked little feathered friends who are a living testimonial to shiftlessness, irresponsibility, and promiscuity. My pasture is their pool hall, and their sudden flight is as you described in the starling poem.

Did I ever tell you that my first book, "The Lady Is Cold" (1929), was dedicated (I thought) to my mother. Turned out I didn't even know her name. I thought it was Janet Hart White, but it was really Jessie. That's how *I* started *my* dedicatory days.

Thanks again for "Poles." There's only one line in the book I don't care for. It's on the last page. "John Updike was born in 1932." This, considering the body of your work, I thought offensive and in bad taste.

Yrs,
Andy White

To JOHN OSBORNE

[New York]
September 26, 1963

Dear Mr. Osborne:

Fowler has a long and spicy section about the word "one," including a distinction between the impersonal "one" and what he calls the "false" or "fraudulent" first-personal "one," which (he says) is employed by journalists who hope to be both personal and impersonal at the same time. As for me, I try to avoid the impersonal "one" but have discovered that it is like a face you keep encountering in the streets and can't always avoid bowing to.

I don't remember whether Strunk had any rule about its being followed by "he." Fowler finds a difference between "One hates *his* enemies" and "One hates *one's* enemies." But I don't know that that answers your question.

Sincerely,
E. B. White

To STANLEY HART WHITE

25 West 43
September 27 [1963]

Dear Stan:

Sometimes I get letters written here just because there is nothing else for me to do in this office anymore except sit around and think about all the things I've ever known. I feel better if I make the sound of a typewriter.

We came to town last week so K could settle a few matters with the clowns at the Medical Center. Her first interview elicited the fact that no surgery is called for at the moment, and this is a relief. . . .

Your life, as reported in your letter written in Santa Fe, sounds relatively spirited and adventurous compared with mine, and I'm glad you are moving around with such vigor. I'll gladly give you the Southwest, though—I don't believe I would ever develop a taste for it, however spectacular it is. (Once I saw it from a train window and was surprised that I felt no desire to get off the train.) I *would* like to see Seattle again, even though I suspect it would be unrecognizable. Nineteen twenty-three was my experience of Seattle.

New York is becoming lost among the enormous glass boxes that are its new buildings. With one or two exceptions there is nothing intrinsically good looking about them, and in clusters they are overpowering and debilitating. I suppose they look quite splashy if you are on the deck of an incoming liner, but I'm not. There's something about these immaculate stone and glass surfaces that destroys all the street-level detail that used to be so much fun. I feel like a spider in a bath-tub—can't get my dragline anchored to anything. (I also walk into glass doors, and take the bruises.)

The Moscow Circus is in town and I saw it the other night. It is a one-ring affair, utterly different in tone from Ringling's extravaganza, very precise and beautiful, almost like ballet. See it if it comes to Denver. The ring curb is bolted to the floor, which enables the fiery little horses of the Cossacks to build up tremendous speed and zing. They go so fast they become almost horizontal, with their feet on the curb instead of on the ground. The bears are great and the clowning is as stylish as you'll ever see. The whole business lacks the smell and the dust and the dung that we associate with our circuses (and that I'm fond of, too) but this is an entirely different medium. Even when they put a bantam rooster into orbit it's different.

We'll probably start back home around the first, which is next week, to dig our potatoes and store the squashes in the attic among the bats. Then we'll try to figure out how to get to Florida, where K's troubles are somewhat modified by warm air and where her doctor thinks it is necessary, now, for her to be. Neither of us is nuts about Florida, but it was helpful last winter. I hope to see Lil before I leave town. Tell me about Clara, when you get the chance. And give my love to Blanche and Janice.

Yrs,
En

• *Judith W. Preusser is a stepdaughter of Conrad Wyvell, White's nephew.*

To JUDITH W. PREUSSER

North Brooklin, Maine
10 November 1963

Dear Judy:

I feel honored that you have brought your problem to me, but I feel a little scared, too. I think I'm probably better equipped to help a lady whose shoe is caught in an escalator than one whose career is caught in a bind. I would have answered your letter sooner had it been plain sailing. At any rate, I'm very glad that you don't regard your indecision as a crisis, but merely as a bother.

You are the second drop-out in my family. Kitty Stableford, our oldest grandchild (my step-granddaughter), did a year in Barnard and then faded away in the middle of her sophomore year. She is now back at work, but in a smaller institution, near her home. Kitty is extremely pretty and also talented (she's a biologist who has already done a lot of experimental work with mice at the Albert Einstein Medical School in New York). I don't know, really, what happened. Her health had something to do with it but I guess it was just a state of mind that she got into—or a state of nerves.

I did *my* dropping out after I graduated. I worked in job after job in New York, unhappy and ineffective, and finally chucked life's race for a while, got into a Model T Ford, and headed west with another fellow who also felt disconsolate. I stayed "out" for about a year and a half and have never regretted a minute of it. I'm glad you are back at college, though, as I strongly believe in the health-giving quality of finishing what one begins.

If you have no deep feeling for literature, and no burning desire to express yourself in writing, you are probably in the same boat with about seventy-five per cent of all the English majors in America, so I wouldn't let it worry you too much. In my case, I majored in English partly because I didn't know what else to do, but mostly because I did have a strong tendency to write. (I was a writing fool when I was eleven years old and have been tapering off ever since.) Because of this desire to write, I was one of the lucky ones. It ought to cheer you up, though, to know that my interest in the world's great literature was woefully anemic; I got very little out of my courses, didn't understand half of what I read, skimped wherever I could, did rather badly, and came away from Cornell without a solid education and have never got round to correcting this deficiency. Primarily, my interest was in journalism, and most of my life has been spent in that arena, tilting at the dragons and clowning with the clowns. Even at Cornell, most of my time was spent getting out the daily newspaper.

I know just how you feel, Judy. Frustration is youth's middle name, and you mustn't worry too much about it. Eventually, things clarify themselves and life begins to divulge a steadier destination. In a way, our lives take form through a simple process of elimination: we discard what we don't like, walk away from what fails to inspirit us. My first job was with the United Press, but I knew within half an hour that my heart was not in it and that I would never be any good at gathering straight news under great difficulties and with the clock always running out.

Your majoring in English was no mistake, even though you do not become a critic or a publisher's assistant or a playwright or a novelist. English and English literature are the rock bottom of our lives, no matter what we do, and we should all do what, in the long run, gives us joy, even if it is only picking grapes or sorting the laundry. "To affect the quality of the day, that is the highest of arts." I agree with Mr. Thoreau, himself a victim of youthful frustration. You seem to me a girl whose head is on straight and I don't worry about you, whether you are majoring in English or in bingo. Joe, my son, majored in English for two years at Cornell, then realized that what he really liked was boats. He transferred to M.I.T., took a degree in Naval Architecture, and now owns and operates a boatyard in Brooklin—hauling, storing, repairing, and building boats. Keeps him busy 24 hours of the day, and keeps him outdoors, where he prefers to be.

We've just had three great gales here and are still picking up the pieces and sawing up the fallen trees. Aunt K is not well, and there isn't much the doctors can do for her, as her trouble is in her arteries.

Thanks for your nice letter—I wish I could write you a better reply, but your question is essentially unanswerable, except by yourself, and you supplied the answer when you said you wanted to live fruitfully and honestly. If you truly want that, you will assuredly bear fruit and be an adornment to the orchard, wherever it turns out to be.

> With love,
> Uncle Andy

To FAITH MC NULTY MARTIN

> North Brooklin, Maine
> 23 October [1963]
> 18 November
> it takes me a long time to
> write a letter

Dear Faith:

I am pleased with the appearance of your mouse and think you lucky to have her.[1] The question, of course, is whether your friend is Peromyscus maniculatus (Deer Mouse) or Peromyscus leocopus (White-footed Mouse). Until you know *that*, you are enveloped in mysticism and are really not free to talk at all—except to the mouse. My book ("Complete Field Guide to American Wildlife") describes you as follows: "Beginners, especially in the Northeast, may find it impossible at times to distinguish the Deer Mouse from the White-footed Mouse. Be satisfied to call it a Peromyscus." To me this is insulting. I don't see why you should be told to content yourself with your ignorant condition. Neither do I see why, just because you live in the Northeastern section of the country, you are less capable of distinguishing between two kinds of mice.

---

1. Mrs. Martin had written White that she was being visited by a fine mouse.

And now to a horrid confession. Not long ago I had a mouse visiting my desk at night. He came because I keep a small crock of water with a sponge in it next to my jar of pencils, and it was obvious that the mouse was visiting this convenient little spring, for a drink. The sponge is yellow plastic, and my mouse would leave his tiny turds in the tiny craters of the sponge. I tired of this after a while, but kept hoping I would catch a glimpse of my visitor. I didn't, so I set a back-breaker trap, baiting it carefully with smoky bacon. Next morning the mouse lay there, his back broken, his eyes wide open, as though incredulous to the last. It was a Deer Mouse, very beautiful in death, and I could have slit my throat from remorse. But then I got wondering how prejudiced a man can get—why was I perfectly prepared to kill a house mouse but not a beautiful Deer Mouse with its soft white underbelly and white feet? I belong in Birmingham among the white supremacists.

I took careful measurements:

3½ body
3½ tail—tail moderately hairy
tail bicolored—greyish brown above, white below
feet white
ears large
whiskers long
Color—brownish grey, faint dark dorsal stripe
Can climb

From the above I deduced that my mouse was maniculatus, and that's the way it stands here at the moment. Once, when I was a child, sick in bed, I had a mouse take up with me. He was a common house mouse and I think must have been a young one, as he was friendly and without fear. I made a home for him, complete with a gymnasium, and he learned many fine tricks and was pleasant company. Enough of mice.

Enough of everything. Hope you are well and that Johnny is thoroughly enjoying Brooks. Katharine is miserable and I'm going to take her to Sarasota to see if that will help some.

Yrs,
Andy

To ROBERT F. KENNEDY

[North Brooklin, Me.]
24 December 1963

Dear Mr. Kennedy:

It was kind of you to write me about the Presidential Medal of Freedom. I was awfully sorry that I was unable to be on hand for the presentation, and to meet you there.

I know President Kennedy must have approached the freedom award list as he approached everything else—with personal concern, lively interest, and knowledge. To find myself on his list was the most gratifying thing that ever happened to me, as well as a matter of pride and sober resolve. The accomplishments of presidents in office are usually measured in rather exact terms, but your brother gave the country something immeasurable and almost indescribable, for which we all will be forever grateful.

Sincerely,
E. B. White

• *Compared with many authors, White lived quite peaceably with his publisher. In 1964, however, Harper got out a new edition of* One Man's Meat *for their Torchbooks paperback line, and when White received an advance copy of the book he was unpleasantly surprised to find that it had an introduction that Harper had not bothered to tell him about. The piece was by Professor Walter Blair, of the University of Chicago. White was annoyed that it had been sprung on him, and he phoned Cass Canfield and told him so.*

Professor Blair, who was caught in the middle, good-naturedly accepted White's suggestions for revision and sent him as a peace offering a copy of a very funny little painting—a self-portrait showing Blair on an imaginary visit with Mark Twain in Elmira.

To CASS CANFIELD

Sarasota, Florida
27 January 1964

Dear Cass:

Thanks for the phone call and for agreeing to the recall of books. I am distressed that this should have happened, but do not feel that I am to blame for it.

I started a long letter to you last night, in which I attempted to set down in detail what I thought was wrong with the Walter Blair introduction. But there is no point in my sending the letter now: instead I'll get to work as soon as I can on the piece itself, so that you can have something in hand. Repairing the piece isn't going to be easy, as some of the stuff that I object to has a sort of built-in quality. Also, it is never easy, or even advisable, to try to evaluate one's own life and work. I'll try to do the minimum of tinkering, and we'll just have to hope that I can come up with a revision that will be satisfactory to

Professor Blair—one that he will be willing to set his name to. I think in general his trouble was that, like many a teacher of English, he felt that to write effectively a man had to be master of certain tricks and devices, had to know the formula. My own belief is that no writing, by anybody, begins to get good until he gets shed of tricks, devices, and formulae.

The factual part will be easy. Professor Blair's picture of my "fashionable" background in fashionable old Mount Vernon, appropriate "preparation" for my activity with the fashionable *New Yorker,* is to me hilarious because it is so far afield. For the first eighteen years of my life I never even knew there *was* such a thing as a dinner party. Nobody got into our fashionable house unless he was kinfolks, and even then he had to beat his way in. I might as well have been living in the Rain Forest.

I'll be in touch with you. And thanks again.

Yrs,
Andy

To **WALTER BLAIR**

[Sarasota, Fla.]
1 February 1964

Dear Professor Blair:

I presume Cass Canfield will be sending you this revision of your Introduction, and I'm writing to say how sorry I am that this incident occurred. Also, I want to explain briefly what I have done and why. Despite the appearance of the manuscript, I haven't done much, and I hope that nowhere in the piece have I done violence to your ideas or twisted your meaning.

First, the opening paragraphs contained a few errors of fact, and these were easily set straight. I was never an editor of *The New Yorker,* for instance. Ross was never Managing Editor—he was the Editor.

Second, I took the liberty of placing Eustace Tilley where he properly belongs, an early figure that was appropriate in the early carefree days of the magazine but whose top hat has been flattened by the events of the world and the sobriety of the periodical. Tilley occurs once a year for sentimental reasons, but his butterfly is long gone.

Third, I have put my dukes up in a few places where I felt that you were making me into something that I'm not or were giving me a stance I had never taken. There was nothing even remotely fashionable in my Mount Vernon phase—I was a middle class public school kid whose parents were not in the swim and didn't want to be. Oddly enough (yet it really isn't odd at all), only two staff people in the early days of *The New Yorker* had a background of Society: Ralph Ingersoll and Fillmore Hyde. The rest of us just popped up out of the subway somewhere.

In a couple of places you had me "aligning" myself with certain writers. I was, in fact, a loner, busy trying to line myself up with me. But like all youngsters I was greatly influenced by my elders—Benchley was one—and I am perfectly sure I imitated him.

In your passage about self-depreciation I removed one quote— the one about hay fever. That piece was pure satire, about Daniel Webster and me, and it hardly qualifies as an example of self-depreciation. I also changed the scarecrow business; I wasn't afraid a crow would pick on me, I was afraid I might appear quite effective to a crow, but not to anybody else.

The part about Thoreau is self-explanatory. My home in Maine resembles the cabin on Walden Pond about as closely as it resembles Buckminster Palace.

On p. 9 of the copy I have added a phrase in order to forestall what might be an unfair implication. You say that nowhere will one "catch me showing a book-learned city man's contempt for farm and frontier ways . . ." This sounded to my ears as though you felt I did feel such contempt but was careful to conceal it, for literary reasons. I not only never felt contempt for my country neighbors, I felt deeply envious of their skills, their savvy, their self reliance, and their general deportment.

I changed "formula" to "technique." In my book, "formula" is a dirty word, and so, as I say, I put my dukes up.

I greatly hope you will find my tampering acceptable to you, and that you will want to lend your name to this Introduction in its revised form. I like the piece, admire the thought and work you put into it, and am grateful to you for having written it. If Cass had just shown it to me before rushing into print with it, all would have been well.

Sincerely,
E B White

To WALTER BLAIR

[Sarasota, Fla.]
14 February 1964

Dear Mr. Blair:

I was relieved to get your letter saying you will sign the piece. The episode was an unusual one for me, and I am sure an embarrassing one for Harper. They have been publishing me, man and boy, since 1929, and should be ready for anything. If, as Canfield suggested over the phone, the recalled books are to be dumped into the East River, I think you and I should be on hand to supervise a modest pyrotechnic display for the benefit of the natives.

Thanks for the very fine view of you and Mark Twain in Elmira. It occupies the second most favored position on my desk, in the lee of a couple of school photographs of my grandchildren, and it has already given me much pleasure. And thanks again for your kind letter and your toleration.

Sincerely,
E. B. White

• *Scott Elledge, professor of English at Cornell University, has been for a long time interested in the life and work of E. B. White, and has a biography of him in progress. In the fall of 1963 he had published in the* Carleton Miscellany *an essay in which he showed that a work of real literary merit such as* One Man's Meat *has none of the characteristics of literary merit as defined in a "test" designed to measure students' appreciation of that quality.*

To SCOTT ELLEDGE

[Sarasota, Fla.]
16 February 1964

Dear Mr. Elledge:

Thank you for sending me the copy of the *Miscellany*, and thanks for revisiting the old book. I was surprised to find it among the survivors and delighted that you could discover in it no signs of literary merit. The only real trouble you got into in your piece was when you tried to spell Katharine. My wife does not take any variations lying down.

I was interested in your remarks about the writer as poser, because, of course, all writing is both a mask and an unveiling, and the question of honesty is uppermost, particularly in the case of the essayist, who must take his trousers off without showing his genitals. (I got my training in the upper berths of Pullman cars long ago.)

Thanks again for your kindness and for your estimate. *One Man's Meat* is the product of just about the best period in my life—best because at that time I could be almost continuously active without fatigue. And that's where the fun is, for me, anyway.

Sincerely,
E. B. White

TO CASS CANFIELD

Sarasota, Florida
21 February 1964

Dear Cass:

Congratulations on receiving the Lasker Award, and in such a noble cause.[1] I don't know just what you're going to do with the Winged Victory of Samothrace, which will simply make Jane[2] uneasy, but I certainly hope you are going to spend the $2500 on contraceptives for the women of China. The figures on the population explosion are frightening, but there are a few things that are going for us, despite all. I'm thinking of the rate of increase of the punched cards that issue from the maws of business machines. It ought not be many years before the civilized peoples die off from suffocation—an avalanche of paper. Tax lawyers are already beginning to look pale and short of breath. . . .

I was very glad to get Walter Blair's letter. My chief reason for kicking up the fuss was on the score of *The New Yorker*. I feel that a man is privileged to say anything he wants to about the magazine, but that he can't use one of my books as a platform. This is known as White's Principle.

Yrs,
Andy

• *In explanation of the following letter, Frank Sullivan said: "Andy was being facetious about Pete Vischer living 'close to the line.' Pete had a luxurious country estate in Port Tabac where he and his third wife lived. . . . Pete sent me a view of his manor and I passed it on to Andy. Then Andy sent me the folder of photos of their grand place at North Brooklin. I enjoyed them and then returned them, as per Andy's request."*

TO FRANK SULLIVAN

North Brooklin, Maine
May 14, 1964

Dear Frank:

My thoughts have often turned to Vischer, down there in Port Tabac, but until your letter arrived I hadn't known how close to the line he was living. The whole place can be encompassed within a single post card, stables and all. I want to extend an invitation to you to visit me and Katharine here in decent surroundings, which are so ample and

---

1. Planned Parenthood, in which Canfield has been active for many years.
2. Mrs. Canfield, a sculptor.

well appointed as to require eleven frames to depict fully. See enclosures. Our house was built by a man who did not sign the Declaration of Independence (an impudent document) and who probably had quite a time signing his own name, which I think was Allen. As for yearlings, I have a pair of yearling orioles that are about to hang their nest from the branch of an elm in our dooryard (Section I, Frame 2). I bought them from the oriole man.

I was on the point of writing Mr. Healey when your letter came. Your courtesy and kindness in consulting K and me about our wishes threw something of a bombshell into my own artifacting operation, which has been under way here for some time. I have never consulted a damn soul about his wishes, and suddenly I realized that I am neither courteous nor kind but merely compulsively tidy. (I'm also fighting a losing battle; more stuff arrives here each day than leaves, and I'm afraid I shall die of congestion of the attic.) First I'd better answer your question—and will answer for K, too.

Send me no artifacts. Since you and I are both in the happy position of emptying our drawers into Cornell, I am quite content to have *you* donate *my* letters, and I will donate yours. They will sleep side by side through the unthinkable ages. However, at this juncture, I'll put on a show of courtesy myself: do you want me to send your letters back to you? I can easily and will gladly do this, if you wish. There, sir! An artifact for an artifact.

I got into the bestowal game two or three years ago as a result of my tax lawyer's tall tales about the Great Worth of manuscripts and other literary shavings. Some of his tales turned out to be not so tall after all. For instance, I gobbled up the manuscript and drafts of "Charlotte's Web," together with a lot of letters pertaining thereto, sent them to Cornell, and that year received a gift allowance of $4800. Correction: $4817.50. The stuff was appraised by John S. Van E. Kohn, of the Seven Gables Bookshop, and I think these appraisers feel that they should end up with some figure other than a round one, to show that they're not just guessing. Anyway, the episode stuck in my mind; if I could pick up forty-eight hundred bucks for a children's book, think what I could do with something written for adults! Vistas opened up, and my step could be heard more frequently on the attic stairs. I have an unusual attic; about thirty-five years ago I discovered that trying to decide whether to keep a letter or throw it away was taking too much out of me, so I eliminated the decision-making thing from my life by the simple expedient of keeping *everything*. My attic is large (Section II, Frames 5 and 6), and the only real trouble I'm in now is that sorting over old papers gives me a terrible sinus condition and most of the letters sound something like this: "Dear Mr. White: I'm taking the liberty of sending you Jane Fetlock's latest novel, which we here at Random feel shows a subtlety of mind that outranks etc." I put this squarely up to Healey, and his reply was, "Send everything." He said modern library procedures had ways of dealing with Jane Fetlock.

In your letter you remarked that your manuscripts ended in wastebaskets "here or at the *New Yorker*." I think you are wrong about the *New Yorker*. As far as I know, every manuscript you turned in to the magazine is still there, in the basement, except manuscripts from the year 1925 to the year 1934. These, too, would be extant had not a patriotic member of our advertising department given way to a burst of emotion in World War II and donated the first nine years' collection to the paper drive. When Ross learned of this he blew all seven gaskets, and there was a goddamming that could be heard as far as a Hundred and Tenth Street. He goddammed for three days without letup. He was in my office a dozen times, venting his magnificent spleen. He would have taken [the patriot] and disemboweled him with a machete, except he didn't have a machete. My desk was so full of goddams I could hardly move a comment into position. But I continued to move them into position off and on, and about two weeks ago they all appeared from the New Yorker's cellar (on my request and after a year's labors on the part of the basement staff), and I now have a stack of Notes & Comment manuscripts, or typescripts, that is, literally, two feet high. This ought to stop Healey, but he seems ready for anything. Actually, the comment manuscript originals are, in the aggregate, as like as two peas. They simply show that I was, in the final draft, a neat typist, that I spelled most of the words right, and that I got almost everything into the confines of a single sheet of yellow paper. (The days of yellow paper, by the way, are over—we now print in Chicago, and we write, or mumble, on slick thick awful white paper. I would rewolt, but my comment writing days are over, so there is not much point in rewolting.)

If you want your original manuscripts, try dropping a line to Daise Terry or Harding Mason or Roger. I truly believe that the manuscripts are there—but it will take a little time. Don't tell anybody I told you.

Your letter contained hints of ill health, and this saddens me. I, too, would like to walk on the waters. Katharine has had three years of almost unremitting woe, of one sort or another. First they said she probably had a brain tumor, then they yanked her appendix on a hot July night, then the brain tumor turned into a blocked artery in the carotid complex, and her throat was slit open in Rochester, N.Y., while I waited patiently for her to be returned to her room (an eleven hour wait with no green stamps for good behavior), then, last December, she developed what appeared to be a mild skin outbreak, and this turned into the worst thing yet. We were all set to repair to Sarasota, and did repair, briefly, but K spent most of the winter in Harkness, shedding her skin, with a confused and attentive army of dermatologists. The trouble, or disease, is still a mystery. But her suffering was real enough, and in a way it has been the worst thing she ever had because it was such a humiliating (for a woman) and lonely time. For a while she could wear nothing, could see nobody (except doctors, nurses, and little old me), and could not even be touched by bedsheets, which had to be supported and held away. I holed up in the Algonquin and commuted between 44th Street and 168th. She was released from the hospital a couple of weeks ago, and flew home here, but the thing has started up again. So that's where we are tonight. Her courage is unimpaired and she will prevail. . . .

I have a brilliant scheme for our joint presentation of artifacts, or, as I now call them, artifarts, to Cornell. My stuff almost fills a pickup truck, and by some miracle of thrift, good management, and chicanery I actually *own* a pickup truck—a lovely thing, grey. When the frost is on the pumpkin, I'll load everything aboard, leaving enough room under the tarpaulin for your mizzling little artifarts, and I'll swing up to Saratoga Springs. Then we two will head west, in bright yellow October, stopping or calling at every likely pub to down a drink and make a little water, and fully loaded in every sense of the word we will draw up, or back up, to Healey's drophole, and call for the boys to turn us over to posterity. When the sun sinks far away in the crimson of the west.

Let me know about your wishes. And stay the same as you've always been, which is good enough for

Yrs,
Andy

• *When White failed to show up in Washington to receive the Presidential Medal of Freedom, President Johnson asked Senator Edmund Muskie to take the medal to Maine on his next trip home and make the presentation. White, accompanied by his daughter-in-law, Allene, drove over to Waterville and received the award in the office of the president of Colby College, Robert E. L. Strider.*

To ROBERT AND HELEN STRIDER

North Brooklin, Maine
30 May 1964

Dear Dr. and Mrs. Strider:

Yesterday was a fine day for me and you had a big part in making it so. Occasions of this sort are not always easy for me and I usually waste a lot of time dreading them, but your warmth and friendliness were so immediately apparent that I felt at home as soon as I arrived. I send you my thanks and gratitude.

I really had not intended to put anyone to any trouble about the medal, which I muffed last December, but Senator Muskie's scheme gave me the pleasure of returning to the Colby campus and of becoming acquainted with you. The only thing that marred the day for me was that Mrs. White couldn't be along. She makes much more sense than I do. But you would have had quite a time prying her loose from that Hugonis rose. She had one and lost it, and she hasn't recovered yet.

I was awfully glad to see Dean Marriner again. I was moved by the Senator's presentation, astonished at the sound of my own voice, touched that it all came about on President Kennedy's birthday, and very proud to strut around your living room in my decorated condition among your delightful company. I hope you both will visit *my* living room when you come down along the coast, and I'll try to find some suitable decoration for you as a reward for yesterday's good conduct. We'll let you look at the spot where the rose was before it died, and at the interesting places in the front lawn where the big Balm of Gilead trees stood before they collapsed. Our place is full of points of interest.

I shall always look back with pleasure on my Presidential day at Colby. Thanks again for everything.

Sincerely,
E. B. White

To ROGER ANGELL

North Brooklin, Maine
June 24, 1964

Dear Rog:

Thanks for the Tom Sawyer—just what I wanted. Remind me to pay up when we meet. I gave it to Steven for camp, but I have an idea he may already have consumed it, as he approaches things directly.

We'll be glad when you and Carol and the girls get here[1]—both of us have had a bellyful of the month of June and would like to go on to pleasanter times. I'm the father of two robins and this has kept me on the go lately. They were in a nest in a vine on the garage and had been deserted by their parents, and without really thinking what I was doing I casually dropped a couple of marinated worms into their throats as I walked by a week ago Monday. This did it. They took me on with open hearts and open mouths, and my schedule became extremely tight. I

---

1. In the fall of 1963 Roger Angell had married Carol Rogge, then a secretary in *The New Yorker*'s fiction department. The girls are Roger's daughters, Caroline (Callie) and Alice.

equipped myself with a 12″ yellow bamboo stick, split at one end, like a robin's bill, and invented a formula: hamburg, chicken mash, kibbled worm, and orange juice. Worms are hard to come by because of the drought, but I dig early and late and pay my grandchildren a penny a worm. The birds are now fledged and are under the impression that they know how to fly. When I come out of the house at 6 a.m. they come streaming at me from bush and tree, trying for a landing on shoulder or cap, usually overshooting me in the fog and bringing up against a wall. This exhausts them and me. But I have proved one thing—a man can bring up young robins if he is foolish enough and hardy enough. My next, and most important job, is to hop about on the lawn with my head cocked on one side, to show them how to get their own living and stop breathing down my neck.

Tell the girls I also have two fine little field mice in the Shipmate stove in the boathouse. They, thank God, have a mother on duty. . . .

Yrs,
Andy

• *Early in September 1964, White got a letter from Cass Canfield stating that Harper would like to publish* One Man's Meat *in their Perennial Library paperback line. The letter went on to say: "The contract for this book provides that on a cheap edition published by ourselves we should pay a royalty of 10% of the wholesale price specified as retail, less 42%. Actually, on this paper edition the average discount will be 47% and I am proposing a royalty of 5½% on retail. This royalty is the equivalent of 10% on wholesale at 45% off."*

White was enchanted. He immediately dusted off his typewriter and hammered out the following reply.

To CASS CANFIELD

25 West 43rd Street
New York
September 11, 1964

Dear Cass:

The prospects for a Perennial One Man's Meat are inviting, and Katharine has agreed to introduce it into her perennial border with the holly phlox and the acrimony. Instead of a royalty of 10% of the wholesale price less 42%, I have been turning over in my mind the idea of a 42% royalty but *without* cross-fertilization, less ten of the little ones. This would be the equivalent (if my mathematics are right) of six long ones, if they're the size I think they are. I am accepting your offer assuming. I mean, I can't not go along with anything that is as exciting and challenging as this except.

Yrs,
Andy

P.S. I saw Zane Grey on the street the other day. He looked awful.[1]

To MRS. GORDON KEITH CHALMERS

[North Brooklin, Me.]
September 23, 1964

Dear Mrs. Chalmers:

Was the adjective "wry"? I've forgotten, too.

Thanks for your nice letter. My wife and I are two little old characters who live in Maine and have nothing to do with the advertising content of *The New Yorker*. But I shall pass your protest along to someone who does. It was good of you to write.

Advertising is always a problem and, of all the magazines that carry advertising, none has waged a longer, sterner fight to keep it within the limits of taste and good sense than has *The New Yorker*. Advertising is the jungle through which winds the thin, clear stream of our discourse. Sometimes it's difficult to tune out the strange cries that come from the forest, but remember, it is the jungle that supports the stream.

Sincerely,
E. B. White

To GEORGE H. HEALEY

North Brooklin, Maine
28 September 1964

Dear Mr. Healey:

Katharine and I were delighted to get your letter, with the news of Frank and the clarification about my papers. Tomorrow or next day I am shipping four more boxes, courtesy of Brooks Brothers and other good box people. (I'm holding back on the patented boxes to conserve my strength.) A list of the contents is enclosed. . . .

I'm glad Professor Keast has been interested in the collection, particularly some of the early *New Yorker* manuscripts. Physically they are rather dull, being only the finished typescript, and if he ever did a

---

1. Harper had a safe full of manuscripts by Zane Grey, which they continued to publish long after his death.

brochure he would have to note that the true collection is in the hands of the world's charwomen—those resolute females who cleaned out from under my desk in the small hours. It is they, not Cornell, I fear, who hold the evidence of my journalistic crimes.

Katharine hasn't committed herself as to her willingness to send along my letters to her, and I am not bringing any pressure to bear on her. For her last birthday I gave her a poem in thirteen cantos, called "Urine Specimen Days—A Backward Glance O'er Rumpled Beds," which is a chronicle of her many hospitalizations. So you can see your chances of receiving anything from her are not good. I'm proud of the title, just the same.

Sincerely,
E. B. White

To SUSAN FRANK

North Brooklin, Maine
15 October 1964

Dear Susan:

I was glad to hear that you got back safely to Ithaca after your wild dash into darkest Maine.[1] The *Sun* has come and I want to thank you and congratulate you on your handiwork. I now think of this type-writer as "old" and when I pass a mirror I glance in quickly, hoping to get a glimpse of the country squire. I think you are the first person to take careful note of what I had on, and this is a step ahead for me. I've always secretly hoped to pass for a country squire, but my friends and neighbors, by and large, have thought that I looked like a trans-planted city slicker who wouldn't know how to whittle a button for a backhouse door and who will probably vote Democratic in the fall. So your remarks were very reassuring to me.

I wish I could congratulate myself on my own piece, which seems to take a long while to say nothing at all. I simply wasn't ready for the tape recorder. If I had known about that I would have had something ready and would have practiced up before your arrival. . . . I never even mentioned Professor George Lincoln Burr, who was perhaps the best thing that happened to me in Ithaca. He led me by the hand through the Middle Ages, and for the first time in my life I learned what men will endure in order to keep alive the fires of freedom when they have been almost extinguished. This opened my eyes and my heart in a way that I have not forgotten. Burr was a tiny little fellow, usually seen hustling across the quadrangle carrying a stack of books higher than

1. Miss Frank was a *Cornell Daily Sun* reporter who had come to North Brooklin, armed with a tape recorder, to get an interview with White.

his head. I live in his debt. And although I can't remember a darned thing about medieval history I learned the meaning of freedom-of-con-science.

Thanks again, Susan, for being such a pleasant visitor, and lots of luck in your senior year and in all the years thereafter. If journalism is to be your career, carry the torch high—it's a nice old torch, much older than this old typewriter.

Sincerely,
E. B. White

To GEORGE H. HEALEY

North Brooklin, Maine
18 October 1964

Dear Mr. Healey:

I wish I could have attended the Convocation, it must have been a splendid sight. Didn't I read that you bore a mace, or a grudge, or some such thing? Miss Susan Frank's visit here set some sort of record for sustained flight. . . . When I got her disentangled from a balky tape-recorder and a large German camera, my thoughts lay scattered all about on the floor. The recorder dutifully picked them up, and Susan rushed them back through the skies to the waiting pages of the Sun. Morris Bishop wrote me that I sounded like Ecclesiastes.

Tomorrow I'm shipping four more boxes. Then, in a week or so, another four; and that will be the end—Box 24. It is a nice number to end on. I shall then formally present the whole works to Cornell with my love and prayers. The gift, I believe, can be made in advance of an appraisal.

This week's shipment relieves my mind about one thing: the strange dearth of early Ross and Thurber letters. I could not understand why my letter files turned up so few of these items. Finally (or suddenly) they appeared. Quite a while ago Katharine and I had rifled the files, extracted the letters, and sequestered them—against the time when we would write a book about *The New Yorker*. So here they all are—Box 20, items 5 and 6. You already have in your possession another envelope of this material. It was in Box 6. At the time, I thought it was the only such collection, but now these others have come to light and I am very pleased.

I was enchanted by the conversation between the scholar and the machine, as reported by Julian Boyd in his address. It has made me wonder about the backstairs gossip among your machines on the sub-ject of the White boxes. Juicy, I'll bet. Did you see the piece in the *Times* not long ago about the M.I.T. computer that writes poetry as good as that composed by a drunken poet? The computer came up with this line: "What does she put four whistles beside heated rugs for?"

Please find attached a list of the contents of the boxes.

Sincerely,
E. B. White

• *Edward Sampson, son of Martin Sampson, White's English professor and close friend at Cornell, was writing a biography of White for Twayne's United States Authors series. The book, No. 232 in the series, was published in 1974.*

To EDWARD C. SAMPSON

North Brooklin, Maine
4 November 1964

Dear Mr. Sampson:

I recently dispatched to the Cornell Library a copy of the Louisville *Herald* containing "Bold son of Runnymede . . . " The paper ran it in a two-column box on the front page, the morning after the Derby. Better sonnets have been written but few quicker ones, and I guess this is the only published sonnet whose author was trying to recover his losses in a horse race.

It was not my first published poem. The *Ladies Home Journal,* around 1910, gave me a prize (a copy of "Rab and His Friends") for a contribution to a column conducted by Aunt Janet. Seems to me it was a poem. I had poems in the Mount Vernon High School's *Oracle,* and, a bit later, in Christopher Morley's *Bowling Green* column. Merit was not in them—but a man can't have everything.

Sincerely,
E. B. White

To DOROTHY LOBRANO GUTH

North Brooklin, Maine
November 10, 1964

Dear Dotty:

What a week last week was, with Vermont and Maine going Democratic, and you bearing a son! Weeks like that don't come along every week in my life, or in yours either. I hope you and Ray did as well as Barry Goldwater—he ended his long campaign a million and a half dollars in the black, a really brilliant defeat. At any rate, I was relieved to get your wire, as I had had no answer to a recent letter inquiring about your health and was beginning to worry about you. Tried to call Jean one evening but with no success. K took the telegram from the

Western Union girl in Ellsworth and for a little while there was a certain amount of confusion, which I had to straighten out. K hollered that it was something about "God's grandchild" and who would *that* be? We don't get messages very distinctly here, they all have to be interpreted.

From one of the department stores (I forget which one) we are sending Raymond Junior a sleeping bag, or bedroll—much the same sort of thing Hemingway worked into his fiction when it seemed to drag. K and I hope this will be useful and will lend a touch of elegance to Tudor Mall on the little boy's outings. Later, when he buys his first sports car and has a girl named Renata, I believe the thing would serve perfectly well as a footwarmer. I plan also to give your baby a Webster's Collegiate Dictionary, a Peterson's "Field Guide to the Birds," and a copy of "Stuart Little," as I don't want him to go through life misspelling words, mistaking the barn owl for the house wren, and failing to realize that his godgrandfather was at one time hard-working. Ray Senior better get busy building a six-inch bookshelf.

I well remember how wonderful it was to have a son of one's own, and I hope you and Ray get as much fun and satisfaction out of it as K and I did, in our East Eighth Street days. Even now, some thirty-four years later, I enjoy looking out of my bedroom window at quarter to seven in the morning and seeing the lad go by in his truck on his way to work, his rifle beside him on the seat.

Write me a note when you get a chance and tell me all about it. Meantime, blessings on the three of you, and

Love from
Andy

To **ROBERT S. PALMER**

[North Brooklin, Me.]
December 4, 1964

Dear Mr. Palmer:

I think when the U.N. was founded there was not, as you indicate, "much support" for a world federal government. There was a small scattering of people who were thinking in those large terms, but these people were not of great influence. The time, apparently, was not ripe for any great revolutionary change in the affairs of men, even though the war was fresh in everyone's mind.

You are right, I think, in saying that a bad side-effect of the present uneasy peace is that it causes people to believe that the nations, independently, will be able to keep the peace indefinitely through the usual devices of diplomacy and power balance. I think the nuclear stalemate has given the world a priceless breathing spell, free of fighting, in which to reshuffle the cards. But except for the test ban treaty, not much progress has been made. The tendency since the end of the war in 1945 has been for nations to solidify their nationalism, rather than build an interdependent world. The parochial streak in people is perhaps the strongest streak in human nature, and I have no idea how it can ever be eradicated sufficiently to allow a better state of affairs.

As for the United Nations developing or evolving into a government, I see no chance of it short of a complete overhaul of the Charter —virtually a total rewriting of it. The Charter affirms and extends national sovereignty in almost every clause. However, the total effect of the U.N. is often quite good, in that its very existence suggests the theme of universal government and the rule of law. It suggests our goal, though it fails to provide the machinery for reaching that goal. Curiously enough, the biggest strides toward unity have been taken in the field of economics, with the common market in Europe showing good health. This is encouraging. It may be that our political structure will take shape from our economic structure—but there will have to be a few great statesmen to lead the world along this road. As long as the Communists are bent on capturing the world in the name of Marxism, the job is doubly difficult and formidable. It is, I think, impossible to contain capitalism and communism under one political roof—there are too many fundamental conflicts. The press is an obvious one.

I discuss some of these things in a chapter called "Unity" in my latest book, called *The Points of My Compass*. You might find something useful in it, if you are pursuing this theme.

Sincerely,
E. B. White

To GEORGE H. HEALEY

Beaufort, S.C.
16 January 1965

Dear Mr. Healey:

The packet containing Mr. Kohn's meditations [an appraisal] has arrived safely, after a quick trip to Maine. Since I did not indulge myself in guessing, and since my confidence in Mr. Kohn's judgment is complete, his evaluation of my papers is correct to the penny, and I am grateful to him for his labors.

In the same mail with the packet, I received an accusatory note from a schoolgirl who was desperately struggling with an assignment from her English teacher. "You are not too well known in Iowa," she wrote. It is from children that one hears the plain truth about one's self, and I wondered whether I should forward the letter to Kohn, in case he might feel in duty bound to knock a couple of thousand dollars off the grand total.

Thanks again for everything you and the other members of the Library staff have done in my behalf. I think one effect of this gift will be to bring me to Ithaca now and then. I've already wanted to consult my "archive" on a certain matter, and this clearly entails a trip to Cornell, where I can lose myself in a study of my own words.

Sincerely,
E. B. White

• *Katharine White's older sister, Elizabeth Shepley Sergeant (Elsie), died early in 1965. She had written several books and she had many friends in literary circles. When the following was written, a memorial service was being arranged, to be held at the Cosmopolitan Club in New York, with Katharine McBride, president of Bryn Mawr, presiding. Much of the work of putting this program together fell to Katharine White.*

To ROGER ANGELL

[Sarasota, Fla.]
3 March [1965]
By the sea

Dear Rog:

I've never half thanked you for all your labors of the past month, which have meant so much to K and me. I am very grateful. For the first few days after Elsie died, when we were still in Beaufort but about to move on, K practically never mentioned Elsie. It was as though nothing had happened, except that she seemed withdrawn and wore a look of quiet interior concentration. Then, when we landed here, work began on the grand design of the memorial service; a secretary named Mrs. Rupprecht came in, mornings, for dictation and copying, and the volume of mail, in and out, grew to almost unbelievable proportions. We've been here for more than a month, and in that time I don't think K has been out of the house for a total of four hours. Her skin erupted, the cortisone had to be stepped up, and for a while she was in a state of near collapse.

But the news is better and I think the corner has been turned. The Club has been engaged for the 12th, and this morning Miss McBride agreed to preside. Paul Nordoff wrote a very nice letter saying he would play the piano. The rest should be relatively simple. At one point I even volunteered to read the Psalms myself, but I've thought better of that.

There's not much news from here of a general nature. A couple of tornados missed us by a decent margin, and the weather in the main has been quite good. The local thespians are offering "My Fair Lady," which showed courage if not judgment. I saw it Monday night and was pleasantly surprised. A history professor from New College played Henry Higgins, and Eliza Doolittle was a mother-of-two from Bradenton. Culture is really the thing here—it's bigger than surfing. Today I visited a service station on the South Trail to get my car greased, and the mechanic kept coming out from under the car, grease gun in hand, to fill me in on the opportunities for lovers of music in Sarasota. He said the last symphony he'd attended was the greatest thing he'd ever seen—the percussionist lasted through the first movement and then went by ambulance to the hospital for an appendectomy, while his under-study took over the drums. Baseball starts next week. I hope K will be willing to go to the Park, as it is her only diversion here, but the damned dermatologist has been trying to keep her away from sunlight. I'm caught right in the middle.

We're so glad that you're going to be in the McCoy cottage. I felt cheated last summer, because of having to go to New York in July, and hope my teeth will stay in this year when you and Carol and the girls are in the land. Give them all my love. And if you hear of a puppy for sale, let me know—I am in the market for a sensible dog.

Yrs,
Andy

• *On April 11, 1965, the* Sunday Herald Tribune *in its magazine section "New York" published an article entitled "Tiny Mummies! The True Story of the Ruler of 43d Street's Land of the Walking Dead," by Tom Wolfe, in which Wolfe gave his opinion of* The New Yorker *and its editor, William Shawn. Although the prose was colorful, the article shocked and angered members of* The New Yorker *staff, who knew and loved Bill Shawn. White immediately wrote this letter to the* Tribune's *publisher. It was published, with several others, in the paper on April 25.*

To **JOHN HAY WHITNEY**

The Tuscany
New York, N.Y.
12 April 1965

Dear Mr. Whitney:

Mr. Wolfe's piece on William Shawn violated every rule of conduct I know anything about. It is sly, cruel, and to a large extent undocumented, and it has, I think, shocked everyone who knows what sort of person Shawn really is. I can't imagine why you published it. The virtuosity of the writer makes it all the more contemptible, and to me, as I read it, the spectacle was of a man being dragged for no apparent reason at the end of a rope by a rider on horseback—a rider, incidentally, sitting very high in the saddle these days and very sure of his mount.

The piece is not merely brutal, it sets some sort of record for journalistic delinquency, for it made sport of a man's physical appearance and psychological problems—which is as low as you can go. If Mr. Shawn is not at ease meeting people in the hall, it should arouse, if anything, compassion, not contempt. And how can Mr. Wolfe, who does not inhabit these halls, state unequivocally that this so-called "shyness" is "deliberate"? The statement is worse than omniscient, it's false.

For forty years *The New Yorker* has employed parody, irony, ridicule, and satire to deflate or diminish persons and institutions it deemed fair game. But I never saw it use brass knuckles, or the rope, or the police dog. The magazine itself is fair game for anyone, and so is its editor, because they are in the public eye, and I have no quarrel with the *Tribune* for taking off after *The New Yorker*. But your departure from the conventional weaponry of satire and criticism is unsettling; it shakes the whole structure of the free press, which depends ultimately on the good temper and good report of the people. There are always a few who will pay to watch some act of particular savagery in the arena, but I would hate to depend on their patronage for the building of a good newspaper.

Long before Harold Ross died, William Shawn was changing the character and scope of *The New Yorker*, and he is still at it. Wolfe's violent attack on him is not only below the belt, it is essentially wide of the mark, in point of fact.

Sincerely,
E. B. White

To PATRICIA GREGER

[North Brooklin, Me.]
May 19, 1965

Dear Miss Greger:

Your letter got sidetracked at Harper's, which is why this reply is so late.

I have encountered two taboos. One was death, the other was monstrosity. In "Charlotte's Web," the spider dies. My editor at Harper's was not very enthusiastic about this development. Apparently, children are not supposed to be exposed to death, but I did not pay any attention to this. In "Stuart Little" an American family has a two inch mouse. This is highly questionable and would be, I guess, bad if it were stated in any other than a matter-of-fact way. A librarian read "Stuart Little" in proof before it was published and strongly urged me not to have it published but I did not pay any attention to that, either.

Television, I think, has more taboos than the book world. But I have had very little experience with television.

Sincerely,

E. B. White

To MORRIS BISHOP

North Brooklin, Maine

28 May 1965

Dear Morris:

You received such a pretty compliment in a letter I had from Susan Frank, I feel impelled if not obliged to pass it along. "Morris Bishop gave one of the finest addresses I've ever heard—in a beautiful English with every sentence turned out just right. I don't think the University will ever find anyone to take his place."

Neither do I. And I like to think of those sentences turned out just right, in their little hats set jauntily on one side and their starchy shirtfronts immaculate.

Yrs,

Andy

To KATHARINE S. WHITE

Hotel Algonquin

New York

[July 1965]

Monday evening

Dear K—

. . . I am pleased with the events of this day; my trip to see Dr. Morse [a dentist] was very worth while, as it shortens by two days my stay here. . . .

Last night was the hottest yet. I dined at the Tuscany, and as I was finishing, in came Hawley [Truax] with Mary Petty and Alan Dunn, so I was summoned over to join them. Mary . . . wore her usual big floppy hat. Alan immediately pressed me about the fire hazard at our house, and was particularly concerned about our using spruce brush to bank the house in winter. Hawley was in fine fettle and was very funny about Blue Hill's resumption of mining operations—he says it occurs in 60 year cycles and that the natives salt the mines, secretly. They all sent you their love. I drank a green mint and left them to their hilarity. Hawley and Althea sail for Europe next month on the Elizabeth.

Lunched today with Milton [Greenstein]. He feels, as I do, that we now have a full blown Fascist movement under way, and under the very most respectable auspices. Yesterday's television, with Governor Wallace's attack on the press and the Federal Court system, and the news reports of Saturday night's riots in Harlem, was the most unsettling series of programs I've ever seen. The city is very strange this summer— alternately deserted and packed, and the nearness of Harlem always in everybody's stomach. And to give it the final touch, we've just had 150,000 Nobles of the Mystic Shrine arrive, with their calliopes, balloons, fun vehicles, and little-boy antics. They look so terribly hot in those fezzes. . . .

I go to the Chair tomorrow, so will end this and climb into bed and hope for some sleep despite the heat. I miss you and would feel easier in my mind if Joe and Allene were there.

Am glad I'll be home in time to see Kitty.

Love,

A

To KATHARINE S. WHITE

[New York]
[July 1965]
Thursday morn

Dear K:

Your letter this morning cheered me because the handwriting was so clear and orderly, and this made me feel that you were on an even keel again. . . .

I've just sent off a card to Forrest at Togus, with a note from both of us.[1] I feel awful about him. He has known for a long time that he had something wrong, but kept putting it off. This may not be as bad as it sounds, though—look at Bob Coates, he had part of his stomach removed and it made him fine again. I love Forrest. He's one of the kindest people I know and always asks about us and our health with the deepest concern in his face. I'll be anxious to hear more news about his condition.

I enjoyed your recital about your thunder-and-lightning-and-social time. Those switches, by the way, do *not* have to be pulled when the power is entirely off, only when the lights go dim and there is still a little current in the line. But I'll soon be back to do it for you. I feel I

1. Forrest Allen, the Whites' mailman, was critically ill in the Veterans Hospital near Augusta.

am over the hump now, and that I can stay on my feet and get back home after this crazy safari. I have devoted myself with religious zeal to remaining upright and keeping the Body in working order, with a strict regimen. Five more days and I'll have it made—it may even be fewer than five, as Dr. Morse holds out some hope that his laboratory man can get the thing [a bridge] built before Monday. But as of now, my last session takes place Monday afternoon at 3:30 and I'll plan to start driving home Tuesday.

Last night was *my* Social Time, two dates in quick succession— cocktails (which turned out to be champagne) at Muriel Spark's, two flights up at Number 112 West 13 Street, the same apartment that Gus and Bob and Mike and I had occupied in the Twenties; then dinner at A——'s, starting with a soup that was blue in color—the only blue soup I ever recall eating. I had spent the day worrying about these two weird engagements and devising a stratagem for getting through them without pouring too much liquor down my nervous throat past the temporary bridge and into the unforgiving stomach. I wrote specific and detailed instructions to myself and placed the instructions in my jacket pocket, starting with "At Spark's, do not *finish* second drink. Thank Mrs. Spark and leave." Not even Eisenhower planning the Normandy invasion took any more pains with preliminary arrangements. A——, whom I had not seen at all since my stay in New York, had showed up in my office two days before with her invitation to dinner "Wednesday evening." A—— can make an invitation to dinner sound vaguely like a counter-revolutionary plot involving some Central American country. I stared blankly at her for a minute and then said, "Why, yes, I would like to come to dinner Wednesday." I added further instructions to my list: "At A——'s take two drinks, mark each drink on slip of paper which keep in pocket, and refer frequently to tally."

I arrived at 112 W. 13 in a slight drizzle of rain, puffing up the two flights and thinking of all the things I had ever known. The place was unrecognizable, except for the stairs. A bar and kitchen counter had been thrown across one end of the living room, a man poured champagne, and Mrs. S. bobbled around in a funny black dress that she said she had got in some Mexican place. . . . Her agent was on hand, and the place crawled with articulate men. The only other female's dress was cut, or slashed, down the front to show her breasts, which I examined carefully. I was escorted into the bedroom by Mrs. Spark to see what time had wrought, and it had wrought a great deal. There is now a terrace, and a full partition between front and back. The back yards, once so scraggly, are groomed. I think Mrs. S. regarded my interest in the place as rather dull sport, which I guess it was, and our conversation soon died, and I couldn't make out what the boys in the front room were saying to each other, and I felt very uncomfortable and out of place in my old home. . . . Shortly after seven, and greatly, I think, to the relief of everybody, I left.

I then proceeded to A——'s. She was in a black pleated skirt, a white pleated blouse, and sandals with pleated toes. There was some background music from a muted radio, and the scuffling of an air conditioner. I ate the blue soup, the individual steak (which was good), refused the green-and-red salad which somewhat resembled pizza, checked off my two drinks on my check list, discussed Goldwater, and departed for the Algonquin and the eleven o'clock news. The place seemed positively homelike, after my Social Time around the town.

Tomorrow I lunch with Bill [Shawn]—our usual lunch, ending with his excruciatingly painful approach to the subject of my writing, or lack of same. . . .

Much love
A

To CHRISTOPHER S. JENNISON

North Brooklin, Maine
August 7, 1965

Dear Mr. Jennison:

Thanks for letting me see the sketch for the cover.[1] It fulfills a lifetime dream of mine: to hold a pencil behind my ear. I've never been able to do it, as my ear sticks out too far.

Quite aside from making a dream come true, the design seems to me perfectly acceptable. The artist has somehow or other made me look as though I had hair on my lower lip as well as on my upper lip. Perhaps his lines should be lightened a bit to correct this false impression. I have a moustache, in the usual place, but have no growth of hair on the chin.

Sincerely,
E. B. White

To JOE BERK

North Brooklin, Maine
October 5, 1965

Dear Mr. Berk:

I would have written you long since, but on the morning the recording of *Stuart Little* arrived, I departed.[1] I headed not north but south, and I was in search not of a bird but of a dentist. When I arrived in New York, I found additional copies of the recording awaiting me in my office at The New Yorker Magazine, but I found no player. And since

1. Of *An E. B. White Reader*. Jennison was the editor in charge of the project.

1. The recording was issued by Pathways of Sound, which Berk heads.

all my friends are now dead, from old age, I did not try to rouse anybody up on the pretext of allowing me to use his record-player.

Now I am home again and have listened to Julie Harris reading my only begotten novel. She does it beautifully and I feel greatly in her debt, and in yours for selecting her. I know that to read a book aloud is a gruelling task, but Miss Harris never gave me any cause for worry. She is as perceptive as she is reliable, and she can read to me any time she wants to. Would you be kind enough to pass along my thanks to her?

My secretary sent me only one disk, failing to notice that they were in sets of two. So I still have the first half of the story to listen to. NBC, you may be amused to know, is at work on a television version of the story, and I feel in my bones that it will end with Stuart's finding Margalo—thus bringing to an abrupt close the quest for beauty in America. As Don Marquis used to say, "Ah, welladay."

Sincerely,

E. B. White

To JOE BERK

North Brooklin, Maine
October 26, 1965

Dear Mr. Berk:

You've already been very generous in handing out records, and I want to pay for this order. . . .

Am enclosing a check for $15.92 to cover the bill. You would be foolhardy to take on my relations. 1 have, at last count, one son, two step-children, eighteen nephews and nieces, eight grandchildren, and a wild assortment of cousins and aunts—some of them impostors. I also have a great many great nephews and great nieces, a godchild and a great godchild. And a Merry Christmas to all.

Thanks for executing this order.

Sincerely,

E. B. White

To CHRISTOPHER S. JENNISON

North Brooklin, Maine
November 22, 1965

Dear Mr. Jennison:

I love the cover. I look just like Festus Haggin, which is good enough for me and should be plenty good enough for my readers.

Am returning it with my blessing. Let the presses roll.

Sincerely,

E. B. White

To CHRISTOPHER S. JENNISON

North Brooklin, Maine
November 26, 1965

Dear Mr. Jennison:

It's delightful to be published by a house whose taste is so elevated nobody has ever turned on "Gunsmoke." That's the kind of publishing life for me. I don't know what you people do with your Saturday nights, but I know what your secretary does with hers. She and I are curled up with the old Dodge City crowd—Kitty Russell, Matt Dillon, Doc Adams, and Festus. Give her my love. Ask her if I don't look just like Festus.

Sincerely,
E. B. White

To JOSEPH T. WEARN

Gainesville, Fla.
7 December 1965

Dear Joe:

I make a practice of swiping one sheet of stationery from every first rate hotel where I stop, like Castle Hill, and this gives tone to my correspondence.

I am writing simply to report a development of the story you told me about the boy who told his schoolmaster that alligators ate herons, pigs, small dogs, and beer bottles. While drifting south this morning on Route 17, trending towards Brunswick, I regaled my wife with this yarn, hoping to relieve the tedium of mid-morning on a national highway. She listened attentively and made no comment. About five minutes later she said, "I wonder how an alligator eliminates a beer bottle." "That's simple," I replied. "He schlitz."

I did not get a very strong response to this witticism, and we knocked off another couple of miles in silence. Then I asked Katharine, "Do you know how an alligator feels after he has passed a beer bottle?" She said, no, she didn't know. "He feels sadder budweiser," I said.

The response was still rather weak, and silence fell upon us again.

A few minutes later, my wife broke the awful stillness. "Pabst he does, and pabst he doesn't."

It seemed necessary to tell you about this, without trying to tell you of our enjoyment of our stay with you, which will come later, if nothing happens to interrupt our southing.

Yrs,
Andy

XIII

THE TRUMPET OF THE SWAN

1966-1970

• *In the latter half of the sixties Katharine's health improved, and White, in addition to writing the occasional Letter from the East and other pieces for* The New Yorker, *went to work on the third of his books for children.* The Trumpet of the Swan *was published in 1970. White also revised* The Elements of Style *and made a recording of* Charlotte's Web.

To ALISON COOK

[Sarasota, Fla.]
January 30, 1966

Dear Mrs. Cook:

Thanks for your note.[1] If my wife's tears seemed to you to indicate a loss of courage or an access of sentimentality, it's because you don't know my wife. She has sailed through seven bouts of major surgery and four of minor without batting an eyelash or losing her nerve. She only cries on small occasions.

Sincerely,
E. B. White

To URSULA NORDSTROM

Sarasota, Florida
February 12, 1966

Dear Ursula:

Thank you for the gigantic postalgram. Everything about the show on Sunday, March 6, is going to be gigantic (except the hero, who is

---

1. After reading White's "What Do Our Hearts Treasure?" in *The New Yorker*, Mrs. Cook had written urging the Whites not to be sad about having to celebrate Christmas in Florida.

quite small). The beans that support the whole business are Green Giants, the audience will be gigantic (20 million), the promotional campaign is gigantic, and my reservations about the TV version are gigantic. Harriet Ames has mysteriously disappeared from the story— just slipped quietly away, probably on the recommendation of the consulting psychologist, a Mr. Charles Winick.

I hope your paper-white narcissus is flourishing, and I hope that you are. I finally forced my wife to give up raising paper-whites on the score that I was having enough trouble from pollenosis without their peremptory challenge. It's a Pyrrhic victory, though. I really loved them.

Sincerely,
Andy

To **JUDITH W. PREUSSER**

Sarasota, Fla.
25 Feb [1966]

Dear Judy:

Thanks for the nice newsy letter—I had been wondering about you, and I'm glad things are going well in your home and in your job.

I can understand how your friend feels, but although I'm sometimes pessimistic about man's future, I don't believe him to be innately evil. I'm more worried about his insatiable curiosity than I am about his poor character: his preoccupation with the moon is disturbing to me, particularly since his own rivers run dirty and his air is getting fouler every year. In Germany during the Hitler regime, there must have been a great many essentially good men who found themselves doing things, or condoning things, that were against their nature. Perhaps your friend's father was one of them. Certainly there must have been a lot of young storm troopers who were caught up in the excitement of the master race theory, and who needed a few more years on their heads to give them a sense of balance and proportion. Youth is headstrong, and with Hitler egging them on, it could only result in brutality and cruelty. The Germans are a disciplined people, and in this case, it was discipline run wild.

You asked whether I ever had "murderous thoughts." Not really. There have been a few people I would have been glad to see dead, because they were causing such trouble in the world. But I don't recall ever being so enraged as to be uncontrollable. I'll have to work on it— maybe I can get madder as time goes on. . . .

Love,
Uncle Andy

To HARRIET WALDEN

[Sarasota, Fla.]
[March 1966]
Sunday

Dear Harriet:

In answer to your direct question, I wasn't satisfied with "Stuart Little" on TV, but I didn't expect to be. It came out about the way I figured it would. By the terms of my contract with NBC, I was entitled to see and approve the script. A year ago, they sent me a script; I edited it (very slightly, but with a few good fixes) and returned it to them with my approval. Weeks later, I was told that they lost or misplaced *my* copy of the script, with my revisions. Then, months later, a brand new script arrived, with the glad tidings that the whole thing was wrapped up anyway, so I never bothered to read it.

It is the fixed purpose of television and motion pictures to scrap the author, sink him without a trace, on the theory that he is incompetent, has never read his own stuff, is not responsible for anything he ever wrote, and wouldn't know what to do about it even if he were. I believe this has something to do with the urge to create, and the only way a TV person or a movie person can become a creator is to sink the guy who did it to begin with. I'm not really complaining about NBC, because by and large they set out to be fairly faithful to the general theme of Stuart, and they did not try to corrupt or demolish it. But there were a hundred places that, if they had wanted to take me into their confidence, I could have bettered for them. It was their choice, not mine. The Johnny Carson narration was straight-forward, but muffed several spots that need not have been muffed. The music was good but in many places overpowering and over-riding. It fought with the words just when it should have been peaceable. I am fairly familiar with the text of "Stuart Little," but when Stuart asked Margalo where she came from, and she replied, "I come from fields once tall with wheat, from pastures deep in fern and thistle" I couldn't hear a damn thing against the musical background. At that particular moment, there shouldn't have been any music anyway, if I may rudely suggest such a departure.

But the filming was ingenious throughout, and it certainly took a lot of dedication and a lot of doing. The sailboat race was pulled off despite great physical difficulties, and the schoolroom scene was effective because of the good faces, even though the script was not right, to my mind. . . .

Yrs,
EBW

• *U.S. Ambassador to Norway Margaret Joy Tibbetts wrote White after reading his piece "The Annals of Birdwatching," about Edward Howe Forbush's* Birds of Massachusetts, *in the February 23 issue of* The New Yorker.

To MARGARET JOY TIBBETTS

[Sarasota, Fla.]
March 29, 1966

Dear Miss Tibbetts:

I consulted Webster to find out how to address our Ambassador to Norway, and if this letter should start "Your Grace," please forgive me. I'm always in some kind of trouble. It was a triple pleasure to hear from a Tibbetts of Maine, an American Ambassador, and a woman whose mother released a hummingbird from a web, all in one.

Your mother's experience differed somewhat from mine in that her bird was caught in an orb web, where there was a practicing spider, and mine was caught in some dusty cobwebs in my woodshed. I have an idea that the "old spider, about the size in diameter of a fifty cent piece" was *Aranea Cavatica*, the common grey spider that inhabits outbuildings. This spider was the one that I wrote about in my children's book, "Charlotte's Web." I rather like spiders; they are not only useful, they are indispensable, and the world would be a frightening place without them, as they are the principal agent that prevents insects from taking over the earth.

When I discovered a hummingbird enmeshed in the cobwebs, I too was surprised that it was unable to free itself. The material spiders use is incredibly strong for its size. I carefully took hold of the bird with one hand, and with the other I plucked the strands of webbing from the bird's wings and from its tiny feet. (The feet of a hummingbird are delicate and weak, they get so little use.) Having cleared the bird of its trappings, I spent a moment admiring it and savoring the pleasure of having a ruby-throat in my hand, and then released it, to take up its life again in the bee balm and the delphiniums.

I'm glad you enjoyed the Forbush article.

Sincerely,
E. B. White

To GEOFFREY HELLMAN

Sarasota, Florida
14 April 1966

Dear Geoffrey:

Thank you for filling in our readers, including me, on Major Bendire.[1] And thank you for your respectful reference to me as "Mr."

1. Hellman had written a "Department of Amplification" about White's piece "The Annals of Birdwatching" for the April 16, 1966, issue of *The New Yorker*. The

E. B. White. This has been long overdue in the pages of the magazine. Someone had to break the barrier and I am glad it was you.

As to your supposition that the Major was where he was from some instinctive knowledge of birds, rather than from an urge to get to the little building, it is anybody's guess. It just could be he was taking a crap. I knew a man once in Canada, in a boys' camp near Dorset, Ontario, who visited a backhouse in darkness and from necessity and without benefit of a flashlight. He was just about to sit down on the hole when he heard a slight noise. Very wisely he returned to his tent, got a flashlight, and when he got back to the little outbuilding of his dreams and shone the light around, he found a porcupine gnawing the rim of the hole for what salt he could get out of it.

It just goes to show.

I was scared as hell to turn in the Forbush piece because of my almost complete ignorance of the subject matter. It occurred to me that I might easily get clobbered by the entire ornithological community, which now numbers millions, including you, of all people. Well, I got out of it with my scalp, and that is all I asked.

I wonder why Bendire (Bender) was kicked out of that theological seminary in Paris. Probably from watching some kind of courtship antics. The cloth wouldn't like that.

Item: There is an active Bald Eagle's nest on the Palmer Ranch a few miles from here. It's in a crotch of a pine, only about a hundred feet from the Tamiami Trail, Route 41. I have kept my eye on it this winter from time to time, and have taken my grandchildren there to visit it.

Yrs,
Andy
Mr. E. B. White

To ROGER ANGELL

North Brooklin, Maine
May 13 [1966]
Cold

Dear Rog:

You are the foremost interpreter of baseball, the unmanly art, and I thoroughly enjoyed your Astro piece[1] and was taken back in memory to the definitive piece on the game you did for *Holiday*. I

---

major, who had once witnessed the courtship of whippoorwills "from a small outbuilding," is one of the dozens of birdwatchers enshrined in *Birds of Massachusetts*.

1. In *The New Yorker*, about the Houston Astrodome.

thought your Texas observations were funny, sound, and good, as well as instructive, and I'm glad you didn't pull any punches with old Judge Pickleheinz or whatever his name is. Baseball is for watching, I know *that* much about the game, even though I seldom understand exactly what is taking place out there. (I had to ask my wife the other day what was the difference between an earned run and a run. She told me a long cock-and-bull story by way of reply, and I am sifting it slowly and carefully.) Eventually I think Texas will have to be thrown away, Pedernales and all, and let the country get along with only Alaska and Hawaii for its oddities. Anyway, thanks for an enjoyable piece. And you were in the same issue with Sissman's "In and Out," which to my mind is the best poem we have published since they invented poets.

No news of consequence here. Dinner at the Parsons' tonight. Six thirty. Grey trousers.

Love,
Andy

• *Reginald Allen, then an assistant to the director of the Metropolitan Opera, and his wife, Helen Howe, were summer neighbors of the Whites. Allen liked to celebrate springtime by sending White a few egg cases of the praying mantis.*

To REGINALD ALLEN

North Brooklin, Maine
June 6, 1966

Dear Mr. Allen:

The egg cases arrived in what seemed to me very good order, the finest gift I have received in a long time. One is sewed to a clematis vine on the south side of the house, the other to a syringa bush on the north side handy to our little grove of frittilaries, which I have just spelled wrong. Fritillaries. Every morning my first tour of inspection takes me to these choice locations, to see if young mantises have broken jail. A warm spell of weather, I am sure, will be the thing that does the trick. Aphids beware the Ides of June!

Thank you for your kindness in supplying me with such an interesting addition to our horticultural scene. I have a pair of Yellow Warblers nesting in the honeysuckle bush by the garage door, so my cup runneth over.

With kindest regards to your wife, and again thanks . . .

Sincerely,
E. B. White

To MRS. ISABEL BAXTER

North Brooklin, Maine

June 9, 1966

Dear Mrs. Baxter:

This letter is for your grandson, whose name is unknown to me. I want to thank him very much for Stuart's skates. They are really ingenious—a good job. I plan to give them to a red-headed girl named Susan Poland who has a model of Stuart. She has him pretty well equipped but I don't think she has any skates for him and I know she will be tickled. Susan is eleven, too.

Will you please convey my thanks to your grandson.

Sincerely,

E. B. White

To MARGARET CHASE SMITH

[North Brooklin, Me.]

August 15, 1966

Dear Senator Smith:

I think the Dirksen amendment on voluntary prayer should be defeated. The Constitution is clear on the subject: there shall be no establishment of religion.

Any religious ceremony in a public school is an exercise in orthodoxy—the orthodoxy of the Christian faith, which is correct for most of us, unacceptable to some. In an atmosphere of "voluntary" prayer, pupils coming from homes where other faiths prevail will feel an embarrassment by their non-participation; in the eyes of their schoolmates they will be "queer" or "different" or "irreligious." Such a stigma for a child can be emotionally disturbing, and although we no longer hang and burn our infidels and our witches, a schoolchild who is left out in the cold during a prayer session suffers scars that are very real.

It should be the concern of our democracy that no child shall feel uncomfortable because of belief. This condition cannot be met if a schoolmaster is empowered to establish a standard of religious rectitude based on a particular form of worship.

Sincerely yours,

E. B. White

• *Stephen White, an acquaintance of White's, wrote from the Carnegie Commission on Educational Television, asking for suggestions. White's reply was included in the Commission's report.*

To STEPHEN WHITE

[North Brooklin, Me.]
September 26, 1966

Dear Steve:

I have a grandson now named Steven White, and I'll bet he can swim faster and stay under longer than you can.

As for television, I doubt that I have any ideas or suggestions that would be worth putting on paper. Non-commercial TV should address itself to the idea of excellence, not the idea of acceptability— which is what keeps commercial TV from climbing the staircase. I think TV should be providing the visual counterpart of the literary essay, should arouse our dreams, satisfy our hunger for beauty, take us on journeys, enable us to participate in events, present great drama and music, explore the sea and the sky and the woods and the hills. It should be our Lyceum, our Chautauqua, our Minsky's, and our Camelot. It should restate and clarify the social dilemma and the political pickle. Once in a while it does, and you get a quick glimpse of its potential.

As you see, I have nothing specific to offer and am well supplied with platitudes, every one of them gilt-edged. But thanks for the chance.

Yrs,
E. B. White

• *Dr. Maurice Root, a physician of West Hartford, Connecticut, is a reader with whom White has exchanged many letters.*

To MAURICE ROOT

North Brooklin, Maine
21 October 1966

Dear Dr. Root:

Thanks for your letter. I hope you saw more eagles last summer than I did. Years ago there was always a fish hawk poised over our cove, ready to dive. Not any more. The flounders and sculpins are gone from the water, the hawk is gone from the sky.

And there always used to be a pair of bald eagles nesting about three miles from here. They would show up in this vicinity and try to rob the hawk of his catch. Not any more. No fish, no hawk-carrying-fish, no eagle robbing the laden hawk. I find this very sad.

I must read the Book of Job, for laughs.

Sincerely,
E. B. White

To MAURICE ROOT

North Brooklin
9 November 1966

Dear Dr. Root:

If I'm down, I suspect it's not as simple a matter as an unhatched eagle's egg. More likely it is that, like many an aging writer, I miss the warmth and the excitement of brooding a clutch of my own eggs. I had become accustomed to the act of creation; now I'm in the moult and my spirit tends to droop. You were extremely kind to remind me of past performances and the eggs of yesteryear. Thanks very much for your letter.

Sincerely,
E. B. White

To FAITH MC NULTY MARTIN

North Brooklin
10 November [1966]

Dear Faith:

I do not consider $9.28 too high for a quart of mouse milk,[1] specially when you think of the hours those little milkmaids put in, on their little stools. I am very pleased to know that I can get a quart of mouse milk for under ten dollars.

I saw a fine thing late yesterday afternoon when I was out gathering wild rose hips for my wife. In a small apple tree, almost directly above my head, I saw what appeared to be a last summer's bird nest. When I looked more closely I saw that I was looking at a little young porcupine whose mother had given him instructions on how to act in an emergency. "If White should come along," she had told him, "simply quit eating your apple and roll yourself into a ball, tucking your feet under you and also your tail, and stay still and don't talk." This is just what he had done. . . .

Hope I can see you in New York, but we will probably skirt around the city on our way to Sarasota.

Love,
Andy

---

1. Mrs. Martin had sent White a newspaper clipping in which it was reported that Swiss agriculturists receive the "high price" of $9.28 per quart of mouse milk.

To CAROL AND ROGER ANGELL

Sarasota [Florida]
January 9 [1967]

Dear Carol and Roger:

You will have forgotten by this time, but at Christmas you sent me a pretty tie and a sad book,[1] and I love them both. I use the tie to push me over the edge when I am at my sartorial greatest, and I use the Nathan Silver book to cry into. It's such a wonderful record. It makes me feel so OLD. You know what they were doing, don't you, the year I was born—they were beginning to demolish the reservoir at 42nd and Fifth to make way for a public library to house the books that little Elwyn White would write when he got big enough to hold a pencil. I saw my first circus in Stanford White's yellow brick Madison Square Garden, holding tight my father's hand. I covered the opening of the Roxy and the Paramount for *Talk*, escorting a girl named Mary Osborn to the Roxy to impress her with what a fellow I was in journalism. I went off to college, a green freshman, aboard a Hoboken ferryboat. I was gliding into middle life when they raised the great Trylon and Perisphere, to make all the other phallic symbols around town look like peanuts. The saddest picture of all to me is the one of the Rhinelander Gardens, on West 11th, the hub of the wheel of my salad days. (There's a metaphor to rassle with!) Well, New York may be lost, but it is not forgotten, and this exciting book will help me keep it in mind. Thank you for choosing it as a gift.

This has been a strange winter, so far, for me—the winter of the wild young dogs. I shouldn't have landed here without a full-time kennelman. These two puppies[2] need about 38 acres in which to let off steam, plus a house that their owner owns free and clear. Here, all is restriction, confinement, frustration, and discipline. I feel so sorry for them in their pent-up exuberance, I tend to spend all my waking hours and a few of my so-called sleeping hours in their company. I rise early and am out early, to get in some brisk work before breakfast. This "private" park, with its clipped cedars, sorrowing doves, well-tended lawns and rose gardens, and faintly stuffy oldsters, is not exactly a paradise for a couple of pot-smoking pups who dream of trips. We are also perilously near a highway (Higel Avenue) that rivals the East River Drive for frenetic energy, so I don't dare be too casual about

---

1. *Lost New York*, by Nathan Silver.
2. Maggie and Jones. White writes: "Jones was a small, poorly shaped Norwich Terrier, a bundle of neuroses. He had been whelped in England. By the time he arrived in Maine he was a nervous wreck, and had to be restored to life. Maggie, a lovable little mongrel bitch, was assigned the task and did it beautifully."

liberty. What I usually do, to start the day, is to put Maggie in leash, and let Jones come along free, as an outrider. He is off like a bullet, but never really separates himself from the hunt proper, and I find I can trust him to return with us, after a quick spin around the Circle. He dashes from one pissing tree to the next, and sometimes raises his leg so high he falls over. Maggie, of course, is furious and jealous. She pulls like a steer, gagging herself and emitting horrible coughs and groans. Jones has a set-piece for an enemy—a tall, dingy, rangy yellow mongrel who emerges at the same hour (7:30 a.m.) from a known driveway. He is a sort of Yellow Dog Dingo. Spotting him, Jones bristles, then starts bouncing straight up into the air, springing from all four legs, to increase his stature. He invariably faces down this yellow dog, and puts him to rout, which he dearly loves. There is another element in it, though. Secretly, Jones wants to explore this dog and hobnob with him, and two or three times this has been accomplished, with sparks flying in all directions. When I return from this exhausting early-morning jaunt, I put both dogs to a hitching post (any handy doorknob) and do a preliminary cleanup of the foul kennels. I have a papier mache chamber pot that I line with sawdust, and I go to work with a trowel. This restores the yards to a semblance of order, and I can go to breakfast. After breakfast, the serious kennel work begins— freshening the beds, patting the pillows, applying new cedar shavings, relandscaping the grounds where holes have been dug, raking the runs, seeding with rye grass, refilling the water pans. And then the brushing and combing and grooming, and the laying-on of hands to discover ticks.

It all takes time. But I have two wonderful puppies, and they are responding, thank God. Maggie is highly emotional and completely adorable. Jones is peppery, scrappy, canny, and semi-obedient. I think I can make a dog of him yet. I have some pictures that I'll send you when I get duplicates made.

Joe's visit with his family turned out well. The weather had chilled a bit, but was bright, and I don't think (or I didn't notice) that any of the White children thought it was anything but very hot, as they swam about five times a day. (I did my swimming about a month ago, when it really *was* hot, and will resume in another month, when heat returns to Florida.) Anyway, it seemed much more like Christmas to have the family here, and they all seemed in good form. I am very lucky and I am grateful for my blessings. Thanks again for your gifts.

Love,
Andy

• *In 1967 the animation team of John and Faith Hubley became interested in acquiring the motion picture rights to* Charlotte's Web. *White knew and liked the Hubleys and was inclined to favor their proposal. Alexander Lindey was the lawyer who represented White in the negotiations, along with Jap Gude, who had become White's agent for film rights during the fifties. From the correspondence it is evident that White wanted more control over the material than movie companies are disposed to grant. A contract was signed, but in the end the Hubleys were unable to get the backing required and the project fell through.*

To ALEXANDER LINDEY

[North Brooklin, Me.]
May 22, 1967

Dear Al:

Your proposed terms of contract sound all right to me, all twelve of them.

I'm not sure I understand 3b. In addition to a fee of $20,000, the Hubleys will share in the alleged profits, won't they? (You'll have to excuse my ignorance in these matters.)

In 4, I don't know what "merchandising rights" means. Does this refer to my right, subsequently, to make other deals, or does it refer to objects of merchandise—dolls, pigs, sweat shirts? Again excuse ignorance.

There should probably be a clause somewhere prohibiting the publication in book form of the screenplay or of any other adaptation of my book. When Disney made "Mary Poppins" he got out a book, "The Walt Disney Mary Poppins." I'm against anything of that sort.

I'm catching the mail with this letter. Tomorrow I'll try to get off another note to you, clarifying my desires about my "right of approval." This seems likely to be the touchiest and haziest of all the elements of the agreement.

Sincerely,
Andy

To ALEXANDER LINDEY

[North Brooklin, Me.]
May 24, 1967

Dear Al:

The purpose of the "right of approval" clause is two-fold: it should protect me from a motion picture version of "Charlotte's Web" that violates the spirit and meaning of the story, and it should protect the Hubleys from obstructive behavior of an author. The movie will be their creation, not mine, and they will naturally want to get on with it in the way they feel it should go. I believe they are sympathetic with and agreeable to my desire to have a look at the screenplay, see sketches of the principal characters, and hear the principal voices. This shouldn't be either difficult or expensive.

I want the chance to edit the script wherever anything turns up that is a gross departure or a gross violation. I also would like to be protected against the insertion of wholly new material—songs, jokes, capers, episodes. I don't anticipate trouble of this sort; the Hubleys have already expressed to me in a letter (as well as verbally) their desire to produce a faithful adaptation, and I believe them to be sincere in this.

This approval business is sensitive, though. Artistic temperaments and pride can easily get on a collision course. In the elaborate papers sent me by Jap Gude, for instance, it says "Owner shall have the right of approval, *not to be unreasonably withheld*." (Italics mine.) I don't know at what point a man's opinion, or stricture, becomes "unreasonable." What may seem reasonable to me may well seem unreasonable to the Hubleys. This is the joker. We will just have to work it out between us as best we can.

I will give you an example of what I call a "gross" violation. In my book, Charlotte dies. If, in the screenplay, she should turn up alive at the end of the story in the interests of a happier ending, I would consider this a gross violation and I would regard my disapproval as reasonable.

Good luck!
Andy

To HOWARD CUSHMAN

North Brooklin
21 June [1967]

Dear Cush:

On this first day of summer (temperature 50°, mean little NE wind from the cold sea, rain falling, Chinese fallout sifting gently down onto bean and broccoli in the neat green rows) I sit cozily indoors, thinking of all the things I've ever known—which includes your unanswered letter about Snow White and the dear dead days. Incidentally, it seems to me that the most damning thing that can be said about Barthelme's piece[1] is that it went completely out of my mind as soon as I had finished reading it, and I haven't thought of it since, except on the occasions when you threw it at me. A writer should take care to be

---

1. "Snow White," by Donald Barthelme, in *The New Yorker* of February 18, 1967.

memorable, and I can't remember Snow White. For that matter, I can't remember Moby Dick, either. I can remember "Men seldom make passes at girls who wear glasses," which should place Mistress Parker ahead of Melville but probably doesn't. The picture is confusing. I never read Joyce and was interested to discover that you hadn't either. Once, when my head was pretty bad, I picked up Ulysses and gave it a go but found out that it was simply making me horribly nervous, and I never went back. And I never understood why the slightest fuss was made over G. Stein, whose contribution to letters strikes me as very close to zero. Barthelme looks like a straight writer compared to her. So every generation has its oddballs, who strike attitudes and often strike out. Most prose today, it seems to me, is not greatly different in style from the prose of our salad days. I've just read "The Secret of Santa Vittoria"; except for a few passages that are more explicit than what was around in the Twenties, the book is straight going and derives from Hemingway, without H's lack of humor.

I think you are worrying the notion that K and I "accept" things that you reject, and that this is because we have lost our balance through overexposure to all kinds of writers and writing. I don't *accept* anything at all unless I happen to like it, and I doubt that I have been exposed to any more litry folks or litry products than you have. I am a non-reader of contemporary poetry in a big way—it gives me a pain in the (excuse it) arse. But I keep my eyes, and I trust my mind, open, and once in a while I stumble on something that I wouldn't have missed for the world, like Sissman's "In and Out"—a fine poem though not in the rigidly lyrical school. Ogden Nash is a gifted poet who has sometimes written lyrically (and well, too) but has mostly written the rambling couplets that made him deservedly (I think) famous.

All of us of our generation feel a great longing for the romanticism and the lyricism and the discipline of the writings that we cut our teeth on. I am in a constant state of lament for the casual yet exciting and disciplined columns of Adams and Morley and Marquis, which were where we could raise our little heads and have our moment of triumph. The day started on a higher level, and we laid down our morning paper exalted if not exulting. Seen in perspective, though, some of the well-loved figures of those days have shrunk with the passage of time. Dotty Parker died on Page 1, but except for a handful of sterling short stories her contribution to letters was slight and she herself knew that she was not much of a poet. I haven't read a word of Dreiser in years, but I have an idea that if I were to return to him and his works I would fwow up. Thomas Wolfe is interesting (to me) more for his correspondence than for his novels. I find his books hard going, but the letters he wrote were revealing and full of immense feeling and the joy of life and the terror of same. Fellows like Woolcott have dwindled till they are almost lost to view. I haven't even spelled his name right. Two l's, wasn't it?

My uneasiness about modern writing is not because of its being experimental but because of its abandonment of the responsibility of good taste and its acceptance of the inevitability of complete disclosure. This I find worrisome. When freedom of expression is abused, and things become disgusting, then freedom of expression is endangered. People will stand just so much, then they want the clamps put on. I think we are getting perilously close to the clampdown. The movies are not going to be happy till they present the sex act in living color, and this is where the trouble is going to start and where the new Victorian age will bloom. . . .

Yr lucid and disciplined old friend,
Andy

To J. G. CASE

North Brooklin, Maine
June 28, 1967

Dear Jack:

Since April I have been wanting to thank you properly for the photo copies of Will Strunk's book. I was enchanted by his markings —so tidy and in the hand that I remember well. As you say in your letter, nothing is heavy or blurred or in any way disorderly. There just wasn't any disorder in Strunk, or any irresolution.

His handwriting seemed to me, a student, admirable, and I made an effort to ape it, but without much success. I wanted to be able to write *frequent* as he wrote it, but still can't manage it. And I was interested in his *rare*, which begins with one kind of an "r" and goes on to another.

One of the markings that I found most satisfying was "Enc. Brit. (without pay)." That has Strunk's imprint, unmistakable. And, in the Charles Lamb, his pouncing on "In a degree beneath manhood," which he changed to "To an unmanly degree."

I hope you are enjoying life along Third Avenue. It was a thoroughfare I found congenial years ago, in my Turtle Bay phase, but on recent visits it has seemed foreign territory and I stroll up and down in a thin cloud of depression laced with diesel oil.

We had no spring here at all and have gone straight into summer. Lilacs and apple blossoms were confused by the whole business and blew their lines. I seized the moment to reactivate my barn; I have sheep, lambs, geese, chickens, and the fastest pig in Hancock County.

My goose has sat for 28 days and is even now hatching her goslings, in a nest in the tieups. The gander, in anticipation of new responsibilities, chose to spend last night at the pond, drinking. And I must make a bedside call right now—a routine check. There is nothing (to me) more delightful than the details surrounding a hatch of goose eggs. The young are as green as grass, and they immediately begin playing their flutes, an enchanting sound.

Please pardon these bucolics, and thanks again for the Strunk items.

Yrs,
Andy

To FRANK SULLIVAN

North Brooklin
Aug 22 [1967].

Dear Dr. Sullivan:

I am enclosing two dollars which I wish you would place upon the nose of a needy horse in the running of The Sullivan ("the run for the posies" as I believed it is called).[1]

I am not fussy about which horse you select for me. I did awfully well on my first bet in 1922, in Lexington, Kentucky. . . . I have done little betting since, as I like to quit when I am ahead. But I have a sentimental interest in The Sullivan that can only be assuaged by naked risk, which is why I am asking this favor of you.

With all best wishes from Katharine S. White and myself on this occasion, and in the hope that the day finds you well dressed, in good health, and good spirits,

Yrs faithfully,
Andy
(Dr. E. B. White)

P.S. If this letter arrives too late for the event, you may spend the money on drink, with all its attendant evils.

To FRANK SULLIVAN

North Brooklin, Maine
September 13, 1967

Dear Frank:

K and I loved your letter. I feel bad that my bet failed to reach you in time for the event—the mails out of here cover the first fifty miles

---

1. The Saratoga Racing Association, at the suggestion of Roger Angell, got up a stake race in honor of Frank Sullivan's seventy-fifth birthday.

by dog-sled, which I believe is pulled by Chihuahuas. I also feel bad that the race was not called "The Sullivan," instead of the Frank Sullivan. Would have been a better name. The trouble with the "Frank Sullivan" is that it suggests that there is more than one Sullivan in this country, which is ridiculous on the face of it. . . .

Your admission that you "can't walk more than a few blocks" makes me feel that you are not challenging yourself enough. When I discovered that I couldn't walk more than a few blocks I immediately broke into a trot—which is what the *Reader's Digest* had been telling me to do all along—and it works very well. Creates a pretty scene on the streets and brings the roses back to your cheeks. You are not running enough, for a man of your years, and very likely you are drawing too many breaths, too. That's another thing I learned from the *R. Digest* —cut breathing down to about four times a minute. I have felt a whole lot younger since I stopped breathing. It drains your strength, breathing does. Along with my philosophy of "challenge" for the elderly, I have instituted a lot of incidental nonsense around here. I acquired a seven-weeks-old mongrel puppy from an adoption home, and there is nothing that beats a puppy for keeping a man's blood coursing in his veins. I have to get out of bed much earlier, for the first feeding, and then I have to clean up the feces, that are often cleverly hidden. I also gave instructions a year ago to have a 20-foot auxiliary sloop built for my use, which was done, and this summer has found me facing the great challenge of fog, wind, and rain at sea, among these treacherous islands and ledges, and usually alone. I don't know why, at my age, I continue to sail a boat under trying conditions, unless it is that I have a secret desire to be knighted by the Queen. Call me not Ishmael, call me Sir Elwyn.[1]

Just read your opening remarks in Corey's new book[2] and enjoyed them. I haven't read the book yet—just poked about to find references to me. I have moments of hoping and dreaming that we will live to see another Golden Age, or at least Silver Age, when writers will be both gay and disciplined and when even newspapers will show an interest in the litry life. But I dream of a lot of things. Anyway, I'm glad I lived when you did, and some others I could mention. It was a privilege while it lasted. Why, it's *still* a privilege!

Life here continues on its accustomed nutty round, with me dipping sheep and Katharine arranging flowers. (Read her upcoming pieces

1. The reference is to the knighting of Francis Chichester on his return to England after sailing around the world single-handed. White's sloop *Martha* was built by Joel White at the Brooklin Boat Yard.
2. *The Time of Laughter*, by Corey Ford.

on flar arrangement in the NYer!) K suffers terribly from the mysterious skin ailment that has the dermatologists baffled and that keeps her, perforce, on a high level of cortisone. She gets tense nervously from the drug, and from not being able to wear the usual female under-attire, but she manages to raise lovely flower borders and occasionally write a piece—which is more than her little husband can say. Hell it is, I just sent a droll thing to the *NYTimes*, for their "Topics" column.[3] Full of fun, 750 words of pure delight. K, I am sure, will write you. Meantime we send our love and best wishes for many happy (and vigorous) returns of the 22nd.

Yrs,
Andy

To HERBERT MITGANG

North Brooklin
5 Oct [1967]

Dear Mr. Mitgang:

You are the most active editor I have known, with the exception of Harold Wallace Ross.[1] Every mail brings a pencil or a paperweight. And the last mail brought the marvelous explanation from Betty[2] (give her my love before I forget it) for the non-arrival of the big hundred-dollar payoff. So I will continue to live in penury until the machine gathers its strength for the October go around, or orgasm.

I figured out today that the *Times* is paying me 13½ cents a word, which is not as good as Calvin Coolidge was getting for the column he wrote in the Nineteen Twenties. He got 50 cents—I remember that. It stuck in my mind. I don't know what they paid Eleanor Roosevelt for "My Day" but whatever it was, she was overpaid. Inflation would bring Coolidge's take well up above a dollar a word—probably a dollar fifty, or two dollars. Coolidge was pithy but uninteresting. I also figured out today that "Topics" fills about 40 square inches in the paper, and would love to know what an advertiser has to pay for his 40 square. The differential would be a fascinating study for a mathematically-minded man like myself. I should have been a computer, with people feeding stray bits of information into me while I belched.

I dare the *Times* to write me a check *today* for $100 using a blank form. What are you? Mice?

E. B. White

3. A piece about computers in banks. It ran in the *New York Times*, September 23, 1967.

1. Mitgang was then a member of the editorial board of the *New York Times*.
2. Betty Pomerantz, Mitgang's secretary.

To CAROLINE ANGELL

Sarasota
17 December [1967]

Dear Callie:

Through Grandma's maneuvering, I think you will receive a copy of "Walden." This is my Christmas present to you in this critical year of 1967. I hope you will get as much fun and instruction from the book as I did, at a somewhat later age.

Thoreau has been greatly misconstrued and been made use of by all sorts of groups and thinkers. He laid himself wide open to this, as you can see by reading his stuff—which is full of contradictions and cryptic utterances. But he was, I think, a good seer and prophet, and many of his sentences cover whole areas of modern life and the modern dilemma.

The way to read Thoreau is to enjoy him—his enthusiasms, his acute perception.

Much love and a Merry Christmas.

Andy

To MILTON GREENSTEIN

[Sarasota, Fla.]
February 3, 1968

Dear Milton:

Please pardon the use of your first name but I feel we should be on a first name basis after the fish we have shared together.

Running "Here Is New York" as a 2-page spread in the *Times* is a flattering project but not, I think, a sensible one, either for Eastern Airlines or for me. Why didn't Mr. Julian A. Rutick seek my permission before putting his agency to the considerable expense of setting the thing in type? Advertising men are surely dreamers. I don't want to appear suddenly in the *N.Y. Times* as a copywriter for an airline. For one thing, I don't fly. For another, I withdrew from the advertising world about forty-two years ago, for what seemed good reasons, and do not wish to return unless forced to do so by circumstances.

Moreover, "Here Is New York" is now a period piece. I re-read it tonight with pleasure but with a strong sense of the passage of time. Very little in the piece captures the city as it is today. I was writing about a city that has all but disappeared; to publish the piece prominently in the Times would be to bewilder or amuse the present inhabitants. When I return to New York, these days, I look around and cry "Where am I?"—like a frightened child.

No, I think Julian (if I may use his first name) should sit down and write his own promotional copy for his airline. When he turns to me he's just looking for an easy way out.

But I appreciate his thoughtfulness and want to thank him for the offer of a job.

Yrs,
Andy

To LELAND HAYWARD

[Sarasota, Fla.]
February 10, 1968

Dear Mr. Hayward:

Perhaps I am deficient in sporting blood, but I can't get worked up over the possibilities of that old doomsday piece for the movies. It strikes me as the wrong tale for these times.

Usually I am reasonably well pleased with what I have written; I was never satisfied with "The Morning of the Day," and I really have no desire to have it made into a film. I respectfully urge you to get it out of your mind, even if you have to read "Anne of Green Gables" to do it.

Sincerely,
E. B. White

• *Ted Weeks, then a consultant and senior editor at the* Atlantic Monthly, *sent White a copy of his new book and, incidentally, asked him what he thought of* Ross, The New Yorker, and Me, *by Ross's first wife, Jane Grant.*

To EDWARD WEEKS

Sarasota
March 12, 1968

Dear Ted:

Many thanks for sending me a copy of "Fresh Waters." I haven't seen the book yet; it is being "held for arrival" in the north. (Katharine and I are sitting out the winter on our favorite sandbar, watching the Gulf of Mexico quietly disappear behind the high-rise buildings.) We've not been back to the Milford House since the summer we encountered you there, but we often think back on it with pleasure and longing, and I look forward to "Fresh Waters."

Jane Grant's book, like almost every attempt to explain Ross and *The New Yorker*, is disappointing. What's more, she played a dirty trick on Katharine and me. She promised us that we would see proof of our hastily-written contributions, and when we returned the proofs with corrections, she allowed our stuff to appear without the corrections. I haven't really read the book—just poked around in it. When she tries to reproduce Ross's speech, I collapse in a fit of ugly mirth.

Charley Morton, although his association with Ross and the magazine was brief and tenuous, somehow managed to evoke the man and the times better than anybody I have read.

Yrs,
Andy

To ANN MORING

[North Brooklin, Me.]
April 16, 1968

Dear Miss Moring:

When I wrote "Death of a Pig," I was simply rendering an account of what actually happened on my place—to my pig, who died, and to me, who tended him in his last hours. There was no "basic premise" in the composition, and there was no "lack of concern" in my ministrations. Had I not been concerned, I'd have never written the piece.

The telephone conversation was recorded word for word, as best I could remember it. I had no reason to be angry at the operator—she was doing what she was supposed to do: cut in to find out whether the connection had been established. Like many incidents in time of crisis or of stress, the conversation seemed funny in retrospect, but I did not introduce it for "comic relief" but because it was a part of the whole story and it kept my narrative moving.

I tend to write about events or circumstances that raise the level of my perception. The death of this animal moved me, heightened my awareness. To confront death, in any guise, is to identify with the victim and face what is unsettling and sobering. As I said in the piece, "I knew that what could be true of my pig could be true also of the rest of my tidy world."

I hope you and your instructor have a nice time unravelling these mysteries.

Sincerely,
E. B. White

To REGINALD ALLEN

[North Brooklin, Me.]
June 4 [1968]

Dear Reggie:

Just want to report a killdeer's nest on the second hole of the Blue Hill golf course. I visited it this afternoon on a tip from Ward Snow, the postmaster of BH. Four eggs, almost the size of bantam's eggs, sharply pointed and the points nicely centered. On bare ground. I watched from my car after a brief observation and saw the hen steal back and settle on the eggs. She had been flushed by an early golfer, wildly swinging. I was almost extinguished by black flies, but am glad I went.

Yrs,
Andy

To STANLEY HART WHITE

North Brooklin
June 9 [1968]

Dear Bun:

I've been wanting to write and thank you for the album you sent. Can you imagine today's youth writing captions like those? Maybe they still do—between puffs of marijuana. I love old pictures of the age of innocence; I remember that age so much more clearly than the recent decades, which tend to blur. Also, I've intended to congratulate you on the medal you picked up from the Mass. Horticultural Society. I studied the photograph of you and decided you looked like Mr. Toad—one of the better fictional characters. I suspect we are all getting to look mildly fictional. I *feel* distinctly fictional. As though I were merely the invention of some rather second-rate mind. Anyhow, I thought your citation was impressive. On the whole, though, medals are a nuisance—dust catchers. I tried to destroy a particularly dishonest plaque once, but only got about half way with it.

I sneaked a look at K's letter to you and was delighted with that sentence about how she is no longer able to write letters. She knocks off ten or twelve a day, of approximately the length of the one you received. Her production staggers me. I avoid writing letters—it resembles too closely writing itself, and gives me a headache. Don't take seriously K's remarks about letters for Cornell; I don't give a damn about this so-called archive. In fact I feel somewhat embarrassed about it since discovering that the stuff I sent them (largely to get it out of the house and to get a tax benefit) now is the largest collection, in the library, of any American writer. I don't think it's highly regarded, but for sheer bulk it's impressive. If you do intend to give away my letters to you, I think it would be a good idea to send them to me first and give me a chance to destroy the worst of the fruitcake. A brother's duty.

The only news here is that we are both gradually folding up like a couple of sickroom tulips. Yesterday I went to a clown who told me I was drifting into a Ménière's syndrome, and that all my troubles were centered in the middle ear. . . . Probably my basic trouble is in the subconscious, and I never allow anybody to invade that region on the theory that there would be enough evidence to lock me up. I don't want to be locked up because I still like to go sailing, and still do, getting all fouled up in the running rigging and having a lovely time of it. The dizzier you are, the more fun it is to sail single-handed. My fingers are now slightly arthritic and refuse to curl strongly around halyards and sheets, grasping them only half-heartedly. And the ringing in my ears is indistinguishable from the sound of bell buoys. I saw a fish hawk while sailing this afternoon—first one I had seen this summer. He couldn't find a fish and gave up and went away. The day of the fish hawk is almost over, I fear.

Best to you both.

Yrs,
En

To DANA W. ATCHLEY

North Brooklin, Maine
June 27, 1968

Dear Dana:

I see by *The Stethoscope* that you have been receiving "signal" honors, and from the looks of that shanty they are throwing up on Fort Washington Avenue in your name the word "signal" seems rather meager. Anyway, I want to send my congratulations to you on this happy occasion and to thank you for being the kind of doctor to whom these honors naturally flow. I miss you every day. And on the days when my head curdles and thumps I miss you doubly. I shall miss you early tomorrow morning ("nothing by mouth after midnight") when I present myself on an empty stomach for a glucose tolerance test that ought to take no more than five hours and prove absolutely nothing except that I can tolerate glucose. I'm always being tested for the wrong thing. They ought to test me for people tolerance, or events tolerance, or gin tolerance, or human stupidity tolerance. And not on an empty stomach.

The Dana W. Atchley Pavilion looks very handsome, and I'm glad it is for the ambulatory—the potential escapees. I also like the photograph of the Kober Medal winner, sitting there pretending to be reading. You must be very proud of this high award, and I am proud to know you. Katharine joins me in this congratulatory message. . . .

It's time to go and mix a martini in preparation for my glucose test. Wish you could join me. Save me a room in your pavilion for my ambulatory, or jogging, days.

Yrs,
Andy

To HARRIET WALDEN

North Brooklin
June 30 [1968]

Dear Harriet:

I'm planning to break up my so-called office at the magazine and distribute the type, or the typos. I think the first step would be for you to gather up the Garth Williams drawings (framed) and send them here to me. I shall give them to the children's room of the Brooklin Library. I believe there are two, but there may be three.

After that is accomplished, the next step will be to empty my locker—which contains a lot of strange books, mostly written by me but in foreign language editions, and an empty (I think) whiskey bottle. Throw the whiskey bottle out of the window so that it will land on the head of a modern poet on 44th Street, and mail the books to me.

As you can see, I am getting ready to die. How sweet it is!

The rest of the stuff in that office consists mainly of two or three shelves of weird books that arrived in the mail addressed to me. I doubt that I'll want more than two or three, and I will select them on my next trip to town. Then there are the desk drawers. These should be easy, and I will do that, too, on my next trip. There is also a framed sketch of frogs, executed by the daughter of an Algonquin waiter. I haven't decided what to do about that yet. Something will come to me in the night probably. It's not a bad sketch of frogs.

Sorry to throw this task at you, but something has to be done.

Yrs,
EBW

To EDWARD C. SAMPSON

North Brooklin, Maine
July 10, 1968

Dear Mr. Sampson:

I can help. In those days I kept a diary—or, as I called it, a journal. When your letter arrived, I turned eagerly to these yellowed, hallowed, mouldy pages.

On Tuesday, April 5th, 1920, I began my duties as Editor-in-Chief of the Sun. My principal function was to write the editorials. Early in May, the Sun published a resolution of Quill and Dagger, one of the two senior honorary societies. It read as follows:

RESOLVED—That we the undersigned senior honorary society will not consider for election to membership in the society at the annual spring bidding members of the junior class who are on probation.

QUILL AND DAGGER

On Monday, May 10, 1920, the Sun appeared carrying a lead editorial (written, but not signed, by me) headed "Honorary Society Eligibility." Following is the text of this editorial.

One senior honorary society has seen fit to cut down its eligibility
list to the exclusion of juniors on probation.

Honorary societies here and elsewhere have only one excuse for
existence, and that is the fact that they represent certain standards.
This is fundamental. When a man makes an honorary society at Cornell, he is looked upon as having done something for the University
which merits special recognition. The badge which he wears betokens
a certain amount of work done: it symbolizes meritorious achievement
in behalf of Cornell. Up to the present time, however, the award has
been open to some men who, purporting to be doing something for their
University, have not even satisfied her first requirement, that of scholarship. Probation has not been a bar to membership in an honorary society.

Regardless of how this change in eligibility is expected to work in
the case of one society or the other, regardless of the objects which
might have been in view by the society which adopted it and made it
public, regardless of the unfortunate bearing which it may have in the
case of certain juniors who are the first to come under the new ruling,
and who, pointing to juniors in the past in whose face was not thrown
the prerequisite of scholarship, feel that they are not getting a square
deal, the move will have an effect on the general scholarship at Cornell
that should prove beneficial.

Achievement in any branch of endeavor at Cornell should run
hand in hand with a reasonable development in the work which the
University offers. This is what the Faculty is continually fighting for.
This is the great cause of all the trouble—Faculty versus Student—
which arises at the end of every semester. The very fact that probation
exists is because it serves as a tool in the hands of a Faculty which
feels it has to maintain its own against an army of pseudo-students
seeking extra-curricular employment. At Cornell there is a definite place
for this kind of activity as well as for the other kind, but until a reconciliation is made between the two, there will still be cause for discontent
on both sides. The one hope for a reconciliation lies in student recognition of scholarship as a basis to work on. There has been a tendency
this year to move in that direction.

This editorial of mine enraged the members of Sphinx Head, the
other senior honorary society. Before the ink had cooled, two of their
fellows appeared in the *Sun* offices in high dudgeon and bearing a
counter-resolution which they demanded be published in the appropriate manner on Page One. I said I would be delighted to publish it. This
was it:

RESOLVED, That we, the undersigned Senior Honorary Society, will not consider for election E. B. White '21, because by so doing, we will be violating the following clause of the agreement between the two senior honorary societies:

"Any undergraduate eligible to election by the societies who shall be shown to have approached other members of his class with a view of influencing their choice, shall not be extended an invitation by either society."

SPHINX HEAD

To this resolution I wrote and added the following sentence, published thereunder:

Action in the above case was taken because of the editorial written by the junior in question appearing in the issue of The Sun, May 10, 1920.

As you can readily see by the documents above, I was learning about journalism fast and the hard way. What I had considered to be a theoretical, philosophical, and detached editorial on the question of honor society eligibility was immediately interpreted as a sinister attempt to influence juniors. This struck me as comical, but informative. I have a fairly clear recollection of the whole business, and I am quite sure that I wasn't trying to influence juniors as to their choice of societies—I didn't give a damn who joined what society and did not possess the kind of political mind that goes with such matters. Sphinx Head's resolution, announcing that I would not be considered for election, seemed to me wildly funny, but I also decided that nobody else would think of it that way. I was wrong. On the morning the Sphinx Head resolution appeared in The Sun, I sat down in Martin Sampson's class in Goldwin Smith. Before the lecture began, I saw Professor Sampson leave his podium. He strode, erect and silent, down the aisle toward me, paused at my desk, and deposited a slip of paper in front of me. Then he turned immediately, and returned to his place at the head of the class.

I have this slip of paper. It is pasted neatly in my journal. Pencilled in his fine hand, it reads:

On account of his editorial of May 10, I shall not invite E. B. White '21 to dinner.

Old Philadelphia Lady.

I have never felt more grateful to anyone than I did to Professor Sampson on that queer morning. His reassurance was more than just friendly, it was subtle and comical, and I felt suddenly reborn. It was the kind of deed, the kind of incident, that, forty-eight years later, could have saved Columbia from the debacle of 1968, if anybody on the campus had been at work in that human area. It is no wonder that the name Sampson is a magical name to me, even after all these years.

Your letter mentioned my "involvement in world peace organizations." I hadn't known I was involved in any. What were they?

Yrs,
E. B. White

To **CAROL AND ROGER ANGELL**

North Brooklin
July 15 [1968]

Dear Carol and Rog:

Your gifts were beautiful and exciting, and I send thanks in abundance. . . .

The weather has looked up lately, and I am waiting for a flush of well-being to overtake me. A clown over in Ellsworth says I am in a Ménière's syndrome and has given me capsules to open the dikes of my middle ear. My own suspicion is that I am dizzy for all the old reliable reasons, inability to write being one. It appears that Arnold Wolfers is dying.[1] The rate at which old friends are falling off is dizzying in itself. . . . Annie Parson, before finishing Winsor, knocked out a 14-page dissertation entitled "Characteristics of E. B. White as shown through his Essays and Children's Books." Annie is a powerful writer. "It is quite possible (she wrote) to believe that Stuart Little *is* E. B. White. Indeed in real life, Mr. White physically resembles a mouse. He is about five feet six inches tall, with a little pointed face and sharp ears." (This puts a new light on my passion for cheese.) . . .

A muskrat showed up in my new pond and stayed around for three or four days, when I think he tired of Jones. Because the pond is so small, the rat looked as big as a beaver. The pond at first looked more like a swimming pool than a wildlife sanctuary, but it is gradually fading into the landscape and is well liked by all. A bittern stops by occasionally, and there are many frogs and tadpoles. No trout yet.

Thanks, Rog, for sending me the Shawn interview.[2] Bill did fine, I thought. And thanks again to the both of you for my birthday presents. So glad Callie landed a job. Love to all.

Yrs,
Andy

---

1. Wolfers was a summer resident of Brooklin, director of the Johns Hopkins Washington Center of Foreign Policy Research.
2. In *Women's Wear Daily*, July 1, 1968.

To EDWARD C. SAMPSON

North Brooklin, Me.
August 4, 1968

Dear Mr. Sampson:

About those world peace organizations, I felt very strongly that I should never get involved with political action groups while I was writing editorials for *The New Yorker*. For one thing, it never seemed to me that my federalist comments truly represented the feelings of the magazine as a whole—Ross himself thought I was nuts, a visionary. But Ross believed in publishing the works or the opinions of nuts and visionaries, provided he trusted the person who wrote the stuff, and he did trust me, I think. Anyway, I used to be propositioned by the action groups, because they knew I was behind the editorials. I do not clearly recall the Mrs. Fisher incident, but it would appear that I went as far as doing a piece of writing for them, but withheld the use of my name and therefore any involvement of *The New Yorker*.

Another reluctance I had was that I seldom saw eye to eye with any of these federalist groups. I wanted to feel perfectly free to express exactly what I felt myself, and was not a mover and doer, except on paper for my favorite weekly. I think I can correctly state that I never involved *The New Yorker* with any organization interested in peace or world federalism. I just wrote my pieces. *Time*, I remember, called them "sententious."

E. B. White

To MRS. N. M. GIBBS

[North Brooklin, Me.]
[August 1968]

Dear Mrs. Gibbs:

Thank you for your letter. I am only one of dozens who have written in praise of Thoreau. Here in America his stature increases as the years go by, and lately he has had quite a vogue among people who find civil disobedience an attractive way of life. I am not fully in agreement with him on civil disobedience, but do greatly admire his ability to make an English sentence do his bidding.

Sincerely yours,
E. B. White

To FRANK SULLIVAN

North Brooklin, Maine
September 20, 1968

Dear Frank:

Elledge visited here, too, thus violating the first rule of the biographer: never make contact with the subject. I'm not sure just what he has in mind—he keeps talking about a "short" book, but I'll believe that when I see it. Probably I never *will* see it: I think all biographers subconsciously hope their man will up and die, clearing the boards and making everything a whole lot simpler. One thing Elledge is bugs on is chronology; he's a fool for the order of events and I have a rotten memory. The years blur. I'm glad you remembered about Ross and Pete Vischer and the extra mouth to feed. I never seem to be able to come up with anecdotes, perhaps because I used to do anecdotes for Talk and got so the very thought of an anecdote tended to bring on the nausea.

News of Pete's death came to me just the other day when I saw it in the Phi Gamma Delta magazine. (They still send me the magazine despite my not having paid any dues in 47 years.) I never made it to Port Tobacco, and never met Wife Three. I had good times with Peter in Ithaca, but we finally clashed one time when he wrote me a long diatribe against Ross—very disciplinary in tone and carrying what seemed to me the implication that the man for the job was Vischer himself. It was a ball that badly needed fielding, and I trun it back.

As a man of the deep country who loses his power with great regularity and often for periods of eight to ten hours, I got a chuckle out of your "shattering experience" when your lights went off and drove you back to Doriden tablets. We have two distinct kinds of power failure here: the nice cleancut kind when it gets wiped out completely, and the fuzzy kind when a small glow still shows in the light bulbs. In the first kind, all you have to do is draw your chair up to the wood stove in the kitchen and pour out a glass of whiskey. In the second kind, you can't sit down in any peace of mind until you've groped your way down cellar and pulled the plugs on every appliance that is equipped with an electric motor: the water pump, the furnace, the freezer, and (upstairs again in the back kitchen) the refrigerator. Most fuzzy failures are caused by young bucks bouncing their automobile off a power pole, or by a windstorm that drops a limb across the wires. . . . Was great to get your letter—wish we ever saw your fabulous face.

Love,
Andy

P.S. Heard last night of the death (at forty) of Rudd Truax, only child of Alethea and Hawley. And of course you know about Al Frueh, the indestructible.[1]

•   *At work on* The Trumpet of the Swan, *White wrote to Howard Cushman, who was now living in Philadelphia, asking him to scout the zoo for him. Cushman paid a visit to the zoo, photographed the trumpeter swans, and sent White a lot of background material.*

To HOWARD CUSHMAN

North Brooklin, Maine
10 October 1968

Dear Cush:

How would you like to do some sleuthing for an aging fiction writer? It would take you, on these golden October days, season of mists and mellow fruitiness, to the Zoological Gardens, there to scan birds and maybe even grill a curator. One of my fictional characters has had the rotten nerve to take me to Philly, and I am severely handicapped, having only been to your quaint burg twice in my life—once in 1920 or 1921 to squire Alice Burchfield to a Penn game, and once in the Fifties to watch the Giants.

I've never visited the Zoo, although I did catch a glimpse of an elephant from a train window. As you know, I am a good deal older than you and am too decrepit to travel to strange lands like Philadelphia in the fall. I look to you for my background information. Now let's take Bird Lake, which is, I believe, where the waterfowl camp out. What does Bird Lake look like? Is it pleasing, ugly, small, big, what? Is there a fence? High? Is it *entirely* caged in? (Oh, dear, I hope not! This would pose a problem that is none of your concern—*I'm* writing this book, not you, Buster.)

Are there any Trumpeter Swans in residence today? How many? Back in 1965, five cygnets were hatched there. I believe they were the first Trumpeters ever hatched in captivity in this country. The Curator of Birds at that time was a Mr. John A. Griswold, and perhaps he still is on the job. He could tell you what I need to know, but don't give me away: I'm a very secretive author, not given to loose talk about my projects.

---

1. Frueh had been *The New Yorker*'s theater caricaturist for forty years.

Have any cygnets been hatched since 1965? How are birds in Bird Lake held captive—cage? wings clipped so they can't fly? Are there the usual complement of waterfowl—ducks, geese, swans? Is there a house they go into from the water? Any shelter? Are they on the Lake all winter, skating around on the ice?

And now a sudden switch. Night clubs! In what general area of Philadelphia would one find a night spot? The only name I know in Philly is Rittenhouse Square. I don't need the name of any club, or anything of that sort—just need to get oriented. For that matter, in what general area of Philly is the Zoo?

By now I'm sure you are thoroughly confused. Is old White at last thoroughly addled? Pay no attention to your qualms and doubts: your reward will come in Heaven, which is probably only a little less idyllic than the Zoological Gardens of Philadelphia. Just pay attention to my questions.

It is very unusual for me to attempt to write about something I don't know about at first hand, but this goddam little fictional character has got me into this, and I could break his arm. Or wing. . . .

So go forth, Old Friend. Case the Gardens for me. Tell me how they smell, what they look like. Examine the swans on Bird Lake. Enjoy this season of mists and mellow fruitcake.

And on November 5th, vote for the best man—whoever *he* may be.

Love,
Ho

P.S. To prepare yourself for this preposterous task, you should probably bone up on nomenclature. A male swan is a cob. A female swan is a pen. A baby swan is a cygnet. (But don't say that I told you.)

• *White met David Dodd, a retired Columbia professor, and his wife Elsie in Florida.*

To **DAVID DODD**

North Brooklin
[October 27, 1968]
Sunday

Dear Dave:

This will have to be a quickie, as I have about one million chores to do in preparation for our migration. But I do want to thank you for the wonderful letter in which you recalled the haying of your boyhood. . . .

My own life with hay has been a mixed dish—I dearly love everything about the cutting and curing of grass and the hauling of the finished product into the delicious upper regions of an old barn. I also have terrible hay fever. I even have an allergy to horse dander. By rights I should never have bought a place in the country and settled down to enjoy the land, because of what it does to my mucous membranes. But I wouldn't trade my barn for the Taj Mahal or Onassis's yacht: and just to go down into my barn cellar at daylight to grain the sheep and pitch some hay down the chutes is compensation enough for all the misery of my silly nose.

My contribution in haying time is to ride the Cub tractor that hoists the load, then back it up briskly to the barn for the next bite of the hayfork. My hay goes into the barn loose, not baled. And that's the way I like it. . . .

Yrs,
Andy

• *When President Johnson appointed James Russell Wiggins of the* Washington Post *ambassador to the U.N., the* New York Times *published an editorial questioning his qualifications. White, who had just borrowed Wiggins' manure spreader and who had had dealings with him about hay, shot off a piece defending his friend and praising his diplomatic ability. (Wiggins is now retired, lives year-round in Maine, and publishes the weekly* Ellsworth American.)

To ROBERT E. L. STRIDER

North Brooklin, Maine
October 28, 1968

Dear Bob:

When I phoned Herb Mitgang at the *Times* and asked whether he'd like a piece on Russell Wiggins, our new Ambassador, Herb sounded crestfallen—if anyone's crest can fall over the telephone. He was afraid I hadn't read the editorial, but I assured him I had. With some reluctance he told me to send the piece in. I guess the management didn't care much for it, but pluck won out.

It was good of you to write. I'm glad you and Helen got some fun out of the thing. I don't really know how well-equipped Russell is for the job he has been summoned to, but he is such a thoroughly cheerful and honest man I think he'll bring fresh air into the chamber. A man whose boss Russell now is wrote me about an episode that took place soon after he arrived. A speech writer submitted a speech for his approval.

Russell read it through slowly, made about one hundred changes, then said: "I'd like to try a different ending. You don't suppose I could have a typewriter in here, do you?" The writer looked alarmed and told the boss that it was a very unusual request but he'd see what he could do. A machine was produced, and the Ambassador settled down happily to his task, in his enormous chair in his enormous office, punching away like the good newspaperman he is. I hope they gave him yellow paper. Did you know that most journalists are incapable of thinking on white paper? I've never been able to—which is why I duck writing letters. . . .

Thanks again for your kind words. Our best to you both, and may you have a good and gentle winter in the groves.

Yrs,
Andy

To HOWARD CUSHMAN

North Brooklin
[October 1968]
Sabbath morn

Dear Cush:

What a friendly fellow you are, and what a fine sheaf of instructive material to help me in the heavy task that lies ahead! I am very grateful to you and Jit. If anything ever comes of this fantastical enterprise of mine, you will be at the very top of the "without whom" set—my beautiful people.

I am having to weigh your report of the swan's voice ("not commanding, sir, at all") against the word of such men as John James Audubon and Edward Howe Forbush, who take a different view of the matter. Your brief "yarp" was probably a polite acknowledgment of tossed peanuts. I can only believe that when Trumpeters are stimulated by the tossed salad of springtime passion, or the giddy sensation of migratory flight (sustained and elevated), they can put an old Reo in the shade with their wild and resonant calling. However that may be, kindly do not go about Philadelphia telling people that White is busy with the Swan—specially that cribbing friend of yours (forget his name) who did such a neat job with a variation of the theme of one of my children's books (forget which). I have what I think is a peachy idea for a tale, and with a little help from God and the great help I've had from you, perhaps I can bring it off.

More later. Thank you, oh good Cushman!

Yrs,
Andy

• *Captain Walter Schirra's irritated exchange with the ground con-trollers of Apollo 7 prompted this reader, who identified himself as a golf pro, to think of White's "The Morning of the Day They Did It."*

To W. M. WELCH

[North Brooklin, Me.]
[October 1968]

Dear Mr. Welch:

I guess we'll just have to hope for the best and blame Schirra's stuffy head cold for the backtalk. It did sound like Obblington and Trett for a few moments there.

As of this writing, the planet earth hasn't broken up yet, and there is always the chance that I am as lousy a prophet as I am a mechanic. I've played golf twice in my life; both times, in order to get any fun out of it, I had to resort to the hit and run. I would hit the ball, then follow it on the run, yelling. I used only one club, a midiron. Played this way, it's not a bad game.

Sincerely,
E. B. White

• *The "Committeemen" of the letter that follows were a group of fourth-graders in Columbus, Ohio.*

To COMMITTEEMEN OF ROOM 24

[North Brooklin, Me.]
[November 1968]

Dear Committeemen of Room 24:

I'm not sure I can explain how to write a book. First, you have to *want* to write one very much. Then, you have to know of something that you want to write about. Then, you have to begin. And, once you have started, you have to keep going. That's really all I know about how to write a book. I've written seventeen of them, and I'm almost ready to quit—but not quite.

Sincerely,
E. B. White

To HOWARD CUSHMAN

The Tuscany
New York
[November? 1968]
Saturday night

Dear Mr. Cushman:

You have shown such aptitude for the kind of work I have been entrusting you with, such zeal, such keen powers of observation, and quick willingness to go direct to the scene, I am inclined to offer you steady work in the challenging field of research. The speed and effectiveness with which you produced excellent color photographs of the swan somehow took me right back to "A Message to Garcia" (The Philistine, 1899) and I realized how proud Elbert Hubbard would be of his fellow townsman. Do you recall that passage about the man "of brilliant parts" (golden balls, I presume) who not only was incapable of managing a business of his own but was absolutely worthless to anyone else, could neither give orders nor receive them. "Tonight this man walks the streets looking for work, the wind whistling through his threadbare coat." Ah, my good friend, what a contrast you are to this heel-dragging knave! What an inspiration to us all!

Next question. Think of small hotels! Think of the old song "In a small hotel." What was the title? Was it "Small Hotel"? Or was it "In a small hotel"? Think of the lyrics. Write them down for me in my terrible need, and without "asking any idiotic questions."

The snapshots from Bird Lake are an inspiration to me and I am encouraged to go on. I would caution you, though, not to underestimate Audubon's familiarity with the Trumpeter. He heard them many times and in many places. Not only that, he and his miller and six or seven of his servants captured one that had been nicked in the wing, and he brought it home for the amusement and pleasure of his wife and children. (It is a lot easier to do something of this sort if you take your miller with you. Anything you undertake for me in the future, take your miller along. Your burden will be greatly eased.)

Address me, kind sir, at 289 Cedar Park Circle, Sarasota, Fla. 33581. I am in this small hotel only for a brief moment.

Yrs gratefully,
E. B. White

To **RICHARD L. LINDELL II**

[Sarasota, Fla.]
December 20, 1968

Dear Mr. Lindell:

I'm not an educator or a pedagogue and have no firm ideas about curricula. But in answer to your question I can only say that if I were teaching an English course, and it had to do with American literature, my students would certainly become acquainted with writers like Don Marquis, who is of the "recent past." Nabokov's memoir called "Speak, Memory" would be required reading.

I think it is true that there is a kind of dead spot, on campuses, in the work of writers of ten or twenty years ago. The students all know about Thoreau, Whitman, Emerson, Pound, Eliot, Hemingway, and Fitzgerald. But then comes a gap. They jump right to Cleaver, over the dead bodies of many a good man.

Sincerely yours,
E. B. White

To **MRS. MAX BRUBAKER**

[Sarasota, Fla.]
December 28, 1968

Dear Mrs. Brubaker:

Celia Summer, of the Scribner Book Store, says you want to know whether I have a book in the making. It is very heartening to know that somebody cares about this.

All writing men have a book in the making; the only question is, what happens. I cannot at this point tell you, or forecast, what will happen. I have in my bedroom a rather heavy, legal-size envelope, and as near as I can make out, it contains about two-thirds of the manuscript of a book. I am 69 years old. It's that last third that I wonder about.

Thanks for the inquiry.

Sincerely,
E. B. White

To **WILLIAM K. ZINSSER**

Sarasota, Florida 33581
December 30, 1968

Dear Mr. Zinsser:

I can't be much help in "assessing" Sid's writing and his influence. I do know that a sentence he wrote about forty years ago still makes me chuckle every time I think of it. I can't quote it exactly, but it was something like: "She had a cow—a Holbein." That's pure Perelman and it stays with you.

Sid, of course, commands a vocabulary that is the despair (and joy) of every writing man. I have to get along with a vocabulary of about fifteen hundred serviceable words that I just use over and over again, trying to rearrange them in an interesting order. Sid is like a Roxy organ that has three decks, fifty stops, and a pride of pedals under the bench. When he wants a word, it's there. Sid even *speaks* with precision —a feat many a writer is incapable of. He and Laura showed up here in Sarasota a couple of winters ago. They had been in an automobile accident—a bad one, the car a complete wreck. Laura came out of it with some bruises, Sid with a new word. The car, he learned, had been "totalled." I could see that the addition of this word to his already enormous store meant a lot to him. His ears are as busy as an ant's feelers. No word ever gets by him.

I'm sure Sid's stuff influenced me in the early days. I recall the pleasures and satisfactions of encountering a Perelman piece in a magazine. Those pieces usually had a lead sentence, or lead paragraph, that was as hair-raising as the first big dip on a roller coaster: it got you in the stomach, and when it was over you were relieved to feel deceleration setting in. In the realm of satire, parody, and burlesque, he has, from the beginning, bowed to none. His erudition is as impressive as his flights of fancy and his sword play. I don't like the word "humorist," never have. It seems to me misleading. Humor is a by-product that occurs in the serious work of some and not others. I was more influenced by Don Marquis than by Ernest Hemingway, by Perelman than by Dreiser. I can't "assess" this, I can merely report it.

But if you're hoping to disabuse people of the notion that there is something vaguely second-rate about humorous expression in literature, I wish you luck. I don't think you have a prayer.

Sincerely,
E. B. White

•   *In the course of his search for material on White, Scott Elledge had paid a call on Mrs. Alice Burchfield Sumner. She had saved White's letters and wrote him of her intention to give them to Cornell.*

To ALICE BURCHFIELD SUMNER

Sarasota, Florida
January 10, 1969

Dear Burch:

It's nice to hear from somebody who lives on Peaceable Street. The street I'm living on, Rancor Alley, is having a sewer laid under it. Men with heavy machinery take their battle stations at seven a.m.

Your letter just arrived. Anything that gets sent to Harper is likely to have a long trip. I apologize for this tardy answer, and I thank you for getting in touch with me before committing yourself to the importunate Mr. Elledge. Scott is a very nice guy. I do not think he has had much experience as a reporter, and whether he can write a "definitive" biography is anybody's guess. I loathe tape recorders and distrust what they do to a conversation, but if you feel like talking to one, it's your choice. I would certainly insist on the right to edit, if you do it at all.

As for letters, a letter belongs to the recipient, and you are free to dispose of letters in any way that suits your fancy. The *contents* of a letter, on the other hand, belongs, under the law of copyright, to the sender—in this case me—and nothing in the letters can be published, by

Elledge or anyone else, without my permission. If you intend to give letters to the Cornell Library, I'd certainly appreciate your letting me have a look at them first, but you're under no obligation to do so and it would be just a courtesy to an old friend. (Old Friend and Early Admirer.)

My attic at home in Maine got so loaded with letters, manuscripts, and assorted papers, I finally started unloading them into the Cornell Library. I presume some of yours were among them, which is what started Elledge on his way to Peaceable Street. He has access, by special permission, to classified material that is not available to the public. And I have an agreement with him that prevents his using any of it without my OK. (The lives of biographers and biographees are miserable lives at best.)

Yrs,
Andy

• *Whenever permission is granted to reprint something by White, the permission includes the proviso: "no changes in text or punctuation without approval. If any biographical or introductory material is used, please submit to us for approval." In this case, Doubleday had evidently failed to comply. Helen Lane is Permissions Editor at Harper's.*

To **HELEN LANE**

[Sarasota, Fla.]
January 24, 1969

Dear Mrs. Lane:

. . . It would appear to me that the use of my material by Doubleday was less an error than a deliberate switch, to accommodate some kind of format or package that the editor desired for the book. The wording of the agreement seems clear enough—three chapters, each with its title. And I assume that Harper stipulated that these three selections be used entire. Isn't this the usual stipulation in such requests?

I am disturbed about the matter simply because I do not like anything of mine rearranged or telescoped to suit somebody's whim or to fit somebody's space. I am aware of the problems of anthologists; I am also aware of the problems of authors, one of which is to keep material intact, free from meddling. I never wrote anything called "Stuart Goes to Sea" and I'll not allow Doubleday to write it just because it happens to suit their fancy. Actually, the title is peculiarly inept or misleading, since there is another episode in the book in which Stuart actually *does* go to sea—but it isn't the sailboat race or the Central Park pond.

Doubleday's suggestion for correcting this "error" seems to me inadequate, considering the terms of our agreement. I would like to have

Harper's opinion about what should be done. I think Doubleday should either use the stuff in the way we agreed upon or drop it entirely.

Incidentally, in the copies you sent me, the first sentence of the book has not been revised in accordance with my request of a long time ago, namely, that the verb "was born" be supplanted by the verb "arrived." This should be carried into all reprints, and it is up to Harper to follow through on it.

I am sorry that this mess has occurred. I think Harper will agree that, from an author's standpoint, it is unwise to let down the bars and allow rearrangements. Pretty soon the rearrangement gains acceptance and becomes standard, and then where does the original material end up? I regard each chapter of a book as a composition, not to be disturbed in the classic design of the Reader's Digest, where sometimes the first four words of Sentence One are joined up with the last ten words of Sentence Twelve, omitting everything that came between. This may be great for a publisher, but for a writing man it is sudden death.

Sincerely,
E. B. White

To ALICE BURCHFIELD SUMNER

Sarasota, Florida
February 17, 1969

Dear Burch:

I'm leaving here on Thursday in an attempt to take Katharine into the hospital in New York while she still is able to walk. She has gone downhill this winter, and her spine no longer holds her up, and it has been a long, cold, grim winter. So, in answer to your question, I'd rather have you wait and send me the letters when we return home to Maine in the spring.

It is very good of you to send them at all—after all, I never sent you yours, and in general acted in a thoroughly high-handed manner with the weird and wonderful and often touching contents of my attic. I *did* go over the things I sent along to Cornell, with certain criteria in mind: I threw out letters from persons who sounded a bit psychotic, or overwrought; I threw out a few letters that were in such bad taste as to afford a later embarrassment to the writer; and I threw out letters that seemed likely to be misinterpreted. My only reason for wanting to see my letters to you is that I have had a little experience in selecting what should be passed on to the mists of time and what had better be discarded. (Of course, an archivist will tell you that *nothing* should *ever* be discarded; but I have developed, over the years, a certain respect for the validity of the wastepaper basket and I use it a lot.) . . .

I started clearing out my attic for cold, mercenary reasons. A lawyer told me I could get a substantial tax relief by doing so, and he was right. But when I started doing it, I became involved in two unexpected developments: a terrific allergy to old moldy papers and documents, which gave me a cracking sinusitis and made the whole business very difficult, and a discovery of the delights and remembrances of the past. It is always sobering and inspiriting to rediscover one's youth in old documents. The exchange of letters between you and me made this very clear. . . .

Good luck.

Yrs,
Andy

To GEORGE H. HEALEY

Sarasota, Florida
February 19, 1969

Dear Mr. Healey:

If you want to provide Helen Thurber with Xerox copies of Thurber's letters to me, please go ahead.

I must remember to buy some stock in Xerox; they seem to be the ones that are coming out on top in this archivistic engagement.

Yours,
E. B. White

To DAN HAVERKAMP

25 West 43
[New York]
April 15 [1969]

Dear Mr. Haverkamp:

Thanks very much for your letter. It seems to be a fairly comprehensive rundown of my literary exertions over the past forty years ("Stuart Little" was begun about forty years ago, as I remember it). I am glad you have enjoyed my stuff and am particularly glad that some of it still seems pertinent to somebody who is sixteen. I have an idea that to the present generation of college students I am too square to be of much account.

I'm in favor of peace but have never been a pacifist, in the usual sense of that word. The active pacifists, over the years of my lifetime, have on the whole been a fuzzy lot, refusing to recognize that as yet no machinery has been developed for defending one's principles except by fighting. Kids nowadays talk a lot about love and brotherhood, but I have little confidence in the brotherhood of man, brotherhood being inconsistent with the nature of the beast. I am pinning my hopes on the government of man—still a long way in the future but the only solid foundation for peace, government being the device for reconciling and resolving the natural hostilities that are latent in every community on whatever level.

Thanks again for writing. I feel encouraged by your letter.

Sincerely,
E. B. White

To MILDRED DILLING

[New York]
April 22, 1969

Dear Miss Dilling:

If I were to be home on April 29, I would certainly drive over to Rockland for your recital.[1] The sad truth is, my wife has been hospitalized here in New York for the past nine weeks, and I am afraid the earliest we can expect to arrive home in North Brooklin is the first of May. She will have to travel by ambulance plane, as she has a spinal fracture along with other serious troubles.

I read her your letter, and she wanted me to tell you about her aunt who married a Japanese and who had a place in Karuizawa. Perhaps you encountered Aunt Poo in my book "One Man's Meat"—I wrote a piece about her. Anyway, having been transported by marriage to a foreign land, Poo wanted to import a bit of New England into her surroundings and wrote us to please dig up a wild rose from our pasture in Maine and send it to her—which we did. This must have been thirty years ago. Poo died during the Second War. As far as we know our roses are still going strong in Karuizawa.

I used to love to hear Harpo play—it was an amazing musical experience. I am so sorry that I cannot hear you on the 29th.

Sincerely,
E. B. White

To FRANK SULLIVAN

North Brooklin
July 14 [1969]

Dear Frank:

The New York Times is mostly an annoyance to me in this house, where it accumulates on chairs and stares accusingly at me as I pass. But when it rouses *you* to the point of flashing a message, I can forgive it its sins. Luckily I took the call myself, after having entrusted a couple to my wretched wife who produced indecipherable greetings on the backs of envelopes; yours came through very nice and clear. And funny.

Israel Shenker's visit to this decadent ranch a couple weeks ago

---

1. Mildred Dilling is a harpist who has many literary friends and numbered Harpo Marx among her pupils.

was not one of those perfect occasions that we all dream about.[1] I greeted him with tachycardia and taciturnity in about even parts, and I guess he left without a story, because I soon received an abominable questionnaire in the mail and had no choice but sit down and answer it. Between the two of us, the Times's celebration of my 70th acquired the taste of stale fruit-cake and reminded me of Morris Bishop's remark some years ago when he read an interview with me by a Cornell co-ed: "You sounded like Ecclesiastes."

. . . The day was punctuated by a lot of phone calls from friends, relatives, and strangers, including a beaut from an unknown ophthal-mologist of Waterville, Maine—unknown to me, anyway. He said he was young and presumptuous but hoped I wouldn't mind his calling; he had tended Dorothy Parker in her last illness and this had aroused his interest in "the Algonquin era." He was just getting into the intricacies of the Algonquin era when our conversation (in which I was taking a mighty small part) was interrupted by the arrival outside the pay booth of an officer of the law, who was interested in the ophthalmologist's illegally parked automobile. From then on it was a three-way affair, ideal for migraine.

K is slowly making a comeback after a winter and spring of assorted tortures of the body and spirit. She fell, broke her back, got shingles, then neuritis, went into Harkness for 13 weeks (osteoporosis from years of cortisone), developed a staph infection on top of her dermatitis, played guinea pig to a drug called Methotrexate for want of a dirtier name, and finally escaped by ambulance plane (piloted by a Mr. Caruso) and now occupies a fine hospital bed (the one with the two little cranks) in White's Nursing Home, North Brooklin. She walks with a walker, gets boosted upstairs and down by my skillful laying on of hands, and is at this moment presiding at the morning ritual of flower arranging. Her borders still bloom, her spirit is still unshattered. The rest of her is in a thousand pieces. . . .

Love, and thanks, Sweet Fellow, for your greeting.

Andy

To RICHARD M. NIXON

[North Brooklin, Me.]
July 15, 1969

Dear Mr. President:

Thank you for your friendly greetings on my 70th birthday. I was very pleased to have them.

I'm afraid your letter crossed a brisk telegram from my wife to

---

1. Shenker went to Brooklin and interviewed White on his 70th.

you demanding that you call off the moon shot. But that's the way life is in this household: something coming in, something going out, all with the best of all possible motives if not with the most sophisticated coordination.

Sincerely,
E. B. White

To PHILIP BOOTH

North Brooklin, Maine
July 20, 1969

Dear Phil:

Joe reports that you will not be in these parts much this summer—all tied up in Oneida. I'm very sorry. You will be missed at the Yard.[1]

Thanks for your letter about the *Times* piece. Shenker did not always make a good choice on what to report, or so it seemed to me. When he asked me how one adjusts to old age, I replied, "I adjust to it by getting up during the night and going to the bathroom and by having a downhaul on my jib so I can lower it without going forward." This failed to register with him.

We had a hot spell last week, but yesterday broke clear and cool with a brisk NW wind, so I bundled my friend Joe Wearn aboard Martha and we went charging into the Benjamin River at low tide, where there were only about twenty drops of water and a lot of wind. It was a fine trip, marred only by my failing to make a mistake in navigation—which would have made it sensational. Years ago, when I summered in East Blue Hill, a fellow there told me of his memories of the Benjamin River when his father, Ralph Long, used to take his coasting schooner into Sedgwick. One dark night, old Ralph wanted to leave the River, because wind and tide were serving him, but he was scared he might bring his schooner up short on the big rock (then unmarked) that lies off the end of the bar. So he sent his son, then just a boy, to row off, locate the rock, and keep lighting matches until the schooner was clear of the hazard. A pleasant memory of boyhood: lighting matches at the rock!

Yrs,
Andy White

---

1. Philip Booth—poet, sailor, and professor of English at Syracuse University—is a summer resident of Castine. He met White on a visit to the Brooklin Boat Yard.

To L. E. SISSMAN

[North Brooklin, Me.]
[July/August 1969]

Dear Mr. Sissman:

Thanks for the letter and for your concern over my journals. The ages can have part of me but not all of me. (There's a lot of me I wouldn't want to palm off on the ages.) Years ago I built a splendid incinerator, a regular brick temple at the edge of a shoddy little piece of woodland. Some day there's going to be a memorable fire down there, and I am going to dance around it, suitably costumed in a burlap loin cloth ornamented with goose quills from my own goose. I'll invite you to the blaze. When exhaustion sets in, we can go back up to the house and have a drink.

Sincerely,
E. B. White

To CAROL ANGELL

N. Brook.
[Summer 1969]
Thursday

Dear Carol:

Tell Rog that I have just sent Joe a note about the mooring, and that it should be in place by August 2.

I am terribly late in thanking you for letters and gifts. (I've lost one of the letters in the great post-Shenker shuffle of mail: I've been deluged, and it is really very hampering, as about 90 per cent of the letters really call for at least an acknowledgment. I've heard from the damndest people—a man today who said he had sailed with me by night in my catboat on the Sound, circa 1924, and I had saved his life by skillfully avoiding a collision with the Boston night boat, which bore down upon us out of the gloom.)

I have *not* lost the shirt, which is beautiful, and which I love, and which is at this very moment in the hands of Virginia Allen, our seamstress, who is very clever at clipping those long Brooks Brothers sleeves off to the right length. Brooks lives in a world of gorillas. Normally, my sleeve length is 33, but to Brooks 33 is just a beginning. It is a lovely shirt, and thank you so much for it. . . .

Joe and Allene and Steven and John are cruising in Stormy. I think they are probably in Friendship tonight for the races. Martha stayed home, with Joy Hooper presiding, to care for the animals. Martha's duck has crossed the road, laid fifteen eggs at the base of a fence post about two feet from the shoulder of the road, and is sitting, while cars whizz by so close it ruffles her feathers. I stopped in day before yesterday, when I heard about this. Nobody was home, but Maggie took me across the highway, pointed the duck, then stuck her head under the cable (guard rail) and rested her chin on the back of the sitting duck, who never stirred.

Fred Parson has been asking for you, and others whom I can't remember. Dean Rusk was a recent house guest of the Russell Wigginses. Haying is over, thank God. Jones is well and very active in the field. My boathouse has had its face lifted, and I can now work down there no matter what the weather is. Donna's baby is beginning to show. Carol Eaton's baby is beginning to show. And come to think of it, my own stomach isn't as flat as it might be.

Everything will be a whole lot better and merrier when you and Rog get here, so hurry up. And thanks again for being so good to me on my birthday.

Love,
Andy

To MARGO TODD

[North Brooklin, Me.]
August 15, 1969

Dear Mrs. Todd:

You were very kind to send me such a detailed accounting. I am, of course, pleased to get the report of your adventures and satisfactions. I like to hear from librarians and to know that my stories are being read to children.

I was alarmed at your idea of suggesting to a child that he model himself after me. Writing is a form of imposture; I'm not at all sure I am anything like the person I seem to a reader. And you certainly wouldn't want to urge a child to model himself after an impostor!

But I appreciate your confidence, which is implied.

Sincerely,
E. B. White

To MARY VIRGINIA PARRISH

[North Brooklin, Me.]
August 29, 1969

Dear Mrs. Parrish:

Writing, which is my way of serving, is hard work for me and usually not attended with any joy. It has its satisfactions, but the act of writing is often a pure headache, and I don't kid myself about there being any joy in it. When I want some fun, I don't write, I go sailing. So I often find it hard to plan the day.

Unlike you, I have no faith, only a suitcaseful of beliefs that sustain me. Life's meaning has always eluded me and I guess always will. But I love it just the same.

Sincerely,
E. B. White

To ROBERT M. COATES

North Brooklin
September 14 [1969]

Dear Bob:

I hope Ashley Pratt[1] has turned up by this time to cut your green stuff. Like you, I'm not on the soil bank and am glad I never succumbed. Most of the "gentlemen farmers" of my acquaintance charge off a loss every year on their tax, but I have never done it and I feel free as a daisy. I don't even accept government lime, for fear somebody in Washington might want to know what I did with it and I would have to tell him I got hungry and ate it.

I was interested to hear that you and Boo were planning to collect algae. I'm not sure I know algae when I see it, but the matter came up the other day when I was over at the grain store talking to the grain store man about my pond, into which I was thinking of putting some trout. I described the pond to the man and he came back at me with a question. "You got any allergy in your pond?" he asked. He said trout got along all right if there was allergy in a pond. I wasn't sure about it, so I bought a small sack of Trout Chow, made by Purina. I now have 27 trout in the pond. I go out of an evening and toss 27 pellets of Trout Chow into the water, one pellet at a time, and you should see the commotion. Sometimes a trout will come clear out of the water, looking pink as a salmon. They were seven inches long when I dumped them into the pond in early summer, and now, after my Chow and my allergy, some of them look like the Loch Ness monster.

. . . I work three or four hours every morning, trying to finish a storybook for children. The first draft is done, but I'm now engaged in the more difficult job of regurgitating it and swallowing it again. I am also greatly handicapped by being unfamiliar with some of the terrain the story unhappily takes me into. I think it was extremely inconsiderate of my characters to lead me, an old man, into unfamiliar territory. At my age, I deserve better.

---

1. A neighbor of Coates's in Old Chatham.

The book will have to net me about half a million dollars, otherwise I won't be able to pay off all the registered and unregistered nurses that tend K every day and every night. They are a nice bunch of girls, but the payroll is fantastic. And Maine has just decided on top of everything else to collect a state income tax. . . . Her heart is acting up, and she has been put on digitalis—foxglove to her. All in all, a sad time. We both send our love to you both.

Andy

To URSULA NORDSTROM

North Brooklin, Maine
October 7, 1969

Dear Ursula:

Thanks for your very generous letter. It frightens me to think that a publishing house is willing to put up large sums of money for something it hasn't even seen, but everything scares me these days.

I can't let you have a copy of the manuscript, as there *is* no copy and I never use carbon paper when I write, and I stay away from Xerox because I don't like the way it smells. I have a title and am pleased with it, but you'll have to wait until I turn the thing in. . . .

About the illustrator, the choice will be up to you. I have no preconceptions but simply want my book to enjoy the best drawings we can get. The ideal way, I would imagine, would be to ask two or three of the likeliest candidates for the job to submit a sketch or two after reading some of the script, and see which fellow comes up with the happiest drawing. But I don't suppose artists—particularly those who are well-established, like Garth Williams—are willing to perform any such antics. Whoever is chosen will have a lot of support and help from me. Garth's Stuart was superb and did much to elevate the book. His Charlotte (until we abandoned everything and just drew a spider) was horrible and would have wrecked the book. I have no idea what Garth is up to, these days. I do not feel committed to him, but I feel grateful to him. I have no reason to want to change illustrators unless you, after reading the script, think you know somebody who could do the job better. More than anything else, the drawings will need someone's touch who is humorous and can make them amusing as well as charming.

May God be with us at all times in this fantastic venture.

Yrs,
Andy

To URSULA NORDSTROM

North Brooklin, Maine
October 28, 1969

Dear Ursula:

If Les Davis[1] wants to explore the possibilities of making "Charlotte's Web" into a movie, I guess his first step would be to get in touch with my agent, J. G. Gude, of Stix & Gude. The address is 30 Rockefeller Plaza.

The reason the story has never been made into a film is because I won't sign a contract unless it gives me the right to see and approve the general shape and appearance of the main characters, and the Hollywood big shots won't sign a contract that *does* give me this right. This has been going on for seventeen years.

Last winter, John and Faith Hubley had the book under option and were most anxious to do a picture. They had no objection to my proviso, but when they went out to Hollywood to raise the money, they met with resistance. Just as soon as a Hollywood producer stumbles on the clause in the contract that gives the author of the book the right of approval, he chucks up his dinner and abandons the deal. The standard procedure in the movies is to knock off the author with one clean blow, and then proceed with the picture. I am just stubborn enough to stand my ground. It causes nothing but trouble, but *somebody* has to stand up to Hollywood. It's such fun. (All it costs me is $75,000—a bargain.)

Yrs,
Andy

P.S. The Disney organization tried for years to beat me down. I didn't beat, and Disney is dead. But he's still trying from the grave.

To DAVID DODD

N. Brooklin
[November 2, 1969]
Sunday

Dear Dave:

. . . I hate interviews and do not regard them as a sensible form of activity or a means of enlightenment. When I was a reporter, on the other side of the fence, I didn't like them. The only interview I recall enjoying was in the very early days of *The New Yorker*, when I was sent to interview Raymond Duncan, brother of Isadora. Raymond was a sort of transplanted goatherd, down from the Grecian hills. When he received me, in

---

1. A young film maker who wanted to know why *Charlotte's Web* had not been made into a movie.

a ratty apartment in the West Seventies or thereabouts, he was wearing toga and sandals. I was in my Brooks raincoat (maybe I've told you all this before). Duncan lay down on a couch to be interviewed, in his toga, so I kept my raincoat on and lay down nearby. Everything in the way of an interview since then has been bathetic.

The event of last week was the attempt of my 27 brook trout to spawn. I found them slatting around in the little brook that feeds the pond, and I didn't know what the hell was going on until I went to the reference books and discovered that brookies spawn in shallow water, in late fall, over a gravelly bottom. They were giving it the old college try, but against considerable odds, as the brook has only two or three inches of water in it and extends from a big culvert under the highway to the pond—a distance of only about a hundred feet. There was a pretty good flow of water and I hadn't provided my fish with a really suitable spawning area, or backwater, where they could get out of the current. It was fun to watch them. In order to get upstream, they practically had to walk on their hands and knees in certain clogged places in the brook—which was full of leaves and other debris. I went out after dark with a spotlight and continued my observations under dark, cold conditions. I never was able to spot any eggs, and have searched in vain for eggs since. But the fish were thrashing about in good shape, and alternately lying very quiet, in three inches of water, with just a barely perceptible movement of their fins. One of them, driven by the relentless lash of love, actually made it through the culvert and to the ditch on the other side of the highway. I just hope he made it back. Jones enjoyed the whole business as much as I did. He is a great trout dog now, and still has hopes of landing one. Mostly, he spends his time treeing red squirrels, with whom he is carrying out a bitter feud. . . .

This is a dark Sunday, a storm brewing, and deerslayers at the ready, waiting for the coming of Monday's first light. Joe is in Lisbon, aboard the schooner, waiting to try the South Atlantic.[1] Jones is asleep. And lunch is ready.

Yrs,
Andy

To URSULA NORDSTROM

North Brooklin, Maine
November 17, 1969

Dear Ursula:

This morning I sent off the manuscript to you by registered mail. It is called "The Trumpet of the Swan" and is about a cygnet that has a

---

1. In late October, Joel White had flown to Lisbon to join the crew of the 52-foot schooner *Integrity* and help sail her to Grenada in the Caribbean.

speech defect—along with some other problems, including a money problem.

If you think the book is promising, let me know. And if you think it's lousy, I would like to know that, too. The Trumpeter Swan, largest of American waterfowl, was once almost extinct but has made a come-back. This book is about a young Trumpeter.

Yrs,
Andy

To CAROL ANGELL

[North Brooklin, Me.]
November 18 [1969]

Dear Carol:

. . . I think I've discovered a misspelled word in the American Heritage Dictionary of the English Language. Vichysoisse. It should be vichyssoise, shouldn't it? I got on to this because of a newsbreak. Webster ducks the whole thing, but my wife spells it "vichyssoise" and so does Betty Crocker. If *I* have turned up *one* misspelled word, my guess is there must be fifty. Good. I like that. . . .

We had a letter yesterday from Joe. The schooner had been headed for Madeira, but changed course and made the port of Arrecife, island of Lanzarote, in the Canaries. There, they took on fresh water and diesel oil. They were a week out of Lisbon and had had light air and head winds and had done some motoring in order to keep going. But the last day, the wind had picked up from the west and they had enjoyed a sailing breeze. Joe said he was learning celestial navigation and that the food was great. . . . On the whole, it was a very good report, and by now the boat should be well on its way on the long jump to Grenada. . . .

Jones, who has had a vibrant fall, is poorly at the moment. I tried to correct this by sprinkling worm powder in his dinner, and he countered by chucking up dinner *and* powder. His interest in red squirrels, normally at a fever peak, lags, and all he did today was attack a mason, rather half-heartedly. Peter Sturtevant's sloop is being strip-planked, the Joel Whites have a new green Pontiac, guns go off every few minutes in the woods from dawn to dark, and it is time for me to go to bed so I can be up in time to hear the first gun. See you soon.

Love,
Andy

To DONALD W. MAC KINNON

[North Brooklin, Me.]
November 25, 1969

Dear Mr. MacKinnon:

Thanks for your invitation to be questioned by the Institute.[1] I'm afraid I shall have to decline.

Recent estimates by an impressive number of scientists give the human race only about fifty years more, at which point Man will join the distinguished company of the Passenger Pigeon and the eastern Heath Hen. Because of this startling development (and because I am seventy and don't have much time anyway), my interest in the creative process is not to explain it but to put it to work, as best I can and with what strength I have left. I find that not one person in a thousand can conceive of Man as a species that faces extinction. If I have any spare moments at a typewriter from now on, I want to use them to spread the alarm, on the chance that our present trend can perhaps be reversed before it's too late.

Questionnaires are not my dish, anyway. I have been pumped dry this year, by interviewers from the *Times*, the Portland *Telegram*, and the *Paris Review*. I am fresh out of answers to questions. But I thank you for your interest in my internal combustion.

Sincerely,
E. B. White

To FAITH MC NULTY MARTIN

North Brooklin, Maine
December 6, 1969

Dear Faith:

No animal is unimportant, and I am glad you are sticking up for the Black-footed Ferret. Further and more, I was glad to hear from you again after such a long time. I crossed the prairies many years ago and saw prairie dogs but do not recall seeing the Black-footed Ferret. According to my Complete Field Guide to American Wildlife, he is a very different sort from me: he is more active at night than by day. He and I are both wary, though. I am even wary at night—I suspect the house is going to catch fire from the glowing end of a Benson & Hedges regular cigarette, tossed to one side by my unwary wife Katharine.

I have just finished a storybook about the Trumpeter Swan, which is less rare than the Black-footed Ferret but a lot bigger and noisier. I find writing quite exhausting. Do you? We are not planning to go to

---

1. Mr. MacKinnon had written on behalf of the Institute of Personality Assessment and Research at the University of California. This was the Institute's second attempt to involve White in their research.

Florida this winter, as K is not able to travel. Her rare skin disease persists. . . .

I was glad to hear you and Johnny get on all right. I would be getting on with Joe all right, but he is aboard a schooner bound from Lisbon to Grenada. It is hard to get on with anybody who is crossing the South Atlantic in a small boat.

K and I send our love, and we look forward to seeing your piece about the ferret. My Guide says, "Today . . . this ferret has become one of the rarest mammals in North America but Faith Martin is not taking this lying down."

Yrs,
Andy

To JOHN KIERAN

[North Brooklin, Me.]
December 7, 1969

Dear Mr. Kieran:

It was a real pleasure, as well as a surprise, to find your new book in my mailbag. Thank you for it and for the generous inscription. I would have got this letter off sooner but have been trying to finish up a book of my own, and I find the work rather exhausting these days. Hell, it was *always* exhausting.

Haven't had time to do more than take a stroll around inside your tome, but it looks great and I look forward to beginning at the beginning and proceeding in an orderly fashion. I discovered—and felt grateful for—the passage in which you paid your respects to the New Yorker writers in the reign of Ross. Even though I happened to have been one of them, I quite agree with you that they were a formidable bunch and the total product is impressive. It is fashionable nowadays to take pot shots at *The New Yorker*, so it pleased me to read a happier (and I think sharper) report by you.

Your house and my house seem to have a certain similarity. My wife is gradually disappearing from view behind a wall of books that are so large and heavy as to stagger the mind and endanger the timbers. Luckily, the fellow who built this house more than a hundred and fifty years ago anticipated something of the sort, for he hewed in the grand manner—12″ x 12″, 10″ x 10″, 6″ x 6″. I guess we are all right for a while, but Katharine's books (mainly horticultural) are a threat. She is not well, has to spend a lot of time in bed with the foot cranked up to take the strain off her spine, and can't lift heavy things. But the garden books keep arriving. I passed by her bed the other day and noticed a new arrival that simply said: *Nightshades*.

I'm not a bookish fellow myself and have not done much reading in my life. (In your list of 100, I think I have read 32.) But I walked right through your "Natural History of New York City" as in a trance. I've read most of the books that have been written about small boat voyaging, but that's the extent of my reading.

Thanks again for "Books I Love," and may you have pleasant holidays, with good health and good spirits.

Sincerely,
E. B. White

P.S. On page 177, you speak of "a collection of light verse" edited by me *et ux.* I think you must mean "A Subtreasury of American Humor." The book contained some verse, but mostly prose. I'd gladly send you a copy but we have no spares.

• *With the manuscript of* The Trumpet of the Swan *in the hands of his publisher, White set about designing a jacket. No artist himself, he persuaded a neighbor, Mrs. Guy Hayes, to do a rough sketch that he could show Harper. Mrs. Hayes, working in watercolor, produced a picture that took everyone's eye and that Edward Frascino followed closely in his illustration for the jacket.*

To DOROTHY HAYES

North Brooklin, Maine
December 10, 1969

Dear Dottie:

It is great that you will do a sketch of the jacket for *The Trumpet of the Swan.* I wish I had more stuff to send you—I am fresh out of swan pictures because I sent everything to Bolognese.[1]

My idea is as follows: An 11-year-old boy is seated on a log by the water's edge of a small wilderness pond. It is a marshy sort of place—reeds, sedges. The time is late spring. The boy has dark hair and dark eyes. His back is toward the viewer, but you will probably want to show part of his face as seen from the rear. He is a quiet, serious boy and is enchanted by what is happening—the lacing of his moccasin is being pulled by a day-old cygnet (baby swan) who has emerged from the water to tug at the lace, bracing himself as a robin braces to pull a worm. One of the cygnet's parents—the old cob—is worried at what is going on. His beautiful head and neck are a prominent element in the design. You can arrange him any way that seems to work, but he should be in an attitude

---

1. Don Bolognese had been commissioned to illustrate the book. Harper, after some disagreements, dropped Bolognese and gave the job to Edward Frascino.

of partial protection for the young cygnet, typical of swans and geese.

The adult bird is pure white, with black bill, black legs, and black webbed feet (three toes). The cygnet is greyish (tanny greyish), with mustard-colored legs. The boy should be wearing a jersey or sport shirt, jeans, and moccasins. He has a hunting knife in his belt.

I can't draw a darned thing and you needn't take my quick sketch too seriously. I haven't even tried to show the little cygnet pulling the lacing. I have shown cattails, but I suspect cattails wouldn't be in blossom when swans hatch in June. Any sort of reedy vegetation will do—tall, thin, wispy. A pond lily in the water would be correct if you also need something like that. My cob appears to be in the foreground, but he should really be more in the background, I think. As for the lettering— any arrangement would be all right, but I suspect that the way I've shown it may work out best. The scene should suggest awe, wonderment, enchantment—not action, except the tiny act of tugging at the lace. The boy should probably be rather hunched over, unsmiling.

Maybe you should pick up, at Scribner's Bookstore, a book called "The Last Trumpeter." It is loaded with swan pictures. I sent my copy to Bolognese.

Love, haste,
Andy

• *Garth Williams' failure to get the job of illustrating* The Trumpet of the Swan *was a severe blow to him and a great disappointment to White, who had found Williams easy to work with and who felt in his debt for the success of the two earlier books.*

To GARTH WILLIAMS

[North Brooklin, Me.]
December 31, 1969

Dear Garth:

Your letter saddened me, but I was feeling sad before it arrived. I had always hoped that Williams and White would be as indestructible as ham and eggs, Scotch and soda, Gilbert and Sullivan.

When I turned in my book manuscript, just before Thanksgiving, I asked Ursula to please get the book out in the spring—not wait till fall, which would have been more to Harper's liking. I think this put some extra pressure on her, and I got a letter back asking about "illustration." I replied, saying that the decision was hers, and that I felt deeply indebted to you, and that she would have to take it from there. An author is not in a position to make a deal with an artist.

The impression I got, after a couple of phone calls, was that, although everybody wanted you to do the book, distance was a controlling factor, and they didn't think—since it is a long book requiring thirty or forty pictures—that spring publication would be possible with you working from Mexico. This is the impression I got, and I held out for spring publication; so the blame, if any blame is to be attached to anybody, belongs with me.

Anyway, I am very sad tonight, the last night of a disturbing year. I'm not entirely happy about the text of the book—I am old and wordy, and this book seems to show it. But my chief source of woe is Katharine's long illness. Our house is rigged up now like a hospital, complete with hospital bed and nurses in white uniforms and off-white shoes. K has had to take cortisone for such a long period and at such a high rate, her bones gave way under the strain.

Although you and I have had very little communication and contact over the years, I have always felt immensely in your debt—particularly for your characterization of Stuart, which really blew life into him and was the start of the whole business. Without your contribution, I don't think Stuart would have traveled very far. Whether my cygnet ever gets off the ground remains to be seen. Whether he does or not, I am unhappy about being separated from you after these many fine and rewarding years. I never expected it to happen, and I never wanted it to happen.

Yrs,
Andy

To **HELEN THURBER**

North Brooklin, Maine
January 9, 1970

Dear Helen:

My ears still ring, and I'm very late in thanking you for our Christmas surprise.[1] It was a terrific gift, and it's a great Thurber—one of the best. I would have written you sooner, spilling out my gratitude on this heavenly blue stationery, but I've been rassling a set of Harper galleys and the work has exhausted this old author. I think the Harper copydesk has found a happy (for them) solution to the problem of punctuation: wherever you see a comma, take it out; wherever none exists, put one in. This is easy to remember, gives a girl something to do with her pencil, and irritates the author. Anyway, I have just finished the awesome task of restoring about five thousand commas to their original position and removing an equal number from some very unlikely crevices indeed.

---

1. An original Thurber cartoon—the one about the woman who had a constant ringing in her ears.

I don't remember that business about the martini in the thunderstorm—it sounds like an invention of the great man himself. I am sorry to say that martinis, if anything, have a muting effect on the constant ringing in my ears, and as five o'clock approaches, my thoughts turn toward the elixir of quietude. Gin stops the bell from tolling. Thunderstorm or no thunderstorm, it is a great treat for me to have an original Thurber sitting on the mantel waiting for an itinerant picture framer to stop by. Oddly enough, this house is almost completely lacking in Thurbers. I have never been a collector, and a few years ago when I was shipping off stuff to Cornell preparatory to dying, I bundled up the "La Flamme and Mr. Prufrock" series (Jim's wedding present to K and me) and sent the pictures along, where they would be preserved under fireproof conditions.

We had a rather odd, uneasy Christmas. Joe had undertaken to help sail a 52-foot schooner across the South Atlantic and we had had no word from him since the Cape Verde Islands. He had expected to be home for Christmas. As things turned out, the passage went well and Joe made good progress while at sea under sail but got stopped cold at LaGuardia on December 26 when our modern flying machines came to a full stop in a NE blizzard. Joe took a train to Boston and found flights still being cancelled, so he continued to Brooklin in a taxi driven by a man who had an artificial foot, which he kept on the seat beside him in case he needed a spare.

K has had a rotten time lately, being high on cortisone. She is trying to write a garden piece but is as tense as an E-string. We have no snow but steady, hard cold. My storybook will probably appear in the spring, I hope, when my goose starts to lay. (I don't want to be the only one around here who's laid an egg.) So far, the book has given me little joy and lots of headaches. . . .

Thanks, thanks for your gift. I hope you are up and around, enjoying the 1970s in good health and good spirits.

Love,
Andy

To CASS CANFIELD

North Brooklin, Me.
January 30, 1970

Dear Cass:

It's good of you to want to bring out "Here Is New York" in a larger format and with photographs. I wish I thought it a good idea, but I'm unable to make myself believe that it is.

You mentioned bringing the book up to date. This would really mean writing a whole new book, and I can't undertake that under the present circumstances. The book as it stands is a period piece belonging to a day long gone and about a city that no longer exists. On my infrequent visits to New York, I am painfully aware that the city I wrote about in the summer of 1948 has changed beyond recognition and that the mood I used to entertain is no longer upon me. To reissue "Here Is New York" in its present text would be unthinkable (the title would have to be "Here Isn't New York"), and to catch up with New York and get it on paper would, for me at my age, be an assignment beyond my powers.

How sad! I would like to feel differently about the matter.

Yrs,
Andy

• *Whit Burnett asked White for an explanatory note to accompany his piece "Death of a Pig," which Burnett proposed to include in his anthology* This Is My Best.

To WHIT BURNETT

[North Brooklin, Me.]
[January? 1970]

Dear Mr. Burnett:

"Death of a Pig" is a straight narrative, and, as I indicated in the opening sentence, I felt a peculiar compulsion to give an accounting. My involvement with suffering and death became great, but I was pursued by the shadow of the irony (or perhaps idiocy) of a man's desire to save the life of a creature he had every intention of murdering. And, of course, I was aware of the farcical notes that seem always to intrude, even in the great theme of death.

Sincerely,
E. B. White

To J. G. CASE

North Brooklin, Maine
February 16, 1970

Dear Jack:

Thanks for your letter.

I don't think the librarians have really surrendered to Stuart Little, but they are retreating in disorder. My new book, by the way, has a character in it who receives a medal. Available at all bookstores, come Spring.

I can't get going on "The Elements" until some of the dust has settled around here. It has been a dusty year in more ways than one. But I am saving stuff in a folder, against the day when I can make a start on revising the book. And I'll need your help, as usual.

I regard the word "hopefully" as beyond recall. I'm afraid it's here to stay, like pollution and sex and death and taxes. I wrote a comment in the *New Yorker* about "hopefully" when it first reared its ugly head, but without any belief that my remarks would act as a deterrent. I heard the word first when I took a very pretty granddaughter of mine to dinner at Le Cheval Blanc. I asked her when she expected to move into her new apartment, and she replied, "Hopefully, on Tuesday." I can't remember what I was stuffing into my mouth at the time, but I remember choking on it.

Yours,
Andy

To JAMES RUSSELL WIGGINS

[North Brooklin, Me.]
February 20, 1970

Dear Russ:

The pollution of Center Harbor by the waste from the Faith School is something the town may have to cope with directly. I attended the recent hearing, when the Environmental Improvement Commissioners were on hand, and I doubt that the State is going to prevent that school from flushing its toilets into our salt water. Even if the State denies the petition to dump treated sewage into the Harbor or the Reach, the School could, I think, file a third petition and continue to pollute. The School has been in violation ever since the first petition was denied, but they continue to flush the toilets, and in about two weeks from now there will be a big influx of students and a corresponding outflow of human waste.

I would like to see the town take this health problem on. The Commissioners are not concerned with public health, they are concerned with a classification of water. It's a different matter, even though the two are related.

Do you see any chance that this question could come up at Town Meeting, or at a special meeting? I think somebody has got to discover a way to put some teeth into health enforcement in Brooklin, Maine. I'm hoping you will get excited about it. I have deep feelings about it, but I can't speak publicly, and I'm not well informed about town structure, and I have serious health problems here at home, with Katharine so ill.

The School petitioned to be allowed to introduce a certain number of gallons of "treated waste" into the salt water. The amount was great. I have been reading about treated waste, and whether the amount is great or small, it is bad news. Our coastal cities have been dumping sludge into the ocean from barges for many years. A recent study showed that all marine life had disappeared from the areas where the waste was dumped. Scientists predicted that within fifty years, if the practice were to continue, all marine life along the coast would be destroyed. Meantime, Brooklin could have an epidemic of hepatitis.

Let's all get together and figure out a way of ending the pollution of Center Harbor. It would be a beginning.

Yrs,
Andy

P.S. I'd like to seize this moment to say that the reincarnation of the *Ellsworth American* is the best thing that has happened to Hancock County in years. My congratulations!

To **DOROTHY HAYES**

North Brooklin, Maine
February 21, 1970

Dear Dottie:

I've owed you a couple of letters for a long time, and I am really ashamed of myself, but I've been drove up lately. My life is too full of goatfeathers at the moment, and it causes me to neglect my friends.

I stopped in to see the twins [lambs], and they are beautiful. Those little white faces—how I love them! And Russell[1] has been here with his sawing machine, and all one morning we listened to that magical sound: the one-lung engine throbbing its heart out, the whine of the saw as it bites its way in, then the slowing and laboring of the engine as it comes to grips with a really big stick, then success and a new burst of acceleration. Our whole house was full of this glad and busy noise, carrying the promise of next winter's warmth.

I don't know how to thank you properly for the interest you have taken in my book and for the real help you gave me. The latest news is that Frascino is switching to wash, so I guess there will be no line drawings in the book. I have seen only one sample of his wash, not counting the jacket, but I think it will be an improvement. It will slow up the production of the book, of course, as he is setting to work and doing everything over. I'm appearing as artist in one spot in the first

1. Russell Smith, a neighbor.

chapter, where Sam, the boy, draws a pencil sketch in his diary. It shows a swan standing at the edge of her nest, gazing down at four eggs. I decided to do the sketch myself, as my ability with a pencil is just about right for an 11-yr-old boy. . . .

Love,
Andy

• *For the recording of* Charlotte's Web, *White had suggested that his friend and summer neighbor Susanna Waterman read the story for Pathways of Sound. His hunch was that her untrained voice would be more effective than the voice of a professional actor. Mrs. Waterman, surprised but pleased, went to Boston and recorded several chapters. Her reading, however, did not satisfy Joe Berk, whose ideas of how something should be read differed markedly from White's.*

To SUSANNA WATERMAN

North Brooklin, Maine
March 15, 1970

Dear Susy:

. . . I've always lived by playing my hunches, and on the whole it has worked well and I have no regrets. My mistake with Pathways of Sound was that I failed to get in touch with you first, before dropping your name. I don't know that it would have made any difference in the long run, but at least you would have had a little time to think about the project and would not have had to field a strange phone call with no warning. . . .

It all started with a letter I had from my agent, Jap Gude, asking me whether I wanted Pathways to record Charlotte. (They had already done Stuart Little, with Julie Harris at the controls, gunning her engine all the way—a fast trip.) I wrote Jap and said I had no objection to having Charlotte recorded, but that I might be more interested in the proposal if the book were read, not by Julie Harris, but by a friend of mine named Susy Waterman. I told Jap that if Joe Berk wanted to consider this suggestion, it would be all right for him to get in touch with you and see if you had any interest in the thing. (At this point I should also have signalled you, but I was busy with many other matters and I rather doubted that Berk would pay any attention to my weird idea anyway. People, in general, pay not the slightest heed to anything I say, and I am always surprised and pleased when someone does.) I knew that Julie Harris had *already* put "Charlotte's Web" on a piece of tape, in the hope that I would make a deal with Pathways. That's another bit of information I should have communicated to you. You perhaps wonder what quirk it is in me that causes me to keep bringing up the subject of your voice with people in the motion picture business and the recording business. It's partly a hunch, partly that I prefer an untrained voice to one that has been trained. Both you and Stan have unusual voices. Stan's has great clarity and a kind of natural elegance. Yours is clear, earthy, humorous, and sometimes has an almost childish sound that I like. But I'm familiar enough with the ways of persons in the performing arts to know that their interest in money is always at fever pitch and that they would rather have the name Julie Harris on the dust cover than the name Susanna Waterman.

Berk phoned me a couple of days ago to report on the Boston affair, and I gathered from our conversation that his idea about how a storybook should be read differs from mine. I gather that he was trying to get you to shift your voice incessantly from the spider to the pig and the rat and all the rest of them. It is no wonder you buckled under the strain. "Charlotte's Web" shouldn't be dramatized for a recording, it should just be read, and the voice should always simply be the voice of the person reading the book. This doesn't mean that the reader shouldn't occasionally put a little English on the ball, but beyond that I think it's wrong to go, and it sounds to me as though Berk were trying to goad you into some sort of theatrics. A motion picture, with actors, would be a different matter—there the spider would have its special sound, the pig his. But not in a reading.

Anyway, Berk said he will send me some tape from Julie Harris and some tape from you. He seemed willing to do this, although I didn't make it a condition of our continuing to do business together. . . .

Meantime I send you my apologies and my

Love,
Andy

• *Greta Lee and Parker Banzhaf are friends and former winter neighbors of the Whites' from Sarasota.*

To GRETA LEE BANZHAF

North Brooklin, Maine
1 April 1970

Dear Greta Lee:

Thanks for your Easter card. Our day was a bit unusual—K was taken quite suddenly with heart failure on Saturday morning and was unable to get her breath. This was right after breakfast. I got our doctor on the phone and he whizzed over here and after examining her put in a call for our local ambulance, which is a volunteer affair. Very soon the Corps arrived, with the old DeSoto and an oxygen tank. They gave K a few whiffs of oxygen, then loaded her into the ambulance. Meantime her nurse and I were wildly trying to assemble all the one thousand things she would need in the hospital.

Once we got there, our doctor gave her three shots and then put her in an oxygen tent. True to form, K wanted to take everything into the tent with her: morning paper, latest *New Yorker*, cigarettes (!! bang bang). Anyway, she responded beautifully to the treatment, slept all night in the tent, and was dramatically improved by Easter morning. There was very little left of me, as I had been sick myself with a spring-time resurgence of the old ulcer. But I was so pleased to see the way she bounced back, I didn't mind, and I felt very lucky that we had been able to get such prompt attention on the Saturday before Easter. The three corpsmen who showed up were (1) the editor of our weekly paper—at the controls, (2) the parson of the Congo church in Blue Hill—oxygen, and (3) the industrial arts teacher at the Academy—heavy lifting. It makes a lot of difference, at such moments, to have your friends drive in and go to work. And our doc was marvelous.

K is on complete bed-rest (she's as busy as a monkey from morn till night), looks well, and will probably be returned to me on Saturday.

Hope the Banzhaf Easter was less turbulent.

Love,
Andy

• *The attempt to record* Charlotte's Web *was an unhappy experience for everyone concerned, including Julie Harris, who had read the book for Berk without White's knowing anything about it. The upshot was that White, after listening to all the tapes, decided to read the story himself.*

To JOE BERK

[North Brooklin, Me.]
May 6, 1970

Dear Mr. Berk:

If we are in a quandary, it is because we differ on the way a story should be read. You tend to throw the job to someone in the theater—Hume Cronyn, Jessica Tandy, Julie Harris. I have listened with the greatest attention to these three talented thespians this evening, in the melancholy quiet of my livingroom, and I hold the same opinion I held before I started to listen. They dramatize a book—especially Cronyn and

Tandy, Harris less so. I think a book is better read the way my father used to read books to me—without drama. He just read the words, beginning with the seductive phrase "Chapter One," and I supplied my own dramatization.

It's really a matter of personal taste. You like the chocolate, I like the vanilla. Nothing wrong with either of them, just a matter of preference.

There's nothing in my letter to you of October 1965 that isn't true. Julie Harris did read "Stuart Little" beautifully, I did feel in her debt and in yours. But that letter did not ramble on, as it might have, into my deeper convictions about the business of reading a book. At that time, such an extension of my ideas would have been irrelevant, if not impertinent. So I just said thank you very much.

Then, when "Charlotte's Web" came up, I assumed the field was wide open and proposed that the book be read by someone who wasn't an actress. This was an attempt on my part to experiment with a new and different sound, and I was naturally surprised when I learned that the book had already been recorded by Miss Harris. I feel reasonably sure you don't want to discard Julie Harris after the work she's put in. As for me, I feel embarrassed, although I had nothing to do with the matter. It would be a snub, on my part, to run Julie Harris down the drain and insist that someone else be substituted. I see no solution to our dilemma. If you see one, I'd like to hear about it.

Sincerely,
E. B. White

To CAROL ANGELL

N. Brooklin
May 28 [1970]

Dear Carol:

Happy, happy Birthday! It must be awful to be forty [she was thirty] but anyway, you are stuck with it now. At 96, I seem to grow younger every day. Jones is feeling his age a little bit, but not much. He is going to feel it more next week when I show up here with a West Highland White Terrier puppy named Susy. I bought Susy from a woman in Southwest Harbor the other day when I was caught in a puppy-buying mood, but I did not bring her home with me—the weather was cold and she will have to live in the barn and I didn't want her first night to be a cold one. Jones is psychic and knows something is going on that will affect him one way or another, probably adversely, and he goes around wreathed in deep suspicion. He was with me in Southwest when I made the purchase, and he smelled a rat.

My next shopping expedition will be to the Rackliffe Pottery or the Rowantrees Pottery to look for a couple of plates which are to be part of your birthday present from K and me. I wish I knew more about what color you would like and what shape. If they are for appetizers, would you like a divided-up plate or a plain plate? I hope to take K with me when I go, but right now her back is so painful she can't get into a car. . . .

The weather has smoothed out and we are in the middle of a beautiful time, crab in bloom, pear in bloom, wild pear along the roadsides in bloom, lilac buds ready to burst, many birds, and blue skies with bright sun. Saturday was a nice day at the Brooklin Boat Yard for the launching of Cachalot, the Peter Sturtevant sloop. It was an *in absentia* launch, but the owner threw a party anyway, and there was a nice crowd, which included old Artley Parson who is 110, with his wife Charlotte. . . . Allene served drinks and fish chowder. Marianne Allen, Henry's daughter, swung the champagne bottle and hit the boat on the second try. Cachalot is strip-planked and is as spacious below as a ballroom. . . .

Joe Berk, from Pathways of Sound, was here last week to talk about recording "Charlotte's Web." He had already got Julie Harris to read the book, unbeknownst to me, and he brought along the tape. I didn't like it and said so, and it ended up by my agreeing to read the book myself, in my famous monotone. Berk and a technician are arriving at the Blue Hill Inn next week and I will read the book in Joe's living room after swallowing a cat pill. Joe and Allene will be away, fetching Steven and Martha. Berk, apparently, is a perfectionist . . . and I am supposed to pause in the narration every time a car goes by on the highway. I don't know what we'll do about the sonic boom or the ducks.[1]

Center Harbor is going to look like Marblehead this summer— lots of boats, including Surfing Seal, back from the Caribbean, and Prudence, the new Williamson boat—a large schooner. Mooring space is so tight, I have been chivvied out of my old location to a less desirable spot closer to the end of the sewer pipe from the Faith School of Theology.

Hope you have a pleasant birthday. Lots and lots of love. See you soon.

Andy

---

1. The recording session did begin in Joel White's home. However, because of continual interruptions from background noise, White managed to read only about half the book the first day. On the second day, the crew moved to the secluded house of White's friend Dr. Wearn and there completed the recording.

To **HOWARD CUSHMAN**

North Brooklin
June 12 [1970]

Dear Cush:

The first copy of "The Trumpet of the Swan" to leave here on the wings of the U.S. Mail is addressed to thee. It goes forth today. Your brilliant work as my operative in the Philadelphia Zoo, your color snaps of Trumpeters, the wealth of material you dispatched a year ago— how can I ever forget! They bore fruit, of a most peculiar sort, but fruit. And I am indeed grateful. If you'd like free copies for your grandkinder or other tots, to sprinkle around at Christmas and birthdays, let me know your needs and I will curb my natural niggardliness and see that you get the books.

The book is too long—which is my fault; I haven't the time to write short these days. The jacket looked quite nice until some genius at Harper decided to paste a green sticker on the boy's crotch. Harper's would gladly put the Good Housekeeping Seal of Approval on the Ten Commandments. It's no use trying to get publishers to do anything sensible, or do anything right.

Sorry about that testy postal card, or, as I call it in my pithy way, post card. I've had enough testiness for three people since about last summer, and I vent my humors on one and all, without fear or favor. I can't even remember what the post card said, but I have no short-memory any more. I presume the blood is not getting to the head, and all the little memory channels are dry and carry no traffic from one point in the brain to another. Ah, welladay! Have you had any news from *your* book yet? Any Lippincouragement? I keep candles burning.

Yr testy friend,
Andy

To **HOWARD CUSHMAN**

[North Brooklin, Me.]
[July 19, 1970]
Sunday

Dear Cush:

Thanks for the Xerox of the Cushman review, and thanks again for writing it. If you need any more copies of the trumpet, let me know. I had my first *visit* from a trumpeter last week—a very pretty young mother from Deer Isle, friend of Gluyas Williams's, showed up in the driveway with her two tots, Jake and Eliza. Jake carried a beatup bugle, adorned with a long, off-white, braided cord. He stood by the barnyard fence and let go with reveille, mess call, and taps, his face wearing a most tortured expression (like the great Armstrong). The notes came out pretty good for an 8-year-old. His mother watched him with affection but not the slightest trace of indulgence, and then, at the end of taps, said to me: "Now you won't know whether to get up, eat, or go to bed."

As the man whom I chauffeured safely across America, daylong and nightlong, you will be sorry to learn that my 55-year stretch of happy motoring came to an abrupt close last Thursday. I fell asleep at the wheel of my car and hit a telephone pole. My injuries are painful but relatively unimportant. My pride is broken, my spirit gone, and my automobile a tangled mass of junk. If you ever feel drowsy at the wheel, stop the car, get out, and lie down under the nearest sassafras bush. And if you ever take an antihistamine pill and follow it with an Old Fashioned, don't drive.

Yrs,
Andy

To J. G. GUDE

North Brooklin
August 28, 1970

Dear Jap:

The eye doctor didn't come up with much. It would appear that my eyes are all right, but on certain days I can't see out of them. Well, often there isn't much to see anyway.

As for those "Charlotte's Web" proposals, here are some thoughts I've had in my more lucid moments:

1. Disney is out. (He's even dead.)

2. I share your doubts about Joel Katz's treatment. It was sketchy and not reassuring. I'm afraid he might get into real trouble with a wholly live adaptation, just as Heinemann got into trouble with that stuffed mouse.

3. The Sagittarius proposal strikes me as the most promising of the lot. If Mr. Edgar Bronfman is president of Seagram's, there must be some money there somewhere. What's more, I sometimes buy Seagram's 7, so I would be helping the whole thing along in my small way. I hold no firm opinion as to whether the story should be totally animated or only partly animated. I think a good and faithful film could be made either way, and I incline to let whoever wants to do the book do it the way he wants to. I remember years ago a letter from Nunnally Johnson,

who said, "Well, maybe animation *is* the way to do it." Or words to that effect. Does Hubley favor Sagittarius?

4. I am pretty sure of one thing: there should be a narrator. This is a story—a story told to children. Children like to hear the words said, and they listen. Certain parts of "Charlotte's Web" would be lost if there were no narrator—the words are there, but they have to be spoken if they are not to be lost. For example, a camera can show a barn. But a camera can't come up with the barn as described in the first paragraph of Chapter III. You need the words. Words are also very useful in transition. "The next day was foggy. Everything on the farm was dripping wet. The grass looked like a magic carpet. The asparagus patch looked like a silver forest." The camera can *show* all that stuff but it can't say "the next day."

Or, "The crickets sang in the grasses. They sang the song of summer's ending, a sad, monotonous song. 'Summer is over and gone,' they sang. 'Over and gone, over and gone. Summer is dying, dying.'" A sound track has no difficulty coming up with cricket-song, but there is no substitute for narration in a transitional passage like that, short of putting the words in the mouth of one of the characters.

5. Music. This story is an old-fashioned story. It's a country story, and it is pastoral in tone. The musical accompaniment should reflect this. I think I'd be against anything very modern in the way of music and would favor old-timey sweet music, plus the sort of music that is typical of country fairs. I recall the music in the old black-and-white film of "State Fair" and it was great.

I'm willing to meet with anyone who wants to come here and see me, and if my health should improve I'm willing to come to New York. Are you acquainted with Campus? And do you think he's a good director? If you have confidence in Sagittarius (I'm Cancer, myself), I think it would be sensible to close a deal and see what happens. I'll help if they want me to and if I'm able to.

Yrs,
Andy

To JAMES A. WRIGHT

North Brooklin, Maine
August 29, 1970

Dear Jim:

I started reading that monthly letter of the Royal Bank of Canada with only a moderate amount of curiosity, but as it progressed I began to hear echoes, and before I got through I discovered that it wasn't just Dostoevsky and Carlyle and Tennyson and Shakespeare he had been reading. He had been dipping into a little book called "The Elements of Style," by William Strunk, Jr., and E. B. White. Take a look at this:

(Royal Bank)	(Elements of Style)
It is no sign of weakness or defeat that a typescript ends up in need of major surgery. This is a common occurrence in all writing, and among the best writers.	Remember, it is no sign of weakness or defeat that your manuscript ends up in need of major surgery. This is a common occurrence in all writing, and among the best writers.

I heard the echo because the words were mine, and I sometimes remember my own words—usually with distaste. Well, I am glad to have helped out an ink-stained wretch of the Royal Bank in his solemn hour of composition. Writing is an ordeal, and in his penultimate paragraph a writer can easily be *in extremis*, as this one evidently was.

I'm glad you liked my kooky little swan story. It took a lot of gall to write it, as I have never in my life laid eyes on a Trumpeter Swan, either in or out of captivity. But I'll tackle anything in a pinch, and I began to feel the pinch more than a year ago when I looked around and discovered that my house was full of day nurses and night nurses at $28 per day. Or night. It runs into money fast. . . .

Yrs,
Andy

To URSULA NORDSTROM

North Brooklin, Maine
September 2, 1970

Dear Ursula:

I have another correction to add to your garland. On page 201, third line from bottom, "ko-hoh" should read "beep." This boo-boo on my part was caught by two alert children who reside at 1010 Fifth Avenue. (All my readers are extremely wealthy.) Their pa wrote me a very nice letter, and I wrote back and also sent the kids a book. Can this mistake be corrected in the next printing?

Yrs,
Andy

To ALICE J. SCOTT

[North Brooklin, Me.]
September 23, 1970

Dear Mrs. Scott:

When I start a book, I never know what my characters are going to do, and I accept no responsibility for their eccentric behavior. Nor do I worry about what children are going to think about the story. I just go ahead and write it the way I see it. As far as Louis is concerned, he was taking Sam's advice, and Sam is very pro-zoo. It doesn't strike me that Louis was insensitive or disloyal, but if that's the way he strikes you, so be it.

Life in a zoo is just the ticket for some animals and birds. Waterfowl usually seem to be having a fine time on their private lagoons. The Philadelphia Zoo, incidentally, hatched some Trumpeter cygnets a few years back when the species was threatened with extinction, and helped save them for the world.

Thanks very much for your letter and your comments.

Sincerely,
E. B. White

To ROGER ANGELL

N. Brooklin
October 24 [1970]

Dear Rog:

Groggy though I be, I'm going to write you this long overdue letter. I've been on an insomnia kick—haven't caught enough sleep the last week to keep a mouse in bad dreams. As a result, I'm light-headed and frail. But at least I've done some reading. Not T. Eliot, top bard, either.

Pleasure, pure naked pleasure, is what I got from a reexamination of your pieces in A Day.[1] It is a terrifically funny book, and good good good. Doog doog doog to you. I have my favorites—Ivy is one, and the title piece. But the whole thing is great and exudes what can only be called class. In some curious way it reminds me of the old Ring Lardner, I think because there is the stratum and the sub-stratum, where you get down into a nice deep dark layer of human experience, far below the surface level of fun and games. For straight parody, the "New York Review of Books" struck me as brilliant at the time, and still does on rereading. Anyway, congratulations on the book, and thanks for sending us this copy. I'm sorry I've been so slow in acknowledging it. (There's a typo on p. 47—"to" for "too.")

Thank Carol for her card about the record album. I am glad my voice sings infants to sleep, and just hope to hell it doesn't sing everybody else to sleep. Somebody at Harper told Joe Berk, the producer, that Harper couldn't get up much interest in it because it sounded "unenthusiastic"—no theatrics. I guess I should have read it against a background of rock music.

A rat has died in our walls—our annual exposure to air pollution.

_____
1. *A Day in the Life of Roger Angell.*

And today the trout are coming up the brook with love in their hearts. The brook has a lot more water in it than it did a year ago on this passionate occasion, when they had to crawl upstream on their hands and knees. Now they can make it by using the breast stroke. And I have scooped out a spawning bed for them, which they may or may not use. . . .

Did you hear about the Maine Maritime Academy tragedy? Four 18-year-old midshipmen were allowed to set out in a Shields Class sloop, name of Phyllis, on a rotten afternoon a week ago. Only one of the four knew anything about boat-handling, and none of the four has shown up since. Only a few battered floor boards off North Haven. The incident has kicked up quite a stir hereabouts, and I'm afraid somebody over at that Academy goofed.

Shawn phoned me yesterday about the piece I turned in,[2] and he sounded so woebegone and melancholy I tried to persuade him to send the thing back. I felt as though I had stabbed him in the back. I'm sure from the tone of his voice he doesn't want to run the piece but is just doing so as a matter of principle. Life is hard.

Am taking K to Bangor on Tuesday for the removal of a skin cancer on her right arm. Her health, otherwise, is about what it was, and she is busy every minute of the day. We still have roses in bloom, but the Christmas orders have gone out long since to Carroll Reed [a mail-order house]. Susy is vibrant and well, Jones is resigned and well. Both have recovered from their surgery. And there is a moose in South Blue Hill. And I guess that about covers the situation. Thanks again, Rog, for the book; it is very impressive. (I thought the endorsements on the back of the jacket were hilarious.)

Love,

Andy

P.S. Another book I'm enjoying is "The Hoopoe" by Christine Weston. I really think she's done it this time. It's a long, ambitious book, wonderful about a girlfriend in India, and, I gather, autobiographical.

To **HAMISH HAMILTON**

[North Brooklin, Me.]
November 11, 1970

Dear Jamie:

My free copies of the British swan have arrived, and I think the book makes a very brave appearance. The glossy dust cover has the elegant appearance of an old but expensive automobile that has been beautifully kept by its owner—plenty of wax. The American jacket seems quite dull by comparison.

2. "The Browning Off of Pelham Manor."

I hope you have good luck with the story. In last Sunday's *Times* it surprised me by busting out in the number one position on the Children's Best Seller list, bumping Charlotte down to fourth place. So there I was, betraying my own best friend, in cold type. Charlotte, by the way, has been sold to the movies, and I am being invaded this weekend by a producer (from Hollywood), an animator from Copenhagen, and another animator from, I think, Prague. All this fuss because of a girl named *Aranea Cavatica*, may she rest undisturbed!

Yrs,
Andy

To MILTON GREENSTEIN

[North Brooklin, Me.]
November 17, 1970

Dear Milt:

It was good to talk to you. I have signed the four copies of the "Charlotte's Web" agreement with Sagittarius, and they are enclosed. Thanks for all your work and for straightening me out last night on the phone, and may good luck go with both of us. And send me a bill. This involves a lot of money, so make the bill in proportion—or, as we writers would say, big.

The director, Gene Deitch, who was here Sunday and whom I got on with fine, listened to a fragment of my recording of the book, and it is possible that he may decide to use my voice in narration. Deitch is American-born, but lives in Prague with a Czech wife and children. He has had 25 years in cartoon film production, worked with UPA, and has scooped up many honors in his field. He did two of the three Bemelmans "Madeline" shorts. I saw the first one and it was beautiful. I feel fairly happy about Deitch—happy as I can ever be in never-never land, which still gives me the shakes.

Yrs,
Andy

To HARRY CLOUDMAN

North Brooklin, Maine
19 November 1970

Dear Harry:

Thanks for your note carrying the sad news. I was aware that Jack [Case] was ailing, but I failed to see the notice of his death in the Times. He was a lovely fellow and I felt good working with him. The letter he wrote me that started the whole thing off was a model of editorial seduction, in the best tradition. I am glad I was seduced and glad that the book did not let Jack down.

Off and on, in recent years, I have been asked by him to bring the book up to date. I always replied, saying that I would and stalling for time. I feel guilty that I've failed to come up with anything.

Yrs,
Andy

To PHILIP BOOTH

North Brooklin, Maine
22 November 1970

Dear Phil:

Thank you for "Margins" and for your inscription. They are lovely poems, and I am late in acknowledging them, but when it comes to poetry I take my own sweet time and allow myself no more than one poem a day. A good poem is like an anchovy: it makes you want another right away and pretty soon the tin is empty and you have a belly-ache or a small bone in your throat or both.

Being a halfway man myself and never quite sure where I am, I liked particularly your first long poem, from a distant land, with its steady rhythms and memorable lines. And I liked "Nightsong," and many others. I can't criticize poetry, any more than I can dissect miracles, so I will fall back on what a little girl told her father. The poor guy was trying to write a review of my recent book for Down East Magazine and in desperation put the matter up to his 6-year-old daughter, who cleared the whole business up by saying, "It's a good story because I like it." Your poems are good because I like them.

We've had a mild and rather wet fall. I had my last sail in Martha on a late October afternoon. The morning had been bright and windless, but after lunch a good breeze came in from the west and although it was cold on the water I took off and beat up the Reach till I closed with the Deer Isle shore, then turned tail and got warm by running back to the Harbor––a fine ending to a slim season for me.

Joe is busy laying the keel for a ketch for Blue Hill's insurance magnate, Merle Grindle. The yard is crowded and busy. He (Joe) was here a few minutes ago, and sends his best. Thanks again for the book.

Yrs,
Andy White

To STANTON WATERMAN

North Brooklin, Maine
December 30, 1970

Dear Stan:

Thanks so much for sending me the clipping from the *Monitor*. It's a very good editorial, I think, on our vanishing humorist. Sid's [Perelman's] marathon departure from these shores reminded me of the Gilbert and Sullivan line—"But you *don't go*."

It seems to me that if a man decides to shake the dust of America and go somewhere else, he would be smart to sneak away with the least possible noise. Then, if he later changes his mind and wants to return to his native land, he can do it without incurring the gibes and jeers of the populace. ("What are *you* doing here?") I liked the sentence in the *Monitor* piece, ". . . an expatriate travels not to find a new home but a new self." A sound reflection.

Nothing that England can offer can match the beauty of the Great Snowfall of Christmas 1970 in Maine. We have more snow here in Brooklin than they have on television, where it snows almost continuously from December 1 to January 1. Christmas Eve was an exciting time—the snow blowing and drifting, the town plows barely visible as they came winking along in the dusk, hurling snow high in the air and effectively plugging up the driveways of one and all, so that when Christmas Day dawned, the highway was a clear open track between high white walls—a track to which nobody could gain access because his car had been effectively sealed in by the bravery and pluck of the tireless plowmen. Long *before* Christmas the snowdrifts in my barnyard topped the fence so the geese could simply walk out to freedom on the snow. And the pink snow-fence in our north field, normally four feet high, now shows up as a tiny four-inch fence such as you might put around a bed of spring flowers to discourage short-legged dogs.

Your description of the reading of "Charlotte's Web" at your house was convincing but did not in any way mitigate my disappointment in the whole business. The voice should have been Susy's, and I think it would have been if I had been present in Boston to get a scissors-hold on Berk so that she could have done her reading without interference from him. I feel terrible about the whole episode. I heard some of the Susanna Waterman tape and the voice came through just as I hoped it would. All it needed was a free rein, and that, I gather, is what it didn't get.

I'm sick abed today with a fierce attack of the Uncommon Cold. If this letter is overlong and rambling it is because I can't write short letters when *in extremis.*

Lots of love to you both from K and me, and all the best for the New Year.

Yrs,
Andy

XIV

IN THE LEE OF THE BARN

1971–1976

• *In 1971, prodded by his friend Reginald Allen, White adapted* The Trumpet of the Swan *for a children's concert, compressing the story into a small fragment but incorporating Sam Beaver's poem about the zoo. Benjamin Lees wrote the score. The Philadelphia Orchestra performed it on May 13, 1972, and it has had a number of subsequent performances by other groups.*

To REGINALD ALLEN

[North Brooklin, Me.]
January 2, 1971

Dear Reggie:

We're gradually digging out, from under the great snows and the weight of bad health. I'm ready and eager to go to work on the Philadelphia Orchestra script if you still think the idea has possibilities and would be acceptable if properly constructed. I have some questions.

1. Is it your idea that the "brief narrative" should tell, in few words, the story of Louis and Serena and Sam? Or should it be much simpler than that? And would it be something like the narrative in "Peter and the Wolf," with musical accompaniment illustrating and heightening the words?

2. You speak of a 12-minute limitation. Does that include the time that Sam Beaver's poem would require? In other words, is 12 minutes the outside limit into which everything must fit?

3. Mr. Smith's letter says: "Such a work (no longer than 12 minutes) could easily be published, and would be performable in all parts of the civilized globe, etc. . . ." In short, a "property" would be created, publication would ensue, and money would change hands. This compels

me to inquire, before getting involved in this lark, what sort of setup do you envision? Whose property is it? Yours? Mine? The composer's? All three of us together? I ask, not because I give a damn but only because, as one of the characters in my book remarks, anything that involves money is complex, and my dream (unfulfilled) is to keep my life simple. I have never had any experience in the great world of music and symphony orchestras and concerts for which admission is charged, and I don't want to blunder into it without knowing in a general way where I am headed and what kind of trouble I am about to get into. Do I have to join ASCAP, and if so, are the rites of initiation very embarrassing to an old man? I don't even know what ASCAP stands for. Just the word ASCAP scares me. Very frightening word.

I am, of course, delighted that the Philadelphia Orchestra Association has taken notice of "The Trumpet of the Swan"; the whole idea sounds great to me, and I feel indebted to you for dreaming it up. Imagine me, sitting down there in my boathouse a year and a half ago, composing the lines of Sam Beaver's poem and not having the slightest inkling that the Philadelphia Orchestra was tuning up onstage. What a life I lead! How merry! How innocent! How nutty!

My bird life, by the way, intensified with the recent storms. I had a catbird hanging around here all fall in the bittersweet vine on the roof of my woodshed. (There were also four robins, rifling the vine, getting stoned on the berries.) One day, shortly before Christmas, after a bitter night, I found the catbird belly up in the snow by our kitchen porch, guarded by Susy, my terrier. We brought her indoors, thawed her out, and I placed her in a cage in the plant room, fed her diced apple and beef stew, and she made a remarkable recovery and became very vigorous and pretty. But then one day I noticed that the toes of both feet were curled up, and she could not hang on to a perch. So I phoned Chandler Richmond in Ellsworth, told him the tale, and he said, "Bring her over—I have a lot of birds here in my cellar."[1] This I did. I've had no report as yet about her progress. I assumed that the curled toes meant that her feet had been frozen, but Richmond said he thought it was more likely a pesticide calamity and that he would massage the feet. There's a man for you—down cellar on bitter winter nights, massaging a catbird's toes! I don't know why I keep referring to this bird as "she." The sexes are alike, and I doubt that anybody can tell a boy catbird from a girl catbird unless he happens to see them coupling. But I hope "she" survives this winter and returns to restore the earth come spring.

We had three storms in a great rush, neatly spaced, Tuesday, Thurs-

1. Chandler Richmond is curator of the Stanwood Wildlife Foundation and the man to whom everyone brings wounded creatures.

day, and Saturday. The result is sensational. The mouth of my main driveway was so plugged I had to hire a loader to lift the snow and carry it across the highway and dump it into the field. There simply was no place to put it on this side of the road.

Yrs,
Andy

To GENE DEITCH

North Brooklin
January 12 [1971]

Dear Gene:

It was generous of you to send me such a detailed report of your scheme for the picture. This afternoon I sent you a few more photographs —they were taken in Canada, but they are close to New England in form and spirit.

You said in your letter (about my script) "how I wish I had the whole thing." You have everything I wrote; there wasn't any more.

I've studied your letter very carefully and find myself in sympathy, or agreement, with most of it. I do hope, though, that you are not planning to turn "Charlotte's Web" into a moral tale. It is not that at all. It is, I think, an *appreciative* story, and there is quite a difference. It celebrates life, the seasons, the goodness of the barn, the beauty of the world, the glory of everything. But it is essentially amoral, because animals are essentially amoral, and I respect them, and I think this respect is implicit in the tale. I discovered, quite by accident, that reality and fantasy make good bedfellows. I discovered that there was no need to tamper in any way with the habits and characteristics of spiders, pigs, geese, and rats. No "motivation" is needed if you remain true to life and true to the spirit of fantasy. I would hate to see Charlotte turned into a "dedicated" spider: she is, if anything, more the Mehitabel type—toujours gai. She is also a New Englander, precise and disciplined. She does what she does. Perhaps she is magnifying herself by her devotion to another, but essentially she is just a trapper. . . .

As for Templeton, he's an old acquaintance and I know him well. He starts as a rat and he ends as a rat—the perfect opportunist and a great gourmand. I devoutly hope that you are not planning to elevate Templeton to sainthood. . . .

An aura of magic is essential, because this is a magical happening. Much can be done by music of the right kind, as when the moment arrives when communication takes place between the little girl and the animals in the barn cellar. This is truly a magical moment and should be so marked by the music. (I hear it as a sort of thrumming, brooding sound, like the sound of crickets in the fall, or katydids, or cicadas. It should be a haunting, quiet, steady sound—subdued and repetitive.)

Even more can be done by *words*, if you are able to use them. (You'll have to forgive me for being a word man, but that's what I am.)

In writing of a spider, I did not make the spider adapt her ways to my scheme. I spent a year studying spiders before I ever started writing the book. In this, I think I found the key to the story. I hope you will, in your own medium, be true to Charlotte and to nature in general. My feeling about animals is just the opposite of Disney's. He made them dance to his tune and came up with some great creations, like Donald Duck. I preferred to dance to *their* tune and came up with Charlotte and Wilbur. It would be futile and unfair to compare the two approaches, but you are stuck with my scheme and will probably come out better if you go along with it. Both techniques are all right, each in its own way, but I have a strong feeling that you can't mix them. It just comes natural to me to keep animals pure and not distort them or take advantage of them.

Interdependence? I agree that the film should be a paean to life, a hymn to the barn, an acceptance of dung. But I think it would be quite untrue to suggest that barnyard creatures are dependent on each other. The barn is a community of rugged individualists, everybody mildly suspicious of everybody else, including me. Friendships sometimes develop, as between a goat and a horse, but there is no sense of true community or cooperation. Heaven forfend! Joy of life, yes. Tolerance of other cultures, yes. Community, no.

I just want to add that there is no symbolism in "Charlotte's Web." And there is no political meaning in the story. It is a straight report from the barn cellar, which I dearly love, having spent so many fine hours there, winter and summer, spring and fall, good times and bad times, with the garrulous geese, the passage of swallows, the nearness of rats, and the sameness of sheep.

K sends her best to you and Zdenka.

Yrs,
Andy

To REGINALD ALLEN

[North Brooklin, Me.]
[January 1971]

Dear Reggie:

I'm just in from tossing snow around, with scoop and shovel—we had another fall yesterday. When the great thaw comes in spring, the runoff should be sensational—like Cairo, Illinois, when the river rises.

Your letter was reassuring, and I'm sure we can set up something workable if I can produce a script that is satisfactory to the Orchestra. Seems to me whatever money may accrue should go to the Orchestra and the Zoo. The book and I will benefit from the publicity. (Incidentally, I just heard that "The Trumpet of the Swan" failed to win the Newbery Award, and that the award went to a book—hold your breath—called "The Summer of the Swan," published by Viking. How's that for a near miss? I just got one word wrong!) . . .

K is deep in seed catalogues, and most of the orders have gone out. I am studying my hatchery catalogue, making the hard choices among the breeds available: Sex-linked Hallcross, Silver Hallcross, Golden Buff, Heavy White Number 7, New Hampshire–Cornish Cross. The old gander has taken to fighting with the young gander. Can spring be far behind? Yes.

Yrs,
Andy

To GENE DEITCH

North Brooklin
February 3, 1971

Dear Gene:

. . . It is all very well to say that "Charlotte's Web was a web of love which extended beyond her own lifespan." But you should never lose sight of the fact that it was a web spun by a true arachnid, not by a *de facto* person. One has eight legs and has been around for an unbelievably long time on this earth; the other has two legs and has been around just long enough to raise a lot of hell, drain the swamps, and bring the planet to the verge of extinction.

. . . As you say, spiders do not talk to pigs, except in the world of the fable. But when conversation does finally take place, in that fabulous and pure world, it is indeed a spider who talks, indeed a pig. It is not a woman in spider's clothing, or a boy in a pig's skin. Be true to animals, O Good Gene, and you will live forever. When you enter the barn cellar, remove your hat. . . .

Yrs,
Andy

To GLUYAS WILLIAMS

North Brooklin, Maine
15 February 1971

Dear Gluyas:

You are absolutely right: it's amazing how many errands can be postponed. If I had put off running that nutty errand last July 16th until I'd recovered from my drowsiness, I would not have crashed into a telephone pole and damn near broken my neck—which still gives me a lot of pain and other queer symptoms. With an automobile at hand, life tends to become just one silly errand after another. . . .

I am not used to celebrating Washington's Birthday on the fifteenth of February, so I walked out early this morning and deposited a sackful of letters in our mailbox. Then had to return and retrieve them an hour later when it dawned on me that the mails weren't moving today, even though George is still locked up tight in his mother's womb and won't emerge for a full week. This country is nuts. The only date I would like to see shifted is December 25, which I would like shifted to February 29, so that it occurs only once in every four years. This would have a profoundly beneficial effect on the nation and would set me back on an even course again.

Eggemoggin Reach froze over this year, and so did Blue Hill Bay down as far as the light, a noble and awe-inspiring sight. The smelt tents in Surry are out in their usual gay colors, but the smelts have quit coming into the harbor because they don't like to travel so far under ice. Gives them claustrophobia. Somebody told me the other day that a gull won't eat a smelt. I don't know whether to believe it or not but am conducting my own survey and will let you know if I learn anything. All the gulls I've ever known will eat anything. Our extreme cold weather has moderated, the light is lengthening, and the vast snow cover is beginning to turn grey and thin. It has been a beautiful winter—quite sunny much of the time—but a confining one. I don't enjoy being housebound. . . . Keep well, and don't run too many errands.

Yrs,
Andy

• *A family named Turner, who lived in a remote spot in British Columbia, had befriended a wintering colony of trumpeter swans. Dolly Connelly, a feature writer living in Seattle, had visited the Turners and written White about young Susan, suggesting he send her a copy of his swan book.*

To **DOLLY CONNELLY**

[North Brooklin, Me.]
[February 16?, 1971]

Dear Miss Connelly:

I shall dispatch a copy of "The Trumpet of the Swan" and a copy of "Charlotte's Web" to Susan Turner of Lonesome Lake. And thanks for your advice.

I couldn't resist writing a poem about Bella Coola when I came across the name.

> I had a girl named Bella Coola,
> And she was full of fun and moola,
> But when I pressed my suit undoola
> It seemed to make my Bella coola.

So much for British Columbia.

I worked for the Seattle *Times* for a year in the far distant past, but they never sent me to Lonesome Lake. Usually they just sent me to fly low over Lake Washington looking for dead bodies. I saw Mount Rainier twice.

Sincerely,
E. B. White

To HOWARD CUSHMAN

North Brooklin
February 18 [1971]

Dear Cush:

Cornellians are great readers of the newspaper. Before your swan clipping arrived, Spud Phillips (Phi Gamma Delta) came through with it—his from the Milwaukee *Journal*. Those Lonesome Lake Turners sure get around. They were in *Life* a while back, I seem to remember. I've already queried Mistress Connelly about my sending a book to young Miss Turner. Just a question, really, of whether any Turner wants to add the weight of a book to the backpack—72 miles of mountain trails. I like the name Bella Coola, anyway. . . .

About this being the glad Spring of our 50th (with you cheating a little on it), I find my enthusiasm for a trip down memory lane something less than wild. Unwild, or tame, is what it is. I suspect that the sight of the campus and the faces of my classmates, those dear dead faces and those unremembered nicknames, would sink me in a pit of melancholy and start me on a round of serious drinking. If I'm going to go somewhere and get drunk, I don't want to be wearing a funny hat and a badge with my name on it. In short, I'm not planning a trip to Ithaca in June. What I *may* do, maybe next spring (1972, which is Hotspur's 50th), is drive to Ithaca in a small wagon loaded with boxes of my so-called literary papers, which are now in my attic and which I have promised to that boxlike library. If *that* journey comes off, you shall go along as navigator, and we will pause at every friendly tavern from here to there, to refresh our tired old selves.

Yrs,
Andy

• *White was increasingly uneasy about Deitch's plans for* Charlotte. *So, it turned out, was Sagittarius. A month after the following letter was written, Sagittarius turned the project over to Hanna-Barbera Productions in Hollywood.*

To J. G. GUDE

[North Brooklin, Me.]
April 10, 1971

Dear Jap:

I saw only a tiny fragment of Deitch's treatment, but it was enough to make me uneasy. And I've been uneasy from the very start because of the Czech locale. Sagittarius has spent enough in airplane fares alone to have offset any gain.

If Deitch plans to make "Charlotte's Web" a picture for adults, then he doesn't understand the story and should be dropped. If he has taken the joy out of the tale, he already has two strikes against him. If he is groping for conflict, he is groping in the dark. If he is phasing Fern out of the story he might as well be phasing Scarlett out of "Gone With the Wind." Fern is built-in, and nobody in his right mind would want to yank her. . . .

The first letter I had from Deitch unnerved me. He seemed to be searching for moral implications. He was analyzing the bejesus out of the story instead of *accepting* it, the way children do. He seemed to want to make the story serve some ends of his own—I'm not sure what. Anybody who can't accept the miracle of the web shouldn't try to film it. . . .

As for music, I agree with you that music is very important, but Deitch seems to want to introduce a lot of songs and turn the thing into a sort of musical. I'm distrustful of this, and the one song he sent me was way off base. You could, of course, weave "Charlotte's Web" into a musical comedy, and maybe some day it will be done. But right now, I think the most promising approach is to keep the story right on course and not interrupt it every few minutes with a song. . . .

Yrs,
Andy

• *Mason Trowbridge is a local physician and long-time friend of the Whites'.*

To MASON TROWBRIDGE

[North Brooklin, Me.]
May 7 [1971]

Dear Mason:

What I really need is a trio of resident internists to look after Katharine and me, and a broody Muscovy duck to sit on goose eggs. I have a young goose that has laid 26 eggs and is still producing. She has seemingly no intention to sit down—likes to be up and around.

But yours is a handsome offer. Right now I wouldn't know how to cope with a trio of Wyandottes, short of constructing a separate condominium for them. My poultry operation is computerized and automated and has no truck with the fancy. I shudder to think what would happen if I were to introduce three fashion plates into my henpen. And of course it would be out of the question to introduce them into my brooder house, whose occupants are only 2½ weeks old.

The rooster whets my appetite, though. I've never employed a rooster with my flock of laying hens, since my eggs go to market (I trade them against my grocery bill). But my hens have always struck me as sex-starved and frustrated, with an occasional outbreak of Lesbianism. I have a neighbor who is an organic enthusiast, and she tells me that fertile eggs don't build up a man's cholesterol count the way infertile eggs do. She has never explained this phenomenon to me, but it appears to be widely accepted among the devout. Anyway, if you still have a Wyandotte male in the fall, when my pullets are housed, I might like to introduce him to the harem. He'd better eat plenty of wheat germ meanwhile, as I usually have 24 young females. (Silver Cross.) Thanks for yr offer. Let us keep in touch. Do you want any goslings?

Andy

• *Efforts were being made to preserve the house on Cornell's campus of Andrew D. White, first president of the university. Professor Henry Guerlac was a prime mover in the project.*

To HENRY GUERLAC

North Brooklin, Maine
May 15, 1971

Dear Mr. Guerlac:

I'll be glad to befriend the Andrew D. White house, and you may use my name. I find it hard to recall the house, after these many years, but if it has a garden and the usual number of mice and will shelter the humanities and yourself, then I am for restoring it. After all, it was President White who, in those happy days, expelled a student for killing a chipmunk with his cane. . . .

With best wishes.

Sincerely,
E. B. White

To MILTON GREENSTEIN

North Brooklin, Maine
May 23, 1971

Dear Milt:

I have just received my second payment from Sagittarius Productions, so I have money to invest. I plan to give some of it away to Worthy Causes, and put the rest to work.

Have you any suggestion for U.S. bonds or Treasury notes?

I tried to spare you this inquiry by buying a book called "What Shall I Do With My Money?" by Eliot Janeway. But although I'm enjoying the book very much, I find that most of my enjoyment comes from mystification of a high order—I just don't understand what he is talking about. But I love to read about E bonds being a "legalized swindle." It's comforting to know that you can be taken, yet still remain solvent.

Now that fish are inedible because of mercury, I'm not sure that money has much meaning any more. I may just recycle my paper money. They can make egg cartons out of it, or cheap letterheads for the Wilderness Society.

Yrs,
Andy

To GENE DEITCH

North Brooklin
June 6, 1971

Dear Gene:

I've delayed answering your letter because I haven't known exactly what was going on in the Sagittarius world. Day before yesterday, Edgar Bronfman and Henry White showed up here bringing with them Joseph Barbera, and I learned that you were out of the picture and that the action had shifted to Hollywood and to Hanna-Barbera Productions. . . .

Even now I don't know what to say except to tell you how deeply sorry I am about what must be for you a disappointing and frustrating experience. As you know from my early letters in answer to the ones you wrote, I was uneasy from the start about certain aspects of your approach to the story and was unhappy about the small fragment of the treatment you sent. I felt that under the circumstances the proper thing to do was to transmit my reactions and complaints to you direct, and that's what I did in those letters. I realized, too, that it would be unfair to judge your finished work on such meager evidence as those few pages of treatment. Then later I learned from Jap Gude that others besides myself were uneasy, too.

I suppose some of my apprehensions and worries arose from my knowing so little about film-making. Some of them came perhaps from a too strong desire to have the book transmitted without change to the screen, even though I know enough to know that this never happens and can't happen. I was also concerned that the story not pick up meanings or implications that simply aren't there.

Anyway, I am truly sorry, Gene, that our brief encounter ends on a sad note. I had not anticipated any such thing, and I did all I knew how to do with my letters of advice and complaint. Perhaps they were more of a hindrance than a help, but they were written in good faith and high hopes, and I was rooting for you as I wrote them. At age 71, there's one thing I understand fully: the creative life is hell more than half the time, riddled with trials and terrors, and paved with woe. I know what it is like to try to bring something into being, as you've been doing the last few months. I know what an unhatched egg does to the spirit.

Katharine and I, sad and sorry, send our best to you and Zdenka, and our congratulations on your Golden Eagle.[1]

Yrs,
Andy

To **D. ANTHONY ENGLISH**

North Brooklin, Maine
June 21, 1971

Dear Mr. English:

. . . I'm not sure I can meet a mid-November deadline, but I'll try.[1] I would like to see the suggestions in Jack Case's file unless the material is bulky or voluminous. If it is, perhaps you'd better just send me a summary.

---

1. An award for excellence in film making.

1. Anthony English had taken over as editor for the revision of *The Elements of Style* after the death of Jack Case.

Another thing I'd like is your own ideas about what needs to be done. The book should not be drastically altered, I feel. This would rob it of its virtue. What chiefly needs doing is to remove certain passages that sound musty and replace them with passages that are in the modern accent. Example: "Winston tastes good" sounds old-hat nowadays—we might be able to come up with something recent and pertinent.

The book carries a word list (Chapter IV), and one obvious task is to add to this list and subtract from it. Any nominations you have will be gratefully received. There are always new, interesting words cropping up in our usage. "Flammable," for instance, should be in the book—a word devised to keep people from getting killed. And there are the new horribles, like "oriented" and "thrust" and "relevant" and "hopefully." . . .

Sincerely,
E. B. White

To **WILLIAM MAXWELL**

N. Brooklin
July 29 [1971]

Dear Bill:

For your kind words in Katharine's letter thanks. I was very pleased that you liked the piece,[1] as I came close to abandoning it after a couple of tries. You were the first person I heard from except Shawn, and I never can tell what Bill really thinks about a piece, he is so polite. One more barnyard story from me and the magazine will have to change its name to the *Rural New Yorker*.

My birds are shedding now, and I'm enclosing two feathers from the young gander; you can make them into pens for Kate and Brookie [Maxwell's daughters] so they will grow up to be writers. Am also enclosing three snapshots, which can be thrown away.

The goose I called Liz in the story hatched eight goslings a week ago. They were immediately adopted by their aunt and uncle, leaving their true parents with nothing but their memories. This was more than I could take in the way of domestic injustice, so I threw the young gander and Apathy in the clink and restored the baby geese to their mother and father. I run a complicated shop here—it makes Baby Lenore seem simple. One of the strange things that happened with the first brood about which I wrote was a return engagement between the old gander and the young gander. This took place on the day when the

---

1. "Letter from the East" (about geese) in *The New Yorker*, July 24, 1971.

little family was making its first trip to the pond—always a hazardous time on account of the cattle. I watched their progress down through the lane, then saw that the old gander, who had been nursing his wounds and broken pride for three or four days, was *also* watching their progress, only he was already down there in the pasture. He has, after all, had years of experience with cattle, and apparently the minute he realized that the young male who had deposed him was about to undertake the job of escorting the goslings through enemy lines, all his old wrath returned. He waited till the whole troupe came through the pasture bars, whereupon he threw himself on the young gander, beat the daylights out of him, reoccupied the throne, and stood off the steers and heifers while the goose and goslings hustled to the pond. As soon as they were safely afloat, he joined them. Oddly enough, so did the young gander after he had dusted himself off, and there was a temporary truce during the swimming hour. When the hour was up, the old boy escorted everybody back to the bars and the safety of the lane, and then returned into exile, reinstating the young leader. It was something. I would never have believed it if I hadn't witnessed the whole thing from start to finish. That old expression crazy-as-a-goose is invalid, without meaning, and void.

I didn't intend to inflict more of my weird tales on you. Just wanted to thank you. Best to Emmy and the girls.

Yrs,
Andy

To **WAYNE CHATTERTON**

[North Brooklin, Me.]
[early August? 1971]

Dear Mr. Chatterton:

Nothing Woollcott did or thought escaped notice.[1] He saw to that. His best writing, it seems to me, was his early drama criticism; his report on a play was usually instructive, clear, and balanced. As a teller of tales, I found him fancy, flirtatious, and repetitious. The one-time head of the *New Yorker*'s make-up department always referred to him as "Old Foolish."

There is a good short estimate of Woollcott in Brooks Atkinson's recent book "Broadway," beginning on page 161. Atkinson points out that he was "famous for his enthusiasms"—a true remark. In later years, when he went on radio, this natural enthusiasm of his rather

---

1. Professor Chatterton of Boise State College, Idaho, had written White for help on a biography of Alexander Woollcott.

got the better of him, and he became the darling of a whole continent-ful of sentimental old ladies, who could hardly wait for the next broadcast.

I'm not a good source on Woollcott—he was a bit before my time, and I did not attend the Round Table luncheons. There would be no point in talking with me about him—there are too many other people around who can speak with so much more authority and in so much more de-tail. All I know about Woollcott is what you can find in any reference library.

Sincerely,

E. B. White

To GRETA LEE AND PARKER BANZHAF

North Brooklin

August 21 [1971]

Dear Greta Lee and Parker:

This morning is hot and sticky, and I'm sitting here in the boathouse thinking of my sins and watching the tide creep in. When it gets to highwater mark where the telltale residue of rockweed shows where the last tide ended, I will walk out on the wharf carrying my rusty thermometer, take the temperature of the flood, and the tempera-ture will be 62°, and I will then walk back, replace the thermometer on its shelf, and resign myself to the idea of not taking a swim. Jones meanwhile will have taken one and will come indoors smelling of Jones.

The summer is all but gone, and it passes so quickly nowadays. Roger and his wife were nearby in a rented cottage in July, and we had many a visit with our new adoptive grandson, John Henry Angell, a merry, agreeable child. He had his first birthday here and is now (we are told) walking. I have allowed myself to be backed up against the wall and saddled with a new project—revising "The Elements of Style" for Macmillan, who want the stuff in time for spring publication, which means a November deadline. The book has grown whiskers and does need some attention, but it's not the kind of work I find easy or pleas-urable or both. Yesterday I worked on it all morning and ended up so dizzy I could hardly find my way through an ear of corn. K is very good about helping me, but in the end it is I who have to get it all down on paper. . . .

Haying is over, the barn swallows are packing their little bags for the trip south, and the race track at the Fair grounds is being groomed for the Labor Day weekend trotting. I have just about quit trying to drive an automobile and have shifted over to a bicycle, which is easier on my head even if harder on my seat. And that's the news—and as you see, there isn't any. Excuse a dull letter. It carries our love to all of you, as ever.

Andy

To HARRIET WALDEN

North Brooklin, Maine
3 September 1971

Dear Harriet:

Thank you for your characteristically prompt, dynamic, thrustful attention to my request for a copy of Bunny Wilson's *Uptight*. I can't thank you enough, but I can at least enclose my meaningful check for $12.20. (And now to remember to do so.) I am sure Katharine will be pleased with the gift, as she has expressed an almost overpowering desire for the book. Wilson is, after all, the Dean of American Letters— it now shows in his face. I am the Hall Porter of American Letters, and it is beginning to show in mine. (Blotches.)

I don't expect to come to New York "to deal with the publisher." The only way to deal with him would be to shoot him, and I don't want to spare the ammunition. The guy who got me embroiled in syntax and rhetoric is happily dead. His name was Jack Case and he was a very nice fellow although I've never forgiven him. This morning I devoted to The Hyphen. Most of what I know about grammar (or anything else) comes from reading newsbreaks, and I am going to explain the Hyphen by citing the sad case of the merger of two newspapers in Chattanooga, which came out to read: CHATTANOOGA NEWS-FREE PRESS. That's my favorite hyphen. It's even better than some of the hyphens in Fowler, if I do say so, and I do.

Mary McCarthy, the writer, stopped by here yesterday with her husband, Jim West, and her friend Hannah Arendt. They brought us some earthenware flower pots and a jar of crabapple jelly. They were on their way to dinner at the Yglesiases.[1]

. . . Thank you again for arranging the book affair. I can't imagine Edmund Wilson stapling a book bag, can you?

Yrs,
EBW

• *Eleanor Gould Packard, known at* The New Yorker *as Miss Gould, has been a copy editor and authority on grammar and style at the magazine for many years. When* The Elements of Style *first appeared, she had*

---

1. Writers José and Helen Yglesias are neighbors of the Whites'.

bought a copy, marked it up as she might mark a raw proof, and slid it into a drawer of her desk. White knew nothing about this—Miss Gould was too shy to admit doing it—but later, when The Elements *was up for revision, White asked her to help him. She agreed, and revealed that she had in her possession a marked-up first edition.*

To ELEANOR GOULD PACKARD

North Brooklin, Maine
12 September 1971

Dear Eleanor:

That isn't a millstone around your neck, it's a milestone. Of course I want to see the marked book. As near as I can make out, practically every grammarian in the land, irritated beyond belief by having an upstart crow like me edit a rulebook, grabbed "The Elements" before it had even cooled off and marked the bejesus out of it. Macmillan has already sent me the inflammatory reactions of *four* of these indignant pros, and I have dutifully sifted their cries of rage and scorn, incorporating a few in the text, hurling the others into the sea.

I would rather have yours than anybody else's, and if I had known that Macmillan planned to pay four teachers to take me and Strunk apart, I would have instantly suggested that they turn first to you. But I didn't know what was going on—they just sprung it on me. Even so, I may be able to wheedle a payment for you if you'll send me your marked copy.

I'm adding quite a few words and phrases to Chapter IV and am deleting a few. In general, I'm trying to hold the little book to its original size. Brevity is of the essence. As Strunk made clear in his introductory remarks, he was not attempting to survey the whole field.

Thanks for your recommendations for the list of reference books. Just what I need. I'm not familiar with the Bernstein books and don't know Bernstein. As for my "having fun with the revision," I would much rather be sorting the dirty clothes.

Yrs,
Andy White

To WAYNE CHATTERTON

[North Brooklin, Me.]
[early October? 1971]

Dear Mr. Chatterton:

I think the proper way for you to get clearance from me on quotes or paraphrasing is to show me the material when you get it on paper. This shouldn't be much of a burden, as my contribution is brief.

I had nothing to do with Profiles, but I know, in general, how they originated. A Profile was simply a sketch of a living person, pithy but in depth. It was a sort of photograph in words. A great many facts had to be assembled, and the facts had to be (and were) checked out. Sometimes, in the case of well-endowed writers, there could be a point-of-view, showing the subject in full color. (One of the great early Profiles was of Mike Romanoff, by Alva Johnston.) Gibbs did a Profile of Woollcott—not well received by the subject, I may add. *The New Yorker* demanded of a Profile writer brevity, wit, knowledge of the subject, and liveliness of expression. There was nothing particularly new or original about the form—it was simply that *The New Yorker* decided to do it better, and did.

I don't recall that Woollcott ever wrote a Profile, but probably he did. I doubt that his ornate style contributed anything to the form. Mostly, *The New Yorker* was trying to keep Woollcott from flouncing around. Ross and Woollcott were wartime buddies, but they had many fallings out. Woollcott was a prima donna, and Ross didn't want prima donnas around the place. Woollcott had mannerisms in writing—he liked to talk about "these old eyes" and he liked words like "reticule" and "tippet" —words that made Ross retch. When Ross decided to run a regular weekly column ("Shouts and Murmurs") by Woollcott, Ross made it clear he would have nothing to do with editing it—turned the whole business over to Katharine White, who, with an occasional assist from Gibbs, managed to keep the peace and get the column into the magazine. It was, incidentally, the only column *The New Yorker* ever ran that was "justified"—that is, made to come out to be a certain length, in this case exactly one page of type. This meant cutting or adding. Only time it ever happened, but Woollcott insisted on it and had his way.

I can't answer your question about the feasibility or value of a biography of F.P.A. I would imagine that any human being is a fit subject for a biography, given a biographer of sufficient power.

Sincerely,
E. B. White

To DAVID DODD

North Brooklin
October 27 [1971]

Dear Dave:

The boathouse is buzzing with flies this morning, warmed to a frenzy by the combined heat of Indian summer and my schoolhouse stove. The flies are hungry and are particularly fond of ankle meat, damn them. But I wish you could see this beautiful day—not a ripple on the bay, sunlight illuminating the maples and birches, which have hardly faded at all. No killing frost yet.

I'll

I have been busier than a monkey lately—in fact have worked every day, including Sundays and holidays, since the first of August, and am getting sick of work and would like to do a little playing. I'm still slugging away at a revision of "The Elements of Style" for Macmillan. I hate the guts of English grammar, but I agreed to revise the text for spring publication. Mid-November deadline. The only fun I get out of it is finding nutty sentences in the New York Times, like the one I spotted yesterday: "The first human sperm bank was officially opened Friday with semen samples from 18 men in a stainless steel refrigerator tank." (Those poor chilly fellows!) And I am also at work trying to get the bugs out of the screenplay of "Charlotte's Web," which was written by a Hollywood character whose knowledge of life on a New England farm is sub-marginal. When I finally can't take any more grammar or screenplay, I hop on my old 3-speed Raleigh bicycle and go scorching up and down the highway to remove the cobwebs. Am considering buying a helmet, against the day of the Great Crash. If I can fall asleep at the wheel of a Mercedes, I ought to be able to go bye-bye at the controls of a bike.

You will be pleased to learn that my trout began spawning yesterday. They are now more than a foot long, and since the brook up which they travel for their amorous sport has a depth of only about two inches, it is quite a sight. Their dorsal fins are fully exposed. But they are nothing if not game. I must try to get a picture to send you. . . .

Enough of this. Back to the grindstone. Love to you and Elsie from the both of us.

Yrs,
Andy

• *White worked over the screenplay for the movie version of* Charlotte's Web *for ten days, annotating it carefully. Hanna-Barbera, however, paid little attention to his suggestions.*

To J. G. GUDE

[North Brooklin, Me.]
8 November 1971

Dear Jap:

I found your letter that I had misplaced. Don't worry about the pig's tail drooping. Droop it does.

The security blanket strikes me as sour. It also seems to be lifted from "Peanuts," where the blanket is almost a daily feature. Do we have to borrow from Schulz? I think not and I think the blanket is not in the spirit of *Ch Web*.

Briefly, my recommendations are

1. Cut out the dream sequence.

2. Transpose the Dr. Dorian visit so it takes place *after* the word has appeared in the web.

3. Cut the corn out of Henry Fussy and his mother and that violin.

4. Play the award scene at the Fair for all it's worth. The pig should faint, Lurvy should dash water on Avery, Avery should clown it up, and the rat should revive the pig by biting his tail. Children know this incident very well indeed and they will feel cheated if they don't get it. Also, it's very lively.

5. Let the story teller say the words that announce the death of Charlotte. It is the last paragraph of Chapter XXI.

As I look back on the screenplay, it strikes me that not enough faith is placed in the barn and the animals and the web, and this results in quite a buildup of Henry Fussy and boy-meets-girl. K had the same reaction, and she feels strongly about it. Anyway, *Charlotte's Web* is not a boy-girl story, it is a study of miracles, tinged with the faint but pervasive odor of the barn. It will stand or fall on the barn. Henry Fussy can't save it.

Yrs,
Andy

To MAURICE ROOT

North Brooklin, Maine
15 November 1971

Dear Dr. Root:

I am sorry this reply is so long in coming. . . .

Does the aging brain function better after it accomplishes something? Well, I have been watching the aging brain out of the corner of one eye for about twenty years, and I don't think I have the answer to that question. . . .

As for writing, I still write—at age 72. My experience is that I have to struggle harder, tire sooner, and come apart at the seams more completely than was the case when I was young. The aging mind has a bagful of nasty tricks, one of which is to tuck names and words away in crannies where they are not immediately available and where I can't always find them. This is extremely annoying to a writer, who wants his words where he can reach them.

When I want to experience a small success these days, I seldom turn to the typewriter; I go out to my workbench and remodel an Express Wagon for a grandson. I find in simple carpentry a chance to slow my aging mind down to a walk. Really the great trouble about the mind, whether aging or not, is that it is always on the go, like a restless person. But, as I say, I can't answer your question. I hope my mind never rusts out completely, but I've already seen the early signs of it, as one sees them on the side of an automobile where a dog has scratched or a coat button struck home.

Sincerely,
E. B. White

• *White had been awarded the National Medal for Literature; it was to be presented at ceremonies at Lincoln Center on December 2. William Maxwell stood in for him and read a prepared speech of acceptance. John Updike showed up and delivered some remarks, as did Cass Canfield.*

To **WILLIAM MAXWELL**

North Brooklin
November 19 [1971]

Dear Bill:

As you've probably discovered by now, I've been tapped to receive the medal of the National Book Committee. I don't feel well enough to make the trip to New York to receive the award on December 2, and when I was talking to Ursula Nordstrom on the phone I had the temerity to drop your name as a possible stand-in for me. This is a dirty trick to play on anyone, and I don't want you to give the matter a second thought if the idea is repulsive to you. I think Roger would be glad to reach out and grab the medal for me. And a letter that has just arrived from Ursula says that somebody had suggested Updike. So there isn't going to be any problem. I just don't want you to feel the slightest obligation in case you get approached. I seldom play dirty tricks on my friends, but I'm not always steady and reliable over the telephone. I don't really think fast enough to be allowed to use the telephone.

Yrs,
Andy

To **JOHN UPDIKE**

North Brooklin
December 11 [1971]

Dear John:

Children, on the whole, have an easier time summing me up than you did. I got a letter from a girl this week, saying, "You are a good writer and I was enjoying your book until our dog, Bella, ate it. It was only a paperback." (Writers have so much to contend with—I now have this dog, Bella.) Another child wrote and said, "It is easy to know what you are from reading your books, you are a veterinary, a teacher, and a nomad." You see? I'm no problem.

Your eulogistic ramble, which gave me immense pleasure and satisfaction, arrived in this house about forty minutes after a stomach bug. That's why you haven't heard from me sooner. I saw my comical wife scratching off a couple of notes to you, to keep your courage up, and I hope you realize how much it meant to me that you went to New York and testified. Bill Maxwell phoned me that same evening to report in. He said you began to stutter, and the more you stuttered the more effective you became. Today, I began brooding happily about the effect of a stutter on those deathless lines of mine: "In the days of my youth . . ." All you had to do was repeat West Twelfth Street a couple of times and I'd soon be up to Thirty-sixth Street writhing with Truth near where the old Rogers Peet used to be. Anyway, I've always liked that poem ["Village Revisited"], when no one was looking, and I'm glad you worked it into the text.

It is difficult for me to believe that your mother bought a farm on the strength of reading "One Man's Meat." It is very scary—to realize what can happen. But if I never did anything in my life but discomfort you with apples and start your wheels turning, I have served American letters as well as any man could hope for. You say you can't remember what I said when Katharine and I showed up at your place in Oxford. I can't either, but I would be willing to bet that I came through the door apologizing for the liveried chauffeur. He was my first liveried chauffeur (his name was 'arry 'unt), and I recall feeling acutely embarrassed at pulling this sort of elegance on a young man who hadn't even had time to write "Poorhouse Fair." I also remember demanding gin at a restaurant where it wasn't readily available. Children are right—I'm just a nomad.

I can't pronounce *oeuvre* and the word has never appeared in my corpus, as I am unwilling to use any word I can't pronounce. (Another word I can't pronounce is *genre*, which I call John; and *genre* has never appeared, either.) So I was glad you worked *oeuvre* in, as it set me right back where I belong, among the flashy illiterates—medalists who ought to turn in their medals. Writers really take their worst shellacking from other writers, like the one you and I took from Rex Stout the other day [in a newspaper interview] when he said you were being pretentious with the title Redux and that although my stuff didn't amount to much I never made a mistake. Wait till Bella catches up with Stout!

And speaking of children, please give my love to your ten-year-old daughter who supplied you with the line I cherish most among all the words of praise you spent so freely and so movingly. I was really touched and heartened by your piece, and particularly by what you said about Katharine, who should get medals but doesn't.

I must tell you about the next oddity that is shaping up in my life. A madman named Reginald Allen, whom you may know, has persuaded the Philadelphia Orchestra to put on a children's number based on "The Trumpet of the Swan." It is scheduled for May 13. I cut the story to four typewritten pages (which should earn me a job with the *Reader's Digest*), and the music is now under construction. Allen told me I would simply *have* to come to Philadelphia for the occasion, and to nip this in the bud I wrote back that I would come only if I were allowed to play a musical instrument with the Orchestra. I figured this would stop him cold. Not at all, he has it all arranged: White on triangle. I can already envision what will happen if I have the bad judgment to accept this larkish invitation. May 13 will be the day the Domino Theory is proved in Philadelphia. I will start drinking early to brace myself for the platform appearance, and just before my one note on the triangle comes due, I will slump forward, dead. My music-stand will catch the bassoonist in the groin, and he will take out all the rest of the wood winds, and the wood winds will take out the brasses and the brasses will take out the strings. It will be like the scene in the book, when the old cob breaks up a music store in Billings. (I keep thinking of good ways to die, and this now heads my list.)

I have taken enough of your valuable time. Thank you, thank you, John, for your kind words of 2 December. They meant a lot to me and always will.

Yrs,
Andy

To WILLIAM MAXWELL

[North Brooklin, Me.]
December 22 [1971]

Dear Bill:

I woke this morning with the horrid feeling that I had never written you a note thanking you for standing in for me and reading that acceptance speech. I'm at the age now when a man suffers from what is called "short memory"—which means he can remember what he did in 1905 but can't for the life of him recall what he did day before yesterday. I can't remember, two minutes after swallowing a pill, whether or not I took the pill. I now keep a chart and make a check mark after a swallowed pill.

Anyway, I do thank you, from the b. of my h. According to Ursula Nordstrom, from whom I've just had a letter, you shone with an unearthly beauty as you stood there. "He stood so quietly, and he looked absolutely beautiful . . . He seemed to have effaced himself completely." Well, I'm glad you didn't thrash about. And everybody knows I picked you for your looks. I trust Emmy still finds you beautiful.

If this is the *second* letter of thanks you've received from me, for God's sake forgive a weavy old man his excesses. And Merry Christmas to all.

Yrs,
Andy

To MARILYN BONDY

North Brooklin, Maine
January 2, 1972

Dear Mrs. Bondy:

Thanks for your very kind letter.

You asked whether Charlotte was modelled after someone I knew. Yes, she was modelled after a large grey spider that I knew pretty well. I used to watch her at her weaving and at her trapping, and I even managed to be present when she constructed her egg sac and deposited her eggs. Her name was Charlotte, and I got quite interested in her, and was sorry to have her go. I also had, on this place, a young pig, an old rat, and some sheep and some geese. Altogether, I was in a very favorable position to write a book called "Charlotte's Web." I'm very glad I did, and I'm very glad you liked it.

Sincerely,
E. B. White

To J. G. GUDE

[North Brooklin, Me.]
January 5, 1972

Dear Jap:

Thanks for sending the record. Do you want it back?

I hope Sagittarius has noted that 1972 is the Year of the Rat. A good omen, considering Templeton's role in our lives.

As for the brothers Sherman and their music, I'll withhold judgment. Some of the songs failed to suggest "Charlotte's Web" to me, and there was a noticeable Irish flavor here and there. I have a few suggestions and queries.

Wilbur sings, "I can talk, I can talk . . ." Well, the ability to communicate is implicit in the book. To make it into a *discovery* strikes me just wrong. I regard this song as not only out of key with the story but embarrassingly suggestive of Rex Harrison, whom Wilbur in no way resembles. If a song is needed in this spot, it should be Fern's song: she sings, very quietly, "I can hear him. He speaks."

What happened to the lullaby "Deep in the dung and the dark"? Lyric by that sweet singer E. B. White. Many composers have dreamed up music for those words, but apparently the Shermans have let the thing lay. Why? I won't go to any movie that doesn't have Charlotte singing "Deep in the dung and the dark." Not even on a free ticket.

The song "Zuckerman's Pig" sounds like the Irish to my ear. Instead, it should carry the lively sounds of a New England country fair.

I liked the melody "How very special are we/For just a moment to be . . ." It stayed with me and seemed on the right track and in the right spirit.

Charlotte's death and, later, the hatching of the young spiders in spring should be turned over to Mozart, for background music. There is an old Columbia Masterworks record that I own and cherish: "Quartet in F Major, for oboe, violin, and violoncello—Leon Goosens on oboe." The adagio movement of that quartet (just a strain or two) would be the perfect accompaniment for the death of the spider, interlarded with the distant music of the Fair. And the rondo is so bright, hopeful, and cheerful it would be perfect for the resurrection—the hatching of the little spiders in spring. The oboe has a flutelike sound that would be just right for this pastoral story. I'll be glad to loan anybody this record, if anybody is interested. Mozart clearly had the "Web" in mind when he wrote "Quartet in F Major."

Take heart! In the Year of the Rat, anything can happen. I could even smuggle Mozart into Hollywood.

Yrs,
Andy

• *Nathaniel Benchley had caught White in a misstatement about their mutual friend the late John McNulty, who had written a song called "Keep Your Dreams Within Reason." White had stated that the song had not got beyond the title stage—was just something McNulty intended to write. Benchley, who had heard the song sung at Barry Fitzgerald's house, wrote to set the record straight.*

To NATHANIEL BENCHLEY

North Brooklin, Maine
January 27, 1972

Dear Nat:

From the depths of my embarrassment I rise to thank you for the correction. It was good to hear from you. The lyrics strike me as something less than deathless, but their author is deathless as far as I am concerned—he pops up almost every day in one form or another, usually when I hear someone say something that I think he ought to hear, would cherish.

A club should probably be formed, membership limited to persons who were taken by McNulty to Barry Fitzgerald's house. I am eligible for this club, even though in my whole life I have spent only about twenty-six hours in Hollywood. In the spring of 1945 I was in San Francisco, observing the formation of the United Nations for *The New Yorker*. John got wind of this and suggested that I return to New York via Hollywood, which I was glad to do because it meant a longer rail journey. John met me at the station, wined and dined me at Chasen's (at I think Chasen's expense), then off to Fitzgerald's and the piano and the tall glasses. I slept at the house of a screen-writer whose name escapes me, and I remember waking with a real stinger and trying to shave while standing on a bathroom rug made of a zebra's hide. McNulty roused himself and took me off to breakfast, where he plied me with eggs. He said he was a great believer in eggs. (At moments like that I believe only in sudden death.)

It seems unlikely that the session at Fitzgerald's failed to include a rendering of "Keep your dreams within reason," but although the title was well known to me the lyrics probably failed to work their way through to my reception center. I wish you would write me a letter telling me that another song of that era got written: one that Thurber dreamed up and that I was supposed to put to music, "You're the sugar in my urine, you're the murmur in my heart." We never did anything about it, beyond enjoying the general idea. It ought to go over big today, with everybody sick and all.

Thanks again. And keep your d. within r., Baby.

Yrs,
Andy

To **DAVID DODD**

North Brooklin
13 February [1972]

Dear Dave:

This is one of those sultry Sunday afternoons when we sit around waiting to see whether it's going to rain or snow. Skies are grey, every bone in my body foretells the approaching storm, the thermometer has inched up to forty, Jones is asleep four feet away on my couch, a small wood blaze snickers in the fireplace, the geese are skating on the pasture pond waiting for the thaw, K has just climbed the stairs to her bedroom for a snooze, and I am marking time until chores, when I will round up the geese, collect the eggs, water the hens, fill the woodbox, empty the garbage, pull the slide in the henpen, load the bird feeder, lay a fire in the living room, feed the dogs, carry the eggs to the arch in the cellar, and lie down for half an hour preparatory to mixing a drink. I figure the best way to mark time is to write you a letter and thank you for your detailed report on Siesta Key [in Sarasota] and for the clippings. I had to laugh when I got to the story of the Arvida hearing,[1] which the Mayor sat out in the Intensive Care unit of the Hospital. If Sarasota had had a modicum of intensive care about thirty or forty years ago, it might be a far fairer city today—and the fishing might be better, too. I miss the early times of Fiddler Bayou, the years when K and I occupied the Achterlonie house and really enjoyed ourselves. There were no condominiums, and everybody had plenty of time of day. And when the sun failed to shine, we lay peacefully listening to the rain.

This morning it was like a spring day here, the ground bare and a definite feeling of change. About ten days ago we had a tremendous gale. Our power was gone most of the night, trees went down, and the Deer Isle Bridge pulled a tendon. It's a lofty bridge, and when it gets slatting around in a high wind it seems to lose its cool. All schools on the Island and in the adjacent mainland towns were closed for a week because parents didn't want their children bussed back and forth across a wobbly bridge. Even now, traffic is limited to a maximum of twenty tons. The designers of the bridge flew on to have a look, and as yet nobody knows just what's going to happen. But there is always *something* happening in Brooklin.

I don't much care for a bare winter like this one. It seems unnatural and uncozy. Last winter, for all its roughness, was more satisfying to the spirit. And there was less sickness when we were under mountains of snow. In one respect, though, we're ahead of where we were a year ago—ten cords of wood have been cut and hauled out. My neighbor, Russell Smith, trailed his saw into the yard a few days ago, and the whole ten cords were fed into the saw while the single-cylinder engine pounded its heart out and the sticks came tumbling off the arbor. Henry [Allen] put on, Russell sawed, and Alan [Smith] took off; and we now have a magnificent pile of wood, ready to be fitted. Susy loves to climb to the summit, for the view.

(Time out for chores)

I also wound the clocks, this being Sunday. Susy has now joined Jones on the couch, and they are tussling. She wants to tussle more than he does, so they compromise. Susy is my barn dog and is allowed in the

---

1. Arvida, a development company, was often the center of controversy.

house only on special occasions and under special surveillance—to make certain she doesn't tear a little hole in K's non-reparable skin.

K is deep in garden catalogues. The south windows in the living room are already abloom with forced freesias—a triumph. My chick order is in, for April delivery. My revision of "The Elements" is in the works, and I learned the other day that Debbie Reynolds is to be the voice of Charlotte in the movie. Whether that's good news or not I do not know. 1971 was a year of pain, pressure, and peril for me, and I'm glad it's over. I've never had such a bad time, never made more money, never done so few things that I wanted to do. Maybe 1972 will level off. I miss fishing with you, which always gave a note of sanity to my otherwise disturbed life. I worry about your infirmities—you always seemed so firm to me compared to myself—and I hope they are quieted down. Glad you've had good weather and hope the fishing will pick up before you have to leave for the north.

K joins me in sending love to you and Elsie.

Yrs,
Andy

To WILLIAM MAXWELL

N Brooklin
March 27 [1972]

Dear Bill:

Sorry I didn't see you on my brief visit [to New York], and thanks for your note. My trip was a complete mess from start to finish. At Back Bay station, where ghosts spend the night, I asked the porter why the train didn't come and didn't come. "They can't find a engine," he said.

Yrs,
Andy

To ROGER ANGELL

North Brooklin
15 May [1972]

Dear Rog:

The tardiness and general inadequacy of this note of thanks for "The Summer Game"[1] can be laid to my being unable to pry the book out of the arms of the author's mother, where it is cradled day and night. She is a baseball nut and devoted parent. The hold she has on the book re-

---

1. A collection of baseball pieces by Angell.

minds me of the way Elsie hung on to her handbag in the hospital—I saw powerful nurses try to get it away from the bed, but they never succeeded. Same way with K and "The Summer Game." I'll get it eventually, though, by some clever ruse or sheer force. I have, of course, caught *glimpses* of the book, and it strikes me that physically it is a beautiful thing. That's a marvelous jacket, and you're lucky, because marvelous jackets don't grow on publisher's trees, in my experience. And I have, of course, pleasant memories of reading the pieces in the book when they appeared, so I'll just go ahead and thank you as though I had been curled up with the book all along.

I liked the Larry Merchant review. And I will be tuned to the Today Show on the 29th to see whether you look as gaunt at that hour as Barbara Walters does. You asked whether an appearance on the show sells books. I don't know for sure, but somebody once told me that when that magical moment comes and the book is actually held up so the camera can see it, it touches off an explosion all over America. I can believe it. There are millions of Americans who feel that it would be a nice thing—a cultural thing—to own a book; but they can't *think* of a book. When they see a real live book on the tube, their problem is solved for them. Doesn't make any difference what the title is, it's a clue.

A couple of magnificent events have taken place here in the last 24 hours. Yesterday morning, out in the plantroom, the egg case of a praying mantis was breached by the inmates and about fifty baby mantises emerged, loaded for bear—loaded, really, for aphids and other tiny pests. Today, right after breakfast, four dump trucks arrived, one after another, and deposited 20 yards of barn dressing (cow manure . . .) at the edge of our vegetable garden. I have been working on this project for a solid month and finally brought it off. The place has an entirely new, authentic appearance, with these battlements of brown dung looming in the north. As for the mantises, I doubt that they'll survive, as there is nothing much to eat out there—K and Henry keep their plants and seedlings so clean. A baby mantis is about three-quarters of an inch long and looks exactly like a common pin that has six legs and a pair of tiny hands clasped in prayer. The ferocity of them is awesome. I produced a tiny fly from the bell of a daffodil and presented it to the hungry hordes. One of them leapt on it like a tiger making the kill—never saw such a bloodthirsty infant.

It's pretty here now, but the spring is late. Hope your baseball trip goes well, and thanks again for the book about same. Love to Carol and JH.

Yrs,
Andy

To W. B. HARRIS

[North Brooklin, Me.]

[May 1972]

Dear Mr. Harris:

Katharine has been having a poor run of health, and she has asked me to write to you, thanking you for the letter and the piece in *Encounter*. When I asked her if she wished to comment on your suggestion about *The New Yorker*, she replied, "No."

I can interpret this response for you, easily and quickly. *The New Yorker* has never been a magazine of consensus—it has always been a one-man show. Under Ross, it was Ross's weekly. Under Shawn, it is Shawn's weekly. Both Katharine and I, who have labored long and hard in the vineyard, approve of this. Dozens of magazines on the newsstands are edited not by a man but by a sort of pulse-machine, and by and large they don't amount to much. *The New Yorker*, for all its crotchets, amounts to a great deal. Neither Katharine nor I would swap it for anything that is going round. This doesn't mean we like everything we see in print, it means we approve of the control by an editor. If you have suggestions for improving the content, send them to the editor. To send them to Katharine is hard on her and, in general, ineffectual, since she is no longer in the counsels of *The New Yorker*.

Sincerely,

E. B. White

To MASON TROWBRIDGE

North Brooklin

November 18 [1972]

Dear Mason:

I was pleased to get your long letter covering wire platforms, debeaking, coccidiosis, Belgian endive, root cellars, perpetual motion, connubial bliss, pernicious anemia, B-12, chicken lettuce, whooping cranes and Scott Nearing. Almost, if not quite, in that order.

You asked, very kindly, how things were going with me. They are going all right, because I am now 73, and a man who is 73 and still up and around is doing all right. I have had a frog in my throat for quite some time now, and of course with me this develops almost instantly into cancer of the larynx, because that's the way I am built. A barium swallow (no relation of the barn swallow and every bit as messy) revealed that I was afflicted with *globus hystericus*. I visited Dr. Gaillard in Bangor under the impression that he would pass a laryngoscope down my throat, but he refused the jump and simply gazed down through his little mirror. He informed me that *globus*, or "frog," could cut off the blood supply to the lining of the stomach, bringing on an ulcer. But I had him there. I already *have* a duodenal ulcer, and therefore am in a position to fight fire with fire. The Bangor *Daily News* says I am dead anyway. In an article about "skipped" beats, or premature ventricular heartbeats, which I now experience, the *News* reported that this condition precedes fatal disturbances. And so it goes. I go cycling every day, not for the exercise but because I enjoy cycling—particularly on ice, which is challenging.

I solved perpetual motion last July when my youngest grandson gave me a guinea chick on my birthday. The chick was only three days old and he, or she, immediately accepted me as his, or her, mother. I still function in that capacity. The guinea is now full grown, in full plumage, and in perpetual motion. He hates my bicycle, mounts me when I kneel, chases cars and trucks, gooses my terriers, and befouls my woodshed. Except at night when he is roosting, his head is never still a minute. And his curiosity is insatiable. I named him Jack, and in another couple of months he will probably be laying eggs—which I won't know what to do with. . . .

Gaillard told me that rather than pay the phone company an extra charge, you dug a hole in your living room floor so Jeem [Mrs. Trowbridge] could hand the telephone down to you when you were in the root cellar. Is that true? I would like to think that it is.

Burn this.

Yrs,
Andy

P.S. Now that you are out of the chicken business, you can savor the pleasures of keeping waterfowl on your place. In the spring I should be in the position to start you off with three or four green goslings from my incomparable goose Felicity, who laid 42 eggs in the 1971 season and 41 in the 1972. Geese are great to have around, because they stir the air. They are sagacious, contentious, storm-loving, and beautiful. They are natural hecklers, delight in arguing a point, and are possessed of a truly remarkable sense of ingratitude. They never fail to greet you on your arrival, and the greeting is tinged with distaste and sarcasm. They take parenthood seriously, are protective of their young but never indulgent. When my young gander is impatient for grain, he seizes the food-box in his mouth and bangs it against the wall, and this racket can be heard all over the place. You've never seen a hen do anything like that. Another fine thing about geese is that they are as easily steered as a modern car—a great convenience. Their bowel activity is, of course, legendary.

To FAY RABINOWITZ

North Brooklin, Maine
December 8, 1972

Dear Mrs. Rabinowitz:

I think less than nothing of some of the letters I get, but yours amused me, and I was glad to know that Wilbur's retort stimulates your jaded math students.[1] I am glad to participate in the great work of education. I sometimes even wish I had an education myself, but it's too late now.

Many thanks for writing.

Sincerely,
E. B. White

• *While hospitalized with labyrinthitis, White received the news of the death, in New York, of his old friend Robert M. Coates.*

To ASTRID P. COATES

North Brooklin, Maine
February 27, 1973

Dear Boo:

. . . The saddest day of all in the hospital was the day K phoned to tell me that Bob had died. I have thought about you a great deal since, even though I haven't mustered the courage to write. The one comforting thing was that I knew you were in the hands of Jap and Helen. I don't know what is going to happen to this benighted world if the Gudes ever disappear, those lovely and indefatigable friends to all those in trouble and in despair. I lay there in the hospital thinking about Bob by the hour, what he looked like, the sound of his inimitable voice, and all the days and times I had known with him from away back—the good days, the early times, the Village years, the Gaylordsville Saturday nights when all was young and gay, and Bob shining like a great red lantern over everybody and everything, with his mind darting about like a swallow in air. I had quite a few friends in those days, and they fell pretty much into two classes—the ones I treasured for one reason or another but didn't particularly want to be with (for one reason or another) and the ones I treasured and could never get enough of. Bob belonged to that second group, and I never remember seeing him approaching in corridor

---

1. In *Charlotte's Web*, Wilbur challenges the phrase "less than nothing": "What do you mean, *less* than nothing? I don't think there is any such thing as *less* than nothing. Nothing is absolutely the limit of nothingness. It's the lowest you can go. . . ."

or street but what my heart leapt up at the sight. Bob looked the way Hemingway would *like* to have looked. One was real, the other ersatz. And I remember how proud and happy I felt the day Bob came to visit me in my cubicle to say that he had liked my piece "The Door" and how pleased he was with the word "ugliproof." I remember that. A young writer doesn't forget things like that, no matter how old he gets. I guess if I had been born a girl I would have fallen madly in love with Bob—I don't see how I could have escaped. For a man of his talents, he had the least side and the most natural modesty I've ever known in a writing man. I shall always miss him and shall always love him in memory. And my love goes out to you and I hope you are well and strong and doing all right. You must have had a terrible time at the last of it, and I think of that too.

We've had bright, cold days lately—a relief. The winter has been mostly a bad one and a bare one. I'm ready for spring, and so are my geese, who can't wait. K is doing pretty well, and sends love, as I do, and a plea for forgiveness at not having written sooner.

Yrs,
Andy

•   *A friend of Reginald Allen's had presented him with twelve wood duck eggs. Allen ended up bringing the eggs to White for hatching. With the help of two bantam hens, White hatched five ducklings, but none survived.*

To REGINALD ALLEN

North Brooklin
March 5 [1973]

Dear Reggie:

You have colored me green. I am a brilliant green with envy over your clutch of Wood Duck eggs. What a prospect! What a promise of spring!

I am writing, though, to sound a gentle note of warning about this broody bantam that is to accompany the shipment of eggs. I have had a lifetime of experience with broody hens, and if there is any more unpredictable female, I don't know what it is. Sometimes, moving a broody as much as fifteen feet from her accustomed location will cause her to become unstuck, and she will take one look at the clutch of eggs and scream, "What's THAT?" Then she will take off into the sunset, scattering your dreams as she goes.

I acquired my first broody hen in 1911, when I was eleven years old, and I can see her now. She was a Black Minorca—in temperament much like a Leghorn, just a bundle of nerves. I had my fertile eggs all ready for her, but I made the mistake of moving her in the daylight hours, and when I placed her lovingly upon the eggs, she rose in a tremendous burst of passionate disgust and disappeared into a neighbor's yard. How I ever managed to corral her and persuade her back onto the eggs will always remain a mystery, but I did, and she hatched the eggs. Ever since that episode I have been at pains always to move a broody under cover of darkness, when she is blind and doesn't know what is happening. Even so, I have not always succeeded.

I am writing all this not to scare you but to comfort you. I have seventeen laying hens, and in the springtime my henpen usually harbors a broody or two. So I want you to count on me as your backup man, in case anything goes wrong. I can come sneaking over to your place in the dead of night, bearing a mesmerized female, all ready to settle down on duck eggs. I also have a neighbor four miles up the road who has a few bantams, and a bantam hen is almost certain to get broody in the spring —also a bantam is a better size for Wood Duck eggs than a standard hen. In any event, I shall not be able to sleep at night until I know that this incubation project is successfully launched. An unhatched egg is to me the greatest challenge in life.

What kind of nest are you planning on? What location? How high above ground level? What nesting material? And what about humidity? All these things should be occupying your thoughts to the exclusion of everything else.

I am at your side.

Yrs,
Andy

• *The letter that follows was in answer to one White received from some students of children's literature, complaining about* The Trumpet of the Swan. *The students said the book contained inconsistencies and contradictions, and lacked "innocence." They didn't like the violence or the emphasis on money.*

To CHILDHOOD REVISITED CLASS

[North Brooklin, Me.]
March 9, 1973

Dear Anne and Meg and Barbara:

I can't speak for other authors. In my case, I got into writing for children ("Stuart Little") by accident, and I persisted because I found it both pleasurable and profitable.

There was no "preparation" for writing "Stuart Little." I did no research. The story was written, episode by episode, over a period of about twelve years, for home consumption. I had nephews and nieces who wanted me to tell them a story, and that's the way I went about it. Book publication was not in my mind.

"Charlotte's Web" was different. I had moved to the country, had experienced the pleasures of a barnyard and a barn, and had introduced sheep, geese, and a pig into the scene. (The rat and the spider moved in without help from me.) I conceived the idea for the story, and by that time I was well acquainted with the principal characters. Before attempting the book, however, I studied spiders and boned up on them. I watched Charlotte at work, here on my place, and I also read books about the life of spiders, to inform myself about their habits, their capabilities, their temperament. It took me two years to write the story. Having finished it, I found I was dissatisfied with it, so instead of submitting it to my publisher, I laid it aside for a while, then rewrote it, introducing Fern and other characters. This took a year, but it was a year well spent.

I can't say whether my style and attitude changed between the writing of "Charlotte's Web" and the writing of "The Trumpet of the Swan." I was almost seventy when I began "The Trumpet." Like Louis, I needed money. Perhaps a man loses his innocence at seventy—I don't know. I had to do a great deal of research for the book because I had never seen a trumpeter swan and, in fact, would not have dared write about the swans at all if I had not been familiar with geese. A man who is dealing in fantasy doesn't worry about contradictions or inconsistencies. It is true, as you point out, that a swan, equipped as he is with an inflexible bill, would be unable to blow a trumpet. But I leapt lightly over that hurdle: I wanted a Trumpeter Swan who could play like Louis Armstrong, and I simply created him and named him Louis. The cutting of the webs between his toes is also fantastical, just as the bird itself is; I introduced it partly to tell a little bit about the horn and its valves, partly because I thought it an amusing incident. It showed, moreover, that Louis was willing to make a personal sacrifice in order to achieve his goal.

I don't think there is any more violence in "The Trumpet of the Swan" than in my other books. You can't have a big bird crashing his way into a music store to steal a horn without stirring up a bit of trouble. The episode is essentially violent in its very nature. As for whether realism and honesty are "good for a young child," I don't pretend to know what is good, what is bad. I go by my instinct. I write largely for myself and am content to believe that what is good enough for me is good enough for a youngster. If "The Trumpet" differs from the other two books, I think it is because perhaps it presupposes a greater maturity in the reader. (I am always distressed when I hear of a second grade teacher reading "The Trumpet" to her class—it really belongs more in the fourth and fifth grade level.) It is a love story. "Charlotte" was a story of friendship, life, death, salvation. "Stuart Little" was a story of a quest—the quest for beauty.

As for the emphasis on money, I think it was Jane Austen who said there were only two things in the world worth writing about—love and money. Louis had both problems. I offer no apology.

Thanks for your letter. I hope I've answered some of your questions.

Sincerely,
E. B. White

To MISS R——

North Brooklin, Maine
March 11, 1973

Dear Miss R——:

That letter may have got out of hand, but it was quite a letter just the same, and I was pleased to receive it.

I still love New York, or rather I love the memory of love for New York as it was when I was young. I don't believe I could live there happily now. When I wrote the piece ["Here Is New York"], in the summer of 1948, the city was already beginning to show a different face from the one I knew and loved. I think the most unfortunate thing that is happening to Manhattan is the steady replacement of small, old buildings (many of which were homes) by large, modern buildings, most of which are offices. If this continues to happen, the city will become simply a vast mercantile house. I don't think any of our mayors have quite come to grips with this problem.

I am old now. It is heartening to see by your letter that New York still has the power to enchant and inspire the young. When a city loses that, it will have lost all that is worth while in a city. I did indeed love it in my day, and it meant a great deal to me as a young man. I loved the little apartments in the Village where I lived and worked. I loved the sounds and the smells. I loved Turtle Bay and its interior garden, with its tulips and daffodils and migratory birds in the spring. As far as I know, the old willow tree still stands there, ready to leaf out at the first sign of warmth.

Many thanks for writing.

Sincerely,
E. B. White

To SUSANNA WATERMAN

North Brooklin, Maine
March 26, 1973

Dear Susy:

Your letter came dashing in just as I had sealed the envelope of a letter I had written Stan. It was a near thing.

I'm sorry that you have been having a sad time with deaths of friends and relatives, and I hope you are not spending too much time assessing your "place in the continuum" but are just out there in the rain with no shoes on as usual. I had to look up "continuum" to find out what it was. My dictionary says it is a continuous succession, no part of which can be distinguished from neighboring parts. The whole thing seems fraudulent to me, because I know perfectly well that I would always be able to spot you no matter how indistinguishable you were trying to be. I could tell you from neighboring parts, in a flash. . . .

Receiving a letter from you is a double pleasure: there is the message itself, and there is the handwriting—which makes each word look as though it had been etched in the ice of a pond by a very fine skater. I shall get your handwriting analyzed some day to see what it means; it must mean *something*. My own handwriting simply means that I have been drinking and had better use a typewriter if I know what's good for me.

Yesterday was a lovely spring day here, with snowdrops in bloom under the brush cover of the borders, and a touch of green showing. So what did I do to celebrate? I fell down. Foot slipped on a tiny patch of frosty ground and down I went very fast and hard. I had a 6-foot rule in one hand, and a clipboard in the other. It shook me up and hurt my back, but I broke nothing and am lucky. The rites of spring!

The movie of Charlotte is about what I expected it to be. The story is interrupted every few minutes so that somebody can sing a jolly song. I don't care much for jolly songs. The Blue Hill Fair, which I tried to report faithfully in the book, has become a Disney world, with 76 trombones. But that's what you get for getting embroiled with Hollywood.

Thanks again, and I hope we will be seeing you and Stan soon, at the edge of summer.

Love,
Andy

To MR. NADEAU

North Brooklin, Maine
30 March 1973

Dear Mr. Nadeau:

As long as there is one upright man, as long as there is one compassionate woman, the contagion may spread and the scene is not desolate. Hope is the thing that is left to us, in a bad time. I shall get up Sunday morning and wind the clock, as a contribution to order and steadfastness.

Sailors have an expression about the weather: they say, the weather is a great bluffer. I guess the same is true of our human society—things can look dark, then a break shows in the clouds, and all is changed, sometimes rather suddenly. It is quite obvious that the human race has made a queer mess of life on this planet. But as a people we probably harbor seeds of goodness that have lain for a long time, waiting to sprout when the conditions are right. Man's curiosity, his relentlessness, his inventiveness, his ingenuity have led him into deep trouble. We can only hope that these same traits will enable him to claw his way out.

Hang on to your hat. Hang on to your hope. And wind the clock, for tomorrow is another day.

Sincerely,
E. B. White

To SOME SIXTH-GRADERS IN LOS ANGELES

[North Brooklin, Me.]
May 20, 1973

Dear Sixth Graders:

Your essays spoke of beauty, of love, of light and darkness, of joy and sorrow, and of the goodness of life. They were wonderful compositions. I have seldom read any that have touched me more.

To thank you and your teacher Mrs. Ellis, I am sending you what I think is one of the most beautiful and miraculous things in the world—an egg. I have a goose named Felicity and she lays about forty eggs every spring. It takes her almost three months to accomplish this. Each egg is a perfect thing. I am mailing you one of Felicity's eggs. The insides have been removed—blown out—so the egg should last forever, or almost forever. I hope you will enjoy seeing this great egg and loving it. Thank you for sending me your essays about being somebody. I was pleased that so many of you felt the beauty and goodness of the world. If we feel that when we are young, then there is great hope for us when we grow older.

Sincerely,
E. B. White

To EDWARD C. SAMPSON

North Brooklin
May 24, 1973

Dear Mr. Sampson:

Have just finished your account of my favorite living writer, and my whole body tingles with admiration for anybody who had the courage to put it all on paper. My marks are in red ink, and are few.[1] They concern, chiefly, matters of fact. My name, for example, is Elwyn, not Edward. Stuff like that.

I think in a couple of places you use the word "forward" for "foreword," but I have lost track of where they are in the manuscript.

I have one bone to pick with you: your characterization of my poem "Commuter" as doggerel. I am not attempting here to build myself up as a poet, merely attempting to get the exact meaning of the word. My Webster defines "doggerel" as "low in style and irregular in measure; mean or undignified." "Commuter," I submit, is none of these. What it is is a rhymed definition, and what you probably don't know is that it came into being because Howard Cushman and I, casting about for a way to stay alive for a few more days, entertained for a short spell the insane notion that we might write a dictionary of the English language in quatrains. Whenever I think of this majestic project, I am lost in longing for the wild dreams of youth. Anyway, Cushman and I set out briskly to produce our dictionary and got as far as about a dozen definitions, as I remember it, before abandoning ship. I apparently started not with "A" but with "C," because I produced "Commuter" and "Critic."

> The critic leaves at curtain fall
> To find, in starting to review it,
> He scarcely saw the play at all
> For watching his reaction to it.

Today, as I think how many times "Commuter" has been reprinted, I wonder whether we shouldn't have plunged on with our ambitious plan. Doggerel it wasn't. Dreamy it was.

On page 41, I have questioned the word "well." You have every right to use it. But to an insider, the story of *The New Yorker* has yet to be *well* told. Many staffers were indignant about parts of the Thurber book. Rebecca West's review of it came close to expressing their feelings. The Kramer book, as I recall it, was simply inadequate.

On page 113, I can fill you in a bit about Fern's being "vital to the story." I found this out to my sorrow, for the story did not contain Fern

---

1. Sampson had finished his biography of White and had sent him a copy of the manuscript for checking.

as I first wrote it. I finished the job and was on the point of turning in my manuscript to Harper when I decided something was wrong, or lacking. I set the thing aside, and then gradually rewrote the whole book—this time with the little girl. It was a lucky move on my part, a narrow squeak.

Thank you again for letting me see your manuscript. I can sympathize with you in your feeling of frustration at being held up so long, and I wish you a fair tide when the book is at last launched.

Sincerely,
E. B. White

To EDWARD C. SAMPSON

North Brooklin
31 May [1973]

Dear Mr. Sampson:

To answer your questions:

I am still doing the newsbreaks for *The New Yorker*. The connection began around 1926, I think, and I am still at it. Not many funny ones come in any more—the days when people knew what was funny seem to be long gone.

My preference would be upper case. *The Lady Is Cold. Here Is New York. Every Day Is Saturday.* I hadn't realized that my titles were so full of the verb *is*. Maybe they should all be changed to *was*.

I am with you in not liking the word "classic." I don't like the word "humorist," either. "Archy and Mehitabel" is, to my mind, a distinguished work in American letters, and whether it is a classic or not, it doesn't deserve the adjective "minor." There is not a minor word in it. The piece about Warty Bliggens is a brilliant exposure of man's startling assumption about his relationship to nature. I have never read anything to beat it.

Sincerely,
E. B. White

To MISS R——

North Brooklin
September 15, 1973

Dear Miss R——:

At seventeen, the future is apt to seem formidable, even depressing. You should see the pages of my journal circa 1916.

You asked me about writing—how I did it. There is no trick to it. If you like to write and want to write, you write, no matter where you are or what else you are doing or whether anyone pays any heed. I must have written half a million words (mostly in my journal) before I had anything published, save for a couple of short items in St. Nicholas. If you want to write about feelings, about the end of summer, about growing, write about it. A great deal of writing is not "plotted"—most of my essays have no plot structure, they are a ramble in the woods, or a ramble in the basement of my mind. You ask, "Who cares?" Everybody cares. You say, "It's been written before." Everything has been written before.

I went to college but not direct from high school; there was an interval of six or eight months. Sometimes it works out well to take a short vacation from the academic world—I have a grandson who took a year off and got a job in Aspen, Colorado. After a year of skiing and working, he is now settled into Colby College as a freshman. But I can't advise you, or *won't* advise you, on any such decision. If you have a counsellor at school, I'd seek the counsellor's advice. In college (Cornell), I got on the daily newspaper and ended up as editor of it. It enabled me to do a lot of writing and gave me a good journalistic experience. You are right that a person's real duty in life is to save his dream, but don't worry about it and don't let them scare you. Henry Thoreau, who wrote "Walden," said, "I learned this at least by my experiment: that if one advances confidently in the direction of his dreams, and endeavors to live the life which he has imagined, he will meet with a success unexpected in common hours." The sentence, after more than a hundred years, is still alive. So, advance confidently. And when you write something, send it (neatly typed) to a magazine or a publishing house. Not all magazines read unsolicited contributions, but some do. *The New Yorker* is always looking for new talent. Write a short piece for them, send it to The Editor. That's what I did forty-some years ago. Good luck.

Sincerely,
E. B. White

• *The collection of essays discussed in the following letter was ready for publication in 1973, but White asked his publisher to hold it until after his book of letters appeared.*

To CASS CANFIELD

[North Brooklin, Me.]
September 24, 1973

Dear Cass:

I'm glad you think the "Essays" are worth publishing in this selected form. I have written Beulah [Hagen] to let her know that I approve the title. I would be happier if there were more new material in the book, but the grim fact is I have not been writing much in the last ten years—too busy trying to stay alive and keep my household afloat.

You asked about an advance against royalties. I think I'll not take any advance on this book—will just pocket the money as it pours in.

You also asked about the extra imprint "A Cass Canfield Book." I am pleased and proud that you want to put your name on the book. This poses, however, a question of exquisite delicacy that I will now address myself to. My preference is for single billing: I like to think of the book as "An E. B. White Book" if only because I wrote it. The pieces go a long way back in time, many of them, and many illustrious and well-loved names have brushed off on them: Harold Ross, Eugene Saxton, Katharine S. White, William Shawn, Cass Canfield. I think I would feel uneasy to have someone's name other than my own on this book, despite your clear claim to the title in your capacity as publisher of the work. That, anyway, is my feeling and my preference—to have the title plain and all to myself. But it is not a matter of great moment, and if it would mean a lot to you to use the extra imprint, I don't want to say no, thereby setting myself up as an elderly curmudgeon. Perhaps I should welcome the chance to "massage an old friend's ego" [Canfield's phrase]; might even set up a massage parlor and charge a fee and incur the displeasure of the police.

I am at work on the Foreword, which will be short. Have you entertained the idea of supplying the book with a Preface by a critical observer—someone who would assay the essays? There may be some merit in the idea. These essays are the result of a lifetime of work on my part and are well thought of by a lot of students of the essay. The advantage of having a Preface would be that it would introduce some new material in the book. You would, of course, have to pay a fee to the Preface writer, but since I am not asking for the ten thousand dollars in advance, you are momentarily in pocket and could afford to hire someone. If you think well of this idea, I might be able to suggest two or three candidates for the job, and I'm sure you can think of many more. This "preface" business is not anything I am firm on, it is just something that occurred to me, as a device for enlivening the book.

Yrs,
Andy

To JILL L——

[North Brooklin, Me.]
February 4, 1974

Dear Jill:

Thanks for your letter—I was very glad to get it. And it is nice to know that you are interested in my stories.

"Stuart Little" is the story of a quest, or search. Much of life is questing and searching, and I was writing about that. If the book ends while the search is still going on, that's because I wanted it that way. As you grow older you will realize that many of us in this world go through life looking for something that seems beautiful and good—often something we can't quite name. In Stuart's case, he was searching for the bird Margalo, who was his ideal of beauty and goodness. Whether he ever found her or not, or whether he ever got home or not, is less important than the adventure itself. If the book made you cry, that's because you are aware of the sadness and richness of life's involvements and of the quest for beauty.

Cheer up—Stuart may yet find his bird. He may even get home again. Meantime, he is headed in the right direction, as I am sure you are.

Sincerely,
E. B. White

• *"Since the emphasis of modern education is tending toward career-oriented goals, we, the concerned Latin students of Hackensack High School, are seeking opinions concerning the relevance of Latin to the school curriculum." Thus began the letter which elicited this reply.*

To MITCHELL USCHER

[North Brooklin, Me.]
[February? 1974]

Dear Mr. Uscher:

I studied Latin when I was in high school. I had a good time with it and have never regretted the experience.

A great many words in the letter you wrote to me had their roots in Latin—a word like "curriculum," for example, or "relevance." And although the skilful writer of English prose tries to avoid words derived from Latin in favor of Anglo-Saxon words, there is, I believe, a great advantage in knowing Latin. It helps you find your way around in the English language, so that when you encounter a common word like "opera" you know that you are dealing with the plural of "opus." Or when you come across the word "interpose," you can immediately dissect it: *inter-*, between + *ponere*, to put or place.

I recommend the study of Latin for today's students in today's world—a world that closely resembles yesterday's world. You speak in your letter of modern education "tending toward career-oriented goals." In my day, fifty years ago, we did not tack the word "oriented" onto everything, but we were just as interested in a career, just as eager to reach our goal, as are the young students of today. Latin is good discipline, good reading, and the study of it makes good sense. When you know Latin, you know enough to say "guts" instead of "intestinal fortitude."

Sincerely,
EBW

• *Geoffrey Hellman was writing a* New Yorker *profile of the American Academy of Arts and Letters and the National Institute of Arts and Letters. He wrote White asking about his and Thurber's connections with the two societies.*

To GEOFFREY HELLMAN

North Brooklin
May 3, 1974

Dear Geoffrey:

You are talking to a man who has never been alone and palely loitering in the vicinity of 633 West 155 Street. It's just an address to me—one that turns up in the mail almost every day on one pretext or another. The Institute and the Academy, whatever else they are, are busy, busy, busy. Someone is always getting tapped, someone is always receiving an Award, votes are always being taken, and poets are always dying and being memorialized. Drinks are served, prizes are won, money is distributed.

I vaguely recall Thurber's refusing the jump, and I remember finding it a bit embarrassing that he named me and my failure to measure up as his reason for not accepting the Institute's invitation. I did not like being the bait the Institute would have to swallow in order to catch Thurber. I think Jim should have accepted or declined without bringing me into the thing. But he did.

I can't recall whether I accepted or declined the first invitation to join the Institute. I did accept the Gold Medal for Essays and Criticism and was pleased to get it. Essayists are thankful for small favors. And this year I accepted, or answered, the call to the Academy but have not been inducted yet. I've never understood the relationship between the Institute and the Academy—I like to think it is an illicit one. Probably you have delved into the matter.

I'm not planning to be present at the Ceremonial this month. Never go anywhere any more.

If you are trying to pin down the date of my entrance into the Institute, I'm sure the Institute's records would show it. Boy, do they keep records!

My non-participation in the ceremonials and gatherings up at 155 Street does not mean that I have anything against these organizations. As far as I know they are worthy and fine. It's just that by nature I don't go in much for ritualistic occasions. . . .

Yrs,
Andy

To DOROTHY JOAN HARRIS

[North Brooklin, Me.]
June 28, 1974

Dear Mrs. Harris:

I've yet to see the book that was effortless to write. They all take it out of you, one way or another. . . .

If you are at the moment struggling with a book, what you should ask yourself is, Do I really care about this particular set of characters, this thing I am doing? If you do, then nothing should deter you. If you are doubtful about it, then I'd turn to something else. I knew, in the case of Charlotte, that I cared deeply about the whole bunch of them. So I went ahead.

May good luck go with you.

Sincerely,
E. B. White

• *In January 1975 Beulah Hagen retired after forty years at Harper & Row, and Corona Machemer became Assistant to Cass Canfield.*

To CORONA MACHEMER

North Brooklin, Maine
June 11, 1975

Dear Miss Machemer:

I'm going to like being edited by a girl who grew up overlooking Snow Pond.[1] I always wanted to try a canoe trip down Belgrade Stream from Long Pond to Messalonski, which according to my map drops only about six feet in ten miles, but I never made it. However, as a very young boy I used to arrive early in the morning at the Belgrade Station with my family, where we were met by Millard Gleason and his buckboard and team, to take our trunks and ourselves over the hills to Great Pond and the Gleason Shore. There have been no adventures since that

---

1. Local name for Lake Messalonski.

equalled it in splendor. You probably don't remember the Salmon Lake House, an old inflammable situated on the stream that connects Ellis Pond with Great Pond. It burned down, just as everybody knew it would. . . .

I hope we can have galleys[2] by the end of June. June is by all odds the most difficult month of the year for me, with its lilacs, its apple blossoms, its timothy, its wild plum, and all the other pollens; and this year it has been made even more difficult by the failure of my heart to stand up to any more pollenosis, so that it has lost its rhythm and now goes one two three four hello-there-everybody! One two three four. Only a set of galleys can get it back in rhythm again.

If Gimbels has let you down, you can bring your dirty clothes here —we have a washing machine that is operational. I look forward to working with you on this highly dubious project. I think publishers are scared of books of letters, and I don't blame them. But once you've got into it, there is no place to go but forward. Onward and upward. It never occurred to me, when I got into this thing, that it was an entirely different kind of exposure to the ones I had been used to as a writer of prose pieces. A man who publishes his letters becomes a nudist—nothing shields him from the world's gaze except his bare skin. A writer. writing away, can always fix things up to make himself more presentable, but a man who has written a letter is stuck with it for all time—unless he is dishonest.

Sincerely,
E. B. White

To **DONALD A. NIZEN**

[North Brooklin, Me.]
October 24, 1975

Dear Mr. Nizen:

Thanks for your letter of October 16 about the Great White Mixup. The *Times* is arriving every day now. For a while we were receiving *two* copies, and this proved oppressive.

You say in your letter that the *New Yorker* magazine owes us a refund. They owe us a refund provided the *Times* has refunded some money to the magazine. Has it?

As nearly as I can reconstruct the events, this is what happened:

1. The newspaper stopped coming, without warning.

2. A form letter from Mr. Innelli arrived, saying that a computer was taking over.

---

2. Of these *Letters*.

3. My wife, disturbed at receiving no newspaper, phoned the New Yorker and asked them to renew the *Times* for us and to pay the bill.

4. Our secretary at the magazine, Mrs. Walden, shot off a letter to the *Times*, dated September 10, enclosing a check for $114 made out to the *Times* by the magazine's accounting department.

5. Not knowing that my wife had done this, I sent the *Times* a check for $114, with instructions to renew our subscription.

6. When I learned that my wife had been busy, and that the magazine had sent you $114, I sent off a check to the New Yorker to reimburse them. That means, of course, that the *Times* got paid twice—you got a check from me, and you got a check from the New Yorker.

7. Two papers began arriving in every mail.

8. I wrote Ms. Zenette Pomykalo, telling her what had happened, and explaining that we were getting two copies of the *Times* and that two payments had been made. I suggested that she cancel one subscription and refund the money. The subscription that apparently got cancelled was the one in the name of Mrs. K. S. White, so I presume that the *Times* refunded some money to the New Yorker. If this has happened, then the New Yorker owes us the refund.

It all goes to show that a husband and wife should check on each other's actions from minute to minute, not just from day to day. Katharine and I ought to know this by now—we will have been married forty-six years come November 13.

Sincerely,
E. B. White

P.S. Today's mail has just arrived, and there are two communications from the *Times*. One is from Mr. Innelli, saying that "only one payment was received," and that "we cancelled the duplicate order which was registered to terminate on September 28, 1976." What Mr. Innelli and the computer can't seem to get through their heads is that one of the two payments arrived at the *Times* in a letter from the New Yorker and that the check enclosed was made out *by* the New Yorker. If we could just convince Innelli of this, we would be making progress. Mr. Innelli also suggests that I forward copies of the cancelled checks. Well, I did that quite a while ago, and you very kindly returned them. Of course, maybe the *Times* will have to see the cancelled check that the New Yorker sent. I'm not sure it will be a simple matter to get my hands on this crucial document, but I'll give it a try if the *Times* insists. I have it on the word of Mrs. Harriet Walden, who is utterly reliable, that a check *was* sent, in a letter dated September 10.

The other item in the mail is addressed to Mrs. E. B. White and is a subscription invoice. It says "Pay this amount − $114." The chances of our sending the *Times* still a third payment of $114 are so slight as to be negligible.

Carry on.

• *Katharine White suffered an attack of congestive heart failure in early November. The following was written to her in the hospital in Blue Hill.*

To KATHARINE S. WHITE

[North Brooklin, Me.]
November 12, 1975

Dear K:

Tomorrow is our 46th, and it is a particularly important one for me because of your having strayed so far away, and then been brought back, and this made me realize more than anything else ever has how much I love you and how little life would mean to me were you not here. Welcome back, and do not ever leave me.

I had intended to drive to Bangor and bring back a piece of jewelry as a wedding gift, but then I thought of a better idea—I want to give you a small greenhouse, for your plants and your seedlings. I think you will find some pleasure and satisfaction in this if it can be set up properly. I am consulting two friends who have had experience with greenhouses—Roy Barrette and Ward Snow—and am planning to benefit by their knowledge. Small greenhouses come in all sizes, shapes, and colors, and they are built of all kinds of different materials. What we need is something that is best suited for this hard winter climate, and that is what I am trying to find out. Henry and I have talked this all over and have agreed on the perfect location for the greenhouse: it should stand just south of the cutting garden, in what is now the clothes yard. This will need a rock wall and some grading to make it level, but that is a simple matter. Anyway, this is my gift to you on this November 13, with all my love and bright hopes for a green springtime in Maine.

A.

To THE EDITOR OF THE ELLSWORTH (MAINE) AMERICAN

[North Brooklin, Me.]
January 1, 1976

To the Editor:

I think it might be useful to stop viewing fences for a moment and take a close look at Esquire magazine's new way of doing business. In

February, Esquire will publish a long article by Harrison E. Salisbury, for which Mr. Salisbury will receive no payment from Esquire but will receive $40,000 from the Xerox Corporation—plus another $15,000 for expenses. This, it would seem to me, is not only a new idea in publishing, it charts a clear course for the erosion of the free press in America. Mr. Salisbury is a former associate editor of the New York Times and should know better. Esquire is a reputable sheet and should know better. But here we go—the Xerox–Salisbury–Esquire axis in full cry!

A news story about this amazing event in the December 14th issue of the Times begins: "Officials of Esquire magazine and of the Xerox Corporation report no adverse reactions, so far, to the announcement that Esquire will publish a 23-page article [about travels through America] in February 'sponsored' by Xerox." Herewith I am happy to turn in my adverse reaction even if it's the first one across the line.

Esquire, according to the Times story, attempts to justify its new payment system (get the money from a sponsor) by assuring us that Mr. Salisbury will not be tampered with by Xerox; his hand and his pen will be free. If Xerox likes what he writes about America, Xerox will run a "low keyed full-page ad preceding the article" and another ad at the end of it. From this advertising, Esquire stands to pick up $115,000, and Mr. Salisbury has already picked up $40,000, traveling, all expenses paid, through this once happy land. . . .

Apparently Mr. Salisbury had a momentary qualm about taking on the Xerox job. The Times reports him as saying, "At first I thought, gee whiz, should I do this?" But he quickly conquered his annoying doubts and remembered that big corporations had in the past been known to sponsor "cultural enterprises," such as opera. The emergence of a magazine reporter as a cultural enterprise is as stunning a sight as the emergence of a butterfly from a cocoon. Mr. Salisbury must have felt great, escaping from his confinement.

Well, it doesn't take a giant intellect to detect in all this the shadow of disaster. If magazines decide to farm out their writers to advertisers and accept the advertiser's payment to the writer and to the magazine, then the periodicals of this country will be far down the drain and will become so fuzzy as to be indistinguishable from the controlled press in other parts of the world.

E. B. White

• *Some weeks after his letter on the Xerox–Esquire–Salisbury arrangement was published, White received a letter of inquiry from W. B. Jones, Director of Communications Operations at Xerox Corporation, outlining the ground rules of the corporation's sponsorship of the Salis-*

bury piece and concluding: "With these ground rules, do you still see something sinister in the sponsorship? The question is put seriously, because if a writer of your achievement and insight—after considering the terms of the arrangement—still sees this kind of corporate sponsorship as leading the periodicals of this country toward the controlled press of other parts of the world, then we may well reconsider our plans to underwrite similar projects in the future." White's reply follows.

TO W. B. JONES

North Brooklin
January 30, 1976

Dear Mr. Jones:

In extending my remarks on sponsorship, published in the Ellsworth *American*, I want to limit the discussion to the press—that is, to newspapers and magazines. I'll not speculate about television, as television is outside my experience and I have no ready opinion about sponsorship in that medium.

In your recent letter to me, you ask whether, having studied your ground rules for proper conduct in sponsoring a magazine piece, I still see something sinister in the sponsorship. Yes, I do. Sinister may not be the right word, but I see something ominous and unhealthy when a corporation underwrites an article in a magazine of general circulation. This is not, essentially, the old familiar question of an advertiser trying to influence editorial content; almost everyone is acquainted with that common phenomenon. Readers are aware that it is always present but usually in a rather subdued or non-threatening form. Xerox's sponsoring of a specific writer on a specific occasion for a specific article is something quite different. No one, as far as I know, accuses Xerox of trying to influence editorial opinion. But many people are wondering why a large corporation placed so much money on a magazine piece, why the writer of the piece was willing to get paid in so unusual a fashion, and why Esquire was ready and willing to have an outsider pick up the tab. These are reasonable questions.

The press in our free country is reliable and useful not because of its good character but because of its great diversity. As long as there are many owners, each pursuing his own brand of truth, we the people have the opportunity to arrive at the truth and to dwell in the light. The multiplicity of ownership is crucial. It's only when there are few owners, or, as in a government-controlled press, one owner, that the truth becomes elusive and the light fails. For a citizen in our free society, it is an enormous privilege and a wonderful protection to have access to hundreds of periodicals, each peddling its own belief. There is safety in numbers: the papers expose each other's follies and peccadillos, correct each other's mistakes, and cancel out each other's biases. The reader is free to range around in the whole editorial bouillabaisse and explore it for the one clam that matters—the truth.

When a large corporation or a rich individual underwrites an article in a magazine, the picture changes: the ownership of that magazine has been diminished, the outline of the magazine has been blurred. In the case of the Salisbury piece, it was as though *Esquire* had gone on relief, was accepting its first welfare payment, and was not its own man anymore. The editor protests that he accepts full responsibility for the text and that Xerox had nothing to do with the whole business. But the fact remains that, despite his full acceptance of responsibility, he somehow did not get around to paying the bill. This is unsettling and I think unhealthy. Whenever money changes hands, something goes along with it—an intangible something that varies with the circumstances. It would be hard to resist the suspicion that *Esquire* feels indebted to Xerox, that Mr. Salisbury feels indebted to both, and that the ownership, or sovereignty, of *Esquire* has been nibbled all around the edges.

Sponsorship in the press is an invitation to corruption and abuse. The temptations are great, and there is an opportunist behind every bush. A funded article is a tempting morsel for any publication—particularly for one that is having a hard time making ends meet. A funded assignment is a tempting dish for a writer, who may pocket a much larger fee than he is accustomed to getting. And sponsorship is attractive to the sponsor himself, who, for one reason or another, feels an urge to penetrate the editorial columns after being so long pent up in the advertising pages. These temptations are real, and if the barriers were to be let down I believe corruption and abuse would soon follow. Not all corporations would approach subsidy in the immaculate way Xerox did or in the same spirit of benefaction. There are a thousand reasons for someone's wishing to buy his way into print, many of them unpalatable, all of them to some degree self-serving. Buying and selling space in news columns could become a serious disease of the press. If it reached epidemic proportions, it could destroy the press. I don't want IBM or the National Rifle Association providing me with a funded spectacular when I open my paper, I want to read what the editor and the publisher have managed to dig up on their own—and paid for out of the till. . . .

My affection for the free press in a democracy goes back a long way. My love for it was my first and greatest love. If I felt a shock at the news of the Salisbury–Xerox–Esquire arrangement, it was because the sponsorship principle seemed to challenge and threaten everything I believe in: that the press must not only be free, it must be fiercely independent—to survive and to serve. Not all papers are fiercely independent, God knows, but there are always enough of them around to provide a core of integrity and an example that others feel obliged to steer by. The funded article is not in itself evil, but it is the beginning of evil and it is an invitation to evil. I hope the invitation will not again be extended, and, if extended, I hope it will be declined.

About a hundred and fifty years ago, Tocqueville wrote: "The journalists of the United States are generally in a very humble position, with a scanty education and a vulgar turn of mind." Today, we chuckle at this antique characterization. But about fifty years ago, when I was a young journalist, I had the good fortune to encounter an editor who fitted the description quite closely. Harold Ross, who founded the *New Yorker*, was deficient in education and had—at least to all outward appearances—a vulgar turn of mind. What he did possess, though, was the ferocity of independence. He was having a tough time finding money to keep his floundering little sheet alive, yet he was determined that neither money nor influence would ever corrupt his dream or deflower his text. His boiling point was so low as to be comical. The faintest suggestion of the shadow of advertising in his news and editorial columns would cause him to erupt. He would explode in anger, the building would reverberate with his wrath, and his terrible swift sword would go flashing up and down the corridors. For a young man, it was an impressive sight and a memorable one. Fifty years have not dimmed for me either the spectacle of Ross's ferocity or my own early convictions —which were identical with his. He has come to my mind often while I've been composing this reply to your inquiry.

I hope I've clarified by a little bit my feelings about the anatomy of the press and the dangers of sponsorship of articles. Thanks for giving me the chance to speak my piece.

Sincerely,
E. B. White

[*Mr. Jones wrote and thanked White for "telling me what I didn't want to hear." In May another letter arrived from Jones saying that Xerox had decided not to underwrite any more articles in the press and that they were convinced it was "the right decision."*]

To **ROGER ANGELL**

[North Brooklin, Me.]
May 20, 1976

Dear Rog:

I thought the closing words of your baseball piece were magnificent, sad and ominous though they were. I have the same feeling about other aspects of American life having nothing to do with sports or baseball, and your expression of this feeling touched me closely. Those quiet slow afternoons in the small parks in the practice season recalled to me the different (and better) pace of the railroad travel that I used to know and enjoy before the Concorde arrived and the trains disappeared. It's not entirely a matter of the great sums of money spent, it seems to be essentially a matter of the spiritual acceptance of What's New, or What's Greater—as though there were something wrong or disappointing about what isn't new or what isn't greater.

Anyway, it's new and exciting to have someone exploring baseball at the depth you have ventured into, and I just want to say that I think it's a great piece . . .

Yrs,
Andy

P.S. An actor named Gary Merrill here today, former husband of Bette Davis. Just popped in to say hello.

ACKNOWLEDGMENTS

I am grateful for advice, cooperation, and assistance from many people, and am particularly indebted to the following:

To Mrs. Luella Adams; the late Everett W. Adams and Mrs. Adams; Mrs. Gertrude A. Turner and Mr. Benjamin A. Adams II, for letters to Professor Bristow Adams and his wife.

To the Department of Rare Books, Cornell University Library, for use of the E. B. White collection; to Donald Eddy, Librarian, and to Mrs. Chris Kreyling, Mrs. Mary Daniels, Miss Martha Crow, James Tyler, Mrs. Jane Woolston, and Miss Ellen Wells.

To the late Professor Morris Bishop and to Mrs. Bishop, for information and encouragement.

To Mrs. Clarence Day, for searching her files with me.

To Mrs. Bernard DeVoto and to the Department of Special Collections, Stanford University Libraries.

To Professor Scott Elledge and Mrs. Elledge for assistance and encouragement.

To Margaret Lieb for permission to quote from her letter to E. B. White, and to Xerox Corporation for permission to quote from W. B. Jones's letters.

To the Fales Library at New York University for use of the Geoffrey Hellman collection.

To the Library of the Hamilton and Kirkland Colleges, and especially to Frank K. Lorenz for the letter to Alexander Woollcott of December 24, 1936.

To the Library of Congress, especially John Broderick, Chief, for the correspondence with Frederick Lewis Allen.

To the Newbery Library of Chicago, and to Diana Haskell there.

To the Manuscripts and Archives Division, The New York Public Library, Astor, Lenox, and Tilden Foundations of the New York Public Library and especially to John Stinson, for letter to Anne Carroll Moore.

To the staff of the 96th Street Branch Library of the New York Public Library for their help.

To the Academic Center Library of the University of Texas for letters to Christopher Morley.

To Mrs. Jean Flick Lobrano for being a literary squirrel.

To Mrs. Doris W. Oliver for help in research.

To *The New Yorker* magazine in general, and in particular to Roger Angell, Milton Greenstein, William Shawn, Mrs. Helen Stark, and Mrs. Harriet Walden.

To Katharine S. White, for much time and trouble and editorial assistance.

To Isabel Russell, the Whites' secretary, for much hard work and patience.

To the Raymond C. Guth family for moral support.

D. L. G.

Names in SMALL CAPITALS are recipients of letters.
Titles without author's name pertain to works by
E. B. White. The following abbreviations are used:

Charlotte	FOR	*Charlotte's Web*
Elements		*The Elements of Style*
Here Is NY		*Here Is New York*
OMM		*One Man's Meat*
PofC		*The Points of My Compass*
Quo Vad.		*Quo Vadimus?*
Second Tree		*The Second Tree From the Corner*
Stuart		*Stuart Little*
Trumpet		*The Trumpet of the Swan*
KSW		White, Katharine Sergeant

By the year 2000, 2 out of 3 Americans could be illiterate.

It's true.

Today, 75 million adults...about one American in three, can't read adequately. And by the year 2000, U.S. News & World Report envisions an America with a literacy rate of only 30%.

Before that America comes to be, you can stop it...by joining the fight against illiteracy today.

Call the Coalition for Literacy at toll-free **1-800-228-8813** and volunteer.

Volunteer
Against Illiteracy.
The only degree you need
is a degree of caring.

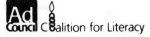 Ad Council Coalition for Literacy